The World of Bribery and Corruption

The Author

Prof. Naunihal Singh earned the degree of M.A. (Economics), M.A. (Sociology), LL.B. (with International Law), Ph.D. (Management) and D.Litt. (International Business). He also obtained Diploma in Industrial Management from the Royal College of Science and Technology, Glasgow, UK; and another Diploma in International Trade from La Sorbonne University, Paris, France.

Dr. Singh taught as Professor of Business Administration at several institutions of USA. A prolific writer, Dr. Singh has authored many outstanding books including *India Betrayed; World of Terrorism; Foundation of Nationalism; International Business: A Strategy for Growth; Scientific Management of Small-Scale Industries; Managing Human Organizations, A System of Governance— Parliamentary or Presidential etc.* in addition to several articles on national and international affairs published in Indian and Foreign journals of repute.

Formerly Director in the Government of India and Member, Board of Governors, Engineering College, Kurukshetra University, India, Dr. Singh has represented India at the United Nations Economic Commission for Asia and Far East (ECAFE) at Addis Ababa. He negotiated trade with Japan on behalf of the Government of India during Expo '70 held in Osaka.

Dr. Singh travelled widely in Europe including England, Canada, Mexico, Brazil, Venezuela, Cambodia, Chile, Japan and other countries in South-East Asia and Africa. A wide spectrum person, currently Dr. Singh is a Member of Parliament (Rajya Sabha).

THE WORLD OF BRIBERY AND CORRUPTION

NAUNIHAL SINGH

MITTAL PUBLICATIONS
NEW DELHI-110059 [INDIA]

First Edition 1998

ISBN 81-7099-709-7

Editorial Office:

H-13, Bali Nagar,
New Delhi - 110015

Phone: 5163610, 5431361

Showroom:

4594/9, Daryaganj,
New Delhi - 110002

Phone: 3250398

Published and printed by Naurang Rai for Mittal Publications,
A-110, Mohan Garden, New Delhi-110059, India.

Phones : 5648028, 5648773
Fax : 91-11-5648725 *Gram* : Mittalbux

Dedicated
to

SHRI LAL KRISHAN ADVANI

a Crusader against
Corruption and Criminality,
a wise Statesman of Sorts
Coupled with Integrity and astute Pariotism,
Aiming at honest,
Progressive and good Governance

"INDIA WAS THE CRADLE OF THE HUMAN RACE,
BIRTH PLACE OF HUMAN SPEECH,
MOTHER OF HISTORY;
GRANDMOTHER OF LEGEND;
GREAT GRANDMOTHER OF TRADITION;
THE ONE LAND THAT ALL MEN DESIRE TO SEE;
AND HAVING ONCE SEEN, BY EVEN A GLIMPSE;
WOULD NOT GIVE THAT GLIMPSE
FOR ALL THE SHOWS OF
ALL THE REST OF THE GLOBE COMBINED"

MARK TWAIN 1896

BUT ALAS! WHAT A DOWNFALL NOW ......

CONTENTS

PART TWO:
INDIAN SCENARIO

REMEDIAL MEASURES

THE FUTURE

ANNEXURES

PREFACE

This book is about bribes and those who take them, give them or condemn them in a variety of cultures from ancient Egypt to modern America. The concept of the bribe at work is the book's theme and matter. It attempts to cover the International scenario; and, in particular, the Indian scenario. By "at work" I mean in use to affect action or thought, conduct or language in criminal prosecutions, in the text of laws, in administrative rules, in political slogans and political campaigns, in confessions, homilies editorials, news stories, and diaries.

Put to work, the concept has had physical, social, spiritual consequences. When, as has happened infrequently, a person has been sent to prison for bribe-taking, all three kinds of consequence are observable. Socially, spiritually, the impact of the bribe is no less palpable when it figures in Chaucer's the *Canterbury Tales*, in Shakespeare's *The Merchant of Venice* and *Measure for Measure*, and in Dante's *Inferno and Pargatorio.*

The core of the concept of a bribe is an inducement improperly influencing the performance of a public function meant to be gratuitously exercised.

The idea is used in postexilic Jerusalem, late Republican Rome, imperial Ravenna, seventh-century Yorkshire, thirteenth century Paris, seventeenth-century London, eighteenth-century Calcutta, nineteenth-century Washington, twentieth-century Tokyo.

Bribery is a legal concept, hence the law determines what counts as bribery in a particular society.

Probing of the various meanings of any law on bribery leads to perception of a tension between it and the morals of any community. Typically, the morals in practice are less demanding than the law on the books and the morals in public expression are more exigent than the law enforced. Often a society has at least four definitions of a bribe that of the more advance moralists; that of the law as written; that of the law as in any degree enforced; that of common practice.

Tourists and journalists are very free in judging that a society is "corrupt" or "very corrupt".

There are no existing sets of figures by which one could conclude the Roman Empire, for example, was more or less corrupt than the British Empire or the United States.

Judgment about corruption in a society need not rest on a statistical basis. But with bribery several factors operate to make unquantified judgment difficult.

First, the act is criminal and consensual; the victim where there is one is not made aware of the arrangement as it affects his case; consequently, a number of acts of bribery remain secret and undiscovered.

Second, accusations of bribery are often politically motivated or are made in order to satisfy certain social or psychic needs; one cannot judge from the accusations alone whether acts of briber have actually occurred.

Third, the amount of legal attention bribery receives is misleading. One society may be uncensorious of most receprocities with its office-holders; there may be no legal response to them at all and the appearance will be given of integrity everywhere.

A different society may define bribes, legislate against bribe-takers, and prosecute bribery in such a way as to suggest that the crime is ubiquitous. A common mistake is to use the number of laws enacted or convictions obtained as an index of corruption.

Fourth, some critics have strong inclinations to exaggerate the corruption of their own day, and others have strong inclinations to denigrate past times or aliens or members of another race, religion, or class.

Their criticisms will then, be used as evidence that corruption is worse now or worse then, or worse with certain groups than others. Impassioned complaint will function as though it were hard evidence.

Fifth, there is the fallacy of the perfectly corrupt man—the belief that vices are linked and that unless a man is thoroughly corrupt in every aspect, he can be no bribe-taker or bribe-giver. Moral judgment is held at bay by the kindly family man or illustrious genius who is also a taker or giver of bribes.

Francis Bacon, Samuel Pepys, Warren Hastings are not merely respectable; they are heroes— respectively the founders, in the view of their admirers, of British science, the British navy and British India.

Bacon was a bribee by the law as actually enforced; Pepys a bribee by his own measure, Hastings a bribee by the law that was being made. Apologists by the score have hesitated to give their bribe-taking its proper name. As for bribers, judgment has always been even more charitable, the underlying assumption being that they are the victims of extortion. When the persons involved have been pre-eminently just, judgment has often been entirely suspended.

Who thinks of Thomas Becket or John Quincy Adams as giving bribes? The fallacy of the perfectly corrupt man prevents seeing bribery in transactions which, measured by at least one of the standards in use in their own time, were corrupt although executed by men or otherwise eminent virtue.

Finally, there is great difficulty in accepting a society's own standards when one approaches the society as a traveller or as a historian. Bribes are a species of reciprocity. Human life is full of reciprocities. The particular reciprocities that count as bribes in particular cultures are distinguished by intentionality form, and context.

What is a bribe depends on the cultural treatment of the constituent elements. The observer outside the culture, like the cynic or rigorist within it, is inclined to see the conventional differences as arbitrary and to reduce all reciprocities of a given kind to bribes—to treat, say, any fift to an office-holder as bribe.

Doing so, the outsider imposes his own standard and reaches a judgment that is unreasonable if the culture's own norms are used.

The fallacy of the perfectly corrupt man; and the reductionism that eliminates conventions and looks only at function—mean that broad generalizations about the amount of bribery in a society must be made with caution and with caveats and without great confidence in their reliability. But evidence of bribery within the law enforcement standards of the day has at times been produced (Oakes Ames's admissions about payment to members of Congress).

Givers of largest to public officials have on occasion furnished documentation of their activities enabling readers of the document to conclude that by some moral or legal standard of their day their donations were bribes (Carl Kotchian's Lockheed Sales Mission).

More rarely, recipients have recorded their receipts in such a way as to show awareness that by their own standards they were taking bribes (the entries of Samuel Pepys in his famous diary).

Confession, autobiographical commemoration, admission against interest occur because the bribe is of significance to the person acknowledging its existence.

As an authority on bribes, St. Augustine does not have the pre-eminence he enjoys in sexual morality, yet a judge in Hippo and a suitor in Ravenna, he contributed to the concept from a life full of litigation.

Of all those who have written on bribes, his known deeds most match his words. Innocent III, ambiguous in his conduct, clear in his standards, was deeply involved in litigation before his curia, Edmond Burke was. a politician who knows the patronage game weel when he moralized on Warren Hastings.

The most celebrated moralist of all on bribery, Cicero, formed his ideas as he worked his way up the slippery ladder of elected office to the consulship. For these men the concept of a bribe-moral rhetoric in their expositions—was also tied to what they had faced in professional practice I draw as much as possible on these moralists seasoned by experience and burndened by responsibility for action.

As a lawyer and a teacher of professional ethics to law students, I have become conscious of the heavy responsibility members of the bar bear for facilitating, disguising, and even delivering bribes, as well as for prohibiting, detecting, and prosecuting them.

As a believer in religion, I have asked how prayer and sacrifice to God are different from bribes.

For Americans generally, bribery has nearly always had a high interest. Treason and bribery are the two crimes mentioned by name in the Constitution charges of corruption have often decided elections. Within the last twenty years one president has been forced to resign after impeachment was voted for offences whose criminal core could be reduced to bribery; another President has been biographically portraved in convincing detail as a habitual bribe-taker and bribe-giver.

One Vice President has been forced to resign after conviction of crimes based on the concealment of bribes; another Vice-President was shown in the hearings in his nomination to practice what was arguably generic bribery by the standard of federal criminal law. Seven members of Congress have been convicted of bribe taking after the most elaborate investigation of legislative corruption ever conducted in any society. Confessions of large American Corporations, solicited by the Securities and Exchange Commission, have produced the most abundant documentation of bribe-giving known to history. One criminal statute enacted in 1970, elevates to the level of federal felony any pattern of bribery in any police department, traffic court, mayoralty, state legislature, or gubernatorial office in the nation.

Hundreds of officials, including four Governors, have in the last decade been sent to prison under this or other federal laws against bribery. Another recent federal statute, unique in the history of the bribe, makes it a crime anywhere in the world for an American corporation to bribe an official of a foreign government. Enmeshed in politics at home, the bribe is now part of an American standard enforced throughout the globe.

At the very time when the concept of the bribe has carried all before it—never were there so many laws against bribery, never were the laws so often enforced by prosecutors, never were there so many convictions of high officials for bribe-taking-at this moment the concept is challenged. There are those who would ignore the moral dimension of bribery as giving the flexibility needed by many political systems.

Typically this counter-concept to the moral notion of the bribe is most boldly applied to the underdeveloped countries. In the same way the argument most subversive of the old concept of usury was first advanced by European moralists in relation to the Chinese. Like usury, bribery could be demoted from a master moral category to a description of a type of economic exploitation.

To look at the bribe at this crisis in its life has the advantage of stimulating comparison with another area of the Western moral tradition in more obvious throes. Here, not a single concept but a duster-chastity contraception homosexually, marriage-has been revamped or reweighed. The relation between bribery and the sexual ethic goes beyond simple comparison.

Metaphors drawn from the vocabulary of sexual sin are used to describe the bribe-taker. Since the time of the Roman Republic "to corrupt" has meant both to seduce a woman and to pay off an office-holder. One "betrays" a lover or an office. One is "faithless" to a spouse or a public trust.

The same religions, the same kind of commandments and examples, the same kind of sanctions have addressed acts of bribery and acts of unlawful intercourse. Taken at a certain level of generality, the same substantive goods are protected and promoted by both ethics. Each sets enormous store by fidelity.

Each lays down the lines that separate a gift, understood as an identification of one person with another person from the manipulative or exploitative use of one person by another person. As the sexual ethic disintegrates, or appears to disintegrate, before our eyes,. we can ask whether the ethic governing bribes will follow suit.

In the time of the prophet Exekiel, violation of the bribery ethic was regarded, like other offences such as intercourse during menstruation, as the cause of national disaster indicated by foreign armies; the impurity of the violations had led to divine punishment. The language in which bribery has been described since at least Roman times reinforces the hypothesis that bribery rules are rules promotive of purity, designed to deter social pollution.

A bribe is "filth" in Roman law. Bribe money in both Latin and English is "dirty". A bribe-taker "soils" his hands. Bribe-givers, aware of the linguistic odium attached to their actions seek to make delivery in "as cleanly a manner as possible", as Sir George Hastings said of his way of bringing a bribe to Francis Bacon. Bags, briefcases, or envelopes regularly put a decent cover over the polluting cash.

To regard the rules on bribery, like the rules on sexual purity, as an tipollutant is not to deny that the specific issues addressed by both sets of rules are important. It is to acknowledge that, as well as fostering fidelity and other specific values, they have an overall order-producing function. Another comparison may seem even more threatening to the objective basis for bribery rules, but is not. This is the analogy, already hinted at, between bribery and witchcraft, a major pollutant of pre-modern societies.

Bribery like witchcraft is often believed to be widely practiced but no one will voluntarily admit publicly to practising it.

Just as accusations of witchcraft sometimes worked to clarify and strengthen the social structure, so have accusations of bribery, as did Burke's indictment of Hastings. Just as accusations of witchcraft sometimes confused and weakened the structure, so have accusations of bribery—such was Bernardino of Siena's implicit judgment of the accusations of bribery so common against the papacy in fifteenth-century Italy.

Where the system is most ambiguous or even at war with itself anti pollution rules multiply. Witchcraft accusations multiply in the fourth century Roman empire and in Elizabethan England. Accusations of ecclesiastical bribery multiply when the Church assumes the highly ambiguous rule of deprecating the accumulation of worldly goods and of amassing them for the service of God; so modern prosecutions begin to bear on legislators who are in the highly ambiguous role of rules and representatives of constituents.

There are other likenesses. Both bribery and witchcraft work in the same way in our modern understanding of them that is, both achieve their effects psychologically. The victim of witchcraft feels tormented. The beneficiary of bribery feels obligated. Response in each case is not to physical pressure but to expectations affecting the mind.

Witchcraft and bribery also have been subject to the same kind of sanctions. Until the twentieth century, although each crime was sometimes prosecuted, regular sanctions for either were social disapproval and supernatural displeasure. No one wanted to be known publicly as a witch; no one wanted to be known publicly as a bribe-taker. The witch was accursed; and from the book of Deuteronomy to the speeches of Edmund Burke the sanction most often invoked against a bribe-taker was divine retribution.

The material harm done by either witchcraft or bribery has often been slight, at times incalculable. No one, for example, showed that the United States as a whole was worse off because the backers of the Union Pacific Railroad bribed the Republican in Congress. The crime was punished not because of material harm done, but because of the affront to intangible ideals of propriety.

As for bribery, the most comprehensive admissions, I have found prior to the ninetheenth century (by Bacon, Pepys, Hastings) all deny that what was called a bribe worked at all-that is, while admitting facts that were socially stamped as bribery, those involved claimed that other factors were decisive for them. If we still conclude that the bribes did work we make a casual connection that depends as much on our own experience, beliefs, and values as did earlier generations' conclusions about the efficacy of witchcraft.

Today, we assume that payment by an interested party to an office-holder is corrupting and we have even changed our statutes so that any such payment is generically bribery—no casual connection showing that the payment obliged the official and influenced his action has to be proved. But it is our desire to be rid of the pollution not a demonstrated correlation between payment and action—that makes the statutes rationally acceptable.

To press these points of resemblance is not to say that the prosecution of bribe-taking officials are witch-hunts and that bribery is in general an imaginary crime. The chief difference is that our experience, as coloured by our beliefs, makes us disbelieve that witches could get supernatural powers in action, while our experience, as coloured by our beliefs, makes us confident that reciprocities can be created and that certain reciprocities conflict with a duty of fidelity we desire to promote. We cannot make an equation of witchcraft and bribery without denying our experience and changing our beliefs and values.

To state summarily what may be best understood by following the story in detail, I take these points to be established:

First, Bribes—socially disapproved inducements of official action meant to be gratuitously exercised—are *abcuebt aknist* as ancient as the invention of scales in Egypt, which symbolized and showed social acceptance of the idea of objective judgment.

Second, the bribe has a history, divisible into discernible epoch. From approximately 3000 B.C. to 1000 A.D. the idea of non-reciprocity struggles against the norms of reciprocation which cement societies whose rulers are both judges and the recipients of offerings.

In the second period from say, 1000 A.D. to 1550 A.D. the anti-bribery ideal is dominant in religious, legal and literary expressions; it's active enforcement is attempted in successive ways of reformation.

The third period of the idea, as far as English speaking people are concerned, begins in the sixteenth century with it's domestication in English bibles and English plays and English law and ends in the eighteenth century with its proclamation as a norm for the English Empire.

The fourth stage is the American when the heirs of the successive reformations and of English politics begin to apply it and then to expand it's sway until it is asserted as an American norm around the earth; and the rest of the world-not merely as a result of American influence but because of the general expansion of the western moral tradition makes at least verbal acknowledgment of the norm.

Third, bribes are today universal; that is, every culture, with insignificant exceptions, treats certain reciprocities with officials as disapproved.

Fourth, the bribe is a concept running counter to normal expectations in approaching a powerful stranger. Linguistic ambiguity in the term for bribe in Hebrew, Greek, and Latin marks the cultural resistance encountered by the concept.

Historically, the limitation of the concept to one class of officials-judges-is a second sign of the resistance. Reluctance to apply the concept against the bribe-giver is a third. Lack of specific sanctions against the bribe-taker is a fourth indication of the precarious hold the concept, historically, has enjoyed.

Fifth, the bribe in its origins depends on religious teaching. Reciprocity is so regularly the norm of human relation that the conception of a transcendental figure, a judge beyond the reach of ordinary reciprocities, was of enormous importance for the idea that certain reciprocities with earthly officials were intolerable.

That conception of transcendental judge was shaped in the ancient Near East. Communication of this image to the West was largely dependent on religion. Accepted as divine revelation, scripture by commandment and paradigm inculcated a teaching on impartial judgment. The concept of the bribe was cast in a biblical mould.

Sixth, Religion—Jewish, Christian pagan—has been, however, profoundly ambivalent in its teaching on reciprocity. The judge beyond influence has been placated by pagans, offered prayers and slaughered animals by jews, and seen by Christians as accepting a special redeeming sacrifice. Religion can be viewed as bribery on a grand scale, organized for the highest end, man's salvation, and practiced to persuade the supreme Authority. Indulgences, systematized no support enterprises from basilicas to bridges, constitute an especially, striking example of this kind of religion. Even in it's most primitive form. Christianity rests on a transaction carried out between God and the son of God which theology labelled the Buy Back, a term in Roman civilization often used to mean payoff to a judge to escape punishment. Job and Jesus himself to the contrary, religion can be read as reinforcement of the iron law, "I give that hou may give" a law requiring reciprocity with every power holder including God.

Seventh, the double message convened by the several religious traditions is paralleled in Western cultures by the elimination of certain reciprocities as bribes and the retention of others as acceptable *quid pro quos*. Words alone seem to mark the distinction between certain acceptable and condemned offerings. . . .

In sixteenth-century Europe payment to obtain a spiritual favour was the sin of simony, a contribution to obtain an indulgence was legitimate. In twentieth-century America, payment to a candidate for his vote is a penal offence, a licenced contribution to a campaign committee is lawful. In some instances, there is only verbal camouflage; in some instances, the verbal destination points to a real difference.

Eighth, although the definition of a bribe depends on the conventions of the cultures, so that ceremony and context form and intention determine whether an exchange counts as a crime or a virtuous act, ultimately the distinction between bribe and gift has become fundamental. Without this distinction the condemnation of bribes appears arbitrary and intermediate offerings such as a tip or a campaign contribution are indeterminately lumped into a single category which includes all reciprocities.

With bribe and gift set a polar opposites, a spectrum with shades of discrimination exists. For out culture-Western culture, now the dominant world culture—the difference between bribe and gift has been most powerfully developed by reflection, theological and literary, on the Redemption.

Ninth, Bribes come openly or covertly, disguised as an interest in a business, as a lawyer's fee or, very often, as loan. Bribes come directly, paid into the waiting hands of the bribee or move commonly, indirectly to the subordinate or friend performing the nearly indispensable office of bagman.

Bribes come in all shapes as sex commodities, appointments, and most often cash. In the shape of sex, bribes have been both male and female; a slave, a wife, a noble boy. As commodities, they have included bedspreads, cups, dogs, fruits, furniture furs, golf balls, jewels, livestock, peacocks, pork, sturgeon, travel, wine-the gamut of enjoyable goods.

As appointments, they have often been rationalized or justified by the merits of the appointee—a double effect, one good, one bad, being achieved by the bribe. As cash they have come as contingent payments and down payments, as payments for the life of the contract and payments for the life of the recipient and as cash on the spot.

They have come at the rate of so much a car towed, so much a prostitute undisturbed. So much a plane purchased, so much a guinea spent, at such a percentage, and at a flat rate. They have been as little as I per cent of contract and as high as 20 per cent or more. They have been as small as 52.50 for a Connecticut voter and as much as $12,000,000 for the Prime Minister of Japan and his associates. A representatives list of prices appears in the Appendix.

Tenth, bribes have included every variety of business, from very small to multinational all the professions: every manner of criminal defendant; and the ordinary citizen in line for an inheritance or in need of a traffic ticket being fixed. Bribes have ranged from constables and sheriffs to the Speaker of the House (U.S. nineteenth century), the Speaker of the House of Commons (U.K. seventeenth century), the President of Honduras, the President of Italy, the Prime minister of Japan, the Prime Consort of the Netherlands, the Lord Chancellor of England (seventeenth century).

Bribe-takers and bribe-givers are not distinguished by any of the characteristics commonly associated with criminality. Sometimes they are oppressed and bribe to escape harassment. Sometimes they are oppressed and therefore, accept bribes.

Often they are possessed of high office and comfortable

income, bribe to maintain or expand their power or wealth, and accept bribes given as tributes to their power or wealth. Their crimes have not been shown to depend on any oedipal fixations, sexual need or malfunction, or uncontrollable instinct. They are not vicious in all respects; they are often otherwise decent individuals. They are of all nationalities and sects and have been in the past more often men than women.

Eleventh, the bribe is ideologically neutral—that is, charges of bribery can be made by an established class attacking a new class (John Randolph pursuing the Yazoo speculators; George Templeton Strong scorning the Tweed Ring); by a new class attacking an old class (the Protestants assailing the papacy; Andrew Jackson censuring Adams and Clay); and in interclass warfare (Coke against Bacon; the Carter administration against the Abscam defendants).

The bribe is a concept which can be effectively evoked by "the center" or existing hierarchy, as fourth-century Roman emperors and popes like Gregory I, Gregory VII, and Innocent III illustrate. It is a concept which is useful to "the border" or sectarian groupings within a society, as is shown by the writings of John Wyclif and Jan Hus.

Twelfth, enforcement of law against bribes has nearly always been a function of prosecutorial discretion. Prosecutions for bribery have been depended on motivations distinct from the desire to punish the bribe. The watershed for widespread federal prosecution of bribery occurred in the 1960s. Whatever social causes account for it, at this time the pursuit of bribery become a national enterprise in the United States.

Watergate is the consequence not the cause of this phenomenon. In the Orwelian prophecy for the year 1984, sexual puritanism is the rule, enforced by electronics. In the actual America of 1984, it is the purity of political reciprocities that is enforced by wire taps, tape recordings, and television cameras.

Thirteenth, the commonest sanctions against bribes are moral—the innovation of guilt before God and shame before society, guilt and shame being equally relied on. Political sanctions—repudiation at the polls, forced resignation from office, loss of promotion—are frequently involved. Sanctions prescribed by law are more often indirect than direct—not the crime of bribery itself but a related offence is usually punished until very recent times application of direct criminal sanctions to highly placed bribe-takers was rare.

Fourteenth, prosecutors, politicians, and journalists are those most attentive to contemporary corruption. Academic lawyers, anthropologists, psychoanalysts, and theologians have had little to say. Political scientists and sociologists, intent on understanding the function of social practices, sometimes give little weight to the moral impact of corruption.

Biographers and historians, despite a tendency at times to act as advocates or apologists, give a kind of secular last judgment on the corrupt. Those who have most powerfully articulated the antibribery ethic are the matters of Western literature—above all Chaucer, Dante and Shakespeare.

Fifteenth, the material injury bribers and bribes inflict is often undemonstrable. Their actions always subvert the trust that accompanies public office and distinguishes office from power. For jews Christians, for those who share their moral heritage, the bribe is not a morally neutral concept.

Writing at this interesting time in the history of the bribe, I venture a prediction that is a projection of my values. That will come at the end. History itself is not prediction but the selection of significant actions, words, and characters to be remembered— drama more than process. "Remember! Remember! Remember!—Burke's incantation after his prosecution of Warren Hastings had ended in defeat. If all that is collected here survive in memory, this account has been worth making.

Focus of the Book

Compared to the macro policy approaches indicated above, the attempt in this volume is more modest and multi-faceted. It concentrates on legal, institutional and systematic charges that would appear to hold the best premise for tackling corruption in the Indian context. On the basis of the research and thought that has gone into the issue involved, it offers prospective proposals which, when taken together, can add up to a strategic agenda for action.

The intention has not been to cover all aspects of corruption, but in planning this volume, the aim was no more than to make a beginning in the formulation of a coherent set of concrete proposals for tackling corruption.

The book aims at dealing with the problem of corruption against a broader canvas of political, economic and administrative reforms. Their specific focus on corruption is oriented towards three broad aspects: preventive, punitive, and promotional. Preventive aspects include curtailing corruption in the political process; insulating public servants from the abuse of political power; strengthening accountability in public administration ensuring transparency in government; enabling access to and dissemination of information; promoting efficiency in the provision of public services; and measures to reduce the role of discretion in administrative law.

The volume concludes with a summary presentation of the specific proposals for tackling corruption. In cases where the authors have not come up with any single view, alternatives have been presented. In a few instances, proposals made have been qualified or elaborated upon . In putting forward proposals, an attempt has been to strike a balance between too much and too little detail. The aim has been to come up with an agenda which is reasonably specific and is, at the same time, sufficiently flexible so that it lends itself to being improved upon in further debate.

The bibliography includes the major contribution to theory, policy and internal experience relating to corruption. Besides helping in a better understanding of the subject, we hope it will stimulate more policy-oriented research on various aspects of corruption in India.

Need for Public Action

While the proposal offered in volume will be useful as an actionable initial agenda for tackling corruption in India, it is clear that no set of proposals, however, well conceived, will themselves be able to bring about the necessary changes. They can only provide a basis for action. They will remain a dead letter unless public action is forthcoming at several levels for winning acceptance for the proposed reforms.

A very encouraging development is that the major Indian

political parties—Bharatiya Janata Party, Indian National Congress, Janata Dal, Communist Party of India (Marxist) and the Communist Party of India—included a number of proposals for tackling corruption in their manifestoes for the 1996 general elections to Parliament. Undoubtedly, this came about in response to the strong revulsion against corruption on the part of the electorate.

The extracts reproduced in the Annexure from the party manifestoes on (a) the Lok Pal, (b) electoral reforms relating to probity of legislators and political parties and (c) other aspects, such as vigilance machinery, accountability, transparency, and preventing abuse of political power would indicate that their is a great deal of convergence as well as a high degree of specificity in the electoral promises relating to the control of corruption.

This opens up an excellent opportunity for public action in the form of a sustained and orchestrated campaign against corruption based on a concrete but evolving agenda. Such a campaign will have to be pursued by a wide alliance against corruption forged among politicians, administrators, legislators, jurists, academicians, journalists, industrialists and other sections of the concerned public.

Meanwhile, citizen groups should be encouraged to tackle corruption at local levels on specific issues. Citizens should be made to feel that as tax payers and consumers of public services, they can demand administrative accountability as a matter of right and entitlement.

The author would feel rewarded if this volume were to help in contributing to such a process.

It was with an intention to focus attention of the intellectuals, politicians, the decision-makers, the law-makers as well as the common man that the book has been written.

Naunihal Singh

INTRODUCTION

Bribery is a legal concept. Hence, the law determines what counts as bribery in a particular society.

Probing of the various meanings of any law on bribery leads to perception of a tension between it and the morals of any community. Typically, the morals in practice are less demanding than the law on the books and the morals in public expression are more exigent than the law enforced. Often a society has at least four definitions of a bribe that of the more advance moralists; that of the law as written; that of the law as in any degree enforced; that of common practice.

Tourists and journalists are very free in judging that a society is "corrupt" or "very corrupt".

There are no existing sets of figures by which one could conclude the Roman Empire, for example, was more or less corrupt than the British Empire or the United States.

Judgement about corruption in a society need not rest on a statistical basis. But with bribery several factors operate to make unquantified judgement difficult.

First, the act is criminal and consensual; the victim where there is one is not made aware of the arrangement as it affects his case; consequently, a number of acts of bribery remain secret and undiscovered.

Second, accusations of bribery are often politically motivated or are made in order to satisfy certain social or psychic needs; one cannot judge from the accusations alone whether acts of briber have actually occurred.

Third, the amount of legal attention bribery receives is misleading. One society may be uncensorious of most reciprocities with it's office-holders; there may be no legal response to them at all and the appearance will be given of integrity everywhere. A different society may define bribes, legislate against bribe-takers, and prosecute bribery in such a way as to suggest that the crime is ubiquitous. A common mistake is to use the number of laws enacted or convictions obtained as an index of corruption.

Fourth, some critics have strong inclinations to exaggerate the corruption of their own day, and others have strong inclinations to denigrate past times or aliens or members of another race, religion, or class. Their criticisms will, then, be used as evidence that corruption is worse now or worse then, or worse with certain groups than others. Impassioned complaint will function as though it were hard evidence.

Fifth, there is the fallacy of the perfectly corrupt man—the belief that vices are linked and that unless a man is thoroughly corrupt in every aspect, he can be no bribe-taker or bribe-giver. Moral judgement is held at bay by the kindly family man or illustrious genius who is also a taker or giver of bribes.

Francis Bacon, Samuel Pepys, Warren Hastings are not merely respectable; they are heroes-respectively the founders, in view of their admirers of British science, the British navy and British India. Bacon was a bribee by the law as actually enforced; Papys a bribee by his own measure, Hastings a bribee by the law that was being made.

Apologists by the core have hesitated to give their bribe-taking its proper name. As for bribers, judgement has always been even more charitable, the underlying assumption being that they are the victims of extortion. When the persons involved have been pre-eminently just, judgement has often been entirely suspended.

Who thinks of Thoms Becket or John Quincy Adams as giving bribes? The fallacy of the perfectly corrupt man prevents seeing bribery in transactions which measured by at least one of the standards in use in their own time, very corrupt although executed by men or otherwise eminent virtue.

Finally, there is great difficulty in accepting a society's own standards when one approaches the society as a traveller or as a historian. Bribes are a species of reciprocity. Human life is full of reciprocities. The particular reciprocities that count as bribes in particular cultures are distinguished by internationality form, and context. What is a bribe depends on the cultural treatment of the constituent elements.

The observer outside the culture, like the cynic or rigourist within it, is inclined to see the conventional differences as arbitrary and to reduce all reciprocities of a given kind to bribes—to treat, say, any gift to an office-holder as bribe. Doing so, the outsider imposes his own standard and reaches a judgement that is unreasonable if the culture's own norms are used.

The fallacy of the perfectly corrupt man; and the reductionism that eliminates conventions and looks only at functions-mean that broad generalizations about the amount of bribery in a society must be made with caution and with caveats and without great confidence in their reliability. But evidence of bribery within the law enforcement standards of the day has at times been produced (Oakes Ames's admissions about payment to members of Congress).

Givers of largess to public officials have on occasion furnished documentation of their activities enabling readers of the document to conclude that by some moral or legal standard of their day their donations were bribes (Carl Kotchian's Lockheed Sales Mission). More rarely, recipients have recorded their receipts in such a way as to show awareness that by their own standards they were taking bribes (the entries of Samuel Pepys in his famous diary).

Confession, auto-biographical commemoration, admission against interest occur because the bribe is of significance to the person acknowledging its existence.

As an authority on bribes, St. Augustine does not have the pre-eminence he enjoys in sexual morality, yet a judge in Hippo and a suitor in Ravenna, he contributed to the concept from a life full of litigation. Of all those who have written on bribes, his known deeds most match his words. Innocent III, ambiguous in his conduct, clear in his standards, was deeply involved in litigation before his curia.

Edmond Burke was a politician who knew the patronage game well when he moralized on Warren Hastings. The most celebrated moralist of all on bribery, Cicero, formed his ideas as he worked his way up the slippery ladder of elected office to the consulship. For these men the concept of a bribe—moral rhetoric in their expositions was also tied to what they had faced in professional practice I draw as much as possible on these moralists seasoned by experience and burdened by responsibility for action.

As a lawyer and a teacher of professional ethics to students, I have become conscious of the heavy responsibility members of the Indian bar bear for facilitating, disguising, and even deliver bribes, as well as for prohibiting, detecting, and prosecuting them.

As a believer in religion, I have asked how prayer and sacrifice to God are different from bribes.

For Americans, generally, bribery has nearly always had a high interest. Treason and bribery are the two crimes mentioned by name in the Constitution. Charges of corruption have often decided elections. Within the last twenty years one American President has been forced to resign after impeachment was voted for offences whose criminal core could be reduced to bribery; another President has been biographically portrayed, in convincing detail, as a habitual bribe-taker and bribe-giver.

One Vice-President has been forced to resign after conviction of crimes based on the concealment of bribes; another Vice-President was shown in the hearings on his nomination to practice what was arguably generic bribery by the standard of federal criminal law.

Seven members of Congress have been convicted of bribe-taking after the most elaborate investigation of legislative corruption ever conducted in any society.

Confessions of large American Corporations, solicited by the securities and Exchange Commission, have produced the most abundant documentation of bribe-giving known to history. One criminal statute enacted in 1970, elevates to the level of federal felony any pattern of bribery in any police department, traffic court, mayoralty, state legislature, or gubernatorial office in the nation.

Hundreds of officials, including four Governors in America, have in the last decade been sent to prison under this or other federal laws against bribery. Another recent federal statute, unique in the history of the bribe, makes it a crime anywhere in the world for an American corporation to bribe an official of a foreign government. Thus, the bribe is now part of an American standard enforced throughout the globe.

At the very time when the concept of the bribe has carried all before it-never were there so many laws against bribery, never were the laws so often enforced by prosecutors, never were there so many convictions of high officials for bribe-taking. At this moment the concept is challenged. There are those who would ignore the moral dimension of bribery as giving the flexibility needed by many political systems.

Typically, this counter-concept to the moral notion of the bribe is most boldly applied to the under-developed countries. In the same way, the argument most subversive of the old concept of usury was first advanced by European moralists in relation to the Chinese. Like usury, bribery could be demoted from a master moral category to a description of a type of economic exploitation.

To look at the bribe at this crisis in it's life has the advantage of stimulating comparison with another area of the Western moral tradition in more obvious throes. Here, not a single concept but a cluster-chastity, contraception, homosexually, marriage-has been revamped or reweighed. The relation between bribery and the sexual ethic goes beyond simple comparison. Metaphors drawn from the vocabulary of sexual sin are used to describe the bribe-taker.

Since the time of the Roman Republic "to corrupt" has meant both to seduce a woman and to pay off an office-holder. One "betrays" a lover or an office. One is "faithless" to a spouse or a public trust. The same religions, the same kind of commandments and examples, the same kind of sanctions have addressed acts of bribery and acts of unlawful intercourse.

Taken at a certain level of generality, the same substantive goods are protected and promoted by both ethics. Each sets enormous store by fidelity. Each lays down the lines that separate a gift, understood as an identification of one person with another person from the manipulative or exploitative use of one person by another person. As the sexual ethic disintegrates, or appears to disintegrate before our eyes, we can ask whether the ethic governing bribes will follow suit.

In the time of the prophet Ezekiel, violation of the bribery ethic was regarded, like other offences such as intercourse during menstruation, as the cause of national disaster indicated by foreign armies; the impurity of the violations had led to divine punishment. The language in which bribery has been described since at least Roman times reinforces the hypothesis that bribery rules are rules promotive of purity, designed to deter social pollution.

A bribe is "filth" in Roman law. Bribe money in both Latin and English is "dirty". A bribe-taker "soils" his hands. Bribe-givers, aware of the linguistic odium, attached to their actions seek to make delivery in "as cleanly a manner as possible", as Sir George Hastings said of his way of bringing a bribe to Francis Bacon. Bags, briefcases, or envelopes regularly put a descent cover over the polluting cash.

To regard the rules on bribery, like the rules on sexual purity, as an tipollutant is not to deny that the specific issues addressed by both sets of rules are important. It is to acknowledge that, as well as fostering fidelity and other specific values, they have an overall order-producing function. Another comparison may seem even more threatening to the objective basis for bribery rules, but is not. This is the analogy, already hinted at, between bribery and witchcraft, a major pollutant, of pre-modern societies.

Bribery like witchcraft is often believed to be widely practiced but no one will voluntarily admit publicly to practicing it.

Just as accusations of witchcraft sometimes worked to clarify and strengthen the social structure, so have accusations of bribery, as did Burke's indictment of Hastings. Just as accusations of witchcraft sometimes confused and weakened the structure, so have accusations of bribery—such was Bernardino of Siena's implicit judgement of the accusations of bribery so common against the papacy in fifteenth-century Italy.

Where the system is most ambiguous or even at war with itself, anti-pollution rules multiply. Witchcraft accusations multiply in the fourth century Roman empire and in Elizabethan England. Accusations of ecclesiastical bribery multiply when the Church assumes the highly ambiguous rule of deprecating the accumulation of worldly goods and of amassing them for the service of God; so modern prosecution begin to bear on legislators who are in the highly ambiguous role of rules and representatives of constituents.

There are other likenesses. Both bribery and witchcraft work in the same way in our modern understanding of them, that is, both achieve their effects psychologically. The victim of witchcraft feels tormented. The beneficiary of bribery feels obligated. Response in each case is not to physical pressure but to expectations affecting the mind. Witchcraft and bribery also have been subject to the same kind of sanctions. Until the twentieth century, although each crime was sometimes prosecuted, regular sanctions for either were social disapproval and supernatural displeasure.

No one wanted to be known publicly as a witch, no one wanted to be known publicly as a bribe-taker. The witch was accursed; and from the book of Deuteronomy to the speeches of Edmund Burke the sanction most often invoked against a bribe-taker was divine retribution.

The material harm done by either witchcraft or bribery has often been slight, at time incalculable. No one, for example, showed that the United States as a whole was worse off because the backers of the Union Pacific Railroad bribed the Republican in Congress. The crime was punished not because of material harm done, but because of the affront to intangible ideals of propriety.

As for bribery, the most comprehensive admission I have found prior to the ninetheenth century (by Bacon, Pepys, Hastings) all deny that what was called a bribe worked at all—that is, while admitting facts that were socially stamped as bribery, those involved claimed that other factors were decisive for them. If we still conclude that the bribes did work, we make a causal connection that depends as much on our own experience, beliefs, and values as did earlier generations' conclusions about the efficacy of witchcraft.

Today, we assume that payment by an interested party to an office-holder is corrupting and we have even changed our statutes so that any such payment is generically bribery—no causal connection showing that the payment obliged the official and influenced his action has to be proved. But it is our desire to be rid of the pollution not a demonstrated correlation between payment and action—that makes the statutes rationally acceptable.

To press these points of resemblance is not to say that the prosecution of bribe-taking officials are witch-hunts and that bribery is, in general, an imaginary crime. The chief difference is that our experience, as coloured by our beliefs, makes us disbelieve that witches could set supernatural powers in action, while our experience, as coloured by our beliefs, makes us confident that reciprocities can be created and that certain reciprocities conflict with a duty of fidelity we desire to promote. We cannot make an equation of witchcraft and bribery without denying our experience and changing our beliefs and values.

To state summarily, I take these points to be established:

First, bribes-socially disapproved inducements of official action meant to be gratuitously exercised are *abcuebt eknist* as ancient as the invention in Egypt of scales which symbolized and showed social acceptance of the idea of objective judgement.

Second, the bribe has a history, divisible into discernible epoch. From approximately 3000 B.C. to 1000 A.D. the idea of non-reciprocity struggle against the norms of reciprocation which cement societies whose rulers are both judges and the recipients of offerings. In the second period from say, 1000 A.D. to 155 A.D. the anti-bribery ideal is dominant in religious, legal an literary expressions; its active enforcement is attempted in successive waves of reformation.

The third period of the idea, as far as English-speaking people are concerned, begins in the sixteenth century with its domestication in English Bibles and English plays and English law and ends in the eighteenth century with its proclamation as a norm for the English Empire.

The Fourth stage is the American when the heirs of the successive reformations and of English politics begin to apply it; and, then, to expand its sway until it is asserted as an American norm around the earth; and the rest of the world-not merely as a result of American influence but because of the general expansion of the western moral tradition makes at least verbal acknowledgment of the norm.

Third, Bribes are today universal; that is, every culture with insignificant exceptions, treats certain reciprocities with officials as disapproved.

Fourth, the bribe is a concept running counter to normal expectations in approaching a powerful stranger. Linguistic ambiguity in the term for bribe in Hebrew, Greek, and Latin marks the cultural resistance encountered by the concept. Historically, the limitation of the concept to one class of officials-judges—is a second sign of the resistance. Reluctance to apply the concept against the bribe-giver is a third. Lack of specific sanctions against the bribe-taker is a fourth indication of the precarious hold the concept, historically, has enjoyed.

Fifth, the bribe in its origins depends on religious teaching. Reciprocity is so regularly the norm of human relation that the conception of a transcendental figure, a judge beyond the reach of ordinary reciprocities, was of enormous importance for the idea that certain reciprocities with earthly officials were intolerable.

That conception of transcendental judge was shaped in the ancient Near East. Communication of this image to the West was largely dependent on religion. Accepted as divine revelation, scripture by commandment and paradigm inculcated a teaching on impartial judgement. The concept of the bribe was cast in a biblical mould.

Sixth, Religion-Jewish, Christian pagan—has been, however, profoundly ambivalent in its teaching on reciprocity. The judge beyond influence has been placated by pagans, offered a prayer and slaughered animals by jews, and seen by jews, and seen by Christians as accepting a special redeeming sacrifice.

Religion can be viewed as bribery on a grand scale, organized for the highest end, man's salvation, and practiced to persuade the supreme Authority. Indulgences, systematized no support enterprises from basilicas to bridge, constitute an especially striking example of this kind of religion. Even in its most primitive form.

Christianity rests on a transaction carried out between God and Son of God which theology labelled the Buy-Back, a term in Roman civilization often used to mean payoff to a judge to escape punishment. Job and Jesus himself to the contrary, religion can be read as reinforcement of the iron law, "I give that you may give" a law requiring reciprocity with every power-holder including God.

Seventh, the double message conveed by the several religious traditions is paralleled in Western cultures by the elimination of certain reciprocities as bribes and the retention of others as acceptable *quid pro quos*. Words alone seem to mark the distinction between certain acceptable and condemned offerings .....

In sixteenth-century Europe, payment to obtain a spiritual favour was the sin of simony, a contribution to obtain an indulgence was legitimate. In twentieth-century America, payment to a candidate for his vote is a penal offence; a licenced contribution to a campaign committee is lawful. In some instances, there is only verbal camouflage; in some instances, the verbal distination points to a real difference.

Eighth, although the definition of a bribe depends on the conventions of the culture, so that ceremony and context form and intention, determine whether an exchange counts as a crime or a virtuous act, untimetely the distinction between bribe and gift has become fundamental.

Without this distinction the condemnation of bribes appears arbitrary and intermediate offerings such as a tip or a campaign contribution are indicriminately lumped into a single category which includes all reciprocities.

With bribe and gift set at polar opposites, a spectrum with shades of discrimination exists. For the Western culture, now the dominant world culture—the difference between bribe and gift has been most powerfully developed by reflection, theological and literary, on the Redemption.

Ninth, bribes come openly or covertly, disguised as an interest in a business, as a lawyer's fee or, very often, as loan. Bribes come directly, paid into the waiting hands of the bribee or move commonly, indirectly to the subordinate or friend performing the nearly indispensable office of bagman. Bribes come in all shapes as sex commodities, appointments, and most often cash.

In the shape of sex, bribes have been both male and female; a slave, a wife, a noble boy. As commodities, they have included bed-spreads, cups, dogs, fruits, furniture, furs, golf balls, jewels, livestock, peacocks, pork, sturgeon, travel, wine—the gamut of enjoyable goods.

As appointments, they have often been rationalized or justified by the merits of the appointee—a double effect, one good, one bad, being achieved by the bribe. As cash, they have come as contingent payments and down payments, as payments for the life of the contract and payments for the life of the recipient and as cash on the spot.

They have come at the rate of so much a prostitute undisturbed. So much a plane purchased, so much a guinea spent, at such a percentage, and at a flat rate. They have been as little as 1 per cent of contract and as high as 20 per cent or more. They have been as small as $ 52.50 for a Connecticut voter and as much as $ 12,000,000 for the Prime Minister of Japan and his associates. A representative list of prices appears in the Appendix.

Tenth, bribers have included every variety of business, from very small to multinational, all the professions: every manner of criminal defendant; and the ordinary citizen in line for an inheritance or in need of a traffic ticket being fixed.

Bribes have ranged from constables and sheriffs to the Speaker of the House (U.S. nineteenth century), the Speaker of the House of Commons (U.K. seventeenth century), the President of Honduras, the President of Italy, the Prime Minister of Japan, the Prince Consort of the Netherlands, the Lord Chancellor of England (seventeenth century).

Bribe-takers and bribe-givers are not distinguished by any of the characteristics commonly associated with criminality. Sometimes they are oppressed and, therefore, accept bribes. Often they are possessed of high office and comfortable income, bribe to maintain or expand their power or wealth, and accept bribes given as tributes to their power or wealth.

Their crimes have not been shown to depend on any oedipus fixation, sexual need or malfunction, or uncontrollable instinct. They are not vicious in all respects; they are often otherwise decent individuals. They are of all nationalities and sects and have been in the past more often men than women.

Eleventh, the bribe is ideologically neutral—that is, charges of bribery can be made by an established class attacking a new class (John Randolph pursuing the Yazoo speculators; George Templeton Strong scorning the Tweed Ring); by a new class attacking an old class (the Protestants assailing the papacy; Andrew Jackson censuring Adams and Clay); and in intraclass warfare (Coke against Bacon; the Carter administration against the Abscam defendants).

The bribe is a concept which can be effectively evoked by "the center" or existing hierarchy, as fourth-century Roman Emperors and popes like Gregory I, Gregory VII, and Innocent III illustrate. It is a concept which is useful to "the border" or sectarian groupings within a society, as is shown by the writings of John Wyclif and Jan Hus.

Twelfth, enforcement of law against bribes has nearly always been a function of prosecutorial discretion. Prosecutions for bribery have been depended on motivations distinct from the desire to punish the bribe. The watershed for widespread federal prosecution of bribery occurred in the 1960s.

Whatever social causes account for it, at this time the pursuit of bribery has become a national enterprise in the United States. Watergate is the consequence not the cause of this phenomenon. In the Orwelian prophecy sexual puritarism is the rule enforced by electronics. In the actual America it is the purity of political reciprocities that is enforced by wire-taps, tape recordings, and television cameras.

Thirteenth, the commonest sanctions against bribes are moral, the invocation of guilt before God and shame before society; guilt and shame being equally relied on. Political sanctions, repudiation at the polls, forced resignation from office, loss of promotion—are frequently invoked.

Sanctions prescribed by law are more often indirect than direct—not the crime of bribery itself, but a related offence is usually punished until very recent times application of direct criminal sanctions to highly placed bribe-takers was rare.

Fourteenth, prosecutors, politicians, and journalists are those most attentive to contemporary corruption. Academics, lawyers, anthropologists, psycho-analysts, and theologians have had little to say. Political scientists and sociologists, intent on understanding the function of social practices, sometimes give little weight to the moral impact of corruption.

Biographers and historians, despite a tendency at times to act as advocates or apologists, give a kind of secular last judgement on the corrupt. Those who have most powerfully articulated the anti-bribery ethic are the matters of Western literature—above all Chaucer, Dante and Shakespeare.

Fifteenth, the material injury bribers and bribees inflict is often undemonstrable. Their actions always subvert the trust that accompanies public office and distinguishes office from power. For jews, Christians, for those who share their moral heritage, the bribe is not a morally neutral concept.

Writing at this interesting time in the history of the bribe, I venture a prediction that is a projection of my values. That will come at the end. History itself is not prediction but the selection of significant actions, Words, and characters to be remembered— drama more than process.

"Remember! Remember! Remember!— "Burke's incantation after his prosecution of Warren Hastings had ended in defeat. If all that is collected here survives in memory, this account has been worth making.

Besides, it would appear that bourgeoning bribery and corruption is a monster which has raised its head high above everything traversing capitalist, socialist and developing societies. It has coloured and conditioned different sections of society differently. Some enjoy the bonanza of this practice and wallow in rich vivaciously. Some taste its bite absorbingly, but disseminate it further sporadically.

A large chunk of people are hard hit by this awesome trouble, captivated in helpless state of affairs and unable to wallope it. In developing countries particularly with the unfolding of development forces and processes, corruption has not been slighted but beefed up and proliferated airily.

Such a societal menace can hardly gounnoticed by any mundane observer. Every thinking mind is fully conscious of the manner it is eating the very vitals of our society. But few have the courage of discussing it publically, much less to raise a plea to curb it.

Until recently, even the intellectuals preferred to maintain studious silence over it. If at any time, this issue was raised, it would be laughed away, dubbing it as global phenomenon. Happily, that situation is no more. People have now begun to discuss it in public and apply their mind how this menace be curbed.

To tackle a societal problem of this type, it is essential that it is examined at three levels-causational, dimensional and remedial. For an insight into the causes that foment it and the different forms it assumes can alone help the society build suitable strategies for its eradication.

The genesis of corruption in such unhealthy social institutions as dowry, consumerism, unemployment and the like could be faced. It may be argued that corruption and the forces which give rise to corruption are not always to be located in the administrative, political and economic institutions and processes.

There are several aspects of our society and several shortcomings of our social structure, attitudes and value systems which provide an impetus to corruption. Political pitfalls, economic failures and administrative loopholes have only worsened the situation.

One would lament that even though remarkable economic growth has taken place over the years, it has had little impact on poverty and unemployment. Instead, inflation and prices have marked an unprecedented escalation which, in turn, has inducted corruption into the system.

However, this ugly phenomenon is attributed to such political factors as the centralisation of power, election process, the practice of doling out fat donations to political parties and, above all, to our failure to develop a suitable work ethics.

Further, it is construed that corruption emanates from the unholy alliance of the politicians, bureaucracy and business. With power as the primary objective of the politician and cultivation of corruption is a logical consequence. From the Marxian perspective, it is held that the capitalistic order of our society is exclusively responsible for all social ills, including corruption.

Not only this but is also considered that the superimposition of rational-legal order (through the instrumentality of the constitution) over a hierarchically structured traditional order created a baffling situation of quality and loyalty for everyone in the country out of this consensus emerged the phenomenon of corruption. A social system which was so used to traditional authority, in it's oriental mode of existence, was clawed with rational-legal authority.

Such a superimposition . . . produced dual loyalties for the supposed custodians of constitutional authority. A machinery groomed in reverential, ceremonial and status ordered conduct could hardly fit in the demands of the impersonal order . . . under the circumstances, it required strong courage of conviction to hold on to the spirit of democracy and constitution of India.

Only a handful could do so, the rest resolved the conflict by subjugating the rational-legal to traditional hierarchical regime. The functionaries of the system started operating as feudal lords paying and receiving tributes.

Whatever may be the cause, the fact remains that corruption has assumed the form of a malignant cancer, and is very swiftly permeating every sphere, every layer of society and is capable of paralysing every organ, rather the very cell of the body social.

It has already sufficiently punctured and extremely hampered the process of economic growth and development. Starting from the political boss to the lowest level of bureaucratic functionary, none seems to be either an exception or immune from its evil effects.

It is lamented that corruption of all sorts has permeated our societal fabric to such an extent that we now have a parallel economy, a parallel state and . . . a parallel morality. Helpless spectators as we are we disgustingly observe that corruption, rather than being exception, seems to be the rule—a way of life which no longer even startles us.

Highlighting the nature of corruption, people consider that corruption has the nature of a malady which is at once individual and social. As an individual malady, it takes the form of loss of sense of duty and of faith in honest individual effort. As a social malady, it appears as institutional decay and chaos which together make for authoritarianism, rendering it more acceptable.

There is hardly an aspect of our life where corruption may not have spread its tentacles. Politics, economy, administration, business and day-to-day social dealings apart, it has engulfed our value-pattern even.

In this context, it is observed that if a few years back some one were to grease the palm of the other he would do so in a highly secret manner. But today the moral qualms of the people are not hurt in any way. Corruption is openly practiced and it would not be an exaggeration to remark here that our morality has degenerated to such a low ebb that people have begun to take pride in boastfully telling their friends and relatives that even if their salaries might be meagre they have many other sources of income to enable them lead an affluent life.

To further attest this fact it is rightly pointed out that what was a crime earlier became a norm. In fact, the trouble is that everyone is bitten by the bug to become rich overnight. To achieve his ambition, one does not mind employing any type of means-fair or foul. The old philosophy of noble means for noble ends is contemptuously set aside by our youngmen and young women. Obviously, when legitimate means fail to answer our needs (as they invariably do) the illegitimate means are resorted to without any compunction. The net result is corruption.

The most deplorable aspect of this appalling situation is that even teachers and doctors-those who shape the man and those who save him from disease and death-have also gone corrupt. It is found that teachers and academics inflate markets and grades, purchase positions and awards for their wards, miss classes and cook research materials. Similarly, doctors and chemists use inferior and sub-standard medicines, charge high fees, and prescribe costly medicines for ordinary ailments. The adverse effects of such corrupt practices may not be measurable in tangible terms, but qualitatively speaking, they are even worse than accepting bribes in grant of a licence or loan.

Now the question is how to cure this malady. The country is frantically looking forward to some remedy which may help it secure a good riddance. For, it has already eaten the very vitals of the system. God alone knows where corruption will ultimately drive us, of course, it is felt that education (as conceived by Plato) the panacea for this and other allied ills is because education, besides emphasising and striking a proper balance among the rational, physical and appetitive aspects of one's personality, seeks to imbibe in the individual compassion, selflessness and devotion into others. When an individual is trained in that manner, such ghastly maladies as corruption would not touch his soul.

It was not long ago that hundreds of our youngmen embraced gallows for the sake of their motherland. They were imbued by the high spirit of patriotism and selfless devotion. That spirit sustained itself even after the Independence as is manifest in glorious accounts (as they, then, dropped in tens, if not in hundreds) of people engaging themselves in nation-building activities and making lavish contribution of money and labour under the aegis of the National Community Development Programme.

Unfortunately, we could not sustain that spirit, perhaps for the reason that large amounts of money that were generated for development and their ready availability to the bureaucracy at all levels, fomented in every mind a propensity to corner a part of those funds. That contagion spread like a wild fire, engulfing the whole society in no time. Now, it is too late to restore that selfless spirit of the by-gone days. No amount of sermons or appeals to the conscience of the people can help improve the situation.

Even reforms in the educational system would be of little avail, partly for the reason that these would not have immediate remedial impact on the too perverted minds, and partly for the reason that they would lack the gnawing effect of the sharp teeth. The grim situation as it is, requires nothing but drastic measures to overcome it. Unless imaginatively-conceived penal measures are devised and (more importantly) they are strictly and objectively enforced, corruption is not going to spare the nation.

The situation calls for two types of measures—long term and short term. The long term measures should include, besides suitable improvements in the educational system, changes in the socio-political order of the nation. As for the educational system, we shall have to think somewhat in more conventional terms.

One fact is quite evident that our educational system neither caters to the day-to-day needs of the society nor does it aim at refining the personality of the man. Despite numerous improvements that we have effected in it since the dawn of Independence, we could not rescue the system from its original moorings. It continues to groom our boys and girls in the old fashion of the clerical world and pays but little attention to equipping them with those modern tools and techniques which may help them effectively tackle their societal problems and earn their bread.

Instead, the knowledge that they acquire is far from practical, with the result that they inflate the ranks of the unemployed. Those of them who have money and other means (obviously their number is very small) get jobs more through underhand means and less through their competence. This system, thus, contributes to the spread of corruption.

The other facet of the educational system is the development of the human personality. This aspect is as much poorly taken care of by this system as the former aspect is. So long as we as a nation do not develop a consensus on the types of values that we should inculcate in our future generations (unfortunately the older consensus based on secularism and nationalism has recently received a serious jolt at the hands of the sectarian, communal and pseudo-nationalist forces) and create the requisite political will not only to socialise the progeny in these values but also to develop and strengthen the educational system through the instrumentality of which socialisation is to be effected—our boys and girls would continue to suffer the sense of alienation and go astray.

Long-term measures also need to be planned with a view to reordering our social system. It makes a sad commentary on our performance that even after four decades of scientific planning we have not been able to banish from amidst us poverty, disease and, above all, illiteracy, though they occupied a top place in our order of national priorities.

Some of the authors hold the political system responsible for this poor performance and even allude to some of its weaknesses to the electoral process; one would also point to the nature of the economy that we have developed over the years and lament over our failure to bring about land reforms and complains of a nexus between the politician, the bureaucrat and business. There may be many other weak spots. Some persons have gone to the extent of suggesting that we should launch the Second Republic by totally discarding the existing Constitution.

Objectively speaking, there is nothing wrong with the institutional fabric that we have woven for ourselves. If the policy has failed to achieve its goals the main reason is that we have not been able to work these institutions properly. Again, the trouble was that when we launched the Republic the rank and file of our populace was both poor and illiterate and, hence, lacked that general intelligence and awareness which exacts from the democratically elected rulers both responsiveness and responsibility. (It may be underlined that there was also not available to us any other option, much less to withhold the introduction of the democratic system till that uncertain day when complete literacy is achieved).

We had hoped that the educated among us, though smaller in number, would help bring about mass literacy and that the growingly literate and economically-improved masses would shape out into responsible citizens, capable of effectively shouldering the burden of democratic responsibilities. Unfortunately, all our hopes were belied. That intelligentsia whom we entrusted the reins of power, betrayed us. Instead of helping their brethren improve their lot, they developed a vested interest in the very illiteracy ad poverty of the latter.

Under such circumstances, we could not expect a performance better than what it is today. If things are to be improved, we must strive hard to banish illiteracy, poverty and disease from amidst the mass of the population. Once the common man becomes an articulate citizen, he would not let the rulers behave the manner they do today and would also not allow his fellow-beings indulge in corrupt practices. The whole socio-political life of the nation would mark a radical improvement. The social order would, then, get automatically reordered.

These long-term measures re good and steps to introduce these measures are urgently called for. But, at the same time, measures of a short-term nature also need to be taken so that some immediate relief from widespread corruption is secured to the common man. Some of the authors have come out with a few worthwhile suggestions.

Holding the public servants responsible for much of this mischief (corruption), the people plead for tightening of the noose over them. They want that there should be instituted a proper system of punishment and reward for them and also that merit should have an edge over seniority in-so-far-as promotion from one rank to another is concerned.

Further, the slant in laws towards the employees be removed and their trade union activities be curbed, and above all, strikes among them be banned. But before such drastic measure are taken, it must also be ensured that due interests of the civil servants and other workers are adequately protected.

In this respect, it is desired to set up a mechanism which may take care of such service matters as automatic periodic revision of the pay structure for all categories of civil servants and their dearness, house rent and other allied allowances; their postings, transfers and promotions (without the least interference of the politicians).

Further, the institution of consultative committees should be strengthened so that the genuine grievances of the individual civil servants are suitably redressed. In this way, the obstructionist role of the trade unions is drastically curtailed. It is also suggested by him that there should be evolved a nation-wide consensus among all political parties that they would not interfere in the selection, postings transfers, promotions and all such interests of the civil servants.

Once the services cease to be pampered, as they are now and the state resumes to itself the onerous responsibility of boldly pulling up the recalcitrant employees, much of the corruption that is prevalent today, will automatically vanish.

Besides we seek to tackle the problem by gearing up the economy and curbing the menace of black money. The measures are also suggested for extension of public distribution system, realistic price policy designed to ensure good return for the expanded public sector output, redefining the role of public and private sectors, improvement in tax laws and their administration, detection of real estate in Benami and prevention of speculative deals in real estate, thereby, checking the production and proliferation of black money, and, above all, framing a suitable development strategy.

Concludingly, it may be observed that a problem of this type that has created a niche for itself in almost every heart cannot be tackled by means of coercion. This method, if applied forcefully, may yield temporary results. But the moment some relaxation is shown this demon would raise its head again.

The best way to fight out this problem is to wage the battle in the minds and brains of the people. They need to be convinced of the desirability to eradicate it. However, it is pointed out that in politics and government, as elsewhere, the most meaningful sanctions are internal, i.e., the sanctions of character, conscience and sense of duty. Only they can enable man to live a consistent and meaningful life in a rapidly changing society.

However, it is admitted that morality and ethics account as the most basic issue of life on which actions are judged and evaluated to be right or wrong. Ethical standards have undergone a change with a passage of time and needs to be redefined in the changed environment as applicable to government and administration. To surmount the catastrophic retribution of corruption, external sanctions can be anti-dote to it but are no substitute for internal sanctions which can go far to get rid of this malady.

However, it is admitted that corruption eventuates into erosion of public morality and ethical standards of individual and group behaviour. Viewing corruption as a compensation for a service rendered in an illegal manner or form, certain factors like process of development, competition among different groups to gain ascendancy in power, social evils and institutions and consumerism add to corruption in society.

We regard corruption as individual and social malady. To enervate it, we should understand the nature of syndrome wherein it flourishes. Capitalism eventuates prosperity and sickness which breeds corruption exploitation and bureaucratization.

In India, the rise of capitalism has been via colonisation which explicates the specific nature and intensity of our problem of corruption. Limited resource but great competition, great poverty but high aspirations, high politicisation but weak influence of public opinion, and weakly neat organisation but powerful leaders cause the acute corruption in our society.

If corruption is embodied in capitalist setting, suppression and wreackage of capitalism becomes inevitable to get rid of the maladies. The autonomy of the individual flowing from the contradiction of capitalism and the organisation of those who have nothing to lose can play the pertinent and called for role here.

Focalising on electioneering, it is construed that populism is practised blatantly to harness electoral victory at the polls by political leaders largely at the cost of moral redemption. Promises to remove poverty, invoking castes bias in the people notwithstanding our secularism, promising employment to the weaker sections on caste basis (i.e. Mandal Commission) and waiving loans (i.e. Tau's slogan) casting down the whole economic balance of the nation are all example of promises made strakly for appeasing sections of populace and enlarging the units of the vote bank. Implicitly, such like promises obstruct and upset the ecological balance of the Indian polity. If the means are bad, can the end be good? One could visibly ask.

Taking corruption as a social reality it is a considered as the tool kit of economics. The 'socialist pattern' of society and the 'traditional authority' produced not Boeke's dualism in India but dual loyalties for the supposed custodian of constitutional authority. The functionaries of the system started operating as feudal lords interpreting, operating and restating the 'rules of the game' in a triumph and manner to favour the predecided party. In nutshell, corruption is utilisation of public organs for private ends.

Earlier, the working of corruption is amplified by taking three situations :

(a) the case of production and administrative permission;

(b) the story of 'selection' and 'suitability' and

(c) making purchases.

Taking cognizance of the derivative inference of all this, the emergence of the corruption pool deity—'Black Money' as the charismatic authority. How can we have Alternative Societal Model devoid of corruption? This remains visibly an open question here. To evolve management strategies to corner corruption in society, we have to develop an integrative perspective. The nature of policy and its aims, crisis of character in it, corruption from political perspective today (i.e. What is not corruption?) and disparity cultivating development path constitute the warp and woof of this perspective.

Axiomatically, the needs of ordinary people are dealt with at the lower rung of administration and it is at this level that corruption looms large and abnormal stage of affairs exists. Accounting for this malady, factors like : inefficiency of administrative reforms, unholy alliance of rich farmers and political elite, buregoning trade unions and associations of workers, growth of bureaucracy as a pressure group and lack of rewards and punishment appears vividly causative. For lack of political will, health environment is considerably wanting for proper functioning of the administration. To surmount this menace and disarray at lower level of administration it is suggested that certain remedial device as, rewards and punishment, curbing the ostentatious living of government officials, urgency in dealing with punitive actions, scrapping the system of promotion by seniority, and 'hire and fire' technique be practiced as well.

Accounting corruption an 'entire family of malpractice, unethical, unlawful an unfair dealing in broad sense whereas 'the acceptance of illegal gratification' in restricted sense, need to probe legal framework and keep into historical perspective. The different forms of corruption, its causes, and administrative set-up be designed for curbing corrupt practices constitute the componental ingredients of this study.

Assessing the impact of Indian planning and the development strategies on overall economic and social growth with equality, we find that it accentuates on the generation of black sector (i.e. black money as tainted money) in India. Taking the bull by its horn, certain devices be designed to achieve overall development emasculating the parallel economy which has almost jeopardised the very foundation of Indian society.

Certain measures, viz extension of public distribution system to curb mass consumption good return for the expanded public sector output, redefining the role of public and private sectors improvements in tax laws and their administration, detection of real estate in '*Benami*' and prevention of speculative deals in real estate will go a long way in checking the production and proliferation of black income in the short-run, but all these problems as poverty, unemployment, inflation and black sectors are inter-related and have to be solved simultaneously by framing a suitable development strategy.

The prevailing malady can be solved only by purging income and wealth differentials among the larger sections of the society. Such a drastic change is not easy to achieve owing to influential vested interest but must be achieved to devolve economic independence to the millions of people who are starving and living below poverty line in India.

As regards corruption in policy formulation and implementation : The Question of Land Reforms in India is vital and it follows Nye's definition of corruption, of course, with slight modifications asserting it as much political behaviour of political elite and public official to subvert the process of land legislations and their implementation to keep theirs and their relatives land intact.

To comprehend corruption appropriately in Indian society, an understanding of the nature of Indian state and its pattern of development is assumed imperative. As a large chunk of Indian people depends on agriculture, the relevance and significance of land reforms is undeniable.

Land reforms were designed to achieve 'the idea of land to the tiller' traversing through abolition of Zamindari, tenancy reforms a ceiling on land holdings. Corruption in policy formulation and policy implementation accounts for the dismal and abominable performance of land reform measures. The idea of 'land to the tiller' remains an unfulfilled goal and the benefits accuring to the landless labourers and tenants did not and could not materialise as such.

Viewing corruption as impairment of integrity, virtue or moral principles and a departure from honesty, integrity or fair dealing, Jaswal and Jaswal hassle about its sociological and legal dimensions. The sociological dimensions are illustrated by dowry problem, seeking employment and electoral system in democracy.

In legal dimensions, provisions to deal with corrupt public servants more effectively in the Indian Penal Code 1860, the Prevention of Corruption Act, 1947 and 1988 are highlighted to surmount corruption.

The provisions of these Acts and their implementation can be anti-dote to corruption in some ways, but they are no surrogate to character building of people to create a good social milieu. However, the trade unions can play a role in combating corruption and injustice in the different countries, and it is considered that trade unions, the interaction of political parties, and public can heat circumspect corruption.

Regarding corruption 'as perversion of integrity by bribery or favour' it is asserted that political theory must deal with ideals. For that Plato's Republic and Charles Dickens' Hard Time should be the guidelines. Not preaching but practising honestly can set on an example for educating others in the society to abjure corrupt practices.

Witnessing the deteriorating standards in politics and administration everyday into the prevalent ethical standards of the elected representatives, political parties, ministers, *vis-a-vis* civil servants. Regarding ingredients of good administration, we should chalk out detailed essentials to rehabilitate the practice of administrative ethics among administrators and politicians viz faith and determination infusing ethics into politics, practice of administrative ethics, ethical commitment to the ideals, effective involvement of the public, character building, emphasis on education and study and practice of true religion.

In fact, we should regard 'political morality' and 'administrative morality' as inter-linked. The enhanced cost of electioneering has engendered and augmented political corruption. We should consider certain measures to curtail political corruption, to prop up administrative efficiency which may mitigate administrators corruption as well.

Considering corruption as a complex phenomenon, we should also probe it from an economic point of view. Dwelling upon a theoretical explanation of corruption in the first instance, we should design certain remedial measures to emasculate and wipe out the malady of corruption from society.

PART ONE:
INTERNATIONAL SCENARIO

1

BOND OF RECIPROCITY

Christianity reads on a transition carried out between God and the Son of God which theology labelled a term in Roman Civilization often used to mean pay off to a judge to escape punishment.

Reciprocity is, in any society, a rule of life, and in some societies atleast it is the rule of life. In a variety of archaic communities, as anthropologists have shown, relations with peaceful strangers are established by an exchange whose essential function is to oblige the offence.

The recipient is bound by receiving. If he does not accept what is offered, he is hostile. If he does not respond after accepting, he is hostile. The requirement of acceptance and reciprocation make exchange risky. Offerings are, however, a necessary way of creating relationships beyond kinfolk and tribe.[1]

That bribery is wrong, that a bribe must distort judgement—assumptions which may seem too obvious to need justification—are not self-evident. Bribery is an act distinguished from other reciprocities only if it is socially identified and socially condemned.

The gods themselves must be approached with offerings that they may be changed from potential enemies to allies. Powerful strangers are to be turned into friends by the creation of family connections or by the acceptance of a present.

Officials are approached with offerings like everyone else. Fault lies not with the giver but with the non-reciprocator.

In an Egyptian story, circa 2000 B.C., a peasant, Khun-Anup, is robbed of his cattle. He seeks redress from Rensi, the chief steward of the pharaoh, and reminds him, "You are the father of the orphan, the husband of the widow, the brother of the divorcee, the apron of him that is motherless." But the pharaoh determines to test the peasant. At his order, Rensi has Khun-Anup beaten.

The peasant persists: "Do Justice for the sake of the Lord of Justice, the justice of whose justice exists. He is again thrashed. The ninth time, the pharaoh has Rensi Judge in his perseverence is rewarded, the appeal to help the powerless is acknowledged. The modern title of the story, "The Protests of the Eloquent Peasant," catches Khun-Anup's dependence on the rhetoric which sets a non-reciprocal standard for the Judge".

The most famous lawgiver of antiquity, Hammurabi, makes it the recommendation of his decrees for Babylon that they are issued so that "the strong might not oppress the weak and that justice might be dealt with the orphan and the widow". The theme by 1700 B.C. is familiar. The claim to protect the help-less goes with the staff of royal authority. The ruler's claim depends on divine inspiration. Hammurabi legislates "by the order of Shamash, the great judge of heaven and earth."

There is, however, a reciprocal relation. It is with the god. The poor are the god's standing. He has, in effect, allotted them his own share. The relation is most succinctly stated, centuries later than Urukagina, in the words of the Wisdom literature of Israel.

He who oppresses the poor insults his Maker;
He who is generous to the needy honours him.

The norm of reciprocity is not abandoned. There is a dis-placement. The ruler's reward is to be from on high, not from the particular poor man he aids.

Every litigant is in a sense a poor, man, subject to being outbid by an unscrupulous adversary. Special solicitude for the poor man flows into a second current of thought, the exalta-tion of objective justice.

Scales had been invented by 3000 B.C., a spendid symbol of objective judgement, once turned to this use. Near the end of the third millennium, between 2200 and 2050, tomb writings refer to "that balance of Re, in which he weighs *Me-at*." Re is the sun god, Ma-at is "Order", "Right", "Truth" "Justice". The scales in which Re weighs truth is now seen as the instrument of determining truth, the means of giving judgement.

From this series it may be learned that the judgement seeker does not come empty-handed nor seek access to the court without gifts, nor does he fail in thankfulness. Reciprocity between judge and judged has not been totally transformed.

The scales' peculiar-conversion of reciprocity into an objective binary form nonetheless remains. In the judgement Hall, at the most decisive moment in a man's life, he does not make an offering to those who weigh him.

Hammurabi does set out a penalty for a judge who changes his decision—he is to be fined, disgraced, and barred from future services. Hammurabi's English editors ask why a judge should change his mind and give one obvious answer: he has been bribed to reverse himself.

Making the assumption that of all possible bribes only this kind of retroactive bribery has been singled out for punishment, they read Hammurabi as threatening permanent retirement to judges bribed to reverse themselves. They entitle this section of the laws of Babylon, "The Corrupt Judge".

Their interpretation is ethnocentrically Western. It overlooks the horror Hammurabi must have had of sheer inconstancy. In the ancient Near East, stability is the mark of a god's decision-making. Inconstancy undermines the divinity surrounding Judgement. The god Nunamnir, in a hymn of Ur-Nammu, speaks of his "life-giving commands and decisions" as "unalterable".

It is the mark of his divinity. For the Egyptians a chief characteristic of Ma-at is immutability. In a Shamash hymn from the library of Ashur-banipal, the god giving a verdict is celebrated because "your manifest utterance may not be changed". Among the Hebrews, Samuel tells the discarded Saul.

> *"God who is the Splendor of Israel does not deceive or change his mind; he is not a man that he should change his mind".* (1 sm 15:29)

In the background of Hammurabi's legislation, there may be judges like Kushshiharbe, the mayor of Nuzi who took 'tatu' and did not reciprocate. A judge who delivers a decision and then changes his mind may be a judge who receives a present, gives the expected verdict, and then reneges. Legislation that punishes such a judge can only confirm a custom of gift-giving, not condemn it.

Hammurabi's editors comment that there is no "known instance of the bribery of a Babylonian judge in legal documents, although there can be little doubt that it frequently occurred; that but Assyrian religious texts imply that it was known when they assert that Samas punishes the judge who accepts a bribe."

The question this comment raises is, by whose standards is bribery determined? If the laws neither define nor punish bribe-taking, what act constituted the crime?" A letter of Hammurabi does read :

"Summan-la-ilu has reported saying an offering (tatu) is present in Durguguru and the man who took the offering and the witness who has knowledge of these matters is there.

(Hammurabi sends an officer to conduct an examination and instructs him:) If an offering is present, set a seal on the money or whatever is offering (indecipherable) and cause it to be brought. And the men who took the offering and the witness who had knowledge shall you send to me.

Each time a form of *'tatu'* appears in this passage it could be translated "bribe". Doing so, a modern translator adds, "From this letter it seems that Hammurabi was anxious to remove corruption from his officials.

Moreover, the successful recovery of any bribe which had been given tended to fill the royal coffers, as we may see from the fact that instructions are given for the bribe to be confiscated and dispatched under seal."[2]

Was it given to influence official conduct? We do not know.

Central to any allegation of bribery of a judge or royal officer would be an indication of the recipient's rank and function. Here the recipient is vaguely a "man" or "men".

The recipients might well have been bribed as witnesses. Nothing shows that they were officials. Nor is it entirely clear that Hammurabi is confiscating the offering to his own advantage; he could be asking for the evidence.

Only by reading in a set of Western assumptions about bribery and proper ways of combating it can, it be concluded that a bribe to an official is meant. If this conclusion should be correct, Hammurabi's investigation is the first known inquiry into bribe-taking; but the conclusion is uncertain.

To move from seventeenth-century Babylon to fifteenth-century Egypt, not only is impartiality exalted, but specifically the rejection by a judge of an offering from a petitioner is upheld as an ideal: the vizier Rekh-Mi-Re in the autobiographical eulogy of himself declares, "I did not turn my brow for the sake of reward (feqa)." In this context, there can be no doubt that an offering to a high official is regarded as undesirable, Rekh-Mi-Re boasts that he has not accepted one."[3]

"He goes on to ask the judges how they can judge others while there is one among you committing a crime against justice" He, then, remits an obligation of members of the official staff to pay the pharaoh a percentage of their income. After this apparently administrative detail; affecting compensation, he continues: "Now, as for any official or any priest of whom it shall be heard.

'He sits among the official staff appointed for judgement to execute judgement, and he commits a crime against justice therein,' it shall be against him a capital crime. "Taking reward from one litigant and not hearing his adversary is inferably the "crime against justice."

Arguably, it is also the "crime against justice" for which he provides capital punishment. If this interpretation is correct, Horemheb's Edict is the first law with a secular penalty for a form of bribe-taking.[4]

The ideal excluding offerings that influence judgement is

clearly stated of the Sun-god who is hailed as He who "places the gods in their places," who is "eternal God, Judge." This judge protects the orphan and "does not put out his hand to the mighty". This "just judge takes no reward." The god's rejection of reward is fused with his function of protecting the poor.

Another eulogy of the god Amon-Re, circa 1230 B.C., declared that he, "the first to be King, the God of the primeval time, the Vizier of the poor, takes no reward from the guilty, and speaks not to him who brings testimony and looks not at him who promises." Amon Re's impartiality is admirable.

That he takes no reward "from the guilty" states a qualification probably understood in other Egyptian texts even when it is not stated only the reward that perverts justice, only the gift that distorts the decision is deplored, no absolute ban on offerings is intended.[5]

Egyptian wisdom literature, six centuries later, contains the same message in the form of exhortation to the judge himself. "The Instruction of Amen-Em-Opet" (circa 650-550) reads :

> *Give not your consideration only to him clothed in white,*
> *Nor give consideration to him that is unkept,*
> *Do not accept the reward of a powerful man,*
> *Nor oppress for him the disabled.*

The ideal of impartiality continues to be unmistakably linked to the injunction against receiving reward. No enforcement mechanism has been developed.

That the god of justice will punish the one who gives reward is neither stated nor implicit. The focus of exhortation on the judge not the litigant. It is no doubt implicit but it is not said, that the god will punish the judge who takes reward to do injustice.

In the style of Babylonian omens, this "Advice to a Prince" sets out an event and what will follow that even as its necessary consequence. Taking an offering that produces an unjust criminal judgement is followed by disaster, divinely produced.

Looking back at the fall of Babylon, a prophet of Eshaddon declares :

> *They were oppressing the poor and putting them in the power of the mighty. There was oppression and acceptance of offerings within the city. Daily, senselessly, they were robbing each other's property." Retroactively, the prophet sees that catastrophe followed a course of oppressive gift-taking."*[6]

Supernatural sanction against the whole class of unjust judges is invoked in a hymn to the sun-god Shamash, also in the library of Ashurbanipal. Shamash is celebrated as he watches over all the people of the world, judging the good and the wicked, heaven and earth, and condemning, among others, these evildoers :

> *The unrighteous judge thou does make to see chains,*
> *The receiver of an offering (tatu) who perverts-thou does make to bear punishment.*
> *The non-receiver of an offering, the raiser-up of the badge of the poor man, is well-pleasing to Shamash, lengthens his life.*
> *The careful judge who pronounces a judgement of righteousness shall prepare a palace—the abode of princes his dwelling.*

Not his country but the judge himself is threatened with supernatural punishment if he receives a gift that perverts his judgement. No more specific retribution exists in the judicial literature of the age.[7]

To summarize : from the fifteenth century B.C. on, there has been a concept that could be rendered in English as "Bribe", the concept of a gift that perverts judgement. It is the hieroglyph fk 3 (feqa) in Egypt. Its Mesopotamian counterparts are *kat-ra* and *tâtu* as these words are used in the contexts quoted above.

The problem in translating any of these terms as 'bribe' is that the ambiguity of the original words is resolved into a clear unambiguous meaning. Tatu, for example, is used for the gifts made by those complaining about Kushshiharbe—the complainants are not saying they gave bribes to pervert his judgement.

The parallel term for the present given to Ashur-aba-iddina is *sulmanum* a word etymologically connected with *sulmanum*, health. Originally a sulmanum meant a present brought by a guest to wish health to his host; it came to apply to any to any offering brought by one in a role subordinate to the receiver. Such offerings are often customary, acceptable, praiseworthy in the eyes of the society in which they are tendered. *Feqa* and *tatu* are analogous—they are, generically, the offerings of subordinates; a negative sense attaches only by context.

The preserve the ambiguity of *feqa*, *kat-ra*, and *tatu* in translation, it is necessary to use terms like 'reward' or 'offering' which often have positive meanings but which can be used ironically to mean somethings improper.

The purely negative terms, 'bribe', 'briber', 'bribery', 'corrupt', and 'corruption' have no verbal counterparts in the ancient Near East. At the same time the concept of impartial judgement and the concept of a subordinate's offering which should be rejected by a judge have been formed. The ideal of impartiality and rhetoric supporting the ideal do exist in Egypt, Assyria and Babylon.[8]

The Bribe in the Bible, neither the Book of the Dead nor a pharaoh's edict nor a vizier's tomb nor Sumerian stele nor Babylonian wisdom furnished the ideas that were to provide recurrent inspiration and directions in later history.

The groupings, the tentative lunges forward, the high rhetoric of Near Eastern literature would have been so many broken shards if the main concepts had not been expressed in Hebrew Scripture.

The Hebrew term that functions in context like *feqa* and *tatu* to express a disapproved payment is shohadh, here translated ambiguously as 'offering'. The first specific criticism of shohadh in a judicial context appears directed at witnesses rather than judges. In the 'Code of the Covenant', circa ninth century B.C., God speaks to Moses on Mount Sinai and after setting out the Ten Commandments gives further instructions for Israel. He ordains :

You shall not spread a baseless rumor.
You shall not make common cause with a wicked man by giving malicious evidence.
You shall not be led into wrong-doing by the majority, nor, when you give evidence in a lawsuit, shall you side with the majority to pervert justice; nor shall you favour the poor man in his suit ......
You shall not deprive the poorman of justice in his suit. Avoid all lies, and do not cause the death of the innocent and the guiltless; for I the Lord will never acquit the guilty. You shall not take shohadh, which makes the clear-eyed blind and the word of the just crooked.

(Ex 23 : 1-3. 6-8)

While the text could be applied to judges, the commands focus on those who make accusation or offer evidence. The Lord is the judge—'I will never acquit the guilty'. Witnesses before the judge, Israelites, are not to lie or take shohadh to slant their testimony.

A story independent of the events on Sinai but eventually incorporated into the narrative of Exodus shows Moses receiving the advice of his father-in-law, Jethro, in appointing judges. Jethro tells him to make leaders or judges those 'who hate loot' (beytza) (Ex 18:21). The term employed is too imprecise to say whether Jethro excluded all reward or merely unusual and exorbitant profit. Exodus contains no distinct condemnation of judges who are willing offerees.

Offerings to the judges of Israel are attacked in the mid-eighth century B.C. when prophets speak out against offerings to God himself.

The rulers have turned 'justice itself into poison' (Am 6:12). The Lord rejects what they offer :

I hate, I spurn your pilgrim feasts;
I will not delight in your sacred ceremonies.
When you present your sacrifices and offerings, I will not accept them, nor look of the buffaloes of your share-offerings

Spare me the sound of your songs.
I cannot endure the music of your lutes.
Let justice roll on like a river and righteousness
like an ever-flowing stream. (AM 5: 21-24)

God 'repudiates the high and mighty . . . . but allows the just claims of the poor and suffering' (Jb 36:5-6). Job must reform himself when he acts as a judge.

In that great work of old age, *The Laws*, Plato says that the contention 'that the gods when they receive gifts can be appeased by the entreaty of wrong-doers is one that no one should admit, and we must try to refute it by every means in our power'. A little later, specifying the kinds of impiety to be punished by the state he classifies as impious the belief that the gods are 'appeased by entreaty'. Probably the qualification 'by wrong-doers' is again understood. The distance between divinity and men is not so ruthlessly and dramatically established as in Job.[9]

At the apex of judgement, at the center of the tradition, in response to the figure who becomes a prototype of Jesus, the Judge is incorruptible because he cannot be bound by anything he has created. Pointless to say that such a Judge does not take shohadh, pointless to qualify the teaching of Amos and Isaiah and say that the Lord rejects only the offerings of the unworthy.

Even the just life of a good man is not enough to bind Him. The bond of reciprocity is rejected, if not forever, at least so seriously that no petty bribes can restore it. At the zenith of Wisdom, *job* is an *a fortiori* statement that offerings intended to influence God are vain.

Vengeance is normally divine. Bribe-takers are among the power-holders in society: that is why they are bribed. In a modern society corporate bribers may be more powerful than the officials they bribe. In an ancient society, power and office are more likely to coincide. To bring the guilty to justice requires strong political backing for their prosecutors.

Bribery is a crime that because of its secret nature is likely to go undetected unless there is incentive to complain about it and a procedure for its discovery. There is a procedure set out in Deuteronomy for the detection and judgement of a bride suspected of unchastity (Dt. 22:13-21). Nothing is provided for the detection of an unlawful offerings.

There is no provision in the Bible that judgements obtained by offerings shall be null, so litigants are given no incentive to object to an offering made by an opponent. Nor is incentive provided for officials to investigate an offering taken by other officials

The absence of specific sanction against bribery stands out even more strongly when bribery is compared with false witnessing. The prevailing assumption of the law in the ancient Near East is that there are only facts to be determined. If the witnesses but speak the truth the facts will be evident.

The judges, agents of the divine, will declare what is manifest to them from the testimony. The fear is that the witness will not testify truthfully. In the Bible the command not to bear false witness against a neighbour is one of the Ten Commandments (Ex 20:16). In the Bible no judgements are corrupted by an offering and no judges punished for receiving one.[10]

Bribery and prostitution are both acts which it takes two to consummate. As a norm teaching what should be done, the rule against shohadh was like a norm against prostitution condemning only the prostitute. If only one can be guilty, the force of the norm is more than halved.

The rule was the more seriously undercut because it had to operate on the more powerful party in the transaction while the less powerful was left unstigmatized. The rulers of the community were asked to consider it wrong for them to receive what it was no sin in others to give.

The ancient writers made no sharp distinction between legislator and judge, but in Israel there were written laws as well as individual judgements. As they were presented to the people, the laws were pronounced by the Lord. As the Lord did not take shohadh, no gift could have influenced their formulation.

It is, however, a mistake to measure law only by the sanctions it imposes, Law is not solely addressed to the bad who must be coerced, but to the good who want to do right and to the puzzled or uninstructed who seek guidance. Without the teeth of sanctions, a rule, a norm, an ideal can both channel conduct and teach what the community expects.

Compare the normative language on sexual conduct. Not only were stories told in which sexual sins were punished, but the principal proscribed act was identified: to commit adultery (Ex 20:14). Not only was the central sin marked off by a name, but a variety of unlawful acts— intercourse with a near relative, intercourse of a man with a man, intercourse with a beast —were verbally identified (Lv 18:6); Lv 20:13; Ex 22:19).

The strength of the sexual norm was confirmed by its metaphorical employment to indicate national apostasy: disobedient Israel was an adulteress or a whore. (1s 1:21; Hos 3:1).

NOTES AND REFERENCES

1. Marcel Mauss, *The Gift*, trans. Ian Cunnison (New York : W.W. Norton, (1967) 31-45; Originally "Essai-Sur Le don", *Lannee sociologue* (1925), 13-14, 30.

2. Leonard W. King, *The Letters and Inscriptions of Hammurabi* (London: Lugac & Co., 1990) 3, 20. King's interpretation follows on p.22 *Tatu* is translated into the German for bribe in M. San Nicolo, "Bestechung," *Reallexikon der Assyriologie*, ed. Erich Abeling and Bruno Meissner (Berlin and Leipizig: Walter de Gruyter & Co., 1938) 2, 19.Kummel, "Bestechung im Alten Orient," in Schuller, Korruption 56, notes that general usage does not support such a translation, but he seems to think it supportable in the context of Hammurabi's letter.

3. ANET 213.

4. Compare "Edict of Harmhab," in James H. Breasted, *Ancient Records of Egypt 3, 31-32 (Harmhab=Horemheb) with Kurt Pfluger, "The Edict of King Harembeb, "Journal of Near Eastern Studies 5 (1946) 265. Breasted has "reward from another",* Pfluger "bribe of another." Wolfgang Helck, "'Korruption' im alten Agypten" in Schuller, *Korruption* 67, has *Geschenke* (gifts). See also Alexandre Moret, "Un procesde famille sous la XIX dynastie, "*Zeitschrift fur Agyptische Sprache und Alterthumskunde* 39 (1901) 39.

5. Ostraka-Cairo 25207, trans, Adolf Erman, "Gebete eines ungerecht Verfolgten und an-dere Ostraka aus der Konigsgrabern," *Zeitschrift fur Agyptische Sprachen* (1900) 38, 23-27 (Prayer to the Sun-god); "Praise of Amon-Re," *Papyrus*

Bologna 1094, trans, Ricardo A. Caminos, *Late Egyption Miscellanies* (London: Oxford University Press 1954) 9.

6. *Riekele* Borger, *Die Inschriften Asarhaddons Konigs von Assyrien,* Supp to vol. 9, *Archiv fur Orientforschung* (1956) 12 (Eshaddon prophet). Borger translates a form based on *Katra* (here translated as "offerings") as *Bestechung* (bribery). "Advice to a Prince" also says, "If the adviser or chief officer of the king's presence denounces them the citizens and so obtains tatu from them, at the command of Ea, king of Apsu, the adviser and chief officer will die by the sword ... "Lambert, 115. Lamabert here translates tatu as bribes where "offerings" would appear more apt; as he himself writes,"Akkadian does not distinguish between 'present' and 'bribe, *Babylonian Wisdom Literature* 320.

7. "Hymn to the Sun-God," trans, Ferris J. Stephens, ANET 388 Emendations in the translation have been made by me on the basis of discussion with Professor Anne Kilmer and consultation of Lambert, *Babylonian Wisdom Literature*, 133, I follow Lambert translating "tatu" as "present", not "bribe". Lambert goes too far in saying that only the judge who takes *tatu* and reneges is condemned by these verses. Lambert translates the lines following those on the judges as referring to investors in"unscrupulous trading missions" abroad, while Stephens translates the lines as condemning usures, making the hymn closer to Psalm 15.

8. On the etymological connection of *sulmánum* with sulman (health), see Kummel, "Bestechung" 61. An Assyrian of the later empire pointedly regrets that he knows no one at the royal court "to whom I might give an offering (sulmanum) to receive me and take up my cause,"Finkelstein, "The Middle Assyrian Sulmanu Texts" 78-79. *Feqa* is used to designate tribute paid to a conquering invader by a rebel vassal of the pharaoh, "The Piankhi Stele," in James H. Breasted, *Records of Ancient Egypt* 4, sec. 802. Akkadian kudrum is Sumerian *Kadra or kat-ra* Kummel, "Bestechung," 61.

9. Plato, The Laws (Loeb Classical Library ed. 1926) 10, 905 D and 10, 908E.

10. In an ancient chapter of the *Book of the Dead the deceased prays,* "May naught stand up to oppose at my judgment. . . nor that which is false be uttered against me before the great god," Egyptian criminal procedure as old as the third millennium focused on the witiness, requiring him to take the "Oath of the Lord" to speak truthfully and often preparing him for the oath by administering a beating. In one especially well-documented

criminal prosecution, the Tomb Robbery Cases, for example, the witnesses were regularly prepared for testimony by the administration of the oath and the bastinado. The laws of Hammurabi set out clear and strong sanctions against false accusers. See *The Book of the Dead—The Papyrus of Ani* 237-238; John A. Wilson, "The Oath in Ancient Egypt", *Journal of Near Eastern Studies* 7 (1948) 135; T. Eric Peet, *The Great Tomb Robberies of the Twentieth Egyptian Dynasty* (Oxford: Clarendon Press, 1930) 20-24; "The Code of Hammurabi" 1-4 ANET 166.

2

PREFERENCE OF THE PROFESSIONS

The concept of bribe was cast in a biblical mould Only Cato, Cicero was to say, could imagine that the Roman state resembled Plato's Republic: those who knew it realistically recognized it as "Romulus' refuse". Reciprocity abounded. Appeals to justice seemed cynical.

What election, what trial occurred without an exchange of favours? Reciprocity was nonetheless more consciously channelled and the reciprocities classified as bribes were more severely censured in Cicero's Rome than in any of the kingdoms of Egypt, Mesopotamia, or Palestine.

To put an anti-bribery ethic into practice in even a limited sphere—as opposed to announcing what it should be—required men professionally interested in the process of judging; it required a corps of men whose skill consisted in the presentation of facts and law and argument.

By Cicero's day in Rome a small corps of politician-orators existed. Professionally their work depended on the presentation of cases. Professionally they were valued highly. Next to generalship, said Cicero, the art most useful to the state was oratory, a skill that could not only check made tribunes and bend the excited mob resist largess.[1]

Whatever dodges orators might use, whatever reciprocities they might invoke, whatever corruption they might connive in, their reliance in the exercise of their profession could not be on cash, for then the courts would be a mere extension of the markets, open to any trader. As courts would be a mere extension of the markets, open to any trader. As orators, the advocates needed a forum in which their words counted as much as, or may be more than money. Professionally, if they were not to be pimps for the judges or panders for their clients, they had to discountenance bribes.

Greek city-states preceded Rome in the use of a political forum in which a charge of bribe-taking was relevant.[2] Professional legal skills were more developed in Rome. Thanks to Cicero's public speeches and private letters, the Roman cases are better documented; and the Roman examples and formulations were of a far greater influence in the subsequent development in the west.

The Staining of Staienus: In 74 B.C. Marcus Tullius Cicero—then thirty two a highly nervous young man with only a half dozen years of practice-was asked by country folk in the provincial town of Larinum to undertake the defense of one Fabricius, charged with complicity in at tempted murder. The trial itself was to be in Rome, a contest between two powerful knights from the provinces who had come to hate each other. The initiator of the proceeding was Aulus Cluentius Habitus and the principal defendant was his stepfather, Statius Albius Oppiancus, to whom he related as Hamlet did to his mother's husband.[3]

The prosecution's case was this: Oppiancus stood to gain a large legacy from his wife if her son, Cluentius, died before she did. Moved by greed, Oppianicus planned to poison him. He contacted Fabricius, a kind of thug-for-hire. Fabricius put to work his freedom, Scamander, and Scamander in turn got in touch with a slave who worked for Cluentius' physician.

Scamander offered the slace a sum of money to do the job. Scamander providing the poison. The slave, however, was honest and reported Scamander's offer to the doctor and Cluentius. They instructed him to pretend to go along. Scamander was captured as he delivered the poison and a sealed packet of money to the slave'.[4]

Publius Cannutius, the prosecutor, was retained—in accordance with Roman usage—by Cluentius himself. Cicero, never a man to under-estimate himself, rated C annutius extraordinarily high —'my equal'.[5] Cannutius proceeded cannily, trying the defendants one at a time and trying is strongest case first.

Cicero, brought in to act for Fabricius, thus, found himself first defending his client's freedman, Scamander, who had no good explanation of why he should have been found in a wood with poison and a sealed packet.

During the course of the trial, however, an incident occurred which Cicero did not mention at the time but which he later brought to light. Oppianicus, the principal target of the prosecution bestowed *dona* and *munera* on one of the judges, Caius Aelius Staienus, turning him into "a more zealous partisan than the fidelity of a judge demanded".

Donum (plural, *dona*) and *munus* (plural, *munera*) both mean 'gift'. *Donum* usually carries no negative implication. In one primary meaning '*munus*' means office or duty; it also means burden and a work or book.

But its range of meanings when used in connection with employment are only background, intensifying the ambiguity of the term when used to describe a type of present. Munus is the equivalent of shohadh. It designates offerings with a string attached. It cannot be simply translated as 'bribe'.

Context determines whether the word is used with a pejorative connotation. In this instance Cicero is contrasting these 'presents and offerings' given in Scamander's trial with what he calls 'the big money' Staienus later got in Oppianicus' own trial. The implication Cicero leaves is that while Staienus behaved improperly after receiving them, there was no absolute barrier to a judge taking small gift. But in this case, to his discredit, Staienus was the sole judge to vote for Scamander's acquittal.[6]

After Scamander was convicted, Cicero prudently withdrew as counsel for Fabricius, who was found guilty too, and Oppianicus went on trial. There was still a gap in the prosecutor's case—direct evidence of Oppiancus' arrangements with Fabricius.

To convict a freedman and a rural thug was not the same

as convicting a knight with Roman connections. Oppianicus had been a power —indeed a hometown tyrant—in the day of the dead, dictator Sulla. The wheel of politics had turned against him, but he was not without friends and resources.

For his advocate he had obtained a tribune, Cucius Quinctius, a skilled and successful politician on his way to becoming praetor. Cluentius could not have been sure that is prime target would be sunk. Much, both sides must have reason, would depend on the thirty-two *indices*.[7]

To have the judges on one's side at the start was obviously a desideratum. 'I have the judges I want,' Cicero reported in the 60's when he was preparing to defend his then client Catiline; and an another occasion, apropos a bill governing the selection of judges in a particular case, he observed.

"Everything was in that". In his celebrated prosecution of Hog a good deal of prosecutorial and defense time was spent on the composition of the court— Cicero's selection of 'good guys' (boni) being met by his opponents' maneuvering to drain his carefully chosen panel for service in another case.

In the defense of Oppianicus, things went badly for the defense. The president of the court, Iunius, was a friend of the prosecutor.[8]

As it turned out, the senators were so closely split that every vote was crucial. Near the end of the trial a vacancy occurred on the panel. The replacement was selected by Iunius, acting in conjuction with the city praetor or law officer.

That officer in 74 B.C. was Hog, the currupt villian of Cicero's later indictment; and it was with his collusion, Cicero was to maintain, that the senator chosen, Gajus Fidiculanius Falcula, came ready to vote for conviction.

Although he had not heard any of the evidence, Falcula so voted. Popular rumour credited him with having received almost 50,000 sesterces for his vote.[9]

At about the same time, Oppianicus made an approach to Staienus whom he had already tested and knew to be responsive to inducements. Now he selected Staienus to be bagman for all the judges he needed bought; Staienus was to be the sequester (fixer) for the others.

A tie was the same as an acquittal; Oppianicus needed sixteen votes. He calculated the cash necessary 'with the precision of an Archimeder' and offered Staienus 640,000 sesterces or 40,000 per judge.[10]

Staienus went to work to enlist his colleagues on the panel. He signed up M. Atilius Bulbus and Tiberius Gutta, promised Bulbus 40,000 and urged him to recruit others.[11] But well into his efforts, Staienus backed off.

The inference is virtually irresistible that he did so when cluentius secretly offered him more money to vote for conviction and to bring colleagues like Bulbus and Gutta with him. According to the charges later made, these men, Falcula, and five other judges were all bought by Cluentius, using Oppianius' bagman as his own instrument.

It is Cicero, defense counsel at the beginning of the trials and eight years later Cluentius' counsel in a kind of replay of Oppiancus' trial who provides the information on the money paid.

As Cluentius' counsel, he did not acknowledge that Cluentius had paid more than Oppianicus; he claimed instead that Staienus' shift was motivated by his desire to keep all 640,000 sesterces for himself.[12]

In 70 B.C. when he was counsel for neither side, he voiced the popular view of what had happened, a view it may be believed he shared. He evoked the image of a corrupt judge by first naming Bulbus-literally 'onion', a godsend to counsel mocking him—and then Staienus.

The 'judgement of Iunius', as the verdict by Iunius' panel was labled, the characterized as "that fullest of crimes . In a devastating sentence in which Staienus was not named but was unmistakably described, Cicero declared that he was "a senator who, when he was a judge, in the same trial received money from the accused which he distributed to judges and from the prosecutor to condemn the accused".[13]

Stained with money from both sides—a veritable mayor of Nippur or Nuzi if these anachronistic comparisons may be allowed—Staienus took money for judgement in a case where life was at stake, political issues muted, counsel active. In this ordinary criminal a trial of a provincial knight money spoke to senatorial judges more effectively than Cannutius or Quinctius.

The Cleansing of Cluentius: Oppianicus, convicted of attempted murder, was not executed or severely punished. Temporarily disgraced, he was even able to make something of a comeback. He trapped Staienus into promising to repay the money he had given him at the trial and successfully sued for its recovery. No law barred him as an unsuccessful briber from getting back his bribe: the ethics of Nippur and Nuzi prevailed.[14]

His counsel, Quinctius, meanwhile protested the verdict. As a tribune of the people, he had a platform from which to denouce the corruption of the court. He did not fail to do so. "This touches each of us," he declared "The courts are nullities. No one who has a rich enemy can be safe." Marcus Caesonius, a judge who had voted against conviction, backed up his denunciations.[15]

Before the Murder Inquiry in Rome, Oppianicus Jr. Charged Cluentius with poisoning his father in 72. In addition, he charged him in the earlier trial with "the encompassing of an innocent man in judgement". The law this charge invoked went back to a statute of C. Sempronius Gracchus in 123 B.C. now incorporated in Sulla's more general murder statute, the *lex Cornelia de sicariis*.

It did not refer specifically to seeking a capital conviction by bribery. The operative verb circumvenire, to encompass or to hem in or to surround, was vague. It could be interpreted to include any scheme intended to bring about the death of another. Specifically, at his trial, Cluentius was accused of encompassing Oppianicus "by false judgement". The gravemen of the case was that he had paid money to the judges to achieve the conviction.[16]

Cluentius had three lines of defense. He had not paid any money. Oppianicus was not innocent. The statute applied only to senators. Untroubled by what he had said earlier about the judgement of lunius as the foulest of crimes, Cicero took all three positions.

"Teach us what money he gave, what he gave it from, how

he gave it. Show us a single trace of money proffered by him." Cicero's challenge to the prosecutor was a classic defense. Cluentius' account books, scrupulously kept, were clean of suspicious payments. As long as he and his agents stayed silent, as long as no paid judge turned informer, the prosecutor had no direct evidence to offer.[17]

The crime charged was to encompass an innocent man. But, Cicero maintained, the deceased had not been innocent. He told three stories to demonstrate his character. In Rome itself Oppianaicus had once been implicated in the murder of a rich young wastrel from Larinum. 'His confederate had been apprehended, brought before Q. Manlius, a triumvir or police commissioner's order. Commissioner and suspect quickly realized that they had mutual interests. Manlius "come to an understanding with Oppianicus and accepted money from him". The case was marked closed.[18]

Within his own family, Oppianicus had used money to induce betrayal of trust. A legacy would fall to Oppianicus Jr. if a child in the womb of a widow were not born. The widow's husband, the testator, had thoughtfully provided that his wife would not get her own legacy unless she gave birth to the child.

Oppianicus Sr. settled the matter by a cash payment to the widow. She "took this price and also many offerings (*munera*) which are disclosed in Oppianicus account books". In short, she "sold the promise which, entrusted to her by her husband, she held in the womb." The child was aborted. Oppianaicus Jr. got the legacy.[19]

A third story : Oppianicus Jr. would have a legacy of 400,000 sesterces if there were not in existence one Marcus Aurius, a young man who had fought in the Social War and had disappeared after the capture of Asculum in 88 B.C.

An informant let his mother know that he was held as a slave by a senator on the Adriatic coast. She died before she could contain his ransom. Oppianicus contacted the informant, "corrupted him by money", found out where the son was, and arranged for his extermination.[20]

Triply guilty of corrupting others, Oppianicus had attempted to corrupt the panel that had tried him. "If it is established that this judgement is corrupted," said Cicero, "it was corrupted either by Cluentius or by Oppianicus."

The implication was that it was a logical dilemma, that both could not have been guilty of corruption. Oppianicus had the character and the motive which made him the probably villain. One or the other, no doubt, had paid off Staienus. "The man who was in danger corrupted him."[21]

Corrupere, "to corrupt", the verb employed by Cicero to describe Oppianicus' action, had been in use before Cicero adopted it. It was a term exact enough to describe the evil act of paying a judge to decide unjustly in one's favour.

It drew strength from its parallel employment in a sexual sense as in the phrase "to corrupt a virgin." The corresponding Greek term, *dekasthṓ,* "to pay ten", focused only on the financial aspect of the transaction with the judge. The Latin word fused disdain for the payment with a significance derived from sexual mores; it implied that the judge had been invaded like a seduced virgin.[22]

No argument could have emphasized more crudely the power politics that affected the Roman courts. Cicero said in so many words to the knights, "Who would dare to judge truly and bravely a man of even slightly greater wealth than himself if he saw that a case might be alleged against him because he conspired or agreed"?

In other, non-Ciceronian words, in a system where money talked, who would dare to be a judge unless he were immune from being tried for his judgement? Only a senator, protected as he was by high political status, should be required to run the risk. Why should the knights endanger their power and influence by enlarging their liabilities?[23]

We cannot tell which line of defense was decisive. But in Cicero's rhetoric we catch the concept of the bribe at work. A partisan, he exaggerates, puts in a bad light, is not scrupulous. What he states as fact can be treated only as allegation.

Nonetheless, what he finds significant about the conduct of Oppianicus Sr. assumes the acceptance by his audience of an ethic deprecating the use of money to bring about betrayal.

The *munera* given to the pregnant widow are viewed negatively; Opianicus Sr. is seen as corrupting the informant who betrayed the enslaved heir; Oppianicus Sr., is a villain when he corrupts the court. The negative force of these incidents rests on shared beliefs.

As to the actual law on bribery we can be less certain. What Cicero declares to be the law must be understood to be his interpretation of the law. He is tendentious in his interpretation. When he takes his first line of defense and insists on Cluentius' simple innocence of making any payment, he plainly assumes that it is important to be able to clear him on the facts —*munera* —giving to judges is not something innocuous which he can concede his nonsenatorial client has committed.

When he takes his third line and asserts that the statute does not apply at all, he is saying that there is no law against bribing two-thirds on the present judges. The social condemnation of bribery to effect betrayal has, if his interpretation is correct, not been very fully incorporated into law. Nonetheless, the sanctions imposed on the nine *muners*-takers of Oppianicus Sr.'s trial show that, circuitously, legal measures support the moral condemnation of the judge who receives *munera*.

Electoral Reform in the Late Republic: Cicero became consul in 63 B.C., and in the year's course of his consulate he sponsored a new statute on *ambitus,* the crime of illegally soliciting votes. Related to our own 'ambition' and 'ambitious', *ambitus* could be committed by any ambitious politician.

Under Cicero's comprehensive statute, *ambitus* became the payments of men to greet a candidate or to follow him, the reservation of places for voters at the public games; the giving by a candidate of banquets open to public; and the sponsoring of gladiatorial contests by a candidate.

Within a year of passage of the bill, L. Licinius Murena, counsul-elect, was charged with *ambitus* by his defeated opponent and by the most uncompromising man in the Senate, Cato. Murena's counsel was ex-consul Cicero.[24]

Gratia, here translated 'clout', was what everyone sought in the system. It was the favour, influence power earned by having an office-holder under obligation to you. Being someone's advocate, being someone's surety, being someone's host, as Cicero implied, were three upper class ways of imposing an obligation and gaining *gratia*.

Gratia as much or more than cash, was what compensated the politician orders who were the professional advocates. The acquisition of *clout*, his speech for Murena assumed, was the legitimate aspiration of everyone. Political loyalty in exchange for favours from the powerful— it was the essence of the republican system.

Ambitus is often rendered in English as "electoral bribery" or simply "bribery", translations that are triply defective. First, the Roman term was deliberately different from any word used in connection with judicial bribery.

Second, it included practices involving no payoff to an individual voter. Third, to an even greater degree than judicial bribery, its meaning depended on shifting legal definitions and political discretion and was vague apart from particular cases.

None of the shame risked by the corrupt judge attended the voter who was the recipient of a candidate's largess; the receptive voter was neither violator of law nor social outcast. The voter was not regarded as exercising a divine prerogative in voting; no divinity hedged in his vote.

No paradigm of uninfluenced voting was appealed to. Without the support of shame, without a divine model to invoke, law alone was too weak an instrument to restrain the normal force of reciprocity.

Clodius' friends, according to Cicero admitted that his crime had been "bought back from the judges." *Redemptam*, "bought back", from the very *redimere*, characterizes the corrupt purchase of release from an obligation. Carrying a tincture of irony, *redimere* is not as precise a term as *corrupere*; in context, its negative connotation is clear.

Significantly in terms of social development, the perjorative verb has its nounal counterpart. The action of buying back a crime had become so common that the linguistic stage was reached where the substantive noun, *redemptio*, designated the corrupt purchase of release from punishment.[25]

Later in the year of Clodius' acquittal, Cato offered a bill in the Senate to condemn all who "took money for judgement". The glaring gap in the law's failure to include two-third of the judges was to be remedied and the bribery law was to be extended beyond capital cases.

Clodius' case no doubt was the immediate inspiration, but as Cicero had illustrated the sanctity of the written law by a polemical comparison between it and ordinary judicial proceedings. He had extolled the written law because "that excessive power which dominates civic life is silent only here. It cannot get to work, approach a judge, signal with a finger."

To the written law, "neither the power nor the clout of anyone can make an approach; and further—to show how great and holy the written law is— a judge in a case of this kind cannot be corrupted even by a price."

A *gratious*—a man with clout—may tell a court, "Judge that this was done or never done; believe this witness; admit accounts"; he cannot dictate a different law.[26]

Cicero deplored the domination of the judges by the wagging finger of a rich man. He felt Clodius' acquittal to have been outrageous. Now when his best clients were threatened, he was not their side.

The knights were angry that their immunity as judges should be removed. They actually preferred the rule of money in the courts to the risk of prosecution of themselves and judges for corruption.

"What more just," Cicero wrote confidentially to Atticus, "than that he who takes money for judgement should come to judgement?"

But the knights "made war" when this was put to them. The war was 'on the Senate, not me, for I dissented'. Cicero's dissent—his opposition to the bill removing the knights' immunity prevailed.[27]

When Cicero had praised the written law as free from the motion of a finger or the payment of a price, the implication had been that the law was fashioned in some higher way than the judgements of courts. Now as a practicing politician Cicero pointed to a different reality as he wryly and candidly acknowledged to Atticus the compromised spirit in which he opposed the bill. At the surface of his consciousness, not articulated, are thoughts about the responsibilities of legislator.

Is a lawgiver corrupt when he responds to the pressures of his constituents? In Rome, as in Egypt and Israel, no law even attempted to regulate the reciprociries at play when law was made by the supreme legislative authority.

Rome was not a theocracy with God as its legislator, but if law in Rome was not seen as tablets handed down on Sinai and, therefore, beyond criticism, still no senator suggested that as legislators he and his colleagues could be as corrupt as they sometimes were as judges.

The Chutzpah of Cicero: A politico-judicial system in which "box money" is paid to election agents and other largess is given the voters, subject only to the lightest and most political scrutiny by a criminal court; in which bagmen and fixers are recognised by generic names and buying off criminal convictions is a practice subject only to a highly politicized judicial inquiry; in which clout is the due of every citizen and the reward of every lawyer; in which gifts with strings attached are so innocent that an advocate can admit that his client gave them to a judge—such is the system, suggested by *ambitus, divisor, gratia, munera, redemption, redimere,* and *sequester.* In such a system, was it really possible to currpt, *corrupere,* a court?

Could corruption be distinguished from customary reciprocity? The difficulty was not unique to Rome. It was to recur in every society where a concept of corruption became current. A man "puts aside the part (*persona*) of a friend when he puts on that of a judge", Cicero wrote primly in Duties, the moral homily dedicated to his son; but he regularly wrote letters to friends who were judges, remarking to them that particular litigants before them were his friends. Despite his usual request for "impartial" consideration of the case, the intended effect of such letters must have been to incline the judge toward the friend of his friend Cicero.

These commendations have been noted by modern commentators as exercised of humanities or civilized benevolence. NO doubt they were conventional and too common to be criticized. But what did a powerful Roman politician expect to happen when he recommended a litigant to a judge?[46]

As for the special friendship represented by relationship, Roman politics were largely conducted on the basis of blood and marriage. The ties of kin were strong in the courts. When the counsul-elect Metellus took steps to stop the prosecution of Hog, Cicero asked in exasperation, "What would you do for an innocent kinsman, if you forsake duty and dignity for an utterly abandoned man, who is no kin?" He implied what must have been the norm—strenuous exertion at every level of office on behalf of an accused relative.

The family connections were inseparable from political connections. If the father of a family was condemned, his son would sometimes wait till be thought the moment politically propitious to avenge his father by prosecuting his father's prosecutor—Oppianicus Jr. is an example of such a son who miscalculated.

Major trials necessarily had heavy political colouring. It was a political act to prosecute a former governor or an incumbent senator or a country big shot like Oppianicus. Although evidence was not convict or acquit. The senatorial judges were making the foreign policy of Rome or scoring in domestic contests for office.

"Most of the time", Cicero wrote, he spent in the law courts-no doubt an exaggeration but true in the feeling it expressed that the law courts were his territory and his home. He had as deep an interest as possible in their good name. Yet, he also expected something from them-in two words, cash and clout. In theory at one time gratuitous, advocay was paid for by money or by the gratitude of a client. "Ingratitude", Cicero wrote feelingly as he contemplated an ungrateful freedma—" in that vice no evil is missing!" Freedom were expected to be grateful. Those for whom an orator spoke were expected to be grateful. Oratory, Cicero exclaimed, was indeed what won "the greatest gratitude".

Ciceo's fine Roman house was due to the generosity of a shady client. The boni, the good buys, whose approbation Cicero sought and whose standards he applauded, were those already possessed of power, whom he hoped to join. Their goodness went with their possession of power. How did they show their goodness to. him except by being grateful for his exertions?

When expectations of reciprocity governed the relations of orators and clients, how could the judges be exempt from tugs of gratitue? In a context that was almost always political, how could they immunize themselves from political demands?

In family-motivated prosecutions, how could they resist the claims of family? "This judge is my friend; that one is the friend of my father," a candid litigant would mutter. Cicero's exclamation, "I have the judges I want", spoke to the kind of impartial justice sought.

In a system in which so many influences other than the evidence operated on the minds of the judges, one could even wonder what the difference was between paying cash and employing an advocate.

> Since nothing ought to be so incorrupt in the state as vote and judgement, I do not understand why he who corrupts them with money is worthy of punishment, but he who corrupts them with eloquence wins praise. Indeed it seems to me that he who corrupts a judge by oratory does more evil than corrupting a judge by money; for no one can corrupt a prudent man by money, but one can by speech.

The passage is attributed to Cicero—an excerpt, preserved while the surrounding context has vanished. No doubt, if we knew the exigencies of the case we would understand why it was spoken. No doubt he would have said that his own eloquence was always on the side of the truth. He knew better.

No one, he remarked defending Cluentius and explaining his earlier negative references to cluentius' purchase of Oppianicus' conviction, should think our speeches to be "our certified opinions. All of them are for the case and the occasion, not for the advocate himself, not for ourselves and men."

But if oratory corrupted, no standard for judging corruption in the courts remained. All was *gratia*, the clout of one's father or a close connection.

And yet. And yet. Cicero's musings on the corrupt orator

were a familiar rhetorical move—to start from what was accepted as evil and to expand the standard by analogy. His intention was not to jeopardize the prime analogate, the evilness of corruption by money, which could not corrupt a prudent man,.

In the end, the line between the use of words and the use of money was distinct. The public conviction persised that the courts were not markets, that reciprocities could be distinguished, that a judge's role was different from a prostitute's. Pieties were offended by cash corruption. Limits to its sway were sought and, if often violated, never forgotten.

Cicero's own self-image did not permit a view of his profession equating him with a sequester of fixer. The letters of Atticus, in which a relative can do prevails, here confirm the stance adopted before a larger public.

Publicly and privately he saw corruption ravaging the courts in terms of which payments to judges were corrupting. It was his sober private judgement—the judgement of a man who knew courts, judges, and clients well —that Cato's proposed law against payments to all judges was utopian.

Yet, standing in what he found to be the filth of the Roman Republic, Cicero had the effrontery to practice advocacy not as an exercise in purchasing votes but as a profession depending on persuasion. In the prosecution of Hog he was given the opportunity to fly his standard.

The Hubris of Hog: When, in 74 B.C., Hog was praetor, or chief Civil law officer in Rome, much came his way. In Sicily in 73 Hog's opportunities multiplied. He took money as before to award legacies. He took money to dismiss judges displeasing to the accuser of a defendant. He took money to let a pirate captain disappear without trial. He took money to let a master retrieve his slave from criminal prosecution.

He took money to let a negligent sea captain escape punishment and money to release senators from duty. He took money in Messana to relax its treaty obligations, in Halaesus to appoint a provincial senator, in Cephaloedium to rig the election of the high priest. He took money to appoint favourable tax assessors.

He took money from prisoners for their necessities and money from their relatives to visit the prisoners; he took money that a man he executed with minimal suffering; he took money that executed men receive burial. The high and the low, the posperous and the bereaved, the living and the dead were those from whom he took.

Hog also indulged in bisexual lust. As a boy he had paid his gambling debts "with the fruit of his youth". His interest in young men continued as governor of Sicily. He was even more passionately interested in women. At the very start of his career, he had caused a riot by his unrestrained craving for a respectable woman of Lampsacus.

In Rome the role of his mistress, Chelidon, had enhanced the disreputableness of his reign as praetor. His governorship of Sicily was stained with promiscuous affairs. Corrupt in judgement, Hog was also lubricious.

Cruelty accompanied his concupiscence for flesh and money. He was also sacrilegious. He did not scruple to steal the property and the images of the gods from their temples. Hog put money down to buy the court. Again "big money" was involved.

He had spent three years in Sicily. The saying went that the first year had gone to himself, the second to his lawyers, and the "very fat, wholly lucrative third year" to the judges.

Sexual corruption was associated with Hog as part of his swinish character. Like many themes of Roman politics, the precedent had been set in Greece. In the classic attack of Aeschines on Timarchus, for example, "the fruits of his bribery" in office. Association of sexual and judicial license played to popular prejudice and envy.

A man license played to popular prejudice and envy. A man like this, Cicero suggested, would do anything and could get away with everything. More fundamentally, the association rested on a psychological assumption: the man who had no care of his integrity in sexual matters would have none in rendering justice. Corrupt in one way, he was corrupt in the other.

The uncleanliness of Hog's activity was reflected in two

kinds of indirection attributed on him. It was usual, Cicero said, for the paid judge to receive his money through an intermediary, an *interpres*, a go-between or fixer. If a court were to accept as a valid defence "I did not receive the money myself", no judge would ever be convicted. In Hog's case.

Cicero's severest word for Hog's action was turpe-foul. From a *Sanskrit* root meaning "to be ashamed", *turpe* had first been applied by Romans to the disgraceful appearance of a man, later to disgraceful deeds. It suggested dirt.

Clodius' acquittal was due to the *sordes iudicum*, "the filth of the judges. "Bribed judges thrived in "Romulus' refuse". The judgement of lunius was "the foulest" of crimes. In the same way, Hog's deeds of selling justice were dirty, filthy, *turpe* or foul.

In Sicily where Hog took "money for judgement", the act was unquestionably criminal —money taken to give a false judgement to condemn the innocent in a criminal case. Cicero dwelt however, not on the illegality but on the turpitude of the act. "To take money for a matter to be judged" was "wicked".

Indeed, "it seems to me"—Cicero speaks for himself and for he listening judges—" of all the things in the world the most foul and the most wicked." The act of the corrupted criminal judge condemning the innocent was the paradigm of evil.

But there was something beyond even that: "How much more wicked, vicious, shameful is it to take money from a man to acquit him and, then, condemn him."

In this negative hierarchy of corruption, violation of the ethic of reciprocity remained the greatest evil. After all, Hog might have said, "The man was guilty. I was wrong to take his money. At last, I was not so wicked as to free him. I did the right in the end, with a reward for my restored virtue."

Next to that act more wicked than the most wicked, more foul than the foulest, was the act of selling criminal justice. To a degree, no doubt, self-interest can explain Cicero's emphasis. If judges were for sale, who needed an orator? The judges, too, had a self-interest to protect.

Their status was endangered if their votes were commodities. The judges Cicero addressed were senators whose status was expressly threatened by the legislation , then pending and later enacted, to reduce their share of judicial seats to one-third.

To preserve their monopoly they had a powerful motive to be just, or to appear to be so, and Cicero appealed to their sense of self-preservation when he made them share in his view that the foulest of acts was taking money for something judged.

"Hold fast, hold fast the man in your city", Cicero admonished them. "Spare him, preserve him, so it may be he who judges with you". The outrageous irony took it for granted that the last thing senatorial judges now would want was the corrupt Hog as a fellow judge.

In a broader context of social expectations, the corrupted judge violated fides-that is, faith and honour and fidelity.

By oath the judges called the gods to witness their fidelity. The devine presence was more than merely supervisory. "You judges" Cicero told the judges of Cluentius, "are as if you were gods" in judging life or death. Divinity went beyond their lawful power over life. Divinity was in them as judges. It was palpable in each man's *conscientia mentis suae,* his inner self, his rational mind. *Conscientia,* Cicero declared, "we receive from the immortal gods, it cannot be torn from us."

To be corrupt was to deny the divine that spoke within. As Cicero put it to the judges of Murena, " All the power of the immortal gods had been transferred to you or at least, it is shared with you." The judges acted for the gods. For this ultimate reason a judge should" not think himself alone not himself free to do whatever he wants".

In the faith that was the foundation of the law and the cornerstone of the courts, the judge depended on divinity. That was why his oath was required. That was why corruption was foul. As in Egypt and Israel, the judge in Rome was the bearer of divinity.

In the peroration of the case against Hog, Cicero broke into prayer,. He addressed the gods and goddesses whom Hog had despoiled—Jupiter and Juno, Minerva, Latona, Apollo, Diana,

Mercury, Hercules, the mother of Ida Castor, Pollux, Libera, and Ceres—and all the other gods and goddesses against whom the insane Hog "had waged impious war."

It was they who should grant his prayer that the senatorial judges not pronounce on Hog a judgement worthy of his unheard of crimes of which the foulest was the sale and resale of judgement.

The Roman gods are giftakers as well as judges. The Romans have no unambiguous word for bribe. The Roman notion of corruption is not comprehensive. The supreme legislative body, the Senate, is never treated as open to bribes in its legislation. The ultimate source of power, the electorate, is subject to no sanction for what it accepts from politicians, and the judgement as to what constitutes too much inducement on an ambitious politician's part is largely political. Even where judges are concerned, the law does not go very far.

Substantial cash payments to a Judge for a vote contrary to the evidence are criminal. Small gifts are tolerated. Payments for a correct judgement are not considered. Influence with the judge is not guarded against. There are no police actions to detect bribe-takers.

There is no statute aimed at bribery as such. The tension between the ethic of reciprocity and an ethic that insists in certain areas of government on non-reciprocity remains high. The newer ethic is still not fully grasped.

NOTES AND REFERENCES

1. Cicero, Pro Murena 24.
2. *Doron* meant gift or offering in Greek. It could be argued to be ambiguous but in the classic orations of Athens, so familiar to educated Romans as a model, a charge of taking *doron* was a charge against one's opponent regularly made in fifth—and fourth—century Athens and as stereotyped in use as "Your father was a salve", or "Your mother was a prostitute." See Hermann Wankel, "Die Korruption in der rednerischen Topik und in der Realitat des classischen Athen", in Schuller, ed. *Korruption im Altertum* 30-35-50. *Doron* in such political context clearly meant "bribe" as in such phrases as "to be charged with *doron*", (Aeschines, Against Ctesiphon 232); to be judged for *doron*" (Lysias, Against Epicrates and His Fellow-Envoys 3),

"to convict of *doron*" (Aristophanes, The clouds 591) The meaning is also found in such compounds as *dorodeketes* (a taker of *doron*) (Job 15:34) and *dorodekeo* (take as *doron*) (Herodotus, History 6, 72). The fourth-century Greek politician Timarchus was accused by Aeschines of consuming "the wages of his prostitution and the fruits of his *dorodokia*" or bribe-taking (Aeschines, Against Timarchus 154). Demosthenes charged Aeschines himself with dorodokia and was told that one who wants to arouse the anger of his hearers over dorodokia must himself refrain from such conduct." (Aeschines, On the Embassy, 3). In other words, a substantive noun denoting habitual acts of bribery exisited in Greek. There was also to dekazein, "the paying of ten", used, for example, by Aristotle, who says"the paying of ten" began with Anytus was successfully "paid ten" to the jury when, in 409 B.c., he was tried for having lost Pylos to Sparta (Aristotle, Athenian Constitution 27, 5) There was also the adjective dorodokos, clearly meaning bribetaking: in Plato's Republic 3, 390, Adeimantus declares, "We cannot let our mean be bribetaking dorodokous) or money-loving." Again, in Plato, Laws 12, 955, where a law is mentioned which says "Do not serve for doroisi", and is backed by the death penalty, the Green word definitely means "bribe".

Nonetheless there are classic Greek texts in which specific words for bribery are not used. Thus, according to a famous story of antiquity, Cambyses, king of Persia, had a judge, Sisamnes, who "received money to give an unjust judgement". Cambyses discovered what he had done, had him killed and flayed and covered the seat of justice with his skin, appointing in his place Sisamnes' son, Otanes, with the reminder never to forgete in what way his chair was cushioned (Herodotus, History 5, 25). The word used for "being given money" is chremasi, a generic verb for being paid.

Another, later example: Aristotle, approving the change in the government of Athens which permitted lawsuits to be decided by large bodies of citizens, observed that "the few are more easily spoiled (*eudiaphthoroteroi*) by gain and favor than the many", Aristotle, Athenian Constitution 41, 2. In a similar vein in the Politics, he defended citizen assemblies judging cases on the ground that" in many cases a crowd judges better than a single individual". He argued, "The many are more incorruptible (adiaphthoroteron)—just like the larger stream of water, so the multitude is more incorruptible than the few", and went on to say that an individual was more easily roused to anger or a similar emotion than was a crowd, Aristotle, Politics 3,

286a. Aristotle, pointedly perhaps, does not meantion corruption by bribery in either work.

The Romans, familiar as they were with Greek examples, did not create Latin equivalents of dorodokia, dorodokos, or to dekazein.

3. The background of the case, Cicero, Pro Cluentio 43-45; Cicero's engagement for Fabricius, ibid, 49-50.
4. Libid 43-47.
5. Cicero, Brutus, 205.
6. *Pro Cluentio* 53-54, 65-67.
7. *Pro Cluentio* 59 (Fabricius' conviction); ibid, 25 (Oppianicus' political background); Erich S. Gruen, The Last Generation of the Roman Republic (Berkeley: University of California Press, 1974) 174, 517 (Quinctius' career).
8. "Judges I want", Cicero to Atticus, 65 B.C., Letters to Atticus 1, 2 ed. D.R. Shackleton Bailey (Cambridge: At the University Press, 1965-1967); Cicero to Atticus, June 61 B.C. Letters 1, 16 ("everything was in that";Cicero, In Verrem 2, 1, 158 (skirmishing on selection of Hog's judges); pro Cluentio 55 (Iunius' ties).
9. In Verrm 2, 1 157 (Hog and Iunius) 1 Cicero Pro Caecina 28-29 (Falcula's blind vote).
10. *Pro Cluentio* 87. Compare the use of sequestra to mean bawd, Apuleius, The Golden Ass 9, 15. Sequester is sometimes the same as interpres, the fixer or go-between who sets up a deal (cf. In Verrem 1, 36).
11. *Pro Cluentio* 69-72.
12. *Ibid.* 71
13. In Verrem 2, 2, 78 (Bulbus and Staienus); ibid. 1, 29 (the judgment of the court); ibid. 1, 39 (the senator-judge who took from both).
14. *Pro Cluentio* 78.
15. *Ibid* 77 (Quinctius); In Verrem 1, 29 (Caesonius).
16. *Pro Cluentio* 148, 151. A common but unproved assumption is that the lex Cornelia not only incorporated the old law but also obliterated it. See, e.g., H. Grose Hodge, "Introduction", *Pro Cluentio*, ed. cited, 211-212. The nontention of C. Joachim Classen that Cluentius is not now being tried for attempted judicial murder by money seems totally mistaken in the light

of *Pro Cluentio* 9, cf. Classen, "Cicero, the Law and the Law Courts", Latomus (1978) 37, 605-606. Two other poisonings also form part of the case against Cluentius, *Pro Cluentio*, 165 and 166.

17. *Pro Cluentio* 124 ("Teach us"); ibid. 82 accounts).

18. *Ibid.* 38-39.

19. *Ibid.* 33-35.

20. *Ibid.* 21-24.

21. *Ibid.* 64.

22. Compare *ibid.* 9: "*Corrupuisse dicitur A. Cluentius iudicium pecunia*" and sed vereor ne mulier me absente hic corrupta sit" (Clinia of the virtuous Antiphilia in Terence, The Self-Tormentor 232). For senatorial usage, see a proposed decree of 74 B.C., which ran, "*Si qui sunt, quorum opera factum sit ut iudicium publicum corrumperetur ...*" (Pro Cluentio 136).

23. *Ibid.* 153.

24. Cluentius, Pro Murena 67; Cicero, Pro Sestio 133-135.

25. Idem: "*rem manifestam illam redemptam esse a iudicibus.*" Other examples: In Verrem 2, 5, 117 (a Sicilian captain): "Metum vigarum nauarchus, homo nobilissimus suae civitatis, Pretio redimit", *ibid.* 2, 2, 186 (on endangered Syracusans): "*Pretio sese redemerunt*", *ibid.* 2, 1, 142 (award): "*Sipupillo opus redimitur,* mihi pracda de manibus eripitur"; *ibid,* 2, 2, 69 (a prisoner's friends): "fuissent auctores redimendae salutis"; Hog himself: "Ut primum 2 provincia rediit, *redemptio est huius iudicii facta grandi pecunia", ibid.* 1, 16. For discussion of the action noun, see David Dauble, Roman Law: Linguistic, Social, and Philosophical Aspects (Edinburgh: At the University Press, 1969) 29-63.

26. Pro Caecina 71-72. The passage is effectively used by John Kelly, Roman Litigation (Oxford: Clarendon Press, 1966) 32-33, to show the force of corrupting factors in the Roman courts.

27. Cicero to Atticus, June 60 B.C., Letters 2, 1, 8.

28. Compare Cicero, De officiis 3, 43, with Cicero, Epistolae ad Familiares, Letters, 53, 55, 57, 58, 59, 61. One apologist for Cicero's Humanitas in the letters is W. Glynn Williams, "Introduction", in the Loeb edition at 5.

3

MORALS OF THE CHRISTIANS

A bribe is "fifth" in Roman Law.

At the same time the concept of a bribe has more scope than in the ancient Near East. The bribery ethic as developed in the ancient Near East and the Mediterranean world rested on the assumption that the judge must be impartial.

The basis for opposing bribery disappeared if the judge could have favourites or be influenced by offerings to change his decree. What the New Testament said on impartiality, redemption, and favour was critical to the moral position of the Christians on bribery.

The problems are more apparent in the fourth century, when the Christians came to power, than in the first century, but for our understanding of the later development it is necessary to look at the way matters stood in the beginning.

Five cases occur in the telling of the stories of Jesus and the early Church where actions are performed which could be related to bribery. The actions and even more dramatically the actors provide possible prototypes for later Christian administration or reprobation.

When Paul selects chastity as a theme, Luke does not report that Drusilla is a daughter of Herod and, according to Jewish law, an adulteress – a divorcee living with a man not her husband; nor does he enlarge upon the moral implications of Felix's position as judge expecting money from his prisoner. The portrait of a weak and corrupt man is made in three sentences, so that it is no surprise that "wishing to offer a favour to the Jews, Felix left Paul bound" (Acts 24:27). The later Christian reader knew that his judicial favour to his enemies was the first step to Paul's death.

Moral indignation is explicitly conveyed in another incident: Simon, a practitioner of magic in Samaria, known popularly as "The Great Power of God," is converted by Philip and baptized.

Peter and John are sent from Jerusalem to lay hands on the Samaritan converts so they will receive the Holy Spirit. When Simon sees this happening, he is moved to action.

Two distinct synonyms are used for money in this short episode *chremata* (money or property), and *argurion*, (money or silver or cash). Attempted exchange of money for power over the Spirit is wickedness, offence against God, an occasion for Peter to curse the offeror and to pronounce this new Christian's separation from the community.

The predicted fate of Simon-poison and fetter-identify him with his evil gift, which itself is bitter poison and an unrighteous chain. His mild reply shows him abashed but not really repentant or aware of the enormity of his attempt.

There is a further aspect of the sin of Simon-of Simon Magician, as he comes to be called-which is memorable. Biblical condemnations of bribe-taking had focused on the bribe-taker. Here the act stigmatized as heinous is the offer. Scripture, when Acts became Scripture, now provided the paradigm of a bribe-giver.

Scripture now showed a person whose name could stand for every evil offeror of money in exchange for what could not be sold.

The scene with Simon Magician was associated, in later commentary, with one saying and one action of Jesus. In Mathew 10:8 when he sends out his disciples on their first mission, he instructs them, "You have taken freely. Give freely, "The iron law of reciprocity is here set out and put on a higher plane. What is received as a gift must be given as a gift." The saying occurs only in Mathew.

The soldiers are the only officials in either Testament portrayed as accepting money for a breach of duty. If we were to apply anachronistically the modern American meaning of bribe, we would say, they were bribe-takers-the only actual bribe-takers in the Bible. A contemporary Roman would have said that they had taken *munera*. The New Testament itself does not supply any concept to cover the transaction.

In the Gospel of John, Judas is described by Jesus as *diabolos* a term meaning "false accuser," "enemy", or "devil". In controversy with Jewish opponents Jesus characterizes the *diabolos* as "a liar and a liar's father". There is a link between the two passages and Judas's act. His betrayal is a lie, a denial of the truth, expectable of one who is the devil. In Mathew, Judas hangs himself.

When the fault of the woman about to be stoned is described, she is said to have been taken "in adultery". When Jesus warns against the lust of the eyes or against remarriage after divorce, "to commit adultery" is the verb he expands to include the condemned behaviour.

The basic sexual sin is well established. No comparable category is available to characterize the acts of the chief priests, Felix, Simon, Judas, or even to identify unmistakably any one of the transactions. Felix asks, the priests and Simon proffer "money", not "a bribe"; Judas gets a concrete sum, not "a payoff." Their actions, disapproved as they are not distinguished as specific sins.

Judge, Buyer, Ransomer, Donee and Donor: A parable, found only in Luke, presents a judge described as "an unrighteous judge" and one "who did not fear God and did not reverence man". He is importuned by a widow asking him to hear her case against her opponent. He refuses to act for a long time, but in the end to avoid a black eye - that is, disgrace—he consents to take up her case. In the background of the story is view of bribery.

The widow is the archetypica suitor who cannot pay. The unjust judge postpones action—what is he waiting for except an access payment? Unjust though he is, he is finally shamed by persistent entreaty; his conduct makes God's response to prayer an a *fortiori* probability. How differently the story would teach about God and man if the Judge acted only when the widow scraped together enough money to make a payment.

The story contains a double message. An adulterer, a homosexual, an incestuous man is never used as an analogue to God: the repugnance to sexual sin is too strong and the sensitivity to possible misinterpretation too great. The acceptability of an unjust man as an analoge implies a degree of tolerance or even respect for him.

The judge gets a measure of sympathy. But his action has been bad - that is the second and dominant part of the message. The parable would lack its bite if it were about a good judge who did not expect a reward for hearing a case.

In this court where no advocates contend and no argument is heard, no room is left for bribery or influence with the judge.

The metaphors of purchase, ransom, and redemption raise two questions. Do they imply a seller as well as a price? Are they inconsistent with the idea of Christ as judge? Neither of these questions are addressed by the New Testament itself.

To raise the questions and to attempt to answer them necessary involves a theology of the New Testament. If one sticks to the texts of the New Testament itself, the questions are merely implicit, present in the ambiguity of meanings of the metaphore as in play.

On the one hand, secular Greek literature furnishes an example of *exagorazein* used to describe the repurchase of Plato by his friends after the tyrant Dionysius had sold the philosopher as a slave—here the idea of buying back is central. *Lutron* and the related verb *lutroun* are frequently found to describe the ransoming of slaves.

There is even an instance in Josephus's The *Jewish War*, published 75-79 A.D., where Lucceius Albinus, the Roman procurator in Judea in 62-64 A.D., is described as Cicero had described Hog - a plunderer of the natives, a tyrannical tax collector, and one who "accepted ransoms (*apelutrou*) from their relatives on behalf of those who had been imprisoned for robbery by local councils or former procurators; the only ones left in prison as wicked were those who did not give. "Ransom here is like *redimptio* in Cicero, an ironic term for payoff.[1]

On the other hand, *exagorazein* was not commonly used in Greek to describe slave redemptions, and *lutron* was frequently used by a first-century A.D. writer like Philo in a very broad sense, for example, "every wise man is the ransom (*lutron*) of a wicked man."

Dóron, the term for gift in ordinary Greek and, in particular, in Mathew and Hebrews, is also the term in Greek for bribe. In each of the places in the old Testament where the

Hebrew used *shohadh* to mean a corrupt gift, the Septuagint exployed *dõron*. Thus, you shall not take *dõron* which makes the clear-eyed blind". God "does not lift up faces and does not take *dõron* and the judges of Israel "shall not take *dõron*, for *dõron* blinds the eyes of the wise"

How then, does a *dõron* to God to liberate us from sin differ from a payment to a judge to release a guilty prisoner? No New Testament author puts this question.

"The preaching and teaching of Christ," objected Volusianus and other members of the Roman ruling elite of a later era, "are in no way suitable for the morals of the state: this demonstrated by the commands to return on one evil for evil, to offer the other cheek to him who strikes one, and to give one's cloak to him who seeks to take one's tunic." The Roman rulers posed a rhetorical question: "Who would not wish by right of war to return evil to the ravager of a Roman Province?"

If the bishop is not of good conscience, said the Syrian *Didascalia Apostolorum*, and takes up a person for a certain foul profit on the offerings which he receives, and spares one who immpiously sins and suffers him to remain in the church, the bishop has polluted his congregation with God and with men.

The teaching uses sexual imagery to convey the rebuke: the bishop "pollutes" as one does by an unlawful genital act. His "lewdness" provides a terrible example for youths and maidens. Such was the experience of third century Christians in Syria.

The Latin version of the *Diascalia* adopted the same vocabulary: the bad bishop takes *turpe lacrum*, "filthy proit." *Inquinavit*, "he has stained," his church. He has been guilty of *intemperantia*, "incontinence."

"Woe to those who say sweet is bitter and bitter is sweet, They say this who in judging do not consider the case but the person. The fruit of Christ, who is justice, who is most sweet, they turn to bitterness. Whosoever in judging is led by kinship, or by friendship, or contrariwise by hostile hatred or by enemity, therefore, perverts judgement of Christ, who is justice, and turns his fruit to bitterness".

Such was the comprehensive condemnation of partiality in judging offered by the fourth century's leading authority on

Scripture. Jerome, here quoting one Old Testament prophet, Isaiah, to interpret another, Amos, and integrating both with Christ, identified as incarnate justice.

Jerome's rejection of those who "do not consider the case but the persons" is common ground for orthodox and unorthodox Christians.[2]

> You hear a case between two men. One of the two is rich and the other is poor; and it happens that the poor man has a bad case but the rich man a good one. Now, if you are not learned in the kingdom of God, thinking to do well for yourself, you will as it were by merciful to the poor man and hide and conceal his injustice. . . .But your God says to you, "Take not up the person of the poor in judgement." We are easily advised not to take up the person of the rich. This every man sees would that every man did![3]

That a judge should not sell his judgements followed as a deduction from the teaching on impartial justice. By his seemingly remote inquiry about the venal judge, Augustine, it appears probable, meant to touch Macedonius. A venal Judge's obligation to make restitution if his sins were to be forgiven was implied but never stated. Why was Augustine so insistent on what justice required in a judge and so reticent on what a sinful judge must do unless he meant to hint to Macedonius that he too had sins?

Explicitly he invoked the analogy of the Lord with the accusers of the woman taken in adultery. The Lord too had charged no accuser directly; a reminder had sufficed. Intermixed with the veiled rebuke to the governor was Augustine's condemnation of any payment to a judge.

In fourth-and fifth-century legislation, good and bad senses are both found. Christian slaves are to be ransomed from Jewish owners; prisoners will be ransomed (*redempti*) from the barbarians; and general legislation deals with ransom (*redemption*) from slavery. Yet guardians may be suspect of being paid off (*redempti*); chaperons may be paid off (*redempti*) to act as go-between; creditors may transfer their rights of action to more powerful claimants and, thereby, buy up (*redimant*) enforcers for their debts. Most spectacularly, in Constantine's basic legislation of A.D. 331 against access payments to provincial governors or to members of their staffs, it is provided,

Let the chamber curtain of the judge not be for sale, nor access bought up". Purchase of this kind, the emperor suggests, is foreign to fundamental equality: "Let the ears of him who judges be open equally to the poorest and the rich." *Redimere* in such legal usage is tied to payment for breach of trust, especially to payment made to a judge, especially to unequal justice.

A Christian theologian, lamenting corruption in the courts, can say, "What can be bought off is not feared - so Cyprian writing in third-century Africa.

"He who is poor and prudent when he sees judgement bought up will be silent in that time, because it is a bad time"—so Jrome writing in Bethlehem about A.D. 400 and speaking against those who "take *munera*".

To apply *redempto* boldly to describe the Christian's liberation from the judgement of god was to attempt a reversal of meaning, a transvaluation of values, to celebrate a paradox where purchase of freedom was rightly bought.

Favour and Favouritism: That God has chosen a people is one message of the New Testament as it is one message of the Old. To choose among several means to favour some. In Greek, what god gives is *charis*; in Latin, *gratia*; in English, "Favour". The celebration of God's choosing of a people and of individual persons runs through the New Testament.

"Hail, highly favoured "the angel greets Mary at the beginning of the Gospel of Luke. The Word, "full of favour," came among us, the Gospel of John begins. "Of his fullness we have all received favour after favour". *Charis*, in Greek, *gratia*, in Latin favour cannot be eliminated from the New Testament without disembowelling surgery.

In the secular law of the fourth century, *gratia* continued to function homonymously. Cicero had employed *gratia* in the sense of "influence" or "clout"—the exercise of pressure by the powerful on the courts. *Gratia* continued to be used in this sense in such legislation as Constantine's of 319, directed to Corsica: any official who has been corrupted by a payment or by influence (*gratia*) and has judged unjustly is subject to suit by the party injured. Similarly, a decrease of 373 of the Senate denounced "the most disgraceful baseness of sycophantic influence" (*gratia*).

Gratia designated not only the influence that unfairly affected judgement. It was also understood as the unjustified act of favourtism itself. A decree of 385 provided for the fine of a judge whose "negligence or favourtism" (*gratia*) had delayed the hearing of a case.

A decree of 398 permitted a bishop to intervene in any judicial case where human life would be taken "through the mistake or the favourtism" of the trier.

Whether it was exercised on the judge or by the judge, *gratia* was objectionable. In these senses, *gratia* was anathema to churchmen as well as lawyers. "Let us not take up a person in judgement. Let favourtism (*gratia*) be banished. Let them decree the merits of the case, "taught Ambrose, bishop of Milan, an ex-judge himself.

When the General Council of Africa met in Hippo in 393 (Augustine, not yet a bishop, a leading spirit in this assembly), the Council referred with scorn to ecclesiastical judges "depraved by cupidity or by clout" (*gratia*). It is these usages of gratia that a modern historian has in mind when he writes. "*Gratia* in common parlance stood for official corruption in the courts, for official hanky-panky of all kinds in public life.

The Roman legal system was honeycombed like the American with a vast array of privileges and exemptions-what tax system is tolerable without them? Do our universities, churches, unions and governmental authorities regard their favoured tax status as corrupt? Yet we are at least as egalitarian in our ideology as the emperors who in 372 proclaimed: "A favour for some is to the injury of the people."

Certainly the artisans (including architects, carpenters, stonecutters, silversmiths, blacksmiths, fullers, potters, plumbers, and furriers), the bishops, the teachers of painting, the imperial officials, the physicians, the professors, and the secret service who were among the beneficiaries of Roman privilege or exemption did not think they were recipients of wrongful bounty. The emperors could declare, "A general regulation must be preferred to a special favour (*beneficium*)"; but special favours could be lawfully sought and were often lawfully granted.[4]

NOTES AND REFERENCES

1. Josephus, *The Jewish War* 2, 273; for the example of *exagorazein* and examples of *lutron*, see Stanislas Lyonnet and Leopold and Leopold Sabourin, Sin, Redemption and Sacrifice: A Biblical and Patristic Study (Rome: Biblical Institute Press, 1970) 80-82 (lutron); 107 (Plato's case).

2. Ibid. 86 (Philo's usage); 90-93 (*Old Testament* usage as to *lutron*, etc.); 110-112 (Old Testament sense of "acquisition"). On God's position as new owner in the Old Testament, see in particular David Daube, *The Exodus Pattern in the Bible* (London: Faber & Faber, 1963) 42-46.

3. Pelagius, *In Epistolam B. Pauli ad Romanos* 2, 1, in PL Supp., ed. A. Hamann 1, 1120 Augustine, *Enarrationes in Psalmos* 32, 1, CC 38, 256.

4. *Codex Theodosianus* 13,1,9, (372). Note that *beneficium*, while used more often than gratia in a positive sense in the Code, is here used in a negative sense; ibid, 1, 1, 4 (393): "Generale praeceptum beneficio speciale anteferendum est. "Implicitly, of course, this decree recognizes that favours have legal status and will be lawfully accorded. Exemptions-with which the *Internal Revenue Code* sec. 503(c) would afford one of numerous comparisons in our legal system-are for professors, physicians, and in some instances for their children, *Codex Theodosianus* 13, 3, 1-19 (A.D. 321-428); for all manner of artisans, ibid. 13, 4, 2 (A.D. 337); for teachers of painting, ibid, 13, 4, 4, (A.D. 374); for bishops, ibid, 16, 2, 1-47 (A.D. 313-425); for officials of the oalace, ibid. 6.35, 1-14 (A.D. 314-425); for the secret service, ibid. 6, 27, 1 (A.D. 354); 6, 27, 8 (A.D. 435).

4

LEST MONEY SHOULD PREVAIL

BRIBES as ancient as The inventions of Scales in Egypt.

Relying on these allegations, one modern historian has suggested that a gift "was probably necessary to gain official attention for the plea." A second has concluded "It is possible that the Africans had strengthened their intervention in a wider circle of the court by bribery." A third has gone further: "On one mission, Alypius had carried with him promise of eighty Numidian stallians, fattened on the estates of the church, as douceurs for the cavalry-officers, whose views on grace had proved decisive." And again: "Alypius, distributing eighty stallions to the Imperial Court, was doing his best, as far as the means of the church of Africa allowed, to live down to the diplomatic methods used by Theophilus of Alexandria against John (Chrysostom)."[1]

In ancient Israel and Rome the judge had appeared as a stand-in for the divine, and corruption was a blinding of the representative of the divine. Imperial response to the problems of corruption may be profitably compared to American legal responses between 1940 and 1975 to air pollution caused by automobiles.

Bribery control is control of a physically observable phenomenon, the payment of money to officials, but what payments are to count as bribes depends on the symbolic function of the official, and what risks of bribery are acceptable depends on political assessments.

Heirs of Cicero, Caesar, and the jurists, the fourth-century emperors legislated to least a dozen times between A.D. 316 and 398 against judicial corruption. Governors are told to conduct trials in public. They shall not "hide themselves in their private council chambers. They shall not judge civil case only at a price."

Opportunities for corruption-appeals, secret meetings, and above all, access payments-are identified and condemned. The fourth-century chronicler most interested in criminal trials. Ammianus Marcellus, notes the presence of corrupted judges on seven principal occasions in the fourteen years between 354 and 369.

Constantine in his decree of 331 had treated court access payments comprehensively as extortion. Draconian legislation addressed to Illyricum about 370 banned under pain of capital punishment eve voluntary "guest gifts or little offerings" to the chief of the department staff and to those serving the governor; that the presents were customary was to be no defence. But Augustine, writing Macedonius in 413, makes reference to no legislation and remarks that lower court officials commonly receive payments from both sides. What they extort immoderately, he observes, can be recaptured in an action for restitution. What they take "by tolerable custom" is not normally sought back.

Martial observes, "The judge asks and the advocate asks"; a litigant might as well pay his opponent and forget about litigating. In Petronius Satyricon the question is put, "What do the laws do where only money rules?" Nowadays, the poem maintains, "Judgement is nothing except public merchandise." Apuleius recalls the story of Paris corrupted by the golden apple and says, since the original judgement between gods and men was sold by the judge for his own profit, it is no surprise that "now so many judges market their own decisions for a price." The negative assessments made by poets and satirists and story tellers show that, from the beginning of the empire, popular and sophisticated belief held that judges were corrupt. The fourth-century evidence appears merely to confirm the long-standing belief.

Modern historians of the late *Emprie* concur. "everyone

steals.. Functionaries traffic in judicial hearings," Writes a French authority. "The whole of the Roman Empire lived in the blind lust for gold....Nothing could be done without *'bakshesh'*, declares a Hungarian historian. "The age was one of venal and corrupt judges and judges' staffs," exclaims an American expert; the "corruption and injustice of the times" were "ubiquitous."

The most recent English analyst of Roman administration joins in: "judicial corruption was normal and systematic in the provincial courts." Provincial governors were "almost invariably venal." Despite "excellence" of Roman law, the judges not applied it "were as a rule venal." Judical corruption was "an endemic evil."

The working of Justice; Ancient critics, popular suspicion, and modern assessment agree. We are back in seventh-century B.C. Jerusalem-all the princes take *shohadh*. We are back in the late republic, Romulus' refuse. Where, however, is hard evidence for the poets, belief that corruption was universal or the historians' belief that it was systematic? The lack of evidence of enforcement of actions has been mentioned. We have found similar lack of evidence of enforcement in Egypt and Israel and Republican Rome. We can infer in each case that the anti-bribery ethic was weak but we are not given quantitative information on the extent of corruption.

But, of course, legislation of this kind is no more than an accusation. Bailiffs, Constantine's decree says, have been taking money from litigants.

Ambiguity, tension, conflict can, no doubt, be found in every society if one probes far. These broad social factors should be seen as contributing to the climate in which the witchcraft accusations flourished without being the sole causes of their popularity and without determining that the suspicion of the day take shape in charges of witchcraft.

In the fourth-century Empire fear of bribery was as rational as fear of sorcery, an in the eyes of those concerned with government, bribery was as good an explanation for success as reference to the occult. The same ambiguity, tension and conflict that account for the climate in which accusations of witchcraft abound also provide the climate in with accusations of bribery occur. In these accusations, too, articulate power affirms the single image of society. The briber is the one who has brought in the unseen to redress the balance of the seen. The briber is the one whose personal skills have succeeded in ways that are unacceptable or difficult to understand and beyond argument, there are real practitioners of bribery.

That all the accusations and suspicions could flourish without some experience of corruption in practice is hard to believe. That a society would have continued to rely so heavily on machinery that was totally corrupt is almost equally incredible.

To enforce the principle, a variety of sanctions were set out. As former law required, governors were to stay fifty days in their provinces after their term of office ended; any governor leaving earlier would be treated as a runaway slave. Appointees were to give an oath that they had given or promised no one anything for patronage and had not agreed to send any one anything from a province and that they would live only on the revenues allotted by the emperor, "keeping their governorship with pure hands and rendering account of it to God and to us; "In particular, they were to swear to be impartial in judging cases.

The oath was to be given before the emperor or his delegate or in the provinces before the bishop, office holders, and inhabitants of the city at the judgement seat of province." If any magistrate violated the edict by giving or taking for office he should undergo confiscation of his property, beatings, torture, and exile. Bishops in the provinces were exhorted to report derelictins to the emperor.

Patriarchs and archbishops were instructed to place the text of the law itself, as a thing "dedicated to God," with the sacred vessels of the church; they would do better if they also had it "engraved in stone on the porticos of their cathedrals." Finally, the judgement of God was also invoked. Those who committed perjury in swearing consented in their oath to be punished "here and in the future world at the terrible judgement of the Great Lord God and Our Saviour Jesus Christ".

NOTES AND REFERENCES

1. These questions are, respectively, from J. Patout Burns, "Augustine's Role in the Imperial Action Against Pelagius", *Journal of Theological Studies,* New Series 30 (1979) at 81; Otto *Wermelinger, Rom und Pelagius* (Stuttgart: Anton Hiersemann, 1975) 199, Peter Brown, *Augustine of Hippo* (Berkeley and Los Angeles: University of California Press, 1969) 362; and Peter Brown, "The Patrons of Pelagius: The Roman Aristocracy Between East and West", *Journal of Theological Studies,* New Series 21, 62 (1970). For the charges against Theophilus, see Palladius, Dialogos, PG 47, 26.

5

THE SAINTS AND THE SYSTEM

Bribe money in both Latin and English is "dirty".

Western Europe, beset by new peoples by the time of Justinian, offered not a bureaucracy to discipline but tribes and nations to initiate into the paradigms breaking the rule of reciprocity. Offerings to the powerful were the norm. Jewish and Roman images of impartiality, Christian emphasis on the gift freely given clashed with native customs. Who had the authority, the desire, the education, the energy to champion the morality of non-reciprocation? If there were those who did, where was a professional class like the Roman advocates with the competence and interest in assuring that in deciding cases offerings did not count more than rhetoric?

A non-reciprocity was, not without struggle, preserved. In select and remarkable instances it was exemplified. Seldom was it enforced.

"Live so your children will imitate you" was Caesarius' theme in "A Sermon Necessary in Parishes." Those who hear cases "should decide them justly and not "take offerings against the innocent, for 'offerings blind the heart of the wise and change the words of the just." While they are gaining money, they may lose their souls." The preacher conveyed the scriptural message on *munera*' his emphasis again was on a supra-temporal sanction.

How frequent was the offence? In "An Admonition to Those Who Frequently Give Alms But Still Commit Robbery and

Adultery Every Day" Caesarius observed that the devil taught them that "although they commit sins every day they believe they buy them back by daily alms-giving. They suppose that God, after the custom of corrupt judges, take money and forgive their sins. In 'On Alms-giving and on the Heavenly Mercy to which we Attain by Mercy on Earth" he preached.

On earth, Caesarius thought, corruption was only a shade less usual than the use of patrons or the trick of forensic advocacy. How seriously did Caesarius struggle against *munera* taking? In the longest and most deliberate of his surviving, writing a circular letter to the bishops of his province setting out major moral rules, he dealt with the subject just after condemning the use of magic and just before condemning the use of abortifacients. "Let no one", he wrote, 'try to oppress a good case by taking offerings. The command was clear, sharp, and stated with a brevity and in a context that gave it attention but not emphasis. It was confined to receivers not extended to givers.

On the Iberian penisula, on June 1st, 572, a council called by King Miro met at Braga under the presidency of Braga's vigorous archbishop, Martin, another former monk in high office. The council recalled the words of Christ on gratuitous giving.

It recalled that both giver and receiver were anathema. It taught that it was necessary to ordain clerics 'not by the favour of offerings (*gratia munerum*) but by careful discussion followed by the testimony of many'. The headnote of this canon ran, 'Let a bishop in the ordination of clerics take no stipend. Stipend (*commodum*) broadly covered all temporal rewards'. In the same vein, the council declared that a bishop should take nothing for the holy chrism, lest he seem to sell, 'as Simon Magician seemed to buy, the gift of God with money. Bishops were not to demand money for consecrating a church, nor priests for baptizing, Many poor people, the council warned, withheld their children from baptism because of clerics who demanded money or a pledge from the needy.

The Ruler of Rome: Three kinds of *munera* or offerings existed: from the heart, from the mouth, from the hand. From the heart comes the service offered by one who is unduly subject or servile - it is commonly called influence. From the mouth comes flattery; its respectable name is glory. From the hand comes money; it is presented as a reward (*pracmium*). In this Augustinian way the monk Gregory analyzed the offerings condemned by the Lord speaking through Isaiah. All were to be rejected by the just man.[1]

A ruler, he wrote, must be 'clean in thought so that no uncleaniness polluters him'. He must have clean hands, which he took care to wash of dirt (*sordes*). He must be careful lest "what he touched with his hands stained anything he touched, lest he pursued what was mud and be held by what was dirt." Isaiah had said, "Be clean, you who bear the vessels of the Lord."

Purity of this kind was freedom from corruption. It paralleled a purity, Gregory insisted on, in sexual matters. Even the married, he taught, 'befouled' copulation by mixing pleasures with it. After lawful conjugal intercourse so Gregory was to instruct Augustine, the missionary bishop he had sent to Canterbury—the spouses would seek "purification" by water and by abstaining from entering a church. "Cleanness" was required to receive the body of the Lord.

The best cleanness was 'the anti-pollution ethic in sexual morals as in government morals reflected a strong impulse 'to become beyond flesh".

Cleanness meant being free from the desire of earthly things. Judging the causes of his subjects "when set in the divine place". The ruler must not let his mind be darkened by the "importunity of dusty desire for terrestrial things".[2]

"The sacred canons"—presumably Gregory meant Chalcedon - had condemned the act of buying God's favour but had no noun to describe the action. Patriarch Gennadius had called it 'bribery' (*dorodokias*). Gregory's teaching on the sale of the spirit could be understood narrowly to apply to the sale of ordination or, as at Chalcedon, to include the sale of any ecclesial officer or, very broadly, to include the sale of justice. Patriarch Gennadius in his encyclical had taught that the canon of Chalcedon embraced all *dorodokias*, all bribery; but it was plain from his context that in fact, he meant only bribery to win office in the Church.

No extension of the canon was made to the sale of justice by judges, even if they were acclesiastical judges. Linguistically there was a difficulty. Chalcedon barred the sale of favour (*charis*).

On the separate track of secular bribery a summation of the ancient standards was offered in Spain.

Wicked judges out of greed "delay or pervert judgements, and do not complete the business begun by the parties until they have exhausted the purses of the litigants". These "judges" are "like wolves in the evening"; and "in the manner of wolves they snatch at everything and leave scarcely anything for the poor." Wounding "their own people" more savagely than the cruelest enemies. The judge who perverts judgement "by favour of kinship or friendship or hatred of enemies" sins "against Christ, who is truth and justice". Such a judge "nerpetrates a fraud against God because justice, which he should impart *gratis*, he sells by taking money". The taking of offerings was "the undoing of the truth."

The rich man "quickly corrupts the judge with offerings". Of Gregory's three kinds of offerings, cash "most easily" perverts the soul. In summary, "human judgement is corrupted in four ways - by fear, greed, hate, and love." On account of these motives justice is "often" violated, innocence "often" harmed.

Classical satire blended with Scripture in Ysidro to set the standard for the judge. His comments on corruption from a small proportion of the total corpus of his work, but the clearly regarded the risk of corruption as real. His anger, his sense that the poor were the victims, was palpable; and the offence to the poor man merged for him with offence to God.

Sellers of justice committed frauds on God by selling what should be *gratis*-so Ysidro adapted to the courts the standard objection to the sale of divine favour; but he himself did not acknowledge the connection, mentioning "the Simonians" only to the identify their name as derived from Simon, the man who "wanted to buy the favour of the Holy Sprit for money". His focus was not the sale of justice.

Everywhere in 798 Teodulfo and Leidradus were met by

crowds, male and female, old and young, rich and poor, all carrying offerings, all believing offerings were essential to win the deputies' favour. Payoffs to witnesses were occasionally attempted; principally the litigants concentrated on the two judges. Offerings were their flying missiles, offerings were their battering rams.[4] Great and small litigants offered in accordance with their means. Linen work, wool, head coverings, boots, gloves, boxes for manuscripts, wax for writing were tendered by the less prosperous. Cordova leather in red or white, coloured clothing of Arabic workmanship, ingeniously embroidered, were presented by the rich. Calves, cows, bulls, even vineyards were promised.[5]

Turbulently, the scene recreates itself: This one promises a crystal drinking vessel and jewellery "if I make him the owner of a farm". That one brings Arabic money "if he may get a house." An ancient vase on which Hercules is depicted in struggle with Nessus is Teodulfo's "if you favour my hopes." Imports from Spain, treasures of the past, local farm products are physically set before the judges. Fruits, eggs, bread, wine, goat, cheese, chickens and other edible birds - all these are put more or less literally in their laps. Openly, unselfconsciously, persistently the litigants take it for granted that reciprocity with the judge is proper. In a word, "all rely on an offering".

Dependent on court attendants, servants, and local assessors who sit with them, the royal judges are handicapped from the start. "Every doorkeeper loves gold; thought Teaodulfo. Not "one in a thousand of them "is honest. The judges' servants are obvious targets. Constant vigilance is necessary to assure their integrity. One or another is ready to say how a case can be decided in a suitor's favour without the judge shouldering "the weight of sin." The servant's words are persuasive, his hands 'loaded with money'. Assessors, drawn from the native nobility, have pleas or gifts ready to press upon the Court. They take their cue from friends in the crowd, wicked at by one man, hand-signaled by another.

Teodulfo reported with gusto the gifts offered and took a stern scriptural view of their propriety. Samuel, Hezekiah, Josiah were examples that showed they must not be taken, "Taking an offering usually turns weak minds from the truth". The judge who accepts "sells what it is fitting that he should give gratis. "A good judge should be looking out for the widow and the orphan, the aged and the sick. He should be helping those "whose voices and whose feet tremble". But with an offering the rich man quickly disturbs the mind of the judge'.

What he did take were 'the little things,' fruit, eggs wine, bread, chickens,. These were offered 'not by a barbarous but a kindly hand'. In this controlled and attenuated form Teodulfo permitted the rule of reciprocity to survive.

For killing a layman, seven years of penance; for the practice of coitus interruptus, two years; for anal intercourse, four years; in this way, for those disposed to receive their discipline, the monks between the sixth and tenth centuries set out tariffs for sin, at once informing confessor and penitent of what acts were sinful and giving an indication of the sin's relative gravity. On the simonian heresy and bribe-taking, a sharp contrast if found between the teaching of Saints Patrick, Caesarius, Martin, Gregorym, and Ysidro and the message of these manuals.

Sins of covetousness fell within the penitentials' purview. From patrick's first encounter with the pagan Celts it was evident that a standard rejecting gifts was new and puzzling to the pious. The custom of secular chiefs expecting payments was obviously engrained. Baptism could Scarcely have erased the habit. Was there not a need to legislate about offerings to judges and bishops? Was there not a necessity to teach about offerings in the discipline enforced on the laity by the monks? The penitentials, by their silence, answered these questions negatively.

Many today are shocked at the crime of Judas as inhuman and wicked he sold his own lord and master and God for money. Yet they do not avoid it. For when they speak false testimony against anyone for offerings they assuredly—for they deny the truth for money-sell God. For he himself said, "I am the truth". By implication only, the passage was a rebuke to judging falsely for a bribe. As to the heresay it drew no lessons. In Latin terminology the sin was 'bought back' by the penance. In Finnian the buy backs were made through personal suffering, not with money. Some sins—for example, kin-slaying, druidism, adultery—were beyond remission of the penance. Buy backs were provided for 'rescuing a soul out of hell'. They consisted in prayers, fasts, and scourging. Cash buy backs were not usual. By analogy, these redemptions of penances were like the redemption of guilt. Basic to each was exchange.

NOTES AND REFERENCES

1. Gregory, *Moralia in Job* 9, 53, ed. Marc Adrien, CC (1979) 143, 494.
2. Gregory, *Regula pastoralis* 2, 2, PL 77, 27 (cleanness of rulers); *ibid.* 77, 102 (conjugal intercourse). Gregory to Augustine, July 601, Registrum 1, 340-341.
3. Teodulfo, *Versus contra iudices* lines 799-809 (witnesses).
4. *Ibid.* lines 212-220, 243-252.

6

SINS OF THE STOMACH

Religion can be viewed as bribery on a grand scale, organised for the highest end, mans 'salvation, and practiced to persuade the supreme Authority.

Reform, a term with a scriptural pedigree, was a theme popular with the Fathers. Renewal, restoration, reassertion of spiritual values were its sense. Multiple in the modes it took, broad in its significance, reform was an idea not narrowly confined to the correction of corruption. Now, however, after one thousand years of Christianity, reform was to become more specific, more connected to concrete corruptions. Invaders, unacquainted with the tradition regulating reciprocity, had continued to despoil Western Europe in the ninth and tenth centuries. Links to Greco-Roman and Mediterranean culture declined. Impoverished, the churches were exploited for personal profit. By 950 the papacy had reached its nadir. A century later, a band of clerics, strategically placed in Rome, raise the banner of reform of the immediate and practical sense of eliminating corruption in the appointments and administration of the Church, Reform was to become the cry of the day. The charge of selling the Spirit was formed around it. Popes came to the office pledged to extirpate the practice and were judged, often harshly, by their own success or failure in living up to the reformers' measure of purity. In the spiritual sphere, no doubt was to remain that reciprocation for spititual office was an evil.

Europeans tendered offerings to those in power. Offerings could not be banned. Yet offerings - *munera*—were exactly what were condemned when given to influence judgement. No unambiguous word for bribe existed. In the canon of the Mass itself, the bread and wine about to be consecrated were described as *dona* and *munera*-gifts and offerings. In the most sacred context, *munera* were still acceptable. As the reform intensified, distinction were to be driven between *munera* that were murderous - that indeed led to murder - and the only *munera* that a Christian could rightly offer.

Three practices were identified by them as evil and applied —concubinage or marriage by the clergy; investiture of laymen with churches; purchase and sale of holy orders. Ten years after the inauguration of Leo IX's reign, a council in Rome summed up their programme: No one was to hear the mass at a price of *gratis,* from a laymen. No one was to be ordained or promoted 'to any ecclesiastical office whatever' by meants of the simonian heresy.

Lay investiture was linked with unworthy, that is, simonian appointments; clerical celibacy was considered a mark of self-control contrary to the looseness and self-indulgence manifested by the venal. Purity-purity both sexual and administrative-was what the reformers sought. If in the Unites States a band of reformers decided that politicians living unchastely should be barred from office, that corporations should not favour candidates, and that no one should be elected to any office who received a campaign contribution from a corporation, the task before them would be comparable.

Political battles, physical warfare lay ahead for the reformers. Our focus will be on the rhetorical and legal combat against bribery itself, a combat centered on 'the simonian heresy'. In this manner of speaking, it is said almost daily that one sells God when he sells justice. "It is evident that neither God nor grace nor justice can be sold although" each can be trampled on for a price.

He who denies the truth for money or speaks false testimony against anyone is proved to deny or sell God. In the context of the same discussion stood the strong text of Ysidro on the judge who seeks a reward for a just judgement. Described as one 'perpetrating a fraud on God'. With it went Ysidro's lapidary phrase. "The taking of money is the undoing of truth".

Interspersed with other texts on judgements wrongly motivated by wrath, Ysidro was quoted, "Justice is quickly violated by gold," and Augustine's letter to Macedonius was recalled, slightly para-pharased, 'Although it may be lawful for an advocate to sell his just advocacy and for a juris consult to sell right counsel, it is not lawful for a judge to sell a just judgement'.

Can alms be given out of usury? "The argument run that what was unjustly acquired must be restored to its true owner. To the contrary, Gratian cited the words to Macedonius teaching that lower officials who by 'tolerable custom' took payments from those doing business with them should give the money to the poor if they changed their lives for the better. This concession to human weakness was surrounded in Gratian's text by the whole paragraph of Augustine declaring that payments to judges where always wicked and giving the rationale that the judge must not be bound to one side.

The father's and emperors' warnings against corruption of the courts were there for all to read. Generations of European law years were to read them.

After seven centuries in which emperors had issued edicts and popes decrees, in which saints had exhorted and homilists denounced, the Concordantia left no doubt in legal theory and legal teaching that neither the spirit not justice could be sold. Still, the preference of academic lawyers has always been to ignore the subjection of rules to the forces of money and influence.

Bribery was a matter to which less than 1 per cent of the Concordantia was devoted. If one went by counting texts the practice was inferably rare and the subject insignificant. Yet, if money spoke more powerfully than texts, the 99 per cent dedicated to exposition of the rules was less important than the 1 per cent directed to preserving the integrity of the judges. If the courts were not incorruptible, no rule of law was beyond bending.

Defenders of the bureaucrats would say that someone has to pay for pen and ink and the daily sustenance of the office-holders, why not the user? John has a double answer. First, these men are not taking routine fees, they are getting "whole pounds". Second, in a well run government, they would have fixed fees and not be expected to make booty of the cases that come their way. They could, John concedes, receive true gifts, *munera* in a good sense, spontaneously offered. Depending on the circumstances of their offering, *munera* 'shine or sully'. These sullied, it is *aximatica* that "to take a benefit is to sell one's liberty". What more shameful for those who are supposed to rule than by taking gifts to become "slaves?" Officials of this sort have indeed sold themselves twice-once in asking, again in delivering.

At this frank and earnest exhortation, John says the pope broke into laughter. He told John the fable the stomach: The other members of the body once complained that they did all the work, seeing, hearing, walking. The stomach did nothing but ate what they produced. The arms and legs and all agreed to abstain from work and to starve the idle greedy stomach. In three days they were faint. Then, they knew that the stomach had to be supplied if anything was to be distributed to them. Further, he said, the Roman Church is like the stomach. John adds no comment. The fable was a very fine defence for the financing of a central organism by levies on its lesser members.

In general, three things were to be considered: the quantity of the offering; the time of its donation, and 'the quality' of the donor and donee. 'Blessed is he who shakes every offering from his hands' was written off gifts likely to 'allure or pervert the soul. In Rome it was not condemned. But it was the bishops of England who could have to risk the king's anger—'when the lion roars, who does not tremble? If they paid anything to Thomas: 'Why do your annual returns mean so much to you, my father, that you want to get them for yourself by the blood of your brothers? Even the Jews, when Judas brought back the money, spurned it because they recognized what was blood-price.

Acting in person, not discriminating among persons, not

taking *munera,* Thomas had been in his last days a true judge. When John wrote his only letter on the circumstances of Thomas's death. This image of his justice came back: he was 'a judge most incorruptible and surely the taker up of neither persons nor gifts'. The generic reform had been accomplished by Christ. It remained for each one, in particular, to be reformed as to the taking of offerings. A pope, the most brilliant of the thirteenth century, was to show how difficult of accomplishment this was at the seat of power.

7

THE QUARTER AND THE ROAD

Religion can be read an reinforcement of the Iron Law, "I give that you may give" a law requiring reciprocity with every power holder including God.

He endorsed the view that even little offerings were corrupting, as Jerome had said. A wife who accepted a small offering from outside her home gave 'a sign of her own corruption;' in the same way, 'from a judge who takes even a small offering, no judgement will issue except a corrupt one'. Let the 'judge in giving judgement have not a friend but only God in mind.'

Under 'Avarice', Robert's inquiring confessor asked, 'Have you ever been corrupted as a judge, witness, advocate, assessor, or arbiter?' If the answer was affirmative, the priest was tó proceed, 'You are bound to satisfy the one you injured as to his loss, his expenses, and his harassment'. Offerings were analyzed in the ancient terms of Gregory the Great munera of the hand, munera of the tongue, and munera of service. Any offerings given for a spiritual good constituted simony.

A judge who sold justice was selling neither a sacrament nor a virtue but his judgement; by implication, he was not guilty of simony. He was, however, guilty of sin and was bound to give what he received either to the poor or to the person injured by his judgement. 'Judges have large incomes so that in their office they can maintain justice, and therefore, they should receive nothing.

The Preacher : Nero in hell was boiling in molten gold when he was surprised to see a group coming: Who should they be but lawyers. The moral for this 'venal race of men' was evident - 'Lawyers, beware, lest you sell your souls to the devil'. The homilist did not specify that lawyers would pay *munera* to win. Their avarice was globally satirized.

A third story: a "poor little woman" was not able to get her right from a notoriously venal judge. She was told, "unless his hands are oiled, you will never obtain justice". She obtained grease from a pig and began to oil the judge's hand in the courtroom. 'Woman, what are you doing?' he exclaimed. 'Lord, it was said to me that unless I oiled your hands, I could not get justice from you'. The judge blushed and was covered with confusion that his ways should be so well-known. The moral: "You, dearest brothers, judging or pleading, conduct yourselves so that you can render a secure account of the talent committed to you before the Supreme Judge, our Lord".

Reforms advocated by Le Chantre - marriage for prostitutes, interest on dowries, abolition of the ordeal, reduction of the canonical gobbledy *goods* on consanguinity and affinity - were to become his reforms.

"You do not attend to the merits of the cases but to the merits of the persons. You attend not to the laws but the *munera*, not to justice but to money". "You"—an indefinite you - "with delay neglect the poor man's case, with urgency you press the rich man's", You - still indefinite—"do not give favour (*gratia*) *gratis* or justice justly". As an adage ran, "Profit in the coffer, loss in the conscience". The measure of the greedy was distorted, their vision was directed at what they could get: "Insatiable is the eye of the avaricious"

To conclude a judgement clearly contrasted with judgements familiar to the author:

> *Wealth will then not avail.*
> *Honors will not be a defence.*
> *Friends will not provide patronage.*

As the Apocalypse puts it, 'He shuts, no one opens. He opens, no one shuts.' Him 'no one can corrupt'. He 'does not swerve from the path or righteousness for prayer or price, love or hate. Always treading the royal road, He will pass over no evil unpunished. He will leave no good unrewarded. The royal Road, designated the path of the just judge.

A certain horrible crime. The tale came from Josephus' history of the fall of Jerusalem. Among the inhabitants reduced to starvation was a mother who devoured her son. What he conveyed was the sense of a vision that rose above material inducements and a progress or process that was like God's because it was free from corruption.

'Filthy profits' (*turpia lucra*, our English 'filthy *lucre*') was already the term used to describe a variety of shameful gains, among them the fee of a prostitute. Filthy profits were what innocent called the litigant-derived compensation of the judges. The term was one of art: it implied wrongdoing, disgraceful conduct, not necessarily injustice. The pope was not saying that every such payment was a bribe; and there was a great deal of litigation where no material object by which compensation could be measured was in contention. But wrongful offerings (*munera*), the pope asserted, could be involved. Judges - delegate were ecclesiastics, assigned benefices by the Church. Innocent said, so "they could live decently". They must impart justice *gratis*.

Another reform: the papal notaries were guarded by doorkeepers from the importunities of litigants in need of documents. To gain admittance one paid. A payment to a door keeper was, so it seemed, different from payment to an office-holder: the old rationalization of access payments had taken this transparent from: Innocent had the doorkeepers dismissed. Most practically, he published a schedule of fees to be paid both the writers who prepared documents and the sealers who sealed them. Not for innocent the costless and impractical justice that Le Chantre had celebrated is St. Thomas of Canterbury. A public schedule would set modest limits. Other acts in the legal process at the *curia* were, the pope added, to be free.

Above all, it was boast that he heard cases in public frequently and in person. In a major case, he took an active part in stating each side. He threw himself into the role of raising the most difficult objections to the advocate of each party in turn, so that each side hearing he would be sure He was on their side. Thus after mature deliberation, he decided. The Lod Chancellor's famous line in Tria 1 by Jury, 'And I, my Lords, embody the law', could have been uttered by him with 'justice' substituted for 'the law'. A friend in power is a friend lost.

NOTES AND REFERENCES

1. *Ibid.*. 15.
2. Lotario, *De miseria*, Bk. 2, chap. 1 ("three big things"); 2, 4 ("woe to you"); 2, 5 ("profit in the coffer"); 2-6, ("insuitable").

8

BUY BACKS

Put aside the corrosive effect of nepotistic example. The legacy of the Innocentian years was a stronger set of standards, sanctions, and institutions hostile to bribe-taking. Innocentian images and rhetoric firmly upheld the ideal of non-reciprocity with judges and with dispensers of the Spirit. The requirement that every Christian confess his sins once a year. In the course of the twelth century, however, papal pardons were extended to those who merely contributed to the expenses of the crusades, and a concrete connection between a cash payment and the pardon obtained was evident.

Royal administration under Edward-I had already taken a strong public stand against bribe-taking. Inquiry had been made at the beginning of his reign, in 1274-1275, into a variety of offences by officials in the justice system.

9

THE POUCHES AND THE PITCH

A bribe-taker "Soils" his hands.

The wolf turns out to be the deadliest of enemies: the *Purgatorio* exclaims,

> *Cursed by you, old wolf.*
> *More than all the other beasts you have.*
> *Prey; for your hunger desires*
> *without end.*

The hunger without end is for wealth, and the wolf's prey are the deeds to which the hunger leads. To speak without symbols, as Dante does in *De monarchia*, the desire for wealth is 'the worst enemy of justice'. In the journey just described one batch of sinners who have been dominated by it are being punished by demons who are themselves remarkably vicious.

Dante does make a distinction between those who surrender to the desire for wealth and those who pursue wealth by unjust deeds. Earlier the travellers had encountered those who had given in to their passions, among themavarice.

Beginning with the Seventh Circle they meet those whose sins include malice - that is, sins of which "injustice is their end". The mark of injustice is this: its accomplishment always "afflicts someone else". Those who have harmed others by violence are in the Seventh Circle. In the Ninth are traitors, who have not only failed to keep a natural love for their fellow men, but have broken faith with those to whom they owed personal loyalty. Between the Seventh and the Ninth are "the pouches" where fraud is punished.[1]

Fraud-*La frode*-is a comprehensive term for the injustice brought about by the wolf's hunger and man's use of his intellect. As Dante teaches in the *Convivio*, justice is "the most human" of virtues. Conversely, fraud-the opposite of justice-is "man's proper vice".[2] For this reason it is worse than violence.

Fraud is also counter to love, to Dante an essential element of justice. In *De monarchia* he writes of "charity or upright love which sharpens and gives light to justice". Over the gate of hell is the inscription:

> *"Divine Power, Supreme Wisdom, Primal Love*
> *Made me."*

"Grafter" is an appropriate term for any kind of official who trades his assent for money-the *barattier*, and "to do *baratteria*" may be rendered, slightly more succinctly than in the Italian, as "to graft."

Accusations of bribery are often political. Accusation is not proof. Accusers may themselves tumble into the pitch. He has made his own bride a harlot-rented her out for money. A fourteenth-century commentator observes. "No greater outrage can a man do to the wife whom he has married than to make her submit for money to him who gives the most."[3]

Not rejecting the institution of papacy, Dante sees its major crime as simony. No reformer, before or since, has made a simpler or more passionate indictment.[4]

Date expects no help from the corrupt papacy. He finds civic corruption published by cruel politicians who themselves get into the pitch.

The bribery of chuochmen and civil leaders in corrected only by God's grace. The terrible indictments of corruption, which could be a call to recollection, end in this prayer.

NOTES AND REFERENCES

1. Inferno, Canto 1, 49-50 (the wolf); *Purgatorio,* Canto 20-10-13 (the wolf cursed); Dante, *De monarchia,* ed. E. Moore (Oxford: Clarendon Press, 1916) 1, 11, 69 ("worst enemy of justice"); *Inferno,* Canto 11,22-24:

D'ogne malizia, Ch'odio in cielo acquisita,
ingiuria e il fine, ed ogne fin cotale
o con forza o con frode altrui contrista.

2. Dante Il Convivio, ed Maria Simonelli (Bologna: Casa Editrice Prof. Riccardo Patron, 1966) 1, 12, 98 (justice most human virtue).

3. *L'Ottimo Commento della Divina Commedia*, ed, Alessandro Torri (Pisa, 1827) 1, 348-349.

4. Writing the six Italian cardinals at nAvignon in 1314 Dante tells them that they despise "the fire sent from heaven" and"strange fire burns on the altars-you sell doves in the temple where those things which cannot be measured .. are made sellable". Eacg has married a wife-covetousness", Dante to the Italian cardinals (circa May-June 1314), *Epistolae,* Letter 9, 131, 133.

10

THE MONKEYS AND THE BEARS

Bribery and witchcraft is a major pollutant of pre-modern society.

In a vision Willian the poet sees a woman in scarlet dress banded with gold and trimmed with the finest fur, a crown on her head, amethysts, beryls, diamonds, sapphires, rubies on her fingers. He asks his guide, Holy Church, her identity, Holy Church, a lady herself, has told him that of all treasures truth is the best, and she now introduces the other woman: "That is Mede the Made," and procedes to delineate her character.[1]

By personification the poet has captured the ambiguity of the basic Latin word for bribe. *Munus* can be the honest return given a labourer or it can be the chief mischief-maker in the pope's places and the corrupt friend of simony, secular law (Cyuille), and jurors. Truth taught by the Church will expose the character in which it acts. In the poem *Munus* is Mede.[2]

Mede has ruined those who love her gifts. She has poisoned popes and corrupted Holy Church and destroyed the king's father. She is "tikil of hire taile", that is, sexually excitable and promiscuous. She is, it is true, respected by jurors, summoners, jailors, and sheriffs. She and Symonye seal the pope's own bulls.

She makes illiterates into bishops and provides livings for priests with concubines and children. At the royal court she does more in one month than the king's privy seal can do in six.

In law court, "She ledeth the lawe as hire list", that is, she decides the law; and a case will not end unless she provides presents or pence (3, 157. 160-161). Poor men have no power to get redress. Mede brings disaster to all honest men.

Never having had joy, he who was created for joy, dares ask joy from his just Judge. A rich man, on the contrary, has been paid by God in advance. He can get another reward after death only if he "rewarde we the pore" (14, 96).

The *Simonie*, whose anonymous author had also found Truth afraid to enter the pope's palace and archdeacons taking made of this one and that one.[3] 'He had fed on the scholastic tradition - for example, the identification of ecclesiastical bribe-taking with simony going back to Pierre le Chantre and his English pupil Thomas Chobhan - and on conventional satire of the curia, satire here handled with great restraint.

Scripture had nourished him most. Out of these public themes, the poet made a personal work - the life project of a man uncelebrated by his contemporaries, a professional acolyte paid for his prayers, with a wife Kitte and a girl Kalote, now old, bald, and impotent if the autobiographical parts can be trusted.

In Piers, a man wrestles with evil, and a large part of that evil as he observes it takes place in acts of bribery in the king's court and the bishop's. No more brilliant analysis has ever been made of the ambiguity of *munera* and the omnipresence of reciprocity in human affairs than the allegory of Mede the maid. The allegory is enriched by full exploitation of the sexual metaphors for the bribe-taker, boldly applied to Mede herself as a bribe-giver.

The concluding world under Antichrist, so far from the kingdom ruled by the Logos, is amazingly bleak-mundane, one might say. Its evils are social. Escape from it is personal and by God's gift. In the time of Antichrist—that is, now 1378 - Resoun and Conscience do not hold sway at the Arches, Westminster, or the pope's palace.[4]

Bishops commit simony when they enter office for temporal profits; when they spend the poor's money on themselves, maintaining large households and grooms for their horses; when they collect money for their services as they do, for example, by charging five marks for the consecration of a holy place; when they wink at charges by their servants (there is even a small charge made by the clerk registering the names of the newly ordained); or when they sell staff appointments like the office of summoner.

To say that what they get is given voluntarily is a sophism; if one did not pay one would get nothing from them. They say they charge only for their labour - they are like vendors who claim to give away some things but actually charge more for the total. Today in England few or no prelates are not simonian heretics.[5]

The evil was left to be redressed by another judge, who could wipe out such a stain which was 'quasi-indelible'? Who could heal a wound which 'had seared so widely'? Where earlier writers could have said "Christ," Wyclif put his trust in the people. The people should reject "the old men" when they are "drunk with avarice" - a remarkably revolutionary note associating age with corruption and making the metaphor of intoxications stand for absorption in wealth.

The people should withhold from the ecclesiastics their offerings, their tithes, their gifts, or their bequests creating endowments. Simony called for rebellion by the faithful, the peaceful rebellion of non-cooperation with the economic system of the Church.[6]

Theological foundation for the traffic in pardons was, Wycliff asserted wanting: no one "can be entirely released from his debt to God". As he put it in other terms, there is an essential connection between sin and punishment, and from it God himself cannot dispense; or as he less rigidly expressed it, satisfaction for sin is part of the *regalia* or royal prerogatives of God, release from which he cannot permit to be performed vicariously.

Moreover, the merits of the saints go to their own account and are not available for distribution. God determines who will profit by the saints' merits. Merits of past deeds cannot be appropriated to help future persons. The whole idea of a treasure of merits gained by suffering and administered by the pope was an invention arising out of "fantastic imagination".[7]

As a campaigner against corruption, Wyclif had done four

things, Bromyard and Fitz Ralph had not; he treated Simonians as heretics; he had attacked indulgences at their root, he had attacked popes by name; and he had called for a kind of layman's boycott of the corrupt establishment. The legacy of Wyclif to those he taught or among whom his works were popularized was a violent sense of abuses in the Church without practical remedies—withholding contributions was about as practical as a tax revolt in the United States today.

"Brybe", the verb, designates the action of the official; it is the equivalent of "extort under colour of office." The summoner goes on to threaten a poor widow with a bogus excommunication unless she pays him twelve pennies. By her curse he is hauled off to hell. A partner of devils, found already in the pages of Bromyard, he is the sinister, story-within-a-story counterpart of the Somonour who is one of the principal pilgrims riding with Frere Hubert, the teller of this tales.

The Pardoner—already described as "a geldying or a mare," like Bromyard's spiritual eunuch he cannot enter the kingdom is told that the Host would prefer his genitals pickled in hogshit.

The bishops say they are selling their Labour not their blessing. They are like innkeepers who serve food free and charge more for beer that the cost of the food and drink combined. And the bishops enter into office simoniacally paying the pope. Many thousand gulden are paid to obtain the archbishopric of Prague.

The annates regularly and openly demanded by the pope from episcopal appointees are simoniac. The pope does not even use "a Gehazi"; he himself has set the rate. Old Nick may say that the pope grants a benefice without any demands being made and that he takes the appointee's money later, so there is no trafficking.

"But Hodek the baker or Huda the vegetable woman would answer Old Nick that when he has bread for sale and someone comes in and in silance lays the money on the counter, either before or after taking the bread, Hodek or Huda concludes that the customer has bought the bread.

The laity are similarly "besmirched" with many kinds of simoniacal practice. At the coarsest level they dispose of ecclesiastical appointments in exchange for money or services; or they make ecclesiastical appointments to a relative or a man who is a good hunting companion. A layman presenting a cleric for a benefice "because of money, gifts, material service, worldly favour, blood or marriage relationship, flattery or to oblige another" is among the Simonians. The sin includes in its sweep those families who send their children to school "that they may become rich, receive honour in the world, and become able to help their relatives." The fathers and mothers send their sons "with evil intent" and their children pursue their studies with "evil intent". Finally, there are the Simonians who cooperate in the commission of simony as its abettors, councilors, and defenders.

A jury of thieves convicting a thief? Since the days of Cicero, scarcely unusual where bribery was the crime. If the exemplary effect of the council's action was weakened by selectivity in the culprits punished, it was even more undermined by the secrecy and haste with which John XXIII was condemned and by the absence of counsel and witnesses for him. The grand example of punishing a pope for simony was also muffled by what was finally done to the deposed pope.

Temporarily imprisoned but not treated like Hus as a heretic, Baldassare Cossa survived to be bishop of Frascati. The proceeding against him at best looked like a grand jury presentment, not a trial, and could be seen as political theater: his submission was not a confession.

Everyone could see the political motive at work: when the Council disposed of one of the two principal popes it had reduced the schism to manageable size.

Finally, in the eyes of Bohemia the Council had made a martyr of the country's most powerful critic of corruption. Constace-the great general council intended to remedy corruption-was compromised, a failure, even before the conciliar flops of the later fifteenth century ended hope in the ability of a council to achieve reform.[9]

As to secular bribery, he had much and little to say:

> There are those who go to steal secretly and with fear, as do thieves who secretly enter homes and steal what they can. Robbers who infest ways and woods and despoil the passers-by are like them, and such are called forest thieves. And there are many others who with open faces under the pretext and insignia of justice, flag flying in the name of common utility, come to office to skin the people. How many extortions, disembowelings, frame-ups, wickednesses, frauds false promises, undue favours, impious terrors and other evil machinations they engage in to draw in money the unhappy peoples who have experienced such things in certain countries know. These are domestic thieves, and they are so much the more pernicious than the forest thieves as among other things they are so much the more secure; for they are not punished and hung as robbers and thieves but defended, praised and honoured by those who are like them, and each becomes an example and a safeguard for the other.[10]

Heartfelt denunciation of crooked politicians set out in a series of lenten sermons, "the Eternal Gospel", this paragraph would appear to be only a prelude to one of Bernardino's masterly dissections of the tricks of a class of crafty wrongdoers. It is a prelude to a definition of *concussio* or shakedown, which, Bernardino says, includes three kinds of acts by officials-extorting money by fear; refusing to carry out a legal duty unless given money; extracting in anyway something beyond salary. The definition encompassed what Chaucer meant by "bribery" and what is often meant by bribery today.

Shakedown and its spiritual counterpart, simony, Bernardino says, constitute one of the four sins arising from avarice for which God beats cities and countries with His anger. Along with the other three sins—robbery, oppression of the poor, and ingratitude for divine benefits—it draws from God the collective punishment of the community. Knowing the unsparing character of Bernardino's denunciation of other sins, one would expect him to give details, to bring the guilt home to those responsible. But the passage says only that these domestic thieves have been experienced by people "in certain countries" No specific suggestion is made as to where such creatures may be found.

"Truth in the world", Bernardino preaches on another occation, "is not defended" because of fear, lechery, or avarice. "Because of avarice," he observes, "many do not defend the truth as they are bound by obligation to do." "He illustrates not by a judge taking a bribe, not by any instance from Siena or any Italian city, but from the court of Herod when Salome asked for John the Baptist's head.

There were "the princes and tribunes and first men of Galilee"—these words are from the Gospel of Mark 6:21—and Bernardino adds,— "They preferred to serve desire rather than stand for the truth." So, "in these times", he continues, there are those "who do not favour the truth, as they are bound to do, lest they give up gain. They have many accomplices in their crime". In a few words, with a slight expansion of the Gospel text, Bernardino has evoked the picture of complaisant courtiers too selfish to risk their positions to speak out for an innocent man. But the scene is far from home; there is no indication of where such courtiers exist in Italy.[11]

In the Lenten series of 1425, preaching in Santa Croce in Florence, he proclaims, "There are twelve evils which undo your city and all others." The first is "the false judge in the consistory," the other is "the avaricious man in office who for money commits every evil and every act of graft. In another florentine sermon of 1425, he declares, "Many of your officials and rulers and other officials have become little tyrants and disgrace your country and your land"; and he sweepingly announces, "Better to live without bread than without justice." Again, at Florence he preaches that the Venetians do not do as the Florentines do. The Venetians remove from office and bar from future appointment any ruler who receives" a single present."[12]

More generally he strikes at bribery in his indictments of avarice and selfishness. In a splendid sermon he apostrophizes "Self or Private Love," as follows:

> *O most cruel beast ....you corrupt all virtues.... You love. no one unless it is reciprocal.... You are distraught if you do not receive....O worst of beasts, in judgements you pervert the just.*

Identifying the requirement of reciprocation as the demand of self-love, Bernardino identifies the central psychological mechanism by which corruption works, he puts his finger on the essential of every corrupt transaction- the demand of a *quid pro quo* by an official bound to act gratuitously and without reciprocity from the one for whom he acts.

Still, he says nothing, or next to nothing, about the political mechanisms by which corruption worked. The problems of restitution arising from the receipt of bribes and the resultant injury to litigants were presumably enormous. Bernardino picks up the problems perfunctorily, invoking Augustine as quoted in Gratian. As to bribes given to judges, Bernardino accepts the view of Alessandro Lombardo, the Franciscan master general in 1313, that if a litigant paid to assure his right, then the judge was bound to return the money to the litigant.

If the bribe was given "to corrupt the mind of the judge," then the repentant judge was bound to give it to the poor. Bernardino's general principles stated elsewhere, required restitution by anyone unjustly causing harm. He makes no specific mention of the obligation of the bribed judge to make up the loss caused by his corrupt decision.

He frees from any obligation of restitution the intercessors paid for their work in obtaining the release of an innocent man. He says the intercessors find merit with God and pays no attention to the shabby network in which they must be a part.[13]

Can a clue to his relative reticence in developing the theme be found in his imagery? A recurrent phenomenon in the vernacular sermons is Bernardino's recourse to animal analogies to describe the corrupt office-holder. A man who leaves his own trade to "despoil the city" is like the cat who sits before a mousehole waiting to seize the mouse who comes out-the mouse is the countryman or poor man.

The avaricious man in office who is prepared to "pluck this one and to plunder that one and to butcher this one" is like a wolf who stuffs himself on a pig. The ruler who does not give justice is like the lion who acquitted the predatory animals and found the lamb worthy of death.

Bad rulers, he tells the Florentines, are the locusts of the

Apocalypse. They are insatiable insects with swollen bodies. "They eat and they bite, these bad rulers, with teeth of iron....They eat their subject."[14]

Pouncing cat, gluttonous wolf, hypocrite lion, iron-toothed locust-the bestial images accumulate. The great beast, Self-Love, takes the form of many different animals, and, in general, Bernardino is not reluctant to point out how sin bestializes man. Historically, tales and images of animals have always been a way for the oppressed or express popular complaint against a ruling class.

The animal images figure prominently in Bromyard's repertoire. When Bernardino employs these similes he is speaking for the oppressed without attacking individual office holders. In one of his most striking stories, told in the Campo in Siena in 1426, he tells of the bear and the monkeys at the French court: The bear, being stronger, ate a baby monkey. The mother monkey ran from one person to another looking into their faces "as if asking for justice." No one responded.

"As no one does justice for the fault of that bear, I will do it myself," declared the mother monkey. She went to the hay-loft where the bear slept, took hay, piled it round the bear, and set it on fire, burning the bear alive. "And she did justice herself."

A final, functional reason: Preaching against bribery was necessarily acusatorial; a preacher could not provide a trial. Accusations of bribery functioned to express social dissatisfaction and social criticism. This function was fulfilled by Bernardino's sustained attack on the multitude of usurious practices. No need for him to duplicate the function that the great sermons against voracious usury already performed.

The story of the monkey and the bear was itself a parable with as much force for the Church as for any secular community. If justice was not upheld in the Church by those appointed to uphold it, Christians would do it themselves. For almost 400 years, reform had been sought by popes and councils, by the passage of statutes and by personal conversions, in the founding of orders and the multiplication of universities.

Reform, if Hus and Wycliff, Chaucer and Langland, preachers and professors and poets could be believed, was still far from realized. Bernardino worked for it from within, without public denunciations of the evils. Others were gathering way-much of it from Bernard, Innocent III, and the canons to be found in Gratian and Gregory IX-for a large conflagration. Sparks from preaching were falling here and there. The bears within the Church were still asleep or at large.

Fire

In all things, look to the end,
and how you will be judged before a strict Judge,
from whom nothing is hidden,
who is not placated by offerings
and does not accept excuses.
but will judge what is just.

These are lines from the great spiritual classic of the fifteenth century. The Imitation of Christ. The austere figure of the Judge at the Last Judgement is drawn in amplicit contrast to human judges who do not judge what is just, who accept excuses, who take *munera*. This kind of piety is not revolutionary but reflects a sense that justice without offerings is an ideal to be realized by divine judgement. Other spiritual authorities looked to reform now.

Even when combined with unorthodox views of the sacraments and the Church, as in Wyclif, the critique of corruption had not been sufficient - absent other conditions-to bring about major changes. The break-up of the papal supervision of the churches of half of Western Europe was a complex concatenation, with multiple causes-among them national and international politics, dynastic calculations, ethnic loyalty, personal greed, spiritual hunger, commercial growth, capital accumulation, new learning, new methods of communication, new concentrations of energy.

"The Reformation was a vast series of events whose religious impact was often liberating for those affected. In the words of a memorable essay by Lucien Febvre, it would be "ridiculous and profoundly puerile" to believe that the spiritual manifestations of the Reformation were caused by impersonal abuses or "by the fairly habitual lack of shame of the merchants of the temple, those eternal parasites of the divine."[15]

Rejection of what once was a stereotype of the Reformation goes too far, however, if it overlooks the part played by the tradition on bribery (including simony), corruption, and reform. In three ways the tradition affected what took placed. First, it had a supportive, if not generative, role in the theology of Redemption which was critical for Luther's thought. Second, it affected the ability of the Roman authorities to reassert themselves. Third, it occupied a prominent place in Rome's perception of the problems posed and channelled much of the Roman response.

Rome itself saw the problems which Luther and his allies posed in the traditional terms where a cry of corruption should be met by measures of reform. The first Roman response, of course, was to defend the general lawfulless of indulgences. After that, as the crisis worsened, a new pope, Adrian Florense, Adrian VI, was elected. An imperial Diet met in Nuremberg holding out the possibility of a settlement in Germany. Writing to his nuncio Francesco Chieragato to convey his views to the Diet in November 1522, the pope declared, "In this Holy See now for some years there have been many abominations.... As corruption has emanated from it into all lower parts, so also from it will come the cure and reformation of all."

"One Hundred Complaints," drafted by the lay estates at the Diet meanwhile reinforced Adrian's confession of corruption. First on the list was "Dispensations Bought Back by Cash" Innumerable obstacles to marriage, the laymen said, had been invented. Money was then able to obtain the favour of dispensing from them. "Money was able to obtain what is freely prohibited to the poor". Complaint number three was "The Burdens of Papal Pardons, "by which the popes were said to have" sucked everything from the simple and too credulous Germans." Indulgences destroyed piety. Every purchaser of them "promises himself impunity in sinning." The fourth complaint was that money so raised was spent "on the luxury of relatives," and the fifth was that the pope reserved cases of absolution to Rome as a way of raising money.[16]

In them the importance of the indulgence issue and corruption generally were given a reading from the Catholic Side: "The heresy of Luther first arose because of the abuses of the Roman Curia, and it grew and spread because of the corrupt morals of the clergy." To meet these evils, SDN (Sanctissimus Dominus Noster-Our Most Holy Lord) should publish "a bull of reformation," and we should call a general council. Specifically, SDN should not appoint non-germans to German benefices, should not takle annates at more than the ancient rate, should not take annates more than once a year even though the benefice becomes vacant twice, should not permit laymen to be dragged before ecclesiastical tribunals in lay cases, and should excommunicated only in grave cases.

Bishops should not permit "nonotrious concubines" to be tolerated, and should, in particular, avoid "the wicked name and fact of toleration where they take money and leave the delinquent unpunished. "Bishops should choose vicars who do not rob the churches, and they should control the preachers.

Pardons "are to be moderated." Scandals have arisen from their collectors, who have used indulgences to pay for hospitality and "what is most foul of all, as a nocturnal wage for wicked women." Germans as well as Romans now bargain over indulgences.

The emperor will not allow indulgences "unless he has a part of the Lord's tunic". Indulgences now are so common that they are sold cheaply. If there were not so many, the pope could raise a bigger subsidy from the German to fight the Turks.

Benefices are a worse problem. Those in Rome traffick in them, getting ten, twenty, thirty benefices—"the patrimony of Christ is set before dogs, pimps, and whores. O gods "In litigation over benefices, fraud is frequent, and wolf agrees beautifully with wolf."

Settlements, savoring of simony, are frequently used to settle benefice cases. Settlements for cash are also the rule with the Sacred Penitentiary, the tribunal handling sins reserved to Rome. "All other kinds of satisfaction are now excluded. Commutation alone remains. Silver and gold only." If a couple has married within the prohibited degrees of relationship and need a dispensation, they are always told. "You must pay, Only pay, and you shall have. I cannot do it for less."

Not surprisingly the office of penitentiary is a salable office, so that its incumbents make money to get a return on their investment and know less of Scripture and the Fathers "than an ass about a lyre"

Confessors of the penitentiary hurry penitents saying." This is nothing. Say something serious'. They are not interested in souls but in getting two or three julians per penitent. To make money the penitentianries release monks from their vows and tighten the canonical way of computing the degrees of kinship and teach proctors of the parties to say what is necessary, 'not caring if it be true or false'.

From Gregory I to Leo X, reform of corruption had been attempted in many ways, direct and indirect, through sanctions and channelling and teaching, by increased centralization of government and active papal intervention in local affairs; by the cultivation of moral theology and canon law in universities removed from some of the pressures of office-seeking.

By preaching, by instruction in the confessional, by personal exhortation; by literature which, reaching its height in Dante and Chaucer, excoriated the bribe-taker, the seller of the spiritual, the corrupt Church. Purity had been insisted on. Accusations had multiplied. No charm had worked. Corruption remained.

The tradition also remained. The tradition so relentlessly established and asserted—theological in its roots and in its ultimate sanction of the Last Judgement; literary in its most effective expositions; political in its implications for judges and rulers on earth—was the embodiment, the ultimate 'work' of all the preaching and legislating and moralizing and exhorting against bribe-takers and Simonians.

This tradition, so formidable in its contributors, its scope, and its bulk, had sustained the recurrent reformation which had gone on since the eleventh century, and that reformation had, in turn, shaped the tradition, making possible - not causing single-handedly the Protestant Reformation and the Catholic Counter Reformation. The tradition needed only to be put into the vernacular to provide a basis for other reformations in the secular governments which were now to occupy center stage.

NOTES AND REFERENCES

1. Modern English writers have rendered Mede as "*Lady Fee*". (J.F. Goodridge, *Piers the Ploughman* Penguin Books, 1959); or said Mede stands for the desire for reward" (Morton W. Bloomfield, *Piers Plowman as a Fourteenth-Century Apocalypse* (New Brunswick, N.J.:Rutgers University Press, 1961) 111, cf. p.6); or identified Lady Mede with graft (Donald and Rachel Attwater, *Piers Plowman* London: J.M. Dent, 1957 ix,202). None of these approximations preserves the ambiguity of munus or mede. The ambiguity is pointed out by Elizabeth Salter, *Piers Plowman* (Cambridge, Mass.: Harvard University Press, 1962) 97, when she says that Mede "is both bribery and reward."
2. Cf. Bloomfield, *Piers Plowman* 38.
3. *The Simonie* 11, 9.16, in Thomas Wright, ed., *The political songs of England* (London: Camden Society, 1839); Elizabeth Salter, "Piers Plowman and 'The Simonie,'" *Archiv. fur das Studium der neueren Sprachen und Literaturen* 203 (1967) 248-250.
4. On the date, Skeat, *Piers Plowman* 2, 274, n. 447.
5. *Ibid.* c. 1, p, 4 (few prelates not heretics) c. 6. pp. 70-83 (Simonians by motives, lifestyle, charges).
6. *Ibid*, c. 7, 94 (stop offerings); c. 8, 101 (old men drunk with avarice).
7. *Ibid*, c. 29, 551 (fantastic imagination); 560 (no release from debt to God); 561 (*regalia* of deity); 564 (past merits not distributable); 568 (God distributes merits); 586 (connection of punishment to sin); see Introduction, xvi, xxiv, on the date of c. 23 devoted to indulgences.
8. Geoffrey Chaucer, *The Canterbury Tales,* ed. F.N. Robinson (Boston: Houghton Mifflin, 1957) F 1517-1520. These abbreviations are adopted: C= Clerks's Tale; F= Freres Tale; MLT=Man of Lawes Tale; P= Prologue; Pers= Persouns Tale; PT= Pardoners Tale; ST= Somonours Tale. Chaucer's use of "brybe" as a verb appears to be a metaphorical adaptation of the *French briber*, to eat greedily, to beg bread; see Randall Cotgrave, *A Dictionary of the French and English Tongues* (London: Adam

Islip, 1632) at *briber*. In making a transformation of the verb, Chaucer's usage begins a new career for the word; in French, the *noun une bribe* meant onbly a piece of bread given to a beggar. The French for one giving a bribe was *un corrompeur par dons,* and the French verb for bribe or corrupt was *corrompre;* see Cotgrave at these words. On the *apparitors* and their blank citations, see Robert E. Rodes; Jr., *Ecclesiastical Administration in Medieval England* (Notre Dame, Ind.: University of Notre Dame Press, 1977) 138.

9. Spinka, *John Hus* 290, 298.

10. Bernardino, *Quadragesimale de evangelio aeterno* 18,3,1, *Opera* 3, 326-327.

11. Bernardino, *Sermones "de diversis",* Sermon 8, art. 3, c. 3 Opera 7, 469.

12. Bernardino, *De christiana religione,* Sermon 39, art. 2, c. 3, *Opera* 1, 508.

13. Bernardino, *le Prediche volgari* 5, 507-508; cf. Bernardino, *Quadragesimale de christiana religione,* Sermon 33, preamble *Opera* 1, 401, on restitution in general.

14. *Le Prediche Volgari*, ed. Cannarozzi, 5, 15.

15. Lucien Febvre, *"Une question mal posee: Les origines de la reforme francaise et le probleme des causes de la reforme", Au Coeur religieux XVIe siecle* (Paris: Sevpen, 1957) 68 Article originally published in *Revue historique* (1929) vol. 161.Cf. G.R. Elton, "Introduction: The age of the Reformation, "*The New Cambridge Modern History* (Cambridge: At the University Press, 1958) 2, 1-22; Steven E Ozment, *The Reformation in the Cities* (New Haven, Conn.: Yale University Press, 1975) 116-120.

16. Lay estates of the Diet, "Centum Gravamina", *ibid.* 133-114.

17. *Ibid.* 115-116.

11

TO RANSOM AND REDEEM, BUT NOT CORRUPT

Bribery like witchcraft is often believed to the widely practiced, but no one will voluntarily admit publicly to practicing it.

Inheritor of a tradition shared for 900 years with continental Europe and conveyed principally in Latin, England possessed a biblical teaching on bribery that theology, preaching and poetry already made part of English culture. No word existed, in Egypt, Greece, Israel or Rome, meaning only 'a corrupt gift'.

The word was found in English. Beyond linguistics, as English drama reached its climax in the early seventeenth century, its greatest playwright was to explore, with a subtlety, force, and focus unequalled by earlier theologians, the relations of a corrupt gift to Christian Redemption.

Good judges today are rare: 'These bribing judges have suffered for a long time: and then it was *quasi non fuisset rex in Anglia.* To suffer this is as much as to say. There is no king in England'. These judges who take bribes touch pitch for 'bribes may be assembled to pitch'.

The Judge Joshva condemned by Cambyses was 'a briber, a gift-taker, a gratifier of rich men, he followed gifts as fast as he that followed the pudding, hand-maker in his office..... Today, '*Omens diligunt munera*': 'they all love bribes'.

Bribery is a princely kind of thieving. They (sic) will be waged by the rich, either to give sentence against the poor, or to put off the poor man's causes. This is the noble theft of princes and magistrates. They are bribe-takers'.[1]

Bribes occur in the administration as well as in the courts, for "Lady Covetousness is a fruitful woman." Offices are bought, and "if they buy, they must need sell." "This buying of offices is a making of bribery; it is an inducing and enforcing and compelling of men to bribery.... This cometh from the devil's consistory, to pay five hundred pound for one office. If they pay so much, it must need follow that they take bribes, that they be bribe-takers."[2]

Bribes occur in the award of benefices. Thirty apples were given one patron, sent to him through his servant. The patron said he had as good apples in his own orchard. Urged to try the presents, he cut one open. It had ten goldpieces within, and so did all the rest. The donor got his benefice. "Get you a graft of this tree," said the patron, "and I warrant you it will stand you in better stead than all the learning of St. Paul."[3]

Bribes occur in secret, yet there are bribes the preacher knows of "He that took the silver basin and a ewer for a bribe, thinketh that it will never come out: but he may know now that I know it; I know it not alone, there be more beside me that know it.

Oh briber and bribery". There is the case he knows where one man killed another and was cleared by a jury who received a crown a piece. There is the case he knows where a woman delivered triplets out of wedlock, killed them at birth, and was found not guilty "through bearing of friends, and bribing of the judge." There are the bribes paid by the king's disbursing officers. Say I have spent 20,000 pounds for the king, "Well when I have laid it out, and do bring in mine account, I must give 300 marks to have my bills warranted." Why? "What needeth any bribes - giving except the bills be false?"[4]

What is the remedy for all this bribery? Like Cambyses' judge, the judges must be skinned. "Surely it was a goodly sign and a goodly monument, the sign of the judge's skin. I pray God that we may once see the sign of the skin in England." On capital punishment of a more conventional kind for bribed judges:

> But I am sure this is *scala inferni*, the right way to hell, to be covetous, to take bribes and pervert justice. If a judge should ask me the way to hell, I would show him this way: First, let him be a covetous man, let his heart be poisoned with covetous. Then let him go a little further and take bribes, and last, pervert judgement. Lo, here is the mother and the daughter and the daughter's daughter. Avarice is the mother, she brings forth bribe-taking: and bribe-taking, perverting of judgement. There lacks a fourth thing to make up the mess, which, so God help men if I were judge, should be *angum tuum, a Tyburn tippet* to take with him, and if it were the judge of the king's bench, my lord chief judge of England; yes, and it were my lord chancellor himself, to Tyburn with him.

"Bribe" and its derivatives had been employed in English since Chaucer, although shaded more to extortion than to voluntary offering. "Made" in the fourteenth century had been a rival. It was a better word for capturing the soft ambiguity of *munus*. If preservation of the amoiguity was wanted. An immense difference existed psychologically between saying, "You give him an offering," where offering could be either a corrupt inducement or gift acceptable to God, and saying, "You give him a bribe". Ambivalence was eliminated. The offering was stigmatized. The new usage no longer tolerated the double meaning words of the classical languages.

"All bribes and unrighteousness shall be put away." Two years later the Mathew Bible, based on Willian Tyndale's unpubulished translation, introduced "bribe" into I Samuel 12:3 "Whose ox have I taken-of whose hand have I received any bribe to blind mine eyes?" Coverdale in 1539, redoing his own work for the Great Bible, followed this emendation. The passage was singled out by Latimer in his preaching before king Edward: "I can commend the English translation," he declared, "that doth interpret *munera*, bribes, not gifts.

When in 1560 the Bible was translated from the Hebrew and the Greek by learned English exiles in Geneva - Calvin's brother-in-law Willian Whittington prominent among them - the precedents set by Calvin might have been followed. The Geneva Bible did still prefer "gift" or "reward" in a majority of cases. Twice, however, it employed "bribes" once (followed the Mathew Bible) at I Samuel 12:3 and once at Psalm 26:10, referring in the singular to one whose "right hand is full of bribes."

Seventy-five years of translation, therefore, had by 1611 established "bribes" as an acceptable although not necessary rendition of *shohadh doron,* or *munus.* "Lady Munera" and "meede", as well as "bribe" were used by Edmund Spenser in The Faerie Queene (1594). But the popularity of the Psalms gave "bribe" a currency beyond other terms. "Now-a-days, Latimer had preached in 1550, "they call them gentle rewards. Let them leave their colouring, and call them by their Christian names, bribes." With the Geneva and King James translations, their Christian names were fixed.

St. Augustine's account of the wife who raised the money for her husband's fine by sleeping with her rich admirer is sometimes cited as a parallel or ancestor of these tales; but the stories are at most distant cousins.

No bribery occurs in Augustine for no official is paid off, and the whole question is whether, arguably, a husband might allow this use of his wife's body. "Barrating" is bribery's synonym, and the bribe-taker is a "barriter," a term so close to barrister-a term already in vogue - that no lawyer could have relished the closeness. The key vary for paying off a low-level official is "grease", a vigorous Englishing of the old Latin term *ungere,* to oil. The earliest documented use of the term is 1526.[5]

Corrupt Judge, Corrupt Generals: For Shakespeare, the verb "to corrupt", and the adjective "corrupt" are recurrent terms. To be corrupt is to be rotted, made evil in a generic way. Joan of Arc upbraids York in Part One of *Henry VI.*

> *. . . you that are polluted with your lusts,*
> *Stain'd with the guiltless blood of innocents,*
> *Corrupted and tained with a thousand vices.*

Pollution and stain are natural accompaniments of this impure condition.

"To corrupt" is to reduce to an evil state as in Sonnet 144:

> *. . . my female evil*
> *Tempteth my better angel from my side,*
> *And would corrupt my saint to be a devil.*

"To corrupt" means specifically to seduce a woman from virtue. Bertram, the married French count in *All's Well That Ends Well*, wooing a Florenting girl, is said "to broke," that is, to be a broker or go-between, "to pimp". Bertram

> "... *brokes with all that can in such a suit*
> *Corrupt the tender honour of a maid*

"To corrupt" also means specifically to seduce an official from duty Cardinal Wolsey in *Henry VIII* begins to speak to Queen Katherin of his *integritas*. She says, "O good my Lord, no Latin." He continues to boast of his "integrity" while he and his Italian colleague advise her to submit to the King's demands. She says:

> *Is this your Christian counsel? Out upon ye!*
> *Heaven is above all yet: there sits a Judge*
> *That no King can corrupt.*

By implication the cardinals' integrity is wanting; they have been corrupted by the king.[6]

Sexual meaning and civic meaning are brought together in *Coriolanus*. A citizen comments after Coriolanus' banishment from Rome:

> *I have heard it said the fittest time*
> *to corrupt a man's wife is when she's fallen*
> *out with her husband.*

Analogously, coriolanus is ripe to be seduced. "To Corrupt" politically is paralleled to "to corrupt sexually. Corruption is also specifically invoked in connection with the sale of indulgences by the pope.

Corrupting is explicitly linked to bribery in *Part III of Henry VI*; but before this happens a scene is presented of a would-be bribe-taker in action. The new king, Edward IV, is approached by Lady Grey, whose husband has been slain in the Yorkist cause and whose lands have, then, been confiscated. York triumphant, she petitions for their restoration. Edward puts her off, hinting and, then, finally saying plainly that she will not have the lands with loss of her honesty. A metaphorical bribe has produced a corrupt effect and the effect is monstrous. That a charge of bribery can do serious political damage, especially to a office-holder who is in jeopardy.

The paradox that tears can be a lawful bribe is played with. Constance says his tears are "in nature of a fee." Like Latin *corrupere* and *corruptus*, "to corrupt" and "corrupt" gain force by invoking a range of images of evil. No progression occurs in Shakespeare in his use of the terms. Whenever they are used they designate what destroys wholesomeness. Development does take place in Shakespeare's presentation of the corruption of justice by bribery. Three plays, *The Merchant of Venice, Julius Caesar,* and *Measure for Measure*, mark the progress.

The *Merchant of Venice* was written between 1596 and 1598. By 1599 Shakespeare had finished *Julius Caesar.* Ironies involving bribery are pressed harder here; a whole scene depicting character depends on their treatment. Brutus and Cassius have been the leaders in the assassination of Caesar.

Brutus speaks not in terms of criminal law but in terms of honour. Bribes are dirty, "base", and "trash". It is dishonourable to be a taker. Brutus would rather metamorphose himself into an animal. Cassius sees himself as a practical fellow. Pella's bribery is an offence too special to be followed up in wartime. Cassius himself has more experience than Brutus in making "conditions", That is, in managing affairs. Yet for Cassius the charge of corruption is unsupportable. That is the first irony. The practical man cannot hear his practice called by its right name.[7]

The "crystal beads"—which were a lawful way of bribing in *King John* have reappeared. The sexual bribe demanded by a ruler to do his office, sketched in Part III of *Henry VI,* is now to be used as the basis of a more profound investigation. When Isabella has gone, Angelo meditates on what he may be given. Like carrion in the sun, he thinks he is becoming "corrupt with virtuous season". When Isabella returns he asks her again:

"Redemption by Christ has been put by Isabella as the model for Angelo, but he has responded by asking her to redeem her brother with herself, and redemption has come to seem, like *redemptio* in much Roman usage, filthy. Paid-for forgiveness stands in contrast to lawful mercy. Differences between a prayer as a bribe and a body as a bribe. and between a body offered as living sacrifice and a body offered for lust, are not stated, but assumed.

Because wealth shields sin (not only bribery but discrimination based on wealth is meant), because men are punishing their own sins in others, there is no place for human justice - "none does offend, none". Yet is this not madness, "matter with impertinency mixed," as Edgar says of Lear's speech? If offences are to be wiped out, more than comradeship in sin is needed.

Angelo is the rascal beadle, engaged in the very act he presumes to punish in another. Yet, like Brutus, he is in his own eyes an honourable man. Like Brutus, he pursures an abstract ethical ideal. Like Brutus, he is self-sufficient yet deficient in love. Like Brutus, he is corruptible. But while Brutus hid from himself his dependence on Cassiu's corrupt means, Angelo sins openly and falls self-consciously.[8]

Measure for Measure goes beyond its predecessors in Isabella's redemptive act. As long as the heroine paid the price for her brother's life by her own sexual submission, she was herself redeemer, corruptor, and corrupted.

Measure for Measure distinguishes gift from bribe, resolves the ambiguity of "ransom", shows salvation won by forgiveness. Images and ideas of the redemption of mankind by Christ are explicit and played with. Isabella's offer of a prayer is "to bribe"; the proposed purchase of her brother with her body is "to redeem."

Concentrating on the lofty parallel, Shakespeare drops the low-level bribery of Phallax. He does not use the pungent but low-level word "grease". More boldly than any major Christian theologian, Shakespeare focuses attention on the similarity in structure of a bribe to God and the redemption won by Christ. Using the "Christian names" of *munera* he asks what is the difference.

Words existed to designate in English the sin of bribery. Was it also a crime? Were denunciations of bribery to be confined to the pulpit and the theater, or could *Measure for Measure* be enacted not on an English stage but at the center of the English system of justice?

12

ANGELO

In sixteenth century Europe payment to obtain a spiritual favour was the sin of simoney

"If you find bribery or corruption, then come boldly; but when I say boldly, beware of coming to complain except you be very sure to prove the justice of your cause.

The lord chancellor, said Crewe, "hath always despised riches and set honour and justice before his eyes." He had judged "out of his noble conscience and integrity of his heart." The "sign of a corrupted estate," a "bribed magistrate," was not to be found here. Yelverton neatly combined repobation of bribery with an appeal for reciprocity: "As justice is not to be recompensed in price, so ought not the scandal hereof to go unpunished."

"I never heard him taxed of corruption." There had indeed been corrupt chancellors-de la Pole and Wolsey; and "if a judge's conscience be oiled and moistened with corruption, then all is naught."

Bribery he had said was against the Ninth Commandment. The lawyer who paid "a gift or a bribe" —Andrews did not say to whom - or who "by any wrong means" sought "to bolster out any matter" fell under the prohibition against false witnessing. As for a judge, without mentioning bribery, Andrews had said he too could transgress the Ninth Commandment: "it is most perilous on his side."

Bacon responded to the Commons presentation of their

speaker to the king. James had graciously agreed that the Commons, besides supplying money, might draw complaints to his attention. The speaker had complemented the king on his judging - "no judges being freer from corruption." Like Cicero confronted by Cato, the chancellor found Platonic perfectionism irritating the illusory.

A striking simile completed his exhortation to moderation: "It is certain that the best governments, yea and the best men, are like the best precious stones, wherein every flaw or icicle or grain are seen and noted more than in those that are generally foul or corrupted." If any icicles were visible on the gems of the Crown, the Commons were not to shake them.

> The vices of authority are chiefly four-delays, corruption, roughness, and facility. . . For corruption; do not only bind thine own hands or thy servants' hands from taking, but bind the hands of suitors also from offering. For integrity used (i.e., practiced), doth the one; but integrity professed, and with a manifest detestation of bribery, doth the other. And avoid not only the fault, but the suspicion.
>
> That "facility", that is, too quick a readiness to please, was worse than bribery, for it was a constant temptation while "bribes come but now and then."

"Justice is a sacred thing," Solomon had said. Continuing the metaphor of the judge as fountain of justice, he had announced that he would water low "at the root". In July 1617, with the king in Scotland, he had charged the judges going circuit, "Do good to the people, love them and give them justice." He had paralleled the famous line of Luke 6:35, *Nihil inde sperantes*, "hoping nothing thereby", so long used as the basis for an absolute prohibition on usury, with another line: "Let it be, as the Psalm saith, *nihil inde expectantes*, looking for nothing, neither praise nor profit."[9]

Bacon's ally Finch, then, intervened, saying that no one "should fall by the testimony of one who had most reason to excuse himself for so foul a fact as the delivery of a bribe."

As all who knew Scripture knew, two witnesses must prove a crime. At this point Coke entered the debate. "You will make bribery to be unpunished if he that carrieth a bribe shall not be a witness." *Particeps criminis*, a participant in the crime, was "often taken for two good witnesses. And, therefore, we have a rule that if an offence be committed in a brothel house, the testimony of brothels shall be admitted."

Unflattering as it may have been to George Hastings to be compared to a brothel, that is, a prostitute, Coke's point was clear and his analogy apt. Like prostitution, bribery was to be proved from the mouths of those who had transacted the business.[10]

To quote Scripture, "Corruption in justice destroyeth the land, "and from Thomas Crewe, a friend of Bacon, "Bribes blind the eyes of the just." It led to speculation as to what the precise offence was in a judge taking a bribe. The crime, it was said, was a kind of perjury, for it was contrary to the oath of a judge; the crime was" against the King," "by falsely distributing the King's conscience, "that is, violating distributive justice. No statute condemned bribery. Like many other crimes, including murder, the offence, if it existed, had to be found in "common law," the precedence to be found in judicial practice.

No particular precedence were reported on this occasion, although Coke, already the acknowledged "father of the common law," affirmed that the criminality of bribery was clear. As Coke pressed the case, the commons agreed to refer the charges to the Lords for judgement.[11]

"Because the world at this time talks so much of bribes, I have just cause to fear the whole body of this House hath bribed him to be a good instrument for you on all occasions. Because he that hath taken bribes is apt to give bribes, I will go further and present your Majesty with a bribe. The bribe would be "a good history of England and a better digest of your laws. The bribe was as spiritual as Isabella's offer to Angelo, and unexpected from Angelo", Bacon concluded with a wit.

NOTES AND REFERENCES

1. Bacon to James I, James Spedding, *The Letters and Life of Francis Bacon* (London: Longmans, Green, Reader & Dyer, 1874) Hereafter Spedding 7, 168-169.

2. Spedding 7, 168.

3. John Donne, Sermon No. 15, Jan. 30, 1620 *Sermons,* ed. Evelyn M. Simpson and George R. Potter (Berkeley and los Angeles: University of California Press, 1962) 2, 313.

4. "Proceedings Against Mr. Wrenham", Star Chamber, 1618, in T. Cobham, ed. State Traials 1, 1059-1086. The statement of the case in the text draws on the accounts of both Wrenham at 1066-1071 and Yelverton at 1066-1069.

5. Andrewes, Sermon No. 10, At the Opening of Parliament, 1621, Ninety-Six Sermons (Oxford: John Henry Parker, 1843) 5, 205-206.

6. *Ibid.* 213, 215, 216.

7. Speaker Richardson's Oration, in Villiers, Hastings Journal 3.

8. Bacon's Speech to the Speaker's Oration, Spedding 7, 178-179.

9. Bacon, Speech, July 1617, Spedding 6, 211.

10. *Ibid.* 2, 240: Christopher Neville quoted in Anon. Journal on the Chancery as labyrinth; 4, 167. William Noy quoted in Pym's Diary on destruction of the land and breach of oath; 5 406: Noy quoted in Smyth's Observations on distribution of king's conscience; 5, 306: Thomas Crewe quoted on blinding bribes.

11. Spedding 7, 215. According to Coke writing in 1628 after Bacon's fall, William Thorpe, Chief Justice of the King's Bench, was found guilty of taking bribes of five felons under Edward III, suspended from office, and deprived of all his lands for having thus "maliciously, falsely, and rebelliously" broken his oath to the king. Thorpe was, however, pardoned and his lands were restored. Coke takes the position that the precedent is not a good one, for Thorpe's offense was wrongly treated as reason. In Coke's view, bribery is neither treason nor felony but "it is a great Misprision, for that it is ever accompanied with Perjury". Edward Coke, The Third Part of the Institutes of the Laws of England (London: M. Flesher, 1644) c. 68, 145-146. Coke also notes that none of the judges charged under Edward I were convicted of bribery. He is left with a single precedent: certain judges who took a "small" bribe of 4 pounds and were fined 4,000 marks under Edward III, *ibid.* 147. The clearest authority he cites is Deuteronomy 16:19.

13

BRIBERY SUPPRESSES CONSCIENCE

Bribes today are universal.

Such are diary entries over two years by Samuel Pepys, clerk of the acts to the Naval Board and member of the Tangier Committee. He had received from those interested in his official actions animals, clothing, food, furniture, silverware, cash, and sex-the mastiff from a ship's surgeon, the mare from Warren; the Japan gown from Abrahall; the cake from Morecooke, the oysters from Barrow, the pork from Grove, the tongue and bacon from Shales; the cabinet from shales, too; silverware from Falconer, Gauden, and warren; the cash from Creed, Deering. Grove, Taylor, Warren and the Tangier victuallers; and the sex from Bagwell. All of these concealments, artifices dodges suggest that taking money for official action was not accounted right and respectable in public.

Pepys "condemned gifts" which obviously operated against the public interest, but not those made merely to expedite business or to establish good personal relations. In fact, "surrounded as he was by the calculated generosity of merchants, he preserved his independence. He had mastered the useful art of receiving gifts without becoming corrupt". These judgements made by men highly familiar with the diary take Pepys at face value in his evaluation of his deals.

More than once Pepys said or hoped his profits were noble," "honest just." His apologists believe they must have been.

The distinction implicit in Pepys's use of the derogatory term "bribes" for Pepys meant payments that brought about substantively wrongful official actions. What he himself got led to nothing wrongful. They were like-he does not use the word-tips, that is, rewards for special service given him with the tacit acquiescence of his superiors. But his insistence in the privacy of his journal on the integrity of his actions is scarcely comprehensible unless he was arguing with a contrary inner voice.

One can hear that inner voice when he recorded on September 10, 1664, that he would make his profit on the Tangiers deal "without the least wrong to the King" and so "with a safe conscience." The entry told his conscience that the transaction was injurious to the Crown. Before his inner judge he customarily claimed to observe two rules: No one was hurt by what he took.

What he got was voluntarily given. He had convinced himself on January 27, 1663, that "there is nothing in the world done with true integrity," but in these inner dialogues he did not make the defence that bribe-taking was customary, the Vice of the age, or what everyone else did. Here he announced his own higher standard.

He would not be unjust, but when he got a payment the money had to come from someone. His theory was that if he had saved money for the king, he was entitled to a percentage. The theory was expressed in the "safe conscience" entry of September 10, 1664. The king had saved 5,000 pounds.

Peppys was taking only 300 pounds. That this 300 pounds was either subtracted from what was spent on the men's victuals, or reduced what the Navy might have saved, was not considered. Pepy's self-contented implication was that the Plymouth syndicate simply cut him into a share of its lawful profit.

That the profit had depended according to his agreement with the syndicate of July 14, 1664, on getting an extra half penny per week per man, Pepys did not mention. In this classic illustration where, by his oral contract with the Plymouth suppliers, his own compensation depended on the victuallers getting the higher price from the Navy, Pepys did not acknowledge that he had made at least 150 pounds by setting up the Navy Board so it would approve the higher price. The emphasis of the diary- "without the least wrong" is telltale.

Only occasionally did he do worse than make an implicit contract and keep it, and each time the circumstances were extraordinary. One was the use of force on Bagwell to subdue her to his use in her own home after her husband had given him dinner shortly before Christians of 1664. But there sex provided an element beyond his usual objectives, and he later did write, albeit ineffectually, two letters seeking to promote her husband.

Another exception was when he received unexpectedly the dress for his wife from a tallow-maker, while already bound to buy tallow from Mrs. Russell. No entry appears as to the return of the dress, no doubt an awkward present as it had caught his wife's eye and came "very opportune." It must be assumed that he somehow made it up to Abrahall.

If the king had abandoned him, would he have fared any better than Bacon? His most basic defence was similar, that he never took money to make a bad decision, or as Bacon had put it, "to pevert justice." The defence was similarly implausible in that, in such subjective matters as the better of a legal argument or the better of good offered, absolute right or wrong is hard to tell, and what is wanted is a judgement uninfluenced by extrinsic considerations affecting discretion. A soccer referee who is bribed but says he made all the right decisions anyway is incredible; so is a judge or a contracting officer.

With this ability at rationalization and self-delusion, he was capable of simultaneously believing that his graft injured no one, that it was voluntarily paid, and that those he favoured owed it to him.

At the back of Pepy's consciousness must have been the size of the amounts involved, relative to the king and relative to himself. On the Tangiers deal, where almost 40,000 pounds was needed for a year's food supply, he took only 350 pounds, not quite I per cent. Apart from Tangiers, the Navy was spending about 350,000 pounds per year. One per cent of the amount was 3,500 pounds. If Pepys helped himself to 350 pounds, he took one tenth of 1 per cent of such expenditure.

Although this amount was insignificant to the king, relative to his own salary and estate it was enormous. He had a salary of 350 pounds as clerk plus the fees and poundage he collected by virtue of his offices. At a time when the mean annual income for a household was under 8 pounds and when not more than 5,000 persons earned over 240 pounds, this income by itself put Pepys in the upper class.

In 1664 if the diary entries are added, close to 300 pounds came to him from contractors, while his net worth rose over 500 pounds. Payoffs made 1664 his first bumper year, the first of his years of great prosperity. The man who began his career as clerk in 1660 with 25 pounds liquid capital, "discoursing of the changes that we have seen and the happiness of them that have estates of their own", became a man possessing over 7,000 pounds by the end of 1667.

As his lawful income had not increased significantly, it must be inferred that his extra-legal arrangements were now paying out handsomely. In his editor's words, at the end of his career he had "grown rich in the service of the state and by investments." When Pepys had first taken the job on August 6, 1660, he had received an offer to buy it from him for 1,000 pounds "which made my mouth water," but he had been advised on August 16, 1660, by his patron Lord Sandwich "that it was not the salary of any place that did make a man rich, but the opportunities of getting money while he is in the place."

Increasing his worth by almost 30,000 per cent in six and a half years, he had realized those opportunities. Engaged in getting an estate of his own, he could no more listen to the voice of conscience than heed the fear of public exposure. The voice became "squeamish;" the qualms were suppressed.

Our focus is not on the man, but on what bribery meant for him morally and socially. The complexity of his consciousness is central. His payoffs were disguised and taken secretly, would not bear public examination, led him to suborn perjury in those who could have testified about them, and made it necessary for him when he wrote the commissioners to assert the contrary of what he had done. His payoffs were, in short, something of which he was ashamed.

They were taken joyfully, industriously, with thin rationalizations and a suppressed conscience. They did come by bargain not true gift. They did work to fatter his discretion and blur his judgement. They were not excusable as the pickings of a poor man making up an inadequate salary. Added to a high lawful income they were the ways of making him rich.

They were, in his own language for others, corruption and bribes. He did not pay a public penalty for them because he was on the politically stronger side, he concealed them, and he was not a judge. The diary, rich as it is in many other aspects, also is the confession of a grafter.

Pepys's consciousness of the gifts he took as somehow significant may be profitably compared with two other kinds of contemporaneous judgement publicly offered: that of professional expositors of a morality more severe than his own and that of Parliament as to its own members.

The Purity of Parliament: Just as the popular handbooks on Christian duty did not address the moral problems of procurement officers, so they left untouched the morals of legislators. Parliament, however, had been at least ready to investigate Pepys. What of Parliament's own standards? John Ashburnham's case is cotemporaneous with Pepys's tenure at the Naval Board.

Non-enforcement of the Criminal penalty, the emphasis on "Dishonour of this House," and the political nature of the proceeding all showed that the application of the anti-bribery rule to a legislator was a novel and difficult business. Pepys, who recorded with such interest Ashburnham's solicitude for the royal linen, did not trouble himself to record the wardrobe keeper's flaw or fall. Ashburnham's disgrace was not a major event like Bacon's. The fall of a courtier in a political context had no larger teaching for Pepys on other servants of the Crown. By Parliament's political standards, Pepys had nothing to worry about as long as he stood in which patrons in with patrons in power.[1]

Pepys was swift of dispatch and easy of access; but his hands could not have been described by the ancient metaphor of cleanliness, and "unbribed" would have been an inappropriate adjective for him. Achitophel—"to all succeeding Ages Curst"—stands as a judge in sharp contrast to the ingenious, busy, conscientious clerk who made such a good thing out of his place and provided the information and the measure by which he himself in the delicate realm of conscience was vulnerable to judgement.

NOTES AND REFERENCES

1. Nearly thirty years later, again as a by-product of a political fracas as an administration fell, the Commons took a formal stand against the bribery of its members-this time against bribery of legislators qua legislators. Sir John Trevor had been Speaker of the House under James II-an ideal selection at the time because he was identified with the militant protestant interest yet was the first cousin of George Jeffreys, James's trusted legal adviser. He had also been master of the rolls while Jeffreys was lord chancellor. In that high judicial capacity he advised his cousin in a judgment by Jeffreys which enriched Jeffreys's son's fiancee by a large amount-Jeffreys behaving as abominably as Portia, and Trevor little better (James McMullen Rigg, "Trevor, Sir John", DNB 19, 1149; H. Montgomery Hyde, *Judge Jeffreys* London: George Harrap, 1940 259 the case of Jeffreys's future daughter-in-law; see also *Baden v. Pembroke, 2 Vernon's Reports* 52 and 213, 23 *English Reports* 644 and 739).

   With great dexterity Trevor had survived the Glorious Revolution, James's flight, and Jeffreys's imprisonment, and by the mid-1690s he was back in his old Jacobite positions, speaker of the House and master of the rolls. No doubt this ability to endure excited envy and distrust.

   When the administration of his patron the earl of Sunder-land, began to crumble, Trevor was fair game. Two new parliamentary leaders, Charles Montagu and Thomas Wharton, began the parliamentary revolt by an accidental discovery that Henry Guy secretary of the treasury, had accepted a sum from a regimental agent to expedite payment of the soldiers' wages, Guy was dismissed and committed to the Tower, Trevor helping the process on. Then Montagu and Wharton turned on Trevor and, doubtless inspired by a discreet hint, demanded that the accounts of the chamberlain of the City of London be inspected (J.P. Kenyon, *Robert Spencer, Earl of Sunderland* London: Longmans, Green, 1958) 269-271).

The inspection almost instantly revealed an order of the London Common Council of Feb. 12, 1694, directing the chamberlain to pay to "the hon. Sir John Trevor, knight, speaker of the hon. house of commons, the sum of 1000 guineas, as soon as a Bill be passed into an act of parliament, for satisfying the Debts of the Orphans and other creditors of the said city." On the back of the order was an endorsement that 1,000 guineas were delivered to Trevor on June 22, 1694, in the presence of two named council men. Testimony by members of the council filled in the background. The City had borrowed from the Orphans' Fund and needed help from Parliament to repay the money. The bill had failed in two or three earlier efforts. The City's solicitor opined that paying Trevor was the only course to take; otherwise, "the Bill would not go." Those acting for the orphans indicated that the bill would cost 2,000 guineas and that they would have to put up what they City didn't. One councilman had protested the City's paying. Everyone else seemed to think it routine enough for a record of the order to be made and kept, although Trevor's name was filled in only at a date later than the date of the order itself. Still, "the discourse at the community was, That the Speaker was the person to whom the sum was to be given." The chamberlain's books revealed that on June 22, 1694, there had also been a payment of 100 pounds to Paul Jodrell, clerk of the House, and 20 guineas to Mr. Hungerford, chairman of the committee to whom the Orphans' Bill was referred (Corbett's *Parliamentary History of England* London: T.C. Hansard, 1809 5, 901-906.

On March 13, 1695, Trevor informed the House he was sick. On March 14, Paul Foley, the chairman of the committee that had investigated the accounts, was elected speaker in his place (House of Commons, *Journal* 11, 272). On March 16, Trevor was expelled from the House "being guilty of a high Crime and Misdemeanour, by receiving a Gratuity of a Thousand Guineas", Ten days later Hungerford was expelled as well (*ibid.* 283).

In the same spirit of reform, the Commons also received the petition of the 400 licensed hackney-coachmen of London reciting that the licensing commission had, "by receiving Bribes, and by other undue means, acted corruptly." Three of the five commissioners were found guilty and were then removed by the king Cobbett 5, 896). The Commons also investigated large-scale corruption-that effected by the East India Company which had been engaged in battle over the renewal of its charter. Production of the East India Company's records showed nearly 90,000 pounds spent by Sir Thomas Cook, a governor of the company, and accounted for vaguely as spent in connection with the charter. The inference was drawn that the money had been spent corruptly. When the Commons tried to track down specific sums, 5,500 guineas were shown to have been paid by Sir Thomas Cook to Sir Basil Firebrace, who in turn delivered them to Charles Bruce, who gave them to John Robart, the Swiss servant of the duke of Leeds, Lord president of the King's Council and the second or third man of the kingdom. Robart fled to the Continent, the duke denied getting the money, the Commons impeached him, the Lords failed to try him. Leeds being already in political trouble, the impeachment marked the end of the duke's political ascendance (Andrew Browning, *Thomas Osborne, Earl of Danby and Duke of Leeds* Glasgow: Jackson, Son & Co., 1951 1, 517).

The penalties meted out for bribery were political and moderate. Leeds lost power but continued as lord president of the Council, Oxford gave him an honorary doctorate in civil law (*ibid.* 523-526). Jodrell, the clerk of the House, was not removed. As for trevor, he did not return to Parliament, but censured for committing "a high crime", he continued as master of the rolls, the second highest officer of Chancery, until his death twenty-two years later; be became a privy councillor in 1702 and died possessing personalty worth over 60,000 pounds (Rigg, "Trevor, Sir John," 1150). The penalty for bribe-taking by a politician in these days of William III was, in a word, political, but political without substantial disgrace. Abstractly considered, to take a bribe was ground for expulsion from Parliament. Concretely, only a failing and disliked politician had to fear this sanction. Other instances of parliamentary discipline for bribery in the eighteenth century were not less political, see House of Commons, journal, vol. 18 (1714-1718) 493, and vol. 19 (1718-1721) 542.

14

BRITISH GOVERNOR OF BENGAL EMBEZZLED PUBLIC FUNDS

Man is conceived in sin, and born in corruption.

Warren Hastings "did not only give and receive bribes accidentally." He "formed plans and systems of government for the very purpose of accumulating bribes and presents to himself." He descended into "the muck and filth of peculation and corruption. He was "not only a public robber himself, but the head of a system of robbery, the captain-general of the gang."

In such and similar language did the most philosophical member of Parliament, Edmund Burke, describe the man, who had for thirteen years, from 1772 to 1785, been the British governor of Bengal. The occasions of his descriptions were public and formal—sessions in the House of Lords in which Burke as the chairman of the managers of an impeachment committee of the House of Commons sought the conviction of the defendant. Of the object of these attacks, Warren Hastings, Burke observed, "Do you want a criminal, my Lords? When was there ever so much iniquity ever laid to the charge of any one?"[2]

Hastings, as portrayed by Burke, had been as cruel as he had been corrupt. Bent on taking all he could, he had instigated, approved, or collaborated with the use of torture to produce the revenues he needed; and he had not stopped at arranging a judicial murder to stifle an accuser. "Do you want a cause, my Lords? You have the cause of oppressed princes, of undone women of the first rank, of desolated provinces, of wasted kingdoms."[3]

Hastings had no doubt as to the model he was being made to fit. He did not wish to sustain "the vile and abhorred character of a Verees." Charles Fox, one of Burke's co-managers, explicity evoked Cicero and paraphrased his appeal to the judges of Hog. Burke himself was wonderfully plain:

We have all, in our early education, read the Verrine Orations. We read them, not merely to instruct us, as they will do, in the principles of eloquence and the laws of the ancient Romans, of which they are an abundant repository; but we may read them from a much higher motive. We may read them from a motive which the great author had doubtless in his view when by publishing he left to the world and to the latest posterity a monument by which it might be seen what course a great public accuser in a great public cause ought to pursue, and, as connected with it, what course judges ought to pursue upon such a cause. In those orations you will find almost every instance of rapacity and pecualion which we charge upon Mr. Hastings.

A "great public accuser" in a "great public cause", "Burke spoke as Cicero and Hastings became Hog.[4] The outcome, however, was different from the classic model. In 1795, after a trial of seven years- a very intermittent trial, for the Lords met thirty-five days the first year, five days the fourth year, etc. - Hastings was formally acquicted.

For thirteen years he was the most important holder of political power in Bengal. But armed with inflexible determination and great resourcefulness, Hastings, usually dominated the government. As the company's employee or servant, to use, the misleading eighteenth-century term, he was responsible to the Company's direction in London. Orders on a variety of matters come from them, but given to distance from which they wrote and the time it took for their commands to arrive (four to five months at the best), Hastings had a latitude of discretion that in practice had few limits.[5]

But relying only on what is established by the records of John Company itself as to bills of exchange and diamonds sent home by Hastings, plus miscellaneous other records referring to him, it has been shown that Hastings, in his thirteen years of office from 1772 to 1785, remitted to England at least 218,527 pounds. This sum was nearly ten times his annual salary, nearly ten thousand times the annual income of a poor gentleman. It is characterized by its modern calculator a student of fortunes made in India, as "extremely large."[6]

Prosecution: As early as 1780, when Lord North was in power, Edmund Burke, then an opposition member of Parliament, had voiced concern, in particular, on Hastings. Burke told Parliament "that he would bring to justice, as far as in him lay, the greatest delinquent that India ever saw."

When Hastings returned in 1785 expecting a peerage, Burke, again in opposition, worked for his impeachment-impeachment in the British sense being a charge by the Commons of violations of "the already known and existing law", tried before the Lords as "the most high and supreme court of criminal jurisdiction." As one who had held a statutory appointment, Hastings was open to impeachment.[7]

After an adjournment and the hearing in early 1787 of further witnesses, pro and con, actual impeachment was voted in May 1787.[8]

The Crime of Corruption: The Preamble of the Articles of Impeachment announced that Hastings had held statutory office, "On the due and incorrupt Execution of which the Welfare of the said United Company, the Happiness of the native Inhabitants of India, the Honour of the Crown of these Kingdoms, and the Character of the British Nation did most materially depend."

The sixth article charged Hastings with having received "presents" and with having thereby" grossly violated the duties of his Station," an invocation of the standard set by the Preamble. Breaching this standard, he was, the sixth article alleged, guilty of "Corruption, Peculation, and Extortion."

"Peculation" was so unfamiliar to English law that it appeared in Blacktone only in its Latin form *peculatus*, defined as the embezzlement of public funds. "Corruption" was the one crime involving the presents where conviction might have seemed possible. But what was "corruption" as defined by English law and applied to acts performed in India"?[9]

In eighteenth-century diction "presents" was a polite description of offerings from a suppliant to a superior; "bribes" were a critical description of the same offerings.

The receipt of the money by Hastings was admitted by him. The accounts furnished by him and on his behalf were, to say the least, unconvincing. Must one infer that he had received the money as a bribe? When a high official of a government acknowledges receiving a large sum of money from an anonymous source and provides no explanation of its purpose except a demonstrably inaccurate one, it is a reasonable conclusion that he received the money for a corrupt purpose.

That there has been a corrupt payment is established by its size, its anonymity, and the payee's attempts to disguise its purpose. Such circumstances existed here. Besides, presents were received from persons from whom receiving presents was generally forbidden.

Hastings's defence had tried to merge the question of bribery with the question of what he did with the money. As Burke put it, "Mr. Hastings confesses it was a sum of money corruptly received, but honestly applied".[10]

A member of parliament taking a bribe for his vote and saying he had given it to a certain Fund.[11]

His figures of speech were more often non-sexual. 'Bribery, filthy hands, a chief governor of a great empire receiving bribes from poor, miserable, indigent people, this is what makes government itself base, contemptible, and odious in the eyes of mankind'; so Burke had said in 1788, employing one of the most basic metaphors for a corrupt official, 'filthy hands'. When he neared the end in 1794 he told the Lords, 'I have had a great encyclopedia of crimes to deal with'. Between those dates, Hastings had been compared physically to a pig: four years he lays down in that style of disgrace, fattening in it, feeding upon that offal of disgrace and excrement.

Minutely examined and marshalled in the final nine days of

oratory, Hastings's faults made him evil personified. The degree of abstraction Burke reached is measured by his ultimate assault on the advice that one should 'hate the sin and love the sinner', paraphased by him as 'hate the crime and love the criminal'. Burke became incredulous that he should be asked to love a Nero or Domitian. 'No', he affirmed, 'we hate the crime, and we hate the criminal ten times more'. The maxim of charity he represented as 'the language of false morality'.

That as a convinced Christian he was required to love his enemies, he put to one side. He could not love the abstract symbol of corruption which Hastings had become. The inevitable correlative of this view of the defendant was an implied sanctity on the part of the prosecutor. Burke once said of an oration of the elder Pitt attacking "any sort of personal connections" that it was "a Speech too virtuous to be honest". Was not the whole prosecution of Hastings too virtuous to be honest?[12]

Social not legal, pragmatic not theoretical, indirect and tempered, not direct and absolute, Hastings was sanctioned for the presents he had taken. Cornwallis declared, 'Every native of Hindustan, I verily believe, is corrupt,' and excluded Indians from all higher government posts.

'Public Errors, Defects, and Abuses': The love of power and the love of money were two weaknesses in human nature that produced 'bribery, corruption, and many other arts.' In our day, love of money predominated.

Ministers took office 'chiefly with a design of filling their pockets, and advancing their families and friends.' They proceeded by 'bribing and buying parliament.' For that purpose they had places to offer in the collection of the customs, excise, and salt-duty in the army and navy; in the church; and as postmasters, surveyors of houses and windows, receivers of land-tax, managers of lotteries, and commissioners of hackney coaches-in a word, in all appointment in the government.

Ministers could also give preferences in loans, subscriptions, and remittances of public money. They could, as they did in 1769, distribute 20,000 lottery tickets to Members of Parliament, giving freely what sold for two pounds a piece. They could award contracts to those 'with the greatest parliamentary interest.' They could use the civil service list and the secret service (a huge cloak thrown over an immense sewer of corruption.) to reward their supporters.

These were the normal practices of the rulers of England the modern plan of government to buy every necessary vote was how a government stayed in power. Charles II had ruled Parliament corruptly, but the art of governing by regularly and systematically bribing the House of Commons came in at the Revolution, that is, with William III. Bribery and corruption, as Burgh uses the terms, are not crimes—at least not crimes in terms of statutes which are enforced. They are moral and political offences condemned by a standard higher than that of most contemporaries. That higher standard was Burke's for Bengal, not Britain.

All political power was, therefore, a trust: and "it is of the very essence of every trust to be rendered accountable". So Hastings must account. On this basis the Articles of Impeachment were framed in terms of the office Hastings held, and Burke could tell the Lords, that "every office of trust, in its very nature, forbids the receipt of bribes."[13]

Burke told Parliament that what gave it an army and a navy and a revenue was nothing but 'the love of the people'. His words, he said he knew, would "wild and chimerical" to "vulgar and mechanical politicians". To Parliament, near the close of his peroration, he addressed words taken from the Latin mass - "the old warning of the Church,' as he described it- '*Sursum corda*!" Only by the members lifting up their hearts beyond the gross and material to the level where love reciprocated fidelity could revolution be avoided and government endure.[14]

Sealing these responsibilities of man was the one law for all, namely that law which governs all law, the law of our Creator, the law of humanity, justice, equity, the law of nature and of Nations."

The Indians without English complexions were his clients because they were made in the image of God. Service to them was based on the imitation of Christ. As he told the Lords in a rare direct evocation of his religion. "When the God whom we adore appeared in human form, He did not appear in a form of greatness and majesty but in sympathy with the lowest of the people and, thereby, made it a firm and ruling principle that their welfare was the object of all government, since the Person who was the master of Nature chose to appear Himself in a subordinate situation." 'That by the example of Christ the welfare of the people was, "the object of all government" was the foundation of Burke's view of the trust that went with office. That becoming rich and remaining innocent in India were inconsistent goals, that serving oneself and the ones one governed were incompatible objectives were propositions he would not have entertained.

What the Commons sought, he had told the Lords in May 1794, was to "see corrupt Pride prostrate under the feet of Justice." What he furnished in his own person was a different image - a politician, an M.P., an orator, suffering in heart and mind and spirit for his failure to achieve the chastisement of corruption. That his posture was more Christian if less comfortable than Cicero's might have occurred to him.[14]

NOTES & REFERENCES

1. Edmund Burke, "Speech in Opening the Impeachment", Third Day, Feb. 18, 1788, Burke, Works (Boston: Little, Brown, 1867) 10, 7: "Plans and systems", Burke, "Speech in General Reply", English Day, June 14, 1794, Works 12, 295: "muck and filth"; Burke, "Speech in General Reply, "First Day, May 28, 1794, Works 11, 175, "captain general of the gang".

2. Burke, "Speech in Opening", Fourth Day, Feb. 19, 1788, works 10, 142.

3. *Ibid.*

4. Burke, "Speech in General Reply", Ninth Day, June 16, 1794, Works 12, 349. See also Burke to William Baker, June 22, 1784, in Burke, *Correspondence,* ed. Holden Furber (Chicago: University of Chicago Press, 1965) 5, 155; cf. H.V. Canter, "The Impeachments of Varres and Hastings: Cicero and Burke," *Classical Journal* 9 (1914) 199; Keith Feiling, Wareen Hastings (London: Macmillan, 1954) 341 ("the vile and abhorred"); Charles Fox, Manager for the House of Commons, *Speech of the Managers and Counsel in the Trial of Wareen Hastings,* ed. E.A. Bond (London: Longman, Green, Longman & Roberts, 1860) 2, 271.

5. See Burke, Correspondence 5, 251, n. 3: passage time to India.

6. Peter J. Marshall, "The Personal Fortune of Warren Hastings", *Economic History Review* 17 (2nd Series; 1964) 284-294; Furber, *John Company at Work* 79-80 (on remittances through Dutch).

7. *Ibid.* 23 ("accidental and temporary"); William Blackstone, *Commentaries on the Laws of England* (Oxford, 1765) 4, 260 (impeachment).

8. Marshall; *Impeachment* 40-50: on Pitt and Dundas; *ibid.* 58: impeachment voted; *ibid.* 62: "idealism and prejudices".

9. Blackstone, Commentaries 4, 9, 2 (*peculatus*); *ibid.* (Chitty's edition 1825), 4, 17, 1 (on the technical requirements of embezzlement).

10. *Ibid.* 10, 62.

11. Charles Fox, Speech, June 7, 1790 *Speeches of the Managers and Counsel* 2, 367-368.

12. Burke, "*Speech in Opening the Impeachment*", Third Day, Feb. 18, 1788, *ibid*, 10, 7 ("bribery, filthy hands"; "staining", "purity");' Burke, Speech on the Sixth Article, Second Day, April 25, 1789, *ibid.* 10, 251 ("sty of disgrace") Burke, Speech in Reply, Eighth Day, June 14, 1794, *ibid.*, 12, 269 (Swfit quoted); *ibid.* 12, 275 (in love with Munni), *ibid.* 12, 277 ("we hate the crime"); *ibid.* 12, 317 ("great encyclopaedia"); *ibid.* 31 (comparison to Satan). James Erskine St. Clair, Manager, Speech, May 30, 1791, Speeches of the Managers and Counsel 2, 477 (unjust steward). The lines of Swift's are from Jonathan Swift, "Phillis, or the Progress of Love." lines 99-100, Swift, Poems, ed. Harold Williams (Oxford: Claredon Press, 1937) 1, 225. Burke to Charles O'Hara, April 24, 1766, Correspondence 1, 252 ("too virtuous to be honest").

13. Burke to Richard Shackleton his lifelong friend, May 25, 1779, *Correspondence 4, 79; Burke, Speech on Mr. Fox's East India Bill, Dec. 1, 1783, Works 2, 439 ("All Political Power"); Burke, "Speech in Opening of Impeachment", Third Day, Feb. 18, 1788, Works 10, 12* ("every office of trust . . . forbids bribes").

14. For comparison and contrast, consider the view of corruption in imperial China under the Ch'ing dynasty as reported in modern works using largely eighteenth-century sources. Administration of justice was the responsibility of the district magistrate, who was also in charge of the collection of taxes and the preservation of order in the area. The magistrate was appointed by the central imperial government, rotated every five years, and chosen from outside the province so that he would not be influenced by family connections. In the eyes of

the uneducated he was the representative of the local god or of the judge of the underworld; he also represented the emperor, the Son of Heaven, Hohn R. Watt, the District Magistrate in Late Imperial China (New York: Columbia University Press, 1972) 17. Usually only acquainted with elementary legal principles, he came with a secretary trained in the law. His staff, provided from the province, consisted in clerks who did the preparation and transcribing of documents and runners who acted as police, bailiffs, process servers, torturers, and jailers. He brought with him personal servants including a gate porter through whom access to him was controlled. From the time of Yung-Cheng (1723) the Central government paid the magistrate *yang-lien yin* ("money to nourish honesty" but this salary was insufficient to meet his public expenses and private expectations. It was taken for granted that he also receive *lou-kuei* ("customary fees"). It was expected that he make money out of the tax collections. Magistrates regularly retired with substantial fortunes, T'ung-Tsu Ch'u, *Local Government in China under the Ch'ing* (Cambridge: Harvard University Press, 1962) 22-31.

The customary fees were not regarded as corrupt, but they were clearly of a kind that could influence the magistrate in performing the many acts that lay within his discretion. They extended to payments to his servants including the "gift for arriving at a post" *(tao-jen li),* the "festival gist", and the "New Year gift"; also the men pao or, gift given the gatekeeper by one wanting to see the magistrate or deliver something to him, Ch'u *Local Administration* 88.

Other payments are classified by modern authors, drawing on imperial edicts and manuals by magistrates for their characterizations, as corrupt. Runners and clerks are said to be habitually engaged in corrup ransactions. Runners are alleged to take payments from criminals not to apprehend them; to shake down the innocent with the threat of arrest; to threaten those they bring to court with chains unless paid "chain-release money" (*chieh-so ch'ien*); to keep persons in uncomfortable imprisonment unless paid; to lighten a sentence of flogging if compensated. Clerks are said to be adept at delaying cases and at altering documents for a price. Specific dodges are noted. A runner will collaborate with a clerk to get official papers in blank; the maes of those singled out for extortion will then be filled in. A clerk will be paid by a defendant to improve a plaintiff's pleadings by clumsy alterations, so that the forgery is obvious and the magistrate believes that it was committed by the plaintiff to aid his cause; the practice is common enough to have its own name, ""cutting out and pasting in." Personal servants are apt to be more controllable than the low-level personnel who constitute runners and clerks; but they too can often be paid for favours. A special provision of law provides for their punishment-the first time they are convicted, the characters tsang-fan ("bribery criminals") are to be tattooed on their arm; the second time, on their face. Official are not to employ tattooed servants. The key servant is the gatekeeper, whose control of access makes his position highly profitable for him in corrupt ways. The secretary, the legal expert, is sometimes, though not often corrupt. Corruption by the magistrate is considered possible but it is not emphasized as a problem, *ibid.* 49-50, 68-70, 88, 92, 256; Watt, The District Magistrate 211, 222.

The Chinese ruling class clearly carried very far the practice of blaming the staff for corruption; one thinks of Chancellor Bacon blaming his servants. The magistrate-an alien in the district in which he presides—is pictured by the sources as buffeted by pressure from the local gentry and as more or less helpless to prevent serious extortion and bribery among his subordinates. In theory the law does punish a magistrate for taking a bribe. There is a scale of punishments ranging from seventy strokes to strangulation depending on the amount of the pribe, Ch'u Local Government 234-235. There is also a set of Disciplinary Regulations providing for a magistrate's removal for" avarice." A magistrate could be dismissed for conniving at a clerk's bribery and disciplined for offering a present "to please" another official, Watt, The District Magistrate 19, 171. The sources give no example of any magistrate being beaten or strangled for bribery. The co-existence of the Disciplinary Regulations, with their far milder penalties, suggest that the criminal sanctions against bribery by magistrates were not regularly employed. Even as to the Disciplinary Regulations, the sources do not supply specific instances where taking a bribe led to removal. Annual review by the central government of a magistrate's performance focused on two things: his ability to collect taxes and his ability to suppress robbers, *ibid.* 174-175. Money and public order were the chief concerns of the central government, not the magistrate's purity. There is no evidence offered that the central government made a serious effort to fix a line between customary fees and bribes or to enforce anti-bribery rules. On the books, for example, the law treated it as bribery for a magistrate to buy supplies at an "official price" well below the market price. In practice, even the most virtuous magistrates did not think they could survive without buying at the "official price", Ch'u Local Government 30.

The imperial government's view appears to have been that there was a great deal of corruption, that low-level personnel was chiefly responsible for it, and that law existed on the books for its correction but could not be enforced. That, beyond the official government position, there was considerable suspicion of corruption on the part of the higher end of the judicial order is indicated by a variety of evidence. When the virtuous secretary Wang Hui-tsu (1731-1807) gave an innovative ruling in an inheritance case, he was believed to have been bribed, Watt, The District Magistrate 218. When two clans litigated against each other before a magistrate, bribery was expected, *ibid.* 219. In the Dream of the Red Chamber, a classic eighteenth-century novel, Chapter 86, an upper-class man kills a surly waiter. He is tried for murder, confesses, and is convicted by a magistrate. The magistrate sends his decision to the defendant's family with an oral message that he knows the family is well off. The family responds by sending several thousand taels to the magistrate, who orders a retrial. The defendant now claims it was an accident; the witnesses change their stories; the clerk alters the foot notes to eliminate evidence of a sustained assault. The magistrate orders the case continued. The defendant's family realizes he will be released if they make a "few more payments" to the magistrate's staff and compensate the deceased victim's family, Tsao Hsueh-Chin and Kao Ngo, A Dream of Red Mansions *The Dream of the Red Chamber* Peaking: Foreign Language Press, 1980 trans by Yang Hsien-Yi and Gladys Yang, 2, 80. This translation from Maoist China is able to rationalize the novel as exposing" the corrupt and reactionary nature of the superstructure in the last period of Chinese feudal society", Publisher's Note, *ibid.* I, VI.

The problem of the access payments to the gate porters recalls imperial Rome and papal Rome. The dodges of the runners recall Chaucer's summoner. "Cutting and pasting" brings to mind the charge against Nanda Kumar. What is conspicuous in China are (1) the absence of advocates, a class with a professional interest in preserving the courts from bribery; (2) a political system that encourages charges of corruption against magistrates; (3) a religious tradition that emphasizes the paradigm of an unbribeale deity.

15

THOROUGH AND MOST ADROIT POLITICIANS

Corruption and Corruptibility one Universal.

Corrupt judges had not been on the revolutionists' mind; corruption by the Executive had. For much of the eighteenth century, English critics of English administrations such as James Burgh had focused on the way the ministry ruled by corrupting Parliament with jobs and appointments. These partisan outpourings had been devoured in America and formed part of the ideology of those who made the Revolution.

As firmly as educated European opinion in the later Middle Ages held the papcy to be corrupt, so it was accepted that corruption characterized British parliamentary rule. What Dr. Johnson took as true in coffee house conversation was also believed by educated colonials.

"Soon after Sir Robert Walpole was made premier he reduced corruption into a regular system", wrote Charles Carroll in 1768; while his son Charles Carroll noted that 'the sweets' of liberty were enjoyed in colonial America in spite of a corrupt Parliament, and added that "the degenerate sons of some future ages" could come to prefer "their own mean lucre, the bribes, and the smiles of corruption."

In revolutionary ideology, corruption of the legislature by the executive was the way in which the people were deprived of liberty. A corrupt and prostituted ministry was what had sought to enslave Americans. Care to prevent such corruption could scarcely not have been a care of the constitution-makers.[1]

Gouverneur Morris of Pennsylvania admitted "corruption and some few other offences to be such as ought to be impeachable, but thought these out to be enumerated and defined'.

He added that the Chief Magistrate may be bribed by a greater interest to secure his trust . . . . One would think the King of England well secured against bribery. He has, as it were, a simple in the whole kingdom. Yet Charles II was bribed by Louis XIV. The Executive ought, therefore, to be impeachable for treachery". He added, corrupting his electors, and incapacity were other causes of impeachment.

James Madison of Virginia stated a commonplace of English politics and Opposition criticism, that the Executive might pervert his administration into a scheme of peculation or oppression and that loss of capacity or corruption was within the compass of the probable events, and either of them might be fatal to the Republic.[2]

The Executive should be impeachable. The Committee on Detail, reflecting the concerns of Mason, Morris, and Madison, specified the ground as Treason, Bribery or Corruption.

No person holding any Office of Profit or Trust under (the United States) shall, without the consent of the Congress, accept any present, Emolument, Office or Title, or any kind whatever, from any king, Prince or foreign State. The proposal passed unanimously and became Article I, section 9, clause 8. Explaining it to the Virginia ratifying convention, John Randolph reported, "this restriction is provided to prevent corruption."

From the first, John Rendolph had proposed that legislators be ineligible for appointment to public office during their term as legislators. The proposal occasioned lively debate especially when Madison moved to limit the ineligibility to offices which the legislator in question had voted to create. The narrower restriction was vigorously opposed. Pierce Butler of South Carolina noted that George II had ruled Parliament by pensions, offices and promotions to the House of Lords.

George Mason referred to Virginia practice where all officers were appointed by the legislature, remarking: Need I add, that many of their appointments are most shameful? Madison's check will soon ease to be any check at all . . . If we do not provide against corruption, our government will soon be at an end; nor would I wish to put a man of virtue in the way of temptation. (Not quite 200 years later the temptation to which the government might subject members of Congress was to be the great question of Abscam).

Elbridge Gerry of Massachusetts observed that during the Revolution a Roman virtue had prevailed. Now in politics we have more land - and stock - jobbers than any place on earth. Gerry whose own name was soon to be incorporated into the word gerrymander to express legislative shenanigans - was not contradicted.

Madison himself declared,

> "My wish is that the national legislature be as uncorrupt as possible. I believe all public bodies are inclined, from various motives, to support members, but it is not always done from the base motives of venality. Friendship, and a knowledge of the abilities of those with whom they associate may profice it. If you bar the door against such attachments, you deprive the government of its greatest strength and support.....The legislative body must be the road to public honour.[3]

A distinctly modest barrier to corruption of Congress was, thus, set up by the Constitution - a barrier designed only to deter the legislature from collaborating with the executive to create or enhance office for the benefit of current legislators. No penalty was set for its violation. It was to be eventually flouted with impunity by Senator Hugo Black and President Franklin Roosevelt, who appointed Black to the Supreme Court after the Justice emoluments had been increased while Black was a legislator.[4]

What was treated as 'corruption' by most participants in the debate was an administration's use of appointments to get votes-the same concept of corruption which had prompted the provision permitting impeachment for bribery.

Great Britain, he observed, showed "the excellence" of judicial appointments lasting as long as good behaviour.[5] Hamilton further supported the jury as a "security against corruption". A standing body of magistrates was always easier "to tamper with" than a jury summoned for a special occasion. Juries could be corruptly chosen by sheriffs or clerks of court, and those "promiscuously taken from the public mass" could be more corruptible than the government's chosen appointees.

Nonetheless a jury must still be a valuable check upon corruption. It greatly multiplies the impediments to its success. If a jury went wrong, the court could grant a new trial. Successful corruption would have to work on both.

By increasing the obstacles to success, it discourages attempts to seduce the integrity of either. The temptations to prostitution which the judges might have to surmount, must certainly be much fewer . . . . Easily and naturally Hamilton fell back upon the ancient sexual metaphors to explicate the dangers besetting a judge.[6]

Sexual imagery was also used by Hamilton when he gave an Aristotelian reason why the Constitution left the election of the President to the people: they were not a small body of men "who might be tampered with beforehand to prostitute their votes".

As for the electoral college, none might be a member who might be suspected to too great devotion to the President in office, and this temporary body, composed of men dispersed over the thirteen states, would not afford time for "the business of corruption" to do its work.[7]

Madison justly held that no man is allowed to be a judge in his own cause, because his interest would certainly bias his judgement, and not improbably, corrupt his integrity. With equal, nay with greater reason, a body of men are unfit to be both judges and parties at the same time; yet what are many of the most important acts of legislation, but so many judicial determinations, not indeed concerning the rights of single persons, but concerning the rights to large bodies of citizens? And what are the different classes of legislators but advocates and parties to the causes which they determine?

The conclusion was not that legislators could not vote. Like Dr. Johnson, Madison accepted the view that 'interest' was inevitable. He did not suppose that the Constitution mitigated its impact even by the elementary rules intended to preserve the impartiality of judges. Interested and biased as they must be, legislators were not provided by the Constitution with any special protection against the temptations of corruption.

Was the virtue of congressmen safeguarded by statute? The first federal law on bribery, enacted in 1789, was part of a general statute directed to protection of the government's most important source of revenue, the customs. Specifically it made it a crime to receive or give 'any bribe, reward or recompense' for making a false entry as to a ship or merchandise. It became criminal to offer or accept money or any other bribe, present or reward, or any promise, contract, obligation or decree of any federal judge.

Draftsman still hesitated to believe that 'bribe alone would cover all contigencies. Thoughtfully, the act extended to promises. Remarkably, no punishment was fixed except for disqualification from federal office. Fine or imprisonment was explicitly left to the discretion of the court. In statutory form the sanction prescribed was that inflicted on Bacon-forfeiture of office and the prospect of office, everything else open to remission.

Only judges—not federal juries, federal district attorneys, federal marshals were protected in this way from corruption. No statute was enacted against bribery of the Executive Branch or by the Executive Branch. Arguably, the common law of bribery covered certain kinds of corruption, for example, buying an appointment, if Lord Mansfield were followed. Lawmakers were not to be inhibited from bribery by law. The only sanction for legislative bribe-takers was to be political.

Assassinated less than six weeks later, Lincoln died on Good Friday. The coincidence was irresistible to many, even extending to the treatment of the assassin, unknown to Lincoln, as a 'Judas'. In Carl Sandburg's summation, 'Over and over again were the parallels drawn of Lincoln and Christ in blood of atonement dying for mankind'. By his death Lincoln legitimated the emancipation and redeemed the slaves already freed by the bargains of congressional politics.

NOTES AND REFERENCES

1. See Bernard Bailyn, *The ideological Origins of the American Revolution* (Cambridge, Mass.: Harvard University Press, 1967) 43, 48, 86; Milton Klein, "Corruption in Colonial America", South Atlantic Quarterly 78 (1979) 57 at 70-71. Charles Carroll of Carrollton to Charles Carroll, Sr. January 29, 1760, and Charles Carroll, Sr., to William Graves, December 23, 1768, quoted in Bailyn Ideological Origins 91-92"; corrupt and prostituted minority", Philadelphia handbill, quoted in *ibid.* 126. For Dr. Johnson's view, see Chapter 14 above at n. 83. Colonial governors in America had often been perceived by Americans as avaricious men, out to make money from their office, see, for example, Stanley N. Katz, *Newcastle's New York* (Cambridge, Mass: Harvard University Press, 1968) 33-35. Relief in England from their oppressions was generally viewed as expensive to obtain (*ibid.* 96). "Connections", "interest; and 'influence' were the ingredients of Anglo-American political infighting", *ibid.* 200. It was against the background of this experience, not on a tabula rasa, that the Americans framed their laws.
2. *Records of the Federal Convention* 2, 65-69 (Madison's Notes for July 20, 1787).
3. *Ibid*, 2, 285-289 (Madison's notes for Aug. 14, 1787).
4. See Gerald T. Dunne, *Hugo Black and the Judicial revolution* (New York: Simon & Schuster, 1977) 52-54. A Legal challenge to Black's appointment was dismissed for lack of standing on the part of the petitioners, Ex parte Leavitt 302 U.S. 633 (1937).
5. *The Federalist*, ed. Henry Cabot Lodge (New York: G.P. Putnam's Sons, 1888). No. 78, 490-491.
6. *Ibid.* No. 83, 522-523.
7. *Ibid.* No. 67, 425.

16

THE CITIZEN CENSORS

All the various forms of corruption should be regarded, nor as fellonies, but as evidence of friction in the process of pouring new wine into the narrow necks of old bottles.

The concept of bribery lived in government. It affected the careers and lives of American officials. It was a political weapon, powerful if skillfully employed. In the interest the idea held for novelists, journalists, concerned citizens, bribery sustained its grip on the American consciousness.

Industrial expansion, increasing accumulation of wealth, immigration by exploitable votes, postwar relaxation of moral standards are supposed to have produced an increase in bribery, and a consequent reaction. Certainly the gross amounts offered as bribes appear to be larger as national wealth increases. But no quantitative data exist to substantiate the belief that the number of corrupted officials increased.

One has only a sense of a greater consciousness of the existence of corruption. Interaction occurs between political events and the bribery tradition inherited from Israel and Rome, Pierre Le Chantre and John Bromyard, Martin Luther and Edward Coke and Edmund Burke. Events are perceived through the spectacles the tradition furnished.

The Caricaturist of Congress: Hot on the heels of the Credit Mobilier investigation, Mark Twain and Charles Dudley Warner published a novel, The Gilded Age - a potboiler, a forerunner in fictional form of the instant journalism that in our time has so often turned congressional scandals into money-making paperbacks; it bore the subtitle, 'A Tale of Today'.

The President of a railroad describe to a stock-holder his expenses in getting an appropriation from Congress:

> A congressional appropriation costs money. Just reflect for instance. A majority of the House Committee, say $ 10,000 a piece - $ 40,000; a majority of the Senate Committee, the same each - say $ 40,000; a little extra to one or two chairman of one or two such committees, say $ 10,000 each - $ 20,000; and there's $ 100,000 of the money gone, to begin with. Then, seven male lobbyists at $ 3,000 each - $ 21,000; one female lobbyist, $ 10,000; a high moral Congressman or Senator here and there - the high moral ones cost more, because they give tone to a measure—say ten of these at $ 3,000 each, is $ 30,000; than a lot of small-fry country members who won't vote for anything whatever without pay-say twenty at $ 500 apiece is $ 10,000; a lot of dinners to members—say $ 10,000 altogether; lots of jimcracks for Congressmen's wives and children - those go a long way - you can't spend too much money in that line well, those things cost in a lump, say $ 10,000.

A newspaperman and old Colonel Sellers from Missouri discuss the morals of the current Congress: "To be sure you can buy now and then a Senator or a Representative; but they do not know it is wrong, and so they are not ashamed of it", says the newspaperman. Colonel Sellers replies that it is "sinful" and "shameful . . . . And yet when you come to look at it you cannot deny that we would have to go without the services of some of our ablest men, if the country were opposed to bribery. It is a harsh term. I do not like to use it."[1]

The Speaker, Laura Hawkins, a country girl turned female lobbyist, tells Trollop: 'Now you seem you had to know one of two things: Namely you either knew that the idea of all this preposterous generousity was to bribe you into future legislative friendship, or you *didn't* know it. That is to say, you had to be either a naive or a well, a fool - there was no middle ground.

You are not a fool,' Mr. Trollop. Colonel Sellers continues to maintain that there is still a very respectable minority of honest men in Congress and that they will investigate corruption. Of course, no one will be expelled: That would not be regular . . . . But all that inquiry is not lost. It has a good moral effect.

Washington Hawkins Laura's naive brother asks, who does it have a good moral effect on? "Sellers answers, Well-I don't know. On foreign countries, I think . . . . it shows that a man cannot be corrupt in this country without sweating for it. I can tell you that"[2] Congress is vindictive, Congress is savage, sir, when it gets waked up once.[3]

The religious imagery interwoven into the story linked it to the inherited learning on bribery. When Bigler calls the high market price of the Pennsylvania legislature 'simony' it is of course a joke—an ironic joke that a lobbyist ready to buy legislators should denounce their high price by the ecclesiastical category. The joke cannot be appreciated without reference to the Old religious meaning; and the novel as a whole cannot be understood without reference to the old denounce their high price by the ecclesiastical category.

The joke cannot be appreciated without reference to the old religious meaning; and the novel as a whole cannot be understood without reference to the old religious tradition. The basic norms measuring what goes on is that of Colonel Sellers. He does not like to use the plain English Christian term for it, bribery, but he does; and when he does, he denounces bribery as "a sin" and "a shame".

A minority of Congress is not corrupted the notion of an elect, a possibly saving remnant, is preserved even as the effectiveness of the elect is being satirized because Congress is going to do little to check the corruption. In the end, evil is defeated and good rewarded. The moral standard is biblical. Even the punishment implied to be condign is from Genesis: Congress is weak and worthless.

Sellers's Jibes suggest, because it merely censures, What it should have done to corrupted members like Mr. Fairoaks is what God did to Adam. Composed of parts of other X men, Ratcliffe is still Blaine, if we may assume, as it appears reasonable to do, that Henry Adams agreed with his wife Clover that Blaine "represents the corruption element as thoroughly as any man can."

From Clover's letters to her father it is evident that she loathed Blaine, and the intensity of her dislike reflected her moral judgement on "the corruption element." But the strength of her feelings against Blaine exemplify a new force in America - the hatred of educated women for the corruptionists. Women had been made the special embodiments of purity in nineteenth - century America.

Democracy used a cliche in treating Madeleine Lee as the guardian of integrity. Women had also internalized the common image. "Surely something can be done to check corruption?. Is a respectable government impossible in a democracy?" Ratcliffe responds, "Purify society and you purify the government. But try to purify the government artificially and you only aggravate failure." Baron Jacobi comments:

> You Americans believe yourselves to be excepted from the operation of general laws. You care not for experience I have lived seventy-five years, and all that time in the midst of corruption. I am corrupt myself . . . Well, I declare to you that in all my experience I have found no society which had had elements of corruption like the United States. The children in the street are corrupt, and know how to cheat me. The cities are all corrupt, and also the towns and countries and the States' legislatures and the judges . . . I do much regret that I have not yet one hundred years to live. If I could then come back to this city, I should find myself very content-much more than now. I am always content where there is much *corrupt and ma parole d'honneur* the United States will then be more corrupt than Rome under Caligula; more corrupt than the Church under Leo X; more corrupt than France under the Regent.
>
> In such a world there should be no guile-but there is a great deal of it notwithstanding. Indeed, at no other season is there so much. This is the moment when the two whited sepulchres at either end of the Avenue reek with the thick atmosphere of bargain and sale. The old is going; the new is coming. Wealth, office, power are at auction. Who bids highest? Who hates with most venom? who intrigues with most skill? Who has done the dirtiest, the meanest, the darkest, and the most, political work? He shall have his reward.

In politics we cannot keep our hands clean. I have done many things in my political career that are not defensible. To act with entire honesty and self-respect, we should always live in a pure atmosphere, and the atmosphere of politics is impure. Domestic life is the salvation of many public men.....

The moral standard by which corruption is condemned is used without reference to redemption. When Redcliffe is thrown overboard, Medeline "rejects American politics into as corrupt Nothing opposes Baron Jacobi's statement that all are corrupt and his apoclayptic prediction of a climax of corruption in America about the year 1976. "The bitterest part of all this horrid story is that nine out of ten of our countrymen would say I had made a mistake."

The bitterest part of all, however, was that *Democracy* used religious criteria and imagery without faith. Unlike Dante, the author did not turn from condemnation of corrupt rulers and a corrupt Church to God. Only the hope-better said, the possibility- of supernatural assistance exists. Actual judgement is on earth. The moral law had expired-like the Constitution.[4]

Novelists reflected the public consciousness of bribery and contributed to that consciousness a sense of its prevalence, effectiveness, and gravity.

> This is a most corrupt and profligate legislature. A legislator who is asked to oppose a lawless and mischievous measure, and who responds by putting his open palm behind him-wide open inviting a little honorarium of greenbacks, is a bad fruit of our prevalent political theories.

The Citizen forecasts revolution:

> Corruption in the legislative bodies, the great corporations, and now even in the state judiciary, and in the sheriffs' office, has at least reached a stage that must produce revolutionary action if no legal remedy can be found. Such things are "in the air". The strongest expressions to this effect received the loudest applause and every condemnation of our accursed elective judiciary system brought down the house. I verily believe it is nearly ripe for a Vigilance Committee. The dishonesty of every man in public office is a violent presumption, and universally recongnized as such. No decent man can take public office without imminent danger of losing caste, unless he compel the respect of a defrauded but corrupt community by the accumulation of at least one or two millions of fraudulent profit. This state of things cannot last much longer without an explosion.

Corruption for the Citizen is a city and state phenomenon, associated with Tammany, "the vital centre of the state Democracy."

"What's biting me?" the citizen could have asked, and answered, "The crimes committed by public officials." The Citizen is within his rights in saying that the crimes done by Tweed and his fellow officials were enough to rouse the wrath of any member of the community.

Those crimes are variously described by the Citizen as "embezzlement", "thievery", and "swindling". The crime of which the Boss the actually convicted, and for which he was sent to jail, was neglect and dishonesty in examining the accounts of the city, a breach of a statutory duty incumbent on him as a member of an audit committee.

Neither this crime nor the others mentioned by the Citizen was the crime of bribery. But bribery was the *modus operandi* of the Boss. Where the voters, the legislature, or the newspapers of New York needed to be won, Tweed was a bribe - giver. Where the city had a say, Tweed took. When the Citizen denounces "corruption" generically, It is this system of payoffs he has in mind. Bribery is central.[5]

Bribery is treason, that is, it destroyed democratic government. When Israel L. Durham, the boss of Philadelphia, asked St. Louis, "Just what is it I do that's so rotten wrong?," Steffens could answer that his crime was "disloyalty"-Durham had sold his neighbour's trust.

"Is democracy possible?" Steffens began his second article on St. Louis. As he looked around the nation and found bribery at levels of government, he began to wonder. On all sides he was told, "That is the way it's done".[6]

Villages were no better than States. Steffens found corruption everywhere. Yankee voters were paid $ 2.50 for their votes, Italian voters $ 2.75. The president himself, Theodore Roosevelt, and old friend from New York, was not exempt from the general evil.

Roosevelt admitted to Steffens that he traded appointments for votes he needed in the Congress. Steffens asked if this were not "the lowest form" of bribery, to buy votes with public office, offering not one's own money but public trusts as payment. Roosevelt would not agree. Steffens then declared that the president did, in fact, engage in bribery.

A split in his consciousness remained. In 1931 he published his autobiography, tracing his conversion from muckraker of corruption to defender of dictatorship. Lenin, he celebrated, because he had founded a new society "without possibilities of riches and poverty, graft, war, injustice, and tyranny." The elimination of graft was still for Steffens a central desideratum.

Yet for his new consciousness, Greek-Christian morality was meaningless. First tentatively-" may be bribery and corruption are acts of God" and "muckrakers, in general, the agents of the Devil"; then decisively "political business corruption a natural, well nigh universal process of change" he concluded that his reforming passion had been misdirected.

Each business, he thought now, bribed only because it had to bribe. The new railroads had had to "tunnel" the old state politics as they had to tunnel the mountains in their way; and so with successive business bribers. Hence, "all the various forms of corruption should be regarded, not as felonies, but as evidence of friction in the process of pouring new wine into the narrow necks of old bottles.

"If you want to know the law and nothing else, you must look at it as a bad man, who cares only for the material consequences which such knowledge enables him to predict, not as a good one, who finds his reasons for conduct, whether inside the law or outside of it, in the vague sanctions of conscience." The bad man would "want to keep out of jail if he can." From his perspective, one could estimate what truly was law, that is, the occasions when public force would be applied by the courts.[8]

Corruption corroded the building blocks. Rules could be set out and reshaped on rational grounds. Corruption was an irrational force. The accomplishments of law professors were in the mind, in argument, on paper. Bribery destroyed confidence in the masses and made the rules the product of sordid bargaining.

No obvious way existed for the law professor to detect the

existence of bribery or to tame its power. George Templeton Strong had written of respectable man losing caste by going into politics, stained as politics was by corruption. The law schools had no interest in their subject being reduced to the low-caste level of politics. Unable to analyze or to control corruption, unwilling to let their field appear to be contaminated, academic lawyers concentrated on more malleable matter.

The theologians. Augustine had analyzed the sin of bribery as had analyzed the sin of adultery. In mid-eighteenth century. Alfonso de'Liguori, summing up two centuries of casuistry in his *Theologia moralis*, still lacked a Latin action noun meaning bribery; he had to use a compound formula of noun and verb and he still lacked a standard, nontechnical, unambiguous word for bribes. The best he could do was to condemn "big *munera*," while still permitting unsought "little *munera*, which are called *xenia*, that is, food and drink". Treated perfunctorily and as it were by rote, bribery received little fresh analysis and sank in a repetition of bromides. Gaps and weaknesses abounded.[9]

Gaps—the omission of explicit treatment of legislators; the omission of explicit treatment of administrators; the omission of explicit treatment of voters; the omission of explicit treatment of bribes by lawyers went back to medieval theology. Even in medieval days the failure to treat expressly—of bribery of the prince qua legislator or to consider licit and illicit reciprocities in city state government left large holes. Liguori, the most representative Catholic moralist of the eighteenth century, still explicitly connected bribery only with judges.

Francis Patrick Kenrick, an Irish immigrant to America, educated at the College of the Propaganda in Rome, was an exception of a sort to the rule. Kenrick taught that lawmakers are sinners if they "waste the Treasury's money in matters of no importance and neglect to complete those things which would bring many advantages to the commonwealth; spend time in useless debates with waste to the Treasury; vote with the hope of reward or with a definite contract already made; take care to make or revise laws for the benefit of their own property with loss to others."

Weaknesses in the moral theologians' analysis of judicial

bribery, inherited from the scholastic tradition, continued. Despite positive law to the country, Liguori and his successors saw it as morally lawful to give *munera* to a judge or his servants "to buy back unjust harassment". This, wrote Liguori, "is not corruption, but insurance that one's own may be given one." The positive laws did not apply, for the laws 'intend to prevent those giving *munera* corrupting the judges, but not their obtaining just judgement.' Although the judge was put under moral obligation to restore the *munera* Liguori left litigants wide scope for rationalizing: most litigants believe, know, are certain that their cause is just.[10]

Another weakness - the theologians' treatment of the obligation of restitution. If the judge received *munera* to give an unjust judgement, wrote Lehmkuhl in the late nineteenth century, he had no moral duty to return what he had received. He had received "the price accepted as the valuation of a dangerous and wicked action".

At work here was the traditional analogy of a corrupt judge and a prostitute. As a whore could keep her hire, so could a judge. The judge did not get off scotfree; he still had the obligation to make up losses he had caused; but if he was paid to give an acquittal, what specific loss was he responsible for? Lehmkuhl neither asked nor answered this question.

In that year John A. MoHugh, O.P. analyzed the sin of 'graft' nothing that it was "so widespread that it can be met in practically every condition of life' and yet was not defined in any treatise of moral theology. Treating it as a synonym for bribery in any context, McHugh went on to state that graft was against commutative justice and against distributive justice; that it was a means of discrimination, that it despoiled the people; that it led to dishonesty and lies; that it contributed to the modern pagan idea which views life as a racket, and that subordinating public good to a public servant's private good, it was against reason and natural law. Custom could not excuse, McHugh sweepingly declared, because graft was intrinsically sinful.

It was Americans who had raised graft to a fine art (the most modest, charitable, and naive of explanations, overlooking entirely the kind of withdrawal from public morals which the Catholic Church in Europe had practised).

Connell himself showed the error in the prevailing view on restitution of a bribe which treated it like a whore's *turpis contractus*. In the case of the prostitute's shameful contract, the right of no third party was injured. In the case of a bribe, either a specific person was damaged and was owed restitution, or the bribe belonged to the state whose agent unlawfully had sold what was not his to sell.[11]

Here and in his more general analysis of graft as violating commutative justice, Connell was aware that "some readers" would think him "over-strict". He did not press the obligation of restitution. He acknowledged the existence of Catholics who 'in perfect good faith' believed they did not sin when they took "honest graft" by bribery.

The old academic disciplines of law and theology showed little taste for the study of bribery. Bribery and Corruption however, do not appear in the index to the *complete Psychological Works* of Sigmund Freud.[12]

Bribery was adopted as a metaphor: neurotics and criminals were said to 'bribe' or disarm their conscience by means of a voluntary acceptance of some suffering".

In a more extensive study, Power, Corruption and Rectitude (1963), Lasswell and Arnold A. Rogow turned to the bribe-taker., dividing politicians into "game politicians" and "gain politicians". The former saw politics as a game in which they obtained power, respect, self-righteousness, and affection in order to compensate for parental deprivations of these goods; the latter, lacking rectitude standards in their early political training, saw politics as a variety of commercial enterprises.

The age of "early political training" was left ambiguous, but the author repeated Lasswell's 1930 thesis that corruption could ensue when early environment promoted severe deprivation. No evidence was offered to demonstrate the relation between corrupt acts and the experiences of infancy and childhood.[13] The implication - not documented by any history - is that bribery would be more readily deterred by punishment than an oedipal crime such as murder.

Bribery, defined as the "purchase of a persons", Simmel stated that a bribee tried to preserve his dignity and hide what he was doing to protect himself against "self - negation and self-devaluation which would result from his sacrificing his personality for a certain amount of money". At the end of the nineteenth century and in Berlin, he wrote as though bribe and bribery were universal concepts, timelessly applicable in every culture.[14]

A significant number of political scientists went further in abandonment of the bribe as a significant concept. Colin Leys, a specialist on modern Africa, wrote in 1965, "what is the Problem about corruption?" and stigmatized as "writers of the moralist school" those who saw corruption as always "a bad thing". Those involved in bribery, he observed, regarded it as "a good thing". For him, he implied, its badness or goodness was a question for investigation. Sometimes corruption led to results not particularly nice but unimportant to society.

On occasion, bribes promoted efficiency and socially useful administration. Frequently, they served persistent integrative needs of society. Examples from Africa, the Soviet Union, and the United States were cited in support of this argument against the uniformly negative evaluation of the bribe.[15]

James Q. Wilson, professor of government at Harvard, writing in the New York Times Magazine in 1968, authored an article entitled 'Corruption Is Not Always Scandalous'. He did not, he wrote, mean to say that corruption was ever right: Corruption by definition is wrong. But he went on to say what was "honest graft"—a concept attributed to George Washington Plunkitt of Tammany in 1900. Honest graft brought a profit to the office-holder and no harm to the public. When done to attract "necessary campaign funds", this was honest graft.

Wilson also distinguished "integrative and disintegrative corruption'—Disintegrative corruption was free-lancing by officials for their own benefit. Integrative corruption was seen in Mertonian terms. It coordinated independent governmental bodies so that the government as a whole could accomplish an objective; it was a way of overcoming fragmented authority. By implication it was close to being good.

In spite of Wilson disclaimer that he was not saying corrupting was right, he treated honest graft, capital formation graft, and integrative corruption in such a way that they appeared to be of little, practical consequence measured against the benefits they bought. Only after these distinctions were made did he observe that some kinds of corruption had 'high symbolic costs', qualifying this apparent concession to the old purity ethic by his agnosticism about the price paid.

In *Comparative Political Corruption* James C. Scott in 1973 took a comprehensive view of corruption in a variety of Third World countries, drawing on unreformed England and machine politics in the United States for analogies. Thailand he found to resemble the England of James I with officials using monopoly concessions and licensing for their own economic and political advantage. In Indonesia under the Guided Democracy of Sukarn, "the corruption market was so disorganized that prices were highly unstable and delivery by "sellers" was highly uncertain."

As the rules of the game and security in office were uncertain officials tried to squeeze as much as possible while in office. A far higher degree of corruption existed than in Thailand; indeed corruption in Indonesia attained truly epidemic proportions.

Haiti under Francois Duvalier was even more corrupt. The government was the only source of wealth; the regime set no limits to its coercive authority. Neither traditional norms, nor an independent authority, nor a commercial class, nor any other institution limited the dictator's power to extract money. If any regime may be said to be fundamentally corrupt, it would be the Duvalier regime.

The fundamentally corrupt Haitian regime was worse than the more gently exploitative Thai government. He noted a number of factors favouring corruption in the Third World: the continuation of traditional gift-giving; the force of ties and kinship; the demand for valuable governmental concessions exceeding the supply; the expansion of governmental functions; the great power of the bureaucracy relative to other sectors of the society; the relatively high status of civil servants, approached by peasants as superiors. Resistance to corruption, he concluded, depended on political authority and the strength of certain political institutions and values.

Invoking 'values', Scott implicity acknowledged the moral element affecting the growth or check of corruption; itself was a value laden word. Normative in his choice of basic concept and in his grading, he simultaneously maintained. Far from being pathological, patterns of corruption and violence may actually represent channels of political demand without which formal societal arrangements could scarcely survive. He quoted the view of Myron Weiner, an authority on India, that American political machines should be emulated in the present state of Indian society; effective politics in the short run depended on 'patronage, favour and bribery'.

American politics were "a morality play" because of the Christian infusions. This mixture of piety and politics obscured the social phenomena. New national problems had arisen which could not be handled by the old structures so 'a new system of national politics had to be devised'. The Guilded Age—America's great age of political corruption was the figment of the gentility's moral imagination.

The academic interest in bribery was tepid, but the true *trahison des clercs* from the perspective of the bribery tradition was its moral abandonment by a major American Novelist. In Theodore Dreser's trilogy, *The Financier, The Titan*, and *The Stoic*, bribery is the essential operation by which the protagonist Frank Algernon Cowperwood, acquires his greater fortune.

The Tradition Reasserted

Among the academicians a spectrum of attitudes toward bribery was descernible, it was a serious social evil. They considered bribe-taking a sin, offensive to God, repugnant to justice. Legal scholars who did not care to investigate bribery still knew that it was a crime and to be shunned.

Psychiatric writers, explaining bribery by childhood deprivations understood involvement in it as a personality disorder. For anthropologist the concept was a zero, a blank. The dominant social scientists found a positive value in some forms of bribery which were necessary to the functioning of the society.

Analogy, the concept of the bribe, used metaphorically in variety of forms.

In casual domestic contexts, 'Bribe' was to be applied to any inducement given a child to persuade him to do what his parents wanted. The idea of a manipulative maneuver by the briber was retained from the classic concept, but the essential element of a breach of trust by the bribee was abandoned. In James both elements of the classic concept are kept, 'Bribe', bribeable, are words of reproach to Chad and Stether because their class has so firmly condemned bribery in the political arena.

The Political Novel : The prime analogate, the corruption of government officials, continued to receive the attention of novelists. The master work of novels treating of bribery was published in 1946; Robert Penn Warren's All the King's Men.

Three arguments or pleas are made for Willie-first, that all judgements of bribery are relative and, in fact, coloured by class: "Graft is what be calls it when the fellows do it who don't know which fork to use". The second is that bribery is a necessity.

The third argument is that corruption and corruptibility are universal - in the country and in the city, in the school board and in the governor's mansion. And Willie says, 'Man is conceived in sin and born in corruption . . . . There is always something.' Illumination is provided through a historical flashback where corruption is analogized to a practice of adultery and its cruel consequences.

Bribery is a class category. What it describes prejoratively is done in all politics and has to be done. Yet, it is evil as adultery is evil. It necessarily produces self-loathing. The shame of it can kill.

Disloyal, mendacious, vulgar, and vindictive, Johnson has only three assets: charm, ability to manage men, and determined energy. The charm is smarmy, the ability to manage reveals the will to dominate, the energy is exercised in ruthlessness. This monster is a master of bribery.

Bribery runs through his rise to power. When he is first elected to Congress in 1937 at the age of twenty-eight, he buys votes - the votes of the rural boxes where the money goes to the sheriff or the country commissioners; the votes of the blacks who are sharecroppers in the country or slum-dwellers in Austin, where the money goes to the blacks' leaders; the votes of the Czech immigrants in the countryside, whose price is higher. He also buys what he needs from the media, paying money for favourable stories in the small town newspapers.

Observing his career, one could conclude that not only were the laws he ignored empty rhetoric but also that in America the anti-bribery ethic itself was dead. Both conclusions would be premature. The portrait of Johnson which Caro painted depends on the bribery tradition. Adulterer, hypocrite, ingrate, liar and traitor in this account, Johnson rises by giving and taking bribes.

NOTES AND REFERENCES

1. The easy pass was discovered before the Ames crowd took over, *ibid.* 117-119.
2. J.B. Crawford, *The Credit Mobilier of America* (Boston, 1880, reprinted Greenwood Press 1969). Despite its author's avowed impartiality, this book is essentially a brief for Oakes Ames.
3. Peter Dey to Grenville M. Dodge, Dec. 8, 1864, quoted in STanley P. Hirshon, *Grenville M. Dodge, Soldier -Politician-Railroad Pioneer* (Bloomington: Indiana University Press, 1967) 109, cf. Select Committee of the United States Senate, Affairs of the Union Pacific Railroad Company, Sen. Report No. 78, 42nd Cong., 3rd Sess., Feb. 20, 1873 hereafter Wilson Committee, 668-669 (Dey testimony, 2/11/73.
4. *Ibid.* 488, 507, 507-508 (Colfax testimony 2/11/73 and 2/19/73).
5. Garfield, Diary 2, 150 (Feb. 9, 1873, on Black's reassurance_; Jeremiah S. Black to James G. Blaine, Feb. 15, 1873,. quoted in *ibid.* 2, 90, n. 249.
6. *Ibid.* 471 (Synder testimony 2/1/73); 287 (Oliver Ames testimony 1/24/73).
7. Ames, *Pioneering the Union Pacific* 326-327 (on the suit and the change in meeting place); Oliver Ames to Major General Grenville Mellen Dodge, May 2, 1869, in Dodge, *Autobiography* (MS, Iowa State Department of History and Archives, 1865-

1871) 943 New York as sink of corruption), quoted in Ames, *Pioneering the Union Pacific* 327.

8. Poland Committee IV, XVIII-XIX.

9. *Ibid.* 2, 155 (Feb. 25, 1873: "more brilliant than solid"); Poland Speech, 2/27/73, Congressional Globe, Appendix 197 ("a class of ingenious lawyers"); Oakes Ames: A Memoir 41 (Ames wept. On Butler, Carol R. Fisk, "Benjamin Franklin Butler", DAB 3, 357-359; George F. Hoar, *Autobiography* of Seventy Years (New York: Charles Scribner's Sons, 1903) 1, 312.

10. Job Stevenson, Speech 2/26/73, Congressional Globe 1819 ("only the outcropping"); Washington Whitthorne, Speech, 2/26/73, *ibid.* 1821 ("purity"); John Bird (Democratic lame duck of New Jersey), Speech, 2/26/73, *ibid,* 1827 ("debasing"; "no other protection"); Poland, Speech, 2/27/73, *ibid.* Appendix 198 ("I quite agree"); *ibid.* 1833 (vote on Ames).

11. *Oakes Ames: A Memoir* 139 (resolution of Massachusetts legislature, April 13, 1883-May 7, 1883).

12. *Ibid.* 45-50 (Scott testimony 5/15/76).

13. *Ibid.* 106 (Blaine testimony 6/1/76); Garfield, Diary 3, 300 (June 1, 1876); 3, 301 (June 2, 1876); 3, 302 (June 4, 1876).

14. Blaine to Fisher, April 13, 1872, *Ibid.* 4, 3607, followed by Baline's "Personal Explanation."

15. Hoar, *Autobiography* 1, 379; Rhodes, History of the United States 7, 207-210.

17

THE IDEAL CRIMINALLY ENFORCED

Corruption is analogized to a practice of poultry and it's cruel consequences.

Federal criminal law against bribery was not, where leaders of the government were involved, enforced by criminal sanctions.

President, Vice-Presidents, Members of the Cabinet, Federal Judges were immune. Legal realists, understanding by the Law, the statutes actually applied, would have to conclude that no criminal law against the bribery of these high officers was in force in the early years of the Republic, in the entire nineteenth Century, or in the first quarter of the twentieth century. Over 140 years of American history elapsed before any one of this rank was criminally convicted as a bribe-taker.

In the late 1920s, the conviction of an ex-cabinet officer for bribery in office changed the prevailing rule or, rather, demonstrated that it was not of iron. In the late 1930s, the conviction of a federal judge while still in office showed that even incumbency was not equivalent to immunity.

Both cases depended on political incentives for their initiation, both were prosecuted with bipartisan cooperation. Read together, the cases were signs of a new seriousness about the criminal aspect of the bribe.

Dewey in 1939 was district attorney for Manhattan. Only thirty-six, he had already run once for Governor, denouncing the corrupt Democratic machines in Albany, Buffalo, and New York City. Ambitious, courageous, outspoken on the tie between organized crime and governmental corruption, Dewey began to investigate Manton. On January 29, 1939, he wrote Hatton W. Summers, Chairman of the House Judiciary Committee, setting out in succinct detail six cases in which Manton had received money from litigants. He made no accusation of crime. He said only that his investigation had been "with a view to possible criminal prosecution under the income-tax laws of the State of New York".[1]

The next day Manton resigned his office—an almost open admission of guilt and if custom were followed a protection against impeachment or a criminal trial. The case Dewey had developed was too strong to be so easily disposed of. The federal government looked foolish for being so far behind. A Democratic administration could not now be seen as protecting its own.

Non-capital offences, committed more than three years previously, were barred by a general statute of limitations. Overt acts in a conspiracy, however, could be introduced in evidence although older than three years, if the conspiracy had continued and if at least one act occurred within the three year period.

Cahill elected to prosecute under the conspiracy statute, even though the maximum penalty was two year imprisonment instead of the fifteen years provided in the law against bribery of a federal judge. The statute prohibited conspiracy 'to defraud the United States' in any manner or for any purpose. Arrangement and acceptance of the bribes were shown as overt acts in the carrying out of the conspiracy.

In the period 1932-1938, Manton had received large sums of money from litigants in at least a dozen cases - six patent suits, three receiverships, two criminal prosecutions, and one stockholders' suit. His payors included two poultry dealers; an insurance salesman; an engineer; a brewer; two lawyers; a fence for stolen bonds; a movie executive (Harry Warner of Warner Brothers); and several presidents of closely in old companies.

The sums were always substantial. In all, not less than

$4,40,000 and, perhaps, as much as $600,000 had been paid. The judge was assisted in these arrangements by two members of the bar, Bill Fallon, a defence lawyer known to professional criminals, and John Lotsch, the president of a small savings bank. Testimony had shown "brokers and brewers and moneylenders lugging the cash into the judge's chambers." Witnesses had painted "an overwhelming picture of judicial corruption."

On appeal, Manton argued that there was no defrauding of the United States and no obstruction of justice, because the cases in which he had been paid were correctly decided in the appellate process. He was only one of three members of any panel. Experienced judges- Harrie Chase, Augustus Hand, Learned Hand, and Thomas Swan - who had sat with him in the cases in question testified that his conduct in conference had in no way reflected bias.

In several of the decisions of the panel had been unanimous. In others, Manton had not written the opinion but only provided a concurring vote. In no appeals case could Manton by himself have produced victory for the litigant bribing him. Now he contended that bribery without harm done by the outcome could not establish the conspiracy of which he stood convicted.[2]

Long service on the federal bench by outstandingly corrupt judges-twenty-five years for Davis; Twenty-one years for Johnson; twenty-three years for Manton - proclaimed the compatibility of public honour and judicial tenure with the secret practice of bribery.

Enforcement of the bribery law against one level of officials did increase in the first half of the twentieth century. Councilmen of cities and selectmen of towns, municipal and state bureaucrats, clerks of court and an occasional mayor of a smaller city were convicted of bribery. Governors, major state office - holders, the mayor of Boston led charmed lives. James Michael Curley was shown, in a civil suit by the city of Boston, to have as mayor accepted $ 35,000 to fix a land damage suite against the city. He was ordered as a faithless trustee to turn his bribe over to the city.

The statute of limitations did not bar prosecution for the

bribery. He was not prosecuted for that crime, nor was he prosecuted for perjury for his lies defending himself in the civil case. His autobiography in 1957, vaguely but defiantly entitled *I'd Do It Again*, portrayed him as the champion of the poor, persecuted bipartisan patricians.[3]

In the late 1960s a modest effort was made to apply the criminal law at higher levels, In 1967 Foster Furcolo, an Ex-Governor, was indicted for arranging to bribe six members of the Governor's Council to approve his nominee for commissioner of Public Works, significantly the money to secure this key public appointment - $ 15,000 or $ 2,500 per councillor - was furnished by a private contractor. Furcolo was acquitted; two councillors were convicted. In 1971, the deputy commissioner of banks was convicted of taking bribes from two big small loan companies (Beneficial Finance Company and Household Finance Corporation) to set the rates on small loans. Also in 1971, the state showed that Commissioner Callahan, now dead seven years, had arranged to have his son-in-law made a partner in an engineering firm doing business with the Turnpike; the son-in-law and the firm were convicted for bribery.

These prosecutions showed that the criminal law was not obsolete and that it did not reach very high or very wide. A special commission on state and country buildings in 1980 investigated the expenditure of 17 billion dollars appropriated since 1968 for public buildings; it reported a 72 per cent failure rate, that is, 72 per cent of the construction had been unusable without repairs. It concluded that 'at those crucial points where money and power come together, the system has been rotten.'

The pattern was "pervasive." In the award of construction contracts for public buildings, corruption was "a way of life in Massachusetts". The commissioner's functions were advisory and reportorial. No major elected officials were indicated. If the commissions's conclusions were true- that the system was rotten, the pattern pervasive, corruption a way of life-the criminal law was scarcely enforced at all.

A paradox: criminal law, federal and state, was infrequently applied to anyone, almost never to those of high status; yet there was continued expansion of the criminal law of bribery. The expansion was statutory and to the extent that the statutes remained unapplied, purely theoretical. The stream of edicts of fourth-century Roman emperors on corruption is an appropriate parallel. Yet, as the sequel eventually showed, the tinkering with statutes could be seen as psychological preparation for hard enforcement. First, however, there were the legislative enactments.

In the late nineteenth century state laws began to criminalize the bribery of private persons. New York was the pioneer, making it a misdemeanour in 1881 to give a "gift" to an agent, employee, or servant. Unlike governmental bribery, consent by the principal was a defence. The states were far from uniform and sometimes whimsical. Statutes were directed at the bribery of specific classes of employees.

The basic crime, as defined by the modern statutes, consisted in conferring a benefit on an employee, agent or fiduciary with intent in influence the recipient's conduct in his principal's affairs. Givers or receivers of such benefits committed bribery.

Unlike any previous society, the United States now had statutes comprehensively extending the criminal law of bribery to almost every class and occupation. Between 1947 and 1960, thirty-two states made it a crime to influence sporting contests by bribes to officials or participants.

In 1600 only judges and witnesses could be criminally bribed, that is, found guilty of a crime for taking money to be influenced. By the eighteenth century the impeachment of Warren Hastings at least acknowledged that administrators fell within a class that could commit the crime. Legislators were a nineteenth-century statutory addition.

By the mid-twentieth century, the usual statute included all officials and employees of government. The expansion did not stop here. Private persons were capable of influencing public decisions.

The model Penal Code of 1962, followed by fifteen states, added the officers and employees of political parties to the bribable class. The Model Panel Code, made any person selling political influence affecting a governmental appointment or transaction guilty of a crime. Political bosses, wives, mistresses, sons and daughters of office-holders, if they exercised their influence for a price, were within the law's scope.

Some state laws restricted bribes to pecuniary benefits. The statutory trend was to define any favour, pecuniary or not, as a bribe. Such a definition on its face encompassed a broad variety of political activity. For example, city councilman A's promise to vote for B as mayor. If B would support A's legislative proposals fell within the definition. Even state senator A's agreement to vote for state senator B's bill if B would vote for A's - logrolling characteristic of most legislatures - was not outside this definition. Read as they were written the statutes extended the bribery rule deeply into political life.

Intent 'to influence' or 'to be influenced' was sometimes hard to prove. Federal bribery law enacted in 1962 treated as bribery a lesser category of offence where intent of this kind did not have to be shown. Bribery was committed if a benefit was sought or offered 'for' or 'because' of 'an official act. The statute embraced the common American practice of giving the mailman five or ten dollars at Christmas; a federal crime was committed because the money was clearly given 'for' the mailman's official service during the year. The criminal law of bribery could establish essential obligations.

On October 11, 1973, Spiro I. Agnew resigned as Vice-President of the United States and pleaded *nolo contendere* to a single count of evading federal tax on income of $ 29,000 unreported by him. When he was governor of Maryland. The prosecutors simultaneously filed in court and made part of the public record a summary of the evidence they had been prepared to offer if Agnew had not abandoned his defence. Their summary showed a man whose willingness to accept bribes had been uninhibited by fear of criminal prosecution.

Common accord existed in the federal judiciary, it appeared, that local corruption was an evil now to be stamped out, almost as vigorously as racial discrimination. That bribery was a great evil had been the contention of American censors since the days of Henry Adams. The federal judges reflected the consensus of concerned citizens, novelists, journalists, Little dissent was heard as the Hobbs Act received a gloss creating a new federal crime of extortion, as mail fraud came to include breach of fiduciary duty to the state, and as the federal courts created a federal common law of bribery.

In 1970, in the second year of the Nixon administration, collaboration between the Democratic controlled Congress and the Justice Department under John Mitchell produced the most comprehensive federal statute ever designed against bribery—the Racketeering Influenced and Corrupt Organization Act or RICO.

RICO, like Dante, treated bribery as seriously as physical violence and indeed as worse than such physical violence as manslaughter and mayhem. Any act indictable under the federal bribery law, the mail and wire fraud laws, the Hobbs Act the Travel Act, was also described as racketeering, so that RICO picked up and, as will be seen, enlarged federal power under all these statutes.

Bribery was obviously only one of several crimes which RICO embraced. Nonetheless, the act's 'Statement of Findings and Purpose' recognized that the money and power of organized crime were 'increasingly used' to 'subvert and corrupt our democratic processes'. A close connection between organized crime and bribery was acknowledged.

Paying bribes, collecting bribes, investing bribes was racketeering. The overwhelming answer of authority was that it had. When a supervisor in the Department of Revenue of Pennsylvania accepted $ 500 a week to permit the smuggling of untaxed cigarettes, the Third Circuit held the department to be an enterprise conducted by racketeering, and the payment of several of the weekly instalments to be a pattern constituting a RICO crime.

The fourth Circuit held the Sheriff's department of Wilson County, North Carolina, to be an enterprise; when Sheriff Wilbur Pridgin accepted pay offs from local houses of prostitution he committed a RICO crime/offence. The seventh Circuit found the sheriff's was convicted of taking $ 50 per week per prostitute from houses of prostitution and $ 6 per car towed from towing companies.

In Louisiana the state agricultural department was treated as an enterprise corruptible by RICO banned acts. In Tennessee, charges that the governor's office in Governor Blanton's time sold pardons were found to be valid RICO counts; the office of the Governor, was an enterprise for RICO purposes.

In South Carolna, state senator John D. Long was convicted of RICO racketeering when he sold his influence to procure state jobs. In cities as far apart as Philadelphia and El Paso, traffic courts were found to be enterprises, and bribe-taking by the employees handling traffic fines was found to be punishable under RICO.

Immunity for actual legislative acts kept a corner of congressional activity free from supervision by the executive branch of the federal government. State legislators, the Supreme Court held, enjoyed no comparable immunity from federal prosecution for their committee actions, speeches in the legislature, introduction of legislation or votes: in a RICO prosecution of a state senator in Tennessee, the federal authorities were permitted to show that he introduced a bill and attended a committee hearing in furtherance of his obtaining of bribes.

Under four different presidents - Nixon, Ford, Carter, Reagan - the application and expansion of federal bribery law went on. Communist ideology stressed the incorruptibility of revolutionary cadres while associating American capitalism with corruption and the support of corrupt regimes. The application of the criminal law of bribery to high officers of the government is an attractive step.

America, Tocqueville wrote in the 1830s, was far stricter than Europe in the purity of its morals - meaning thereby the public sexual morals of the Americans. The rules for sexual purity in a society may be read as a way of securing important enterances and exits, a way of avoiding ambiguities. One overall function of such rules, it has been argued anthropologically, is to impose order on the chaotic flux of existence.

In the United States in the 1960s, the rules on sexual purity underwent a marked decline in public acknowledgement and public acceptability, a decline marked by the repeal of many statutes on sexual behaviour and eventually reflected in the late 1960s and early 1970s at the highest public level by the

United States Supreme Court obliterating many of the traditional legal distinctions between the married and the unmarried.

Americans, once so proud of their chaste superiority to most European nations, war no longer distinguished by public insistence on sexual virtue. If rules on purity-rules against social pollution have an essential orde: - maintaining function entirely apart from their specific content, it may be supposed that as one type of purity regulation declined, a compensating increase took place in insistence on the purity of governmental conduct.

The ancient parallel between sexual corruption, bribery and civic corruption, and the use of sexual metaphors to describe bribery, can be seen as confirmatory evidence that the bribery ethic has always had an anti-pollutant effect with one function analogous to the purifying function of the rules on sexual conduct. In the 1960s this function became dominant. In the late 1960s anti-corruption law began to be criminally enforced more often than ever before.

In the period 1970-1977, 43 mayors, 44 state judges, 60 state legislators, and 260 sheriffs or local police officers were federally indicted for corruption; most were convicted. In all, 369 state officials and 1,290 local officials were found guilty of corruption. There was no way of knowing whether more corruption existed in the 1970s than at earlier times in the United States. What was clear was that corruption was being investigated and punished on a scale unknown before.

No statute with regard to bribery applicable to Congress existed before 1852. No convictions were obtained before the twentieth century. At the height of the Progressive Era, when muckrakers were denouncing the corruption of the Senate as 'treason', the Roosevelt administration dusted off the Civil War statute against a member of Congress accepting 'compensation' in any matter before a government department when the United States was a party.

Theodore Roosevelt's administration did convict and jail two natives in national politics. Joseph R. Burton, a first-term Republican Senator from Kansas, was found to have agreed to receive $ 2,500 from the Rialto Grain and Securities Company to stop a mail fraud investigation. Edmund H. Driggs, a Democratic ex-congressman from Brooklyn, was found to have been paid 12,500 by the Edward J. Brandt-Dent Company to use his influence while in Congress to secure a contract for the purchase by the United States of 250 cash registers.

In the 1920s, John Wesley Langley, a veteran Republican represe··:ative from Kentucky, was prosecuted by the coolidge administration and convicted of accepting $ 11,700 for his influence in obtaining permits for whiskey shipments into Kentucky. His formal conviction was for conspiracy to violate the Prohibition Act. In the 1930s, two congressmen were convicted violating a statute enacted in 1926 against accepting money to procure a federal appointment. Harry E. Rowbottom, a recently defeated Republican from Indiana, for selling post office appointments in Indiana; and Joh H. Doeppel, a second-term Democrat from California, for selling for $ 1,000 a nomination to West Point. George E. Foulkes, a recently defeated Democrat from Michigan, was convicted of conspiracy to assess postmasters for political contributions.

In 1949, J. Parnell Thomas, a Republican congressman from New Jersey, was convicted of a practice not unknown before of taking what were euphemistically called 'kickbacks' from the salaries of staff members, in effect continuous bribes for their appointments.

As of 1970, then ten members of Congress had been convicted of crimes generically bribery. In summary, the laws relating to the bribery of Congress were enforced in a non-partisan way, sporadically and symbolically and very mildly. The major sanction was political oblivion.

Three members of Congress were actually charged with bribery. Under the Nixon administration, Frank J. Brasco, Democrat of New York, was indicted for conspiracy to receive bribes to influence truck-leasing contracts from the Post Office; he was convicted in 1974. Also under Nixon, Senator Daniel B. Brewster, Democrat of Maryland, was charged with soliciting bribes; ultimately in 1975, he pleaded no contest to a charge of receiving payments for his official act, a crime under the illegal gratuities section of the bribery statute.

During the Carter administration, Daniel J. Flood, Democrat

of Pennsylvania, Chairman of the Labour HEW Appropriations Sub-Committee, wad indicted for conspiracy in receiving bribes to influence his actions as Chairman of the Sub-Committee; after one trial resulted in a hung jury, Flood pleaded guilty to defrauding the government.

Compared to the past 180 years, the amount of attention to congressional bribery in the 1970s was remarkable. Like the Justice Department's supervision of the states, it antedated Watergate: Brasco, Brewster, and Podell were cases begun under Nixon, Culprits ranged from powerful incumbents like Flood to lame ducks like Brewster. Democrats predominated, impartially prosecuted under Democratic and Republican administrations alike. Sentences continued to be light-Brasco received three months, Eilberg and Flood were put on probation, Brewster was merely fined. Political death was the true sanction.

The culmination of all the efforts to curtail and punish bribery among legislators occurred near the end of the 1970s in the police operation known by its governmental code name of Abscam. It could not have taken place except in a society drenched in the anti-bribery ethic. No comparable anti-bribery effort had ever been mounted by any nation against criminal bribe-takers among its own lawmakers.

Reciprocity remained central to politics. Federal prosecutors would decide which reciprocities were criminal. Federal judges would decide if the prosecutors' distinctions should be upheld. Definers of what exchanges constituted bribery, these prosecutors and judges were unlikely to forego their new power. Employing means that would have been criminal if employed by private persons, the executive branch was in a position to supervise every government official in the country from traffic court clerks to senators.

The judicial branch was in a position to approve or disapprove this supervision. Enforcers of the anti-bribery ethic by the criminal law, these prosecutors and judges had become the guardians of honest government, local, state, and national. At the centre of this supervisory system created by the Hobbs Act, the Travel Act, the Internal Revenue Code, the Mail and Wire Fraud Statutes, the conspiracy statute, and RICO, and the federal common law' based on these acts, was the crime of bribery.

A new stage in the use of the concept of the bribe had been reached. This epoch, which began about 1968, caused unprecedented pressure for the creation of a clear line between what could lead to disgrace and prison and the voluntary contributions that were the fuel of politics in a democracy.

NOTES AND REFERENCES

1. *Ibid.* 519.
2. Twain and Warner, *The Gilded Age* 487. on Pomeroy, see Justin Kaplan, *Mr. Clemens and Mark Twain* (New York: Simon & Schuster, 1966) 166.
3. *Ibid.* 25 (the 1852 editorial); 104 (The rings running New York); 116 (Hoffman and the Tammany Ring; the Corporation Ring); 117 (the Ring of the Board); 119 (the famous Tammany Ring); 127-128 (the Lunch Club Ring; the City Hall Ring); 137 (Tweed elected Grand Sachem). According to Samuel J. Tilden, *The New York City "Ring". Its Origin, Maturity and Fall* (New York, 1873) 11, "a ring" also implies the notion of encircling men in both major parties.

18

THE DONATIONS OF DEMOCRACY

Bribe and bribery were universal concepts timelessly applicable in every culture.

Democracy does not work without campaigns for office. Campaigns require money. Unless only the rich are to run, the money must be raised. If the governments supplied it, the danger of manipulation by incumbents would be great. If the money comes from citizens, they give it to candidates they expect to vote, on at least some issues, in accordance with the donors' desires.

Normally, at any rate, money is given to an office seeker whose views on important issues coincide with the giver's. The money is given with the hope, expectation, purpose that particular views will be translated into particular votes. A tacit reciprocity exists. How is money given a candidate different from a bribe?

Nineteenth-century usage made the very "to contribute" and the noun "contribution" central to the answer to this question. As early as 1829 New York passed a statute entitled "An Act to Preserve the Purity of Election" forbidding anyone" to contribute money" for an election except for printing. The law was interpreted in 1842. An entrepreneur who had performed a contract to build a long cabin on Broadway to promote the presidential campaign of Willian Henry Harrison was denied payment of the contract price of $1,000.

The case struck a theme that would recur and become stronger. Preservation of purity could lead to total prohibition. The statute-not heard of again in New York politics-was a linguistic benchmark. "Purity" was its aim. "Contribute" was the normal way of designating a politics payment. "Contribution" in the New York courts" opinion was the normal noun for the action contributing and the normal noun for what was contributed.

The verb "to contribute" was employed in the same sense in a federal statute of 1867 : government officials were not "to require or request" the employees of naval yards "to contribute or pay any money for political purposes." To contribute "here was in effect to offer a quid pro quo for keeping one's job with the Navy : Pepys would have understood. But a request to a working man to contribute was condemned not as extortion or as a request for a bribe it was condemned as a distinct practice deserving special statutory attention.

Unless stigmatized by a specific law, a contribution was marked off from a bribe, which was criminal, and at the same time subtly distinguished from a gift, which was gratuitous. The word was the American equivalent of contribution, the Latin term the fifteenth century had used to distinguish a lawful payment for a pardon from a sinful bribe or a free gift.

A contribution was that one made, in other contexts, to a partnership or a charity. It was, if not precisely an investment, something shared with another whose purposes agreed with one's own, who was in the process of furthering those purposes, Who responded to the contribution by using it for those purposes.

A contribution in politics, wrote Theodore Roosevelt, that most practical if progressive Republicans, was received by him "without any kind of promise, expressed or implied." In the same sentence he asked that he accepted it on the principle that the one making it had "no end to serve except to assist the cause he is championing."

Roosevelt did not acknowledge the tension between his absence of a promise and the donor's desire to assist a cause. The donor gave, replying on the candidate to furnish the assistance. Did not reliance depend upon, or create, reciprocation? And if one gives to get reciprocation in office, is one not giving in order to influence official conduct?

Roosevelt, however, had mentioned "corrupt practice acts." "Corrupt practice" was a standard phrase in America by the 1840s the English had enacted a Corrupt-Practice Act in 1883. In 1910 Congress added its own "Federal Corrupt Practices Act," a statute requiring the reporting of all contributions to national elections. A corporation that made a contribution and concealed it was now guilty of two crimes, and national party committees receiving corporation contributions were under a criminal obligation to report them. The next year, 1911, the law against corporate giving was extended to include primaries. But in 1913 a gap was allowed to develop.

The Seventeenth Amendment providing for the popular election of senators was adopted. The provisions of the law against corporate gifts were such that they applied only to the election of senators by state legislatures. For a dozen years nothing was done to fill the hole. In 1921 another hole was opened.

The Supreme Court held that Congress had no constitutional power to regulate spending in any primary. In 1925, in the wake of the Fall affair and other scandals of the Harding administration, an amended Federal Corrupt Practices Act patched up the statute, include, within its scope the direct elections of senators, eliminating primaries, and expanding "money contribution" to "contribution".

Gulf Oil Corporation in 1973 had assets of about twelve billion dollars, gross revenues of about eighteen billion, and a net income of about one billion. Claude C. Wild. Jr. vice-president and head of its "Government Relations Office,: conducted its legislative programme in Washington. In July, 1973, Wild informed Gulf's chairman and chief executive officer. Bob R. Dorsey, that he had given $100,000 of Gulf funds in cash to the Committee to Re-Elect the President.

Gulf at once retained outside counsel, who advised confession to the Watergate prosecutor. This was done. Return of the money was demanded by the company. The money was obtained from the committee. Gulf's board of directors, up till now unadvised of the gift, was summoned to a special meeting, and told.

The cash received was distributed by Wild personally or by his staff, which included an assistant for "legislative liaison" and regional vice-presidents of Gulf's Government Relations Department. The money was usually distributed in plain envelopes. The recipients were officials, usually legislators or members of their staffs.

Those getting the cash were both Democrats and Republicans. Next to the $1,00,000 given the Committee to Re-Elect the President, the largest amount was $50,000 delivered over several months to Lyndon B.Johnson, then a senator and majority leader of the Senate, through his assistant, Walter Jenkins. The next highest recipient of cash- $25,000 delivered to "a personal confidant"—was Hubert Humphrey, then a senator campaigning for vice-president.

Cash was also dispensed to state officials. William H. Avery, governor of Kansas, received an envelope at his office. Another envelope was delivered to Preston Smith governor of Taxas. George Bloom, a Pennsylvania utility commissioner, received an envelope. Various Pennsylvania state legislators got from $1,000 a piece, with one republican leader getting $7,000 to be split among other politicians.

Interaction of the ancient concept of corruption and the modern law of securities regulation produced the Gulf-report. The Securities and Exchange Commission had no general policing function and no special charge to prevent corruption. Its mission was to prevent fraud on investors in a company with stock registered under the Securities Exchange Act.

Since corrupt practices were a crime, they had, therefore, to be hidden on a corporation's books, a corporation committing them had to engage in fictitious accounting and fraud under the securities laws.

The interest of the SEC in accurate accounting created for it an interest in discouraging corruption and illegal political payments, it was the SEC's that had finally flushed out Gulf's system of illegal disbursements.

Suppose an intelligent and cynical investor said, " It is to my interest and the company's interest that bribes be paid on occasion. I don't care if the amounts are buried on the corporation's books if, comparatively speaking, they are not too large. Four hundred thousand dollars an year spent for political purposes in less than one-tenth of one per cent of Gulf's income.

It is an infinitesimal amount, certainly an amount of no material significance to me as an investor. It was being spent in the wise discretion of experienced corporate officers for corporate purposes. It did not help my appraisal of Gulf to have the payment ;of these sums disclosed. When the SEC decided to force disclosure, it acted as a policeman or the holder of a roving commission. It departed from its statutory purpose.

It is always fraudulent to take money, however small the amount, on the pretext of lawful business and, then, use the money to break the law.

That answer might satisfy a conscientious law-abiding investor puzzled by the SECs concern about payments in violation of domestic law. But suppose bribes were paid overseas? Are investors and corporations citizens of the world, called on to be obedient to the law of every country? And suppose a bribe abroad is no crime but the custom of the country? The Gulf report implicily raised these questions.

Gulf in 1966 had $200 million invested in plastic and fertilizer plans, shipping, and a large refinery in South Korea, with the encouragement of the American government, Korea was preparing for a democratic election. The incumbent party though its expenses in a democratic election would be high.

The incumbent party turned to foreign investors, especially American ones, to finance its campaign. A high official in the secretariat of President Park asked Gulf for $ 1 million dollars. The request was "accompanied by pressure which left little to the imagination." Gulf President Bob Dorsey in Pittsburgh approved the payment. It was recorded at headquarters as a transfer to Bahamas Ex.

Four years later, 1970, there was a much heavier election challenge to the incumbents. S.K. Kim, a leader of the incumbents, summoned Korean Gulf Oil's "vice president for governmental relations" to his office and told him that Gulf must contribute $ 10 million. Gulf's answer was postponed until Dorsey, on his way to Korea on other business, arrived. He atonce informed Kim that the request "was almost preposterous." Kim said, in effect, although "substantially more roughly," "I'm not here to debate matters.

You are either going to put up the god damned money or suffer the consequences." Dorsey left in anger but eventually agreed that Gulf would contribute $3 million. He was, he said later, not afraid of nationalization. The payment a profitable business, without unwarranted and inhibiting government interference, required it." The payment was recorded as a transfer to Bahamas Ex. and the funds were, then, routed through a Swiss bank account. From it, nine checks for $200,000 a piece, and $ 1,199,790 in cash went to make up the sum in Korea.

The large payments supplemented a second kind of off the-books arrangement in Korea, the "Gray Fund, " amounting to about $ 10,000 a year. The purpose of the Gray Fund was not to pay for "specific administrative or legislative favours but "to ease access" to government agencies and "to obtain expeditious but routine action."

The explanation for its existence was the low salaries of the bureaucrats who needed "gratuities" to supplement their income. Payments here were remarkably like those St. Augustine had discussed in the context of the Roman Empire in Africa and had treated as distinct from unjust yet the sort of thing a devout man would avoid taking.

Italy was .a country which Gulf entered after World War II. Of 5 particular interest, given the common belief of Americans in Italian corruption, there was here a large gap between most rumours about Gulf's activities in Italy and credible evidence. The Gulf review committee examined of Gulf's Milan refinery and $ 1,200,000 spent for rights to a pipeline. The committee concluded that both expenditures were made in legitimate commercial transactions.

But an off-the-books fund was run by Gulf in Italy, formally known as the "Special Account" and informally called the Fondo Nero or "Black Fund." In Korea, the review committee had noted the excuse of Gulf that cash tips had been used to expedite the flow of business "through the bureaucracies of a relatively inexperienced government," as though lack of experience was a relevant factor.

No one could have said that Italian bureaucracies were inexperienced. Payments were, nonetheless required. For example, in the 1960s Gulf was expending its marketing in Italy, acquiring gas stations from other companies and opening new ones. It needed permits to operate the stations. For this purpose cashier's checks paid for by the Black Fund were sent to Gulf district managers, who then disbursed the cash among the bureaucrats.

The amount spent was comparatively trivial $ 23,000 over a decade or no more that $ 2,300 a year.

On occasion Gulf also distributed gas coupons to officials. The giving of such *omaggi*, or gifts, the committee concluded, " to lubricate the sluggish machinery of petty bureaucracy, was and is an accepted way of life which did not involve significant sums, considering the nature and volume of the Government contacts."

Regular corporate accounts as well as the Fondo Nero were drawn on to provide the cash. The practice, the committee reported, "was characterized as tipping rather than bribery and was not considered unlawful.

Gulf's political contributions in the United States, one might urge, represented a similar conformity to local mores. Federal law made the contributions criminal, but federal lawmakers, often of great respectability, accepted them. The payments were morally no worse than political contributions to President Park's party in Korea or *omaggi* to Italian bureaucrats.

They were the custom of the country. If management hid the practice from the directors it was from fear of the need for explanations. There was nothing wrong in the contributions in themselves. The anti-bribery ethic distorted their treatment by requiring that they be hidden.

In Buckley V. Valeo- the court upheld the restrictions on contributions. It said, "To the extent that large contributions are given to secure a political *quid pro quo* from current and potential office holders, the integrity of our system of representative democracy is undermined."

Bribery statutes were not in themselves sufficient to reach the evil: "Laws making criminal the giving and taking of bribes deal with only the most blatant and specific attempts of those with money to influence governmental action." Less blatant, less specific attempts to exchange money for response by an office-holder could be prohibited by the laws limiting campaign contributions.

Under the Nixon administration, a federal prosecution challenged a committee that had collected over one million dollars from members of the Pipe fitters Union and contributed to federal campaigns. Union officials ran the committee. Union members paid the committee regularly. Often they were under the impression that they had to pay if any were to remain in the union. The union was convicted of violating the Corrupt Practices Act.

An analogy with an old moral issue appeared relevant. In the analysis of usury advanced by theologians of the thirteenth century it was a sin for the lender to lend expecting or hoping for specific gain by a gift from the borrower; but it was no sin if the lender merely believed that his borrower might be generous. A very fine line separated sinful usurious intent and blameless awareness of the likelihood of reciprocity. It was a line too fine to be maintained except in the interior judgement of a soul. A similar mental line seemed to distinguish the lawful gift to a candidate from a bribe.

19

CORPORATE BRIBERY

Bribes come in all shapes as sex commodities, appointment and most often cash.

"In Intelligence operations, money is an essential ingredient; even where other motives arise-as patriotism or ideological affiliation-money, however little, or its equivalent, must be dropped in, like a touch of bitter in a mint julep, to validate the deal. Only when money had passed is the mystical union fully established." Thus, in certain circumstances, the passing of money had to be engineered in such a way that it seemed to happen of itself, which in seduction terms, was the equivalent of lolling or reaching out an arm as though by accident.

"There is an implicit moral criticism in his comparing his bribing activity to seduction. The critique is muted. It is taken for granted that intelligence activities will go on; that governments will bribe the officials of neutral foreign governments; that the techniques are standard and the practice universal.

The ethical connotations of bribery operated as a restraint, as did, ever more, an awareness that all civilized countries had some laws on bribery-the bough officials could not be publically identified. Discretion but not moral objection, accompanied the payment of overseas bribes.

Necessity, the rationale for bribery during war or for intelligence, was equally present for any nation dependent on foreign commerce when commerce was protected or obtained by bribery.

Lockheed did a large part of its business with foreigners. A substantial part of its revenue came from the sale of military and commercial aircraft abroad.

As Lockheed's payments abroad to the officials of foreign governments became public before a global audience, the main questions present in any historical presentation of bribery were implicitly raised: If these payments were to be called bribes was it by application of American law or by application of American ethics or by application of foreign law or foreign ethics?

If the law of any country was chosen, was it law as announced or as enforced? If an ethical standard was used what group's standard was to be chosed ? Without formally addressing these questions, the accountants, lawyers, and directors of Lockheed, the Emergency Loan Guarantee Board and the Securities and Exchange Commission, two committees of the Unites States Senate, and governments from Japan to the Netherlands struggled with answers to them.

To a striking degree, once the payments were public-one, so to speak, the money was out on the table-there was agreement about their ethical status. Ethically the concept of the bribe was now universal or almost universal. The upshot of the Lookhead affair and similar disclosures by other American corporations was to be an effort by the United States to give the concept universal legal significance.

Lockhead does not defend or condone the practice of payments to foreign officials. "We only say the practice exists, and that in many countries it appeared, as a matter of business judgement, necessary in order to compete against both U.S. and foreign competitors." Necessity, it appeared, was Houghton's justification.

Lockheed payments in Iran, the Philippines, and elsewhere were publicity exposed. Lockheed's relations with Dasaad Musin, its intermediary in Indonesia under Sukarno, were, for example, explored at length. Dasaad rated by Lockheed as being in "a unique position" with Sukarno, customarily took a 3 per cent commission. When, three years after Sukarno's fall, Dasaad finally lost his influence, he was eliminated as an agent. The commission rose to 5 per cent ant Lockheed found itself dealing directly with Indonesian military officers

Dasaad's operations paled besides those of Lockheed's representative in Saudi Arabia, whose name might have been extravagantly invented by Dickens. Adnan Khashoggi was a Standford-educated Saudi who first came to prominence in arranging the Saudi purchase of tanks from France. Also employed by Northrop, he had been Lockheed's agent since 1964. In the five years looked at by the committee, 1970 to 1975, commissions paid by Lockheed on Saudi sales amounted to $106 millions.

A kickback was "where you have something for me, and I will return to the buyer." He continued, "A bribe to me is where you go to somebody and say I would like for you to do something for me, and I will pay you. Now that is the way it comes through to me.

Lockheed correspondence referring to the payments was often encoded. The code for "consultant" was "locust." The senators inquired how the word had been chosen. Senator Church said, "Even the computer had a conscience." Senator Case told the story of a man convicted of cheating his clients; the judge asked if he was not ashamed of cheating those who trusted him; the criminal asked, " whom else can you cheat?" This subversion of "people who necessarily have to put their trust in you."

Two days later Lockheed's president, A Carl Kotchian, was put on public display. He testified about the off-the-books account in Switzerland, then about a million dollars paid to "a high government official in the Netherlands." Senator Church asked if Kotchian wouldn't call the million dollars a bribe Lockheed's management still resisted the characterization. Kotchian answered, "I think, Sir, that as my understanding of a bribe is a *quid pro quo* for a specific item in return.... I would characterize this more as a gift. But I don't want to quibble with you, sir.

Unprecedentedly, governments around the world had been told by American senators in the most public of forums, a Senate hearing, that they had been bribed. Disclosure of the payments and their denunciation as bribery put each affected government on the spot : would it look further? Implicitly the Church committee asked other governments to cooperate in enforcing a universal ethic. Would they respond? Reactions in the Netherlands, Italy, and Japan were representative.

No names were mentioned when Kotchian told the Church Committee about $ 1,000,000 paid to a high official of the Netherlands and declined to quibble as to whether the million was a bribe or not. Almost immediately a leak from the committee revealed the name of the recipient. It was His Royal Highness, Bernhard, Prince of the Netherlands, consort of Queen Juliana. In Holland, Bernhard, formally informed the prime minister that Kotchian's testimony was untrue. The Prime Minister four days after Kotchian's statement was made, created a "Commission of Three" to determine the truth.

The conditions were two. The prince was required to resign all the functions that had caused him to confuse his interests with the nation's. He was required to resign every military polition and every business directorship, and did so. The second condition was that the prince apologize to his countrymen. A public statement set out his confession.

> I have not been critical enough in my judgement of initiatives presented to me.
>
> I have written letters that I should not have sent.
>
> I have not observed the caution in this matter which is required in my vulnerable position as consort of the Queen and Prince of the Netherlands.
>
> I admit and sincerely regret this.

The Italians were "not all that surprised" by the revelations about Lockheed bribery because "envelopes of varying thicknesses are such an everyday part of Italian life."

The Italian police moved quickly to arrest suspects, and Luigi Gui, a Christian Democrat, Mario Tanassi, a Social Democrat, and nine others went on trial for "aggravated corruption" in connection with the purchase of fourteen Lockheed Hercules planes in 1970-71. Bribery in short, was punished, and punished criminally, and about as quickly and incompletely as was usual in America where high government officials were concerned.

Japanese Politicians and Prosecutors: It took no longer for the news from Washington to be transmitted to Japan than for suspicion there to be pointed at ex-Prime Minister Kakuki Tanaka and for the connections of Lockheed's agent Kodama with ex-Prime Minister Kishi to be noted. Another Prime Minister, Takeo Miki, who came from Kishi and Tanaka's party, the Liberal Democrats, announced, " I will make it a point of honour for Japan to investigate the Lockheed contribution and to clarify the issue for our people." His statement used the preferred term of American politics "contribution" and combined a bold promise to investigate with a nicely ambiguous pharase "about" clarifying the issue.

Arrests, resignations, indictments, and trials followed. A prime Lockheed agent, Yoshi Kodama-Known in Japanese terms as a kuromaku or black curtain, that is, one exercising control behind the scenes had a stroke, which dispensed him from testifying before Parliament, but he was indicted in March 1976, and his assets were seized by the tax authorities.

In June 1977 he went on trial for tax evasion and breaking the foreign currency laws in connection with the Lockheed payments. In his opening statement to the court, he said he received $ 178,571 per year from 1969 to 1976 as a Lockheed consultant and received nothing else from Lockheed in these years.

On July 26,1976 Itoh-the recipient of the "Peanuts" and Marubeni's contact with Prime Minister Tanaka—was indicted. Japan was "stunned" by the arrest of Tanaka himself. The Marubeni men were charged with paying Tanaka 500,000,000 yen in four instalments; Tanaka was charged with having received this bribe " in connection with his duties" as Prime Minister. He was also charged with violation of the Foreign Exchange and Foreign Trade Control Law.

The case against the former prime minister was proved, he was liable to three years' imprisonment for the foreign exchange offense, to five years' imprisonment for bribery, and a fine of tribble the bribe and confiscation of the bribe by the tax authorities, a potential liability of two billion yen.

The criminal law of Japan was plain. It was a crime to give or to receive a bribe. Bribe—takers in Japan were, in fact, sometimes prosecuted and even occasionally imprisoned.

Approximately 500 corporations came forward to confess to the canonical offence of making unreported, questionable payments overseas. Characterized as "questionable" rather than as bribes-the father confessors here being indulgent to the qualms and scruples of the penitents- the payments very often were sums paid to government officials to influence their official acts. As a percentage of American corporations doing business abroad, the number of penitents was not large less than 1.5 per cent.

Lockheed confessed to using a number of devices to conceal the payments: backdated contracts: multiple contracts for a single transition; false invoices; shell corporations; straw payees; the regular use of bearer checks or cash. It confessed to departures from standard accounting practice to accumulate the money used; an off-the-books accounts in Switzerland opened in the name of two lawyers; a deposit box in Geneva containing at times over $300,000 in cash; transfers through Swiss subsidiaries not recorded on the subsidiaries books.

It confessed to transporting large amounts of cash in unorhodox ways-huge amounts of yen for Japan, for example, were picked up physically by couriers in Hong Kong and delivered to Lockheed's man in Japan bundled in newspapers. It confessed to having no protection against its own employees taking a share of a payment made to a foreign official by a side arrangement that part of the cash they paid be returned to them.

It confessed that the normal beneficiaries of its country were the employees of national airlines, foreign political parties, and the officials of governments around the world. It did not treat every commission to a middleman as questionable: if it, had it would have had to include in it's tally the whole $106 million paid on Saudi sales.

Adopting a more liberal rule, by which a substantial part of Khashoggi's pay was legitimate, it still reached a remarkable sum of the five years, 1970-1975, covered by the report. Lockheed confessed to paying in those years over $30 million which it called questionable.

THE CRIMINAL STANDARD MADE UNIVERSAL

Unethical perhaps but not criminal under American law was the self-characterization of the confessants to the SEC disclosing their payments. Yet they needed to confess only because the SEC took the position that to have hidden the payments was a species of securities fraud. Confession was the alternative to prosecution.

Two statutes caught the means often used in making foreign bribes. The Bank Secrecy Act, in force since 1970, required the reporting of transfers of more than $5,000 cash in or out of the country. The penalties imposable became serious-five years' imprisonment and a $ 500,000 fine-if the law was broken to further the commission of any other federal crime, a condition arguably met by many transfers for bribery overseas. The general conspiracy statute made any agreement to defraud the United States a felony. It could be applied to a plan to deduct bribes will fully in violation of the Internal Revenue Code.

Lockheed too pleaded guilty and was fined $647,000 for false statements on the financing of its overseas sales and for their fraud on payments channelled through a front in the Cayman Islands. Its chief American competitors, Boeing and McDonnell-Douglas, were eventually convicted to crimes in the sale of planes abroad: McDonnell-Douglas pleaded guilty to wire fraud and false statements, and paid $55,000 in fines and $1,200,000 in civil damages; Boeing pleaded guilty to false statements and was fined $400,000. Tactfully, in none of the cases did the prosecutors invoke. RICO.

No law specifically criminalizing bribery abroad existed. All the statutes violated had been peripheral, related to the means or to the reporting of bribes. Nothing explicitly prohibited an American from paying for a favour overseas. No such law had ever been framed in this country or anywhere else. It now existed.

In some ways the Foreign Corrupt Practices Act (FCPA) was like any law on domestic bribery. The FCPA went a good deal further than domestic anti-bribery law in its financial sanction —a possible one million dollar fine for the company. The five years' maximum imprisonment provided for company directors, officers, or employees was severe but not unusual.

"The word 'corruptly' connotes an evil motive or purpose, and intent to wrongfully influence the recipient." Old-fashioned and eliminated as obsolete in many modern bribery statutes, "corruptly" meant "by bribes" inescapably an American court applying the law would have to decide whose standard measured "evil motive, "wrongfully" or "bribes."

In some ways the Foreign Corrupt Practices Act was less stringent than laws already applicable to American bribes overseas. To violate the FCPA, the bribe had to be for the purpose of getting or keeping business.

Enforcement was assured by requirements as to accounting, requirements intended, so the committee said, "to operate in tandem with the criminalization provisions of the bill to deter corporate bribery." Corporations were required to keep books reflecting their transactions "accurately and fairly" and "in reasonable detail."

They also had to maintain internal accounting controls good enough to provide "reasonable assurances" that transactions were executed in accordance with management's instructions; managements were not to have the excuse that it did not know what its bribe-giving employees were doing.

In theory, no doubt, if it became criminal for an American to corrupt a foreigner, it became criminal for the foreigner to conspire with the American to arrange for his corruption. For the first time, a country made it criminal to corrupt the officials of another country. America's ambassadors that is, its businessmens were to show American purity throughout the globe. Secular requirements had never so comprehensively embraced and extended the bribery ethic.

20

COUNTRIES WIN FAVOURS BY PAYING U.S. POLITICIANS

BRIBES are "dirty", "lease, and "trash"

—Brutus in Julius Caeser

Is the electoral process in the world's most trumpeted democracy being subverted by foreign money?

Yes, if you believe the bogey being raised by the Republican Party about political contributions by foreign nationals in the US. Here's the take: under current American Federal election laws, foreigners who are permanent residents of the United States (Green Card holders), are not allowed to vote but they can contribute to political parties and candidates.

Current disclosure laws also do not require individuals to identify themselves as foreign nationals.

Some Republicans say that foreign countries and conglomerates are taking advantage of this "loophole" to funnel money to American politicians and win favours.

In the latest case, they suggest that a $ 5 billion Indonesian banking and real estate conglomerate - Lippo Bank - may have channelled $ 450,000 to President Clinton's Democratic Party through a low level intermediary.

The money was contributed to the DNC by Arief and Soraya Wiriadinata, an Indonesian couple who lived modestly in a Virginia suburb before they left home for Jakarta last year.

Soraya Wiriadinata's father was a major investor in Lippo,

whose chairman, Mochtar Riady, is a friend of president Clinton.

And what's in it or Lippo? Clout in the US political system, access to the White House, fat contracts in Indonesia and elsewhere.

This is not the first time the campaign finance reformers in the US have cried foul about foreign money. A prominent case reported in these columns some months back involved an Indian political gadfly.

Maryland Democratic Party fund-raiser Lalit Gadhia pleaded guilty in May to funneling more than $ 46,000, handed out to him by an official of the Indian Embassy. The money was directed to nearly 20 Congressmen who were seen as sympathetic to Indian causes.

The contributions were made by workaday Indian immigrants, including cooks, busboys and students, who were subsequently reimbursed by Gadhia with money paid by the Embassy official.

The issue raised a stink with the State Department taking it up with the Indian Embassy and ticking off the Ambassador. Gadhia is currently awaiting sentencing.

The episode, combined with other dubious donation controversies, has generated a momentum for campaign finance reform in the U.S.

There are now 10 million foreigners who are permanent residents in the United States and increasingly countries are known to rally their nationals for political causes. Moreover, there are also foreign special interest groups who lobby for their own survival and benefits.

The American Association of Physicians from India (AAPI), for instance, got President Clinton to address their convention in Chicago last year after making a handsome contribution to his campaign kitty. A 26,000-doctors strong organisation, AAPI keeps a close tab in Washington on legislation affecting foreign health care professionals.

Foreign companies are also allowed to contribute to the US political parties through their American subsidiaries as long as the money is deemed to have been generated in the U.S.

Most recently, the Democratic Party was forced to return $250,000 from Cheong Am, a Korean company, after it determined the money wasn't generated by its U.S subsidiary.

The money, in fact, was raised by a political activist who formerly worked with Lippo and is now with the Democratic Party.

The *hoopla* about foreign donations suits the Republican platform of stemming immigration. Conservative think-tankers have lately drummed up visions of a 'White minority" in America.

California is supposed to lead the way with the Whites being reduced to a minority in the state in the next decade. According to one study, at current immigration levels, the U.S itself will be a white minority country in the next 50 years.

PART: TWO
INDIAN SCENARIO

21

GENESIS OF CORRUPTION IN INDIA

Bribery rules are rules promotive of purity, designed to eradicate deeper social pollution.

As regards Indian scenario is concerned, among the various developments (good as well as bad) that have taken place in post-Independence India, the one that deserves the utmost attention of everyone of us is the acute degeneration of moral standards that has set in every walk of our life. Tragically, the old values that innumerable generation of this country had so ungrudgingly imbibed both in their private and public conduct, have worn away in less than four decades.

The mad race for quick acquisition of wealth, power and status in society that has overtaken all of us, has made us ruthlessly trample under foot all those virtues (as for instance honesty, selflessness and fellow-feeling) which once beaconed our way through thick and thin.

Now we have stooped ourselves so low that we no longer make a distinction between good and bad, the fair and the foul. Whatever contrivance helps us achieve our goal quickly and effortlessly is good and fair. The net result is corruption, more corruption and profligate corruption.

Some aspects of social interaction are confined to small groups of people and do not, therefore, impinge upon society as a whole. But politics and administration are, by nature, so pervasive and penetrating that no individual can ever escape their influence, even remotely.

Unfortunately, it is in this realm that corruption rules the roost and the harm that it has, thus, been doing to social fabric is perhaps beyond repair. It was, however, observed that until recently, men in authority even though felt hurt and aggrieved over this ugly phenomenon, would not take congnisance of it, much less discuss it in public. Happily, that phase is over. Now every same person is exercised over its menacing growth and openly clamours for curbing it.

In the background of the characteristics, causes and cost of corruption, we could move on to the specificities of corruption in the contemporary Indian context. It would appear that most of the political, economical, sociological and cultural factors that generally account for corruption operate in India to a greater rather than a lesser degree. India is a low-income developing country in which there is intense competition among both the affluent and the poor for scarce resources in an environment of rising expectations.

It is an active democracy in which the high cost of electoral politics has been a major factor in fuelling corruption in the electoral process and, subsequently, governance. In recent decades, there has been a great deal of political instability as reflected in frequent elections and changes of government, especially in the States, which has accelerated corruption. Divisions based on region, caste and language are the other factors that have promoted corruption, nepotism, and patronage.

India has not been free of corruption, whether in ancient times (at least as far back as the Arthasastra), the immediate precolonial period, the British rule or the decades following Independence. Gandhiji was concerned with corruption in the provincial Congress Ministries formed after the 1935 Act.

A number of cases of corruption in the States have been documented during the critical decades after Independence when Nehru was Prime Minister; nor were cases of corruption absent in the Centre itself.

It was in response to the concern expressed in Parliament on 'the growing menace of corruption in public administration' that the Government of India set up a Committee of MPs and officials, under the chairmanship of Shri K. Santhanam in the closing years of the Nehru period, to undertake a comprehensive inquiry into the problem.

A Crisis of Corruption

Neither the incidence of corruption in India nor the concern with it are, thus, new. However, the current state of corruption in the country is not just a linear continuation of the experience in the 1950s and 1960s.

Beginning with the 1970s, changes in the level, trend, nature and spread of corruption in the 1980s and 1990s have been such as to suggest that corruption has assumed critical proportions.

In other words, it might not be an exaggeration today to talk about corruption in terms of a crisis or a cancer endangering India's society, polity and economy.

Consider the following :

1. There has been a distinct increase—in terms of the number and amounts—in transactions in which the presence of corruption has been substantiated. At the Centre, these have included, but have not been confined to, defence contracts (e.g., Bofors, HDW submarines), civil contracts (e.g., railways), telecommunication contracts, commodity imports (e.g., fertiliser and sugar), privatization (e.g. Bailadilla mine), housing allotments, the financial sector (e.g., the Bank scam) and violations of the Foreign Exchange Regulation and Income Tax Acts (Hawala cases).

2. A number of Ministers and Governors of State have had to resign on account of being legally charged with corrupt transactions. Leading politicians belonging to different political parties have been charged in the Hawala proceedings related to violations of the Foreign Exchange Regulation and Income Tax Acts.

   In more than one instance Prime Ministers have been tainted with suspicion though investigations against them do not seem to have been expeditiously or effectively pursued. In any event, it is not credible that widespread Ministerial corruption would have been possible without the acquiescence, if not the involvement,, of the head of the government.

3. India has acquired the uneviable reputation of being among the most corrupt countries in the world. A careful poll taken among business interests and financial journalists by Transparency International (TI), the reputed anti-corruption non-governmental organisation, placed India 9th from the bottom in its 1996 list of 54 countries. India scored 2.63 on a scale with a maximum of 10 for the totally corrupt-free country.

4. In a number of States, Chief Ministers and Ministers have been implicated in major corrupt transactions relating to liquor regulations, real estate approvals, large government contracts, allocation of scarce materials, transfers of public servants and so on. Similarly, on the basis of proven cases, well substantiated allegations and reliable internal information, it would appear that corruption among ministers in the States is widespread. This again cannot be the case unless it is countenanced by the heads of government in the states.

5. In both the Centre and States, evidence points to an increase of corruption in the higher bureaucracy. A sizeable proportion of higher level civil servants are believed to be either corrupt on their own and/or to be acting as accomplices, conduits or agents for corrupt Ministers.

   A large proportion, while keeping themselves clean, have had to be silent witnesses to corruption among Ministers and their peers in the civil services. Some of them have been induced or intimidated into going along with financially irregular decisions and corrupt administrative practices.

   Yet, others have eased themselves out by taking early retirement. Many have paid the price for maintaining integrity by being exiled to posts which are not commensurate with their seniority or experience. Only very few have taken a principled stand in resigning from the civil service in a protest against corruption.

Correspondingly, the transfer of civil servants in many States has been aimed at positioning pliable officials in posts with a high potential for corruption, moving out honest officials to innocuous post and frequently transferring those who have refused to oblige their political masters in corrupt transactions. The result of all this has been immense damage to morale, motivation and efficiency in the public services.

6. Concerning the lower levels of the bureaucracy, corruption mostly takes the form of speed money for expediting approvals and the demand for bribes for providing (or not withholding) legitimate services (e.g., in utilities such as telephones, electricity boards and civic services).

   Corruption is also rampant in the administration of welfare schemes, the public distribution system, the police, revenue, and irrigation departments and several other sectors in which the people come into daily contact with the administration. The higher bureaucracy seems to be unwilling or unable to tackle corruption at its subordinate levels.

7. Of grave concern is the interlocking or 'vertical integration' of corruption at various levels of the governmental hierarchy-elected politicians, higher bureaucracy and lower bureaucracy.

   The normal assumption is that the 'principals' at each of the higher levels would be committed to ensure that their agents at respective lower levels would act according to standards and norms of probity. In a situation in which the principals and agents collude with each other in corruption, the problem of tackling it becomes much more intractable.

8. In the public domain, corruption is not confined to the executive government. It has spread to legislatures, the judiciary, media and the independent pro-

fessions (such as lawyers, doctors, chartered accountants and contractors). Through mutual interaction, such a horizontal spread of corruption has entrenched it further in government and made its prevention and control much more difficult.

9. Mechanisms to prevent, monitor, and punish corruption are not adequate nor have they proved to be effective to the extent that they exist. At the national level, India still does not have an Ombudsman-type, *Lok Pal* legislation and machinery to deal with corruption among ministers and the higher bureaucracy.

In general, governments at the Centre and in the State have been tardy, at best, and insincere, at worst, in investigating and pursuing corruption. Commissions of Inquiry established for the purpose over the years have not been able to effectively prove or punish corruption. Corruption has been politicised just as politics has been corrupted in the sense that cases of corruption have been used for partisan political purposes rather than with any serious intent to objectively tackle the problem.

As is to be expected, opposition parties in Parliament and State Legislatures have played a role in agitating issues relating to corruption but, by and large, their efforts have not been effective. Judicial processes under normal anti-corruption laws are dilatory although in recent times the Supreme Court, in response to public interest litigation, has intervened to enforce the law.

Investigative journalism has helped to expose corruption but, given its nature, media coverage has been episodic rather than sustained. A number of activist groups have taken up local issues of corruption. However, their contributions have varied widely over different parts of the country and have not assumed the critical mass required to generate a popular movement against corruption.

The Response to Corruption

Despite the fact that corruption is pervasive and has gone largely unchecked and, indeed, perhaps because of it there is now a strong demand by the public for effective punitive and corrective measures to tackle the problem. That corruption is a national concern in the consciousness of the people has been demonstrated by the fact that it was the most important issue in the general elections to Parliament in 1989, 1996 and in several elections to State Legislatures. Essentially, the challenge that concerned citizens face is to translate the widespread public sentiment against corruption into effective public action.

What needs to be taken into account at the outset is that the very scale and spread of corruption has generated helplessness, at best, and apathy, at worst. These, in turn, tend to be rationalised in terms of cynicism or in arguments that tend to acquiesce in corruption.

The first task is to generate the confidence that India is not doomed to live with corruption forever and that in India—as has happened in many other countries—it is possible to mobilise public pressure for reforms aimed at containing and rolling it back. As corruption intensifies and spreads its tentackles, it tends to reproduce and perpetuate itself on an increasing scale.

No time should, therefore, be lost in undertaking all possible efforts to put a brake on the process. At the same time, there is need for the sober recognition that it would not be feasible to eliminate corruption altogether. Tackling corruption is not achieved in one stroke but through a continuous and cumulative endeavour. In addition, it carries its own costs. All that can be aimed at is to progressively move toward a state of affairs in which corruption is the exception rather than the rule.

It is possible and legitimate to approach the problem of tackling corruption from different angles. Generally speaking, four approaches can be distinguished. One consists of fundamental changes in the Constitution which would, like a Presidential system, insulate executive authority from legislatures and include appropriate checks and balances against the abuse of political power.

The second would emphasise thorough deregulation and

privatisation of governmental activities so as to reduce the role of the sate as much as possible along with reforms aimed at enhancing efficiency.

The third would argue for an extensive decentralisation of governance so as to promote accountability and transparency at local levels in order to check corruption. The fourth would rely on an increased development of moral values along among the people at large beginning with youth and focused on politicians and officials in particular.

Each of these approaches is doubtless germane to the problem of tackling corruption, they are necessary but not sufficient. They cannot be relied upon singly for each has its limitations. There can be much debate about the pros and cons of fundamental constitutional changes and, in any event, they would not appear to be readily feasible. Nor can there be the assurance that the replacement of parliamentary democracy with an executive government, notwitstanding the checks and balances that might be introduced, will not prove to be a remedy worse than the disease. Similarly, deregulation and decentralisation, for which there is already a wide consensus, cannot be a panacea.

The state cannot be whisked away, not can it be expected to wither away. Corruption can continue under different forms in a largely privatized economy, likewise, it can itself get decentralized, persisting in less visible ways under local authorities. The upgrading of moral values is of fundamental importance but a moral revolution cannot be expedited on the basis of rhetorical appeals that urge its necessity. It can be promoted and sustained only around a series of concrete incremental measures which demonstrate that reform is possible and can cumulate. This is the surest way to strengthen and channel the moral impetus for a more honest polity.

India infamous for Corruption

The approach presented here is not so much on individual sectors of the economy or on specific departments of the government, but rather on the overall legal, institutional and behavioural aspects of the government that are critical to corruption control. The focus is on the need to redesign and improve the underlying framework of our basic public institutions that serve all sectors, their structures and systems in order to achieve corruption control.

In view of the vehemence of corruption, there is a need for amendments to the laws and constitution of the country, to specific steps for improving the working of the public institutions with which citizens interact.

There is, however, a need for a major restructuring of the way in which the government functions, both at political and bureaucratic levels. Such a need is perfectly valid given the urgent need to improve the efficiency and effectiveness of different public institutions and governmental functions.

Such reforms will also create a favourable setting for tackling corruption. Thus, improved recruitment, career development and reward systems in the civil service will go a long way in institutionalising a more efficient and responsive bureaucracy that will also be less corruption prone.

Implementation of the National Police Commission recommendations (1977-81) will, for instance, improve the morale and accountability of the police who are responsible for enforcing laws including those pertinent to corruption control. Systematic reforms of the laws, regulations and institutions are essential for the orderly progress of the country. There is no doubt that the quality of governance in our society will improve significantly as a result of administrative reforms.

Corruption, however, is a multi-faced and complex phenomenon; interventions on many fronts and the collaborative efforts of may people are required to control it. Numerous proposals are added to for action emanating from other quarters to the recommendations, the task may seem daunting to any government, or for that matter, to any society. From the standpoint of controlling corruption, focus on comprehensiveness may, thus, become counter productive for several reasons.

Firstly, when taken together, these reforms may cause such an overload on government that scarce public resources and attention would be spread thin.

Secondly, all reforms are not equally critical to the control of corruption. An improvement in efficiency or quality by itself need not necessarily reduce corruption.

Thirdly, more often than not, comprehensiveness in the arena of reform can make prioritisation extremely difficult.

A more strategic approach that links together a select set of proposals covering both the institutional and behavioural dimensions of corruption control is, therefore, in order.

Accordingly, an outline of a strategic agenda for action to tackle corruption is presented. The agenda is based largely on the specific recommendations. Such a strategic agenda may give our policy makers and other key players a sense of the critical interventions necessary to combat corruption and a greater appreciation of the inter-relationships between the parts.

The propensity for corruption in any society can be controlled only by systematically reducing the incentives and opportunities to engage in corrupt practices. An agenda for action to control corruption must identify the key interventions to minimise such incentives and opportunities in the Indian society.

Four action areas are presented as the essential building blocks for a national agenda for corruption control :

(a) reform of the political process,

(b) restructuring and reorienting the government machinery,

(c) empowerment of citizens, and

(d) creating sustained public pressure for change.

The political process needs reform at strategic points in the order to create an enabling environment that is conducive to the control of corruption. Effective implementation of new initiatives will occur only through a restructuring and reorientation of key public institutions of the country and their bureaucracy.

Pressure for these changes much also come from citizens who, in turn, need to be enabled to play this role through access to information and other means of empowerment. Finally, public pressure for change can be sustained only through the active intervention of civil society institutions such as the media and a variety of non-governmental organisations at both local and national levels.

Action on the recommendations presented here will call for initiatives and collaborative efforts by numerous players and organisations. In many cases, the recommendations are inter-related and will reinforce each other.

By highlighting selected areas for action, and combining the institutional and behavioural dimensions of the reforms required, we are essentially underscoring their priority and mutual reinforcement, and their potential to trigger off other initiatives and behavioural changes in society that can also contribute to the control of corruption.

Strategic Interventions for reform

Reforms of the political process is the most sensitive area in our agenda and is of fundamental importance. It is not uncommon to find anti-corruption efforts at the micro-level being subverted by corrupt political leaders at higher levels.

The power over resources, information, patronage and decisions that the political leadership in India enjoys is so vast that it is imperative to set right the process by which they come to appropriate this power.

This is not to expect that the qualities of political leaders and representatives could be rigidly specified or to ask for a different form of government. Even within the confines of existing system of government, it should be possible to reform the process by which representatives get elected and rise to power. If this process can be improved at strategic points, it is possible that persons with greater integrity and commitment to public service will be attracted to the political arena.

The objective, then, should be to get political parties to commit themselves to a set of practices, discipline, and values which together can create an environment that is more conducive to the control of corruption.

Thus, the leaders shown up by political parties that are dependent largely on funds from big business or other interest groups will tend to be of a different orientation and value base compared to those whose election is financed by small contributions from the people at large or State funding without strings attached.

The latter set of leaders, when elected, are likely to be less vulnerable to *quid pro quo* arrangements and co-option by powerful organised groups in society. If they are less corruption prone and are not motivated in similar practices can also be expected to decline. The financing of elections to political offices, is thus, a central issue from the standpoint of corruption control.

A similar case exists for improvements in the functioning and management of political parties. If parties are not governed by generally accepted norms of good management and are not transparent and accountable as public organisations ought to be, how can we expect them to lead the country and it's government in terms of efficiency, accountability and transparency?

Maintenance of audited accounts, compliance with income tax guidelines and public disclosure of information are practices that have to be insisted upon in order to make political parties more accountable and less susceptible to the pressures of corruption.

When leaders brought up under this discipline assume power, their values and orientation, and the signals they give their colleagues and subordinates, are likely to be more supportive of corruption control than would be the case otherwise. Hence, the need to take a close look at the way our political parties are managed.

A third aspects of the political process that has a bearing on corruption is the code of conduct governing the behaviour of elected representatives and political appointees and related issues in terms of their compensation and privileges. When monetary compensation is limited, there is an understandable tendency to sell privileges.

Incentives to engage in corruption are stronger when penalties for the abuse of power are weak and poorly implemented. Corrective action here may call for a modification of laws and regulations governing the conduct of elected representatives and other political appointees, and their treatment when charged with misconduct.

An important area for reform pertains to defections or floor crossing by elected representatives which, in many cases, are believed to be the result of corrupt influences. The final authority for determining disqualification under the Anti-Defection Law may need to be vested in the Election Commission rather than in the Speaker of the House or Chairman of the Upper House.

22

CORRUPTION: A SOCIOLOGICAL PHENOMENA

In twentieth Century America, payment to a Candidate for the vote is a penal offence.

In every society and at all stages at growth and development and in all ages there is corruption in one form or the other. This is because the urges to ego corrupt and circumstances providing an incentive to corruption are universally prevalent. Only the extent, form and style of corruption may vary.

Nevertheless, corruption in a developing society and in newly-independent states is so rampant and has pervaded all professional walks of life that its visible effects are too serious to be ignored. The entry of corrupt practices into areas on which the whole health of social life and polity rests, results into all erosion of public morality and ethical standards of individual and group behaviour. It is from this angle that the subject of corruption in India is too grave to be ignored.

As popularly understood, it is giving or accepting some kind of compensation in the form of money, office or position etc., for a service rendered in an illegal form, or by over-stepping one's legal authority. It is a kind of reward promised or taken, or compensation expected for a service which is rendered even in the course of fulfilment of one's normal administrative or other lawful duties.

Defined in this sense, corruption is held distinct from the tips which are genuinely felt and legitimately expressed tokens of appreciation of the services rendered legitimately by a person. The dispenser of a tip is under no pressure to pay tips, nor does he expect some extra favour from the receiver in return for it.

All the same, distinction between a tip and bribe, which is clearly a case of corruption, has only a very thin and delicate wall of separation. A tip given once for a service rendered with expectation that the receiver will oblige the giver at a later occasion or favour him with some extra service does, of course, lead to corruption. This is because the tip serves the purpose of extracting some additional service at a later date or time.

Corruption in administration and in the political spheres impinge maximum on public life and has a clear reflection on the efficiency of the bureaucracy and indeed on the body polity. This is because it is the bureaucrats and the political office-holders, who are in authority to disburse socio-economic goods, rewards and political values. The disbursement of these values has a direct impact on the day-to-day life of the people and even a bearing on their socio-economic status.

For example, purchasing a railway ticket by paying an extra buck to the Ticket Collector; buying a cinema ticket at an inflated rate; getting an application processed at a quicker pace; procuring a contract for the construction of a building project, a license for the establishment of an industrial unit, a loan from the Bank, all on payment of bribe; are clear-cut cases of corruption. Both the giver and the receiver have indulged into an activity which is both illegal and immoral, and degrading as far as the standards of public life are concerned.

Such cases of corruption have been too well-known in our country since independence. As a matter of fact these acts and activities have indicated such an upward turn that people have almost taken it for granted that bribes will have to be paid. So much so that the rates of bribes are fixed accordingly to the monetary benefit that a person is going to derive out of a particular service. The larger and more important a service, bigger the bribe.

As for the corruption at the higher political levels rewards and bribes are not always in the form of cash or kind. Corruption takes more subtle forms as the stakes are too high. It is probable, this phenomenon of corruption which one is witnessing in increasing proportions with the growth and spread of what one might describe as political democracy. One hears of corruption in the distribution of election tickets and in the change of political affiliations of the members of the political parties.

Therefore, while corruption among traders and businessmen motivated out of pecuniary designs may be understandable, even though not justifiable, corruption in the distribution of political offices and in shifts in political ideologies and loyalties may perhaps be least desirable of all.

What is equally deplorable is the corruption among the teachers and academics, lawyers and doctors, in the public recruitment agencies and judicial services and so on. Teachers and academics awarding inflated marks and grades, purchasing positions and awards for their wards, missing classes and cooking research materials; doctors and chemists using inferior and sub-standards medicines; charging high fees and prescribing costly medicines for ordinary ailments; judicial officers depending justice under social to political influence; can all be described as case of corruption.

Indeed, it is these areas of public life which have been infected with the bug of corruption in the recent decades and which has started eating into the very vitals of the public life in our society. We should examine what are the social factors which have, and are, indeed, promoting corruption in India.

First, the process of development must be held responsible for abetting corruption in India. A developing society becomes amenable to corruption in many ways. The neglected parts and sections are motivated to derive the fruits of development through illegal means. Corruption, therefore, becomes a remedial step to correct the imbalances left in the developmental process.

Secondly, in the newly emergent States, especially, if they have adopted a democratic set up of government, competition among different groups to gain power is intensified. Consequently, to succeed in this competitive activity the use of money power finds a new role resulting into the use of malpractices both in the political and economic areas of social life.

By virtue of holding these coveted political positions the new groups strive for not only betterment of social status but also for increasing political influence and power. Use of money power in elections, promises of incentives and disincentives through which votes are collected, and what has now become legendary of Indian polls, booth capturing, are all the manifestations of this type of corruption.

Thirdly, in India there are prevalent several social evils and institutions which have added further fuel to the fire of corruption. For example, the dowry custom in India. The demand for dowry is increasingly affecting both the middle and lower classes where economic constraints are real. For those who make these demands, it is the quickest way to improve standard of living.

For those who go beyond their permissible limits to give dowry it is a question of maintaining a respectable status in the society. Therefore, irrespective of the legislative measures, one does not see the system of dowry-making an exit of our society. On the contrary, one finds, and, particularly, in the lower sections of the middle class, that people will not mind paying even through their noses because giving handsome dowry is after all a symbol of their status in the society.

What, therefore, is required, is a change in social attitudes and values so that for the same only of false prestige people will not perpetuate such an unhealthy institution to maintain which they have to indulge in unethical practices.

Fourthly, it is consumerism and the values attached with it which have also helped in the increase of corruption. Indeed, consumerism can very easily be described as the principal cause of unhealthy increase in the dowry system in India. Love for consumer goods motivates a person to own and even hoard, to an extent, which is least desirable.

It is the love for these goods out of which the practice of profittering grows. As more goods of consumer use and pleasure flow into the market, the urge to own and use them also increases. Persons with meagre means even wants to posses them. If their income earned through lawful means is not enough, they will be encouraged to employ corrupt means to do so.

Sociologists have argued that consumerism is mere a trait of a middle class in society. Consequently, larger the middle class more of consumerism. In India, there is a very large and extensive middle class. The previous few years budget adopted by the Government of India tended to cater to the needs of the middle class more than of any other class in the society.

Smuggling of foreign goods of consumer interest, electronics and many contraband goods can be attributed to this consumerism and to the existence of a very large middle class in the Indian society.

One can say without any hesitation that media in our country has played a very vital role in the increase of consumerism, apart from industrialisation and productive system. Daily newspapers carry consumer columns and consumer coupons; there are special issues of magazines which are consumer special numbers. Surprisingly, even the government—controlled media, both Air and Doordarshan, are leading agencies of propagating goods of consumer interest.

Day-in and day-out, there are advertisements of textiles and dress materials, chocolates, wafers and chips, soft drinks and coffees, shoes and garments which urge people to go in for more and variety of them.

A survey carried in Delhi market a week later revealed that the sale of horse grams of the pavement dwellers sitting near the local bus stops in the Capital had gone up by almost 50 per cent. Such is the powerful impact of Doordarshan in India on the spread of consumerism.

Scarcity of goods and shortages are so common in our society that uncontrolled consumerism plays a negative role. Sometimes shortages are manipulated by the businessmen and traders to make money through black sales. Therefore, in a society like India, it is questionable if uncontrolled consumerism needs to be preached to the extent it is being done at the moment.

Fifthly, in India it is no longer so important to earn and enjoy a good reputation. In the absence of social disapproval, the premium on corruption has gone up. There are some known forms of corruption which are now rated as "honest businesses"

Sometime back, an owner of a new Maruti car will proundly declare that he had paid a premium of Rs. 25,000 on it, since he wanted it immediately. A tax paid on the house or shop of a businessman or trader may upset the family for a short while. Very soon, he gets it settle with the use of money power and his children walk across the street and in the neighbourhood in an uprightly manner.

There are no traces of any strain on him and society seems to go along with him in his explanation of the entire incident. As a matter of fact as the social relations become more and more impersonal the fear of social verdict grows weaker. In the absence of social pressures, therefore, corrupt practices will have the tendencies to grow.

Finally, Indian society is a highly stratified society. The divisions in the society are not only on economic lines but there are several other basis on which the society is cut into groups and categories. There is caste, there is religion, there is a language, region and so on.

In such a situation the levelling process is sought to be achieved through corrupt means, as the legitimate remedies are found wanting. Hence, there are some in built weaknesses in Indian Society which give rise to corruption.

In the end, it may be argued that corruption and the forces which give rise to corruption are not always to be located in the administrative, political and economic institutions and processes. There are several aspects of our society and several shortcomings of our social structure, attitudes and value systems, which provide an impetus to corruption. Political pitfalls, economic failures and administrative loopholes have only worsened the situation.

23

CORRUPTION AND CRIMINALISATION OF POLITICS

This Chapter is divided into two sections. The first section deals with the theoretical aspects of the ethical standards and their decline into corruption. The second part deals with the issue within the context of Indian politics. No one can deny that during elections, the candidates under the banner of their respective political parties, make promises to the people.

But the question is, how ephemeral can the promises be? Can the candidate only make promise for the moment and then, forget about its accountability? Also how far do the false promises contribute the fall of ethical standards in Indian politics?

What is ethics? Ethics holds the key to the man's ascent towards the spiritual pinnacle. But there is nothing religious about ethics. Any contact between ethics and religion is purely coincidental.

Whenever religion and ethics come together, it is because both aim for the spiritual improvement of man. Among the religions, this fact is more evident in Hinduism. But, then, more than being a religion, Hinduism is a philosophy of life.

The rich Indian culture, over the ages has stood on the portals of "*Dharma.*" Literally speaking, *"dharma"* means duty. To an individual, it implies personal obligation, while as a doctrine, it stands for a moral code of conduct. Every historical period inspires its own ethical conduct.

Yet, in the society of electronic nineties, rampant complaints are voiced about the decline in morals. In politics too the complaint against declining morals becomes more vocal.

In administration, declining ethical standards are seen more easily; corruption and various forms of bribes move the wheels of administration faster.

Without ethics, man would be reduced to an automation. With it, man is able to transcend great heights of wisdom. Without it, men will stand on a brink and may collide to bring chaos in society. Without it, then, we cannot hope for a secure future for our posterity.

The whole problem is that in today's fast moving world, the ethical norms are believed to be in clash with self-interest. In the past decade, a great deal of research has been done on moral development—viewed particularly as the aspects of socialisation, that is, learning to conform to the rules in situations that arouse impulses. Various theories and researchers have stressed three aspects of socialisation: the behavioural, the emotional and the judgemental aspects of moral action.

The behavioural criterion refers to conformity motivated from within, or simply resistance to temptation. Such a conception is implicit in the common sense notion of 'moral character' as a set of culturally defined virtues, such as honest. The second criterion is the emotion of guilt i.e. self-punitive self-critical reactions of remorse and anxiety after transgression of cultural standards. And the third aspect implies the capacity to make judgements and to justify maintaining that judgemental standard to oneself and to others.

These three aspects, together involve the *moral development* of people. The individual, then becomes the pivot of all system—political, social and psychological. Given the fact the individual is the central point of all thinking he must, then, be affected by, in twin effect of the environs.

The pact of the individual on political life may be seen in the following statements made by the Presidents of U.S.A. in 1966 and 1988. Both have a common under—current running through them, both touch the soft chord of the human - the individual. One can safely say that, even today when the world is moving speedily towards technological developments, the human factor cannot be overlooked. In fact, in order to click, the human factor has to be stressed.

In his inaugural address when the President of the United States of America, John F. Kennedy said in 1961, "ask not what your country can do for you, ask what you can do for your country", he was appealing to the individual for self-sacrifice.

Appealing to the individual, George Bush in his inaugural address in 1988 said, "America is never wholly herself unless she is engaged in high moral principle, we as a people have a purpose today. It is to make kinder the face of the nation and gentler the face of the world", (emphasis added) This statement aimed to the level to bring the level of the national purpose to that of the individual.

All aspects of society are dependent on and reflect man's nature. But man is himself a complex being. Sir Isiah Berlin delving into the individual's mind pointed out, "Men are not merely objects in nature, governed by discoverable casual laws". Further, he stated, "To understand human behaviour one needs to understand how men interpret themselves, and conceive their relations to others, how they see themselves in the world, what they think their relationship to be to past and future; to nature and above all to one another". Man, thus, is a reasonable being and a balanced blend of idealism and self-interest can alone retain decorum in the political life of both citizens and men in governance.

Is Corruption a part of Human Psyche?

We are all susceptible to corruption in some form at one time or another in life. In fact, it can be safely said that the question of magnitude of corruption is directly proportional to the opportunity or situation one finds oneself in. Since corruption stems from the individual, the only solution of improvement lies with the individual himself, a gigantic task a task almost impossible for the state to undertake.

Needless to say, it must be done at the basic level i.e. family—school, etc. Because in the end what is going to matter is what we imbibed as we grow and what we inculcate in others, perhaps our progeny.

Needless to say, the decadence of morals in the society is reflected in the government apparatus. Clearly, this is so, because men in the government form a part of the society and are risen in the society. It is a different matter that once they form part of the governmental apparatus they seem different (This is so because their environment changes).

But as the men may cover difference towards the political life in the government, they imbibe from all that is happening in society. Thus, if there is evidence of decaying ethical standards in the society, it is bound to be mirrored in the men who run the system.

India became independent in 1947 with the high ideals evinced in the constitution. But a perusal of the last forty years shows a steady decline of ethical standards in both politics and administration.

On the political scene, the selfless dedication of pre-independence patriots is missing. This may be attributed to the fact that the morality of purpose of independence being over, the ethical standards have fallen in the post-independence era.

The decadence in moral standards was abetted by the period of transition in India where the agricultural conventional society was moving towards a mechanised, industrial and a echnologically advanced one. Money and tax morals are not necessarily accompanied by each other. But in case of India where tradition was unfolding into modernity, the cultural standards changed abruptly within a short span of time.

What was a crime earlier became a norm. Within the vortex of speed, some of our norms submerged completely, others got eroded. But now that India has reached a firmer ground, we can stop a while and ponder. The pinnacle of this moral decadence may be seen in its crystallised form in the politics and administration in India since the eighties.

Perhaps we can console ourselves that in modern times the decadence of ethical standards is more or less as international phenomena. In modern times, one major factor which contributes to the fall of ethical standards is: 'alienation'. Alienation of the individual may be viewed as essentially solitariness of the modern man who thinks for himself alone or for his immediate ones first.

The concept of the good of totality comes later. In India, too, this concept of ethical behaviour has percolated to all aspects of social and political life. Elections are an important factor in the political arena.

Election time is a promise-making time. Election manifestors are pledges which the political parties promise to seek if they are voted to power. Since these are addressed to the all sections of people within the society, their aim is to please everyone, consequently, many of the promises made at the election-time are misleading. They are deliberately couched in rosy assurances as they are meant to attract wide range of people.

A large percentage of the Indian population is poor. Some even below the starvation level but each adult has a right to vote as result of adult franchise. Therefore, the election manifestos include clauses which directly appeal to the individual.

The manifestos of major political parties vouch to-

(a) foster reinforcing sound economic programmes by reorganising agrarian and urban economies to ensure higher growth rate with greater social justice,

(b) maintain a close vigil on prices,

(c) liquidating poverty by checking the population growth,

(d) removing social disabilities of the scheduled castes and improving their economic conditions,

(e) protect rights of minorities,

(f) protect peasants, agricultural labour, weavers and artisans,

(g) equal implementation of laws for women,

(h) tapping the youth, students,

(i) improve education system,

(j) transfer technology to under-developed rural sector,

(k) retain the ecological balance with environment,

(l) bringing administration closer to the people,

(m) defend and strengthen foreign policy,

(n) establish a new International Economic Order based on equality.

At the election—time depending on the situational context and the mood of the people, the political parties lay great stress on the issue which is most relevant and most capable of yielding best results.

During Jawaharlal Nehru's time, Congress won largely due to the image of the party which had been instrumental in getting the independence. In the post-Nehru era, when the generation of politicians who had made personal sacrifice (like Nehru, Gandhi, Patel and many other luminaries) were gone, the focus of election strategy changed. The more the country moved away from independence, the more the focus of electioneering underwent a change.

Electioneering became more and more hectic. Political parties began to make fresh promises with an aim to encompass as wide a section of people as possible. This may also be attributed to the fact that the social and economic scene in India was undergoing a transformation. Living in democratic system, the people became conscious of their rights and duties.

Therefore, the Indian electorate has not hesitated to vote out of power a political party, whenever it lost credibility with the people (the outstanding example is the defeat of Congress in the 1977 elections.

The party leadership evolves a strategy and directs field operations either themselves or through their managers. Elections are an expensive process. Large amounts of money are collected to fight the elections. Collection of election funds gives rise to corruption. Although there is a legislation which places ceiling on the funds at election, yet, it is not adhered to in real practice. The ceiling imposed by Election Commission for Lok Sabha elections varies from Rs. 1,20,000 to Rs. 1.50 lakhs for Assembly election, it is Rs. 35,000. Now, in 1998 elections has increased to Rs. 15 Lakhs and Rs. 6 Lakhs respectively.

But this ceiling becomes meaningless as it does not include the expenses incurred by political parties and friends of the candidate. In order to have large election funds, the finances have to be tapped from the moneyed section. Financial assistance comes from them, but, naturally, it is accompanied with a 'string' or a 'catch' which becomes a major source of political corruption. If political corruption is to be ended, then the Government must take steps in this direction. The Election Commission has itself recommended that the Government should provide funds to the genuine candidates either through political parties or otherwise.

This system is followed in seventeen countries including West Germany. Another suggestion sets a limit donations by the companies. The Companies Act, it is suggested, may be amended to limit donations to a political party to certain reasonable limit. Political parties have a crucial role in maintaining objectivity and impartiality of the electoral process. Unfortunately, during the past two decades, the Indian experience has not been positive.

Defection adds a dimension of uncertainty to the polity. Indian politics had been deeply affected by the defection politics till the Anti-Defection Bill was finally passed in 1985. The severity of this political malaise is indicated by the fact that the politics of defenction resulted in the fall of sixty-six state governments and one Central government between January 1952 and 1982, and necessitated the imposition of President's Rule seventy times.

The defections during 1967-1972 are different from earlier ones and stand out in their volume. In 1967 alone, 438 legislators defected (In the previous years since independence, the number of defections was 542). In fact, the defections took place too rapidly and some MLAs defected more than once. Ram Dhari Gaur of Haryana defected twice in a single day. In the defection process in 1967, nearly 200 (20%) defectors were rewarded with ministerial and other offices. No doubt, such treatment to the defectors gave an impetus to the defection politics in India.

The sole aim to many politicians was to gain power at any cost. This resulted in floor-crossing and various combines were formed - the rightist and leftist, the secularist and communalist, the progressive and conservative. The formations openly invited defections from the party in power by offering ministerial posts well in advance. During the operation of defection politics the politicians become expensive marketable commodities. The politician at state level in 1967 took Rs. 20,000 while performing the role of 'Gaya Ram' and Rs. 40,000 for the role of 'Aya Ram'—the return trip, thus, amounted to Rs. 60,000 or more.

Within a span of three years between 1977 and 1979, eleven State governments went out of office as a result of defections. Out of them, four were Congress ministries, two belonged to Janata, two to CFD, one to AIADMK, one of Assam Janata Dal and one to Peoples' Conference. In 1978, President's Rule was imposed in Mizoram and Pondicherry and again in 1979 in Manipur.

The Seventh Lok Sabha Election of January 1980 returned Congress (I) to power with a thumping majority at the Centre. Once again there is a history of accurations after Congress (I) came to power. During February 1980 and February 1982, seven State Governments fell and two State governments shifted their loyalty to Congress(I).

After the eighth Lok Sabha elections, the Anti-Defection Act was passed in 1985. It became the fifty-second Amendment and added a new Tenth Schedule to the Constitution. It is clearly pointed out that the anti-defection law will be applicable only in those cases where a member deliberately disobeys the party whips or if he voluntarily resigns his party membership. But this disqualification is not applicable in case of split of the party or in case of party merger. This clause has given fresh lease to defections in Indian politics. In order to circumvent this clause, defections are carried out enbloc instead of on individual basis.

Populism

Populist slogans are coined in order to have a mass appeal. Populism refers to an attitude that favours the interest of the ordinary people. As an ideology, populism among the several elements includes the tendency to make speeches placating the people, without meaning much. It also involves adoption of some measures that are substantially insignificant but which are "popular" and mean a lot to the people.

Nationalization of Banks, abolition of privy purses of the former rulers of Indian States, '*Garibi Hatao*' programmes (all by Mrs. Indira Gandhi) or "genuine non-alignment" (by the Janata Government) or Mr. Rajiv Gandhi's slogans such as "A government that works faster" or "race into the 21st century" are all examples of populism followed in Indian politics.

It cannot be denied that populism is a form of moral corruption because it promises much more than it can ever achieve. One may even argue that populist slogans are employed by all political parties the world over at the time of elections. But populist slogans when reflect sectarian and communalist colour are suspect and dangerous for the Indian polity.

Sectarian populism assumes special importance in a country which had planned to resolve the difficulty of different religions by giving them an equal status under secularism. India, even before independence, had decided to become 'secular'. Accordingly, with adoption of the Constitution in 1950, India formally became secular.

To say that there is no place for religion in a secular government is incorrect. Secularism, in fact, has no disregard for religion (as Indian scholars are at pains to explain this). It is neutral and treats all religions equally.

The 1984 elections had the pro-Hindu, anti-Sikh backlash which brought Rajiv Gandhi to power. A micro-analysis would indicate that by the year 1984 the nation was drifting into corruption and Mrs. Gandhi's firm decisive leadership was being shaken by the emergence of new power brokers. The opposition, inspite of its disunity, stood to gain in the elections.

But in the post—assassination period the Congress won as a result of the sympathy wave. Many interpretations reveal that the Congress won, ironically, partly due to anti-Congress vote - because Rajiv appeared to represent action, change and cleanliness. By that context the 1984 vote was also a public outcry against national drift and decay.

The vote bank theory holds that while Hindus make electoral judgements on the basis of several factors (such as prices, corruption, ideology, stability etc.). Muslims and other minorities are guided by the communal consideration. While it cannot be denied that the minorities generally give some weightage to their communal identity (which is, perhaps, a safety measure to retain their separate identity) but it is certainly not the only overwhelming factor. In fact, research conducted in this direction by various political scientists has indicated that there is no such thing as Muslim vote and they certainly do not vote en-bloc.

Paul Brass studied the voting patterns of Muslims of Kanpur in 1957 and 1962 and found it to be non-communal. Myron Weiner studied the Muslim vote in 1977 and 1980 and found that although Muslims returned to Congress fold in 1980, but, then, voting pattern was in no greater proportion different than other communities. There is evidence which shows that Muslim vote does not exist. In other words, there is no Muslim vote, only muslims who vote.

This is so because in the end, it is the system rather than individual which is the most vulnerable. The Home Ministry document notes that "No single issue has so adversely affected communal harmony between Hindus and Muslims as the *Ram Janam Bhoomi* Babri Masjid Controversy" and that the growing temptation to communalise politics, has become a strong impediment to the normalisation of communal relations. No political party can be absolved of whetting the communal appetite among a people, who ironically have declared themselves secular only a forty years ago.

The Spread of Communal Violence

According to conservative estimates, about 340 people died in incidents of communal violence between January to September 1989—a little before the November 9th Lok Sabha polls. The dominant trend of communalism indicates that this number is increased.

The Union Home Ministry sources reveal that 611 communal riots took place in 1988. Bhagalpur, Sitamarhi, Darbhanga (Bihar), Badaun (U.P.), Ratlam, Indore, Mhow (M.P.), and Kota (Rajasthan) are some of the places where communal flare-ups took place. Most disturbing fact is that most of these places did not have a history of inter-religious strife.

The B.J.P. has been accused of using the Hindu card - L.K. Advani in an interview: "Whenever I'm accused of being communal or my party described as a Hindu Party, I invariably recall that prior to 1947, the Congress was a Hindu Party. Muslim leaders in the Congress, the Maulana Azad and Rafi

Ahmad Kidwai were showboys of the Congress. I cannot forget that when Gandhiji died in 1948, the tribute paid by Pakistan's Mohammed Ali Jinnah: "A great Hindu leader has passed away". So if today the BJP is described as a Hindu Party, I do not mind it."

But in the ninth Lok Sabha polls, all political parties are guilty of this charge. Each political party has, its somewhat permanent vote base, but at the time of elections each one angles for the floating vote (this refers to undecided voters) as also the minority vote The aim of a large party is to be able to tilt towards itself the minority vote en-bloc. In Indian politician, this task is rendered simple by invoking the caste basis and, thereby, fanning the communal fire.

No matter what the campaign rhetoric and advertisement campaigns unless they match the reality, the Indian voter has, again and again, cast his lot against corruption and does not hesitate to take a chance on a new face. In 1984, the Indian voter turned to new hopes offered by Rajiv Gandhi. By that count, the 1984 vote was also a public outcry against national drift and decay. In 1989, the voter accused him of breach of faith and unhonoured promises and gave a chance to Mr. V.P. Singh and his promise to expose the corruption.

An opinion poll conducted by *Marg* (a leading market research company) for India Today on all-India basis, indicated corruption as the major problem faced by the people, only second to inflation.

Most Important Problem?

	Communalism	*Terrorism*	*Prices*	*Corruption*
All India	11	13	54	22
Men	14	15	46	25
Women	8	10	63	19
				25

Dont's know's excluded. All figures in %age

Loan Waiver Issue

Another issue which may be considered within the parameters of ethical standards is that of loan waiving. The basic promise of such-like promises of waiving loans (National Front in 1989

Lok Sabha Polls) or promising employment under Jawahar Rozgar Yojna (Congress-I) in the same election is suspect, firstly because the aim of such promises is to lure the voter. Secondly, such over-riding promises are made by political parties without working out the modalities. This leads to gross difficulties. The pursuit of loan waiving, for example, has seriously affected the bank's liquidity position and profitability and adversely affected their future loaning programmes.

The loan waiver issue has brought to the fore a serious implications. The National Front at the time of elections promises to waive (if voted to power) loans to farmers and artisans upto a sum of 10,000 rupees. Loans worth Rs. 1,000 crore are understood to have been waived as a result of government order to give directions to the banks by the Reserve Bank of India. The burden will be shared directly by the banks and indirectly by the customers, without the Finance Minister having to adjust the amount in the budget.

Waiving of loans have an impression to the people that they could get their loans waived again. This is clear from the concern expressed by the Reserve Bank of India only advising the defaulters. The Reserve Bank has warned that the entire rural credit system of the country will be choked. Unless the money is recovered from the loan beneficiaries after the debt relief has been implemented. Otherwise, fresh defaulters will give rise to a situation of deficit financing leading to a further rise in inflation. With the rate of inflation on the increase, the country cannot afford any more deficit financing. In other words, deficit financing will, in future, means a loss for the depositors in the commercial and co-operative banks.

Rural credit cannot be tempered with, as the process depends on the smooth flow of funds. Credit taken much before harvest must be repaid after the harvest in order to pave the way for future loan. Otherwise the circular flow of rural credits is broken and this can be retrieved only by a method which leads to further deficit financing and inflation.

A similar situation of deficit financing would have emerged, in all probability, had the Congress returned to power with its promises like Jawahar Rozgar Yojna. Clearly, the political parties must steer clear of making any electoral promises without working out the modalities.

The implementation of Mandal Commission Report promising an increased reservation for Scheduled Tribes and Castes, OBC may also be seen in this light. The students protest was not merely a protest against shrinking job opportunities, but also aimed at questioning the perverse values of politicians who are unable to look beyond the very narrow electoral compulsions.

That such promises will lead to dangerous results is evident from the fact that the student agitations gained momentum all over the country. The agitations marred with sporadic violence threatening the very emotional integration of India. A deep schism within the society is likely to emerge as a result of tension between pro-reservationists and anti-reservationists.

In a democracy like ours, the criminalisation of politics is steadily destroying the fabric of the political system. And all political parties are equally to blame for the Muscle power and availability of money has run hand-in-hand in politics for those who have made money available have always had a last say. Thus, the inevitability of the role of muscle in our politics.

The new power centres which emerge as new entrepreneurs arise, give rise to new codes of conduct which clash, or atleast, run divergent to the other already existing codes. This leads to a dichotomy of response from peoples - and a segregation within a person. The deeply religious one-half allows on mixing with the other-half which abides by new codes of the new power centres. The resultant water-tight compartments provide answer to the querry: "how can he do it when he is so God-fearing?"

Corruption breeds corruption. When it sets in, it grows like weeds in a garden and the whole world is facing the problem of corruption. There is no known antidote for it except exposure and punishment for corruption stems from the individual and correction must be within him alone.

Inspite of the dismal picture of false electoral promises, the money and power axis, communalisation of politics and even a compartmentalisation of individual there is yet some hope in the Indian polity.

A ray of hope is seen in the Indian voter who has, again and again, cast his lot against corruption. Thus, alongwith the deeply passimistic scenario in the Indian electoral politics, one the plausible optimistic ones. On the whole, men abide by moral values. But there are always pockets and events which reflect otherwise. There can, however, be no indicators of the ethical standards of people. We are perhaps passing through the best of times and worst of times.

Criminalisation of Politics

The recent move by the Election Commission to debar candidates convicted for criminal offences (under Section 8 of the Representation of the People Act, 1951) by the trial court from contesting elections, even if their appeals against conviction are pending in a Superior Court, though widely welcomed has raised many questions.

According to the Election Commissions sources, out of the 13,952 candidates who contested the last general elections about 1500 had a criminal record of murder, dacoity, rape extortion etc.

In the Eleventh Lok Sabha, 40 members had criminal background. At legislature level, 700 M.L.As were involved in criminal cases. The Vohra Commission report referred to politician-criminal-business nexus. At a recent conference at Srinagar, the then Prime Minister strongly supported the Central Law preventing criminals from contesting elections. The subsequent Parliament session has also identified criminalisation of politics as the main evil of Indian politics. In this background, the Election Commission passed an order on August 28, 1997, towards this objective.

Referring in the Preamble to the judgement of the Madhya Pradesh High Court in the *Puroshotham Lal Kaushik Vs. V.C. Shukla* case, the Commission concluded that the disqualification for contesting elections came into effect on the date of conviction by the trial court irrespective of whether the convicted person was released on bail or not during the tendency of the appeal. It directed all Returning Officers at the time of scrutiny of nominations to take note of the above legal position and decide accordingly on the validity or otherwise of the candidature of the contestants disqualified under the Section 8 of the R.P.A.

The Returning Officer should request the candidate to furnish the information asked for in an enclosed proforma and file an affidavit stating that, the information furnished by him is true and nothing material has been concealed. The proforma clause (1) asks the candidate to state whether he has been convicted in court and remaining clauses refer to details of convictions, appeal, revision and bail.

Though the Commission's order was generally welcomed, its validity or reasonableness has been questioned on several grounds.

The then Lok Sabha Speaker Mr. P.A. Sangma observed that both the Constitution and the R.P.A. needs amendment. Legislation alone won't plug the hole and political parties should be educated about the need to cleanse the electoral process. He also expressed apprehension over the misuse of the legislation to harass political rivals.

Some feel the order goes against the basic tenets of the law that no person could be presumed guilty unless proved otherwise, particularly when the conviction was challenged in appeal or revision.

Another objection is that it makes no distinction between political and other offences.

Article 102 (1) of the Constitution lists the grounds of disqualification for being chosen and for being a member of either House of Parliament. Clauses (a) to (d) mention specific grounds of qualification, if a person is so disqualified by or under any law made by parliament.

There is a similar provision for disqualification in regard to the State Legislature. Hence, it is clear that there is provisions in Article 102 and 191, read with the R.P.A. for dealing with disqualification of candidates of election.

The Election Commission's order does not interfere with the disqualifications under the several provisions of the R.P.A. It merely states that on a proper interpretation of the provisions according to court decisions, the disqualifications continue, notwithstanding an appeal or revision to a higher court or bail being granted. It therefore, follows that there is no need to amend the constitution or the R.P.A.

The Indian Penal Code doesn't make a distinction between political and other offences. While the R.P.A. makes a distinction between electoral and other offences, it does not make a distinction between political and other offences. On the other hand, if such a situation is made, the order may be attacked on the ground of discrimination between the two sets of offences apart from being inconsistent with the provision of the R.P.A.

The basic tenet of criminal law is that a person is deemed innocent until he is proved guilty. There is no basic tenet that if a person is found guilty by the trial court, he must still be presumed innocent until an appeal or revision petition preferred by him is disposed off.

The Election commission has rightly relied on the decisions referred to in the preamble that a bail granted or sentence suspended does not have the effect on wiping out the conviction.

The following observations are relevant to the current situation:

> It is only the execution which is suspended and nothing more with the result that the sentence awarded is not to be suffered during the pendency or the appeal even though it subsists and the appellant is released on bail.
>
> There is no indication in Section 8(2) of the R.P.A. that the disqualification remains in abeyance during the pendency of the appeal against conviction.
>
> On the other hand, Section 8(3) gives the contrary indication by laying down an exception in the case of sitting members.

Then, the judges proceed to rely on the Supreme Court decision in the *Sarat Chandra case* for the proposition that a reprieve is a temporary suspension of the sentence which does not wipe out; all that it does not have an effect on the execution of the sentence.

When the whole objective is to break the nexus between the politicians and the criminals, it doesn't make sense to say that it must be left to the political parties to decide on breaking that nexus.

Under the circumstances, and in view of the Government's reluctance to bring forward any measure to root out criminalisation, the Election Commission rightly stepped in and passed the order in exercise of it's powers under Article 324. The order is not inconsistent with the R.P.A. On the other hand, it seeks to give effect to the provisions of the R.P.A. as interpreted in the court judgement referred to in the preamble.

The disqualification continues to be the same as the R.P.A. Hence, there is no need to define the disqualification more precisely.

Regarding the apprehension that rival parties may be harassed, it should be stated that even if innocent persons are charged with a crime, that is not sufficient ground to disqualify them. It must result in a conviction. Our courts are independent, impartial and competent and there is no reason to fear they will convict an innocent person.

It is heartening to note that in the recent bye-elections to the Council the candidates willingly signed the proforma and the affidavit suggested by the Election Commission.

24

DISCRETION BREEDS CORRUPTION

Helpless spectators as we are, we disgustingly observe that corruption, rather than being exception, seems to be the rule—a way of life, which no longer even startles us.

There is no denying the fact that corruption being endemic to the political system that we have built over the years, can be eradicated only if major steps of fundamental nature are taken. Yet some small steps here and there by way of a little improvement in the structural pattern of the system can go a long way to provide some meaningful relief to the common man.

The menace of black money or the electoral malpractices are too big issues to be appreciated by him. What is of greater concern to him is: whether the lower level functionaries he generally interacts with day in and day out are responsive to his needs and expectations?

Do they give him a good treatment? Do his papers in the government offices move automatically and swiftly or is he required to give speed-money for the same?

To him, it is the behaviour of such government officials which provides an index to the overall functioning of the administration and the government. It is, therefore, imperative that all efforts need be made to ensure that administration gets more efficient and responsive.

The tinkering with the administrative structure does not by any means rule out the possibility or the desirability of initiating the reforms of the political system at large or grappling with the bigger issues of a more fundamental nature from where corruption actually emanates. Both the processes can go on simultaneously.

It may, however, be underlined that in so far as the bigger issues are concerned, they involve too powerful vested interests to be easily extirpated. This fact thus renders this type of reform somewhat difficult to be initiated. On the contrary, smaller measures of reform at the lower rungs of the administration are comparatively easier to be taken.

It may further be added that the attempt to reform the administrative structures would not be an unusual effort on our part. Instead, it will be a part of the on-going process of administrative reforms which has been under way since the Independence. In fact, it would mean a significant step ahead towards the goal of providing an efficient and responsive administration to the nation.

Why does our administrative structure portray such a dismal picture? The following causes appear to be mainly responsible for it.

First, with establishment of the welfare state after the dawn of the Independence, the administrative structure witnessed an unprecedented degree of expansion both horizontally and vertically. This expansion took place so rapidly that it became virtually difficult to maintain the standards of efficiency and integrity. Though some administrative reforms were effected, these proved too ineffective.

Second, the induction of the half-baked politicians into the crucial decision-making bodies made the bureaucracy all the more head-strong. Little conversant with the intricate processes of policy formulation, these politicians began to heavily lean upon the bureaucracy, with the result that a nexus came to be built between the two. The big business and the rich farmer who support and finance the politician, jumped into the fray and joined this caucus with a view to protecting and advancing one another's interests. This unholy alliance put the bureaucracy in a position strong enough to hoodwink the common man and spread corruption.

Third, the vastness of numbers coupled with the high level of political consciousness made the rank and file of the officials (both high and low) organise themselves into unions and associations. Over the years, these unions have accumulated to themselves so much strength that they are now powerful enough to virtually coerce the state to accept their demands.

An assessment of their power and influence can be had from the highly inverse proportion of their salary and their output of work. Our bureaucracy particularly its lower rungs are very well paid, notwithstanding the poverty ridden conditions of the country.

Yet another cause of the growingly pampered nature of the bureaucracy is that its numerically large strength, combined with its spread over the length and breadth of the country, has made it emerge as a very powerful pressure group. Motivated by mutual interests, it lends its support to the politicians.

Posted in every nook and corner of the country, the officials help the contesting candidates in various ways. The political umbrella that they thus procure to themselves saves them from all types of rough weather.

If at all some one happens to be under a cloud, his union would come forward to his rescue. More often than not, the higher authorities do not run the risk of earning the displeasure of their (recalcitrant) subordinates lest they should land them into difficulties. Obviously, such a situation would promote indiscipline and corruption. On the top of all this comes the absence of the system of rewards and punishment. What a great irony that those who are ardently committed to their work cannot be rewarded because of the iron law of promotion by seniority, while the recalcitrants cannot be punished.

If by chance some one is caught even redhandedly, he is at best put under suspension. For months together, the inquiry is not instituted. At long last when the committee to look into the allegations levelled against the official concerned is set up and goes into action, the long and circuitous procedure hampers its task.

The inquiry generally stretches itself over months and years. If ultimately the official concerned is indicted (though such cases are far fewer in number), he goes into appeals, one after another. By this time the whole case is forgotten and he is finally declared innocent and is reinstated.

This happens more often than not, partly for the reason that the laws are so much full of loopholes that somewhere some point is definitely found out to save the person. Also partly for the reason that everyone right from the trade union down to the courts of law tends to lean towards the appellant out of the general attitude of sympathy toward him and also due to our inability and loathsomeness to take hard decisions. Thus, what we find is that the number of those who are finally 'fired' is much too small than those who are acquitted.

It may not be out of place to mention that suspension from work which was earlier considered to be a disciplinary measure as also a social stigma to punish the recalcitrant officials, has begun to be looked upon as a boon in disguise, for, on the one hand the official is acquitted honourably while, on the other, he is given the salary in lump sum for the period he remains under suspension. Besides, during the period of suspension when officials are not supposed to do any official work, they generally engage themselves in other lucrative tasks.

It is widely observed that most of this type of officials utilise this interugnum to set up and groom up their business. But the time they are reinstated they have developed an additional source of income.

When our rules and procedures are so lax, why should the officials feel sore over their suspension from the service? In fact, in most of the cases, they even welcome such a 'punishment' and in some cases go to the extent of 'procuring' it.

The net result of all these factors and forces is that the bureaucracy which is secure both politically and organisationally is spt to be unresponsive, corrupt and, thus, irresponsible. This is too dangerous a trend.

For, bureaucracy occupies so cardinal a position in a political system that one it becomes corrupt, it not only lowers the prestige of the system but also alienates the common man from it. Reform in the functioning of the bureaucracy must, therefore, occupy a high place in our order of priorities.

Administrative reforms with an eye on the eradication of corruption are further desired in order to ensure that the tax-payers money is put to the right use. Instead of finding its way into the pockets of the men who matter as happens today, it should be carefully utilized for the welfare of the nation.

The urgency to curb corruption may further be stressed on the ground that this menace has been doing irreparable harm to our body politic in the sense that it has weakened the moral fabric of our society.

Those days are gone when corrupt practices were frowned upon by the people. If a few unsocial elements were to grease the palm of someone, they would do so in a highly guarded manner. But today the moral qualms of the people are not hurt in any way.

Corruption is openly practiced and it would not be an exaggeration to remark here that our morality has degenerated to such a low ebb that people have begun to take pride in boastfully telling their friends and relatives that even if their salaries might be meagre, they have many 'other sources' of income to enable them lead an affluent life.

The legitimacy that corruption has, thus, acquired in our society has highly degenerated the standards of our politics and administration. We have come to such a pass that no one can be relied upon particularly in terms of the honest discharge of the official duties.

If taxes are not realised in full, if official papers do not move swiftly in government offices, if law and order in the country has virtually come to a stand-still.

If the various social development measures are not being properly executed, if newly-constructed buildings, bridges, dams and the like collapse immediately on their completion, if our public undertakings are going in perpetual loss.

Above all, our defence secrets are leaked out-corruption alone is responsible for every undesirable act. If this menace is not suitably tackled sooner than later, the country would land itself in chaos of the worst kind.

To come to the practical aspect of action, it may once again be emphasised that though total eradication of corruption is possible only if it is tackled at its root, some improvements in the administrative structure and processes will also go a long way in providing immediate relief to the exasperated people. We confine ourselves to these smaller measures of improvement.

Before we spell out those measures, we may refer to those basic conditions which, if not satisfied, may (in fact, are bound to) frustrate all measures of reform. It is both the government officials and the society at large which must mutually agree to accept and implement those conditions.

The first condition is that the government officials should not be equated with the layman in the street in so far as the rights and privileges, accruing from society, are concerned. There is a basic difference between the two.

While the government official has entered upon a contract with the employer (the government) and has, thus, entitled himself to certain benefits and a status in society and has also bound himself to certain obligations, the other person is free from such encumbrances.

Obviously, the former cannot be equated with the latter, for his contractual obligations will come into conflict with his civic rights and in such a situation contractual obligations should have precedence over other rights.

This point needs to be thoroughly brought home to the government officials. Today, the position is the other way round, with the result that indiscipline is rampant in the government services.

It is not difficult to effect this measure of reform. The Constitution has also provided scope (vide Article 33) to restrict the fuel and unhindered enjoyment of fundamental rights to the members of the Armed Forces and other forces, engaged in the maintenance of law and order, in the larger interests of the efficient discharge of their official duties. This Article may be amended so as to include all the civilian employees.

Another fact that needs to be highlighted is that all laws,

rules and regulations that govern the conduct of the government officials are highly favourable to the latter. Take the case of the Constitution (Article 311, in particular) or the Indian Trade Union Act.

They so unduly safeguard the interests of the worker that if at any time his conduct is found prejudicial to the interests of the organisation/department or the state at large, they would generally uphold him rather than the latter. This undue protection that these laws give to the worker is perhaps one of the main causes of his having become so much pampered

Why are all the laws of the land so much favourably disposed toward the worker? History has word of explanation to offer. All these laws were framed at that point of time when the workers were poorly paid and shabbily treated and, above all. they were unorganised.

It was with a view to giving due protection to them against the repression of the employers that the laws were provided a heavy slant toward them.

But over the years the whole perspective has undergone a radical change. Today the workers are both well looked after and well organised. They no longer need the protective hand of the state, for their unions are so well-organised and (hence) so strong that they can coerce the state to do anything for them.

In this changed perspective, it is not the worker but society and the state who are in need of protection.

Thus, the need of the hour is to bring about a change in our basic approach to this issue. Once this attitudinal change is effected, our task of securing to the contractual obligations (accruing from one's employment in a government office or even in a private undertaking), paramount position over one's personal rights as a citizen, is completed.

How to effect a change in the general approach of the rank and file of our population to this vital issue? Though it is a highly momentous task as every attitudinal change involves, yet some steps here and there can facilitate it.

Before anything else is done we must create a permanent mechanism to efficiently deal with the common problems of the government officials.

The structural aspect of this problem apart, what is of the topmost priority is that we must develop suitable salary norms for every category of the employees and, accordingly, determine their salary structure.

We have, of course, been doing this for a number of years through the instrumentality of the pay commissions. This process can continue. But what is of greater importance is that we must ensure that we have a periodic review and revision of the pay structure.

Our endeavour should always be that the workers unions are not afforded an opportunity to lead an agitation to secure this periodic review. The whole process should go on automatically on the same lines as we have done with regard to the release of the periodic instalments of the dearness allowance.

This is now practised by Central Government as dearness allowance is increased twice a year in January and July. Some of the State Governments also follow this practice on the pattern of Central Government.

One corollary of this suggestion is that they pay structure of the government officials should, by and large, be uniform throughout the country. Though it is difficult to do so in a federal set-up, for the reason that the Central Government cannot compel the autonomous State Governments to follow its dictum, particularly under the present poor financial conditions of the state governments.

Corruption means taking gratification for the exercise of a public function. The range of such gratification varies between a bribe which a petty civil servant takes for rendering a service or exercising power in favour of or against someone to granting a largess or conferring a privilege on a minister or highly - placed civil servant. Gratification may take diverse forms such as money, property, a woman, wine, a job, educational facilities for the son, daughter or near relative or a foreign trip for the official or his near ones.

There are various types of corruption:

(1) When services or actions in favour of or against another person are required urgently, gratification, oth-

erwise known as speed money, is given for expediting it.

(2) When an authority has power which he or she chooses to exercise in favour of or against a person in return for some money or such other consideration, it is a bribe; examples of this would be giving employment or admission to professional education or ministers taking bribes for making appointments to public offices

(3) When an authority has discretion to do or not to do a thing or to choose one person out of those who seek a privilege and exercises such discretion for an illegal consideration, it is an abuse of power; granting of licences, permits, exemptions or monopolies, dealerships, etc., in favour of a person on consideration other than merit falls into this category. All cases of abuse of power and *mala-fide* exercise of power are cases of corruption.

A person who accepts illegal gratification is punishable for offence under the Indian Penal Code as well as the Prevention of Corruption Act, 1988 (which replaces the Prevention of Corruption Act, 1947). These penal sanctions operate only after the corruption actually occurs.

Since there are penal sanctions, the guilt of the person must be established beyond reasonable doubt. This is often difficult and so there are few convictions; moreover, where high officials are involved in corruption, criminal proceedings seldom succeed.

People do not come forward to give evidence. There is the possibility of the matter being hushed up. A good deal of evidence gets lost due to delay. Moreover, corruption can be successfully punished only if its incidence is minimised through preventive measures.

Further, more benign methods of giving justice than those used in the criminal justice system would be preferable for introducing accountability on the part of those who exercise power. We have to turn towards administrative law for this purpose.

There are various types of administrative action available:

Administrative law has been described as the law relating to the control of governmental powers.[1] It deals with the following questions:

(1) What are the powers of the administration?;

(2) What are the limits of such powers?;

(3) What are the ways in which the administration is kept within those limits?;

(4) What procedures does the administration have to follow in the exercise of its powers? and

(5) What remedies are available to the individual against the illegal acts of the administration?

An administrative action may be of three types:

(a) quasi-legislative,

(b) quasi-judicial and

(c) administrative.

Where the administration announces a policy in accordance with which it would exercise its discretion through a government resolution, circular or notification, it performs a legislative function.

Though the exercise of quasi-legislative power, the administration is continuously circumscribing its discretionary power. Where an administrative action is likely to result in deprivation of a right or has an adverse effect on an interest the action is required to be preceded by a fair inquiry in accordance with a procedure governed by the rules of natural justice.

Discretion and Rule of Law

The possibility of the abuse of discretion is, however, much greater when it is part of a non-quasi-legislative or non-quasi-judicial administrative action. Discretion means freedom to act or not to act and freedom to choose one or a few among many who are applicants for a privilege, licence or other such largess.

A *writ of mandamus* is not issued where an authority has

the discretion to compel it to act in one way rather than another. A writ may be issued to complete it to act where such an authority is bound to act.

Where the discretion is not merely regarding how to act but also regarding whether to act but also, no compulsion can be made by a court to the authority to act. Discretion is often conferred by statutes through phrases such as 'if he is satisfied' of, 'is of the opinion of,' or ' has reasonable grounds to believe' which give it the freedom to act as well not to act.

Prof. A.V. Dicey, in his monumental treatise on Constitutional Law, described discretion as being inconsistent with the rule of law.[3] Many years later, Prof. Wade said that if the existence of discretion negated the rule of law, there could not be rule of law in any civilised democratic country.[4]

The emergence of the welfare state increased the functions of the State and with it the powers and particularly the discretionary powers of the administrative authorities.

Today, although we conceded to Prof. Wade's point and admit that discretionary power cannot altogether be eliminated, we also share Prof. Dicey's apprehensions about the inconsistency between administrative discretion and the rule of law.

Therefore, the courts have been most reluctant to concede absolute discretion to an administrative authority. The courts of England as well as India have acted vigilantly while reviewing the exercise of discretion.

Discretion and Judicial Review

The courts in England took a passive attitude towards discretion before the end of the *Second World War. Liversidge Vs. Anderson* was the highest watermark of judicial restraint. Under the defence of the Realm Act, regulation 14B provided that if the Home Secretary had 'reasonable grounds to believe' that a person was of hostile origin (i.e. German), he could be held in preventive detention.

The House of Lords was invited to interpret that provision. There were two possible interpretations: one was that the Home Secretary must have 'reasonable grounds to believe,' thereby, implying that the reasonableness of the grounds was justificable, and another that if the Home Secretary believed that there were reasonable grounds, the court would not examine whether the grounds were reasonable.

The majority of the Lords adopted the latter interpretation, thereby, giving the Home Secretary the last word on whether the grounds were reasonable.

Lord Atkin, in his memorable dissent, admonished his brothern for being more executive-minded than the executive and spoke the following words: 'In this country, amidst the clash of arms, the laws are not silent.

They may be changed, but they speak the same language in war as they speak in peace.' The courts in England, however, have not adopted such a positivistic interpretation of regulation 14B in subsequent cases. Judicial restraint shown during or before the Second World War was slowly abandoned by the English courts during the post Second World War years; lately, they have become much more jealous of the Executive's discretionary powers.

Possibly, the honeymoon with the welfare State ended, and the courts became more critical of discretionary powers and their exercise.[5] Absolute discretion has been held to a constitutional monstrosity, and the courts have insisted that the exercise of such discretionary power must be subjected to the strictest judicial scrutiny.

In India, the written Constitution with a declaration of Fundamental rights gives the courts much greater power of judicial review than what the courts in England possess. A court in England cannot strike down a law as being unconstitutional due to the doctrine of parliamentary sovereignty.

The Supreme Court of India and the High Courts can declare any law or administrative action void if it is inconsistent with, takes away or abridges any of the fundamental rights guaranteed by Part-III of the Constitution. The courts have used this power to control not only the exercise of discretionary power but also the grant of discretionary power.[6]

The Supreme Court of India has held that if a law vests unguided or absolute discretion in the Executive, such a law would be held to be violative of the right to equality guaranteed by Article 14 and an unreasonable restriction on the rights guaranteed by Article 19 of the Constitution.

The fact that the executive is required to exercise such discretion in a quasi-judicial manner may be one of the mitigating factors which may save the grant of absolute discretion from being held unconstitutional.

Although the Court has laid down a sound policy with regard to the grant of discretionary power to the Executive, the courts have generally leaned heavily in favour of the legislature, and upheld the grant of discretion when there was a broad statement of policy. The courts usually avoid striking down legislation and prefer to entertain a complaint regarding the improper exercise of discretion.

The courts have insisted that the discretion must be exercised strictly in accordance with the parameters laid down in the Act concerned. An administrative action may be struck down if the power is not exercised for the purpose for which it has been given or if it is exercised *mala-fide*.

When the exercise of discretion is contingent upon the satisfaction or opinion of the administrative authority, the courts want to find out whether such satisfaction is based on relevant considerations (Barium Chemicals Ltd. vs. Company Law Board).

All the cases regarding the grant of petrol pumps to the relatives of the ministers, the transfer of a customs official who insisted a minister pay customs duty for the contraband articles imported from abroad or the waiving of arrears on rent payable by retired ministers or government officials, which recently came up before the courts, were cases of alleged abuse of discretionary power.

One important bottleneck to penetrating judicial review is the inaccessibility of the materials on the basis of which the administrative decisions were made. For a long time, the government frustrated such judicial probes by pleading its privilege not to disclose certain documents is given to the Government by Sections 122 and 123 of the Indian Evidence Act.

The Supreme Court has now held that any claim of privilege to withhold disclosure of documents is reviewable by courts to make sure that it is not unnecessary (*S.P. Gupta vs. Government of India*). Another difficulty is that rarely are such decisions made through reasoned orders.

In a recent decision (*Mohd. Zafer vs. Government of India*), Justice P.B. Sawant castigated the government for merely writing the reasons in its file but not communicating them to the person concerned. This was a case under the Unlawful Activities (Prevention) Act where an association had been declared unlawful.

The law required the government to state the reasons. Justice Sawant wondered what would be the use of the government merely stating the reasons in it's file but not communicating them to the organisation concerned. The government order was, therefore, held unconstitutional. Also, the reasons recorded in the file were not always intelligible.

The grant of discretion is so omnibus, and the methods of abuse of discretion are so subtle and sophisticated, that judicial review is bound to play a marginal role in tracking down the abuse of discretion.

There are two reasons for this: (i) by its very nature, judicial review exercised by the High Courts under Articles 226 and 227 of the Constitution and the Supreme Court under Articles 32 and 136 of the Constitution tends to be sporadic and peripheral; (ii) the information required for proving the allegations of corruption or abuse of power is not easily available because it is locked up in government files.

Nature of Judicial Review

Judicial review tends to be sporadic and peripheral because it does not envisage determination of questions on merit by the courts.[7] It is supposed to merely stop the administrative authority from acting beyond their powers and in violation of certain minimal procedural norms.

The basic rule of judicial review is that the courts should not substitute their decision or view for that of the administrative authority whom the legislature has thought to be fit and proper to decide that matter. In administrative law, there is a celebrated quote which says that administrative authorities can decide rightly as well as wrongly as long as they are acting within their powers.

The courts of England and India have shown a tendency to convert any error of law into an error apparent on the face of the record (*Anisminic Ltd. vs. Foreign Compensation Commission*).

Thus, they have increased the scope of judicial review and have subjected administrative actions to critical scrutiny. Judicial activism of this type is a feature of almost all countries of the Anglo-Saxon System.

We have a few cases in which administrative actions were held invalid because of *mala-fide* exercise of power or abuse of discretion. Further, barring the solitary instance of A.R. Antulay, no minister was ever prosecuted for corruption.[8]

It was only because of the public interest litigation undertaken by some public-spirited citizens that cases of corruption against ministers and high officials have come up before the courts.

Readers will recall how persistent enquiries had to be made by courts in matters involving allotment of petrol pump, LPG and kerosene agencies, the transfer of a customs official, Ms. Shakuntala, who had demanded customs duty from a minister for articles imported from abroad, or out-of-turn allotments of government houses by ministers.

This research could not have been achieved through the effort of an ordinary citizen. Moreover, given the costs of judicial processes and technicalities of the adversary procedures, the chances of abuse of discretion being successfully prosecuted are rare. Power can be abused without much likelihood of being legally caught.

Abuses of Discretion

There are potential sources of corruption by politicians and civil servants. One of the most significant and fertile areas of corruption is the urban property. Corruption takes place when agricultural land is converted into non-agricultural land.

When the stakes are so high and the discretion so absolute, such discretion is susceptible to abuse. With real property in urban places being so expensive, it is no wonder this power has become a source of corruption.

Although power is vested in the collector, he is often made to use it according to the wishes of the higher-ups.

In fact, in districts where land prices are very high, only those persons are chosen to be Collectors who would agree to quietly use their power according to the wishes of higher-ups. Such corruption would be difficult to prove in a court of law, much less in a review court.

Government Contracts and Corruption

The government contracts has the greatest prospensity for corruption. The modern welfare State is required to enter into contract for the supply of goods as well as services. Sometimes, these contracts are with multinational corporations. The Supreme Court has laid down the law regarding judicial review of such contract-making to ensure that

(a) the terms and conditions of such contracts are not detrimental to public interest; and

(b) contracts are granted after giving equal opportunities to all potential competitors to bid. The principles of government contract were laid down by the Supreme Court in *R.D. Shetty vs. International Airport Authority.*

Since then, in a number of cases, the Court has insisted upon transparency in government contracts. Such contracts often contain secret clauses and commissions are paid by traders to clinch a deal. Here again, the limitations of judicial review become quite obvious.

A review court does not go into the merits of the terms and conditions of a contract but merely satisfies itself as to whether tenders and quotations were invited from all eligible competitors and whether they were accepted or rejected by giving reasons. Even if such requisites are satisfied, there can be an invisible exchange of favours.

Discretion made Accountable

The administrative law developed by the courts highlights

how discretion should not be exercised. If an authority acts *mala-fide*, decides without applying his mind, takes irrelevant considerations or does not take relevant considerations while deciding a matter, the decision is held to be vitiated and is, therefore, void.

But not enough has been said about how discretion should be exercised. In this section, hence, it is proposed to examine what reforms need be made in order to make the exercise of discretion more predictable and objective.

Administrative Instructions

One way to minimise the abuse of discretion is to minimise the unpredicatability of the exercise of this power. This could be done by laying down, through administrative instructions, the policy in accordance with which such discretion is to be exercised.

A book containing a statement of policy is often issued in respect to discretion under the Import and Export Control Act. Administrative instructions have the advantage of greater flexibility than any legislative instrument.

The Government may change its policy and, therefore, replace one set of instructions with another. Though such instructions do not have the force of law in the sense that they cannot be invoked for obtaining a *writ of mandamus* for their enforcement,[9] they doubtless provide parameters for judging whether the discretion has been properly exercised.

Sometimes, administrative instructions contain guidelines as to how Government largess is to be distributed. An administrative instruction provided that a person whose spouse, father, mother, brother, sister, son, daughter, son-in-law or daughter-in-law already possessed a dealership, would not be eligible to apply for one, was held to be valid by the Supreme Court in *Mahinder Kumar Gupta vs. Government of India.*

It had been contended that the above restriction on eligibility to apply violated the fundamental right of a citizen to carry on any trade or business guaranteed by Article 19(1)(g).

Such a restriction may be necessary for preventing concentration of such largess in a few hands but it is sufficient to prevent the allocation of scarce resources on considerations other than merit?

In fact, it could legitimately be asked why a person could be disqualified because some other relation has a dealership. If getting a largess because of a family relationship is bad, is not denial of an opportunity to compete because of family connections also bad?

The crux of the whole issue of corruption is that such largess should be distributed equitably as well as impartially. The administrative instructions could lay down who would be preferred and why, and the decision-making should rest with an independent and impartial body.

Being a relation of a minister would not be objected to if the decision is taken not by the minister but by an independent body on considerations of the candidate's suitability for the largess.

The criteria of such suitability ought to be clearly laid down through administrative instructions. All decisions regarding the distribution of largess should be in writing with reasons, and be accessible to anyone who desires to verify its proper allocation.

Principles of Natural Justice

Administrative actions which entail adverse actions against others resulting in a loss of privilege, right or adversely affect some interest are required to be exercised after complying with the principles of natural justice.

This means that the person against whom such an action is likely to be taken must be informed of the grounds on which the action is proposed to be taken; also, he must be given an opportunity to say why it should not be taken against him. As much as possible, the authority taking a decision must give reasons.

The rules of natural justice tend to make administrative decisions transparent and objective. These rules are, however, not relevant where the decision does not result in the infringement of a right or does not have adverse effect on an interest.

For example, it was held that before giving sanction [illegible] prosecution of a public servant for an offence under the Prevention of Corruption Act, 1988, the concerned public servant need not be given an opportunity of being heard (*Superintendent of Police (CBI) vs. Deepak Chowdhury*).

The requirement of sanction has been provided with a view to protecting the honest civil servant from vexatious proceedings which ultimately subserves the cause of good administration.

The requirement of sanction to prosecute is a matter of public policy and not the right of a public servant. If the sanction to prosecute is refused, such refusal could be challenged on the ground that the power was exercised *mala-fide*. In another case (*India vs. W.N. Chadha*), it was held that the accused could not claim a right of hearing before a court issued a letter rogatory to a foreign court (latter rogatory means a request by an Indian court to a court abroad to take the testimony of a person residing within its jurisdiction and transmit the same to it).

An accused does not have a right to say what evidence should be collected against him during investigation of crime. He, of course, would get an opportunity to rebut any evidence produced against him by the prosecution.

Reasoned Decisions

Although the rules of natural justice, which include the two principles, (i) that no one who has interest in the disposal of a matter should hear that matter; and (ii) no one should be condemned unheard, are applicable only when the action is quasi-judicial.

It is desirable that the first of the two rules become applicable even in respect of the discharge of the discretionary functions. In fact, in administrative law, greater flexibility in the application of such principles is being injected through decisional law.

Although the selection of persons for jobs or higher posts is not a quasi-judicial function, the Supreme Court held that a person who was himself a candidate for such promotion could not sit on the selection committee for recommending persons for such promotion (*A.K. Kraipak vs. India*).

A person is disqualified to be an examiner in the university examinations if any of his near-relations are appearing for such examination. This is because a mere likelihood of bias would disqualify a person from being a judge of someone's suitability for an entitlement. This principle, in our submission, should now apply to all decisions involving the exercise of discretionary powers. Further, all such decisions must be reasoned decisions. Reasoned decisions are necessary for satisfying the respondent's right to information and making the administration transparent.

Right to Information

Although the Supreme Court has held that the right to information is included within the right to freedom of speech and expression, yet it is emphasised that the right to information emanates from a number of constitutional provisions other than the right to freedom of speech and expression.[10]

For example, Article 22(1) of the Constitution says that no person who is arrested shall be detained in custody without being informed, as soon as may be, of the ground for such arrest.

Right to information is to be found in a number of constitutional provisions such as Article 311(2) which says that no government servant shall be dismissed or removed or reduced in rank without being informed of the charges against him and having been given an opportunity to contradict those charges. Even the principles of natural justice, by implication, recognise the right to information.

But the citizen's right to information about how decisions are taken by ministers, how largess is allocated, on what basis are contracts made for the supply of commodities or services, how regulatory agencies such as the Pollution Control Boards or the Securities Exchange Board of India (SEBI) Act need to be specifically guaranteed and enforced. Such a right will make the administration transparent.

The right to information about these matters emanates directly from the citizen's right to a good and honest government which is implicit in his right to vote. A comprehensive legislation providing for such a right, specifying limitations thereupon, is urgently required. The right to information is subject to the right to privacy, and the scope of the right to privacy also needs to be delineated.

The Supreme Court has held that the right to life and personal liberty guaranteed by Article 21 of the Constitution includes the right to privacy as an aspect of personal liberty (*Kharak Singh vs. U.P.*). The Supreme Court has recently drawn limits of the right to privacy that could be claimed by public functionaries. We shall consider these cases briefly.

In *R. Rajagopal vs. Tamil Nadu*, the petitioner was the editor, printer and publisher of a Tamil weekly. He had agreed to serialize an autobiography of one Shankar who had been convicted of murder and sentenced to death.

The autobiography was to reveal the close association of some police officers in the crimes committed by him. The police authorities issued a warning to the petitioner against publishing this book because

(1) he had no authority to do so since Shanker could not give him the power of attorney since such attorney could be given only through the prison authorities and that had not been done;

(2) his action of publishing the said autobiography would amount to attempt to blackmail and would be liable to action.

The petitioner, therefore, urged the Court to restrain the police from interfering with publication of the book which was his fundamental right to publish. In their counter affidavit, the respondents said that the publications of the above book would compromise the right to privacy of various police officers who were likely to be referred to by the author in his book.

The relevant question for the Court's determination was whether the police officers could invoke their right to privacy for stopping the magazine from serialising the autobiography.

The Court was, therefore, required to go into the scope of the right to privacy available to persons performing public functions in respect of matters which fell within the domain of their public duties.

Justice B.P. Jeevan Reddy, in his judgement, traced the decisional laws in the United States and India on the right to privacy as being part of the right to personal liberty. The learned Judge held that the petitioner had a right to publish, what he alleged to be the life story/autobiography of Shankar insofar as it appeared from public records even without his consent or authorisation.

If he went beyond such records, he might be violating the right to privacy of the person concerned i.e., Shanker. If such a person voluntarily gave information about himself, he would have forfeited his right to privacy to that extent.

However, others who were affected by the disclosures contained in such an autobiography might sue the author as well as the publisher for defamation or infringement of privacy. Such persons, whether government officials or the Government on their behalf, could not impose any prior restraint against the publication of such an autobiography. They could, however, sue them for defamation. Such a remedy, however, could be availed of by the public/officials figures only after publication and would be governed by ordinary law.

The Judge, however, further circumscribed the scope of the remedy in respect to public officials or the public figures as follows:

> "In the case of public officials, it is obvious, right to privacy, or for that matter, the remedy for action for damages, is simply not available with respect to their acts and conduct relevant to the discharge of their officials duties. This is so even where the publication is based upon facts and statements which are not true, unless the officials establishes that the publications was made (by the defendant) with reckless disregard for truth. In such a case, it would be enough for the defendant (member of the press or media) to prove that he acted after a reasonable verification of the facts; it is not necessary for him to prove that what he has written is true."

This changes the law of privacy insofar as public figures or officials are concerned. The press or the media would not have to establish truth in their defence if they have written about the public acts of the public figures.

It will be enough if they prove that they took reasonable care to verify that what was written was authentic. The Court made it clear that it had not gone into the impact of Article 19(1)(a) on the law of defamation contained in Sections 499 and 500 of the IPC. That might have to await a proper case.

The above observations, however, mean a significant empowerment of the media against the public officials/figures in respect of their public acts. The Court, after persuing the decisions of the United States Supreme Court in which it had been held that the constitutional guarantee contained in the first Amendment prohibited a public official from recovering damages for a defamatory falsehood relating to his official conduct unless he proved that the statement was made with actual malice, observed that the citizen had a legitimate and substantial interest in the conduct of such public officials and that the freedom of the Press extended to engaging in an uninhibited debate about the involvement of public figures in public issues and events.

Another significant case on freedom of speech and expression was *Gadakh Yashwantrao Kanakrao vs. Balasaheb Vikhe Patil.* The election of Gadakh had been held invalid on the ground that he had committed corrupt practice as defined in Section 123(@) of the Representation of the People Act, 1951.

Sharad Pawar, the then Chief Minister of Maharashtra, was also named for being guilty of such a corrupt practice and served with notice as per the requirement of the RPA.

Section 123(4) declares that publication by a candidate or his agent, or by any other person with the consent of the candidate or his agent, of any statement which is false, and which he either believes to be false or does not believe to be true, in relation to the personal character or conduct of any candidate, or in relation to the candidature or withdrawal of any candidate, being a statement reasonably calculated to prejudice the prospects of that candidate's election, as a corrupt practice.

Both Gadakh as well as Pawar had accused Vikhe Patil of

giving money to the voters and Pawar went to the extent of saying that even if the rival candidate offered *moneu*, the voters should accept it but vote for Gadakh. Ashok Desai, who argued on behalf of one of the appellants, said that, in view of the fall in the ethical standards of political people in general, such allegations were not likely to prejudice the electoral prospects of a candidate. Ram Jethmalani went further and said that such allegations were desirable because they educated the electorate about the malpractices which were not uncommon in elections.

Justice Verma, speaking on behalf of N.P. Singh, N. Venkatachala JJ and himself, observed that "the growth of this unhealthy trend (of malpractices mentioned above) is a cause for serious concern" for the proper functioning of democracy.

His Lordship, however, described the lament of Gadakh and Pawar about the financial might of Vikhe Patil as being 'farcical and comical in view of their own considerable resources'. The Judge also deplored the speeches but held that they did not constitute corrupt practice.

The Judge said:

> "It is clear that every statement of fact in relation to the personal character of any candidate does not amount to a corrupt practice under Section 123(4) unless all the requirements of the provision are satisfied, notwithstanding the fact that such a statement may be defamatory in character. The additional requirements to constitute a corrupt practice are obviously to maintain the delicate balance between the freedom of speech of an individual and the public interest of giving full information to the electorate of the candidates".

It is submitted that the balance is to be maintained not between freedom of speech and the right of information of the electorate, because both are aspects of the same freedom and not poised against each other. The balance is to be maintained between freedom of speech and decency in elections. Section 123(4) imposes a reasonable restriction in the interest of decency on freedom of speech and expression guaranteed by Article 19(1)(a) if all the requisites mentioned therein are satisfied.

The primary requirement of Section 123(4) is that the statement should be of a fact which is false and which the maker either believes to be false or does not believe to be true; that it should relate to the personal character or conduct, etc. of any candidate and that it should be reasonably calculated to prejudice the prospects of that candidate's election.

Unless all these requirements were satisfied, the statement did not become a corrupt practice under Section 123(4) of the RPA. Unlike in the law of defamation, the falsity of the statement is not presumed but is required to be proved by the candidate against whom it is made.

Both the cases discussed above expose public persons to greater public criticism and scrutiny and deny them certain presumptions of law which are available to an ordinary person. The public persons cannot now invoke the right to privacy against acts which they do as public functionaries and cannot allege a corrupt practice on the part of their rival in an election if he uses false stories against them, unless they show that they were false, were believed to be false by the maker and they were likely to prejudice their chances in the election.

We hope the Court will in the near future explain the scope of the law of defamation in relation to political or public persons so as to make it consistent with the freedom of the Press which includes the people's right to know.

Other Administrative Agencies

All decisions regarding economic benefits or social benefits should, as far as possible, be taken by autonomous administrative agencies which will be directly accountable to Parliament. While their policies will be subject to the government's approval, the Government shall not interfere in the day-to-day administration.

The Chairman and members of such regulatory bodies shall be experts in the respective subjects and they shall be appointed by the government subject to approval of the Upper House of Parliament. We are not in favour of having such appointments made on the recommendations of a selection committee consisting of the Prime Minister's nominee, a nominee of the Leader of the Opposition, the Speaker and the

Chief Justice of India, which is usually considered as a panance against improper appointments.

Some statutes like the Protection of human Rights Act, 1993, contain such a provision for the appointment of the Chairperson and members of the commission. It is believed that such a provision could become a mere ritual and might not prevent undesirable appointments.

Therefore, the only way to reinforce poor group control is to make such appointments more transparent and subject to legislative control. Such legislative control should not only be restricted to the appointments of the personnel but should also extend to the work and recommendations of the concerned administrative agency.

For example, the recommendations of the MRTP Commission regarding the monopolitic character of a business organisation are at present submitted to the Central Government, and the Government is not bound to abide by it. The reports of such a Commission should be laid on the Table of each of the Houses of Parliament and the Government must give an adequate and convincing explanation as to why it disagrees with the Commission's recommendations.

All important regulatory authorities such as SEBI, Reserve Bank of India and Environmental Control Authority should have autonomy; and their reports annually submitted must be published and made available for modest price.

One would wish to make it clear that all such administrative agencies should have autonomy, not independence, from the Government. They will have to be accountable to the Government which, in turn, must be accountable to Parliament or legislature. We say to because often the words 'independent' and 'autonomous' are used interchangeably but the two concepts are distinct.

The need for an independent and autonomous regulatory authority to regulate the use of airwaves was stressed by the Supreme Court in Secretary, Ministry of Information and Broadcasting vs. Cricket Association of Bengal.

The Court observed that the broadcasting medium is subject to the freedom of speech and expression guaranteed to the citizen of India. Hence, monopoly of the medium whether by Government or an individual body or organisation is unacceptable.

The citizen must have the benefit of plurality of opinions on all public issues. Unlike trade or business which can be monopolised by the State (Article 19(6) (ii) broadcasting or telecasting which is subject to freedom of speech and expression cannot be monopolised by the State.

However, the electronic media needs to be regulated so that the airwaves which are a public property are used for the maximum public good. The electronic media should be under the control of a public as distinguished from a governmental authority. The Court observed:

> "The broadcasting media should be under the control of the public as distinct from Government. This is the command implicit in Article 19(1)(a). It should be operated by a public statutory corporation or corporations, as the case may be, whose constitution and composition must be such as to ensure its/their impartiality in political, economic and social matters and on all other public issues."

What it true of the broadcasting or electronic medium regulatory authorities could also apply to the other regulatory authorities which have to apply standards of efficiency in public interest to other trades like insurance and banking, which are also now open to private enterprise.

Such bodies have to be autonomous but can they be independent of the Government? They cannot be independent in the sense that the judiciary is independent. The judiciary has to do justice in accordance with the law and the Constitution.

It is independent in the discharge of that function. However, the judges are liable to be removed by Parliament (Article 124(4), Article 217(1) Proviso (b)) and appointments of the judges are made by the President. (Article 124(2), Article 217(1)).

No authority which is performing a legislative or administrative function can be totally independent of the Government and Parliament. Such independence would be contrary to the system of Parliamentary Democracy.

We do not know what the Court means when it says that the media regulatory authority should be subject to public control but not governmental control. Public control, after all, is exercised through the Government which is elected by the people. It is respectfully submitted that in our enthusiasm to weed out corruption, we should not think of setting up bodies or authorities which would be accountable to no one.

Punishing Corrupt Officials

Civil servants and political persons accused of corruption must be fairly tried before an independent judicial authority. The standard of proof required for the conviction of a persons in a criminal case is far higher than that required for holding him guilty in a disciplinary enquiry.

In a criminal case, the accused officer must be held guilty 'beyond reasonable doubt'. In departmental actions, the probability of his being guilty may suffice. Criminal law punishes a person whereas the administrative law merely relieves the administrative powers of an officer whose integrity is suspect.

The civil servants are protected under the Constitution from arbitrary actions resulting in their dismissal, removal or reduction in rank by a provision which assures that a government servant would not be so punished unless he is informed of the charges against him and given a reasonable opportunity of being heard in respect of those charges (Article 311(2)).

Although in exceptional cases, an enquiry before dismissal can be dispensed with (Second Proviso to Article 311 (2)) an elaborate procedure for such enquiry has been prescribed. In spite of this, arbitrary actions might take place. While there should be adequate protection against arbitrary action, there should be enough deterrence against those who indulge in corruption.

At present, a civil servant can approach an administrative tribunal set up under the Administrative Tribunals Act, 1985 against a decision of the departmental authorities. The Administrative Tribunal was set up as an alternative to the High Court and it's jurisdiction restricted to the writ jurisdiction of the High Court (*S.P. Sampath Kumar vs. India*). An appeal against the decision of this Tribunal lies only with Supreme Court.

This works to the great disadvantage of the civil servant because going to the Supreme Court is extremely expensive for him. Since the Administrative Tribunal does not decide matters on merit but confines itself to the threshold questions relevant to judicial review,[11] he is helpless against the arbitrary actions of his department. The appellate jurisdiction of the Supreme Court is also not broad enough to include an examination of the allegedly wrong administrative actions on merits.

It is necessary to develop an internal appellate procedure, may be in the form of a service tribunal, which will consider his case on its merits. Such a tribunal may consist of an experienced civil servant with a good background in law.

The procedures to be followed by such a service tribunal will not be adversary as are followed by courts but may be inquisitorial like the administrative courts in France.

Ombudsman and the Administration

The *ombudsman* is a Scandinavian institution through which administrative actions are overseen by an independent authority with a view to ridding them of mal-administration and abuse of discretion. Such an authority had been recommended by the Administrative Reforms Commission in 1966 and a Bill was accordingly passed by the Fourth Lok Sabha.

The Bill lapsed on the dissolution of the Lok Sabha in 1970. Since then it has reappeared several times but in a variety of forms. The original concept of *ombudsman* seems to have been replaced by a permanent Inquiry Commission against high placed public persons.[12]

The *ombudsman* essentially advises the administration to avoid taking wrong decisions and only when the administration is not amenable to its recommendations does it report to Parliament.

This is how the institution functions in England under the name Parliamentary Commissioner. In India, if we were to replicate the English model, the *Lok Pal* would make recommendations to Parliament.

The cases involving allegations of *mala-fide* exercise of powers, such as those involving preference of a party for a government contract on ulterior considerations or with unfair terms, or the transfer of an official of CBI with a view to frustrating investigation of a crime involving high dignitaries, or preference to the kith and kin of ministers in the allotment of largess are cases which require in depth probes which might not be possible through the adversary judicial processes.

What the Supreme Court of India is doing at present is really the function of an *ombudsman*. The setting up of the office of the *Lok Pal* may relieve the Supreme Court of dealing with cases of that type. The office of the *Lok Pal* will, however, become meaningful only if Parliamentary control over the Executive becomes more active and vigilant.

A person held guilty by the *Lok Pal* may not be sent to jail that can happen only when a competent criminal court convicts him of an offence but such a person should lose his political legitimacy.

India may have to transplant the continental system of administrative justice to its soil without disrupting the common law system of judicial process. A combination of tribunals following inquisitorial processes and *ombudsman* may be the right solution for preventing and minimising corruption.

Conclusion

1. Discretion given in broad terms must be narrowed by administrative instructions stating the policy in accordance with which such discretion is to be exercised.

2. Decisions involving exercise of discretion must become transparent and accompanied with reasons.

3. Authorities taking decisions regarding the allotment of largess should be independent and should not be disqualified on the ground of bias as understood in administrative law.

4. An Act specifying various aspects of the right to information should be enacted. The limits of the right to privacy must be clearly stated. This will have to be done consistently with the law laid down by the Supreme Court in respect of the right to privacy that could be claimed by persons holding public office.

5. An Administrative Appellate Tribunal should be set up for hearing appeals against the decisions of the administrative authorities, including ministers in respect of the grant of exemptions, privileges or largess.

   These tribunals should follow inquisitorial procedures. No appeal shall lie from the decision of the tribunal to any court. The decision of the tribunal shall, however, be subject to judicial review under Article 226 and 227 of the Constitution.

6. Service tribunals manned by senior civil servants should be set up to hear appeals against the departmental actions against civil servants resulting in transfer, demotion, reduction in rank, removal and dismissal on merit.

   These tribunals should follow inquisitorial procedures. An appeal shall lie from the decision of the tribunal to the administrative tribunal set up under the Administrative Tribunals act, 1985.

7. The present Administrative Tribunals Act should be amended to confer administrative tribunals appellate jurisdiction over the decisions of the service tribunals in the above matters. These tribunals should in addition continue to possess the powers of a High Court under Article 226 of the Constitution.

8. *Ombudsmen* should be set up at various levels and the office of the *Lok Pal* may be set up at the apex of such a network of *ombudsmen*. The *Lok Pal* and other ombudsmen should deal with cases of mal-administration, abuse of discretion, delays or callourness which are not within the purview of the courts.

The *Lok Pal* should not merely be a recommendatory authority as in other countries but ought to be given specific jurisdiction in matters which do not fall within the purview of the courts.

Corruption in the Administration is not a phenomenon peculiar to India, but its ramification are so large and pervasive in India that it has corroded the administrative machinery and retarded efficiency and progress

The phenomenal expansion of governmental activities and institutions has not led to efficiency and economy in the administration. On the contrary, the administration has become a growing field of corruption in India. It is true that even in countries like the U.S. and Great Britain, there is corruption. In fact, no country is free from the evil. "Power corrupts and absolute power corrupts absolutely". Sometimes a distinction is made between personal corruption and administrative corruption.

As a result of deliberate misuse of power and improprieties committed by the two former Chief Ministers of Orissa - Biju Patnaik and Biren Mitra, the State Government incurred a loss of about 20 crores of rupees, late Lal Bahadur Shastri, as Prime Minister, declared that no proof of any pecuniary benefit had been established in the two cases.

The fact in these cases was that, these transactions were made with firms with which the wives of the Chief Ministers were directly and actively connected. It is interesting to remember that Sardar Pratap Singh Kairon of Punjab was asked to quit office, not because any direct charge of corruption was proved against him, but because former Chief Justice S.R. Das, who investigated into allegations made against Sardar Pratap Singh Kairon, held that he connived at the doings of his sons, who amassed wealth.

In the present day society, political leaders hold very responsible positions and people look to them for leadership. The administration is also influenced by these political leaders and politicians. This is not to say that no corruption existed during the British days and this is a new development. Corruption prevailed during the British days, but the opportunities for it were not many, and the highest level, the steel frame was secured, well-paid and disciplined; Administration was utterly impersonal and was not responsive to the people. In fact, it had no direct relationship with the people. The people did not have any say in the administration - it was imposed upon them.

This makes a great difference. The top executives are answerable to some higher-ups who were equally authoritarian and die-hard. The scope for corruption during the British days was much less and the opportunities were very low. It cannot be said that there was no corruption at the lower level of the administration.

But, there was no mal-administration during British days. In present day administration, corruption and mal-administration have increased immensely and are a great strain on our democracy. It will be proper to quote here a passage from the Santhanam Committee's Report in regard to the integrity of the ministers and the political and governmental leaders (which constitute a basic source of corruption in India). The Committee observed:

> "There is a widespread impression that failure of integrity is not uncommon among ministers, and that some ministers who have held office during the last sixteen years have enriched themselves illegitimately, obtained good jobs for their sons and relations through nepotism. The general belief about failure of integrity among Ministers is as damaging as actual failure".

We have inherited an out-dated administrative system. Though the same machinery and paraphernalia continue in the administration, its basic integrity has greatly declined. The Indian Civil Service was accused of being the steel frame of alien rulers. That is replaced by the Indian Administrative Service. But it has to be admitted that like the politicians, their standard has also gone down. They tend to become a hand-made of the politicians, and as has been revealed by the Kairon Enquiry Commission.

One does not find, barring a very a few exceptions specially amongst the younger recruits, independence of approach and action amongst the civil servants. Rather, some try to win favour with the new rulers and specially in the states some ambitious civil servants almost indulge in party and partisan activities. They "swim or sink" with unscrupulous politicians and even share the booty.

At the lower level, interference in the day-to-day administration from the politicians has almost become a normal feature. This being the state of affairs at the top level both official and non-official—it is impossible to expect honesty and incorruptibility at lower level. Today, the political and administrative leadership is the real fountain head of corruption.

The Santhanam Committee further observed:

> "Corruption can exist only if there is someone willing to corrupt and capable of corrupting. We regret to say that both this willingness and capacity to corrupt is found in a large measure in the industrial and commercial classes". The ranks of these classes have been swelled by speculators and adventures of the worst kind. To these, corruption is not only an easy method to secure large unearned profits, but also the necessary means to enable them to pursue their vocations or retain their positions among their own competitors.

This is a realistic analysis of the prevailing position in the administration and it shows how the relationship is established and the dubious manner in which it is done, between the officials and the business community. Added to this the fact that the legal enactment permitting business houses and companies to give donation to political parties. This gives the former an enormous opportunity not only to influence political parties and the administration but influence decisions of the Government as well.

Nepotism and favouritism has crept into the recruitment to public service commissions both at the Centre and the States. Bright young men and women holding high positions in universities hardly feel confident to get into a post according to their merit and qualifications, on opportunities that are readily available.

In any developing society, it is not only the resources and planned programmes of development, but also the enthusiasm and idealism of the younger generation which are the greatest asset. But in such a polluted atmosphere characterised by insecurity and frustration, they tend to become cynical.

It is not necessary to go into details as to how in different departments of the Government, corruption and nepotism prevail almost in an organised and systematic manner.

In Western countries, they have been able to check petty corruption, practically it is non-existent. The sale of newspapers without a hawker and the sales in big departmental stores without a shop-assistant do indicate the type of honesty that exists in Western Countries.

Business morality might not be so high in some of the comparatively backward countries in the west. By and large, this evil is looked down upon and has become rare. Of course, supply and demand are the main cause of this malady. In a democracy, if this tendency goes unchecked, it will cut at the very roots of a democratic system.

Not that our people are unaware of these evil practices. A majority of the people might be illiterate, but they have a power of discrimination and, in their practical life, they understand and experience these evil practices much more than other persons.

In this country, service, suffering and sacrifice have always had a great appeal. This is in conformity with our traditions. It cannot be denied that the unexpected debacle that the Congress Party suffered during the 1967 general elections was mainly due to the failure of the partymen to conform to certain standards of public behaviour and morality.

The connivance of the party in power in shielding the real culprits was not unknown to the common man who felt disgusted and threw them out of power in mere disguest. They were disillusioned and wanted an end such malpractices. Gandhiji generated an atmosphere of service to the downtrodden. He popularized spiritual and moral incentives to take the place of monetary incentives. But the national life is once again at the mercy of those values which led to its downfall.

The above brief description of the state of affairs in our society and administration is enough to cause an alarming concern to all those who are sincerely committed to nation-building and development. India is fighting an uncommon battle; democratic progress through peaceful means, as against dictatorship. It has to prove by action and institutional devices that the progress of a democratic society cannot only be faster, but better than a dictatorial country.

Without infringing upon the individual rights of the citizens, and without any recourse to violence or coercion of any kind.

This task has to be achieved within a definite period of time so that India does not lag behind other countries of the world. The task is difficult, no doubt, but it has to be achieved all the same and there is no short-cut to freedom, progress and change by any other method.

This path has been chosen deliberately and has to be a success. It needs a moral regeneration as moral and psychological factors play a vital and decisive role not only in making the society move forward. It will also be a source of strength for this country in her socio-political and economic development. How to deal with such a situation and to break through the quagmire of stagnancy is the question at issue.

They real remedy for this evil lies in creating an atmosphere against these practices. The moral side of it has the greatest importance in this matter. After all, our administrative machinery has to function in the midst of our social climate. Even, nor our society imposes a certain kind of moral authority over persons and unsocial acts such as rape, theft, etc., are looked down upon. This is not to say that such acts have become rare; but the very fact that society would not approve such action necessarily puts a great restraint on those who might be tempted to commit these acts.

Indian society has not yet been completely westernised or modernised in the sense that its moral fabric has been completely broken to give place to purely materialistic values. This has to be nurtured and given a proper recognition in our behaviour, social and political, which was being done by Gandhiji.

Every person who holds a prominent position in the political, social, religious and even educational sphere has to follow a certain standard of conduct, a life of austerity and simplicity and imbibe the good values of our society.

These are not ideals, these are practical ways of meeting the present deterioration and degeneration of our society. In this, the political parties can play a very important role. They have to conduct their affairs and follow such norms of which would help this process of creating a healthy atmosphere.

It has to be admitted that the exposures made in the highest people's forum - the Parliament of the misdeeds of the ministers, high government officials and influential business houses and their collusion with political leaders holding administrative jobs and such other acts of corruption have made the country and the people more vigilant.

The very appointment of the Santhanam Committee known as the committee on the Prevention of Corruption by the Home Affairs Ministry in June 1962 was the result of the raging campaign in the Lok Sabha in the matter of what is popularly known as "Serajuddin Affair" and the such exposures made in the Parliament.

Not that various measures to deal with this evil were not suggested. As early as 1951, in the election Manifesto, the Socialist Party had advocated the establishment of a statutory Anti-corruption Commission with independent authority and power like the Supreme Court and the Election Commission to deal with all matters of corruption including those in high places.

Later on, C.D. Deshmukh also suggested the establishment of an independent tribunal. But this was resisted by the powers that be, specially Jawaharlal Nehru was against the establishment of any such authority.

After the report of the Santhanam Committee some measures have been taken to eradicate this evil in the administrative machinery. Some of the recommendations of the Committee for disciplinary rules, preventive measures, establishment of a Central vigilance commission and rationalisation and reorganisation of the Special Bureau of Investigation have been accepted and implemented.

One would really like to place on record the commendable work done by the C.B.I. in very difficult cases of corruption specially concerning very highly-placed and influential leaders. These orgainsations should be given more freedom and no executive pressure or influence should be exerted on their investigations. The Government have so far not agreed to put on the table of the Parliament the report of the C.B.I. on the influence of foreign money on the general elections of this country.

Whether there is sufficient evidence to proceed against any party or individual in a court of law or not, it would throw sufficient light on this question and such exposures are always a good deterrent than any penal action when it relates to political parties and individuals. Some statutory or other suitable procedure should be adopted wherein the accounts of political parties should be made public and all sources of their income should be disclosed.

The administrative steps taken so far, are very halting and half-hearted. While a few procedures recommended by the Santhanam Committee are accepted, the very important recommendations of the Committee in regard to ministers and public men have not been accepted.

It recommended that if specific allegations against a minister at the Centre or of a state are made by ten members of the Parliament or a State Legislature, prompt measures should be taken to investigate and that a national panel should be created to consider these allegations.

After a *prima facie* case has been established, a commission of enquiry should be appointed and during pendency of the enquiry, the Minister concerned should resign from his job. This has not been accepted by the Government. It also suggested a code of conduct and certain standards of behaviour for the members of Parliament and State legislature. It is regrettable that the Government have not accepted these recommendations.

NOTES AND REFERENCES

1. Wade and Phillips, *Constitutional and Administrative Law* (Edited by A.N. Bradley) 9th ed. 1978. p. 4.
2. Sathe, S.P., *Administrative Law* (5th ed. 1991), N.M. Tripathi, Bombay. p. 6.
3. Dicey, *Introduction to the Study of the Law of the Constitution*, 9th Ed. (Macmillan, 1952).
4. Wade and Phillips, No. 1 above.
5. De Smith, S.A. Judicial Review of Administrative Action, Stevens & Sons 1980, pp. 31-35.
6. Sathe, No. 2 above, p. 7.

7. De Smith, No. 5 above, p. 3.
8. Baxi, Upendra, *Liberty and Corruption: The Antulay Case and Beyond*, Eastern Book Company, 1989.
9. Sathe, No. 2 above.
10. Sathe, S.P., *The Right to Know*, N.M. Tripathi, Bombay, 1991.
11. Sathe, S.P., *Tribunal System of India* (in Press), N.M. Tripathi, Bombay, 1996.
12. Dhavan, Rajeev, 'Engrafting the *Ombudsman* Idea on a Parliamentary Democracy - A Comment on the *Lok Pal* Bill, 1977', *Journal of the Indian Law Institute*, Vol. 19, p. 257, 1977.

25

BLACKMONEY MENACE

Corruption has already sufficiently punctured and unfriendly hampered the process of economic growth and development.

Corruption is a complex phenomenon. Its origin can be traced to a multitude of factors. Corruption can involve payment in cash or in kind. Corruption can also involve payment in terms of provision of a return service (lawful or unlawful) if the party benefiting from such an act happens to be directly or indirectly connected with some other branch of administration.

The payment can be immediate or delayed, direct or round about. Again, corruption can be *adhoc* or it can be institutionalised. Further, corruption can appear both in public as well as private institutions.

The prevalance of corruption in an organisation can be due to social, economic, political, personal and many other factors. This chapter tries to study the problem of corruption purely from an economic point of view.

Theory of Black Marketing

Broadly speaking, the phenomenon of corruption is similar to the phenomenon of black marketing. As such, it is desirable to start with the theory of black marketing itself. The following diagram explains how a black market in commodities appears.

Black market for a commodity appears when the govern-

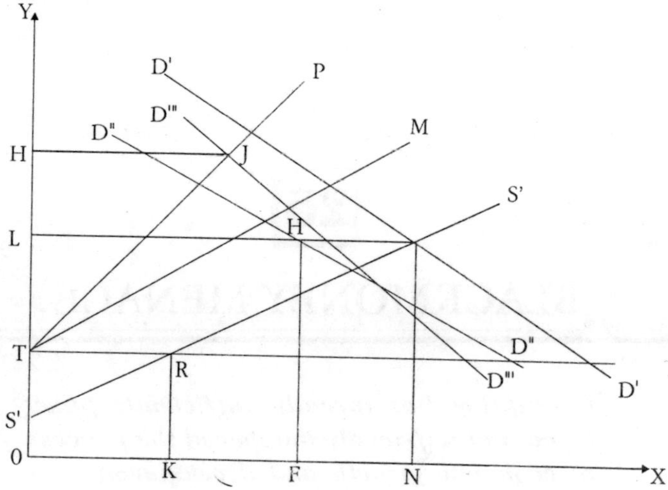

Fig. I : Determination of Price in the Black Market

ment fixes a price for it which is below that determined by the market forces of supply and demand and at the same time does nothing to regulate the supply and demand for the concerned commodity. In the diagram, in the absence of price control, with *S S* as supply curve and *D D* as demand curve, the price will be *O L*.

Suppose the government fixes OT as the price of the commodity. The producers, in such a case, will be willing to supply OK units of commodity. Assuming that out of TN amount of the commodity demanded, TR (= OK) is actually supplied at price OT. Then, the supply curve TM and the demand curve D"D", (both moving toward Y - axis by the amount TR), should appear as supply and demand curves relevant for the black market and the price in the black market will again be equal to OL, the market price determined in the absence of price control.

In actual practice, however, events do not move as simply as is indicated by the foregoing assumption. The supply curve for the black market is likely to be steeper than TM due to various reasons, firstly, before price control each unit of the commodity was sold at price OL.

After the price control, a part of the commodity supplied is sold at a lower price, i.e. OT. Loss in total profits due to this, is likely to be recovered by the producers through the sale of the Commodity in the black market.

This loss in profit, becomes a part of the cost of production and, thus, makes the supply curve for the black market steeper. Secondly, the supply curve becomes still steeper because of the fact that the sale of the commodity at a price higher than the controlled one is unlawful and is punishable. Any insurance by the producers, against any penal action will make the supply curve steeper.

Some reservations may be expressed even about the way the demand curve has moved towards Y-axis by the amount TR. It will be a movement horizontally paralled to the original demand curve, only if the consumers in the top bracket demanding upto TR commodity, are able to purchase this commodity.

If these people move out of the market, the demand curve will shift in the way, described above. However, this is only an exceptional case. Some consumers in the lower bracket too are expected to be able to purchase the commodity at the controlled price.

The demand curve for the black market will then, no doubt, move towards the left, but movement will be slower at the top, gaining moment as it moves downwards, and will complete the shift towards left by TR amount only when the price becomes OT. The demand Curve for the black market will, thus, becomes steeper.

The whole Demand Curve can shift further to the left if there is a fear of punishment for purchasing the commodity in the black market. However, as the situation is the shift in the demand curve to the left, as a result of the fear of punishment, will not be as much as of the supply curve. Normally, the sellers of the commodity are considered to be the bigger culprits.

The two curves for the black market, under competitive conditions may be, thus, represented by TP and D"D" and DH is the black market price. The price in the black market is, thus, likely to be higher than that which would have prevailed if there were no price control.

The social gain from the price control will be the maximum if commodity at the controlled rate is supplied solely to the lowest bracket of consumers. However, in that case, the black market price will be the highest because the demand curve in the black market will become as steep as it can be.

Above conclusions are based upon the assumption that perfect competition prevails in the black market. If market is monopolistic or oligopolistic in character, its impact on the black market price will be magnified.

Further, it is also possible that in such a market structure price discrimination practiced by the producers may enable them to charge from different consumers, as high a price as the latter can pay.

Theory of Corruption—A Derivation

We may note here that the theory of corruption, as we shall realise at the end of this section, could be developed independently, from first principles as well. However, we followed the present approach because of two reasons.

Firstly, corruption is not a kind in itself but a species of a large genus, one of the other species being the black marketing. In broad terms, both call for the same type of analysis.

Secondly, to us, black marketing is the leading species of the genus. Introduction to corruption, through the analysis of black marketing will enable us to focus our attention on some finer points which would have been ignored if the analysis of corruption had been carried on independently.

To us, as indicated earlier, corruption implies some sort of black-marketing in the supply of services. The above theory can, accordingly, be applied to the provision of services flowing from a particular source.

I would, in this section, confine my analysis to the lawful services to be provided by the government. Further, I consider only those services which can be quantified in terms of units of similar nature.

Some Modifications: As a service is different in nature from a commodity, the theory of black marketing pertaining to a commodity will need some important modifications. The fact that the service, under consideration, is provided by the government will necessitate some other modifications as well. These modifications are as follows:

(a) Whereas in case of a commodity, the producer himself is the supplier of the commodity, in case of a service provided by the government a distinction is to be made between the producer of the service and the agency supplying the service. The government is the producer of service while the administrator is the final supplier of the service.

    This, in fact, also implies that it is not the institution that is corrupt. Rather, it is a functionary in that institution who is corrupt. He is corrupted because of the control that he has over the flow of service provided by the government.

(b) After the government has decided to make available a service to the public, it will determine the number of units of service to be supplied to the public. The units of service in some cases is fixed in number as in case of issuing certain permits or setting up of certain supply outlets or admission to certain courses.

    In other cases, these can be unlimited in supply, e.g. in case of service involving renewal of driving licences. By the terms 'unlimited' we mean that the service units to be supplied are as many as the public wants.

(c) There may be a change in the cost of production per unit of a service when the quantity of the unit SS produced changes. However, the government normally announces to change a fixed price for a unit of that service.

On the basis of modification (b) and (c), we come to the conclusion that the supply curve for a service offered by the government is not upward sloping, as has been shown in

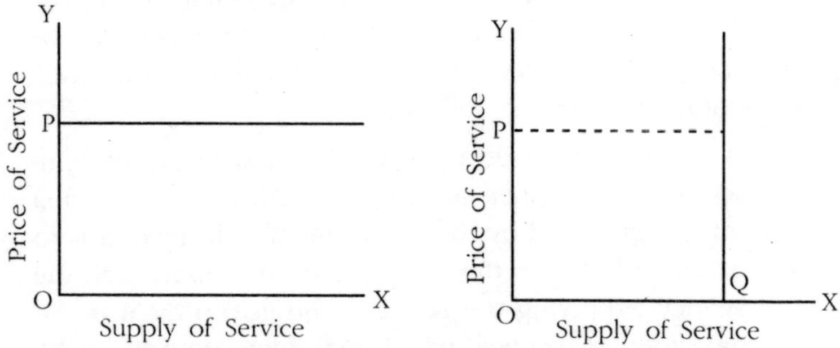

Fig. 2(a) and 2(b) : Supply Curves of the Service

diagram 1, but will be either completely horizontal or vertical as shown in the diagrams 2 (a) and 2(b).

Diagram 2(a) shows the unlimited supply of a service at OP Price fixed by the government whereas diagram 2(b) shows the fixed units of service supplied at that price.

Before we are able to examine all other differences between the theory of black marketing and the theory of corruption we may superimpose the demand curve for a service on the supply curve for the service.

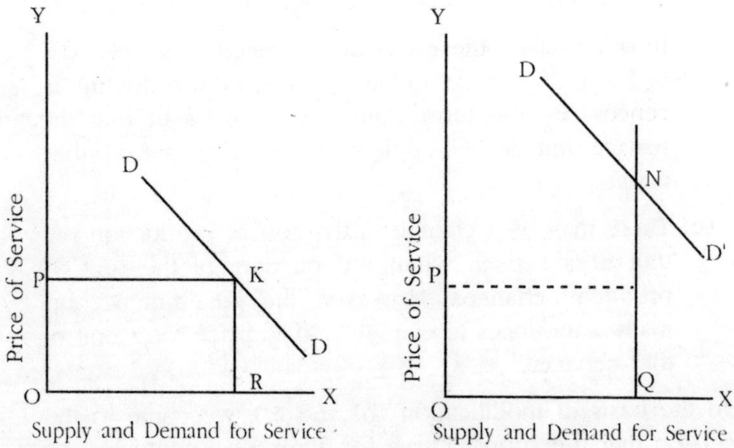

Fig. 3(a) and 3(b) : The Equilibrium Price and the Announced Price of the Service

The exercise will result in the following diagram

Diagram 3(a) shows the interaction between demand and supply of a service whose supply is perfectly elastic while diagram 3(b) shows interaction between supply and demand for a service whose supply has been fixed by the government.

An important difference: Comparison of diagram 3 with diagram I brings out an important difference. It can be described as follows.

In case of price control by the government, flow of the commodity in the open market is reduced as determined by the supply curve and a part of the amount of commodity produced moves into the black market. A new demand curve for the black market also appears.

In case of a service supplied by the government (fixed or unlimited in supply) at a predetermined price the supply curve will not be split into two parts i.e. one for the open market and the other for the black market. The price is already fixed and the government has announced the amount to be supplied (fixed or variable) at that price.

Thus, the supply curve remains unchanged whether the transaction takes place in the open market or in black market. There is to repeat no separate supply curve for the black market. Same is the case with the demand curve.

The demand curve is already based upon the information that the government is supplying the commodity at the fixed price. So, no new demand curve will emerge as is the case with diagram 1 (i.e. that pertaining to black marketing).

Both supply and demand curves, thus, in fact, represent the curves which are relevant for the open market, and the price that will be determined after the intersection of supply and demand curves will be the price of the service that will prevail if free operation of the market forces was allowed.

From diagram 3, it will appear that in case of a service with competely elastic supply, (Diagram 3(a), the market price will be OP and it will be ON if the supply of service is fixed at OQ.

And now enters into the picture, the role played by the

price of the service as announced by the government. The price as determined by the free operation of the forces of supply and demand does not always equal to the announced price.

In case of a service with perfectly elastic supply, the determined price is equal to announced price (OP) whereas in case a service with fixed supply, the determined price is higher than the announced price.

Scope of corruption is indicated by the difference between the price of the service as determined by the free operation of market forces and the announced price of service. The determined price is the price which the consumer of the service are willing to pay, at the given level of supply of that service. If the announced price is lower than the determined price, surplus can be pocketed by the person through whom this service flows to the public i.e. the administrator.

If somehow or other, the service flow could be regulated by the constitutional entity, i.e. the government in its impersonal form, the service would have been actually sold at the announced price and there would have been no corruption.

However, when the service, though initially originating from an impersonal entity, is supplied to the public through the agencies of an individual, the economic motive of that individual is likely to come into play. He will get some unearned income and at the same time, the government will get the price fixed for the service.

In accordance with the preceding analysis, in the present case, we can say that possibility of corruption exists from the very beginning in a situation where the government announces the supply of fixed units of service at a fixed price (diagram 3(b). Where the number of units of service to be supplied are according to the requirements of the public under normal circumstances, there are no chances of corruption (diagram 3(a).

In case of such a situation the administrator will try to obstruct the flow of the service so that the supply again falls short of the demand and a surplus over the fixed price can be generated and pocketed.

This is generally done by the administrator by showing to be a stickler for rules, over-worked, awefully busy and sometime, by suggesting to the members of the public to pay for jobs shown to be ancilliary to the main service.

One more point needs to be noted. If the administrator is completely an economic man, the difference between determined price and the fixed price will indicate the minimum level of corruption for a unit of service. The level can be higher also if the administrator starts dealing with members of the public on individual basis.

There will be many members of the public who are willing to pay a price, even higher than the determined price. The administrator can ask them to pay more. Such a possibility of price discrimination always exists in case of the supply of direct services. From this angle, environment for corruption exists even in case of a service with perfectly elastic supply.

Conclusion

Corruption does not imply a black market in service There is only a black market price for the service otherwise supplied openly. The service itself is to be supplied openly. This is because the government insists as such. No part of the supply of service itself is to be diverted into the black market and, as such there are no two supply curves—one for the open market and the other for the black market, as shown in diagram 1.

As a result, the analysis of corruption from the economic point of view, becomes simpler. From the economic angle, corruption is the result of excess demand for service, at the price fixed by the government, and the surplus offered by the members of the public over and above the price fixed by the government for the service, is the economic indicator of the extent of corruption that can take place in the supply of the given service.

Some Remedies as suggested by the supply and demand Analysis

The above analysis explains why corruption comes into existence. An excess demand situation is a favourable breeding ground for corruption.

Measures to correct the imbalance between the supply and demand will obviously reduce the scope for corruption. This suggestion, in turn, implies that the supply of the service should be increased and the demand for the service should be reduced.

We can think of various measures which can be used to influence the supply or demand for service in the desired direction.

Following measures influencing the supply of service can be examined.

(a) Supply of Service

(1) *Creation of Additional Units of Service*—of course, the above analysis of corruption altogether assumes away this suggestion. In one case, it is already assumed that the supply or service is fixed and in the other case, it is assumed to be completely elastic. However, this is not to deny the fact that greater the number of units supplied, less will be the chances of corruption.

(2) *Measures to minimise demand for Extra Payment:* Even though the increase in the supply of service is ruled out, measures can be taken to ensure that the suppliers of service do not demand a price for service which is higher than the announced price.

These measures are concerned mainly with the regulation of the flow of service. Regulation of the flow of service is of utmost importance in cases where the service supplied is announced by the government to be perfectly elastic but the administrator creates artificial hindrances in the flow of service. Various measure can be adopted. Some of these are as follows:

(2.1) *Simplification of Procedures for Getting the Service*: Power to hinder the flow of service seems to have a positive association with the complexity of procedure to be followed for availing of the service.

(2.2) *Increase in the Number of Outlets for the Supply of Service* : Such a step will divide the consumers of service into many sub-groups. This will, in turn, reduce the rush on a particular outlet. The bargaining power of the person controlling the flow of this service (considered to be completely elastic at each outlet) for extra payment, though hindering the flow of service, will go down.

In fact, if consumers of service are not attached to a specific outlet and are allowed to buy it from any outlet, a sort of competition for attracting consumers (though for getting extra payment only) will ensue among the controller of various outlets of service. This will reduce the interruption in the flow of service.

(2.3) *Payment of a Bonus:* Inversely related to the number of pending cases with reference to a particular norm) - is also likely to regulate the flow of service.

How far is the Penal action against the controller of an outlet of Service useful: To us, fear of penal action against a controller of an outlet of service can work both ways.

On the one hand, it can completely dissuade a person from indulging in corrupt practices (in the present case, to demand a surplus over announced price in part or in full).

On the other hand, if he is bent upon getting some extra payment from the consumers of service, he will ensure against the risk of penal action by adding something to the minimum that he would have otherwise demanded as the surplus money.

In fact, this is the argument which Boulding puts forth for the ineffectiveness of penal action against the suppliers of the commodity in the black market. The supply curve for the commodity in the black market becomes steeper because of the fear of punishment and the black market prices rise further, as a result.

3. Where the number of units of service to be supplied

are fixed and there is a single outlet for the supply of the service, a joint control by a group of independent administrators will reduce the scope for extra payment. The best results will be obtained if the group does not delegate the control of the outlet to a sub-group.

(B) Demand for Service

Measures to influence the urge to pay more than the announced price on the part of the users of the Service : Measures ot influence the demand side are more relevant in those cases where the number of units to be supplied at the announced price are fixed. It is in this case that the equilibrium price is higher than the announced price. Two measures can be easily suggested. These are :

(i) Excess payment should not guarantee that the service will be supplied to the person making this payment. Distribution of service units among the eligible demanders of service through lots can help achieve such an objective.

(ii) *Penal Action :* Though we are not certain about the outcome of panal action against the controllers of service outlets, there is no doubt that penal action against the demanders of service will definitely reduce the level of corruption. Fear of penal action, in fact, shifts the existing demand curve towards the left. The reason is as follows. The existing demand curve shows the maximum price that the consumers are willing to pay for the given number of units of service.

If a penal action is announced for the consumers of service indulging in corruption, they would like to ensure against the penal action and they would deduct the national cost of insurance from the price they are willing to pay to the suppliers of the service. In other words, the maximum which the consumers are willing to pay for the service will go down or we can say that the demand for the service will go down.

The equilibrium price and, therefore, the scope for corruption will go down.

Penal action against the persons paying the surplus amount will, thus, be more effective and certain measure to check corruption than a penal action against the suppliers of service.

In fact, this conclusion also suggests a penal action against those purchasing commodities in the black market, smuggled and pilfered goods or those purchasing the unlawful services etc.

Some Measures of General Nature

The foregoing measures are directly aimed at the suppliers and users of a service to dissuade them from indulging in corrupt practices, as defined above. However, some other measures affecting the economy as a whole can also influence the level of corruption.

These measures aim at reducing the capacity of the people to make the extra payment while purchasing a service. The target of these measures is the richer section of the society. From this angle, imposition of direct taxes on the richer section of the society, measures to improve the distribution of income, and control over inflation (as inflation makes the distribution of income more unfair), will be helpful.

Conclusion

In conclusion, one can say that the measure, suggested above, will reduce the scope of corruption. But to say that corruption will totally disappear if these measures are successfully implemented is to say too much.

Corruption is not confined only to the two categories of services discussed here. Further corruption is not solely an economic phenomenon. Much also depends upon the personal character of the individuals in the administration, and that of the members of the public and the general atmosphere in which they operate.

Ending Black Money

In recent years, corruption has emerged as the issue of greatest concern to ordinary people. Not only are there daily fresh revelations of corruption in high places, but also the person on the street has to grapple with corruption in virtually every aspect of daily work and living. If systemic answer are not found to this malaise, faith in democratic institutions and processes is likely to collapse beyond repair.

In this quest for systemic answers, we must identify systematic sources of corruption within the character of the bureaucratic machine. These include lack of transparency, accessibility and accountability, combersome and confusing procedures, proliferation of mindless controls, and poor commitment at all levels to real results of public welfare.

Most government officials typically present as picture of a client public bewildered and harassed by opaque rules and procedures and inordinate delays, constantly vulnerable to exploitation by employees and touts.

Side by side with resoletely confronting corruption wherever it occurs, attempt should also be made to systematically address systemic causes of corruption in office functioning, such as lack of transparency.

It is important to understand that information is power, and that the bureaucracy at all levels attempt to withhold information to increase it's power for control, patronage, arbitrariness, nepotism, corruption and lack of accountability.

Therefore, demystification of rules and procedures, complete transparency and pro-active dissemination of this relevant information amongst the client public is potentially a very strong safeguard against corruption.

Ultimately, the most effective systemic check on corruption would be where the citizen himself or herself has the right to take initiative to seek information from the state, to enforce transparency and accountability.

It is in this context that the movement for right to information is so important. It secures for every citizen the enforceable right to question, examine, audit review and assess government acts and decisions, to ensure that these are consistent with the principles of public interest, probity and justice.

It promotes openness, transparency and accountability in administration, by making government more open to public scrutiny. The right to information is expected to improve the quality of decision-making by government agencies in both policy and administrative matter, by removing unnecessary secrecy surrounding the decision-making process.

It would enable groups and individuals to be kept informed of the functioning of the decision-making process as it affects them and to know the kinds of criteria that will be applied by government agencies in making these decisions.

It is hoped that this will enhance the quality of participatory political democracy in giving all citizens further opportunity to participate in a more full and informed way in the political process.

By ensuring access to relevant information and knowledge, the citizens would be enabled to assess government performance and to participate in an influence the processes of government decision-making and policy formulation on any issue of concern to them.

Information is the currency that we all require to participate in the life and government of our society. The greater the access we have to information, the greater would be the responsiveness of our governments to community needs.

Alternatively, the greater the restrictions that are placed on access, the greater the feelings of 'powerlessness' and 'alienation' of the ordinary citizen.

There are numerous ways in which government information is already accessible to members of the public. The parliamentary system promotes the transfer of information from government to Parliament and the legislatures, and from these to the people.

Members of the public can seek information from their elected members. Annual reporting requirements, committee reports publications of information and administrative law requirements increase the flow of information from government.

Today, there is a wide acceptance, in principle, that the right to information is an indispensable instrument for increasing citizen control over exercise of executive power, and for enforcing transparency and accountability.

The debate has shifted to the practicality of legislation that would guarantee such a right to the ordinary citizen and which would lay down time limits as well as penalities in case information is not provided on time.

Opponents of such a proposed legislation argue that government is unable to cope even with the demands for information of a few hundred legislators and parliamentarians. It would be paralysed and swampted if every citizen would enjoy the freedom of demand bulky and even irrelevant information.

It is important to allay such fears by pointing out that most of the information relevant to a citizen is already being collated and compiled within government.

There is very little authority that is exercised in government which is at least in theory not accountable to a higher level. The vital difference is that documents, reports and other information which at present is available only to superior supervisory levels would be now also become available to the ordinary citizen.

Looked at in this way, it would become clear that the burden of additional workload which would be generated by the right to information would not be in the collection and collation of fresh information, but only in making available copies of information already available somewhere within the system.

Given the ready availability of technology of photocopying machines and computers generating additional copies of information at a price would be no means be unbearably burdensome to the system.

We may also identify in the first stage some examples of such information that may be easily made available to the ordinary citizen on demand, but which would be momentous in its cumulative impact on control of corruption and the arbitrary exercise of power.

Such information may broadly be classified under the following heads:

(i) All information related to development programmes, including estimates, sanctions, physical progress and expenditure.

(ii) All information related to the award of licenses, permits, contracts and selection of beneficiaries.

(iii) All information related to selection for any appointment in government service or a public undertaking. Land records.

(iv) All information related to curtailment of liberty and crime control.

(v) All information related to impacts and the environment.

All illustrative list of such information is given below:

— Copies of the allotment register and distribution register under PDS.

— All estimates, sanctions, bills, vouchers and muster rolls.

— Criterion and procedure for selection of beneficiaries for any government programme, list of applicants and list of persons selected.

— Per capita food eligibility and allotments under nutrition supplementation programmes, in hospitals, welfare and custodial institutions etc.

— Allotments and purchase of drugs and consumables in hospitals.

— Rules related to award of problems, licenses, house allotments, gas, water and electricity connections, contracts, etc., list of applicants with relevant details of applications and list of those selected, conditions of award, if any etc.

— Rules related to imposition of taxes such as property tax, stamp duty, sales tax, income tax, etc., copies of tax returns and reasons for imposition of particular level of tax in any specific case.

— Copies of all land records.

— Statements of revenue, civil and criminal case work disposal.

— Details of afforestation work, including details of land/ sites, species and numbers of plants, expenditure on protection etc.

— List of children enrolled and attending school, availing of scholarships etc.

— Rules related to criterion and procedure for selection of persons to appointment in Government, local bodies or public undertakings, copy of advertisement and/ or references to employment exchange, list of applicants with relevant details, and list of beneficiaries selected.

— Prescribed procedure of sending names from employment exchanges, relevant, details of demands from prospective employers, list of candidates, registered and list referred to specific employers.

— Rules related to criterion and procedure for college admissions, list of applicants with relevant details, and list of persons selected.

— Food adulteration samples - in addition to the three samples currently taken, a fourth sample should be placed in a transparent jar, available for public inspection, and copies, chemical analysis report should be available to citizens.

— Copies of monthly crime report.

— Air and water emission levels and content of all manufacturing units with rights of citizens' committees to check the veracity of these figures; copies also of levels declared safe by the Central Pollution Board relevant in each case.

What we urgently require is a Bill to ensure the right to information, a reform which is regarded by many as the most significant reform in public administration in the last 50 years.

The importance of the Bill is that it provides an enforceable right to access to government-held information. It enables members of the public to obtain access under the law to documents that may otherwise be available only at the discretion of government.

Without information people cannot adequately exercise their right and responsibilities as citizens or make informed choices. Government information is a national resource. Neither the particular government of the day nor public officials create information of their own benefit.

This information is generated for purposes related to the legitimate discharge of their duties of office, and for the service of the public for whose benefit the institutions of government exist, and who ultimately (through one kind of import or another) fund the institutions of government and the salaries of officials.

It follows that government and officials are 'trustees' of this information for the people. The time has come when the trustees must share this resource with the people, to enable them to control the corrupt and arbitrary exercise of state power.

26

LAND OWNERSHIP PATTERN BREEDS CORRUPTION

From the Marxian perspective it is held that the capitalistic order of our society is exclusively responsible for all social ills including corruption.

Epidemic corruption seems too malevolent in its nature and implications which has equally encompassed the capitalistic and socialistic societies in the world. In the developing countries (i.e. Third World), corruption has attained exorbitant ascendancy.

In a country like India, this malignant trouble has sufficiently punctured and extremely hampered the process of healthy economic growth and development. Starting from the political bosses to the lowest level of bureaucratic functionary, none seems to be either an exception or immune from its evil effects.

Such an assertion does not denote that everyone is corrupt but simply highlights the sad prevalent plight of affairs. Even a sacrosanct person finds himself sufficiently circumscribed to yield under it's vociferous pressure and tastes the bitter bite of this panic in divergent walks of life.

An honest and sincere official performing his job efficiently loath to converge with the corrupt channels is swiftly shifted and replaced by a convention convenient official in the genuineness of public interest.

Over-temptation, too much greediness and craze for material possession has degenerated the individual in society to fall prey to corrupt practices. Instead of abhorring, rejecting and condemning the ill-earned possession, the established societal norms have accorded full recognition to such illegal gratification of the individuals.

Consequently, corruption seems to have been unequivocally legitimised in the societal norms. In the context of eroding ethical standards of public life, minor innovations will render no help and a total transformation and complete overhauling is essentially called for to save the individual/ society from his/it's present degeneration.

To probe the phenomenon of corruption in a proper perspective, certain general observations seem enormously pertinent. What is the nature of Indian State? What is the pattern of development followed in our country? What is the meaning of the concept of corruption in the context of this chapter?

To comprehend the nature of Indian State, we need to look toward the political institutions and processes which vastly resemble the western liberal democratic nations. President, being the constitutional head, we have followed Parliamentary System of Government wherein all powers are exercised by the Council of Ministers headed by the Prime Minister in practice.

The permanent executive provides a sense of continuity in the administration and adds to the rationality of the governmental decisions. Ministers are accountable to the elected members of Parliament at a regular interval of five years.

The present day parliamentary democracy has eventuated elitist democracy wherein various elite groups compete for power loath to and indifferent from the political education of the masses. They aspire only to win people on their side through cheap tactics and appeasement.

The true nature of Indian State is reflected in Gunner Myrdal's observation as a 'soft state'[1] on account of its failure on the front of policy measures. The term denoted to highlight the hazardous limits and inability of the state to implement policies and place obligation on the people.

After achieving Independence in 1947, the immediate task was to meet the revolution of rising expectations of the masses through speedy developmental process. Capitalist model of development practiced in the West and the Socialist model of development followed in the socialist countries were the two available methods for guidance.

Considering their extremity and inapplicability to the Indian conditions[2], our political leaders patronised a middle-path of development called mixed economy wherein public sector and private sector were destined to operate in close co-operation and in collaboration with each other.

Despite endeavouring to harness the possible gains of both available models of development genuinely emerged out to be capitalistic in character and contents. A.R. Desai's research works[3] confirm enormously such an assertion. The most valuable goal in capitalism seems material wealth which promotes fetishism of commodities, particularly conspicuous consumerism.

Even social prestige and social status of a person corresponds to his position in the material domain. Inferently, though we tried to design our own model of mixed economy, yet 'we could not give the cultural input so very essential for our indigenous path of development to make it a success'.[4]

The concept of corruption does demand a sense of specificity for its probing and some scholars have dwelt upon it. Oxford English Dictionary defines corruption 'as the perversion or destruction of integrity or fidelity in the discharge of public duties by bribery or favour'. Andreski considered corruption 'as the use of public power for private advantage in ways which transgress some formal rule or law.'[5]

While exploring corruption in Zambian politics, Morris Szeftel observes, 'corruption is behaviour which deviates from the norms, rules and duties governing the exercise of public role or office for private gains, it may do this by ignoring prohibitions against certain acts, or by fulfilling obligations to act or by exercising legitimate discretion to act, as long as it does so for private advantage or for private regarding motives.'[6]

Corruption typically denotes the abuse of public office for

personal gain as J. Nye states 'corruption is political behaviour which deviates from the formal duties of public role, because of private regarding (personal, close family, private clique) pecuniary or status gains, or violates rules against certain type of private regarding influences.'[7] I am adopting here this Nye's definition of corruption with slight modifications.

In this context of present chapter: corruption is such political behaviour of political elite and public officials to subvert the process of land legislation and their implementation to keep theirs and their relatives land in tact; to ensure that the idea of land to the tiller did not materialise and the benefits occruing to the tenants and land-less labour through the land legislative measures were unequivocally hampered.

In India the pertinence and the pivotal position of land reforms seems undeniable as a large chunk of it's population depends on agriculture as a way of livelihood. In recent years, the concern for these reforms has augmented due to a let down in expectations of the impact of Green Revolution. The hope of increased productivity leading to an era of rural affluence, benefiting everybody from it, had been belied.

Rich landlords have garnered all the gains and 'the rich have become richer and the poor poorer. The pre-existing pattern of land ownership and socio-economic structure flowing out of it has skewed the distribution of benefits in favour of the rich.'[8]

Thereupon, land reforms have been brought into the mainstream of rural development activity under the Seventh Five Year Plan 1985-90. It observes: 'Land reforms have been recognised to constitute a vital element both in term of the anti-poverty strategy and for modernisation and increased productivity in agriculture.

Re-distribution of land could provide a permanent asset base for large number of rural land-less poor for taking up land-based and other supplementary activities.'[9] (emphasis added).

While thinking about modern India, the conspicusos reality seems to be that this is an overwhelming rural and agrarian society. In its social and economic setting, the dominant issue for India's past and present has been who owns or does not own the land? Who gets what from whom and on what terms, on the land?

In this context, Bernard Cohn remarks aptly that 'the control of land and the distribution of the product of the land were and are central to the social relation and the social structure was and is, not only about ownership of land, rents and taxes, but about kinship, marriage, ritual, status, prestige, power and authority.'[10]

To understand the evolution of agrarian relations in India, a brief historical retrospect of land relations during the pre-Independence period is imperative. In British India, it's land tenures 'were adapted and modified to suit the economic and political requirements of the British economy'.[11]

In their attempt to reorganise India's agrarian structure, the British rulers established three types of land system in the country, viz. the Zamindari Settlement; the Mahalwari Settlement; and the Ryotwari Settlement.[12]

The distinction between these land systems was mainly historical as the 'practice of sub-infeudation in effect, repeated subleasing has grown up,[13] thereby, establishing a hierarchy of non-cultivating landed interests. At the apex of the agrarian structure was the landlord class with 'Superior' property right in the soil, which permitted them to lease out land to lesser tenants, sub-tenants, or cropper and to extract from them a surplus in the form of rent.

The creation of a long chain of middlemen or rent receivers, has led to the emergence of a parasitic class of absentee land-owners whose only interest in agriculture lies in realising a certain amount of rent, i.e. a share of the profits from agricultural production.'[14]

Within this parasitic class there were two broad groups, which existed in all parts of India, but one or the other of which predominated in any particular region. The first was a class of large usually absentee landlords who tended to hold land in more than one village and were mostly to be found in Zamindari regions. These were the classic intermediaries between the government and the peasants even whose tenants often sublet to others.'[15]

Secondly, there was a class of smaller normally resident proprietors, who typically held land in one village, who were in ryotwari and mahalwari areas, and who, like their wealthier counterparts, would sub-let the land.[16]

Since the landlord class was interested only in higher rents and not in agricultural production, there was a built-in depressor in Indian agriculture leading to the deterioration of the conditions of the peasantry. P.C. Joshi observes rightly, 'The concentration of land in the hand of rentier land-owners enabled them to extract high rents from the tenants......

The land-hungry and rack-rented peasantry constituted the vast army of unemployed manpower from whom high rents could be squeezed by leasing them lands on the most exploitative terms and conditions.'[17] Being in commanding position of the national economy, the British Government allied with the landlords and traders and made them to be cogs of its own massive machinery of economic and political exploitation.

In short, the pre-Independence agrarian structure of the country was characterised by the exploitation of the peasantry in the form of exhorbitant rent; uncertainty of the lease hold and repressive nature of the land tenure.

Ever since the National Movement acquired a true national character, the historic resolution of the Karachi Session (1931) of the All India National Congress had, *inter alia* promised to work for the reduction of land rent, thereby, relieving the peasantry of much of its back-breaking burden.[18]

A 'Kissan' Conference held at Allahabad in April, 1935, under the Presidentship of Sardar Patel, also passed a resolution which among other things recommended 'the introduction of a system of peasant properietorship under which the tiller of the soil is himself the owner or it and pays revenue to the government without the intervention of any Zamindar or talukdar.'[19]

As the Congress contested election under the Government of India Act of 1935, it reiterated it's declaration made at Karachi and accorded in its manifesto an important place to land reforms. The Congress Government formed in certain provinces tried to tinker with this problem. But limited in competence, they could not do much.[20]

With the dawn of Independence, the Congress Agrarian Reforms Committee, headed by J.C. Kumarappa, was set-up to formulate, in more precise terms, the policy of the Congress in the matter of land reforms. This Committee recommended that 'there was no place for intermediaries and declared that land must belong to the tiller.'[21]

For a correct agrarian policy the Committee suggested

(1) provision of enough opportunity to develop the farmer's personality,

(2) no scope for exploitation,

(3) maximum efficiency of production, and

(4) the scheme of reforms must be within the realm of practicability.[22]

The Committee favoured neither a capitalist agrarian structure nor collective farming but an agrarian pattern of intermediate-size, village based cooperative association as the best safeguard for the legitimate interest of both the individual and community.

The Committee favoured family farming (with a ceiling on individual ownership of land); and joint farming (for all uneconomic farms) where all such uneconomic holdings were to be amalgamated in joint cooperative farms.

The Report candidly expressed the hope that all land in the village would ultimately come under joint cooperative management, and that family farm would gradually disappear after an indefinite period of transition.

Even some amount of coercion by person of proper perspective[23] was favoured for establishing the new agrarian pattern-the scheme of compulsory joint farming. These recommendations of the Kumarappa Committee were made the basis of the comprehensive programme of land reforms in the country.

The mass of illiterate tenants farmers and landless labourers were though dimly aware of the exact recommendations for changes in the land tenure system, yet could hope for a major improvement in their condition as a result of the establishment of a popular government.

In 1951, the era of planned development ushered in. The land reform programme outlined in various Five-Year Plans constituted an integral part of the agricultural development and rural reconstruction.

It's objectives was to remove such motivational and other impediments as stood in the way of the enhancement of agricultural production arising out of the agrarian structure inherited from the past; to create conditions for evolving an agricultural economy element with high level of efficiency and productivity; and to eliminate elements of exploitation and social injustice within the agrarian system.

With these objectives in view, the policy of land reforms to be followed in the states, as part of the national plan, was outlined in the First Plan and, further, elaborated in the Second and Third Plans.

"Land to the tiller was adopted as the main plank in the scheme of land reform, which contemplated that owner cultivation should be established on the widest possible scale and all cultivators should come into direct relation with the State (emphasis added).[24]

Ryotwari system was supposed to have been one of peasant proprietorships, but in actual practice leasing out of land was wide spread. Most of these leases and sub-leases were oral and terminable.

Legislative efforts had been made before Independence, to provide a measure of security to the tenants.[25] But for all intents and purposes, it was a stop-gap arrangement, providing immediate relief to the highly oppressed farmers.

As stated above, in the proposed post-Independence set-up (i.e. land to the tiller), there was to be no need for any such legislation. However, in the initial stages the older policy was continued, presumably again as a stop-gap arrangement. The important guide lines laid down in the Five-Year Plans for the reform of tenancy were:

> First, that rent should not exceed the level of one-fifth to one-fourth of the gross produce;
>
> Secondly, the tenants should be accorded permanent rights in the land they cultivate subject to a limited right of resumption to be granted to landowners; and
>
> Thirdly, that in respect of non-resumable land, the landlord-tenant relationship should be ended by conferring ownership rights on tenants.[26]

With the passage of time, tenancy reforms became a recognised area of land legislation bringing in it's purview such new issues as that of the ceiling on land holdings.

In order to narrow down the gap between the 'haves' and 'have-nots' the idea of putting a ceiling limit on the size of one's land holding had been mooted right since the inception of the era of land reforms in the country.

About the idea of the ceiling on landholding, D.R. Gadgil, observes rightly, "It has been developed not in the context of checking future possibilities but, in that, of granting immediate relief.

It had it's origin in land where very large landlord estates existed side by side with diminutive peasant holdings and in which there remained some vestige of serfdom or in which the memories of a serf society were yet alive. The situation created a land hunger and also suggested a not unwelcome manner of satisfying it."[27]

Spelling out this policy, the First Five-year Plan observed, 'In relation to land, individual property in excess of any norm that may be proposed has to be justified in terms of public interest and not merely on ground of individual rights or claims.

We are, therefore, in favour of the principle that there should be an upper limit to the amount of land that an individual may hold'.[28] In May, 1955, the Planning Commission set-up a Panel of Land Reforms and a Committee was formed to report on 'size of Holdings' Accepting family as a unit for fixing the ceiling limits on land holding, this Committee observed:

"This policy of imposition of ceiling would be able to make a contribution towards fulfilling the following objectives:

(i) meeting the widespread desire to possess land;

(ii) reducing glaring inequalities in ownership and use of land

(iii) reducing inequalities in agricultural incomes; and

(iv) enlarging the sphere of self-employment.'[29]

In continuity, the Second Plan also emphasised the need of taking steps in each state to impose ceiling on existing holdings. But on the question whether the ceiling should apply to holdings of individuals or to holdings of families, the Plan surprisingly enough did not make any definite recommendation.

It was left to the discretion of State Governments as the Plan went to say 'according to it's special conditions and other relevant factors, each state may determine whether the ceiling should apply to individual holding or to holding of family.'[30]

Such a discretion to the State Governments led to the frustration of ceiling measures as the landed gentry was in strong hold of its control over the decision-making apparatus of the State structure.

The policy performance of land reform programme needs to be seen on three fronts:

(i) the abolition of intermediary tenures like Zamindaries, Jagirdari and Inams which covered almost 40 per cent of the land in the country;

(ii) the imposition of ceiling on land holdings and distribution of surplus land to the poor peasants and landless labourers; and

(iii) providing security of tenure to tenants and regulation of rents.

The task of abolition of intermediaries was started in late forties and without loss of much time, all the States passed pieces of legislation abolishing all such institutions as Zamindars and intermediaries and, thereby, vesting the proprietory rights of acreage in those who tilled it.

The task of abolition of intermediaries was completed by early sixties and through this a large body of tenants, estimated as 20 millions, have been brought into direct relationship with the State....The social and economic position of tenants has candidly improved.[31] It was, indeed, a big leap forward.

To ameliorate the conditions of tenantry, tenurial reform measures were enacted. Legislative provisions have been made in most of the states to determine fair rents from tenants. Laws have also been made in most of the States for conferring security of tenure on tenants.

Provisions have also been made in extensive area of the country providing for conferment of ownership rights on tenants or allowing cultivating tenants to acquire ownership rights on payment of a reasonable compensation to the landlords.

Under these measures, the magnitude of tenancy[32] (in terms of proportion of operated leased in area) has declined from 35.7 per cent in 1950-51 to 20.34 per cent in 1953-54 and, then, to 10.7 per cent in 1961-62. It has come down to 8.80 per cent, as reported in 1970-71.

In effect, however, tenancy legislations have had adverse effects. This set into motion process of mass eviction of tenants, sub-tenants and share-croppers, through various legal and extra legal devices.

Under the influence of landlord class, the state laws have invariably juggled with the key concepts. Evictions of tenants can still take place, but on the ground of 'personal cultivation'.

Personal cultivation does not require personal supervision of farming activities or residence in the village where land is located. Consequently, large-scale evictions have taken place which have converted the tenants to farm labourers.

Further more, the law left the way open for owners to operate agricultural holdings either with hired labourer or through disguised tenancies like share-cropping partnership between owner and cultivator. As such, the produce continued to be shared between the share-cropper and landlord in the ratio of 50 : 50.

Provisions regarding voluntary surrender have further helped the landlords in resuming land for personal cultivation and displacing tenants. Voluntary surrenders are often accompanied by threats and even the use of brute force to which the weak and unorganised tenants usually succumbed.

As the voluntary surrenders tended to defeat the purpose of tenancy legislation, the Third Five-Year Plan recommended that

(a) Surrenders should not be regarded as valid unless they were duly registered with the revenue authorities; and

(b) even where the surrender was held to be valid, the landowner should be entitled to take possession of land only upto the right of resumption permitted by law.[33]

Although village records showed little change in the distribution of land ownership between 1954 and 1961, striking differences were noticeable with respect to leased-out land. The number of cultivators reported to be operating 'mixed' holdings of partly—owned and partly-leased in land had declined from about 23 per cent in 1954 and 15 per cent in 1960 while those classified as pure tenants fell from 17 per cent to 8 per cent.

The only logical explanation for the sharp decline in recorded tenancies is the eviction of tenants from their holdings and resumption of land for personal cultivation. There seems little reason to believe that the actual tenancy decreased. Rather, it appears that registered leases were simply converted into informal, oral agreements that effectively deprived the cultivator of any protection under state tenancy acts.

The policy performance in this area remains far from satisfactory. Tenants, by and large, still do not enjoy security of tenure. They are either tenants-at-will or subject to the landlord's rights or resumption or enjoy temporary protection only.

There has been leasing of land on considerable area and such tenancies are generally of an informal nature without written documents or record which makes it difficult to arrive at a correct assessment of the extent of the tenancy problem.

A number of documents by India's Planning Commission also substantiate such a view-point on tenurial reforms. The Third Plan Mid-Term Appraisal notes, 'In most states rents are payable generally as a share of the crop....and share crop rents are difficult to enforce.[35]

In it's Memorandum on the Fourth Five-Year Plan, the Planning Commission reported that 'there is a considerable number of informal tenants. Such tenants are not recorded in the revenue paper and are not recognised as such, and invariably, they pay high produce rents and enjoy no security of tenure.[36]

A review by the Land Reform Implementation Committee of the National Development Council gives a detailed information on this and states, in particular, that 'substantial areas in some regions of the country were still cultivated through informal crop-sharing arrangement, ejectment of tenants still go on through the device of voluntary surrender.[37]

Policies for achieving greater equality in the agrarian structure were directed towards determining ceiling on land-holdings and re-distributing surplus land made available among the landless.

These policies were aimed at solving the problems of step inequalities in land ownership. In this context, land ceiling measures were first enacted in late fifties and early sixties by the different states. These were revised after national guidelines were issued in early 1970's.

While looking into the policy performance on this front, it is clear that these legislations went by lapse. During the first phase between 1958 and 1971, in the 16 Indian states which implemented land ceiling legislation, 'only 0.99 million hectares had been declared surplus representing only 0.7 per cent of the net cropped area.'[38]

In the second phase (i.e. after 1972) the policy performance is reported in the Sixth Five-Year Plan (Draft document) as under on 31st July, 1977:

> The Estimated Surplus Area: 5.32 Million Acres
> The Area Declared Surplus: 4.04 Million Acres
> (Source: Sixth Five Year Plan - Draft Document Para I, p. 68)

How much this declared surplus was below the expected

level could be gauged from the estimate as worked out by the Planning Commission on the basis of National Sample Survey data (26th Round 1970-71).

It had worked out the surplus as 22 million acres.[39] The poor performance of ceiling measures was also underlined by the, then, Union Minister for Agriculture, Shri Buta Singh, in his inaugural address to the Conference of State Ministers for Revenue on May 18, 1985 while giving the following figures.[40]

The Estimated Surplus Area: 23.54 Lakh hectares
The Area Declared Surplus: 17.46 Lakh hectares

Furthermore, the unsatisfactory policy performance of ceiling measures is explicit from the existing gap between the area taken possession of and the area distributed to the landless labourers or poor peasants. According to the Draft Plan the figures are given below:

The Area taken possession of : 2.10 Million Acres
The Area distributed is: 1.29 Million Acres
(*Source*: Sixth Five Year Plan: Draft Document Para 7, p. 68)

Since the area distributed remains less than one-fourth of the estimated surplus, the ceiling measures did not have much impact on the general pattern of size and distribution of land-holding in the country as a whole.

In a nutshell, the poor policy performance to tenurial reforms and ceiling measures did not ameliorate the much deteriorating conditions of the tenantry and poor peasantry, in general, and the rural poor, in particular. Theodor Bergmann remarks aptly that these measures had no visible impact on the distribution of rural property.[41]

To say succinctly in summation, corruption in the policy formulation and implementation seems an inevitable corrollary of the nation of 'soft state' and capitalist pattern of development in our country.

On the question of land reform,[42] the gap in the policy logic and policy performance reflects the prevalent corruption due to which the land reform legislations did not and could not do much to ameliorate the conditions of the tillers of the soil and the landless labourers.

REFERENCES

1. For details see Gunnar Myrdal, *Asian Drama: An Inquiry into the Poverty of Nations* (London: Allen Lane & Penguin, 1968), pp. 66, 277 & 895-900.
2. For details see Franciene Frankel, *Indian Political Economy* 1947-77 (Princeton: Princeton University Press, 1978), pp. 2-4.
3. For details see, A.R. Desai, (ed.) *Rural Sociology in India* (Bombay Popular Prakashan, 1969).
4. Krishan Kant, "A 'Civilisation' battle" *The Tribune*, 11 October, 1990.
5. See Article of Andreski in Michael Clarke (ed.), *Corruption, Causes and Consequences* (London Frances Publisher, 1983).
6. Morris Szeftel, "Corruption and the Spoil System in Zambia" in Michael Clarke (ed.) *Corruption, Causes and Consequences, op. cit.*
7. J. Nye, "Corruption, and Political Development: A Cost Benefit Analysis", *American Political Science Review*, 61 (1967, p. 419.
8. Kuldeep Mathur, "Policies and Implementation of Land Reform in India" in Inayatullah (ed.), *Land Reform: Some Asian Experience*, Vol. IV (Kuala Lampur: Asian and Pacific Development Administration Centre, 1980), p. 159.
9. *Seventh Five Year Plan*, Vol. II (New Delhi: Govt. of India, Planning Commission), p. 62.
10. Bernard S. Cohn, "Comments on Papers of W. Hauser, J.R. McLane and T.E. Metcalf on Land Tenure", *Indian Economic and Social history Review*, Vol. I No. 2., Oct-Dec. 1963.
11. P.C. Joshi, "Land Reforms in India", in A.R. Desai (ed.), *Rural Sociology in India op. cit.* p. 444.
12. For details of these land tenure system See Robert Eric Ferykenberg" Introduction", in his (ed.), *Land Tenure and Peasant in south Asia* (New Delhi: Orient Longman, 1977), pp. 7-8.
13. M.L. Dantawala, "India: Progress in Agrarian Reforms", *Far Eastern Survey*, Vol. XIX No. 22. December 20, 1950 pp. 239-40.
14. K. Mukerjee, *Land Reforms* (Calcutta: H. Chatterjee & Co. 1952), p. 63.
15. In this context Robert Eric Frykenbery observes, "A Zamindar's tenure was, therefore, a form of political and socio-economic

authority or control; moreover, his 'tenants' and 'subtenants' and 'sub-subtenants' all held similar kind of 'settlement or agreement." Robert Eric Frykenberg. "Introduction in his (ed.) *Land Tenure and Peasant in South Asia Op. cit.*, p. 8.

16. Daniel Thorner, the *Agrarian Prospects in India* (Bombay: Allied Publishers, (1973), pp. 4-5.
17. P.C. Joshi, "Land Reform In India" in A.R. Desai (ed.) *Rural Sociology in India, Op. cit.*, p. 446.
18. For details see B. Pattabhai Sitramayya, *The History of the Indian National Congress* vol. I. (Bombay: Padma Publication, 1946), pp. 465-66.
19. H.D. Malaviya, *Land Reforms in India* (Delhi: All India Congress Committee, 1954), p. 59.
20. For details see K. Mukerjee, *Land Reforms Op. cit.* pp. 49-56.
21. H.D. Malaviya, *Land Reforms in India op. cit.*, p. 83.
22. *Ibid.*, p. 83.
23. *Report of the Congress Agrarian Reform Committee*, (New Delhi: Indian National Congress, A.I.C.C. 1949) p. 125.
24. *Fourth Five Year Plan—A Draft outline* (New Delhi: Government of India, Planning Commission-1970), p. 25.
25. For details see K. Mukerje, *Land Reforms, op. cit.*, pp. 49-56.
26. P.S. Appu, "Tenancy Reform in India". *Economic and Political Weekly* vol. XNos. 33, 34 & 35, August 1975, p. 1341.
27. D.R. Gadgil, "Agrarian Reform" in his (ed.), *Planning and Economic Policy of India* (Poona: Gokhale Institute of Politics, 1972), p. 61.
28. *First Five Year Plan* (New Delhi: Government of India, Planning Commission, 1953), p. 189.
29. Report of the Committee of Panel on Land Reform (New Delhi: Government of India, Planning Commission, 1959), p. 99.
30. Second Five Year Plan (New Delhi: Government of India, Planning Commission, 1956), p. 206.
31. *Report of the Committee of Panel on Land Reform Op. cit.*, p. 12.
32. For details see Kuldeep Mathur, "Policies and Implementation of Land Reforms in India" in Inayatullah (ed.), *Land Reform*....op.cit., p. 161.

33. *Third Five Year Plan* (New Delhi: Government of India, Planning Commission, 1960), p. 228.
34. *The Hindustan Times*, April, 28, 1964.
35. *The Third Plan—Mid Term Appraisal* (New Delhi: Government of India, Planning Commission, 1963), p. 100.
36. *Memorandum on the Fourth Five Year Plan* (New Delhi: Government of India, Planning Commission, 1964), p.37.
37. *Implementation of Land Reform: A Review* (New Delhi Government of India, Planning Commission, 1966), p. 16.
38. G. Thimmaiha and Abdul Aziz, "The Political Economy of Land Reforms in India" in A.R. Rajapurohit (ed.) *Land Reforms in India* (New Delhi: Ashish Publishing, House, 1984), pp. 18-19.
39. For details see Kuldeep Mathur, "Policies and Implementation on Land Reforms in India" in Inayatullah (ed.) Land Reform....*op. cit.*, p. 166.
40. Buta Singh, "Land Reform and Poverty Alleviation" *Mainstream* Vol. XXIII No. 41, June 1985, pp. 11-13.
41. Theodor Bergmann, *Agrarian Reform in India* (Delhi: Agricole Publishing Academy, 1984), pp. 32-33.
42. For details see S.K. Sharma's Land Reforms in India: An overview", *Asian Affairs* Vol. X, No. I January-March 1988, pp. 1-16; "Land Legislations in India: Shifting Trends", *Asian Profile*, Vol. 16, No. 6 December 1988, pp. 515-528; and *Politics of Land Reforms in Haryana* an unpublished Ph. D Thesis Panjab University, Chandigarh, 1987.

27

CORRUPTION IN PUBLIC SERVICE AGENCIES

Against bribes, political sanctions, repudiation at the polls, forced resignation from office, loss of promotion are frequently invoked.

Corruption in the public agencies that regulate or deliver services to the people is seldom monitored or widely debated in India. But 'retail' corruption of the kind that is associated with public services also needs to be taken seriously because it impacts the lives of large numbers of people.

Politicians who have to raise funds for their elections may try to recover their investments by auctioning off jobs in public utilities and other agencies under their control.

In a government elected by the people, all public officials are expected to act as agents for the citizens. An agent who has the power to allocate resources may sell his decisions or services for personal gain, thus, sacrificing the interests of citizens. Corruption in any form, thus, entails a conflict of interest.[1]

Conflicts of interest can arise in a government's purchase and sale of goods and services, its regulation of economic and/or other activities and the supervision and control of its assets and organisations. Correspondingly, the potential for corrupt practices exist in all these areas. The growing size and complexity of governments and the impersonal relationships between bureaucrats and citizens have steadily expanded the scope for corruption.

Thus, my focus will be on corruption in the services that the government provides its citizens through its various departments, agencies and enterprises. They include public utility services such as water and power, a wide range of civic services and regulatory activities such as taxation and law enforcement. I shall, therefore, examine the major factors that contribute to corruption in public services.

It would appear that in a highly-regulated and slow-moving economic environment, corruption enables economic actors to cross barriers and move forward. If speed money is not paid, decisions are delayed and services are denied. Corruption is the price to be paid to cut through these problems. What is ignored here is the adverse impact corruption may have on the efficient and equitable allocation and distribution of resources.

It is understood that licences, permits and tax benefits may not go to the efficient, but to those most willing to bribe or use the power of connections. When politicians take money for the appointment and transfer of officials, the resultant allocation of personnel may be far from efficient or equitable. When credit and other services for the poor are allocated based on the influence of corruption, neither efficiency nor equity will be served.

Besides, it is true that the potential for corrupt practices increases with the severity of shortages. What is often overlooked, however, is the fact that corruption prevails even when no physical shortage is present.

Many regulatory services (e.g. driver's licence, registration of land sale, etc.) do not involve any shortages in the supply sense. Regulatory controls are used to simulate shortages or create delays, but this is a far cry from shortages that are beyond the control of the authorities concerned.

Low government salaries may encourage corruption and a tendency to sell favours. Implied here is the hypothesis that corruption would disappear once government compensation policies are reformed. This is difficult to accept for the simple reasons that grand corruption is associated with those with high incomes and assets. It would seem as though the appetite for more goes up with one's income level.

There is a tendency, however, to conclude that corruption is a manifestation of the socio-economic backwardness of a country. The socio-economic transformation of a society will no doubt have a bearing on the behaviour of its public officials and citizens. In our own life-time, Singapore, which was known for its corruption, has substantially eradicated the problem.

Chile, though surrounded by several countries known for widespread corruption, is known for its relatively non-corrupt public services and institutions. This shows that leadership, economic reforms and proper incentive structures to reduce corruption need not wait for socio-economic backwardness to disappear in order to make an impact.

The first significant factor that contributes to corruption in public services is a monopoly in the supply of public goods and services.[2] Absence of competition tends to create opportunities for corruption either by restricting supply deliberately or through inefficiency.

This can occur in both public and private sectors. Monopoly is natural in some sectors for reasons such as economies of scale. The inherent monopolistic nature of some of these services create a fertile environment for corrupt practices which an individual citizen cannot easily monitor or fight.

A second contributory factor is the discretion that monopolistic public agencies enjoy in their decision-making and allocative roles. This situation creates opportunities and incentives for those involved to engage in corrupt practices. Often the decision-makers, their supervisors and clients collude and take advantage of the discretionary facility.

A third factor is the relative lack of accountability of the service providers except in the nominal sense of presenting annual audited accounts to Parliament or other superior authorities. Part of the problem here stems from the collusive tendencies referred to above. When those who are expected to supervise the agents are themselves party to collusion with the latter, the enforcement of accountability becomes extremely difficult.

The problem is exacerbated by the difficulties in measuring the performance of the agents and the outcome of their decisions. The lack of proper reporting systems and supervisory controls add to the severity of the problem. Last, but not the least, accountability is viewed as hierarchical with little attention paid to the need to be accountable to the clients (citizens).

In addition to these three factors, which Klitgard also highlights in his work, we need to add a fourth, the role of information barriers in contributing to corruption. Corruption involves both givers and takers. Existing legislation in India contributes to this situation as public agencies are not required to divulge information concerning specific decisions or actions to the public.

Citizens, having been brought up in this tradition are not used to demanding information. They are often unaware of heir rights vis-a-vis service-providers and of the remedies available if justice is denied to them. That the right to information is a fundamental right of citizens and consumers, whether it be in relation to the attributes of the goods they buy or to the benefit schemes provided by the State, is not a notion fully accepted by Indian leaders and representatives. Under these conditions, information barriers tend to create a setting in which incentives and opportunities for corruption gain strength.

These factors taken together explain a substantial part of the phenomenon of 'retail' corruption in India. But monopoly, wide discretion in decision-making, poor accountability systems and information barriers are more proximate causes and may offer valuable insights into the kind of reforms that could make a difference.

For example, it is well known that most public services are delivered by mostly state-owned monopolies. That they are often insensitive to customers and withhold information to the detriment of the latter is also widely observed. We also know that their decision -making processes, rules and practices are seldom transparent and probably lead to the abuse of the discretionary powers vested in them. Information such as this points to the directions of change required to improve public services and reduce the scope for corruption.

Monitoring the Problem

A number of State governments have established the office to *Lok Ayukt*, comparable to an ombudsman, while the Central Government has yet to appoint a Lok Pal, the counterpart of the Lok Ayukt. Citizens can take their complaints to the Lok Ayukt. Ministeries and departments of both Central and State governments have vigilance officers who are expected to monitor and deal with corruption complaints.

Many of the larted public utilities also have their own vigilance officers. In serious cases, these agencies may set their own inquiry commissions or ask the *Lok Ayukt* in their state to investage specific cases.

Transparency international, a non-profit group that monitors corruption across countries, has stated that India, along with Indonesia and China, is among the most corrupt countries in the world.[3] The study was based on a survey of those who do business in various countries.

It is reasonable to conclude that the phenomenon assessed is a mix of 'grand' corruption and 'retail' corruption. Nonetheless, it is difficult to generalise on the severity or extent of the corruption in public services alone based only on the country rankings given by Transparency International.

There are very few studies that have attempted to quantify corruption in India. A recent study analysed the complaints on corruption received by the Anti-corruption Bureau, Vigilance Commissioner and Lok Ayukt in Karnataka and compared them with similar data in some other States.[4]

The findings of this study confirm that retail corruption arising from the transactions of public service providers with citizens is the most pervasive form of corruption. For Karnataka, the study concluded that the departments of revenue, police, education, health and public works accounted for nearly three-fourths of all corruption complaints in recent years. The study further noted that corruption in local bodies was increasing and that in departments like commercial taxes, excise, road transport, weights and measures, etc. corruption had remained steady. Of the different types of complaints corruption in the issuance of certificates, licences and permits occupied the first position (15% of the total), followed by bribes for the use of certain facilities and allied services like admission to public hospitals, appointments and transfers, and the release of grants and passing of bills in the education department (11%). There are fixed rates for certain services and favours, and the study gave examples of how the bribes are shared within the public hierarchy.

Complaints in Karnataka were much higher compared to those in Andhra Pradesh, Madhya Pradesh, Uttar Pradesh, Maharashtra and Bihar. This may, however, merely mean that people are more indifferent and are unable to access the anti-corruption bodies in their respective States.

The study also found that over two-thirds of all complaints received were from urban areas. In addition, many aggrieved persons avoid lodging complaints, and are afraid of retaliation from officials and of the high costs of pursuing their cases.

The cities of Ahmedabad, Bangalore, Madras, Pune and Calcutta were surveyed on a variety of public service related issues including corruption. Feedback through personal interviews with citizens was obtained from slum dwellers as well as the general population (non-poor).

Table 27.1 presents a comparative picture of the extent of retail corruption in these cities. It shows, for example, that in Madras, every fourth person in general population ends up paying a bribe when dealing with agencies such as the urban development authority, electricity board, municipal corporation and telephones.[5]

In Bangalore, it is one in eight persons, in Pune, it is only one in seventeen that pays a bribe. With respect to slum dwellers, Madras and Bangalore lead other cities in the matter of retail corruption. The average amount paid as bribe per case was also estimated. Bangalore led in this regard (Rs. 850), followed by Ahmedabad (Rs. 500), and Pune (Rs. 350).

Table 27.1: The Speed Money Phenomenon

(% of persons who paid)

City	*Among the urban poor*	*Among general households*
Ahmedabad	20	10
Bangalore	33	14
Calcutta	12	2.4
Madras	26	22
Pune	6	4

Even the poor living in slums is not spared, In Bangalore, every third slum dweller claims to have paid a bribe for getting a service or solving a problem with a public agency. In Madras, every fourth person pays a bribe. Pune, again, reported the lowest incidence of this problem.

It is reasonable to conclude from this evidence that corruption is a pervasive phenomenon in India's public services. Others might add that this statement applies equally to rural areas even if systematic surveys have not been conducted there.

Though the practice of corruption is widespread, the proportion of people who consider it abhorrent ranges from two thirds to four-fifths. Over half the respondents in these cities claim that bribes are demanded of them by officials.

The feedback given by the respondents in the five cities confirm that they face a moral dilemma when faced with corrupt demands and that they would rather avoid having to pay bribes and would prefer to pay a little more officially provided they get efficient service from public agencies.

Even when higher prices for services are charged, public officials have found ingenious ways to practice corruption. The Telephone Department has a "*Tatkal*" Scheme to enable customers to get new connection within a short period on a payment of Rs. 30,000. The only qualification is that the staff have to first ascertain the feasibility of installing a telephone in the location requested.

There are cases where the staff would inform the customer that feasibility can be checked out only after the full deposit is made. The customer is naturally concerned that his money will be blocked if the finding is negative. Agents are available to see that the feasibility test results in a positive finding. This, of course, calls for an extra payment.

Remedies: Proposals for Action

It is proper that we review what the government has done so far to tackle the problem of corruption in public services. A good example is the Consumer Protection Act of 1986 and the establishment of district consumer courts. Similarly, the Lok Ayukt Act provides for cases of corruption in public services to be dealt with along with wider forms of corruption.

Nevertheless, the media, public interest groups and other non-governmental organisations can play a proactive and facilitating role by putting these ideas on the agenda for public debate and encouraging citizen groups to understand the issues involved and cooperate with the government when corrective measures are taken.

The proposals discussed below can be divided into two categories, preventive and curative. Preventive actions are steps that can be taken in advance so as to minimise the emergence of opportunities for corruption in public services. These measures therefore, endeavour to deal with the underlying causes to the extent feasible.

Preventive measures may not always fully succeed in eliminating 'retail' corruption. Hence, there is the need to track and respond to corruption cases once they surface. This is comparable to curative or corrective measures since the mechanisms are activated only after the problem has been detected. A combination of both preventive and corrective actions will doubtless be more effective in curbing retail corruption than either approach alone.

Preventive Measures

1. Deregulation and Elimination of unnecessary Controls

The process of deregulation initiated by the Government of India has focused largely on industry and trade. It has had a positive impact on the corruption front despite the irritants that remain. These reforms, however, have not yet been extended to the State and local levels where the maximum interaction between public officials and citizens take place.

Legislation on public utilities has created public monopolies, but they are exempt from responsibility for services or outputs. These are major problems that often create opportunities for corrupt practices. A systematic review of the laws and regulations governing public utilities and municipalities with a view to simplyfying them and improving their transparency deserves early attention.

As pointed out earlier, the existence of monopolistic conditions tends to create favourable conditions for the practice of corruption. Where there is competition, people have the option to choose more efficient and less corrupt service-providers. The presence of competition can, thus, dampen the spread and the severity of corruption.

Even in service sectors that were considered natural monopolistic, there is now evidence that competitive options can be made available to citizens. The long distance segment of telecommunications, electricity and transport are services where multiple service providers are able to operate in many countries.

A systematic attempt to encourage multiple providers to enter the public utility arena in India, wherever it is feasible, may not only generate efficiency gains, but also discourage the practice of 'retail' corruption.

2. Decentralise services and involve citizens in Monitoring them

This applies, in particular, to municipal and other local bodies services for which people pay taxes or user charges. The creations of ward officers in large cities can make officials more accessible to the residents. Although decentralisation cannot possibly be expected to eliminate all forms of corruption, but at least in respect of many day-to-day service-related problems that people face, the scope for the severity of corruption may get reduced. Still, decentralisation of services has yet to be reduced. Still, decentralisation of services has yet to be seriously attempted in India.

It is often argued that decentralisation tends to strengthen the hands of the local elites who may use their proximity to decentralised power centres to engage in corrupt practices even more effectively. While there is some validity to this arguement, centralised control is also vulnerable.

3. Modify the Official Secrets Act

The Official Secrets Act has been used to hide abuses of power, and according to knowledgeable observers, it is a convenient spawning ground for corruption. In the area of public services, it has enabled officials to withhold information from the public even when no security or concern for national interest is involved.

Perhaps, the most damaging consequence of this legislation is the generally secretive behaviour ('discretionary secrecy') it has instilled in the Indian bureaucracy. India inherited this tradition from the U.K. which has been behind other developed countries with respect to access to information.[6]

But U.K. has, of late, moved forward in it's stance on access to information while we in India have yet to recognise the need for reform in this areas.

The Consumer Education and Research Centre, Ahmedabad (CERC) recently prepared an Access to Information Bill, comparable to Right to Information Acts in other countries, which CERC hopes will be introduced in Parliament in the near future.

Initiatives of this nature deserve to be widely debated and supported. A more open government, while it cannot guarantee the end of corruption, will at least create an environment that is more hostile to corruption.

4. Service-providers should be permitted to charge Higher fees to customers who wish to have speedy services

The role that the pricing of services can play in reducing the scope for corruption is not well understood by most people, including administrators. The provision of free services in the name of equity or other laudable goals has often had the perverse effect of creating excess demand for such services and attracting corrupt middlemen and other well-connected persons who divert these benefits to less deserving people.

This is not an argument for abolishing all free or subsidised public services. The conditions under which free services are provided must be more tightly stipulated so that incentives to divert these benefits are eliminated whether free or highly subsidised services are what the poor need also deserves to be assessed.

It is well known by now that subsidised credit often does not get to the intended persons and costs them much more than was anticipated. Through the imaginative use of pricing, these credit agencies have effectively cut down the scope for corruption and diversion of benefits in this socially important activity.

An important reason for the presence of corruption in some of the public services is the failure of service providers to match services to the differing needs of users and their ability and willingness to pay for such services.

When services are rigidly standardised, those with special needs tend to exert undue pressure or bribe officials to get what they want. Thus, unofficial multiple tracks of services are created resulting in corruption or the abuse of power in the process.

Whether governments need to pre-empt most services and facilities through liberal quotas is itself a moot point. Even if the case for some pre-emption is accepted, the question still remains whether or not providing services to meet the varying needs of customers in terms of urgency or special features is justified, both in terms of meeting the objectives of efficiency and resource generation as well as reducing the scope of for corruption. It is typically argued that dual or multiple tracks of services will lead to the neglect of services for the ordinary citizen.

The challenge is to think creatively about the relevance of this option in as many services as possible so that the incentives and opportunities for corruption are reduced. The basic point to note is that when services are poorly matched to customer needs or are given free or at subsidised prices, there will be a strong tendency for public officials and middlemen to collect 'rents', a euphemism for corruption.

Dual or multiple track pricing of services is one way to reduce the load on service-providers while meeting customer needs more effectively. The underlying assumption here is that those who need services with special characteristics or urgency are more vulnerable to the use of influence and speed money. All the citizen feedback studies done so far have reaffirmed the willingness of customers to pay higher official fees than bribes provided services are more efficiently delivered.[7]

This is especially relevant to business enterprises that need to obtain documents, permits and authorisations on an urgent basis. Singapore, for example, is well known for innovatice applications of this approach. Specified time frames such as 24 or 48 hours are announced for getting certain services. In India, too, dual pricing has been tried out in some services such as telephone and cooking gas.

But, as noted above, the terms and conditions of the dual track's working needs to be carefully designed so that they are not exploited by interested parties to extract bribes on top of the increased fees. In the *"Tatkal"* Telephone case, there should be no ambiguity about the technical feasibility condition when customers are asked to pay a substantially higher amount.

The dual-track pricing approach merits attention because of its potential to reduce the pressure on citizens to pay speed money. It encourages the flow of speed money or at least a good part of it into public coffers.

In brief, dual track pricing should be viewed as a means to provide wider choices to customers and reduce the incentives and opportunities for corruption. However, it should not become a suitable tool for serving one set of customers at the cost of another.

5. Every service-provider or regulatory agency should widely disseminate information on its standards of service

It is a common attitude of our public agencies that they do not feel any obligation to inform and educate citizens on how to transact business with them efficiently. The time required for service delivery, the conditions and sequential steps to be met and remedies available in the event of unsatisfactory agency responses are usually unavailable. In contrast, standards for over 1,500 services offered by government agencies in the United States have been widely disseminated.

In the U.K., Citizen Charters have defined standards for most service-oriented departments of the government. The British Government's Competition and Service Utilities Act of 1992 provides new statutory powers for regulators to set and monitor standards for specified public services, help make customers aware of standards, provide for compensation when guaranteed standards are not met, improve the complaints procedure, and facilitate greater competition in the provision of water and sewerage services. In the process, it encourages citizens to demand greater accountability from public officials.

A serious problem in India is that the legislation governing most public utilities does not require the authorities to lay down measurable standards of service and ensure the proper dissemination of this information to the public. It is left to those in-charge of these organisations to specify standards, review and update them periodically and disseminate information as they deem fit.

As a result, there is considerable unevenness in the actions taken on this front by the responsible authorities. It will be a major step forward if service—providers are required by law to specify their standards of service and to make this information easily acessable to the public. Ready access to this information will strengthen the hands of the users of services to resist extortionary tendencies of public officials.

It is recommended that every public service—provider be required to take the following steps:

— Survey its customers to understand what problems they face in their transactions with the agency and identify the kinds of information that can minimise these problems.

— Define the standards which the agency will maintain in the provision of it's services and the conditions customers should fulfil in order to qualify for the services.

— Specify who can provide additional information or clarification if customers require such assistance.

— Announce the remedies and appeal procedures available if customers are dissatisfied.

— Display the above information and guidelines clearly in agency offices and disseminate the same widely and periodically to the public through the media and other forums.

Corrective Measures

1. Major Public utilities should appoint independent *Ombudsmen*

Corruption cases are today reported to the agencies them selves or to other bodies, such as the *Lok Ayukt*, which are part of the executive arm of the government. A recent development is the appointment of *ombudsmen* by the Reserve Bank of India with a mandate to investigate complaints about banking services in different geographical areas.

If the banks fail to comply with the decisions of the *ombudsmen*, there is provision for the R.B.I. to use its regulatory authority to direct banks to implement them. The same model should apply to all other public utilities. To begin with, an *ombudsmen* may be appointed for all the public utilities in a state if the total load is modest. Depending on the nature and extent of the complaints received and after periodical reviews, a state may decide to appoint additional *ombudsmen*.

2. Creating constitutionaly protected authority to entertain complaints about corruption

Some States have appointed "*Lok Ayukts*" and "*Lok Pals*" for this purpose. Experience has shown that this institutional mechanism has not been very effective. This mechanism will work only when it can act as a quasi-judicial authority, with citizens having the right to lodge complaints, lead evidence followed by public hearings and speaking orders, and directions to provide not only for the punishment of corrupt officials, but also award compensation for loss or injury suffered by the aggrieved.

This quasi-judicial authority will be comparable to the Election commission in terms of its independence. There should be one such authority in each State, and it's performance reviewed every two years. To minimise the politicisation of appointments, there should a panel nominated by the Chief Justice, Chairman of the State Consumer Protection Council and similar high level persons least vulnerable to political influence. This panel should identify suitable candidates to be appointed to the proposed commission.

NOTES & REFERENCES

1. M. Naim, 'Corruption Eruption', The Borwn Journal of World Affairs, Summer, 1995.
2. R. Klitgaard, Controlling Corruption, University of California Press, Berkeley, 1988.
3. Transparency International, National Integrity System: The T.I. Source Book, Berlin, 1996.
4. S.N. Sangita, 'Institutional Arrangement for Controlling Corruption in Public Life: Karnataka Experience', Indian Journal of Public Administration, Vol. XLI, No. 1, January-March, 1995, pp. 45-67.
5. S. Paul, A Report Card on Three Indian Cities, : A View from Below, Public Affairs, Centre, Bangalore, 1995.

   S. Paul, Public Services for the Urban Poor, Public Affairs Centre, Bangalore, 1995.

   S. Shekhar, Public Services and the Urban Poor: A Comparative Assessment Based on Citizen Feedback from Five Indian Cities, Public Affairs Centre, Bangalore, 1996.

6. R. Chapman & M. Hunt (eds.), Open Government, Croomhell, London, 1987.

7. S. Paul, 1995 (see No. 5 above).

28

INFORMATION BE A FUNDAMENTAL RIGHT

"It has been established that more the effort at secrecy the greater the chance of abuse of authority by the functionaries".[1]

The Shah Commission had good cause to make this general observation, which its three reports bear out. Ironically, only a couple of years later, the Chairman of the Press Council of India, a former and highly respected judge of the Supreme Court, Mr. Justice A.N. Sen, described the situation at a Seminar organised by the Gujarat Daily Newspapers Association on December 20, 1987 at Ahmedabad in graphic detail. He said:

> *"The major constraint on the freedom of the Press, as I see it, is the lack of a proper recognition of the right to information by the press. The right of information which is ancillary and incidental to the fundamental right of freedom of press ....*
>
> "Unfortunately, however, important information is at times sought to be withheld by the authority in power on the plea of the bar of the Official Secrets Act even in matters where the Act may not have any application at all, causing a great deal of harassment to the journalists and imposing improper curbs on the freedom of the press. In various places, regional newspapers have complained to me of the very great harassment they have to suffer in the matters of collection of

> information from the authority concerned. In some States, only particular officers in districts and towns are authorised to brief Press. The gentlemen so authorised in the districts are usually District Magistrates and the Superintendents of police. Journalists come from far away places to get particular information, and it so happens that on very many occasions these officers are not available and the journalist have to go back not only without getting the necessary information but also having incurred expenses and lost some very valuable time. Press Council. Of India had occasion to deal with complaints protesting against such harassment as a result of the power to give information being placed only in some select hands. It may be expedient on the part of any State Government to authorise only responsible persons for dissemination of information and news but the whole thing has to be so organised that information is not, in any circumstances witheld and the journalists in the matter of furnishing legitimate information may amount to undue interference with the freedom of the Press. I feel that appropriate legislative measures should be adopted in our country not only for the right of the press to information but also for proper implementation of this right."

Section 5 of the Official Secrets Act, 1923 is a replica of Section 2 of the British Official Secrets Act, 1911, a statute that was revised after two decades of agitation in Britain by the Secrets Act, 1989. But there is no sign of a serious effort to reform that law in India, let alone one to facilitate access to information.

The Congress (I)'s Election Manifesto for the general Election in 1991, said : "Freedom of information is another precious right. The Congress will make a law in this behalf". The promised law was never so much as proposed. There were also no moves for a dialogue with the opposition parties on the subject. They are no less culpable.

The National Front's Government was none too active in this sphere during the brief months it was in power in 1990. Its manifesto for 1991 said:" The National Front reaffirms its pledge to inscribe the people's right to information as a fundamental right in the Constitution. From this solemn pledge shall follow the National Front's commitment to replace the present Official Secrets Act by such legislation as shall protect confidentiality in matters of national security in conformity with the adherence to the principle of open government."

It is always open to the opposition in a parliamentary democracy—indeed, incumbent upon it—to urge Parliament to adopt its policies. No such bill was moved, however.

In this context, Secrecy in Government in India, Prof. Shriram Maheshwari recalled the moves towards "open government", which were made in the wake of the emergency".

The Janata Party made a special mention of promoting 'openness' in government in its manifesto of 1977. By way of fulfilling this commitment, the then Home Minister Charan Singh, constituted in 1977 a working group comprising of officials from the Cabinet Secretariat, the Ministry of Home Affairs and the Ministries of Finance and Defence to find if the Official Secrets Act, framed in 1923, could be modified so as to enable greater dissemination of information to the public. The working group laboured for months to reiterate the soundeness of retaining without change or abridgement the statute of 1923.

It is argued that there was nothing in the Official Secrets Act, 1923 which stood in the way of flow of necessary information to the public. The very composition of the working group ordained the kind of verdict which ultimately emanated from it. Secrecy is a well-known device which bureaucracy presses into service to strengthen its power position and to minimise criticism of its action.

Bureaucracy revels in secrecy. The 'no change' recommendation made by the working group serves only to confirm that ancient truth. Indeed, any other kind of recommendation would have been a surprise."[2]

On August 30, 1978, Mr. Jyotirmoy Basu asked whether the Government 'would bring an Act to guarantee access to all official documents other than the highly sensitive genuine ones dealing with national security.?

The Government's answer was that, 'The provisions of the Official Secrets Act, 1923 are designed primarily to safeguard national security and not to prohibit legitimate access to official documents and, therefore, no legislation to guarantee access to official documents, other than those dealing with national security, is considered necessary."[3]

On June 4, 1979, it was announced by the government of India that a working group which reviewed the Act had come to the conclusion that it needed no amendment as, in its view, it did not impose the flow of information to the people. The group comprised exclusively of officials from the Cabinet Secretariat and the Ministries of Home, Defence and Finance. The States, predictably, endorsed their views. Thus, ended the efforts of the Janata Government.

On Government 17, 1987, the Minister of State for Internal Security, Mr. P. Chidambaram, informed the Rajya Sabha that amendments to the Act were at an 'advanced' stage of preparation and a bill incorporating them would be brought before parliament 'as soon as possible'. The Congress Government did not propose any such legislation in the remaining two years of its tenure in office.

On December 20, 1989, President R. Venkataraman said in his address to the joint session of Parliament, that 'a participating democracy required an enlightened and informed electorate. An open Government functioning in full public view will minimise wrong doing. The Official Secrets Act will be suitably amended so that people have increased access to information. Legislative measures will be taken to have the right to information enshrined in the Constitution and to ensure free flow of information to the people'.

Two distinct, though related, pledges were made, viz. amendment of the Act in order to remove the impediments in the exercise of the right to know, and recognition of that right by constitutional amendment.

A 25-member Committee, headed by Mr. B.S. Lali, Joint Secretary in the Union Home Ministry, was set up. It was reported to have recommended appropriate amendments and a guarantee of the right. Askari H. Zaidi, a correspondent for the Times of India, noted :

> "The Lali Committee has recommended, among other things, that barring a few sensitive areas like defence, intelligence and some financial matters, all other areas should be opened to public scrutiny which is the hallmark of democracy.

"The ministry is supposed to prepare a note based on the recommendations of the committee which will be presented for cabinet approval. Then the fate of the report would depend on the political will of the government. Both the National Front and the ruling Congress have promised right to information in their election manifestoes. The Congress manifesto says : "Freedom of information is another precious right. The Congress will make a law in this behalf."

"Unlike the present system, where even highly secret information having bearing on national security is leaked and most innocuous information is hidden from citizens, the Committee has recommended strengthening of the mechanism to protect leakage of information on the areas vital for the country's security and integrity.

"But it says that these areas should be limited in number so that all other spheres of government functioning could be made open to citizens. On payment of a nominal fee, ordinary people should be allowed access to government documents except those classified as vital, report says.

"In case the government seeks to withhold certain information to a citizen on the pretext that it may cause injury to public interest, a pretext notice too often under the system, the Lali Committee report makes it mandatory for the government to specify how a certain information would be injurious to public interest. The committee has also recommended setting up of a tribunal type body".[4]

On the other hand, *The Hindu's* special correspondent reported that a Special Task Force had been set up "over one and a half years ago, on the subject, submitted its report" some time last week "and had recommended sweeping changes in the laws on five counts."[5] The correspondent proceeded to give details :

"These are an enactment of a statute on freedom of information, modification in the totality outdated Official Secrets Act, 1923: a close and comprehensive look at the issues relating to personal privacy, a more purposeful information dissemination system and appropriate changes in the related areas of record-keeping and archives.

"Sources said the Union Government has circulated copies of the two-volume report to the Ministries of Home, Defence and Information and Broadcasting for their comments on the various issues raised by the Task Force. The ministries are expected to submit their response to the recommendations which specific reference to their bearing on the security and other related matters latest by December 19.

"On receipt of the comments from the various ministries, the Union Government is expected to process them and forward it to the Law Ministry for further consideration. 'The process might take a few months. The ultimate result might fall far short of expectations. But the commitment of the government on this issue can no longer be doubted,' said an official who is engaged in the exercise.

"Sources said there should not be any major hurdles in the acceptance of majority of the recommendations of the Task Force, as its report was the outcome of the inputs from the major ministries under the Union Government. The Task Force, though headed by a special Secretary in the Union Home Ministry, had members from all the important ministries of the Government.

"The first volume of the Task Force report primarily deals with the status report in India on freedom of information and records the experience of various advanced countries on the subject. Examples from the European Economic Community (EEC) member countries, United States of America, United Kingdom, Germany and Japan have been quoted.

"The second volume of the report deals with the recommendations of the Task Force which seeks to make freedom of information a reality in India within the security framework of the country. There is emphasis on the need for a comprehensive mechanism for dissemination of 'purposeful' information.

"Some of the issues discussed in the report give an idea of the changes desired to realise the goal of 'freedom of information'. For instance, there is reference to a legislation which would make it obligatory for the government to give information to any citizen on demand within a minimum period of one week to a maximum of one month.

"The report also makes reference to the legislation in the United States under which all government documents are deemed to be declassified or made open to public with a lapse of 12 years from the time of their coming into existence. Of course, there is an amendment to the legislation which provides for making certain categories of information or documents to be inaccessible in the national interest.

"The Task Force has dealt with issue of granting immunity to citizens from disclosing the source of information. Under the present legal frame-work, citizens in India have no immunity protection in the court of law. Such immunity, if granted, would be a boon to journalists".

Four years have rolled by since without the legislation over which considerable public time and money had been spent. In the light of these reports by responsible correspondents, it is clear that the sole obstacle to reform is lack of political will. The civil servants are agreeable and, more so, the soldiers. Lt. Gen. Depinder Singh made a powerful plea for reform of the Act.[6] In his Foreword to the book, Field Marshall Sam Manekshaw urged greater facilities for Press coverage of "the theatre of operations"[7].

The Government's position was made plain in the Rajya Sabha on March 16, 1994 by the Union Home Minister, Mr. S.B. Chavan, in reply to an unstarred question. 'Some suggestions/ recommendations for amending the Official Secrets Act, 1923 have been received. At present, there is no proposal to amend the Act".[8]

A report entitled 'Freedom of Information and Expression in India', published in October 1990 by Article 191, The International Centre on Censorship London noted : 'Actual applications of the Officials Secrets Act well demonstrate its potential for abuse'. Faced by criticism of the Narmada dam, which required the relocation of tens of thousands of indigenous people, the Gujarat government simply declared the whole dam area to be off limits under Section 3 of the Official Secrets Act.

It, thus, became impossible for journalists and activists to learn what was happening at the construction sites. When 8,000 people demonstrated in the area in January 1989, 5000 were arrested, including journalists, and 18 were actually charged. Only after sustained and intense pressure from activist groups was the Act's application to the area lifted in March, 1989.

'In 1986 several members of the Bhopal Information and Action Group were arrested under Section 5 of the Act for taking notes in an open and public meeting of scientists and doctors concerning the medical measures that should be taken for the rehabilitation of the Bhopal gas victims. The government has still declined to disclose information concerning the way in which the settlement of monetary damages for victims was reached".

On December 13, 1994, the Supreme Court ordered the Madhya Pradesh Government to publish the Jayant Patil Committee's Report on the Sardar Sarovar Project, Belatedly, on December 16, 1994, the Government of India agreed to deposit into Parliament's library the Gyan Prakash Report entitled 'Preliminary administrative inquiry into the sugar shortage 1993-94' and that as 'a precedent for the future' according to Mr. V.C. Shukla, the Minister for Parliamentary Affairs. The Report was not laid on the Parliament and, thus, not published for the nation.

Abuses in the States are common. A circular of October 30, 1995 issued by the Punjab Government to all senior civil servants stated : 'The Chief Minister has desired that except with his prior approval, no administrative secretary or head of department should issue any statement on Government policy. These instructions should be complied with immediately'.

As the correspondent Ms. Aunohita Mojumdar noted : 'This, in effect, means that there is to be no interaction between the press and bureaucrats . . . .'[9] It look some time for the circular to become known to the press.

A similar edict was issued by the Government of Tamil Nadu in 1981 as the *Indian Express* reported (June 16, 1981). It said :

> 'Firstly, the government instructed the city police control room not to give any information to the press. Since April 22 when the city police revolted and indulged in an orgy of violence, the control room has become silent.
>
> 'The police control room advises newsmen to talk to the public relations officer for any information.
>
> Secondly, instructions were given to all the police stations and senior police officers not to talk to reporters.
>
> "Then the government opened a control room at the Circuit House Annexe manned by the personnel of the Information Department. It was from this control room that the government doles out information to the Press about the daily law and order situation."
>
> "Since the information given out to the press at these official briefings was found too inadequate, the reports used to get details about incidents of violence and arson from hospital and civic sources."

Vasant Sathe criticised the Tamil Nadu Government's order restraining its officials and employees from furnishing any information to the Press, AIR, Doordarshan. The Minister for Information and Broadcasting said that the Central Government believed that officials must share information fully with the Press to prevent misunderstanding on any issue.

Such orders are obviously unconstitutional. In *Pells vs. Procunier 4174 s. 817 (1974)*, Justice William O. Douglas asked :

> 'Could the government deny the Press access to all public institutions and prohibit interviews by all government employees? Could it find constitutional footing by expanding the ban to deny access to everyone?" Justice William Doughlas' questions were obviously rhetorical. He was emphatically denying the

> government's right to impose a ban on information by simply asking public servants not to give any information to their masters, the public through their surrogates, the Press.

He was aware of this possibility though he considered it most unlikely in the United States. But the potential remained:

> 'A state might decide that criticism of it's affairs could be reduced by prohibiting all its employees from discussing governmental operations in interviews with the media, leaving criticism of the state to those with the time, energy, ability and inclination to communicate through the mails.'

The Supreme Court of India has ruled more than once in the last two decades that the citizen's right to know flows directly from this fundamental right to freedom of speech and expression guaranteed in Article 19(11)(a) of the Constitution. With this constitutional precedent, the provisions of the Official Secrets Act, 1923 would not survive. In the *State of U.P. vs. Raj Narain A.I.R. 1975 S.C. 865,* Mr. Justice K.K. Mathew said :

> "The people of this country have a right to know every public act, everything that is done in a public way, by these public functionaries. They are entitled to know the particulars of every public transaction in all its hearings. The right to know, which is derived from the concept of speech, though not absolute, is a factor which should make one wary, when secrecy is claimed for transactions which can, at any rate, have no repercussions on public security".

In *Maneka Gandhi vs. Union of India, AIR 1978 S.C. 597,* Mr. Justice P.N. Bhagwati said that 'freedom of speech and expression carries with it the right to gather information'. In the famous High Court Judge's case, *S.P. Gupta vs. Union of India A.I.R. 1981 S.C. 149,* the Court struck a powerful blow for open government. In interpreted Section 123 and 162 of the Evidence Act to restrict severely the area of privileged secrecy and asserted the power of judicial review in deciding between competing claims of privileges against disclosure and the public interest in the disclosure.

The government test was whether the public interest would be harmed by the disclosure, Mr. Justice Bhagwati said : 'The concept of an open government is the direct emanation from the right to know which seems to be implicit in the right of free speech and expression guaranteed under Article 19(1)(a)'.

More recently, the right to know was affirmed in *Secretary, Ministry of Information and Broadcasting vs. Cricket Association of Bengal and others. (1995) 2 SCC 161.*

It is not widely known, although it should be, that a freedom of Information Act exists already in an embryonic form in a colonial statute which is a masterpiece of its kind. This is the Indian Evidence Act, 1872. Section 74 defines public documents as (1) documents forming the act or records of the acts (i) of the sovereign authority, (ii) of public officers, legislative, judicial and executive, of any part of India or of the Commonwealth, or of a foreign country, and (2) public records kept in any state of private documents.

Section 75 says that 'all other documents are private'.

Next comes the important Section 76. It reads : 'Every public officer having the custody of a public document, which any person has a right to inspect, shall give that person on demand a copy of it on payment of the legal fees, therefore, together with a certificate written at the foot of such copy that it is true copy of such document and such copies so certified copies'.

The italicised words are crucial—'*which any person has a right to inspect*'. Who decides whether the person concerned has a right or not? The custodian of the document, the government or the bureaucrat? The person aggrieved by a refusal can, of course, take the government to court. It will be for the court to decide whether he has 'a right to inspect' or not. A simple *writ of mandamus* is all that is required. A civil suit also lies.

The court will be able to construe Section 76. So far, there are few decided cases on it. Judicial creativity has a fine opportunity to express itself here.

But, of course, this statute risks being curtailed by a later one, the Act of 1923. Therefore, a reform of the Secrets Act is imperative. It is important to bear in mind it's background in order to appreciate its provisions. Structures on its British model not only have direct relevance but added force. In India, the politician in power decides on whether or not to prosecute; in Britain, the Attorney General alone makes the decision.

As Lord Shawcross pointed out in a letter to The Times (November 19, 1970), 'Although the Attorney General is a political appointee, his actions as Attorney General and the way in which he exercises his discretion are entirely non-political. I know of no instance (since the Campbell case) in which the Cabinet has been called upon to decide whether or not a prosecution should take any such decision on political grounds.' In India, the executive controls the launching and, as recent experience shows, even the withdrawal of prosecutions.

The background of the Official Secrets Act, 1923 shows that replication of British Law on the subject was a practice faithfully followed over the years. An analysis of its provisions confirms this. It is necessary intrinsically for two reasons. First, to know what the law is and, next, to consider its effect on freedom of the Press and it's validity in the light of the provisions of the Constitution. Debates in Britain on comparable provisions in the law are relevant in so far as they throw light on the scope of the provisions in our statute.

The Background

No sooner had Britain passed it's first Official Secrets Act in 1889, than the Indian Official Secrets Act was passed by the Imperial Legislative Assembly, the same year. Section 5 of the British statute provided that if 'the legislatures of any British possession' made provisions which appeared to the Crown 'to be of the like effect of those contained in this Act' the crown could by Order in Council suspend the operation of the British statute in that colony.

Already, by then, the Indian Press had asserted it's right to reveal information of public interest even if it was classified as secret. In October 1889, the Amrit Bazar Patrika published the full text of a memorandum by the Foreign Secretary Sir H.M. Durand dated May 6, 1888 , opposing the British Resident in Kashmir Mr. Plowden's proposal to annex Gilgit. The paper teasingly wrote that the Viceroy Lord Lansdowne would find the original of the document in the Foreign Office.[10]

The publication was used as a pretext for a secrets law. Four years later, the Viceroy, Lord Curzon, set about improving the Act. The result was the Indian Official Secrets (Amendment) Act, 1904. It was trenchantly criticised in the Imperial Legislative Assembly by Gopal Krishan Gokhale, Asuthosh Mukherjee and others whose comments have a strong contemporary relevance.

Gokhale's reaction was: 'The proper and only remedy worthy of the British Government is not to gag newspapers as proposed in this Bill but to discourage the issue of confidential circulars. . . . The criticism of the Indian Press is the only outward check operating continuously upon the conduct of a bureaucracy possessing absolute and uncontrolled power'.

Asuthosh Mukherjee remarked: 'A journalist may obtain most innocently, important information relating to civil affairs; before he can publish it, he must satisfy himself that it will not be treated as an official secret under this Act; in other words, that it will not be regarded as of such a confidential nature that the public interest would suffer by its disclosure.

So far as I know, he has no means of ascertaining this with any degree of certainty, and he must either face the risk of a prosecution—be the prosecution ultimately successful—or, unsuccessful what is more within the range of probabilities, he will think it safer to leave the subject alone.

Meanwhile, in 1911, the British Parliament passed the Official Secrets Act, 1911 which held sway till 1989. Like it's predecessor of 1889, Section 11 of this Act gave the colonies the option either to legislate not 'like effect' or be governed by the British Act. It was amended in 1920 in light of experience gained in World War-I.

The Indian Official Secrets Act, 1923, as it was originally called, was a repliça of the British Acts of 1911 and 1923. Like them, it is directed against two distinct acts : espionage (section 3) and unauthorised communication of information to outsiders (section 5)

A great jurist, Sir Hari Singh Gour, attacked it's provisions in the Central Legislative Assembly : 'Your provisions are so wide that you will have no difficulty whatever in running in anybody who peeps into an office for the purpose of making some enquiry, it may be entirely innocent, enquiry as to when there is going to be, the next meeting of the Assembly or whether a certain report on the census of India has come out and what is the population of India recorded in that period'.[11] The Act of 1923 is still in force, however, as amended by Act 24 of 1967.

Analysis of the Official Secrets Act, 1923

The Act deals with espionage as well as the unauthorised disclosure of official information to outsiders. Only the latter part is discussed in this chapter since its aim is to consider primarily the impact of this statute on the right to information.

In this context, the most important provision is Section 5 of the Act which is virtually a replica of the infamous Section 2 of the British Act of 1911, as amended by the Act of 1920. The texts of the two provisions are set out herein below to facilitate comparison :

Section 2 of the British Act of 1911 (as amended) :

"(1) If any person having in his possession or control any secret official code word, or password, or any sketch, plan, model, article, note, document or information which relates to or is used in a prohibited place of anything in such a place or which has been made or obtained in contravention of this Act, or which has been entrusted in confidence to him by any person holding office under Her Majesty or which he has obtained or to which he has had access owing to his position as a person who holds or has held office under Her Majesty, or as a person who holds or has held a contract made on behalf of Her Majesty or as a person who is or has been employed under a person who holds or has held such an office or contract—

"(a) communicates the code word, password, sketch, plan model, note, document, or information to any person, other than a person to whom he is authorised to communicate it, or a person to whom it is in the interest of the State his duty communicate it; or

"(aa) uses the information in his possession for the benefit of any foreign Power or in any other manner prejudicial to the safety or interests of the State.

"(b) retains the sketch, plan, model, article note, or document in his possession or control when he has no right to retain or when it is contrary to his duty to retain it, or fails to comply with all directions issued by lawful authority with regard to the return or disposal thereof; or

"(c) fails to take reasonable care of, or so conducts himself as to endanger the safety of the sketch, plan, model article, note, document, secret official code or password of information;

that person shall be guilty of a misdemeanour.

"(1A) If any person having in his possession or control any sketch, plan, model, article, note, document, or information which relates to munitions of war, communicates it directly or indirectly to any foreign power, or in any other manner prejudicial to the safety or interests of the State, that person shall be guilty of a misdemeanour.

"(2) If any person receives any secret official code word, or password, or sketch, plan, model, article, note, document, or information, knowing or having reasonable ground to believe, at the time when he receives it, that the code word, password, sketch, plan, model article, note, document, or information is communicated to him in contravention of this Act, he shall be guilty of a misdemeanour, unless he proves that the communication to him of the code word, password, sketch, plan, model article, note, document or information was contrary to his desire."

Its Indian replica, Section 5 reads thus :

(1) If any person having in his possession or control any secret official code or password or any sketch, plan, model, article, note, document or information which relates to anything in such a place, or which is likely to assist, directly or indirectly, an enemy or which relates to a matter the disclosure of which is likely to affect the sovereignty and integrity of India, the security of this Act; or which has been entrusted in confidence to him by any person holding office under Government, or which he has obtained or to which he has had access owing to his position as a person who holds or has held a contract made on behalf of Government, or as a person who is or has been employed under a person who holds or has held such an office or contract—

"(a) wilfully communicates the code or password, sketch, plan, model, article, note, document or information to any person other than a person to whom he authorised to communicate it, or a Court of Justice or a person to whom it is, in the interests of the State, his duty to communicate it; or

"(b) uses the information in his possession for the benefit of any foreign power or in any other manner prejudicial to the safety of the State; or

"(c) retains the sketch, plan, model, article, note or document in his possession or control when it is contrary when he has no right to retain it, or when it is contrary to his duty to retain it, or wilfully fails to comply with all directions issued by lawful authority with all directions issued by lawful authority with regard to the return or disposal thereof; or

"(d) fails to take reasonable care of, or so conducts himself as to endanger the safety of, the sketch, plan, model, article, note, document, secret official code or password or information; he shall be guilty of an offence under this section.

"(2) If any person voluntarily receives any secret official code or passwords or any sketch, plan, model, article, note, document or information knowing or having reasonable ground to believe, at the time when he receives it, that the code, password, sketch, plan, model, article, note, document or information is communication in contravention of this Act, he shall be guilty of an offence under this section.

"(3) If any person having in his possession or control any sketch, plan, model, article note, document or information, which relates to munitions of war, communicates it, directly or indirectly, to safety or interests of the State, he shall be guilty of an offence under this section.

"(4) A person guilty of an offence under this Section shall be punishable with imprisonment for a term which may extend to three years, or with fine, or with both."

A comparison of Section 5 of the Indian Act with Section 2 of the British Act shows the following points of departure:

(1) The words in Section 5(1) referring to "information", etc. and "or which is likely to assist, directly or indirectly, an enemy or which is likely to affect the sovereignty and integrity of India, the security of the State or friendly relations with foreign States" were inserted by the Amending Act 24 of 1967. The expression "friendly relation with foreign States" is particularly liable to be abused to prevent disclosure which expose mistakes in the conduct of foreign policy by the regime of the day.

(2) Use of the word "wilfully" in clause (a) of Section 5(1) to qualify communication of information *is one of the few welcome departures from the British Act* as is the exception "or a court of justice" in the same clause. However, the clause was drafted in light of Sections 123 and 124 of the Evidence Act, 1873 on privilege as to evidence relating to the affairs of State and official communications. In recent years, the Supreme Court has narrowed the scope of the privilege.

(3) Clause (b) refers only to "the *safety* of the State" whereas Clause (aa) of Section 2 of the British Act refers also to "*the interests* of the State".

(4) *Clause (d) of Section 5(1) is not found in the British Act.* It is vaguely worded. A person who has in his "possession or control" any "information" or document of the kind mentioned in the provision and "fails to take reasonable care of it" or "so conducts himself as to endanger the safety" thereof will be guilty of an offence.

(5) Section 5 (3) is an exact replica of Section 2(1A) of the British Act. The definition of "munitions of War" in Section 2(5) of our Act is identical to that in Section 12 of the British Act. It is wide enough to include any ship or aircraft "intended or adopted for use in War". To take a concrete case: if a person who has any "information" about the Bofors gun communicates it, "directly or indirectly" in a manner prejudicial to the "interests of the state", he will be guilty of an offence.

(6) The remaining parts of Section 5 and Section 2 are identical. The former retains all the latter's features which have been authoritatively criticised in Britain in recent decades—its "catch all quality", its self-serving nature for the men in power, and the like. It is relevant in this context to note that under Section 8 of the British Act of 1911, a prosecution for an offence under the Act can be instituted only by, or with the consent of the Attorney General who it is well settled, acts with his own discretion in such cases. Under Section 13(3) of the Indian statute, prosecution can be launched only with the sanction of "the appropriate Government" or some officer authorised by it. In relation to any offence under Section 5 "not connected with a prohibited place or with a foreign power", it is "the State Government" which is "the appropriate Government".

Section 14 empowers the court to order trial in camera on

an application by the prosecution "but the passing of sentence shall in any case take place in public".

Section 15 refers to offences by companies. It makes "every person" in "charge of, and was responsible to, the company for the conduct" of its business liable unless he proves absence of knowledge or exercise of "due diligence to prevent the commission of such offence". Since most dailies and periodicals are owned by limited companies, Section 15 would apply to the staff, editorial and managerial, of the company which is concerned with the actual publication of the impugned matter.

On the crucial and fundamentally important question of the scope of judicial review, Section 5 is identical to Section 2 . Is it open to one charged with the offence to contend that he communicated the information or document 'to a person to whom it is, in the interests of the State, his duty to communicate it' construing the expression "the interests of the State" to mean the interests of the nation, as distinct from those of the men in power?

It is pertinent to recall the views expressed by the two Press Commissions, the Press Council of India, and some judicial precedents.

In 1948, the Press Laws Enquiry Committee said: "We are unable to accept the contention that the application of this Act should be confined to a national emergency or war emergency, and that the scope of the definition of document, information, etc. in Section 5 should be narrowed down to the documents or information likely to imperil public safety in times of emergency .... We have no doubt that the Government must be the sole judge in this matter; and we trust that popular democratic government in India would utilise the provisions of this Act only in case of genuine necessity and in the large interests of the State and the public".

Two members, Mr. S.A. Brelvi and Mr. Kasturi Srinivasan, dissented and opined that "the application of the Act must be confined, as the recent Geneva Conference on freedom of information has recommended, only to matters which must remain secret in the interests of national safety."

The AINEC initially took a bold stand but retreated from it

later. It argued in its memorandum to this Committee that "while the Press cannot claim any right to publish information likely to be useful to the enemy in times of war and confidential government information likely to imperil public safety in times of emergency, it cannot accept the claim that every circular or note or instructions becomes a prohibited secret because it is marked 'secret and confidential'.

The Press claims the right to publish Confidential Government information when publication is in the interest of the public and the two limitations mentioned above do not apply. Indeed it would be a matter of professional honour and distinction for a newspaper to expose secret moves when public interests justify such exposure'.

Only a few years later, the AINEC changed its position when the First Press Commission was appointed in 1952. 'In view of the international tensions and consequent need for ensuring that secret policies are not divulged, they did not recommend modification of the provisions of the Act'. (Para 1046 of the Press Commission's Report. It noted that the AINEC had 'modified' it's opinion).

The Commission reported in 1954 that 'in view of the eminently reasonable manner in which the Act is being administered we refrain from making any recommendation for an amendment of the Act'.

Eighteen years later, in 1982, the Second Press Commission opined that 'one of the chief obstacles to the free flow of legitimate information to the people is the existence of certain provisions in the official Secrets Act, 1923' (para 47). It mentioned in particular Section 5 which, in its view, 'has a chilling effect on the freedom of the press'.

It added that : 'there can be no doubt that the Section 5 as it stands can prevent any information about that any affairs of Government being disclosed to the public and there widespread public opinion in the country that the Section has to be modified or replaced and substituted by a more liberal one' (para 50). However, it is important to note that in its view '*mens rea* (the guilty mind) is a necessary ingredient of an offence under the Act' (para 49).

The Commission urged the repeal of Section 5, instead of it's amendment, and it's substitute by provisions which would meet both the needs of 'national security and other vital interests of the State as well as the right of the people to know the affairs of the State affecting them' (para 52).

The Press Council of India commissioned a study by the late Dr. S.N. Jain jointly with the Indian Law Institute of which he was Director, and adopted a draft of Section 5 to replace the existing provision.

The draft embodies this very essential defence: 'Nothing shall be an offence under the Section if it predominantly and substantially subserves public interest unless the communication or use of the 'official secret' is made for the benefit of any foreign power or in any manner prejudicial to the safety of the state.'[12]

In Britain, it came to be universally recognised by the early '70s that Section 2 of the Act of 1911 was wholly inappropriate in a democracy. In 1971, the Sunday Telegraph, it's editor and two others along the chain of communication were prosecuted when the paper published a confidential assessment of the situation in Nigeria written by the Advisor to the Britain High Commission in Lagos. They were all acquitted in February, 1971.

In the course of his summing up, Mr. Justice Caulfied made the memorable remark that Section 2 should be 'pensioned off' soon, there were demands for its repeal. The British Government adopted the classic remedy of appointing a Committee that year. It was headed by Lord Franks and comprised distinguished civil servants, diplomats, MPs and a leading CQC Brian Neill (Departmental Committee on Section 2 of the committee (Cmnd. 5104; HMSO London).

The Franks Report, submitted in August 1972 condemned Section 2 in unequivocal terms :'The main offence which Section 2 creates is the unauthorised Communication of official information (including documents) by a Crown servant. The Leading characteristic of this offence is its catch-all quality. It catches all official documents and information. It makes no distinction of kind, and no distinctions of degree.

All Information which a Crown servant learns in the course of his duty is 'official' for the purposes of Section 2, whatever it's nature, whatever it's importance, whatever it's original source. A blanket is thrown over everything, nothing escapes. The Section catches all Crown servants as well as all official information.'

Correspondingly, anyone, whether a newsman or lay person, who receives such information is liable to punishment once it is proved that he either actually knew or had reasonable ground to believe that the information was communicated to breach of the Act. Both the giver and the receiver of the information are liable to imprisonment for a term which may extend to three years.

There is an additional issue to which the Franks Committee drew pointed attention : 'Ministers are, in effect, self-authorising. They decide for themselves what to reveal. Senior civil servants exercise a considerable degree of personal judgement in deciding what disclosures of official information they may properly make and to whom'.

Such communication is regarded as 'authorised' communication. The result is that while official leaks, a fertile source of disinformation, are protected, their exposure by unravelling the whole truth is forbidden. Lord Devlin's censure of Section 2 is very apt : 'It installs as the judges of what ought to be revealed men whose interests it is to conceal.'

Two English decisions bear directly on the issue of judicial review. One decided by the House of Lords, is *Chandler vs. Director of Public Prosecutions (1964) A.C. 763* Six members of the Committee of 100, part of the Campaign for Nuclear Disarmament, were convicted under the Act for organising a sit-in at an airfield.

Bertrand Russell led the defence witnesses to explain the purpose of the campaign, to make known the horrors of nuclear warfare. The evidence was excluded as being irrelevant. The defence that aircraft armed with nuclear bombs were not 'in the interests of the State' was rejected. But the expression divided the lords.

Lord Reid warned about 'what can happen if you personify and almost deify the State'. He said the state 'does not mean the government or the executive' and it cannot have 'the last word' about what is or is not in the public interest. Lord Devlin took a similar view.

'The fact to be proved is the existence of a purpose prejudicial to the State—not a purpose which 'appears to the Crown' to be prejudicial to the State'. Lord Radcliffe and Pearce differed while Lord Hodson avoided the issue.

Prof. Harry Street and other jurists criticised the Lords for 'the dangerous doctrine that whatever is Crown policy is necessarily in the interests of the State'. Though Lords Reid and Devlin had clearly rejected the doctrine, they upheld the conviction because they rejected the defence on the grounds immobilising an airfield for hours cannot be in public interest.

However, official deception can make disclosure of an official document an act 'in the interests of the State' albeit not in those of the Government. A high authority on constitutional law, Prof. H.W.R. Wade, testified at the Ponting trial that if a civil servant was convinced of deception by the ministers it 'might be in the public interest for him to give his information direct to parliament' as is done by accounting officers. 'For, the Government of the country could not be run as it does now if Parliament was consistently fed with information.

In the case of Mr. Clive Ponting, a senior official of the Ministry of Defence, the trial judge, Mr. Justice Mc. Cowan, in his summing up to the jury interpreted the words 'in the interest of the State' to mean 'the policies laid down by those recognised organs of Government and authority.'[13]

The jury rejected the interpretation and brought a verdict of 'not guilty'. In the House of Lords, Lord Denning welcomed the verdict and criticised the Judge's interpretation. In his view, the words mean 'the interests of the country or realm.'[14]

In the changed climate of opinion, the views expressed by Lords Reid and Devlin are likely to prevail should the issue be decided today. The following extracts from their rulings delivered a quarter century ago are, therefore, relevant. Lord Reid said :

> "Next comes the question of what is meant by the safety or interests of the State. 'State' is not an easy

> word. It does not mean the Government or the Executive. '*L'Etat c'est moi*' was a shrewd remark, but can hardly have been intended as a definition even in the France of the time.

And I do not think it means islands. Again, we have seen only too clearly in some other countries what can happen if you personify and almost deify the State. Perhaps the country or the realm are as good synonyms as one can find and I would be prepared to accept organised community as coming as near to a definition as one can get.

"Who, then, is to determine what is and what is not prejudicial to the safety and interests of the State? The question more frequently arises as to what is or is not in the public interest. I do not subscribe to the view that the Government or a Minister must always or even as a general rule have the last word. But here we are dealing with a very special matter interfering with a prohibited place which Wethersfied was'.

The titled the decision against the accused. Lord Devlin said:

> "The fact to be proved is the existence of a purpose prejudicial to the State—not a purpose which 'appears to the Crown' to be prejudicial to the State. Words of that sort could have been written into the statute. In emergency legislation they frequently are. Inexceptional cases they can be implied : *Liversidge vs. Anderson*. But there has been no suggestion that they are to be implied into this statute. Their place cannot be filed by common law. There is no rule of common law that whenever questions of national security are considered by any court for any purpose, it is what the Crown thinks to be necessary or expedient in fact. If there were, the reasoning in *Liversidge vs. Anderson* would, in effect, be part of common law instead of the exigencies of an emergency regulation.

"Consequently, the Crown's opinion as to what is or not prejudicial in this case is just as inadmissible as the appellant's. The Crown's evidence about what its interests are is an entirely different matter. They can be proved by an officer of the

Crown wherever it may be necessary to do so. In a case like the present, it may be presumed that it is contrary to the interests of the Crown to have one of its airfields immobilised just as it may be presumed that it is contrary to the interest of an industrialists to have his factory immoblised. The thing speaks for itself, as the Attorney General submitted. But the presumption is not irrebuttable. Men can exaggerate the extent of their interests and so can the Crown.

The servants of the Crown, like other men animated by the highest motives, are capable of formulating a policy *ad hoc* so as to prevent the citizen from doing something that the Crown does not want him to do. It is the duty of the courts to be as alert now as they always been to prevent abuse of the prerogative. But in the present case there is nothing at all to suggest that the Crown's interest in the proper operation of its airfields is not what it may naturally be presumed to be or that it was exaggerating the perils of interference with their effectiveness."

In July 1978, the British Government published a White Paper on "Reform of Section 2 the Official Secrets Act 1911" (Cmnd. 7285) followed by another, in June 1988 with the same title (Cm. 408). It divided offences relating to the disclosure of secrets into two categories. One was the absolute category where disclosure itself is an offence; for instance, information supplied in confidence by another government.

The defence of 'serious injury' to the nation, recommended by the Frank's Report, was rejected; so was one of revealing wrong doing. In the other category, proof of harm was necessary, but proof of public interest was not relevant. The upshot was that the Official Secrets Act, 1989, which is an advance on the previous law, falls short of what is desired in a modern democracy.

It studiously omits the defence of 'public interest' in the disclosure. The White Paper of 1988 had said that motives are relevant only in sentencing. The offence itself turns 'on the nature and degree of the harm which their acts may cause' The new element of 'damage', thus, introduced, is applied in different ways.

Even in the clime of 1972, the Frank's Report had recommended that 'the citizen should have the defence that he did not know, and had no reason to believe that disclosure of the document might cause serious injury to the interest of the nation, 'as distinct from damage simpliciter.

A devastating critique of the White Paper was made by Richard Shephered in an article in The Times (London) of July 18, 1988 entitled, Secrets : Freedom at risk. He pointed out that 'revealing iniquity would be no defence' and 'the possible benefit to the public interest could not be argued'.

The criticism was ignored and the Official Secrets Act, 1989 became law. It covers disclosure of information concerning security or intelligence, defence (which, however, is precisely defined in Section 2); international relations (including relations with international organisations); and crime investigation (also precisely defined). Section 5(2) makes it an offence for a person into whose possession has come such information or document to disclose it without lawful authority 'knowing or having reason to believe that it is protected against disclosure by the Act'.

Note that mere unauthorised receipt of an official secret is no offence unless the receiver, in turn, discloses it. The prosecution must prove that the disclosure was 'damaging' and was made in the knowledge or with 'reasonable cause to believe' that it would have that effect. The offence by the original communicator of the official secret is open to the same defence.

As Geoffrey Robertson, Q.C., pointed out, the defence that 'the benefit of revelation outweighted any damage which might be caused by it' is denied by the law. For example, under it the Hindu would have been liable to prosecution for publishing the Bofors documents.

Mark his word :'disclosure of a public scandal— such as corruption in naval procurement ... will be a criminal offence if it is 'damaging' as defined by the Act the virtue of the disclosure and the social value of its consequences will be irrelevant.'[15] Publication of the same information abroad was no defence, either.

Revelations about any aspect of intelligence work by persons engaged or formerly engaged in it are absolute offences. Information obtained by telephone tapping or burglaries authorised by the Home Secretary's warrant is protected absolutely. 'It will not only be an offence to blow the whistle, but even in some cases to hear it.'

After this Act became law in the U.K., the Press Council of India (PCI), now headed by Justice R.S. Sarkaria, did the incredible: It back-tracked on its own draft of 1982 and propounded, a new one in 1990 based on its own draft of 1989. It said that 'fresh thinking was initiated *in the matter in 1989 with official support*.[16] It's recommendations were communicated to the Government of India in August 1990.

It urged the repeal of the Act of 1923 and the enactment of a Freedom of Information Act making 'privacy' a ground of exemption. It said that 'a constitutional amendment incorporating the right to information is not absolutely necessary at this stage, as this been upheld by the Supreme Court to be implicit in Article 19(1) (a). However, such an amendment can be made at a later stage to make explicit in Article'.

The PCI proposed new draft amendments as Section 5, 5A, and 5B of the Act of 1923 which were far worse than the PCI's own draft of 1982. The defence of the public interest, ironically, is denied to a person who reveals an official secret in respect of three matters of the greatest public interest :

> 'the sovereignty and integrity of India' (itself an expression perilously vague as compared to 'defence'), 'the security of the state' (which acquires by juxtaposition with the first formulation, a vague connotation); and 'international relations'.

In effect, the Press Council discarded its liberal draft of 1982 and enthusiastically endorsed the Thatcher Government's conservative law of 1989. In one vital respect, the Press Council rendered its draft worse than the British law.

Under the latter, the prosecution needs to prove that unauthorised disclosure of relations was in fact 'likely' to endanger or obstruct the promotion of the interests of the United Kingdom abroad or the safety of its citizens.

But the Press Council, in its zeal, went one step further by introducing a legal fiction, a deeming clause, to shut out the defence thus: 'Any matter which another State or with an international organisation, shall be deemed to be 'likely to damage international relations.' The Thatcher law penalised the offender only if there was a real probability, a likelihood, of damage.

The Press Council forcibly identifies mere possibility, or capability with probability and would have a man sent to prison on the mere possibility of a disclosure on foreign affairs causing damage.

Any officer from the Ministry of External Affairs can step into the witness box and testify that the disclosure had such a capability. Deprived of the defence of public interest, the accused would be convicted even if he exposed a gross betrayal of national interest in foreign affairs by the regime of the day.

The other interests which the Press Council's draft protects are public order and preservation of the confidentiality of information held in confidence. Only on these two is the defence of public interest allowed, albeit in a qualified form.

Again, unlike the 1989 British law, the Council's draft would punish a person who consciously received an official secret in breach of the law even if he keeps that secret to himself.

It is pathetic to see a body entrusted by statute with the duties 'to preserve the freedom of the press' and to keep a vigil on 'any development likely to restrict the supply and dissemination of news of public interest and importance' suggesting a new law which will effectively curb that freedom, especially in the vital realm of international relations, and impede the dissemination of new of public importance.17

On June 30, 1993, the PCI formulated Guidelines for Investigative Journalism in a case decided on a complaint by Mr.R.C. Bhargava, Chairman of Maruti Udyog, against the Statesman. One wonders that guidance a guideline such as this can provide the press :

'There being a conflict between the factors which require openness and those which necessitate secrecy, the investigative journalist should strike and maintain in his report a proper balance between openness on the one hand and secrecy on the other hand, placing the public good above every thing.

There are a number of laws, such as Section 5, Official Secrets Act; Sections 123, 124, Evidence Act, 'which stare the journalist coldly in print.' As far as possible, the investigative reporter should avoid a head-on collision with the consequences, for the sake of overriding public interest and benefit, without prejudicing the chances of fair trial to the subject (i.e. public figure) whose conduct he investigates."[18]

On July 15, 1993 the British Government published a White paper on Open Government (Cm. 2290). It left the law alone but promised relaxation of executive control in many fields, e.g. public records.

In the light of the censures of the law by judges and committees in Britain and by the Press Commission and PCI in India, the questionarises whether Section 5 of the Act of 1923 is at all constitutionally valid.

In his Endowment Lecture 1984 at the Advocate's Association, Bangalore, Mr. Justice E.S. Venkataramaiah, later a Chief Justice of India, commented on the constitutional validity of Section 5.

He said :

> "There is the question of constitutionality of the catch-all provision of the Official Secrets Act under Article 19(1) (a) (2). Without passing any judgement on the same, let me mention the American Supreme Court decision in the *Landmark Communications, Inc.* Vs. *Commonwealth of Virginia*. In this case, a newspaper owner was tried and convicted in the Circuit Court of the city of Norfolk, Virginia, for violation of a Virginia statute making it a crime for any person to divulge information regarding proceedings of the Virginia Judicial Inquiry and Review Commission—an organisation authorised to hear complaints concerning the disability or misconduct of judges—which proceedings are declared to be confidential by the Constitution and statutes of Virginia. The basis for the newspaper's conviction was the rejection of its

contention that the Virginia criminal statute violated the First Amendment. On appeal, the United States Supreme Court reversed the judgement of the Supreme Court of Virginia and remanded the case. In the judgement of Chief Justice Warren E. Burger, joined by Justices White, Marshall, Blackmun, Renquist and Stevens, it was held that the First Amendment which guaranteed freedom of speech and press did not permit the criminal punishment of third persons, including the news media, who were non-participants in the Commission's investigative proceedings for divulging or publishing truthful information regarding the Commission's confidential proceedings, such encroachment on the first Amendment not being justified either on the ground that the absence of criminal sanctions would undermine the objectives of the State's statutory scheme for confidentially or on the ground of Virginia's interests in protecting the reputation of its judges and in maintaining the institutional integrity of its courts. Justice Stewart wrote a concurring Judgement."

An analysis of Section 5 in the light of the authoritative comments on it in India and on Section 2 in Britain establishes that :

(1) Section 5 is incontestably unreasonable as restriction on the fundamental right to freedom of speech and expression. In *R.S. Nayak vs. A.R. Antulay (1984) 2 SSC 1983* (decided on February 16, 1984), The Supreme Court ruled that 'reports of the committee which preceded the enactment of a legislation reports of joint parliamentary committee information leading to the enactment are permissible external aids to construction'.

These observations are even the more relevant when it is the Constitution, and not a mere statute, which is being construed. No court will ignore the reports of the Press Commission, the Franks Committee, recommendations of the Press Council or the two White Papers published by the British Government on *Re-*

forms of Section 2 of the Official Secrets Act, 1911 in July 1978 and June 1988.

(2) For the same reasons, Section 5 is violative also of Article 21 of the Constitution. The definition of the offence is impermissibly vague.

3. Constitutionality apart, like any provision creating an offence, Section 5 must be construed strictly. The Second Press Commission observed in para 49 of Chapter IV of its report that 'the only redeeming feature is that *mens rea* is a necessary ingredient of the offence under the Act'.

   It must be proved that the person giving, or the persons voluntarily receiving the information knew or had reasonable grounds to believe that such information was being given in contravention of the Act. All the elements of the breach will have to be proved beyond reasonable doubt.

4. The defence of 'public interest' should be available to the accused. Correspondingly, the prosecution will have to establish that the disclosure is 'Likely to affect . . . . the security of the State', etc., or was made or obtained 'in contravention of the Act' and was communicated 'wilfully' to a person other than one to whom he is authorised to communicate it.

   The likelihood of harm to the public interest or 'the interests of the State' is an essential ingredient of the offence. Here, the observations of Lord Reid and Lord Devlin are relevant.

(5) Judicial review is always available in respect of each ingredient of the offence. A provision which bars judicial review will, per se, be unconstitutional. The fact that the fundamental rights alleviate the vigour is no reason for not repealing the Act.

The Second Press Commission commended Part-II of the British Freedom of Information Bill 'as a model in framing the new provisions' after the repeal of Section 5. It's text is reproduced in Volume II of the Report (p. 113).

Part II was to be a replacement of the Act of 1989. Part I of the Bill provided for 'Access to Official Documents'. The Press Commission said that Part I 'can be studied with the profit and our legislation modelled on that part with appropriate changes.'

A major effort was made in the Right to Know Bill, moved by Mr. Mark Fisher, a Labour MP. It was supported by MPs from all parties, had it's second reading in the House of Commons on February 19, 1993 and was referred to a Committee for detailed examination. On March 24, 1993, however, Mr. Robert Jackson, Parliamentary Secretary for the office of Public Service and Science, told the Committee that the Government would not support the Bill.

The U.S. Freedom of Information Act, 1966, an amendment to the Administrative Procedures Act, was improved by the Act of 1974 and is one of the most successful of it's kind. The specific document need not be mentioned. It is enough for the request to 'reasonably describe such records.'

It is also sufficient to request all the documents on a specified matter. The documents can be had for inspection. A search free of $ 7.50 is payable although this is waived by some agencies if the request is for disclosure in the public interest rather than for personal reasons. Photo copies can be had for a fee.

There are nine categories of matters which are exempted from the duty of disclosure. They are, first matters which are specified by the President, 'to be kept secret in the interest of national defence or foreign policy'.

The court can, however, examine the records for itself, incamera, if need be, to ensure that the refusal does not exceed the terms of the Presidential Order. On this point, the court can also require considerable preliminary disclosure to the lawyer for the applicant.

The eight other exempted categories relate to matters concerning internal personnel rules, inter-agency memoranda, personal and medical files, trade secrets, certain records compiled for law enforcement purposes, records of agencies responsible for supervision of financial institutions, geological and geophysical data concerning wells, and matters specifically exempted from disclosure by other statutes.

The Act confers jurisdiction on the Federal District Court to hear complaints against refusals of disclosure. 'In such a case, the court shall determine the matter *de novo,* and may examine the contents of such agency records *in camera* to determine whether such records or any of the exemptions set forth in the Act.' However, 'the burden is on the agency to sustain its action.'

In India, an effort in this direction was made in the Karnataka Freedom of Press Bill, 1988 (L.A. Bill No. 12 of 1988). Clause 2 conferred on journalists 'Immunity from disclosure of source of information'. Clause 3 provided a detailed procedure for the exercise of 'right to access to a public document.'

The PCI, headed by Justice A.N. Sen, made detailed comments on the Bill recommending changes in order to improve the procedure. It opined : 'In the Council's view it would be eminently desirable if the Parliament chooses to pass such a Bill which will have effect throughout the country. The fact that the Parliament has not chosen to pass any such Bill may not constitute any bar on any State (Legislature to the passing of the Bill.'[19]

One last category of publishers of information deserves special mention—'the whistle blower'. The U.S. Civil Service Reform Act, 1978, known as the 'whistle blowers Act' protects civil servants from any form of retalisation, legal action or demotion if they disclose to Congress or to the Press any evidence of violation of the law, mismanagement, gross waste of funds, abuse of authority or any substantial danger to public health or safety.

In Britain, on July 4, 1988, a few days after the publication of the White Paper, the 35th Report from the Committee of Public Accounts was published. It was on the 'Ministry of Defence, Procurement Irregularities.' It recognised the role of the 'whistle blower'. Is a member of the intelligence services who blows the whistle on a gigantic fraud in defence purchases to be published, then?

However, the civil servants right to 'blow the Wishtle' is more appropriately dealt with in the service rules as it has been in the U.S. Act of 1978. What is needed in India is drastic reform of the Official Secrets Act plus a freedom of Information Act.

Conclusions

(1) The Official Secrets Act should be reformed; not on the lines of the draft proposed by the Press Council of India in 1990 but on the basis of its recommendations in 1982; specifically Clause (2) of draft Section 5 which made 'public interest ' a good defence. This might well protect the 'whistle blower' in the public services from prosecution; disciplinary action apart.

The draft listed only six categories of official information for protection. Information relating to defence or security, foreign relations, monetary policy, foreign exchange policy, etc. But only 'where premature disclosure may harm the national interest or provide interests'; information likely to facilitate commission of crime, affect prison security, impede crime detection or apprehension of offenders; private information given to the State in confidence and trade secrets.

(2) A freedom of Information Act, as well as Part-I of the U.K. Bill commended by the Second Press Commission, the U.S. Act of 1966 can be drawn upon the basic structure is more or less the same. The right of access to official documents is explicitly guaranteed, subject to the provisions of the law. Procedure for the access is laid down by application to a prescribed authority and on payment of a reasonable fee.

The rule of the matter lies in the categories of documents exempt from disclosure. The Schedule to the UK Bill delineates six categories to be exempt from disclosure —matters relating to the defence, foreign affairs; crime detection etc.; matters otherwise privileged in law; matters affecting the privacy of any individual and Cabinet Papers.

The Karnataka Bill followed the same pattern. The documents exempt from disclosure were ones relating to defence; foreign relations, those privileged under Section 123 and 124 of the Evidence Act; Union—State or inter-State correspondence; trade secrets; private information given to government in confidence and 'monetary policy' (using the formulation in the Press Council's draft).

The Bill laid down the procedure for access— 'application to the competent authority in the department concerned' in a prescribed form; a decision there on within 20 days of its receipt; failure to notify the same to be treated as refusal; expeditious access in the event of its acceptance. Refusal would, of course, be subject to court jurisdiction.

It is, however, imperative that the decision to decline access should be notified to the applicant and the reasons for the same set out clearly enough. An appeal could also be provided for.

NOTES AND REFERENCES

1. *Report of the Shah Commission of Inquiry* (Third and Final Report), Controller of Publications, Government of India, 1978. p. 231.
2. T.N. Chaturvedi (Ed.), *Secrecy in Government,* Indian Institute of Public Administration. 1978. p. 126.
3. T.N. Chaturvedi, no. 2 above p. 127
4. *The Times of India, August* 15, 1991.
5. *The Hindu,* December 13, 1991.
6. Lt. Gen. Depinder Singh, *The IPKF in Sri Lanka,* Trishul Publications, New Delhi.
7. See A.G. Noorani, 'In Defence of Openness : The Armed Forces and the Media', *Frontline,* February 25, 1994.
8. See *The Hindu,* April 19, 1994, for an informed resume of the Background.
9. *The Statesman,* January 11, 1996.
10. William Digby, *Condemned Unheard: The Government of India and H.H. The Maharaja of Kashmir,* London: 1890, pp. 99-112.
11. T.N. Chaturvedi, no. 2 above, p. 123.
12. See N.M. Tripathi P. Ltd., *Official Secrecy and the Press,* 1982; p.p. 43-44 for the text of the Press Council's recommendation in the form of a draft of a new Section 5.
13. *The Times,* February 2,1985.

14. *The Guardian,* March 21, 1985.
15. Geoffrey Robertson, *Freedom, the Individual and the Law,* Penguin Book, 1989, pp. 139-144.
16. See Press Council of India, *12th Annual Report, April 1, 1990-March 31,1991.*
17. A.G. Noorani, 'Shelter in Secrecy', *Frontline,* December 6, 191.
18. Press Council of India, *15th Annual Report 1993-94.* p. 139.
19. Press Council of India, *10th Annual Report (Chapter V-Press Bills)* , p. 288.

REMEDIAL MEASURE

29

EDUCATION: A PANACEA TO CORRUPTION

It is construed that corruption emanates from the unholy alliance of the politicians, bureaucracy and business.

Bofors Scandal, HDW Submarine Scandal, Land Grab Scandal something is really rotten at the core of government and administration. Corruption, rather than being an exception, seems to be the rule—a way of life which no longer even startles us.

According to Oxford Dictionary, corruption is the perversion of integrity by bribery or favour. Whether the period we are living in is the proverbial 'Ram Rajya' for which thousands laid down their lives? Is it totally futile in such an atmosphere to think of such utopias? I think not.

In the eighth and ninth book of *The Republic* Plato seeks to judge and measure actual states by the degree to which they deviate from the ideal. The various states are a perversion of the ideal state, to a lesser or greater degree. Thus, he describes the successive stages of corruption.

The point which he emphasizes and which I would like to highlight is that the ideal state is the perfect product of a perfect mind and that the degradation of state proceeds from within and not from accidents or external factors.

Plato remarks, in the eighth book that this will happen, when the individuals lose this best safeguard, which as per him is "A properly trained mind . . . . That is the only thing that will preserve the character of its possessor intact throughout life."

Corruption of the state, implies a corruption of the character of its citizens. States are made what they are by the type of mind they represent.

The ideal state is ideal because it represents the type of mind in which a perfect adjustment of the faculties has been achieved. A corrupt state is corrupt because this balance has been disturbed.

The extent of corruption depending upon the degree to, which the balance has been disturbed. But, such readjustment can be affected by education.

In fact Plato instead of conceiving education as a consequence of the existence of government, and as one of the functions of government, conceives government as the consequence of education. In fact, education and education alone can help us fight this menance of corruption.

According to Plato the ideal state was based on harmonious union of the three elements of reason, spirit, and appetite, in which the reason was dominant. In a corrupt state appetites dominant. Here, Plato distinguishes between necessary and unnecessary appetites. The satisfaction of necessary appetites is essential and beneficial.

The unnecessary appetites are the appetites of wild beast within us. In a corrupt state, the unnecessary appetites dominate. A corrupt democracy becomes the government of a community by professional politicians, at the expense of the well-to-do, and in the interest primarily of themselves and incidentally of the masses.

Rousseau was right when he commented that *The Republic* is "the finest treatise on education that ever was written." In fact, it would not be wrong to say that ideal education is the very life-breath of Plato's ideal state. Justice is the goal of an ideal state. Education is the means by which this goal can be achieved.

The community for its excellence must train its members to excellence in the discharge of their function. Education is a social process, by which the units of society become instinct with social consciousness and learn to fulfil all social demands.

It is clear from his views that Plato regards education as a way to social righteousness and not to social success. In Book Two, Plato remarks:

> That is what I meant by saying that we start to train the mind before the body. And the first step, as you know, is always what matters most, particularly, when we are dealing with those who are young and tender. That is the time when they are taking shape and when any impression we choose to make leaves a permanent mark.

The teacher has to bring out the best in his pupils. Education, is Plato's metaphor, results in the turning of the 'inward eye' towards the light; and it does so because the teacher sets the light to catch the eye.

Education is concerned with the reaction of the soul on it's environment. The soul can no more live without food for its activities than can the body and, therefore, as long as the soul lives, there is need of education to supply its nutrient. Education is continuing process.

In its second and higher state, Plato no longer talks of suggestion and plasticity of the soul, but of illumination. There is now the slow turning of the eye to pure light and the gradual dawn of wisdom through arduous effort and strict self-discipline. The fullness of human experience is, therefore, the curriculum and subject-matter of education.

Plato's view on individual and society are startlingly modern and scientific. The state is what it is because it is composed of the individuals of whom it is composed. "The states are as the men are . . . They grow out of human character."

Plato, thus, assumes, somewhat like Herbert Spencer, that the character of the aggregate depends on that of the units. Like Charles Darwin, he believes in the evolution of better citizens and societies. He remarks in Book four of *The Republic*.

> "And once we have given our community a good start . . . . the process will be cumulative. By maintaining a sound system of education you produce citizens of good character, and citizens of sound character, with the advantage of a good education, produce, inturn, children better than themselves and better able to produce still better children in their turn, as can be seen with animals."

From Plato to the nineteenth century is a long way and yet the basics remain unaltered. In the nineteenth century I would like to take up Charles Dickens in this context. A great story teller and humorist Dickens was deeply concerned about "The condition of England."

England in the nineteenth century was at the zenith of its imperial glory. Rapid industrialization, urbanization and colonization had also made it an extremely rich nation. But, as a humanist Dickans could see beyond this power and glory to the slum-like industrial towns and dehumanization of society.

Its interesting to remember that Dickens had been a parliamentary reporter in his earlier years. In fact, he was there when the first Reform Bill was passed. He was disgusted by the slowness of the parliamentary procedure and the flood of varbiage and the self-centred members of parliament.

In his masterpiece *Hard Times*, he terms the parliamentary process "a little noisy and rather dirty machinery and members of parliament "national dustmen". (H.T. 238).

Mr. Gradgrind, the honourable member of Parliament :

> Mr. Gradgrind, apprised of his wife's decrease, made an expedition from London, and buried here in a business-like manner. He, then, returned with promptitude to the national cinder heap, and resumed is sifting for the odds and ends he wanted, and his throwing of dust about into the eyes of other people who wanted other odds and ends—in fact, resumed his parliamentary duties. (H.T. 230).

The guardians of people are busy looking after their own interest. The state is rotten. The society is dehumanized. The reason—the state of education. As a social novelist Dickens was deeply concerned with the moulding of human plastic into an iron mould. In a speech on November 5, 1857, Dickens said :

> "I don't like that sort of school— and I have seen a great many such in these later times-where the bright childish imagination is utterly discouraged, and where those bright childish faces, which is so very good for the wisest among us to remember in after life, when the world is too much with us early and late, stare gloomily and grimly scared out of countenance where I have never seen among pupils, whether boys or girls, anything but little parrots and small calculating machines."

Dickens's interesting schools and education extended beyond his writing. Many of his lecture readings were for the benefit of educational institutions. He visited more than seventy schools in England, Europe and America. This is addition to the twelve to which at one time or another, he sent his own children. In his fiction, the interest in education is deep and constant, Dickens sent this fictional children to some thirty schools.

I shall only take a couple of illustrations to show the dismal state of education, which according to Dickens was responsible for the dismal state of affairs in the society. As a child, he had been sent to Wellington House Academy, the spectres of which haunted him all his adult life. In one of his speeches he remarked :

> "I don't like the sort of school to which I went myself, the respected proprietor of which was by far the most ignorant Man I have ever had the pleasure to know, who was one of the worst tempered men, perhaps, that ever lived, whose business it was to make as much out of us and to put as little into us as possible..."

Almost every kind of education, then existing in London gets a mauling at Dickens's hands, because he believes that this wrong education is responsible for all the ills of society

But, as story-teller it is his forte to sugar-coat the biter pill.

There is a, for example, the hilarious description of a dame school in Great Expectations. Dickens gives a beautiful word picture of the "horrible din" called education.

It is one of the fine and funniest of his scences. The humorist in Dickens makes the painful not only bearable but almost enjoyable, till, of course, one shakes out of the sheer magic of the scene and wakes upto the fact of what one has been laughing at. Dickens's account of the unqualified teacher is no exaggeration.

Many of the teachers could not write and some were unable to read. In many instances parish clerks and chapel cleaners once they were incapacitated for their regular service took up teaching. In one town a man was appointed school master when age made him incompetent to take care of pigs!

But Dickens objection does not stop with merely having trained teachers.The crucial point remains—what do they teach? The so-called trained teachers choked the children with facts. The Gradgrind system of education in *Hard Times* is no exaggeration.

Dickens has taken it from the Birkbeck schools, founded by Willian Ellis, a Utilitarian and a close friend of John Stuart Mill. His intention was to equip the poor for social function in an industrial society.

The novel clearly reveals how the utilitarian education connived with rapid industrialization to rob man of his humanity. The syllabi of these schools was dominated by the science of social economy. In other words, the relationship of man to man was interpreted in terms of cash—nexus, the applied form of self-interest.

The brightest pupil of such an institution Bitzer, who significantly is also the villain of the novel, declares unashamedly that the guiding principles of his life is self-interest and declares", ... the whole social system is question of self-interest. What you must always appeal to, is a person's self-interest.

"It is your only hold. We are so constituted. I was brought up in that catechism when I was very young ..... (H.T., 303) Bitzer's villainy is that he has learnt his lessons too well. The function of the whole plot is to expose the crisis of an ironically retard education.

The three movements of the structure are "Sowing", "Reapring", and "Garnering". The Biblican overtones of the three books remind us that "he who sows the wind shall reap the whirlwind."

By a negative implication, Dickens gives us a theory of education with very clear-cut outlines. We have to be very careful in what we sow, because we have to reap what we sow. I must emphasize that here education must be taken in its widest connotations.

What the child is taught in the class-room, at home and in the world. Parents, teachers and leaders must always remembers what Thoreau said. Henry David Thoreau, the great author, who influenced Mahatma Gandhi's thought and work, remarked that there are only three ways to teach a child (1) Example (2) Example and (3) Example.

The leader exhorts the people to work honetly and diligently and gives the largest contract to his favourite nephew. The teacher lectures the students to work hard, but refuses to take his class because he is, not in the mood.

The father tells his child soul-stirring tales of honesty, but pinches brown paper from his office to cover his school books. All of them share the *onus* for the whirlwind of corruption that will follow.

I shall sum up with the views of Plato because I think the education state nexus presented by him has not been improved upon. He felt that a society where an ideal education has been imparted will need neither doctors nor lawyers because there will be neither disease of the body nor of the mind.

Sounds like a castle in the air. Nothing is amiss, all that we need to do is put foundations under this castle. True knowledge is the basic anti-dote to corruption. True knowledge, according to Plato, is philosophy.

I conclude in his words, "Until philosophers are kings, or the kings and princes of this world have the spirit and power of philosophy, cities will never have rest from their evils."

30

AUDIT TACKLES CORRUPTION

The commonest sanctions against bribes are moral, the invocation of guilt before god and shame before society.

By corruption, we commonly mean bribery, i.e., the payment of a sum of money to a government official, public sector official or politician for something which is in his or her power to do or refrain from doing, or for indirectly bringing about a desired result.

Whether the payment is demanded or offered and whether it is meant for the private gain of an individual or goes to a political party or other organisation, are questions which make no difference, it is still corruption.

The payment can, of course, be in kind rather than in cash; it could take the form of costly gifts, paid holidays, entertainment, alcoholic drinks, provision of services including sexual services, and so on.

There are many other kinds of improprieties or wrongdoings in our public systems, and the word 'corruption' itself is used in a wide range of senses such as degeneration, decay, putrefaction, moral deterioration, perversion of an institution or system, gross deviation from original purpose or rationale and so on.

Indeed, in the widest sense of the word 'corruption', practically all the evils of our administrative and political systems and institutions, and of our society as a whole, can be brought under that rubric.

However, such a wide coverage will not facilitate purposeful discussion or the prescription of specific remedies. Here, the reference is to corruption in the narrower sense. An attempt is made to examine whether or not constitutionally mandated audit machinery can be pressed into service as a useful and effective instrument to curb corruption in the public domain.

An Overview

CAG : Our Supreme Audit Institution (SAI)

The audit machinery referred to above is the Indian Audit Department (IAD) presided over by the Comptroller and Auditor General of India (CAG). The financial accountability of the Government, and the observance of 'regularity' (i.e., conformity to rules and procedures) and propriety in public financial transactions must be confined by the CAG. An important feature of Indian quasi-federalism is that there is a common CAG for both the Union and the States.

The CAG is appointed by the President of India by the warrant under his hand and seal; he is given a term of office of six years and cannot be removed except in the same manner as a judge of the Supreme Court, i.e, by an impeachment process. His salary and other terms and conditions of service are fixed by statute and cannot be varied to his disadvantage after his appointment.

The administrative expenses of the office of the CAG are 'charged' on the Consolidated Fund of India i.e., they are not subjected to a vote of Parliament. After his term, the CAG cannot be appointed to further office under the Government either at the Centre or in any of the States. Thus, through a variety of provisions, some symbolic and some substantive, the CAG's status and independence are ensured.

An important point to bear in mind is that the CAG, at the time of appointment, takes an oath similar to that taken by the judges of the Supreme Court, to 'uphold the Constitution and the laws', whereas a minister has to swear an oath only to act 'in accordance with the Constitution.'

The CAG is our Supreme Audit Institution (SAI). There are SAIs in the form of CAGs, Comptrollers-General, Audit Commissions or Courts of Audit in different countries with diverse systems of governance. In the USA, the General Accounting Office (GAO), headed by the Comptroller General of the United States, has been declared to be a part of the legislative branch. In the UK, after the enactment of the National Audit Act of 1983, the CAG is an officer of the House of Commons.

In contrast, the CAG of India is not formally an officer of Parliament, though he assists Parliament and the State Legislatures in ensuring the financial accountability of the executive government. However, his duties and powers are laid down by Parliament.

Article 149 of the Constitution says that the CAG 'shall perform such duties and exercise such powers in relation to the accounts of the Union and the States and of any other authority or body as may be prescribed by or under any law made by Parliament'. In pursuance of this, Parliament has enacted the CAG's (Duties, and Conditions of Service) Act, 1971.

The organisations subject to the audit of the CAG are all government departments and offices, Central and State, including departmental commercial undertakings such as the Indian Railways and Posts and Telecommunications, government companies, Central and State (under special provisions relating to their audit in the Companies Act) and statutory corporations where the relevant statute provides for an audit by the CAG; a number of non-commercial autonomous bodies and authorities, owned or controlled by the State and Central Governments; and a large number of authorities and bodies substantially financed from Union or State revenues.

The CAG also ensures uniformity in accounting; the accounts of the Union and the States are kept in the form prescribed by the President on the advice of the CAG. He continues to be responsible for the compilation of the accounts of many of the State Governments though this responsibility has been taken over by the Governments at the Centre and in some of the States.

CAG's Audit

The word 'audit' has not been defined either in the Constitution or in the CAG's Act, and has, therefore, to be understood in the light of common usage ('to make an official examination of accounts to ascertain their accuracy'—The Oxford English Dictionary), and the actual practices which have evolved over time. The CAG's audit has a wider scope than that of chartered accountants in the private sector. For instance, in the case of expenditures, the CAG's audit examines :

- — the availability of funds for the expenditure which has been incurred (budget provision, a vote by the legislature, a valid re-appropriation order, whether the item constitutes a 'New Service' or 'New instrument of Service' requiring a fresh vote, etc.);
- — the existence of proper authority for the expenditure (a valid sanction order by a competent authority); and
- — procedural correctness and proper documentation and vouching ('regularity')

It goes one step beyond this when it scrutinises a sanction order itself for legality and constitutionality. It also examines whether an expenditure was avoidable, infructuous or clearly more than the object warranted. It goes even further when it examines the prudence or propriety of an expenditure or a financial decision.

The Audit of receipts would include an examination whether the relevant law is being properly applied; whether there were reasoned grounds for all decisions; whether the interpretations of the law, if any, are based on existing case-law and rulings, or if new, are tenable; and, of course, whether the receipts have been correctly brought to account.

Accounts-Related, Records-based

Most SAIs tend to interpret their audit functions expansively. In some cases, the extensions get written into the relevant statute. For instance, the National Audit Act, 1983 of the U.K. specifically enables the CAG to carry out examinations of economy, efficiency, and effectiveness (though, in fact, he had begun doing this earlier than 1983).

The functions of the GAO of the USA have been expanded enormously over the years, and cover programme evaluations of the most diverse kind. In India, too, there has always been a tendency to stretch the audit function.

Much of the 'stretching' (e.g. sanction audit, propriety audit, 'value-for-money' audit) remains within the bounds of what may be properly called 'audit', but in some cases (e.g. comprehensive 'appraisals' public enterprises; reviews of governmental decisions or programmes which verge on 'Policy audit'; reports on economic subject such as public debt or the management of the balance of payments), there may be room for doubt whether or not the bounds of audit have been overstepped.

If so, did the IAD have any special expertise in the areas in question or even a constitutional mandate for the activity? Without entering into that debate and confining ourselves to the essential concerns of this chapter, we need to note two points :

(i) The first is that audit is essentially an activity relating to accounts and finance. Irregularities other than those relating to accounts or improprieties of a non-financial nature do not come within the purview of audit unless they also happen to have an accounting or financial aspect.

(ii) The second point is that the examination is with reference to vouchers, books of account, registers, ledgers, and other documents and related files. An audit can raise queries arising from that examination, ask for substantiation, draw attention to inconsistencies or evident improbabilities, seek clarification, explanations, further information, and so on; it can judge whether the replies and materials provided in response are adequate or warrant a comment.

However, it does not, under the Indian System, undertake its own investigation of facts in the world outside those books, files and documents.

Keeping these two points in mind, we can examine how the audit processes can assist in controlling corruption.

Audit and Corruption

Corruption : Contexts and Forms

Corruption can occur in a wide range of contexts including but not limited to the following :

— ordinary governmental housekeeping (petty office purchases or minor works, passing of medical, travelling and other allowances and claims of government servants, allotment of government accommodation, etc.);

— administrative approvals (appointments, postings, transfers, etc.);

— major governmental or public sector contracts (large public works, purchases of commodities or equipment, project consultancy or construction, etc.);

— administration of tax laws (assessment, questions of classification, allowances and disallowances, applications for refunds, etc.);

— economic clearances/approvals, regulatory activities, etc.;

— provision of certain services to the people and related billing etc.

Tell-Tale Marks

In all such cases, any illegal gratification in cash or mind will necessarily be clandestine and is likely to take place outside the account books of the department or public enterprise concerned; it will, therefore, not come squarely within the purview of audit like the fraud or misappropriation of public funds might. However, the private occurrence of corruption might have some consequences in the public domain.

Illegal gratification is aimed at securing a particular desired result and the effort on the part of officials or politicians to bring about that result, as a *quid pro quo* for favours received, could lead to deviations from the prescribed procedure, specious reasoning, special pleading in favour of a particular choice, course of action or manifestly erroneous, arbitrary or perverse decisions.

There could be an exercise of undue patronage, the favouring of particular individuals or groups, failure to ensure adequate competition, excessively generous terms for a contractor, failure to safeguard the interests of the government or the public enterprise adequately and enforce penal clauses, poor choices in technology or equipment which subsequently give rise to problems, and so on. These are some of the tell-tale marks which could lead one to the possible presence of corruption.

Role of Audit

Procedural correctness and perfect documentation do not preclude the possibility of corruption. Procedural and documentational deficiencies do not necessarily warrant an inference of corruption.

All that can be said is that corruption is probably facilitated when there is procedural laxity and imperfection in documentation than when there is perfect conformity to all requirements, and in-so-far-as corruption introduces an extraneous consideration into decision-making, there is a distinct possibility that the decision may be adversely affected. In drawing attention to procedural lapses or other ill-considered decision-making or mismanagement, Audit can provide pointers to the possibility of corruption.

Should Audit proceed beyond the kinds of query or comment indicated above and undertake further investigations of possible corruption on its own? The answer has to be 'No'. Its constitutional mandate does not warrant this.

Moreover, when we proceed from an examination of procedural lapses and internal inconsistencies in the world of accounts to an investigation of the possibility of corruption, the nature of the activity changes and demands a different kind of expertise and experience from what auditors possess.

They could certainly acquire that expertise and experience,

but they would, then cease to be auditors; nor is there any need for them to do so, since specialized agencies which can investigate corruption are available. Corruption can be best controlled and investigated when Audit performs its own mandated and professional functions diligently and, then, leaving it to other specialised agencies to pursue further inquiries into possible corruption.

Selection of CAG

It is clear that if the audit machinery is to be used as an instrument (along with others) in the battle against corruption, it needs to be a strong and effective one. Unfortunately, it suffers from serious limitations, some external and some internal.

Absence of System

The first of these arises from the very system (if it can be so described) of selecting the CAG. Any institution, however exalted, is only as good as the incumbent. In singing a litany in praise of this high office we take it for granted that great care goes into the selection of the most suitable person for it.

Unfortunately, the actual selection processes do not inspire confidence. They are entirely internal. No one outside the government has any knowledge of what criteria are applied, how names are short-listed, and how the final selection is made.

Effectively, the choice is in the hands of the government of the day, i.e. the Prime Minister and the entrenched bureaucracy in the form of Cabinet Secretary and Principal Secretary to the Prime Minister, both officers of the Indian Administrative Service (IAS); it would appear that bureaucratic considerations play an important role in the selection process.

This is hardly reassuring. We hypnotise ourselves with pious incantations of constitutional and statutory provisions and unctuous quotations from distinguished leaders of the past extolling the virtues of this high office, but the reality does not warrant such celebration.

One may almost say that the CAG of the Constitution is a

mythical creature, like the unicorn, which does not exist in reality, and that the current system of selection can only yield a pale simulacrum of that shining image. If, in fact, some CAGs have been not unworthy of their office, this is not because of but despite the system of selection.

The fact that the last three CAGs (and the newly appointed CAG) came from the IAS, has some functional implications which need to be noted. We are not concerned here with inter-service rivalries or resentments. No one can argue that the post of CAG should be treated as reserved for the Indian Audit and Accounts Service (IAAS); it is not even necessary that the CAG should be a former bureaucrat.

However, by the year 2002, the Audit Department would be under IAS officers continuously for 24 years; from the point of view of the IAAS, this looks like the systematic exclusion of that Service and the virtual absorption of the post of CAG in the IAS cadre.

That view, right or wrong, has had a demoralising effect on the IAAS. The self-esteem of the Department, the firm belief in the virtues of an independent audit and the pride in performing constitutionally mandated functions, which used to be quite marked in the early years, are now much less in evidence. In its place, a spirit of cynicism seems to be growing.

This is bound to affect the commitment and courage with which the audit function is performed. The answer to this morale problem is not to give any special voted rights to the IAAS over the post of CAG, but to ensure that the appointment processes are such as to leave no room at all for a sense of unfairness or suspicions of impropriety. Also, the selected person, drawn from whichever source, should be of such unquestionable suitability as to command respect both within and outside the Audit Department.

Need for a high-level selection committee

It is clearly necessary, then, to rescue this high constitutional and federal office from the hands of the ruling party and the entrenched bureaucracy by creating a wider field of choice and an objective selection process.

In the U.K., the CAG is appointed by the Crown on an address presented by the House of Commons, and the motion for such an address is made by the Prime Minister acting in agreement with the Chairman of the Public Accounts Committee.

In the USA, the President appoints the Comptroller General subject to Senate confirmation, but under a new system introduced by the GAO Act of 1980, the President is expected, though not mandatorily required, to make a selection from a list prepared by a special congressional commission.

In India, a pattern is available : The Protection of Human Rights Act 1993 provides for the appointment of the Chairpersons and other members of the National Human Rights Commission to be based on the recommendations of the Committee consisting of the Prime Minister, the Home Minister, the Leaders of the Opposition in the two Houses of Parliament, the Speaker of the Lok Sabha and the Deputy Chairman of Rajya Sabha.

In the case of the CAG, considering the high constitutional position of the office and the nature of its functions, the Committee could include the Finance Minister instead of the Home Minister, and it may be appropriate to include the Chief Justice of India. The final selection and even the preliminary step of compiling a short list should be the responsibility of that Committee.

The short list should include outstanding civil servants from the IAAS, IAS and some other Services as well as some distinguished names from sources outside the bureaucracy.

Criteria needed

In this context, it is necessary to lay down in advance the criteria that should govern the selection of the CAG. Unfortunately, a write petition to this effect, filed by H.D. Shourie, was not admitted by the Supreme Court. It is regrettable that the Supreme Court, which has lately been playing an 'activist' role and going into all kinds of issues—including industrial pollution, removal of city garbage, and so on—did not choose to interest itself in helping to determine the manner of selection of a high constitutional functionary.

As such, the selection committee suggested above will have to lay down the job specifications and the selection criteria first before proceedings with the actual selection.

At the time of writing, a new CAG has just been appointed, and so there will be no new selection for another six years. Nevertheless, the reform proposed is an important one and needs to be debated by those who have public interest at heart.

Reorientation of I.A.D.

The second limitation on the effectiveness of the audit function is one of orientation. From the very beginning, there has been a tendency in the IAD to regard the conventional audit activities such as the check of procedural correctness, proper documentation, and so on as routine or formal functions. There has been a constant search for higher functions.

Perhaps, the officers of the IAD derive greater satisfaction from writing reports on subjects such as public debt, undertaking appraisals of public enterprises, questioning decisions taken at high levels in government, or vanturing into policy audit rather than commenting on ordinary irregularities.

Possibly, these activities were a defensive reaction to the usual criticisms of an audit as being 'wooden', 'unimaginative', 'pettifogging', etc. One wonders whether the Audit Department itself has become somewhat uncomfortable about its basic duties and tries to maintain its self-esteem by doing 'higher' things.

Whatever the explanation, and however, justified the extended and 'higher' functions, we have to recognise that it is an audit proper, and not the 'higher' activities, which could be of some assistance in curbing corruption.

The basic audit function needs to be restored to a position of importance in the internal thinking and value system of the IAD. Other SAIs may take the prevalence of certain standards of integrity and probity in public administration and public life for granted, and concentrate on administrative audit, efficiency, value for money, and so on.

Given the situation in this country, it seems reasonable to suggest that our SAI should pay special attention to the national problem of corruption, and give a special orientation to audit activity in order to remain on the watch for any incidence of corruption. As mentioned earlier, corruption may leave a trace or a smell and auditors need to develop a keen sense for this.

In operational terms, what does this mean? One is not advocating a presumption that the slightest procedural defect must be *mala fide*, the acceptance of a bid other than the lowest is necessarily indicative of corruption or every judgement or discretion has questionable motivations. That would paralyse the administration and place a premium on safe rather than sound decision-making.

What is being suggested is that the possibility of corruption should be kept in view while carefully examining procedural lapses and deficiencies as well as exercises of judgement and discretion; there should always be a readiness to listen to explanations. A combination of rigorous scrutiny with an appreciation of the urgencies and compulsions of administrative and managerial decision-making is essential.

That is no doubt a difficult combination to practice. It would be easy to slip either into undue suspiciousness and a wooden insistence on correctness or into an excessive readiness to accept plausible explanations for lapses and deviations. Both of these dangers have to be carefully avoided, but their presence does not invalidate the undertaking proposed or reduce its importance.

Role of Detectives

Clearly, this will call for a major reorientation of attitudes in the IAD. An important element in such a reorientation would be to stress a forgotten aspect of the audit function, i.e., discovery or detection.

An auditor is supposed to bring to light things which would otherwise have remained hidden. An audit notices errors, omissions, deficiencies, discrepancies and other oddities; it burrows deeper, asks for explanations.

As a result, what looks innocent on the surface can turn out to be something more sinister; a fraud or misappropriation.

Even a case of corruption could come to light. Yet, in recent years, it is difficult to recall instances of a major scandal having been ferreted out by the audit process.

There was, indeed, one such case some years ago; the Kuo oil deal case which came to light as a result of audit queries. However, in recent years, most of the cases which have figured in public debates have come to light in other ways.

Audit reports on the Bofors case, the securities scam, disinvestment in public enterprises, etc. were written long after the cases had been debated extensively in the media and Parliament. One almost wonders if the IAD picked up the cases from newspaper reports and discussions in Parliament.

Perhaps that is not a fair comment, it is for the IAD itself to undertake an honest and objective self-examination on this matter. But it is not unfair to suggest that there is need for the Department to re-discover the role of auditors as financial and accounting detectives.

Strengthening Audit

The effectiveness of the CAG's audit is greatly impaired by a number of factors and circumstances beyond its control. First replies to audit objections and queries are often not received or only after long delays and several reminders. Most replies are grossly inadequate or evasive; sometimes, the replies are of an obfuscatory kind.

Secondly, when Audit suspects that the reply is untrue or misleading. It is often handicapped in formulating a firm and sharp comment because of the aforementioned tradition that it does not undertake an external cross-check on its own.

Thirdly, even when Audit clearly finds a particular expenditure or financial decision to be unacceptable or improper it has no power to impose a sanction; it can only include a selective commentary in the ensuring Audit Report. Audit objections, thus, have no disagreeable consequences, in other words, audit lacks bite.

Even, when an adverse comment is included in an Audit Report, it may be long after the event and, therefore, have little impact; furthermore, it may not get picked up for discussion by the Parliamentary Committee concerned. It is necessary to see whether these weaknesses can at least partially be remedied. Three possible measures suggest themselves.

Power to Summon Officials

When the Accountant General (AG)— or by whatever title the head of the audit office is known—finds that he is not receiving a reply at all to his queries or that the reply is inadequate or misleading, it should be made possible for him to issue a notice to the departmental official concerned summoning him or her to appear in person and give evidence.

Limited External Checks

As mentioned earlier, Audit raises questions and objections to find contents of the accounts, vouchers, contracts, correspondence and files that come before it, and does not undertake its own investigation of the facts behind those documents externally. That is a sound principle, but it need not be allowed to become a crippling constraint on the effectiveness of audit. A limited and judicious recourse to external checks and the obtaining of information from sources other than the office being audited seem worth considering.

Ordering Recoveries

Where it is clear that an irregularity has occurred —e.g. an advance drawn has not been adjusted, the sanctioned amount has been exceeded, the unspent balance out of an advance has not been surrendered, a sanctioning authority has clearly exceeded its powers or has deliberately split a single work in order to bring it within its powers, pay and allowances have been overdrawn, there are elements in a claim which have to be disallowed as not being in accordance with the rules, and so on—it should be made possible for the AG to issue an order for the recovery of the appropriate amount from the official or officials concerned.

Power of S.A.I.'s

These are not novel suggestions. SAIs in certain other countries have powers of summoning witnesses and taking evidence; undertaking the physical verification of assets, stories, etc.; calling for information, material and witnesses from sources other than the offices under audit; ordering search and seizure; ordering recoveries or imposing financial penalties; demanding the institution of remedial or disciplinary measures; and so on.

In some countries, failure or refusal to provide information and other material to the audit authorities, impeding or obstructing the audit process, etc., have been made offences punishable by fines or imprisonment. Diverse provisions of these kinds will be found in the statute books of France, Sri Lanka, Bangladesh, Kenya Indonesia, the Republic of Korea, the Gambia and Zimbabwe.

The laws and systems in those and other countries need to be studied and some of the features considered for adoption in this country through suitable amendments to the CAG's Act, other relevant statutes or even the Constitution.

However, it may be possible to introduce some limited measures, e.g., asking departmental officials to appear in person to provide information or clarification, undertaking limited 'external' inquiries, etc., through decisions by the CAG even without statutory amendments.

The Collapse in Bihar

At this stage, we should look at the appalling state of affairs in relation to finance and accounts in Bihar, because it highlights, among other things, serious sicknesses in the audit function.

Massive financial irregularities have been present in certain departments of the Bihar State government for some years now. What has become known as the Animal Husbandry Department scam or the fodder scam has often been in the news in the recent months. The case appears to be one of misappropriation of government funds, but the possibility of corruption, also being involved, cannot perhaps be ruled out.

In any case, the kinds of lapses, deficiencies and deviations from procedure which rendered the misappropriation possible could also have facilitated corruption. A study of the case could, therefore, be instructive in respect to the role of audit.

However, we shall have to wait for the CBI's investigations to be completed to obtain a full picture of the scandal and the details of its *modus operandi*. *The* CBI will no doubt consult the IAD in regard to the budgetary, accounting and procedural aspects of the matter. Yet, even at this stage, three main features stand out.

Excesses Over Grants

First, year after year there were substantial excesses over the voted grants under various heads of expenditure, making a mockery of the basic system of the legislature's financial control over the executive.

Excesses over voted grants do occur elsewhere too, but the magnitude of the excesses in Bihar is staggering. In theory, there is a procedure for regularising this; the excess has to be reported to the legislature and voted by it as an *expo facto* grant.

That would provide an opportunity for the legislature to take the executive to task, pass strictures, ask for responsibility to be fixed, and so on. However, the underlying assumption is that such cases would be exceptional and that the excess would be of a small order. If there are continuing and massive excesses which are, in some cases, as high as multiple of the voted grant, what is the purpose of retrospective regularisation?

Funds Drawn Freely From Treasuries

Secondly, it has been possible for various departmental authorities to draw funds freely from the treasuries without any limit and fail to account for sums drawn. Apart from the procedural slackness which facilitated this, it is clear that it would not have been possible without the collusion and active participation of large number of officials at all levels in numerous government departments and agencies; the network of collusion must have been vast.

Accounts not Rendered

The rendering of accounts by several treasuries to the Accountant General (AG) seems to have been in arrears for years not only making audit virtually impossible, but also seriously affecting the accuracy and reliability of the State accounts as a whole. In the absence of treasury accounts, the AG can only make a simple observation ('accounts not received'), and cannot offer detailed comments on the accounts. That elementary failure can cover a multitude of sins as is evident in the case of Bihar.

Failures

The AG has, no doubt been writing letters to the State Government at various levels regarding these matters, and they might also have been mentioned in the Audit Reports placed before the legislature.

It may, therefore, be claimed that the Audit Department had in a technical sense discharged its responsibility, but the situation seems far from satisfactory. What, then, can be done in such a situation? The following is an attempt to explore some possible lines of action :

(i) The non-receipt of treasury accounts was evidence that the treasuries in question were not functioning properly. The AG could, perhaps, have undertaken in-depth and extensive inspections of treasuries and made special reports. Such inspections might have brought to light not only weaknesses in the treasury administration but also any dubious activities.

(ii) Excesses over budgetary allocations are possible in the Indian system because we do not have the kind of 'exchequer control' system that exists in the UK, wherein, immediately after the budget is passed every year by Parliament, the CAG authorises the various Departments of the Government to draw funds from the Consolidated Fund up to the limit of the voted grants. In such a system, excesses over the vote would be impossible.

During the debates in the Constituent Assembly, such a system was envisaged as a future possibility in this country, and the term 'Comptroller' was added to the designation of the Auditor General.

Unfortunately, it has remained purely ornamental. The idea of exchequer control was given up fairly early because of certain perceived difficulties. Since then, there has been a separation of accounts from audit and the departmentalisation of the former at the centre and in some States.

Departmentalisation has been accompanied, at least at the Centre, by the further step of placing the departments in accounts with commercial banks. Thus, we have two payment systems; through cheques issued by departmental or centralised Pay and Accounts Offices or through old-style treasuries.

In either case, the voted grant gets distributed over a large number of offices spread far and wide; that is the real difficulty in the introduction of exchequer control based on the UK model.

However, it cannot be an insuperable one. In any case, it is absolutely necessary to obviate the possibility of an excess over the vote rather than allow excesses to occur and, then, go through regularisation procedures.

Serious thought needs to be given to this problem which has assumed staggering proportions in Bihar. (Even under the present system, the AG is expected to conduct an 'appropriation audit' and issue warning memoranda if expenditure seems likely to exceed the appropriation. It is not clear whether that procedure was operating in Bihar or was rendered difficult by the non- receipt of treasury accounts).

(iii) In regards to the evil of funds being freely drawn from the treasuries, there are two possible explanations. First, the vouchers and other documents might have been submitted, in which case the question arises whether or not this could have been detected in the treasuries or later in the AG's office.

Secondly, funds could have been drawn on abstract contingent bills and not adjusted later through detailed bills. A simple remedy for this would be to insist that unless an earlier withdrawal has been adjusted no further funds can be drawn.

If this is not considered feasible, an alternative check of some kind will have to be established. It is the responsibility of the CAG to ensure that this loophole is plugged.

(iv) This case is not a series of minor infractions but a massive complex of religious failures of a fundamental nature. It would not be an exaggeration to describe this as a virtual breakdown of the machinery of the State : it is not merely the failure of the law-enforcing machinery that merits such a description.

Considering that the CAG swears an oath to 'uphold the Constitution and the laws', a possibility which suggests itself is that faced such a collapse of the constitutionally ordained financial system the CAG could have gone beyond letters to the government bureaucracy or even the Chief Minister, and made special reports to the Governor of the State and perhaps the President of India for such action as they might have deemed appropriate.

These reports could also have been simultaneously released to the Press. In the normal course, the CAG does not go to the Press with his findings. His reports become public only when they are placed before Parliament or the State legislature. However, this applies only to the regular Audit Reports. A report to the President or Governor that the constitutionally ordained financial system is not functioning is not an audit report in the ordinary sense.

It is a special report detailing a breakdown. By making it public, the CAG would not be violating any provisions of the Constitution. On the contrary, he would be living up to his oath to uphold the Constitution.

Appraisal of IAD

The above suggestions, based on suppositions of what might have happened in Bihar, may have to be reviewed and perhaps modified when detailed examinations by the CBI and the IAD are complete. However, what has already come to light is so shocking in terms of magnitude and implications that it could not be ignored in this Chapter.

It seems fair to say that while there were massive failures on the part of the State Government departments and offices, the IAD cannot escape its share of blame for ignoring the grave irregularities which have occurred, particularly when we note that there is no separation of audit and accounts in Bihar and that the accounting function remains with the CAG.

The Bihar revelations go to corroborate two points made earlier in this Chapter:

(i) the IAD has shifted its focus away from its main business, and

(ii) the effectiveness of the IAD has been reduced by a number of weaknesses.

We have ready made some suggestions for improvement, such as a restoration of the importance of the basic audit function in the activities and internal value system of the IAD, and a strengthening of the hands of the department through the adoption of some of the features present in the SAI statutes of other countries.

In addition, there is an urgent need to substantially reform the audit function in India based on a thorough, comprehensive and independent appraisal of its performance. The CAG himself should set up a high-level committee or commission for this purpose, and draw upon external consultants to provide it with expert assistance.

Follow-up Arrangements

We can now return to an earlier point regarding special institutional arrangements for a follow-up on the pointers indicating corruption, fraud, misappropriation, or the breakdown of a system emerging from an audit.

Clearly, such pointers need to be taken note of quickly, examined further, investigated and remedial and/or punitive measures promptly instituted. This would require

(i) a system of reporting

(ii) co-operation in investigation (net-working) and

(iii) dissemination, i.e. making serious developments widely known.

Early Identification

The first thing to do is to establish a mechanism for an early identification of matters which need prompt further investigation. There should be a unit for this purpose in each State Accountant General's Office and the important Principal Audit Offices at the Central level.

Perhaps, a small special cell consisting of hand-picked experienced persons could review the results of the audit on a monthly basis and pick out all those cases which seem to warrant further investigation by the appropriate agencies.

Once a month, the head of the audit office could write a letter to the government at the highest level (prime minister/ chief minister) containing brief accounts of such cases. Simultaneously, a copy of the communication could also be sent to the Central Vigilance Commission or the corresponding functionary at the State level as well as the *Ombudsman* if one has been established. It would, then, be for the *Ombudsman*, CVC or another authority to have the cases investigated further.

There may be nothing to report in certain months in which case the letter will say so, but a regular system of monthly reporting will provide an occasion to highlight matters that need attention before becoming serious problems. A question may be raised whether the CAG can report to anyone other than the President/Governor in terms of the constitutional provisions,.

The monthly letters suggested above would not be 'audit reports' but communications which would facilitate investigations. Further, so far as one knows, the constitutional provisions do not bar a working relationship between the government and the CAG.

Network

The role of the Audit Department does not necessarily end with reporting. Its expert assistance may continue to be needed in the course of the investigations by the CVC, CBI or other agencies. If corruption, fraud and other grave irregularities are to be effectively dealt with, close collaboration among the various investigative agencies is essential.

This kind of networking is perhaps best secured through a special committee for checking fraud and corruption, consisting of representatives from the CVS, CBI and other such agencies and committees at the State level. The CAG should have no hesitation in associating his representatives with such a committee. The governmental investigative agencies are entitled to expect the CAG's co-operation in such an important task and the CAG should not withhold that co-opeation on the basis of a narrow interpretation of what his constitutional position entails.

The committee should meet periodically, say, once a month, and review the progress of the investigations. In this context, it is interesting to note that in the UK there is an office known as the Serious Fraud Office, set up under the Criminal Justice Act, 1987, which is responsible for all the functions of detection, investigation and prosecution in relation to serious fraud cases. It is vested with special powers, including access to bank accounts, which would enable it to obtain information quickly and efficiently.

It functions through multi-disciplinary teams including lawyers, accountants, police officers and support staff. In India, there may be need to establish a similar Fraud and Corruption Office either as a separate new institution or as a sepcialized part of the CBI.

In either case, the CAG should both depute personnel to such an organisation and co-operate fully in its functions of detection, investigation and prosecution.

Dissemination

Apart from reporting and networking, the widest possible dissemination of the results of the audit is essential for the enforcement of accountability. The present arrangements leave much to be desired. The CAG reports only to the Government, and it is the Government which lays the reports before Parliament or the State Legislature; it is only, then, that the reports become public. Delays take place at every stage.

By the time the reports are released, the events and transactions to which they relate would be at least a year old. Further delays can take place during the processes of consideration by the Parliamentary Committee concerned (the Public Accounts Committee and the Committee on Public Undertakings). The discussion, when it does take place, is very selective, and large numbers paragraphs, and even entire reports, may not get discussed at all.

There are even more delays in the finalisation of the reports by Committees, the Government's responses in the form of 'Action Taken Notes', their consideration by the Parliamentary Committees, and their further observations. Such a protracted and dilatory process greatly reduced the meaning of accountability.

The irregularities and improprieties reported in the CAG's audit reports should be taken note of promptly, discussed in the House and appropriate remedial and disciplinary actions taken without delay, and the information and outcome made readily available to the general public. How can this be ensured?

Special or Concurrent Audit

In the first place, audit reports themselves need to be expedited. This is linked with the compiletion of the accounts, which is a major subject in itself, but not our primary concern in this chapter.

However, we need not take the linkage with the accounting process as ineluctable. We have already suggested that there should be a monthly letter regarding cases which need investigation.

What this implies is a delinking of audit findings from the accounting cycle and we can carry this further. There can be special audit reports throughout the year when important audits are completed. Some special audit reports are already being submitted. but the practice needs to be expanded.

The more concurrent the audit process becomes, the more effective it will be (By concurrent' we mean 'as soon as possible after the action or decision', and not 'during the course of executive action or decision-making'; audit must necessarily remain an *ex post facto* check.

In respect of major purchases, works, projects or consultancy contracts, prompt completion of audit reports on the contracts themselves and periodical reports on their operation later may be among the most effective checks on corruption.

This would also apply to the audit of other major decisions, such as the leasing of oilfields or mineral deposits for development and exploitation, the selection bids for 'telecom' operations, raising of funds abroad, disinvestment of equity in public enterprises, and so on.

Such reports need not necessarily be 'thematic'; there could also be regular monthly or quarterly audit reports embodying the results of an audit of particular expenditures, receipts, sanctions contracts or other decisions having financial implications as distinguished from the audit of accounts.

In other words, there would be an annual audit report on the accounts containing the CAG's comments and a series of reports throughtout the year on particular cases and special themes. When necessary, there could be special reports on serious accounting failures.

These monthly or quarterly or special audit reports will be presented to the President/Governor in the same way as conventional annual audit reports. However, all these will be taken note of by the Fraud and Corruption Office referred to earlier which will identify cases needing further investigation.

Such cases will be included in the monthly letters suggested earlier, and will come within the purview of the investigative agencies and the committee to check fraud and corruption.

Making Reports Public

That still leaves the question of dissemination. Should the monthly letters, periodic audit reports, etc. suggested above, be released forthwith to the Press? There is much to be said for this. Everything should be in the public domain as much as possible. Transparency is the best safeguard against corruption, fraud and any other form of wrong doing.

In the USA, all GAO reports, unless classified for national security reasons, are available to the Press and the Public immediately upon issue, or within a few weeks. We must move towards that position.

Audit on Request

The special reports referred to above are those decided upon by the CAG. Should the CAG also undertake special checks at the request of others? It is possible that a department or ministry in the government may suspect the possibility of fraud or misappropriation or corruption and feel that a special audit is necessary.

Similarly, Parliament or one of its Committees and another investigative agency may desire that certain matter should be looked at with the expertise available in the IAD.

Thirdly, a member of the general public, voluntary organisation, or investigative journalist may propose a special examination by the CAG. In a sense, this would be similar to 'public interest litigation' in the legal domain. What should be the CAG's response to request?

Requests from Parliament will surely be on a special footing. The CAG may not be 'under' Parliament, but he is bound to give due weight to any suggestion emanating from that body. This would also apply to State Legislatures. Similarly, he is also bound to give due consideration to requests for special audits by the government.

Requests or suggestions emanating from individuals, voluntary organisations or the media may not carry the same weight but these too should be given proper consideration.

The CAG is no doubt a high constitutional functionary, but

it does not follow that he should refrain from responding to suggestions or requests for special audits received from outside. It would certainly be for the CAG to consider the material submitted to him and decide whether the matter warrants further examination.

If he decides in favour of a special audit, it could be undertaken as a regular departmental activity and not as a job taken up on behalf of another agency. It is understood that in the USA, in the context of the widespread concern arising from some emerging scandals in the late 70's, the GAO set up a nationwide tool-free 'hot line' through which federal employees or private citizens could communicate information regarding alleged instances of federal waste, fraud or abuse; a small special staff was established to follow up, investigate, and where appropriate, initiate action on the basis of such calls.

Once the CAG has decided that a matter which has been brought to his notice needs to be examined, his report on the subject will be submitted in the usual manner to the government and not to those who had suggested the examination.

Expertise to be made available

There is another aspect to this. The IAD is not merely a constitutionally mandated watchdog agency; it is also a specialised professional organisation with certain skills and capabilities which might be of value to other bodies.

When Parliament or its committees including Joint Parliamentary Committees set up for special purposes, or investigative agencies such as the CVC or the CBI undertake investigations into certain matters not necessarily arising from audit objections or reports, they may feel the need to enlist the expertise and experience available in the IAD for a thorough examination of the financial and accounting aspects.

There should be a readiness on the part of the CAG to respond positively to such cases without compromising his right to comment on the matters in question later on in the discharge of his constitutional responsibilities.

Similarly, if as a part of the effort to reform the electoral process, it is considered necessary to require political parties to get their accounts audited by the CAG, it seems desirable that the CAG to accept such a responsibility.

Needless to say, in all these cases, the undertaking of an examination by the CAG would be on the basis of an agreement by him to do so, and not as, a responsibility cast on him by another agency.

Speeding up Audit Reports

How can we ensure that Parliament and the State Legislatures take note of the CAG's reports and insist on appropriate and prompt remedial or punitive action being taken by the government? It is difficult to suggest procedural remedies.

It is really for Parliament and the State legislatures to enforce the accountability of the executive. If there is a lack of interest in this on their part, there are no answers left except perhaps public interest litigation by earnest persons or voluntary agencies who are deeply concerned about probity in public life.

The only positive step that can be thought of is to ensure that the CAG's reports reach the public domain as early as possible. In this scenario Parliament may conceivably come under some degree of public pressure to take notice of the reports.

As the reports become public only when they are placed before the Parliament or State legislature, it is necessary to see that they reach those bodies without delay. This can be achieved by laying down that all reports from the CAG should be placed before the Parliament or State legislature within three weeks from the date of their receipt by the President or Governor.

This would apply only to proper audit reports whether monthly or quarterly or annual, and not to the monthly letters which we had suggested earlier in this chapter, those would merely be communications for the purpose of facilitating an early start on investigations by the appropriate agencies, and it would be premature to give publicity to them at that stage.

Meanwhile, one possibility seems worth considering. There is now a vast accumulation of audit reports both at the Centre and in the States, and only a fraction of the reported matters have been discussed in Parliament, the State legislatures or the media.

It may be useful if the CAG could have all those reports carefully reviewed by a special team of officers, and a small, compact volume (one for the Centre and one for each of the States) brought out which selectively brings to notice the significant deficiencies, irregularities and improprieties which deserve attention despite the passage of time.

Such an effort could perhaps salvage at least a part of the valuable work done during the last several years and provide the basis for a useful debate in Parliament and elsewhere.

Recommendations

A number of suggestions and recommendations have been made in this Chapter. Some may require legislation or even constitutional amendments; some would need governmental decisions and orders. Others would call for decisions by the CAG and internal instructions within the IAD. A summary statement showing the necessary action need, and by whom, is appended below:

Points made	*Addressed To*	*Nature of Action*
1. Selection of CAG : High level Committee (on the analogy of the NHRC law) to slect CAG out of a wide field of choice, after laying down specific criteria for selection.	Govt. of India/ Parliament	Constitutional Amendment (Article 148)
2. Re-oreintation of IAD : Restore focus on basic audit function; re-discover role of auditors as financial/ accounting detectives.	CAG	Internal orders and guidelines in the IAD
3. Strengthening the hands of Audit: Empowering the Audit Office to summon officials to appear in person; judicious recourse to external checks and to information from sources other than 'auditee' offices; empowering the Audit Office to order recoveries or impose penalties.	Partly CAG; partly GOI, Parliament	Instructions by CAG; amendments to the CAG's Act (based on study of SAI statutes in other countries).
4. Bihar revelations:		
(a) Weaknesses in Audit Office and in State Govt. Dept. (control and check of treasuries, inadequacies of appropriation audit);	CAG/State Govt.	Enforce existing orders and procedures; tighten performance in IAD.
(b) Obviate excesses over voted grant through exchequer control or other measures;	CAG/GOI/Parliament	Work out a system; amend CAG's Act.
(c) Massive financial break down: special report by the CAG to Governor/President and release to press needed;	CAG	Decision by CAG
(d) Independent appraisal of IAD, with external consultancy.	CAG	CAG to establish a Committee; engage external consultants.
5. Pursuing pointers to corruption		
(a) Establish special cell in audit office to identify cases needing investigation; monthly letter to PM/CM, with copy to CVC/*ombudsman*;	CAG	Internal decisions in IAD.

Points made	Addressed To	Nature of Action
(b) Co-operation in investigations; a committee like the Serious Fraud Committee of the UK	GOI/State Govts/CAG	Order by CAG to Audit Offices; Government Resolution or Legislation establishing Committee. Internal decisions in
(c) Delinking audit reports from accounting cycle; monthly/quarterly concurrent audit reports.	CAG	IAD.
6. Audit on request		Decisions by CAG (if necessary, amendments to CAG's Act.)
(a) Need for positive response	CAG	
(b) Expert assistance needed by CVC, CBI, JPC, etc.	CAG	
7. Impact of Audit Reports:	CAG	Internal action in IADs
(a) Speed up ARs		
(b) ARs to reach Parliament/Legislature within 3 weeks after submission by CAG; make them public early.	Parliament/Legislatures; Govts—Central and State	Understanding between Govt and parliament (parallel action in States); amendments to Constitution (Art. 151)
(c) Special review and compendium of past reports	CAG	Internal action in IAD.

31

TRADE UNIONS: COMBATING CORRUPTION

The difference between bribe and gift has been most powerfully developed by reflection, theological and literary, on the Redemption.

Trade Unions perform several functions. One of the major function of Trade Unions is to raise a voice against injustice and corruption. Political parties, trade unions and public—all the three interact with one another in their fight against corruption.

Several patterns of trade unions exist. The British pattern forges an organic link between the trade union and the Labour Party. Other less institutionalized and more flexible arrangements exist in Norway, Belgium and several other countries.

Trade Unions in the socialist economics follows the function of a Transmission Belt between the party and the working people. The trade unions transmit the policy of the party to the working classes and take part in its preparation and implementation. Unions develop into, "a school of administration, a school of economic management, a school of communism".

The rate of unionization in these countries is 94% to 98%. In this system the major function of the trade union is to see that the principles and morals of the society are strictly observed, while anti-social acts are prevented from occurrence.

In developing economies, trade unions have adopted different approaches. In some African countries having a one party system, workers' organization receive guidance and protection from the parties. In countries where there is a multiple party system, trade unions help the parties with electoral and financial help.

In some Caribbean countries where trade unions have been historically associated with major political parties, payment of dues to the political parties give workers automatic trade union membership.

In India, for example, almost every political party has a trade union wing. Before independence, there was, by and large, a single union structure. This was mainly because the objective, various political parties namely, the Congress, the Socialist, and the Communist, was to attain freedom from the British rule.

For this a united working class was a necessary pre-condition. However, after independence such political compulsions ceased to exist and along with it, uniformity of organisation also came to an end.

This nexus between the trade unions and political parties have to explain a lot about the objective of social change. Trade unions have worked for the change of corrupt political system. Russian revolution, engineered by the working class, was the reaction to Czar's corrupt rule. Similarly, solidarity, a workers organization, in Poland played a significant role, in harbingering the democratic structure in that country.

A similar role was played by the trade unions in Romania and other Eastern European countries. Trade unions are playing a very significant role to check several malpractices of the capitalist countries.

They put a check on the excessive profit earning tendencies of the capitalist and force them to give the legitimate dues of these working class so to lessen their exploitation.

An individual may not be adequate to put a curb on the corrupt practices of a bureaucrat, businessman or politician, but trade unions as a group prove effective to restrain them. Trade unions, as anti-dote to their excessive power, endeavour to check their wrong doings by different techniques.

In a factory, Trade unions would vehemently oppose an out-of-turn allotment, recruitment or promotion or any other misuse of official position. Outside the factory the trade union itself would fight against corruption or help those forces which are fighting against corruption.

Trade unions in India and abroad have exposed several scandals especially in the government. Or public sector institutions. A bureaucrat, involved in wrong doings, may not be afraid of an individual but he is afraid of trade union as a group and may desist from doing a wrong act.

Thus, trade unions, the world over, have not only been successful in overthrowing the corrupt rulers and their system, but have also proved successful in checking the day-to-day corrupt practices and injustices.

Moral pressure of the society is the major mechanism to check corruption. Since a man, being a social animal, wants to be accepted and appreciated by the society, he would dissuade himself from the corrupt practice if he fears that the society's wrath will certainly fall upon him if he does a wrong act.

If the whole majority of the society gets corrupt and all the wrong acts get acceptance by them and are not resisted by the society no amount of law can check corruption.

There is a competition among people to possess consumer goods through methods-fair and foul. To enlighten the society on right path and to awaken masses against corrupt practices, trade unions have a major role to play.

From the point of view of corruption a society may pass through the following six stages.

Stage I People, by and large, are not corrupt but jobs and positions are few. There is lot of social resistance to any corrupt practice. Earnings through honest effort, though lower, are appreciated. Society puts a lot of check on corrupt people. Corrupts are afraid of the criticism of the society.

Stage 2 Again people, by and large, are not corrupt. Some of the leaders, who emerge as a chance factor misuse their power and get corrupt. They have abundant wealth and roll in comforts and luxuries. Their corruption is resisted by the general public and primarily due to social pressures some of these leaders are dropped.

Stage 3 Corrupt leaders/bureaucrats start incorporating a larger number of people in their clan so as to ensure their survival. They lure people and incorporate or destroy those who endanger them. The fear of society yet continues. These leaders/bureaucrats continue to give a posture of honesty.

Stage 4 Corruption perculates to lower ranks and start getting social acceptability. Because of their luxurious living they get respectability. Their develop *mafias* in each and every sphere and generates a white collar gangsterism.

The political, the bureaucrat, the businessman, the intellectual feed each other and form a click to check any opposition which disturbs their march towards amassing power and wealth.

Whole of the effort of the working class/peasant is channelized to fill their coffers. A majority of the expenditure of the Government directed to ameliorate the state of the poor is cornered by them. The *pseudo* trade union structure also help their members to follow this line. They get gains for their members at the cost of unorganized workers and peasants.

Stage 5 The gap between the exploiter and the exploited increases. The exploited start understanding the game of the rich and get united to fight back.: Owners of property could not sleep soundly in their beds. This fight continues, gets sharper and ultimately the downtrodden win the battle after facing several set-backs.

Stage 6 Again, distortions emerge in the new system. Those who remain in power for long start searching more and more of personal comforts. The process of fighting against the corrupt of the system restarts and continues till the human society learns to live equally and with dignity for all.

To bring about this change from a complete corrupt to a complete honest system, there is a need to generate social awakening so as to create social pressures. Trade unions are to play a significant role in this process of change.

Genuine trade unionism by definition requires a leader to be honest and sacrificing. Union leader should be a crusader for the rights of workers and ready to sacrifice personal gains to fight against the corrupt and exploitative management practices.

Corruption can be checked by persons/institutions only if they themselves are not corrupt. For example, political parties and their leadership in India,. before independence had an image of honesty.

The All India Trade Union Congress, also had a similar image and helped the political parties to achieve their objective i.e. to fight the British out and attain independence for India.

Both political parties and trade unions could get response from the public as they had leadership which was honest and sacrificing and their objective was noble.

Thus, honesty of the leadership and the nobleness of the objective motivated the people to join hands and they were successful in overthrowing the corrupt and ignoble foreign rule.

However, the scenario changes after independence. The power went to congress party. Leaders, who were in the forefront of freedom movement, by and large, got incorporated in the corrupt system, and started working in the interest of their families.

It encouraged corruption in every walk of life. Next generation of these freedom fighters, by and large, become 'Open Corrupts'. Since their fathers forgot the lessons of sacrifice, they threw them to the winds.

Indian National Trade Union Congress (INTUC) which was an affiliate of Congress Party; also, by and large, helped these leaders in their design. INYUC'S Leadership, by and large, also got itself involved in sharing the booty. The party and the union, which started with Gandhian ideals became a party/ union of the power seekers and corrupt persons.

A very long rule by the Congress party at the centre and the states further strengthened these forces, INTUC got acceptance from the management because of the patronage of the congress rule in the state. It, by and large, helped the management and opposed those forces which wanted to fight out the injustices and corrupt practices of the authorities.

As explained earlier, India, after independence, had a multiple union structure. Union belonging to opposition parties such as AITUC, CITU, HMS, BMS, UTUC started rasing their voice for the working class.

However, they could not unite themselves for the unorganized and poor. They remained more keen to serve their membership and utilized them for the political struggles to wean away the power from the Congress Party. Trade Unions were their major source of funds and cadres.

Whenever, a political party belonging to opposition came to power in centre/states trade unions affiliated to them behaved like INTUC to congress-ruled states. For examples, strikes launched by left unions are very few in West Bengal than in the Congress-ruled states.

Trade unions belonging to the ruling party did not play the role of conscience keeper of the ruling party and led to a system of corrupt union leadership which is unable to work for social change or work for the system which helps the downtrodden. Therefore, it is not surprising to find that degree of unionization in India is below 10%.

However, to change the scenario, we need to change the way to administer things. There is a need to create awareness amongst the poorest of the poor to organize. They should build mass movements and change the existing social order. Dignity of each person be protected and every one should get equal status in the society.

Democratic functioning should be encouraged at the grass root level. There should be improvement of quality of work life with a willing cooperation between labour and management to achieve high standards of production.

To fight corruption and injustice in the society, it is very essential that trade union leaders should work for high ideals and should not themselves be corrupt.

Trade unions have always played a significant role for the peace and prosperity of the world. They should continue with their spirit and work for the removal of social evils and achieve economic justice for all.

32

ESTABLISHING INQUIRY COMMISSIONS

Corruption of all sorts has permeated our social fabric to such as extent that we now have a parallel economy, a parallel state and a parallel morality.

India is, perhaps, the only democracy whose constitutional, legal and political systems do not ensure accountability to law by men at the helm of the nation's affairs despite having a Constitution which is based on the rule of law.

The void in politics, stemming from the failure to evolve an effective party system and the absence of democratic functioning within the parties, among other things, is concerned with the legal and constitutional aspects of the problem.

Some of the drawbacks are common to all parliamentary democracies. In actual practice, the executive controls the legislature, and not the other way around, as theory ordains. One of the most eloquent and best-known critiques of this distortion was delivered on October 14, 1976 by Lord Hailasham in the Richard Dimbleby Lectures on BBC:

"The checks and balances which in practice used to prevent abuse have now disappeared," he wanted. An "elective dictatorship is a fact and not just a lawyer's theory. Party discipline has become more strict. The power of whips has increased. Back-benches count increasingly for little"!

Hailsham said "All other free nations impose limitations on their representative assemblies. We impose none on ours." In contrast, India's Constitution does impose precise limitations on its legislatures, but the polity has none of the other checks which operate in other democracies and is not sustained by a culture of autonomy.

For example, in India, both the police and the prosecution machinery are firmly under executive control, despite judicial pronouncements on the independence of the police.[2]

It needs to be emphasized, at the very outset, that this flaw alone can vitiate any institution that may be devised to ensure accountability, be it the Commission of Inquiry or the *Lok Pal.* Both depend on the police. As two authorities on constitutional law, Geoffrey Marshall and Barry Loveday, point out:

"The impartiality of the police is one of the main components of the rule of law. In recent times impartiality has been seen as guaranteed by the doctrine that all police officers have a degree of independence guaranteed by the law that is enjoyed by no other central or local executive officer."[3]

This is certainly not true of India. Interestingly, while British works on constitutional law invariable discuss the legal status of the police force. Indian works on the subject do not.

Nor does India have any of the other checks such as an informed and assertive public opinion, well-organised political parties and a powerful Press although there has been considerable progress in these fields of late. The result is that a disproportionate burden has falled on the judiciary.

As the debates in the Constituent Assembly show, the farmers of the Constitution of India were well aware of the rise in corruption among ministers, civil servants, and the society in general.

On one occasion, December 31, 1948, Dr. B.R. Ambedkar urged disclosure of assets by ministers at the time of assumption as well as demission of their office.[4] But no institutional checks were devised.

Corruption in public life goes back to the days when the freedom movement was in full swing. On a complaint by the Governor of Bengal, the Private Secretary to the Viceroy, G.F. de Montmorency, wrote to the Home Member of the Viceroy's

Executive Council, Sir James Crerar, on August 16, 1924 about "actual payments made to members of the Legislative Council of Bengal to vote with the Swaraj Party."[5]

The premier political party, the Indian National Congress, tended to treat corruption as a party matter and the approach of it's leaders was often politically selective.[6] The most striking instance of this is the Party's treatment of the Bihar Molasses Scandal. The Congress President, Dr. Rajendra Prasad, sent a colleague, Shankarrao Deo, to Bihar "to look into the matter".[7]

Prasad complained to Home Minister Vallabhbhi Patel, on January 17, 1949 about Prime Minister Jawaharlal Nehru's omission to institute an inquiry.[8] The tendency persisted for over a decade after Independence. A party inquiry in 1958 exonerated the Chief Minister of Pubjab, Pratap Singh Kairon, of charges of corruption.[9]

One case, in particular, that aroused much disquiet was "the Jeep Scandal" in which grave charges were levelled against India's High Commissioner to the U.K., V.K. Krishna Menon. It was dealt with first by a Sub-Committee of the Congress Parliamentary Party which reported on April 9, 1951, and next by the Public Accounts Committee in it's Ninth Report. It recommended inquiry by a "high-level committee consisting of one or two High Court Judges." The Government of India refused to do so and declared the case to be closed on September 30, 1955.

In 1951, A.D. Gorwala, a civil servant with high reputation for integrity had bean asked by the Planning Commission to consider in different fields the question whether the present administrative machinery and methods were adequate and could meet the requirements of planned development. His report had a whole section entitled, Integrity.[10]

Now, nearly half a century later, the report still makes poignant reading. Gorwala wrote: "Parliamentary government is in it's infancy in the country. Accordingly, this is the proper time to lay down and observe conventions, so that with the passage of years they may consolidate into traditions which, those who come hereafter, will accept instinctively knowing that, based as they are on the wisdom of their fathers, they will serve their turn well."

Recalling the Sanskrit proverb, "*As the king, so the people*", he stressed that it was the conduct of those at the top which shaped the country's development. By 1951, the situation in this regard had deteriorated enough for Gorwala to record the following:

> ". . . during the past few years there have been various instances in which grave allegations of a specific nature have been made by responsible parties against persons occupying the position of Ministers of Government. Such allegations have on occasion been the subject of debates in the Legislatures. The ministry, as a whole, and the party which has put it in power having thrown their weight behind the minister complained against, the debates have either been inconclusive or have ended in a vote in his favour. Thereafter, the matter has generally been ended. Enquiries into the allegations have sometimes been made by senior all-India leaders of the principal political party: occasionally, their reports have been made public, but often they have remained secret. Some of the reports have exculpated those complained against and some have, in effect, condemned them. In any case, no action has been taken. It is not surprising that when grave allegations by responsible parties are made against people holding positions of high authority and they remain in power without being cleared of the accusations, the public feel that the influential always escape punishment."

Gorwala, therefore, urged that: "arrangements must be made that no one, however highly placed, is immunce from enquiry if allegations against him are made by responsible parties and a *prime facte* case exists."

This is the crux of the matter; the initiation of an investigation into crime or an inquiry into charge of corruption or mal-administration must not depend on the wishes of the men in power. If it does, it ceases to be government according to the rule of law.

Gorwala, obviously influenced by the Lynskey Tribunal in Britain which had found John Belcher, Parliamentary Secretary to the Board of Trade, guilty of grave misconduct (1948), remarked:

> "There is no reason why similar tribunals could not work satisfactorily in this country, considering the high standard of our judiciary. All facilities for directing investigation, obtaining evidence, examining documents, etc., would have to be placed at the disposal of the tribunal. The authority responsible for setting up the tribunal might, for the Central Government, be the President, and for State Government, the Governor acting in consultation with the President. They, in either case, on being satisfied that there was *prima facie* evidence, would appoint a tribunal. An alternative would be to vest the power of appointing such tribunals in the Supreme Court."[11]

This was, probably, the first official document to discuss corruption by politicians in power. The tendency hitherto was to treat the vice as an affliction of the civil services or businessmen.

The Report of the Corruption Enquiry Committee appointed by the Congress Government in Bihar, on April 8, 1938, for instance, was confined to "the crying evils of bribery and corruption believed to be prevailing in the various public services of Bihar." The report, submitted on November 30, 1938, left corruption elsewhere alone.

The British model was emulated by Parliament in 1952 when it passed the Commissions of Inquiry Act 60 of 1952. Hitherto, Commissions of Inquiry were appointed under executive order. Their remit generally concerned police firings or railway and other accidents.

The Act was not intended specifically to provide a standing machinery for investigation into charges of misconduct against ministers or civil servants but simply to be a ready mechanism for inquiries with statutory powers "to enforce the attendance of witnesses and the production of documents." The first Commission of note to be appointed under the Act was the Press Commission on October 3, 1952.

The Act left the appointment of a Commission at the sole

discretion of the Government or the Lower House of the Legislature, Central or State; in other words, the party in power. Section 3(1), as originally enacted, reads thus:

"The appropriate Government may, if it is of opinion that it is necessary so to do, and shall, if a resolution in this behalf is passed by the House of the people or, as the case may be, the Legislative Assembly of the State, by notification in the Official Gazette, appoint a Commission of Inquiry for the purpose of making an inquiry into any definite matter of public importance and performing such functions and within such time, as may be specified in the notification, and the Commission so appointed shall make the inquiry and perform the function accordingly."

Two features of the Act Stand out. One is that the appointment of members of the Commission was also left to the discretion of the Government (Section 3 (2)). There was no provision for consultation with the Chief Justice of India or the High Court and the Leader of the Opposition. The other is that the scope of the remit was defined in words of the widest amplitude: "Definite matter of public importance."

The Central Government was free, as the "appropriate Government" defined by Section 2(a), to appoint a Commission to make an inquiry into any matter relating to any of the entries enumerated in any of the lists of topics for legislation in the Seventh Schedule to the Constitution. The power of the States was confined to List II or III.

A significant change was made by Section 2 of the Commissions of Inquiry (Amendment) Act 19 of 1990 in Section 3 of the Act of 1952. For the words "the House of the People or, as the case may be, the Legislative Assembly of the State" were substituted with the words "each House of Parliament, or as the case may be, the Legislature of the State".

This would enable an opposition - dominated Rajya Sabha or Legislative Council in a State to appoint a Commission of Inquiry even against the wishes of the Government. However, it's composition would, none-the-less, be determined by the Government, not to forget the dependence of Commissions of Inquiry on the official machinery.

Article 44 of the Basic Law of the Federal Republic of Germany enables one-fourth of the members of the *Bundestag* (the Lower House of Parliament), to institute an inquiry. Article 44 is instructive and reads thus:

"(1) the *Bundestag* shall have the right, and, upon the motion of one-fourth of it's members the duty, to set-up a committee of investigation which shall take the requisite evidence at public hearings. The public may be excluded.

"(2) The rules of criminal procedure shall apply *nutatis mutandis* to the taking of evidence. The privacy of posts and telecommunications shall remain unaffected.

"(3) Courts and administrative authorities shall be bound to render legal and administrative assistance."

The Commissions of Inquiry Act, 1952 endows Commissions with the powers of a civil courts to ensure attendance of witnesses, requisition of documents and receipt of evidence on affidavits, etc. (Section 4). The Act was reviewed by the Law Commission of India in it's Twenty-Fourth Report in December 1962.

In 1971, the Act was amended by the Commissions of Inquiry (Amendment Act 79 of 1971 to empower Commissions to utilise the services of Government officers or investigation agencies under a newly inserted Section 5A which reads thus:

(1) The commission may, for the purpose of conducting any investigation pertaining to the inquiry, utilise the services;

(a) in the case of a commission appointed by the Central Government, of any officer or investigation agency of the Central Government or any State Government with the concurrence of the Central Government or the State Government, as the case may be; or

(b) in the case of a commission appointed by the state Government, of any officer or investigation agency of the State Government or Central Government with the concurrence of the State Government or the Central Government, as the case may be."

The officer or agency is empowered to summon witnesses, requisition records etc., and report to the Commission. As Section 5A(5) says: "The Commission shall satisfy itself about the correctness of the facts stated and the conclusions, if any, arrived at in the investigation report submitted to it under Sub-Section (4), and for this purpose the Commission may make such inquiry (including the examination of the person or persons who conducted or assisted in the investigation) as it thinks fit."

Thus, the Commission may not employ a private investigation agency or individual. The appointment depends on "the concurrence" of the Government. In practice, the Commissions of Inquiry depend on the CBI or the State police.

The Amendment Act of 1971 also added provisions for the protection of the reputation of persons likely to be prejudically affected and obligates the Commissions of Inquiry to give them "a reasonable opportunity of being heard." Section 8B and 8C confer detailed rights of participation on such persons.

The Amendment Act enjoined "the appropriate Government" to lay the Commission's Report before the Lok Sabha or the State Assembly, as the case may be, "together with a memorandum of the action taken thereon within a period of six months of the submission of the report by the Commission to appropriate Government" [Section 3(4)]. This provision has been honoured more in its breach than in it's observance.

For two decades from 1958 onwards, the Commissions of Inquiry Act, 1952 served as a fairly effective instrument for investigation into charges of corruption, abuse of power and the like; in each case, however, because the government established it whether of it's own free volition or under force of circumstances.

The first notable Commission of Inquiry to be appointed under the Act to inquire into a public scandal was the one comprising the Chief Justice of Bombay, M.C. Chagla, on the Life Insurance Corporation of India's (LIC) purchase of shares in certain companies controlled by Haridas Mundhra. It was appointed on January 7, 1958 and submitted a report on February 13, 1958. This record of despatch has not been equalled. There was no evidence on affidavit.

All the witnesses deposed orally on oath in open proceedings. They included Feroze Gandhi, MP; T.T. Krishnamachari, Union Finance Minister; H.M. Patel, Principal Secretary to the Finance Ministry; H.V.R. Iyengar, Governor of the Reserve Bank and G.R. Kamat, Chairman of the LIC. M.C. Setalwad, Attorney General, appeared for the government but acted independently and made no attempt to act as defence counsel for the Minister. He performed the same role as tradition ordains for the Attorney General in Britain and as was performed by Sir Hartley Shawcross before the Lynskey Tribunal in 1946. In the circumstances, there was no counsel for the Commission.

Another noteworthy, feature was that the Commission was not asked to probe into charges in a memorandum or, for that matter, debates in Parliament on a particular day. The Commission was required to inquire into three main questions:

"(i) Whether the purchases were in accordance with normal business principles or practices;

(ii) the propriety of the purchases; and

(iii) the person or persons responsible for the purchases."

Justice Chagla, however, took the unusual course of personally examining the witnesses first, leaving it to the Attorney General to "supplement the evidence in any manner that he thinks proper."

In January 28, Haridas Mundhra's application for legal representation was rejected by the Commission, though he had been summoned to give evidence and grave charges had been levelled against him earlier in the proceedings. The Attorney General also opposed Mundhra's pleas.[12]

Justice Chagla found that there was clear acquiescence on the part of the minister in the role played by Patel with regard to the transaction of June 24, 1957 and the lack of repudiation by the minister supported Patel's case that the minister had approved of the transaction in Bombay.

Having rejected Krishnamachari's version on the basis of the evidence, Chagla stated the legal position as follows: "In my opinion, in any case, it is clear that constitutionally the Minister is responsible for the action taken by his Secretary with regards to this transaction. It is clear that a Minister must take the responsibility for actions done by his subordinates.

He cannot take shelter behind them. Nor can he disown their actions. The doctrine of ministerial responsibility has two facets. The Minister has complete autonomy within his own sphere or authority. As a necessary corollary, he must take full responsibility for the actions of his servants."[13] T.T. Krishnamachari resigned from the Union Cabinet.

As late as June 3, 1960, the Congress working Committee passed the following resolution:

"Whereas complaints are received occasionally about misuse of authority by responsible Congressmen, it is advisable to have a permanent machinery to examine the merits of such complaints."

For this purpose, the President is authorised to appoint a Panel out of which he may nominate one or more persons, wherever he considers such action necessary, to inquire into such complaints and to report to him." The Act of 1952 was not even mentioned.

Nor was it invoked when, in 1963, charges were levelled against Union Minister for Mines and Fuel, K.D. Malaviya, in the Serajuddin affair. Instead, Prime Minister Nehru referred them to a sitting judge of the Supreme Court, Justice S.K. Das, rejecting the advice of the Attorney General, C.K. Daphtary, for a full inquiry. He told the Lok Sabha on May 7, 1963:

> "There is going to be on judicial inquiry as such.
>
> This matter essentially is a matter for the Prime Minister to decide on the advice of eminent persons. It will naturally be a quasi-judicial inquiry because there is a Supreme Court Judge.
>
> It is not a normal judicial inquiry, it is not that with judicial procedures and all that. It will be upto him to decide,, of course."[14]

On August 17, 1963, the results of the inquiry were announced in the *Lok Sabha*. Two of the six charges were upheld. The report was not published. Malaviya resigned from the Cabinet. He expressed great dissatisfaction with the procedure followed by the Judge. So did the Opposition.

The procedure satisfied nobody. Such an approach to inquiries set a tradition of stalling on inquiries even when they were called for on the facts. Nehru's note recommending an inquiry dated October 25, 1963 to President S. Radhakrishan on the Kairon case, was written in the wake of certain strictures on Kairon by the Supreme Court.[15]

A memorandum of charges against Kairon had been presented to the Congress President, U.N. Dhebar, as far back as May 4, 1958, but nothing came of it. Another was presented to his successor on August 14, 1960 with similar results. Only the Supreme Court's strictures against the Chief Minister of Punjab for not responding personally and on sworn affidavit to charges made against him forced the Centre's hands.

On November 1, 1963, the Government of India appointed a commission of Inquiry, consisting of Justice S.R. Das, a former Chief Justice of India, "to inquire into the allegations made against Kairon by Devi Lal and others in a memorandum presented to the President of India on the 13th July, 1963". The inquiry was held on the basis of affidavits and not oral evidence.

The report recorded: "The Commission took the view that where the affidavits taken and read together were reasonably clear and unambiguous and the Commission was able to hold, without any reasonable doubt, that a *prima facie* case had not been made out in respect of one or more of the charges.

The persons making or supporting such charges could not be permitted to have another opportunity to adduce fresh evidence or to cross-examine the person charged on the off-chance of being able to make out a case which in legal parlance may be said to be sufficient to go to the jury.

Likewise, if a *prima facie* case had been out in respect of one or more of the charges the person charged could not be permitted to claim another opportunity to clear himself by adducing fresh evidence or cross-examining the persons making the charges.

The Commission was of the opinion that where the affidavits were so evenly balanced that it could not come to a firm conclusion, then and then only, could the Commission say that it was necessary to record oral evidence."

The Commission accepted that it's inquiry had neither prosecutor or plaintiff, no accused or defendant. "There is no list of charges to be adjudicated upon......it's function is only to inquire."[16] But, in effect, the Commission converted itself into a court trying specific charges in the memorandum and cast the *onus* of proof entirely on the memorialists.

It rejected their submission that "it was the duty of the Commission to collect all available evidence by the exercise of its own powers."[17] The Commission ruled "that an individual must be presumed to be innocent until the contrary is proved beyond reasonable doubt by dependable evidence freely given and publicly ascertained or by the irresistible probabilities of the Case."[18]

The two are not identical. The former is the standard of proof required in a criminal case and the latter is required in a civil suit. Several charges were upheld. Prime Minister Lal Bahadur Shastri published the report in view of Kairon's reluctance to resign. Kairon resigned at once.

The Das Report was published on June 11, 1964. Shortly before that, on March 31, 1964, the Committee on Prevention of Corruption set-up by the Government of India in 1962 submitted its report.

The Committee was headed by K. Santhanam and it's members were Santosh Kumar Basu, M.P., Tikaram Paliwal, M.P., R.K. Khadilkar, M.P.; Nath Pai, M.P.; Shambu Nath Chaturvedi, M.P.; L.P. Singh, Director, Administrative Vigilance Division and D.P. Kohli, Inspector General, Special Police Establishment. The terms of reference dealt mainly with government servants.

Only one term of reference was general enough to bring ministers within it's ambit, viz, "to suggest measures calculated to produce a social climate both amongst public servants and in the general public in which bribery and corruption may not flourish." The Committee considered the aspect of ministers in the chapter entitled, Social Climate.

The Committee's assessment of the "climate" was no different from Gorwala's little over a decade earlier. It said:

> "There is a wide-spread impression that failure of integrity it not uncommon among Ministers and that

> some Ministers, who have held office during the last 16 years, have enriched themselves illegitimately, obtained good jobs for their sons and relations through nepotism, and have reaped other advantages inconsistent with any notion of purity in public life. The general belief about failure of integrity amongst Ministers is as damaging as actual failure.......
>
> "It is pity that neither the Congress authorities nor the great leaders who took over the Government of India realised that importance of evolving a suitable machinery and procedure for preventing and dealing with such corruption."[19]

The Committee proceeded to make two recommendations in this regard. One was a code of conduct for Ministers. The other was a defined procedure for investigation into charges against them:

> ". . . .If a formal allegation is made by any ten members of Parliament or a Legislature in writing addressed to the Prime Minister or Chief Minister, through the Speakers and Chairman, the Prime Minister or Chief Minister should consider himself obliged, by convention, to refer the allegations for immediate investigation by a Committee, as has been suggested later in this Section.

This would be in addition to the responsibilities of the Chief Ministers of States to take note of minister and chief allegations made in the Press or which otherwise come to their notice. In respect of such allegations also the Prime Minister and the Chief Ministers should be free to refer the matter to the proposed Committee.......

> "We consider that the appropriate course would be for the President to constitute on the advice of the Prime Minister a national panel. Whenever allegations against a Minister require to be inquired into an *ad hoc* Committee should be selected out of this nation's panel by the president.
>
> The Committee may consist of three persons one of whom, at least, should have held or should be holding

> a high judicial office. It should be the duty of the Committee to ascertain whether there is a *prima facie* case. The Committee should have the power to direct the Central Bureau of Investigation, in suitable cases, to investigate and report.
>
> If the Committee wishes to make any inquiries, otherwise then through the Central Bureau of Investigation, it should be given all the necessary facilities and assistance including free access to all documents, files, etc., without being hampered by any claim of privilege.
>
> On the completion of the inquiries either through the Central Bureau of Investigation or otherwise, the Committee should consider the available material and advise as to further action, if any, that may be necessary. It may advise that a regular case be registered for investigation with a view to prosecute the Minister concerned or a Commission of Inquiry be appointed under the Commissions of Inquiry Act, 1952.
>
> If the Committee makes such a recommendation, the Minister should resign as a matter convention and should remain out of office till the completion of the proceedings. If the Minister is found guilty of the allegations or is found to have been corrupt, he should be dismissed and should also become ineligible for becoming a Minister or for holding any elective office.
>
> The necessary legal instruments for giving effect to this provision should be brought into existence. Until such time as the necessary legislation is made, there should be convention which would give effect to this provision."[20]

The core of the second recommendation is the initiation of an inquiry at the request of any ten legislators regardless of the wishes of the Government in power; initially "by convention" and eventually, under a "legal instrument." The *ad hoc* Committee's function and duty would be "to ascertain whether there is a *prima facie* case."

This would effectively deprive governments of the standard pretext, which has been almost invariably advanced whenever memoranda of charges are delivered viz., that they do not disclose a *prima facie* case. The Committee would be assisted by the CBI. If a *prima facie* case is disclosed, it could advise either registration of a case for investigation or appointment of a Commission of Inquiry.

It is a matter of opinion whether a Committee of three persons, one of whom should have held or should be holding a high judicial office, is necessary for so limited a function. It is very much the duty of the police, in law, to act on any information about commission of an offence laid before it and to investigate into it diligently and expeditiously.

As for the appointment of a Commission of Inquiry, as will be pointed out at the conclusion of this survey, an effective arrangement can be arrived at so as to activate whether a Commission of Inquiry or the *Lok Pal* and leave it to either to pronounce on the charges.

The governing test would not be the existence of a *prima facie* case but, as the Salmon Commission put it, "a nation-wide crisis of confidence" which warrants the appointment of a Commission. In other cases, the charges should be inquired into by the *Lok Pal*.

The Commission of Inquiry that followed tended, by and large, to follow the precedent set by the Das Commission and inquire into specific memoranda of charges. They did not act as inquisitorial bodies.

Justice N. Rajagopalan, a former Judge of the Supreme Court, was appointment on a Commission of Inquiry set-up by the Government of Jammu & Kashmir on January 30, 1965. Its terms of reference were in two parts. One concerned "the nature and extent of the assets and pecuniary resources" of Bakshi Ghulam Mohammed, members of his family and named relatives in October 1947, when he became Minister, and in October 1963, when he resigned as Chief Minister of the State.

The second part of the terms of reference directed the Commission to inquire whether, during the same period, Bakshi Ghulam Mohammed and members of his family and other relatives "obtained any assets, pecuniary resources or advantages or other benefits by Bakshi Ghulam Mohammed abusing the various official positions held by him or by the aforesaid members of his family, his other relatives and persons exploiting with his consent, knowledge or connivance the various official positions held by him."

In making this latter inquiry, however, the Commission was asked to consider only the thirty-seven specific allegations listed in the Second Schedule to the terms of reference.

The Commission relied on affidavits and official records. The State Government adduced such evidence in support of the charges, but did not lead any oral evidence to explain contradictions although it was afforded an opportunity to do so.

The standard which the Commission adopted was proof so "overwhelming" as to rule out "any alternative innocent explanation". The *onus* of proof rested on the government. A good many charges were upheld.

Bakshi had been arrested on September 22, 1964, in order to prevent him from moving a motion of no-confidence against the G.M. Sadiq Ministry, and was released in December 1964. Despite the adverse findings in the Commission's Report submitted on June 30, 1967, he was given the Congress (R)'s ticket for the *Lok Sabha* elections in 1971.

Meanwhile, in 1967, the State Government persuaded the State legislature to adopt an amendment to the Representation of the People Act disqualifying persons found guilty by the Commissions of Inquiry.

Since there is no corresponding provision in the Central law on the subject, viz. the Representation of the People Act, 1951, the result was that Bakshi could be an MP, but not an MLA. He could aspire for the Prime Ministership of the country, which was well beyond his reach, but he was effectively barred from ever becoming the Chief Minister of the State, which was well within his reach then.

Despite a CBI Report dated November 15, 1964 recommending "further inquiries" into charges levelled by the Opposition against the former Chief Minister of Orissa, Biju Patnaik - who had resigned as such in 1963—and his successor, Biren Mitra, no Commission of Inquiry was appointed.

Instead, the charges were examined by a Sub-Committee of the Union Cabinet. It found "the improper use of authority by leaders of the Government" but opined against the setting up of a Commission of Inquiry.

It was only after the General Elections of 1967 when a non-Congress Ministry came to power that a judicial inquiry was set-up. On October 26, 1967, the Singh Deo Ministry appointed H.R. Khanna, who was, then, a Judge of the Delhi High Court, as the Commission of Inquiry to inquire into charges against Patnaik, Biren Mitra and thirteen other Ministers, including Sadasiba Tripathi, Leader of the Opposition. Justice H.R. Khanna submitted his report on January 15, 1969. The Commission found Patnaik and Biren Mitra guilty of some grave improprieties.

The terms of reference required the Commission to inquire into the conduct of named persons between June 23, 1961 and March 8, 1967 from which "it appears" to the State Government that they had "committed various acts of misconduct, misappropriation", etc.

The Commission observed that "as the precise particulars are missing, the respondents cannot be said to have notice of the factual allegations they have to meet and rebut."

It cited the provisions of the Code of Civil Procedure on civil suits and the Code of Civil Procedure on the particulars required in a valid charge. The State Government thereupon filed the particulars, as directed by the Commission, which upheld certain charges and rejected others. Again, this was more a trial than an inquiry.

In a related case, a former Judge of the Supreme Court, justice J.R. Mudholkar, was requested by the Chief Minister of Orissa, R.N. Singh Deo "for a preliminary verification" of charges made in a memorial to the President on June 26, 1967 alleging acts of corruption and improprieties against Minister who held office between 1947 and 1961.

The Chief Minister's letter of May 3, 1966 outlined the remit to Justice Mudhollar, who proceeded thereafter to style himself as "Special Judge for Inquiries." In his report dated September 26, 1968, Justice Mudholkar found a *prima facie* case against Harekrushna Mahtab on various counts.

On January 8, 1971, the Orissa Government appointed Sarjoo Prasad, a former Chief Justice of Rajasthan and Assam High Courts but, then, a practicing advocate at the Supreme Court, as Commission of Inquiry, only hours before the Singh Deo Government fell as a result of Mahtab's withdrawal of support to it.

Sarjoo Prasad took oral evidence. The memorialists made themselves scarce, "may be due to changes on the political stage," the Commission remarked. The State Government filed detailed particulars in support of charges, some of which were upheld in a Report dated May 25, 1972.

A similar course was adopted in the Bihar inquiries, Justice T.L. Venkatarama Aiyar, a former Judge of the Supreme Court, was appointed to a Commission of Inquiry on October 1, 1967 by the United Front Minister of Bihar to probe into allegations of abuse of power and corruption against six former ministers of the State belonging to the Congress. The Commission directed the State "to file a statement specifying the charges" against them. The inquiry was held on affidavit evidence.

It ruled that "the burden is undoubtedly on the State to establish the charge, beyond all reasonable doubt". The Report upheld several charges.

The United Front Ministry fell on January 25, 1968 when the Assembly passed on a no-confidence motion against it. A new Ministry was formed by the Soshi Dal headed by B.P. Mandal with the support of the Congress Party. Mandal and others of the Dal had defected from the Front earlier in August 1967. Mandal's ministry did not last long.

On March 18, 1968, it succumbed to a motion of no-confidence, but not before it had appointed, on March 12, another Commission of Inquiry to inquire into charges against the Ministers of the United Front Ministry. Justice Mudholkar conducted the inquiry.

Here, again, "formal charges were formulated by the State against the respondents and filed before the Commission." It ruled that a "notification (under Section 3 of the Act) which permits an inquiry to be made into the conduct of an unnamed person would rob it of definiteness. It must, therefore, be characterised as ultra vires."

Kerala is a classic case of the use of the Commission of Inquiry as a political weapon. The High Court struck down on January 20, 1970 the notification appointing one such Commission on the ground of *mala fide*.[21]

One Commission of Inquiry, headed by Justice S. Velu Pillai, was appointed by a resolution of the State Assembly on October 17, 1969 in respect of four ministers. His remit comprised "the allegation of corruption and favouritism raised on the floor of the House and those submitted to the Hon'ble Home Minister by some Hon'ble Members of this House".

The Commission held: "A vast area of accusations made in the Assembly was left uncovered by the statements of the parties in the inquiries (the memorialists). I did not conceive it to be proper or within my province in holding an inquiry of this nature, fact-finding though it be, to act as an investigator myself or to devise a machinery to investigate the truth of those accusations.

At the same time, I could not simply shut my eyes to them, for want of pleading as in a civil action. Such accusations had, of course, to be tested; for this purpose, as no material was furnished by members of the public pursuant to the public notification and to the individual letters addressed, I had to rely for the most part on government files".

In law, the Commission is very much required "to act as an investigator itself." The standard of proof adopted was the same as in a criminal trial - proof, beyond reasonable doubt.

The Interim Probe Machinery Order of December 12, 1969 enabled any citizen to set in motion the process of accountability. Once, Justice R. Sankaranarayana Iyer found that a *prima facie* case existed against P.K. Kunju, following the procedure laid down in the Order, Justice Velu Pilai was appointed as Commission of Inquiry by the State Government in 1970.

He was asked to ascertain "the extent of debts" of Kunju when he became Minister and "the portion of the debts repaid "by him when he was Finance Minister, "the sources of funds," and a specific charge of nepotism.

A.N. Mulla, was a former Judge but a practicing counsel

when he was appointed as Commission of Inquiry on October 18, 1969 to inquire into charges made against M.N. Govindan Nair and T.V. Thomas in two memoranda. Oral as well as documentary evidence was received.

Justice P. Govinda Menon was appointed as Commission of Inquiry on December 16, 1970 to inquire into the charges levelled against B. Wellingdon in the Kerala Assembly on three specified days. The report was submitted on March 24, 1972.

Thus, all the Commissions of Inquiry that inquired into charges of corruption or misconduct against ministers followed the precedent set by the Das Commission in 1964 and functioned as courts of law trying specific charges rather than following an inquisitorial procedure.

After an interval of eight years, the Central Government appointed on October 16, 1971 what proved to be precursor to a series of Commissions of Inquiry against ministers of State governments run by political parties who were opposed to the ruling party at the Centre. Kairon's was the last case of a Central Commission of Inquiry against a member of the ruling party.

This time it was against former ministers of Pubjab, including P.S. Badal, former Chief Minister, in respect to charges made in memoranda and letters to the president plus "further allegations....that may be referred to the Commission by the Central Government." The Government did not produce any evidence, however.

Initially, Justice D.S. Dave, former Chief Justice, was appointed to conduct the inquiry, but he was unable to proceed much further. On January 20, 1973, Justice L.N. Chhangani, a former Judge of the Rajasthan High Court, succeeded him. He made plain his rejection of the standard of proof adopted hitherto by previous Commissions, viz., one of proof beyond reasonable doubt.

But he did not propound his alternative in clear terms beyond saying that "the approach in such inquiries should be non-doctrinaire, pragmatic, realistic and imaginative rather than doctrinaire, mechanical or wooden."[22] As in Kerala, the Commission's work was hampered by the indifference of the memorialists once the Commission was set-up.

Into the same genre falls the Sarkaria Commission. It was quintessentially an off-shoot of the Emergency. Memoranda against the Chief Minister of Tamil Nadu, M. Karunanidhi and his colleagues had been submitted to the President as far back as November 1972.

Prime Minister Indira Gandhi sought his explanations that month. He responded in December 1972. By 1973, the process of rejoinders by memorialists and replies thereto was over.

On January 31, 1976, President's Rule was imposed in the State. On February 3, the Government of India appointed Justice R.S. Sarkaria, a sitting Judge of the Supreme Court, as Commission of Inquiry to inquire into allegations contained in the memoranda submitted to the President in 1972 and on December 1, 1975, on April 12, 1976, the Commission invoked Section 5A of the Act and sought the assistance of the investigating agencies of the Centre and the State.

The Commission ruled that "the task of the Commission is essentially inquisitorial". The memorialists are not "*dominus litis*. They cannot stop the enquiry by abandoning their allegations" before the Commission.

There is grave doubt as to the correctness of the Commission's rejection of the respondent's plea for oral examination of deponents of affidavits, especially on matters on which affidavit evidence is intrinsically inadequate; for example, charges of receipt of illegal gratification. Karunanidhi and most of the other respondents withdrew from the Commission as had the Punjab Ministers from the Chhangani Commission.

Similar problems arose in the Commissions set-up in the post-Emergency days on how to ensure that rights of persons charged with misconduct and summoned to appear before the Commission and the fairness of procedure generally so as to command public confidence in it's proceedings and the findings in its report.

The most famous of these, the Shah Commission, had to suffer the ignominy of having it's proceedings in respect of the Prime respondent, Mrs. Indira Gandhi, and her colleague, Mr. Pranab Mukherjee, declared "void and *ultra vires*" on December 20, 1979 by Justice T.P.S. Chawla of the Delhi High Court for non-compliance with the statutory safeguards (Sections 8B and 8C) of the Act based on principles of natural justice. Although the judgement ranged far and wide on a host of issues, on the crucial issue of observance of those safeguards from the very inception, it was, with. respect, clearly right.[23]

On May, 28, 1977, the Government of India appointed a Commission of Inquiry consisting of J.C. Shah, a retired Chief Justice of India "to inquire into the facts and circumstances relating to specific instances of subversion of lawful processes and well-established conventions, administrative procedures and practices, abuse of authority, misuse of power, excesses and / or mal-practices committed during the period when the proclamation on Emergency made on 25th June 1975 under Article 352 of the Constitution was in force or in days immediately preceding the said Proclamation".

Also included were acts of misuse of powers of arrests or issue of detention orders; atrocities on detenues; use of force in the implementation of the family planning programme and the demolition of houses during this period.

The Commission utilised the services of investigation officers of the Government. The Commission submitted it's First Interim Report on March 11, 1978; the Second on April 26, 1978; and the Third and Final Report on August 6, 1978.

The Commission received over 48,000 complaints and a mass of official records The inquiry was held in two stages as laid down in a ruling on September 29, 1977. At the first stage the Commission would consider whether on a "preponderance of probability that it is necessary to probe further into the matter...." if so, it would at the next stage hold an inquiry and apply sections 8B and 8C of the Act which read thus:

"8B. If at any stage of the inquiry, the Commission:

(a) considers it necessary to inquire into the conduct of any persons; or (b) is of opinion that the reputation of any person is likely to be prejudically affected by the inquiry. The Commission shall give to that person a reasonable opportunity of being heard in the inquiry and to produce evidence in his defence: provided that nothing in this section shall apply where the credit of a witness is being impeached.

"8C. The appropriate government, every person referred to in Section 8B and, with the permission of the Commission, any other person whose evidence is recorded by the Commission

(a) may cross-examine a witness other than a witness produced by it or him;

(b) may address the Commission; and

(c) may be represented before the Commission by a legal practitioner or, with the permission of the Commission, by any other person."

Case summaries were read out in public proceedings involving individuals and testimony recorded before Sections 8B and 8C were applied. As will be pointed out, there is a better procedure for ensuring fair play.

The Commission of Inquiry to probe into charges against three Chief Ministers set up during this period, followed precedent. In response to a Memorandum of Charges against the Chief Minister of Andhra Pradesh, J. Vengala Rao, presented to the Prime Minister on April 6, 1977, the Government of India appointed on May 19, 1977 a Commission of Inquiry consisting of Justice J.R. Vimadalal, a former Judge of the Bombay High Court.

It was well-known that he had been transferred to the Andhra Pradesh high Court in 1976 as a punishment for his rulings in cases of detention. Honest and able as the Judge was, one would have thought that he was not the best judge for such a task though he did conduct the proceedings fairly.

He rightly rejected proof, beyond reasonable doubt, as the right standard to be adopted, but applied the test of "preponderance of probability, though, what should be the extent of that preponderance must....depends upon the gravity of the consequences of its finding..." on a particular issue. On the standard of proof, his discussion remains the most instructive. With the exception of two charges relating to Sanjay Gandhi's visit, all the others were rejected.

The Commission was appointed, though no *prima facie* case existed, in respect of those charges. But it helped to allay public disquiet and resolve a "crisis of confidence."

The Government of India led no evidence, the task was left entirely to the memorialists. The Commission had it's own counsel and an investigation team comprising police officers.

On may 23, 1977, the Government of India appointed a Commission of Inquiry consisting of Justice A.N. Grover to inquire into the charges made in a memorandum presented to the Prime Minister on April 11, 1988 against the Chief Minister of Karnataka, Devraj Urs.

Excluded were matters covered in the terms of reference of a Commission of Inquiry, consisting of Justice Mir Iqbal Hussain, a former Judge of the Karnataka High Court, set up by the State Government on May 18, 1977. Justice J.N. Shelat and K.S. Hegde for the appointment of the Chief Justice of India.

Under the circumstances, it was not a wise appointment. His First Report was submitted on January 10, 1978 and the Second and Final Report...On two points, the Final Report contains highly relevant observations.

One relates to the need for an independent investigation agency for Commission on inquiry and the other to the use of investigation reports under Section 5A of the Act. They should not preclude inquiry by the Commission itself. The Government of Karnataka's challenge to the validity of the Commission's appointment was rejected by the Supreme Court.[24]

On June 14, 1977, Justice P. Jaganmohan Reddy, a former Judge of the Supreme Court, was appointed as Commission of Inquiry to inquire into "all matters" relating to specified transactions of the Government of Haryana when Bansi Lal was its Chief Minister in order to ascertain whether any impropriety was committed. A Director of Investigation with staff was appointed.

Three reports were submitted on November 30, 1977; March 23, 1978 and June 4, 23, 1978. Like Justice Grover, Justice Jaganmohan Reddy also stressed the "need for a permanent investigating agency to serve the Commission of Inquiry". He suggested an alternative, "a separate wing be added or attached to the investigating agency with permanent staff for conducting investigation to assist the Inquiry Commission." He also opined against inquiries by Commission once criminal proceedings had begun.

The Commission of Inquiry on Maruti Affairs, set up on May 30, 1977, consisted of a sitting Judge of the Supreme Court, Justice A.C. Gupta. The core issue was whether "undue favour" was shown to the three Maruti concerns floated and run by Sanjay Gandhi.

The matters for inquiry were clearly specified. The report submitted on May 31, 1979 is a model of brevity, impartiality, and thoroughness. A large number of witnesses were examined and a mass of documents perused by the Commission.

Of a fundamentally different kind was the inquiry conducted in 1979 by Justice C.A. Vaidyalingam, a retired Judge of the Supreme Court, into charges against the families of Prime Minister Morarji Desai and Home Minister Charan Singh. He was not appointed as Commission under the Act of 1952 but styled himself a "Special Judge". His authority, such as it was, derived from the two letters to him dated April 27 and May 2, 1979 by the Union Home Minister, H.M. Patel.

His remit was "to go through the debate on the motion adopted in the Rajya Sabha on August 10, 1978 and advise the Government whether any *prima facie* case in respect of any of the charges referred to in the debate which pertain to the period after the present Government took office is established against the family members of the Prime Minister and those of the, then, Home Minister, Charan Singh, so as to justify a formal inquiry under the Commissions of Inquiry Act."

None of the MPs who levelled charges during the debate assisted the inquiry despite "repeated request". No one paid any attention to the Report, dated January 25, 1980, on its publication, either. It was a wholly irregular and futile exercise.

The '80s saw Commissions of Inquiry completely discredited, as a credible mechanism for accountability. It was all over in a period of five years. It began on February 17, 1982 with the appointment of the Kudal Commission to inquire into "the working and activities, including publications and sources and misuse of funds" of four named Gandhian bodies including the Gandhi Peace Foundation.

It was headed by Justice P.D. Kudal who had a long and controversial record as a Congress politician before his appointment as Judge of the Rajasthan High Court. Justice Ranganath Misra's conduct of the Commission of Inquiry into the Delhi riots in 1984 added to the disillusionment.[25]

The political inquiry was not an altogether new phenomenon, though a sitting Judge of the Supreme Court, Justice K.K. Mathew, was appointed as Commission of Inquiry on February 10, 1975 to inquire into the explosions at Samastipur on January 2, 1975 which resulted in the death of the Union Minister, L.N. Mishra.

He declined to answer the main query as to "the facts and circumstances pertaining to the explosion." But he went out of his way to devote a whole Chapter (V) on "the extent of the right to dissent in our democracy."

It was a thinly veiled attack on Jayaprakash Narayan and the movement he had launched in Bihar against corruption. (The Chapter ended with a recommendation for the establishment of a *Lok Pal*).

Justice Mathew's appointment as Chairman of the Second Press Commission and the Law Commission; his Report as Commission of Inquiry on the Chandigarh question, under the Punjab Accord of July 24, 1985, did much to wreck the accord.

Justice M.P. Thakkar was a sitting Judge of the Supreme court, when he was asked to conduct an inquiry into Mrs. Indira Gandhi's assassination. The Commission of Inquiry was formally constituted on November 20, 1984. The report was published in 1989 after extracts from it appeared in the Press.

Justice Thakkar simply abdicated his task and refused to hold an inquiry. Having done that, he proceeded to do something worse- he aired freely, wild suspicions and asked the Special Investigation Team to chase them. This is what he said: "The Commission cannot itself hold an inquiry into the facts and circumstances of the matter which will be more in the nature of a trial". His own "observations" were "made on the basis of the material gathered in the course of the investigative exercise which precedes an inquiry proper and not on the basis of an inquiry".

This was so far the simple reason why he had declined to hold an inquiry. Thakkar asserted categorically that "this report is based on the pre-inquiry investigative exercise and not an inquiry under Section 8B of the Commission of Inquiry Act, which is neither feasible nor practicable. The rest has to be done by the investigative agency". All the same, he freely displayed some "needles of suspicion".

The rest was accomplished by Justice Thakkar and another sitting Judge of the Supreme Court, Justice S. Natarajan, as Commission of Inquiry on the engagement of the Fairfax Group Inc. in the United States by the Finance Ministry. It was appointed on April 6, 1987 and the report was submitted on November 30, 1987.

It rushed to examine Bhure Lal, Director of Enforcement, on May 5 even before it had acquired a staff (May 7), it's offices (May 25), or it's counsel (June 3). It "began functioning", the Report records, on June 4, Bhure Lal was not given time to engage any counsel. His examination was violative of Sections 8B and 8C of the Act. There were other violations of the law.

The Thakkar-Natarajan Report was a blatantly political document. On December 14, 1987, V.P. Singh, former Union Finance Minister, revealed in the "Rajya Sabha how these judges were selected for appointment on the Commission.

A Union Minister, P. Shiv Shankar, brought along a list of the desirables to the office of Prime Minister Rajiv Gandhi, out of which the two Judges were selected.

Well before that, public disenchantment with Commissions of Inquiry was complete. When the Bofors Scandal broke out in 1987, hardly anyone demanded the setting-up of a Commission of Inquiry. The demand was for a Joint Committee of Parliament (IPC).

The Government and the Opposition could not agree neither on it's terms of reference nor it's powers. In consequence, the opposition declined to participate in the JPC that was set-up by the motion adopted by the *Lok Sabha* on August 6 and by the Rajya Sabha on August 12, 1987. The JPC's Report was presented to both Houses of Parliament on April 26, 1988. It was a command performance.

It rejected all the charges against the government as well as Bofors and was exposed to increasing ridicule with the publication of each instalment of the Bofors papers in The Hindu, shortly thereafter.

Far more successful was the Joint Committee to enquiry into Irregularities in Securities and Banking Transactions set up by a resolution of the *Lok Sabha* on August 6, 1992 and the *Rajya Sabha*, the next day.

To no small extent the success was due to the personality of it's Chairman, Ram Niwas Mirdha. The report, submitted on December 11, 1993, necessarily represented a compromise arrived at among the JPC's thirty members.

In varying degrees of severity, four Union Ministers, several senior officers and a number of public sector undertakings were criticised. The Committee's warning of the consequences "if a system be devoid of the moral quotient" was widely noted.

It appeared all too clearly from the Action Taken Report (ATR), which the government submitted to Parliament on July 25, 1994, that it had not accepted the JPC's recommendation in several key areas. Revised paragraphs of the ATR were submitted by the government in December 1994 in order to silence criticism.

The then JPC was in truth a retrograde move. The Commissions of Inquiry Act, 1952 is modelled on a British statute, the Tribunals of Inquiry (Evidence) Act, 1921, which was subjected to a careful review by the Royal Commission on Tribunals of Inquiry (1966) headed by Lord Justice Salmon (Cmnd. 3121; HMSO, London).

The Commission noted that from the middle of the 17th century until 1921, the norm was inquiry by a Select Parliamentary Committee and occasionally by a Commission of Inquiry.

In 1912 in the UK, there occurred what became known as the Marconi Scandal involving several including Lloyd George and Rufus Isaacs. A select committee of fourteen members, excluding the Chairman, was appointed "to investigate those rumours."

It split along party lines in 1913; so did the House of Commons When, in 1921, grave charges were made against officials of the Ministry of Munitions, Parliament enacted the Act of 1921.

By 1966, there had been four major inquiries in post-war Britain of which three were under the Act-the Lynskey Tribunal (1948), the Parker Tribunal (1957) on improper disclosure of information on the bank rate, and the Radcliffe Tribunal (1962) on a spy scare.

The Denning Inquiry (1963) into the Profumo affair was not set-up under the Act nor was the recent Scott Inquiry on arms to Iraq. There had been considerable criticism of the damage to reputations of individuals by the proceedings of the Tribunals.

The Royal Commission said:

> "We recommend that no Government in the future should ever, in any circumstances whatsoever, set up a Tribunal of the type adopted in the Profumo case to investigate any matter causing nation-wide public concern. For the reasons we have stated, we are satisfied that such a method of inquiry is inferior to, and certainly no acceptable substitute for, an inquiry under the Act of 1921....."
>
> "We are strongly of the opinion that the inquisitorial machinery set-up/under the Act of 1921 should never be used for matters of local or minor public importance, but always be confined to matters of vital public importance concerning which there is something in the nature of a nation-wide crisis of confidence. In such cases we consider that no other method of investigation would be adequate." (Para 27, of the Report, p. 16)

It's observations on the essentially inquisitorial nature of the Tribunal's word are noteworthy. "The Tribunal directs the inquiry and the witnesses are necessarily the Tribunal's witness. There is no plaintiff or defendant, no prosecutor or accused; there are no pleadings defining issues to be tried, no charges, indictments, or depositions.

The inquiry may take a fresh turn at any moment. It is,

therefore, difficult for persons involved to know in advance of the hearing what allegations may be made against them." (Para 30; p. 17)

The Commission propounded safeguards which are essentially the same as those in Sections 8B and 8C of the Act of 1952. One point of difference deserves to be noted. The person summoned as witness "should have the opportunity of being examined by his own solicitor or counsel and to stating his case in public at the inquiry" (Para 32; p. 18)

He should have the right "in the first instance" of being examined by his own counsel before he is examined or cross-examined by others (Para 57; p. 24). Also, immediately after the opening speech by counsel for the Tribunal, counsel for the witnesses should be permitted to make brief speeches giving their version to the Tribunal and, thus, to the public.

Section 1 of the Act of 1921 permits appointment of a Tribunal only in pursuance of a resolution by both Houses of Parliament "for inquiring into a definite matter described in the Resolution as of urgent public importance". The Royal Commission opined that no Tribunal should be set-up to probe into "a nebulous mass of vague and unspecified rumours."

The terms of reference of British Tribunals are far less precise than those of the Indian Commissions. The Lynskey Tribunal was appointed "for inquiring into a definite matter of urgent public importance, i.e. whether there is any justification for allegations that payments, rewards or other considerations have been sought, offered, promised, made or received by or to Ministers of the Crown or other public servants in connection with licences or permissions required under any enactment, regulation or order or in connection with the withdrawal of any prosecution and, if so, in what circumstances the transactions took place and what persons were involved therein."

Among the questions it considered was "whether there were allegations of the nature set out in our appointment." In other words, the Tribunal itself ascertained and defined the allegations and proceeded to consider them. This is in glaring contrast to Indian Commissions which are provided precise charges, as if they are trial courts.

The Lynskey Report said:

> "The first question we had to decide was one of procedure. A Tribunal appointed under the Act of 1921 is itself responsible for the collection of evidence, taking statements from witnesses, presenting their evidence, then, resting its accuracy and, finally, finding the facts. In a simple case, it might be convenient for the Tribunal itself to carry out these responsibilities, but where there are a number of transactions to be investigated it would not merely be inconvenient, but physically impossible, within a reasonable time, for the Tribunal to undertake these tasks."

> "The services of the Treasury Solicitor, Sir Thomas Barnes, and his staff were placed at our disposal. We also had the assistance of Superintendent A.J. Thorp and other officers of the Metropolitan Police. The Treasury Solicitor with the assistance of the police interviewed all persons whom they thought might be able to give useful information to the Tribunal, and statements were taken from them. These statements were, then, placed before us and we directed what further inquiries should be made and eventually decided which witness should be called to give evidence before us." (Cmnd. 7616; HMSO, London; p. 1)

The Radcliffe Tribunal was asked to inquire into possible breaches of security as well as allegations that the First Lord of the Admiralty and his Service Chiefs knew of a spy other than the one who was detected and "any other allegations which have been or may be brought to their attention, reflecting similarly on the honour and integrity" of ministers and civil servants.

The report records that in order to find out "what was being said," the Tribunal drew on "Parliamentary criticism and press criticism". (Cmnd. 200g; HMSO, London). This is why the Press accused Prime Minister Harold Macmillan of launching a witch-hunt against it.

Every newspaper report on the matter was scanned. Much of the Press criticism was exposed to be false. The leading newspapers were represented by a counsel before the Tribunal.

Apply this to allegations of misconduct against ministers in India, and the limitations of the Commissions of Inquiry become obvious. They are self-imposed since Section 3 of the Indian Act of 1952 is not much different from Section 1 of the British Act of 1921.

The Das Commission set a wrong precedent. Justice J.R. Mudholkar opined in his Report on the U.P. Ministers that "the conduct of an unnamed person cannot lawfully be inquired into." (p. 281 of the Report).

The Supreme Court rules in the case of the Bihar Minister that "if the charges were vague or speculative suggesting a fishing expedition we would have paused to consider whether such an inquiry should be allowed to proceed." These remarks are clearly obiter.[26]

In the State of *Madhya Pradesh vs. Arjun Singh & Ors.* (1993) 1 SCC 51 at p. 54; (para 8), the Court said that the State Government was free to appoint any Commission of Inquiry after "applying it's mind to any fresh or further material placed before it" and added:

"Such formation of opinion depends on the subjective satisfaction of an appropriate Government but should be based on an objective or real material and not merely on some vague allegations or hearsay evidence or to make fishing inquiry".

These too were, in the context, obiter. The Court has had no occasion yet to consider fully the model on which the Act of 1952 is based nor the manner in which it has worked. Commissions of Inquiry in India need to be set firmly on the track of inquisitorial work if they are to perform their tasks properly.

The Commissions of Inquiry Act, 1952 was reviewed by the Law Commission in it's 24th Report submitted on December 26, 1962. It did not deal with the issues that have arisen recently.

A Joint Committee of Parliament reported on November 9, 1970 on the Commissions of Inquiry (Amendment) Bill, 1969 which was enacted in 1971. The Committee strongly opined against leaving it to the Government to discontinue a Commission "before it has completed its task". (para 14).

Suggestions

In the light of the foregoing, it is suggested that:

(1) There should be a comprehensive review of the Commissions of Inquiry Act, 1952 in the light of experience gained since its enactment.

This review should be undertaken by a Committee that commands public confidence and it should particularly consider the abuse of the Act by governments and also it's violation by the Commissions of Inquiry.

(2) No Commission or Committee of Inquiry should be appointed except with statutory sanction. The S.K. Das, Mudholkar and Vaidyalingam inquiries were highly irregular.

(3) A Committee of Parliament, other than those established under the Rules of Procedure of each of it's Houses, such as the Public Accounts Committee, is ill-suited to undertake inquiries of the kind undertaken by the Commissions of Inquiry, e.g., the JPCs on Bofors or Securities and Banking transactions.

While in Britain, the Ministers, Lloyd George and his colleagues, were grilled by the select committee, the Indian JPC cannot summon ministers and is hopelessly dependent on the Speaker under the Rules of Procedure of the *Lok Sabha*.

He appoints it's Chairman (Rule 258), determines disputes as to the relevance of a witness or a document (Rule 270) and on "Procedure or otherwise". He can also issue directions to regulate the procedure and organise the committee's work (Rule 283). A Parliamentary Committee is intrinsically susceptible to political influence.

(4) There is now a new "culture of appointments" as

reflected in the Press Council Act, 1978 and all the four *Lok Pal* Bills. The Government no longer has the sole discretion on appointments of persons in high judicial or quasi-judicial positions.

The Supreme Court only upheld the Special Courts Bill, 1978 when the Government agreed to it's suggestion that the presiding Judge would be a sitting judge of a High Court and he would be appointed with the concurrence of the Chief Justice of India (In re: the Special Courts Bill, 1978; (1979) 1 SCC 380).

It is of vital importance that suitable amendments should be made to Section 3(2) of the Act and the Governments unfettered power of appointment of members of a Commission of Inquiry be curtailed by requiring consultation with the leaders of the Opposition in both the Houses of Parliament, their presiding officers and the concurrence of the Chief Justice of India.

(5) Likewise, the unfettered power of refusal to appoint a Commission of Inquiry should be abolished. It is highly desirable that one-third members of the legislature should have the power to move for the establishment of an enquiry, on the lines of Article 44 of Germany's Basic Law.

It is necessary to assuage public concern once there is a "crisis of confidence", quite regardless of the existence of a *prima facie* case, as is the practice in Britain demonstrated, most notably in the Radcliffe inquiry.

The solution suggested, tentatively, is to allow executive and legislature to have their way in the decision to appoint Commissions. Neither is likely to abuse the power since the composition of the Commission will be subject to the concurrence of the Chief Justice of India, besides other consultative checks.

(6) There should be a separate, independent investigation agency to serve the Commissions of Inquiry, the *Lok Pal* and the *Lok Ayukts*.

(7) The inquisitorial character of Commission of Inquiry should be restored.

(8) Justice J.R. Mudholkar suggested in his Report on the United Front Ministers that the representation of the People Act, 1951 should be amended to disqualify from candidature *inter alia* anyone found guilty of corruption and the like by a Commission of Inquiry. Such a provision exists in Section 24F of the Jammu and Kashmir Representation of the People Act, 1957.

However such a provision should be inserted in election law only if, the Act of 1952 is so amended as to render abuse of its provisions by the Government and arbitrariness by Commissions of Inquiry well nigh impossible.

(9) Sections 8B and 8C of the Commissions of Inquiry Act, 1952, should be recast in the light of the observations in the Salmon Report.

(10) The two institutions, *Lok Pal* and Commission of Inquiry, should be so meshed together, apart from a common investigative staff, that the *Lok Pal* could *suo moto* set in motion procedures for the establishment of a Commission of Inquiry if a public scandal has surfaced, e.g., the Bailadila, the Bihar fodder scam and the Orissa party funds scandals.

(11) The Centre's right to appoint Commissions of Inquiry against Chief Ministers was challenged by Mr. M. Karunanidhi in 1971 23 (vide the writer's Ministers Misconduct, pp. 392/394 for the text of Mr. Karunanidhi's letter of December 14, 1972 to Prime Minister Indira Gandhi) and by Mr. Devraj Urs in 1977.

The constitutional position is not free from doubt. Entry'45 in the Concurrent List in the Seventh Schedule to the Constitution empowers both the Union and the States to legislate on "Inquiries and statistics for the purposes of any of the matters specified in List II or List III."

It is concurrent power. Justice Kailasam, in his dissenting judgement, opined that Entry 45 should not be construed to give the union power to appoint Commissions of Inquiry against Chief Ministers. It militates against the federal principle, he ruled.

The best course is to amend the Act to bar the Union from instituting such inquiries unless the conduct of the State Ministers has been of such a magnitude as to make the scandal a matter of national or inter-State concern, e.e. the fodder scam in Bihar. This proviso should be written into the Act in clear terms.

Certainly, the practice of the Centre receiving memoranda of charges against Chief Ministers, demanding explanation from them and setting up a Commission of Inquiry to probe into them is violative of the federal principle and is liable to abuse; indeed, it has been abused and should be abandoned.

The *Lok Ayukts* should deal with the charges and, in any case, one-third members of the State Assembly should be able to have a Commission of Inquiry set up.

The 'Sarkaria Report' noted (page 65; para 2.22.24 and 25) that one "startling result" from the Supreme Court's construction of Entry 45 in List III would be to empower the State also to appoint Commissions of Inquiry against Union Ministers.

It, however, opined that the potentiality of abuse of the power "is no ground for amending the constitution". It suggested two safeguards against abuse of the power by the Union-a resolution passed by both Houses of Parliament and prior approval by the Inter-State Council set up under Article 263. These safeguards should be written into the Act, it said.

Neither safeguard is altogether satisfactory although both can serve as deterrents. The best course is to define in the Act, precisely enough, the gravity of the matter which can warrant a probe, while excluding it explicitly merely because memoranda have been submitted to the Union against Ministers in a State. It must be "a matter of national concern which has created a crisis of confidence."

(12) Finally, it is highly important to formulate guide lines for protecting the rights of the accused if a Commission of Inquiry and a trial concerning the same matter proceed simultaneously.

The Madon Commission on the Bhiwandi riots (1970-72) was able to avoid any conflict by not compelling the accused to depose. Contrary to the impression in some minds, a trial should not prevent the setting up of a Commission of Inquiry.

As Justice Y.V. Chandrachud observed, in his Report of October 20, 1970, as Commission of Inquiry on the death of Deen Dayal Uphdhyaya: "The scope of this inquiry is wider than the scope of the sessions trial.

I must determine why the murder was committed- a question that has wider ramification than the question before the session court; namely' whether the accused before it were guilty... I can conduct a probe into the real truth."

James Hamilton, Assistant Chief Counsel to Senator Sam Ervin's Committee on the Watergate affair recorded in his book "The Power to Probe" that Senator Ervin believed that "exposing the true nature of the scandal to the country was even more crucial than convicting a few high administration officials for their crimes."[27]

Justice K.K. Mathew opined to the contrary and in error in his report on the death of Mr. L.N. Mishra as a result of the explosion in Samastipur in 1975. He refused to probe into the circumstances of the death on the ground that a trial was in progress.

One fundamental consideration must be borne in mind as it concerns the very nature of such inquiries. They are set-up in the belief that their findings will form public opinion and lead to action.

In his definitive work Trial By Tribunal, Prof. G.W. Keeton observed that "the function of this fact-finding organisation was found increasingly to establish what the facts are, and to leave the final verdict on the propriety of what has been done to public opinion".

This essential character of Commissions of Inquiry should be retained. The follow up to their Reports should be left to the *Lok Pal* or *Lok Ayukt*.

NOTES AND REFERENCES

1. *The Times*, October 15, 1976.

2. Vide Second Report of the National Police Commission, Government of India, August 1979, para 15-40, p. 30.

3. Vide their essay 'The Police: Independence and Accountability' in Jeffrey Jowell and Dawn Oliver, *The Changing Constitution*, Oxford University Press, Third Edition; 1994, p. 295.

4. Constituent Assembly Debates, Vol. 7, pp. 1187.

5. Salil Kumar Nag, *Evolution of Parliamentary Privileges in India till 1947*, Sterling, 1978, p. 212.

6. Vide G. Rudrayya Chowdari, *Prakasam: A Political Study*, Orient Longman, 1971, pp. 158-86 on the Congress High Command's treatment of T. Prakasam's acceptance of purses of money presented to him and Durga Das (ed.), *Sardar Patel's Correspondence* 1945-50, Navajivan Publishing House, Ahmedabad, Vol. 2, pp. 243-50.

7. See Durga Das (ed.) (No. 6 above) Vol. 9, p. 51. vide pp. 512-520 for the text of a draft unsigned report to The Congress President on the scandal.

8. *Ibid*, p. 51.

9. A.G. Noorani, *Minister's Misconduct*, Vikas, 1973, p. 44.

10. See A.D. Gorwala, 'Report on Public Administration,' *Planning Commission*, pp. 12-27.

11 *Ibid*, p. 16.

12. 'Mundhra inquiry: The Full Story', Free Press Journal, Bombay, 1958.

13. *Ibid*, p. 80.

14. Lok Sabha Debates, Vol. 18, April 25 to May 7, 1963, 4th Session, 3rd Series, col, 14211.

15. *S. Pratap Singh vs. State of Punjab,* A.I.R. 1964, Supreme Court 72.

16. 'Report of the Commission of Inquiry', New Delhi, June 11, 1964 p. 18.

17. *Ibid*, p. 12.

18. *Ibid*, p. 285.

19. 'Report of the Committee on Prevention of Corruption', Government of India, Ministry of Home Affairs, 1964, pp. 101-102.

20. *Ibid*, pp. 102-103.

21. *P.K. Kunju vs State of Kerala & Ors.* A.I.R. 1970 Kerala 252, for details of other such commissions, see A.G. Noorani, *Ministers' Misconduct* (No. 9 above), Ch, 7 on Azhimathi in Kerala.

22. *Report of the Commission of Inquiry into the allegations against certain former Minister of Punjab*; Mr. Justice D.S. Dave, Mr. Justice L.N. Chhangani, New Delhi; pp. 184-185. This report was submitted on April 26, 1975. Another followed on September 30, 1975.

23. *Smt. Indira Gandhi vs. Shri S.C. Shah*, ILR (1980) 1 Delhi 552. Vide *Kiran Bedi vs. Committee of Inquiry* (1989) 1 SCC 494 for an authoritative and detailed exposition of the law on the subject.

24. *State of Karnataka vs. Union of India* (1977). Of the seven members of the Bench, Justice P.S. Kailasam alone held 4 Supreme Court cases 608, that it was not open to the Centre to appoint a Commission of Inquiry against a Minister in a State Government. He raised points on the federal aspect which deserve closer examination than they have received.

25. For detailed analyses, see A.G. Noorani, *Indian Affairs: The Constitutional Dimension*, Konark, 1990, pp. 338-353 and 362-366.

26. *K.B. Sahay & Ors. vs. Commission of Inquiry & Ors.*, A.I.R. 1969, S.C. 258.

27. James Hamilton, *The Power to Probe, Random House*, New York, 1976, p. 129.

33

NEED FOR INDIAN *OMBUDSMAN*

> ***"Law has reached its finest moments when it has freed men from the unlimited discretion of some ruler, some civil or military officials, some bureaucrat, Where discretion is absolute, man has always suffered. At times, it has been his property that has been invaded; at times, his privacy; at times, his liberty of movement; at times, his freedom of thought; at times, his life. Absolute discretion is a ruthless master. It is more destructive of freedom than any of man's other inventions".***[1]

It has been amply seen that above-mentioned ideal cannot be attained by the classic institutions provided by democratic forms of government; legislatures elected by the people in free elections held periodically with executive heads responsible to them, or themselves elected directly by the people.

An independent judiciary and a free Press are only the barest minimum essentials for the functioning of a democratic polity.

These institutions themselves are sorely in need of reform, especially in India. However, even at their best, they ensure neither the government's accountability to the people nor an effective mechanism for the redress of grievances. An 'elective despotism' is how the British system has been commonly described in recent years.

What Michael Meacher, Labour Party's social security spokesman, said of that system on May 26, 1992, applies to the Indian system with far greater force. The Prime Minister, he said, now had more untrammeled power than the King before the Revolution of 1988. Meacher said "the corrupt proliferation of patronage, the opium of the elite; the rise of unelected confidants in the No. 10 office who can be more powerful and less accountable than elected Ministers; the all-pervading blanket of secrecy around most sensitive decisions, which excludes even Cabinet members - all these should be reduced or ended.[2]"

In June 1969, a UN Seminar held in Stockholm on Ways of Safeguarding the Rights of Individuals against the Abuse of Administrative power discussed five principal means of ensuring such protection:

— Parliamentary Commissions of Inquiry;

— Procuracy of the Soviet Type;

— Judicial Remedies of the English legal System;

— The French Counsel D'Etat; and

— The *ombudsman* of Scandinavia.

By then, the *ombudsman* had already acquired a reputation in India. Addressing the All-India Congress Committee at Jaipur, on November 3, 1963, Prime Minister Jawaharlal Nehru said he was fascinated by the idea of an "*ombudsman*" who should have the authority to deal with the charges against the Prime Minister and command respect and confidence from all.[3] But, he added, it was beset with difficulties in a large country like India.

Interest in India was aroused by a report published in 1961 entitled "The Citizen and Administration: The Redress of Grievances'. It was written by Sir John Whyatt, a former Chief Justice of Singapore, for 'justice,' the British section of the International Commission of Jurists.

It recommended a large extension of the system of the

administrative tribunals to consider complaints against the discretionary actions of administrators, a large extension of the system proposed by the Franks Committee Report on Administrative Tribnunals and Enquiries (1957) and the establishment of the British equivalent to an *Ombudsman* to look into complaints of mal-administration.

The Whyatt Report has been described as "one of the great non-state papers" and testifies to the efficacy of studies conducted by non-governmental organisations provided they are based on thorough research and cogent reasoning.[4] The result was the Parliamentary Commissioner Act in 1967.

It is unnecessary to trace the evolution of this institution or those of its counterparts elsewhere.[5] Three decades of study and experiment in India have helped enormously in defining the problems and the needs of the specific situation in our country and the tests of effectiveness which an Indian *ombudsman* must meet. The problem, broadly, is two-fold: mal-administration and corrupt. Abuse of power is implicit in both.

There are five requirements which the Indian "*ombudsman*" must satisfy - accessibility to the ordinary citizen; jurisdiction wide enough to reach the most powerful executive in the land; independence from executive power and influence; power fully requisite to the task; and sanctions which make the institution worthwhile.

It is trite to say that no office or institution can function in isolation from the rest of the society. It cannot but reflect its mores, strengths and failings. In India, the remark is not trite. It only describes a grave problem.

The many "*Lok Pal*" Bills moved in Parliament in the last three decades and the *'Lok Ayukt'* Acts enacted in the States over the last two decades reveal dependence on two other institutions; neither of which is in good shape - the superior judiciary and the police force.

Unless the procedure for judicial appointments, recommended by the Law Commission, is reformed on the lines of the Bill moved in Parliament in 1990 by the, then, Union Law Minister, Dinesh Goswami, for the appointment of a National Judicial Commission, no "*Lok Pal*" will inspire much public confidence.

Likewise, it is imperative that the professional autonomy and integrity of the police force is ensured by implementing the reports of the National Police Commission.

In India, the State not only enjoys exclusive power to decide whether or not an inquiry is to be instituted on grave charges of mal-administration or corruption on the part of its ministers and civil servants, but also vast powers on the disclosure of information.

The rise of investigative journalism has alleviated the situation but the exposure of wrong has not ensured redress. Witness the scandals of recent years alone - HWD submarine, Bofors gun, Airbus deal, ABB loco deal, securities, sugar scam, Jain Hawala racket and telecom scandals.

But there is not the faintest sign of any serious move by the Government of India to establish a "*Lok Pal*" at the Centre nor have the opposition parties pressed seriously for the establishment of the institution although it is nearly three decades since a high-powered body recommended its establishment.

The Administrative Reforms Commission (ARC), headed by Morarji Desai, was set up by the Government of India on January 5, 1966. It is highly significant that its first major action was the Interim Report on Problems of Redress of Citizens Grievances which was submitted on October 20, 1966. It recommended the setting up of two institutions, the *"Lok Pal"* at the Centre and the "*Lok Ayukt*" in each State.

After an able and concise survey of the working of the "*Ombudsman*" in other countries, the report said: The following would be the main features of the institutions of "*Lok Pal*" and "*Lok Ayukt*":

— They should be demonstrably independent and impartial.

— Their investigations and proceedings should be conducted in private and be informal in character.

— Their appointment should, as far as possible, be non-political.

— Their status should compare with the highest judicial functionaries in the country.

— They should deal with matters in the discretionary field involving acts of injustice, corruption or favouritism.

— Their proceedings should not be subject to judicial interference and they should have the maximum latitude and power in obtaining information relevant to their duties.

— They should not look forward to any benefit or pecuniary advantage from the executive Government.

It would be true to say that the report set the basic pattern for all similar legislation that has been proposed or enacted since, though some departed from certain essentials. The "*Lok Pal*" would have the same status as the Chief Justice of India and be appointed by the President on the Prime Minister's advice after consultation with the Chief Justice of India and the Leader of the Opposition.

He 'would be free to choose his own staff' and would 'have the powers of a court with regard to the calling of witnesses, documents etc.' The investigations would be in private. He would report to the legislature. The "*Lok Ayukts*" would have similar status, powers and functions.

The Report made an important point which has been overlooked in all subsequent discussions for reasons not difficult to understand. It said that 'for the "*Lok Pal*" to be fully effective and for him to acquire power, without conflict with other functionaries under the Constitution, it would be necessary to give a constitutional status to his office, his powers, functions, etc.'

That, it added, was no reason for delaying the legislation. "The "*Lok Pal*", we are confident, would be able to function in a large number of cases without the definition of his position under the Constitution. The constitutional amendment and any constitutional modification of the relevant statute can follow".

There is, however, another consideration besides the ones the ARC mentioned. The entire edifice of the "*Lok Pal*" can be brought down by a mere ordinance, as the Press Council was in 1975 during the Emergency.

As in the case of the Election Commission and the Comptroller and Auditor General, it is highly essential that similar provisions are made by a constitutional amendment to endow the institution of the *Lok Pal* with constitutional status and the holder of the office with the security of tenure leaving it to Parliament to legislate the details.

Since, however, there was never any real earnest at the Centre in this matter, the thought of constitutional amendment never troubled anyone's mind.

Appended to the report was a draft Bill running into thirteen clauses. It covered 'Ministers' as well as 'Secretary'. The Prime Minister was not excluded. The "*Lok Pal's*" main function was to "investigate any action by these persons *suo moto* or a written complaint by a person (i) who claims to have sustained injustice in consequence of mal-administration in connection with such action, or (ii) who affirms that such action has resulted in favour being unduly shown to any person or in accrual of personal benefit or gain to the Minister or to the Secretary, as the case may be."

It, thus, covered cases of both mal-administration as well as corruption. There followed many exceptions and exemptions where he had no discretion- action in respect of which the person had a remedy before a tribunal or a court of law unless, in the latter case, the *Lok Pal* was satisfied that it was 'not reasonable to expect him to take or to have taken such proceedings.' He was endowed with discretion not to investigate if he was of the view that 'a remedy for the injustice alleged to have caused, thereby, exists."

Eight other matters, as well as existence of legal remedies, were excluded from the *Lok Pal*'s jurisdiction:

(a) Action taken in a matter certified by a Union Minister as affecting the relations or dealings between the Government of India and any foreign government or any international organisation of States or governments.

(b) Action taken under the Extradition Act, 1962 or the Foreigners Act, 1946.

(c) Action taken for the purpose of investigating crime or protecting the security of the State including action taken with respect of passports.

(d) Action taken in the exercise of power in relation to determining whether a matter shall go to a court or not.

(e) Action taken in matters which arise out of the terms of contract governing purely commercial relations of the administration with customers or suppliers, except where the complainant alleges harassment or gross delay in meeting contractual obligations.

(f) Action taken in respect of appointments, removals, pay, discipline, superannuation or other personnel matters.

(g) Grant of honours and awards.

(h) A decision made in exercise of his discretion by an administrative authority unless the elements involved in the exercise of discretion are absent to such an extent that no discretion has been exercised at all.

Several of these were adopted in State Laws and the Central Bill of 1971.

Information or documents could be withheld from disclosure if the Cabinet Secretary certified that it-

(a) might prejudice the security or defence or international relations of India (including India's relations with the Government of any other country or with any international organisation), or the investigation or detection of crime, or

(b) which might involve the disclosure of proceedings of the Cabinet or any Committee of the Cabinet.

Additionally, a blanket power to suppress material was conferred: "A Minister may give notice in writing to the *Lok Pal* with respect to any documents or information specified in the notice or any class of documents so specified that in the opinion of the minister the disclosure of the document or information or of documents or information of that class would be contrary to public interest and where such a notice is given, nothing in this Act shall be construed as authorising or requiring the *Lok Pal* or any officer of the *Lok Pal* to communicate to any person any document or information specified in the notice or any document or information of a class so specified".

The Official Secrets Act was extended to the *Lok Pal* and his staff. Publication of 'proceedings relating to an investigation' was punishable by the Supreme Court 'as if it were a case of contempt before that court'.

It was only a beginning. The report recorded: 'The problem was thrown up in bold relief and in it's full impact on the citizens in the very first round of our discussions with the Ministers of the Central Government and the Congress President; its importance, urgency and dimensions have been increasingly impressed upon the author, by the large, volume of both official and non-official opinion consulted so far.

The Commission was so impressed by both the unanimity and the strength of the popular demand on this subject that it decided to devote itself to this problem rather than form a separate group for the specific purpose of devising a scheme to enable the citizen to seek redress for an administrative injustice-The more the Commission considered this issue, the more was it convinced that the problem brooked no delay.

Thirty years later, one sees little interest in the establishment of a *Lok Pal* by the government or by the opposition. Although, as many as five Bills for this purpose were moved in the Parliament, none of them could reach the statute book.

The first step for the establishment of the institution came with the introduction of the *Lok Pal* Bill in the Lok Sabha on May 9, 1968 to implement the recommendations of the Administrative Reforms Commission (ARC).

The Bill was referred to a Joint Committee and was later passed by the Lok Sabha on August 20, 1969. But while it was pending in the Rajya Sabha, the Lok Sabha was dissolved and the Bill consequently lapsed.

The Bill, as passed by the Lok Sabha, was reintroduced in the Lok Sabha on August 11, 1971. This also lapsed on the dissolution of the Fifth Lok Sabha.

The new Government which came to power in March, 1977, introduced a Bill on *Lok Pal* in the Lok Sabha on July 28, 1977. The 1977 Bill was considered by a Joint Committee of the two Houses of Parliament.

The report of the Joint Committee incorporating certain amendments in the Bill was placed before the Lok Sabha on January 20, 1978.

However, before the Bill could be considered and adopted by the Parliament, the Sixth Lok Sabha dissolved and the Bill lapsed. No Bill on the subject was considered by the Lok Sabha (1980-84).

Yet another *Lok Pal* Bill was introduced in the Lok Sabha on August 26, 1985.[6]

However, this new Bill was withdrawn by the Government itself on specious grounds in November, 1988.

The National Front Government introduced the *Lok Pal* Bill, 1989 in the Lok Sabha on December 29, 1989 within days of assuming office. It lapsed with the dissolution of the Lok Sabha in 1991.

The four bills of 1971, 1977, 1985 and 1989 varied greatly in their ambit and scope. (The 1971 Bill was similar to the one of the 1968.) To give an overview at the outset, the 1971 and 1985 Bills excluded the Prime Minister from their purview while the 1977 and 1989 Bills did not.

The 1971 Bills alone covered both grievances in respect of 'mal-administration' and allegations of misconduct. The 1977 Bill was confined to allegations only but it defined the term 'misconduct widely to cover improprieties as well as corruption.

The 1985 Bill omitted grievances altogether and restricted the *Lok Pal*'s jurisdiction to offences 'punishable under Chapter IX of the Indian Penal Code (offences by or relating to public servants, such as bribery) or, under the Prevention of Corruption Act, 1947.'

In the joint note of dissent dated November 1988 on the withdrawal of the Bill by the Government, the Opposition members pointed out that 'of various versions of the *Lok Pal*

Bill presented till then, the 1985 Bill seemed to us the most anaemic in content and the most restricted in scope'.

While the 1989 Bill contained certain improvements on earlier Bills, its jurisdiction clause was the narrowest. It covered only offences 'punishable under the Prevention of Corruption Act, 1988' Even offences punishable under the Penal Code were excluded.

On August 3, 1995, the Minister of State for Personnel, Mrs. Margaret Alva, informed the Rajya Sabha that the Government had already circulated the two draft Bills on *Lok Pal* of 1985 and 1989 to all political parties seeking their views

Forty-nine MPs were requested to send their suggestions to bring about a consensus on the *Lok Pal* Bill. Only five of them had responded till July 28.

They were Chaturanan Mishra (CPI), E. Ahmed (Muslim League) Jaswant Singh (BJP), Chimabhai Mehta (Ind.) and Mr. Dil Kumari Bhandari (SSP). She recalled that the Prime Minster Mr. P.V. Narasimha Rao had assured the House that the office of the Prime Minister as well as those of the Chief Minister would be brought within the purview of the Bill. She also mentioned that Jaswant Singh had even suggested that the matter be left to next Lok SaBha.[7]

Mrs. Alva's allusion was to the Prime Minister's statement in the Rajya Sabha on December 15, 1994 that he was not averse to the inclusion of the Prime Minister's office within the scope of the Bill.

On December 6, 1995, Mrs. Alva revealed in the Lok Sabha that the Union Home Minister, S.B. Chavan, had held discussions with the political leaders on this subject the day before. She added that the proposed Bill did not envisage any separate investigative machinery for the *Lok Pal* set-up to enquire in high places.

Mr. Saifuddin Chaudhary (CPM) said that there was no need for a *Lok Pal* if the Prime Minister was exempt from his jurisdiction.[8] (As a senior correspondent, Pushp Saraf rightly pointed out, Mrs. Alva 'was speaking a half-truth when she stated that the poor response to her efforts to evolve a conscience was one of the reasons for the delay in bringing forward the legislation'. The government was none to serious about it either.[9])

Meanwhile, several States went ahead with establishing their own version of the ARC's model. There is no uniformity in the width of their jurisdiction, independence or effectiveness. It is doubtful if any of them can be said to have caught the public imagination or carved a place for the *Lok Pal* in the consciousness of the ordinary citizen. Even so, that is no reason for writing them off as useless.

Their work is conducted away from public gaze. The annual reports do not provide the details and receive little publicity. Citizens' bodies can activate the office and also help citizen to file complaints.

There is, moreover, the incontrovertible fact that heads have rolled in a few cases, thanks to the labour of some *Lok Ayukts*, and, in some others, Chief Ministers have been dragged before the *Lok Ayukts*.

Two recent cases illustrate this. It has been estimated that every third member of the Madhya Pradesh government, headed by Digvijay Singh, and including the Chief Minister himself, is facing charges before the *Lok Ayukt*.[10] Copies of complaints to the *Lok Ayukt* are freely published in the Press.

The Madhya Pradesh *Lok Ayukt*'s 13th Annual Report for the year 1994-95 was released to the press on December 12, 1995.[11] But apparently it was not tabled in the State Assembly.[12] As many as three Ministers were indicted according to reports in *The Hindu* and *The Telegraph*. The Deputy Chief Minister, Subhas Yadav, was indicted for corruption. The Minister of State for Higher Education, Mukesh Nayak, was censured as being "incompetent to hold the office of an independent minister".

In another case relating to the allotment for setting up a petrol pump on government land to Devendra Kumar Sadho, brother of Ms. Vijaya Lakshmi Sadho, Minister for Tourism, Culture, Science and Technology, Public Enterprises and Implementation of 20-point Programme, the *Lok Ayukt* observed that Sadho's application for the allotment of land at a concessional rate should have been rejected because there was no policy or order permitting allotment of land at concessional rates to anyone for commercial purposes. "Even assuming that in future the Cabinet may approve so such a policy, it will be highly improper to begin implementing a policy for the benefit of a close relative of a Minister," the Report pointed out.

Another case figuring in the *Lok Ayukt*'s Report related to the former Minister of State for Forest, Environment and Mineral Resources, Dayal Singh Tumrachi, against whom a probe was conducted for giving abortive appointments as forest guard to two persons. Tumrachi's resignation was later sought and accepted by the Chief Minister on the recommendation of the *Lok Ayukt*.

In this case, the *Lok Ayukt* had said in an earlier Report that "if a minister bypasses the Secretariat and sends his order or direction directly to the officer by whom it is to be complied with, he cannot throw on the shoulders of that officer the responsibility of examining the legality or otherwise of his order or direction. If such an order or direction is carried out and it turns out to be illegal, the minister will have to own full responsibility."

Apparently, this is the only case in which the Chief Minister acted on the recommendation of the *Lok Ayukt*. The *ombudsman* is essentially an officer of the legislature to whom he reports. His effectiveness depends considerably on the people's consciousness of their rights and that of their representatives in the legislature.

Experience in the States can help considerably in drafting legislation for the *Lok Pal* at the Centre. The State laws fall into two broad patterns. Most sought to follow the *Lok Pal* model. Three preferred to innovate like Uttar Pradesh, Kerala and Tamil Nadu.

The States of Orissa, Uttar Pradesh and Maharashtra were the first to create the institution. The Orissa *Lok Pal* and Uttar Pradesh *Lok Ayukt* Act, 1970, received the assent of the President of India on February 8, 1971, whereas the Maharashtra *Lok Ayukt* and Uttar Pradesh *Lok Ayukt* Act, 1971 was assented by the President on December 10, 1971.

Two years later, the Bihar *Lok Ayukt* Act, 1973, and the Rajasthan *Lok Ayukt* and U.P. *Lok Ayukt* Act, 1973, were brought on the statute book. The Bihar *Lok Ayukt* Act received the assent of the President on January 16, 1974. Appreciating the importance of this institution, a few other States followed suit. The Uttar Pradesh *Lok Ayukt* Act, 1975, received the assent of the President on September 7, 1975 and was enforced with effect from July 12, 1977. The Madhya Pradesh *Lok Ayukt* Act, 1981, received the assent of the President on September 16, 1981.

About two years later, the State of Himachal Pradesh enforced the Himachal Pradesh *Lok Ayukt* Act on June 1, 1983 and the Andhra Pradesh *Lok Ayukt* Act, 1983 was enforced with effect from November 1, 1983.[13] The Karnataka *Lok Ayukt* Act, 1984 replaced the Karnataka *Lok Ayukt* Ordinance 1 of 1984.

It received the President's assent on January 16, 1985. The Acts of Andhra Pradesh, bihar, Maharashtra Rajasthan and Uttar Pradesh do not cover the Chief Minister while those of Himachal Pradesh, Karnataka and Orissa do.

The three State innovations are the Uttar Pradesh Public Men Inquiries Ordinance promulgated on October 21, 1967 by the Charan Singh Government; the Order of the Kerala Government, dated December 20, 1969, for 'setting up of an interim machinery to enquire into allegations against public men', (replaced by the Kerala Public Men Prevention of Corruption Act, 1983), and the Tamil Nadu Men (Criminal Misconduct) Act, 1973.

They merit for greater attention than they have received. There will, however, be a certain overlap between the function of a *Lok Ayukt* and those of a Commission of Inquiry, especially if the Kerala model described later in this chapter is followed.

It is proposed to discuss the salient features of the four Central Bills of 1971, 1977, 1985 and 1989 and, then, the two categories of State laws in order to formulate the basic principles to which any legislation for an Indian *ombudsman* should confirm to make the institution worthwhile.

The *Lok Pal* and *Lok Ayukts* Bill, 1971 sought to give effect to the recommendation of the ARC in so far as they relate to matters within the purview of the Union Government. Except for modifications of a formal nature, the Bill was identical with the *Lok Pal* and *Lok Ayukts* Bill, 1969, which was passed by the Fourth Lok Sabha on August 20, 1969.

In its scope, the Bill differed from the draft Bill proposed by the Commission in two major respects. It did not extend to public servants in the States. Secondly, it did not confine itself to ministers and secretaries alone. In other words, the bill sought to provide a statutory machinery to enquire into complaints based on actions of all union public servants including ministers but excluding the Prime Minister.

Its definition of "public servant" was, apart the odious exemption of the Prime Minister, comprehensive. It included ministers, officials of government, local authorities in any Union territory, public corporations, government-owned companies and registered societies under government control.

Two classes of cases were covered. One related to "maladministration". This was defined to mean "action taken or purporting to have been taken in the exercise of administrative functions in any case, (1) where such action or the administrative procedure or practice governing such action is unreasonable, unjust, oppressive or improperly discriminatory; or (2) where there has been negligence or undue delay in taking such action, or the administrative procedure or practice governing such action involves undue delay".

The other category was defined in the term "allegation". It meant any affirmation in relation to a "public servant" that he "has abused his position as such to obtain any gain or favour to himself or to any other person or to cause undue harm or hardship to any other person, (ii) was actuated in the discharge of his functions as such public servant by personal interest or improper or corrupt motives or (iii) is guilty of corruption, or lacks of integrity in his capacity as such public servant".

The *Lok Pal* was to be appointed by the President, after consultation with the Chief Justice of India and the Leader of the Opposition, for a five-year term. *Lok Ayukts* were to be appointed in consultation with him to assist him in performing his duties under his "administrative control".

They would all enjoy the security of tenure. Neither the *Lok Pal* nor a *Lok Ayukt* could be removed except on the ground of proven misconduct or incapacity after an inquiry by a sitting of a former Judge of the Supreme Court and an address by both Houses of Parliament adopted by a special majority.

The powers of a civil court for production of documents or summoning of witnesses were conferred by Clause 11(2). Only two classes of information or documents were exempt, cabinet proceedings or such as might "prejudice the security or defence or international relations of India (including India's relations with the government of any other country or with any international organisation), or the investigation or detection of crime". The "public interest" *carte blanche* clause of the ARC Bill was reproduced.

If an "allegation" was proved, the finding was communicated to "the competent authority", e.g. the Prime Minister in the case of a minister—for action which he was to report to the *Lok Ayukt* within three months. The term was one month in cases of mal-administration in respect of both the public servant concerned and "the competent authority."

If the *Lok Pal* was satisfied with the result, the case was closed. If not, he would report to the President who was bound to lay it before Parliament. He was free also to make available to the public the facts of the cases disposed of.

Investigations were to be conducted in private treating the identities of the complainant and the public servant confidential as a rule. They could be held in public if the *Lok Pal* so desired.

The exemption Clause (8) aroused controversy. Some topics were excluded for obvious reasons; viz., if the complainant had any legal remedy though even here the *Lok Pal* could waive the bar or matters referred for inquiry with his consent, under the Public Servants Inquiries Act, 1850, or the Commissions of Inquiry Act, 1952.

But the list in the Third Schedule (read with Clause 8(1)(a)) was of a different kind. It reads thus:

(a) Action in a matter certified by a Secretary as affecting the relations or dealings between the Government of India and any foreign Government or any international organisation of States or Governments.

(b) Action taken under the Extradition Act, 1962, or the Foreigners' Act, 1946.

(c) Action taken for the purpose of investigating crime or protecting the security of the State including action taken with respect to passports and travel documents.

(d) Action taken in the exercise of powers in relation to determining whether a matter shall go to a court or not.

(e) Action taken in matters which arise out of the terms of a contract governing purely commercial relations of the administration with customers or suppliers, except where the complainant alleges harassment or gross delay in meeting contractual obligations.

(f) Action taken in respect of appointments, pay, discipline, superannuation or other matters relating to conditions of service of public servants but not including action relating to claims for pension, gratuity, provident fund or to any claims which arise on retirement, removal or termination of service; and

(g) Grant of honours and awards.

When, in 1973, Jayaprakash Narayan launched his crusade against the fast rising spiral of corruption in the country, he trenchantly criticised these provisions of the bill in an article in his journal.[14] J.P. wrote "if the *Lok Pal* Bill and the Maharashtra *Ayukt* Act, which is claimed to be patterned after the former, were carefully scrutinised, it would be discovered that the action of these vital officers is severely limited and hemmed in by the restrictive provisions.

It is in many ways a case of giving by one hand and taking away by the other.....a fertile and well—known source of corruption at the State level, which embraces MLAs, local party functionaries and even ministers, is the matters of transfers, postings and promotions of subordinate and higher government servants of all departments. Not only is this a source of corruption, but it also occupies most of the ministers.

The remedy for this also is institutionalization of the system. J.P. contrasted the lethargy on this measure in contrast to 'spectacular' activity on some others.

As Union Home Minister in the Janata Party Government, Charan Singh showed the same enthusiasm on this subject as he had done a decade ago as Uttar Pradesh's Chief Minister. His *Lok Pal* Bill, 1977 did not include grievances in respect of mal-administration for which separate legislation was intended.

It's prime concern was to combat corruption, 'misconduct by a public man'. Both terms were widely defined; 'Public man' was defined to include any member(s) of the Council of Ministers for the Union, MPs and Chief Ministers. 'Public servant' was given the same meaning as in Section 21 of the Penal Code.

'Misconduct' received the widest definition possible in Clause 3(1) : 'A public man commits misconduct-

(a) if he is actuated in the discharge of his functions as such public man by motives of personal interest or other improper or corrupt motives; or

(b) if he abuses or attempts to abuse his position as such public man to cause harm or undue hardship to any other persons;

(c) if he directly or indirectly allows his position as such public man to be taken advantage of by any of his relatives or associates and by reason thereof such relative or associate secures any undue gain or favour to himself or to another person or causes harm or undue hardship to another person. Explanation: For the purposes of this clause, 'associate' in relation to a public man includes any person in whom such public man is interested; or

(d) if he fails to act in any case otherwise than in accordance with the norms of integrity and conduct which ought to be followed by the class of public men to which he belongs; or

(e) if any act or omission by him constitutes corruption as made punishable under Chapter IX of the Penal Code or under the Prevention of Corruption Act, 1947.

The jurisdiction was also wide:

(1) Subject to the other provisions of this Act, the *Lok Pal* may inquire into any matter involved in, or arising from, or connected with, any allegation of misconduct against a public man made in a complaint under this Act.

(2) No matter in respect of which a complaint may be made under this Act shall be referred for inquiry under the Commissions of Inquiry Act, 1952, except on the recommendation or with the concurrence of the *Lok Pal*.

Allegations against civil servants were outside the purview of the Bill. Any persons other than a public servant could make a complaint to the *Lok Pal* alleging misconduct against a public man in the manner prescribed.

For the rest, the provisions of the 1971 Bill were drawn upon with certain changes. For example, instead of the Leader of the Opposition, the presiding officers of both Houses of Parliament were to be consulted in the appointment of the *Lok Pal*.

As in the 1971 Bill, he would have his own staff, but 'as may be prescribed' by Rules made by the President (i.e. the Government). He could secure the services of any officer or agency of the Central or State Government or 'of any other person or agency'.

The *Lok Pal* was to enjoy the security of tenure of a judge of the Supreme Court. His sanction was the same report to the competent authority and eventually to the President. There was a special provision regarding the Prime Minister.

The 'competent authority' to deal with him was the Council of Ministers. Clause 18 required him to report to it 'without delay' any complaint made against him to the *Lok Pal* which the latter had transmitted to him for his comments as well as the report of the *Lok Pal* on the complaint.

This can be a meaningful check only if the Council of Ministers functions as such and not if it is an instrument of what Richard Crossman called the Prime Ministerial Government which the country witnessed under Prime Ministers Indira Gandhi and Rajiv Gandhi.

It was in a badly battered shape that this Bill emerged in the Report of the Joint Committee of Parliament presented on July 20, 1978. Chief Ministers were totally omitted from its purview. Legislators were given special treatment.

The definition of 'misconduct' was greatly restricted in Class 3 of the revised Bill: 'A public man, other than a legislator, commits misconduct-

"1. (a) if he is actuated in the discharge of his functions as such public man by corrupt motives; or (b) if he abuses, or attempts to abuse, or knowingly allows to be abused, his position as such public man for securing for himself or for any of his relatives or associates any valuable thing or pecuniary advantage; or (c) if any act or omission by him constitutes corruption.

2. "A legislator commits misconduct if he abuses, or knowingly allows to be abused, his position as such legislator for securing for himself directly or indirectly any valuable thing or pecuniary advantage".

There was nothing vague about the original definition. The definition of the misconduct in the original Bill was fully adequate. As well as including corruption, as made punishable under the Penal Code and the Prevention of Corruption Act, it covered failure on the part of a public man "to act in any case otherwise than in accordance with the norms of integrity and conduct which ought to be followed by the class of public men to which he belongs."

This was not "too wide" and no reason was advanced for dubbing it so at all. It was more "amenable to different interpretations" than the word "reasonable" which is used to restrict the fundamental rights embodied in Article 19 and is otherwise commonly used in legal parlance without much difficulty.

Section 45 of the Army Act 1950 makes it an offence for

any officer, junior commissioned officer or warrant officer to behave "in a manner unbecoming of his position and the character expected of him." Section 35 of the Advocates Act, 1961 renders an advocate liable to disciplinary proceedings, if he has been guilty of professional or other misconduct.

These expressions have not been defined by the Acts because they are not susceptible to precise definition. On the other hand, the norms of conduct expected of an advocate or of an army officer are fairly well known. So, indeed, are those expected of a public man, thanks to the various Commissions of Inquiry.

It is illustrative of the difference between the approach of the farmers of the bill and the joint committee that while the original bill included within "misconduct" any conduct on the part of a public man in the discharge of his functions which is actuated by "motives of personal interest or other improper or corrupt motives", the Committee deleted "personal interest or other motives" and confined the scope to "corrupt motives" alone. Thus, for all practical purposes, abuse of power, gross impropriety and the like were made completely exempt from the *Lok Pal*'s jurisdiction.

The original definition, besides being comprehensive, was realistically flexible in that it covered violations of norms "which ought to be followed by the class of public men to which he belongs". This would have endowed the *Lok Pal* with ample discretion in applying the correct norms to members of parliament who, unlike other public men, wield no executive authority. Undoubtedly, the concept of misconduct cannot be the same for an MP as for a minister.

The Bill took good care of that, but the Committee deleted a salutary provision and proceeded to tackle a problem of its own creation.

Instead of the Union Council of Ministers, "the competent authority to the *Lok Pal*'s Report on the Prime Minister, was one who is virtually a single appointee of his, viz., the Speaker of the Lok Sabha, as in the case of any Member of Parliament."

The procedure for the *Lok Pal*'s appointment was improved by empowering the presiding officers of both Houses of Parliament to consult leaders of various parties. It, however, speaks for the approach of the Committee that it took away from the *Lok Pal* completely the discretion whether or not to hold an inquiry in private or in public. If a legislator was involved, the inquiry had to be *in camera*.

The *Lok Pal* Bill, 1985 was far worse than either of its predecessors of 1971 or 1977. Introduced in the Lok Sabha on August 26, 1985, it was unceremoniously dropped by the Government itself in November 1988 on the ground that it did not cover grievances, a flaw by no means fatal and one which was of its own making. The remit was the narrowest possible. The *Lok Pal* was empowered by the Clause 8(1) to "inquire into any matter involved in, or arising from, or connected with, any allegation made in a complaint".

This had to be read with the definition Clause 2(b) which defined 'complaint' as one alleging that a 'public functionary has, while holding any of the offices mentioned in Clause (e) committed any offence punishable under Chapter IX of the Indian Penal Code or under the Prevention of Corruption Act, 1947.'

If that was all, the Bill was utterly redundant. These statutes were enforceable by the court of law and the police, any way. The sanctions provided in the Criminal Procedure Code, 1973, could have been relaxed to facilitate the filing of a private complaint, a right which the Supreme Court had ruled in 1984 belonged to a citizen.[15]

'Public functionary' was, in turn, narrowly defined to cover only ministers. The Prime Minister was excluded as were civil servants and officials of the State Corporations. The only concession was the inclusion of Parliamentary Secretaries. The sole 'competent authority' over all of them was the Prime Minister.

There was a retreat from previous Bills all along the line. The Chief Justice of India was to be consulted in the appointment of the *Lok Pal*. His security of tenure was diluted. Address by both the Houses of Parliament was dispensed with.

The only safeguard was the inquiry by the Chief Justice of India or any of his colleagues chosen by him. The Executive's say in the appointment of his staff was made more explicit (as the President may determine) Not that it was absent in earlier bills ('as may be prescribed'), i.e. by rules made by the President.

As in previous bills, any person other than a public servant could file a complaint. Since the remit was only to enforce two panel statutes, the possibility of a conflict in between police investigation and the *Lok Pal's* inquiry was inherent in the situation. Clause 13 empowered the *Lok Pal* to direct the police to defer the investigation, unless it was made pursuant to an order of any court.

There was one change in favour of openness. A provision to Clause 14(4) empowered the *Lok Pal* to question the certificate issued by a Secretary to the Government that a document or information is of the exempted category (defence, etc.) order disclosure, examine it "in private for scrutiny' and 'declare the certificate to be of no effect.' This is noteworthy.

Clause 21 contained a draconian provision penalising disclosure of the identities of the parties or the particulars of the complaint before it is dismissed or the case is closed.

It was made triable by the *Lok Pal* himself summarily and liable to a six months' prison term or a fine of Rs. 10,000 or both. Appeal lay only to the Supreme Court. There was no requirement of *mens rea* The liability was absolute.

If the *Lok Pal* was dissatisfied with the action taken by the 'competent authority' (the Prime Minister) on his findings, he had no power to submit a special report to the President.

The Note of Dissent dated November 29, 1988 signed by some members of the Parliamentary Committee protesting against the withdrawal of the Bill recorded in detail the time and the labour expended over it: 'The Committee had visited 23 different States and Union Territories.'[16]

Barring some changes, the thirty-three clauses of the National Front Government's Bill of December 29, 1989 were an exact verbatim reproduction of the thirty-three clauses of the 1985 Bill. One would have expected it to draw from the salutary features of the 1971 and 1977 bills and combine them into one. It chose a different model.

Three departures from the 1985 bill were in the liberal

direction. Most notably, the inclusion of the Prime Minister within the sway of the *Lok Pal*. Secondly, in the event of his findings that any of the allegations against the Prime Minister have been 'substantiated either wholly or partly, 'his report went to the Speaker of the Lok Sabha to be laid before the House within ninety days of its receipt (Clause 16(3).

In contrast, Janata's *Lok Pal* Bill, 1977 provided that the report went to the Prime Minister himself who was enjoined to place it 'without delay before the other members of the Council of Ministers.'

Thus, what the Janata Bill reduced to a private affairs was made a matter of national concern to be dealt with publicly by the Lok Sabha and the nation at large.

Lastly, the 1985 Bill provided that the President shall after consultation with the Chief Justice of India, appoint, as *Lok Pal*, 'a person who is or has been, or is qualified to be, a judge of the Supreme Court'. The last category can include any advocate of ten years practice. The 1989 Bill restricted the qualification to two categories alone, viz. serving or retired judges of the court.

Besides, all the previous bills provided for a single-member institution. In 1989, a three-member *Lok Pal* was proposed to be set up with a Chairman and two other members and all three were to be either serving or retired Supreme Court judges.

Yet, all that this high-powered body could be asked to do was to probe charges of offences under the Prevention of Corruption Act, 1988—and no more. This narrow limitation was a hangover of the 1985 Bill which ignored precedents completely.

In one respect, the remit of the 1989 bill was narrower than that of it's model of 1985, in that, unlike the latter, it was confined to offences under the Prevention of Corruption Act, 1988 omitting those under Chapter IX of the Penal Code.

Clause 21 of the 1989 bill was a replica of Clause 21 of the 1985 bill. This provision did not figure either in the 1971 or the 1977 Bill. There is everything to be said for the confidentiality of proceedings before the *Lok Pal*.

But, it is indefensible to provide for summary trial by the very person who is aggrieved and for offences to be widely defined excluding the elements of intention, public harm or prejudice to the proceedings.

Such a provision is a threat to press freedom and is clearly violative of the fundamental right to freedom of speech and expression embodied in Article 19(1)(a) of the Constitution of India.

Any legislation that will be drafted for adoption by the new Lok Sabha must take cognizance of these bills. There has been ample discussion in the past. Only policy decisions are required to combine the best elements of the 1971 and 1977 bills and, indeed, to profit by the experiments in the various States.

The Maharashtra *Lok Ayukt* and *Upa-Lok Ayukt*'s Act, 1971 was based entirely on the Central Bill of 1971. The first *Lok Ayukt* appointed under the State's law was a former Chief Justice of Bombay High Court, Justice S.P. Kotval. His annual Report for the first year (October 25, 1973) listed the flaws in the statute. The Report is, therefore, of enormous help, Jayaprakash Narayan wrote his article, in Every Man, after a full discussion with Justice Kotval.

The Report noted : "It is to be regretted that in several cases notwithstanding that a complaint had merit or justice on it's side, the *Lok Ayukt* or *Upa-Lok Ayukt* have had to refuse to investigate because of technical grounds such as want of jurisdiction under Section 8(1)(a) or because another remedy is theoretically open to the complaint, [Section 8(1)(b)], without going into the merits of the case.'

Not all the limitations were unwarranted. Those listed in the Third Schedule - itself a replace of the Third Schedule of the 1971 Bill minus matters exclusively of Union concern - were open to serious objection.

The police enjoyed 'complete immunity' because of two limitations: 'action taken for the purpose of investigating circle' and 'action taken in the exercise of powers in relation to determining whether a matter shall go to a court or not'. Even if the police refuse to act on a complaint for improper reasons, the *Lok Ayukt*'s jurisdiction is barred; for 'action' includes 'failure to act'. Of the 903 complaints received in the year, 101 were against the police department.

Next as to Clause (c) of the Third Schedule, it refers to action taken in matters which arise out of the terms of a contract governing purely commercial relations of the administration with customers and suppliers. This will exclude from the jurisdiction of the *Lok Ayukt* and the *Upa-Lok Ayukt* the scrutiny of the implementation of all contracts of the public works department, of the excise department, all lease and licence, (e.g., contracts for building, grant of licences for liquor shops), the exploitation of forest produce or contracts for removal of *lac* or *tendu* leaves etc.

The exception contemplated in the clause does not materially affect the above limitation. The exception is 'except where the complainant alleges harassment or gross delay in meeting contractual obligations.'

The report added: the *Lok Ayukt* and *Upa-Lok Ayukt* have no separate investigating agency of their own for conducting investigations under the Act.' He had requested the Anti-Corruption Bureau of the State Government to investigate a complaint against a minister 'but the experience of the *Lok Ayukt* in this respect has not been happy. In important cases especially against a minister, investigation has either not been made or inordinately delayed.'

It was not possible to utilise the service of 'any person or agency' besides that of the State, 'without financial sanction and creation of posts under Section 13(3)(1)', which required the government's approval. The Union refused to lend the services of the C.B.I.

Justice Kotval made detailed comment, advisedly. First, because the Central Bill was on the anvil and was open to modification. 'Secondly, after the Maharashtra *Lok Ayukt* and the *Upa-Lok Ayukt* was passed, other States have undertaken similar legislations but they have not adopted its provisions and have instread considerably modified them, particularly provisions like Section 8 or the Third Schedule.

In fact, very recently on the 27th March, 1973, the state of

Rajasthan passed the Rajasthan *Lok Ayukt* and Upa-*Lok Ayukt* Act, 1973 (Act 9 of 1973), and it is in respect of the very points which we have made that the Rajasthan Act has modified it's own statute and made it more effective.

The salient features of the Rajasthan Act are:

(a) The definition of grievance in Section 2(d) of the Maharashtra Act has been omitted. The result is that the distinction sought to be drawn in the Maharashtra Act between an allegation and a grievance has been abolished as unnecessary. (This is not a matter for praise. It is a blemish (emphasis author).

(b) There is no provision like section 8(3) of the Maharashtra Act in the Rajasthan Act so that the bar imposed on investigating grievances in respect of public servants mentioned in Section 2(k) (IV) of the Maharashtra Act has been taken away.

(c) Most important of all, there are no provisions in the Rajasthan Act imposing limitations such as laid down in Section 8(1)(a) and (b) of the Maharashtra Act and the whole of the third schedule has been omitted.

He reported an encouraging public response and recommended that full publicity be given to the new remedies provided to the citizen. The Second Annual Report (1973-74) noted that a copy of the previous report had not been laid before the legislature though a year had elapsed since its submission.

On June 17, 1977, Justice S.P. Kotval was obliged to make a special report to the Governor because Chief Minister S.B. Chavan had failed to act as 'competent authority' on the *Lok Ayukt*'s findings against two Ministers, H.G. Vartak and N.K. Tirpude. The episode is instructive of what can fail the institution if the government proves obstructive.

The report was sent to Mr. Chavan on July 1, 1976. He replied negatively and only through the Secretary to the Chief Minister on December 23, 1976. The *Lok Ayukt* re-read the papers and wrote again to the Chief Minister on April, 14, 1977 but received no reply. Instead, Chavan spoke to the press on June 16, 1977.

State laws vary. The Karnataka *Lok Ayukt* Act, 1984 includes the Chief Minister, ministers, MLAs, civil servants as well as officials of State Corporations, companies, registered societies, co-operative societies, universities and local authorities. The 'competent authority' discretion.

The *Lok Ayukt* could be appointed only after consultation with the Chief Justice of the High Court, presiding officers and leaders of opposition in both Houses of the legislature. The qualification was raised to one who had held the office of a judge of the Supreme Court or that of the Chief Justice of a High Court. These were all highly commendable; but the Bill took over the Third Schedule (of exception) whole-sale.

The Andhra Pradesh *Lok Ayukt* and *Upa-Lok Ayukt* Act, 1983-which had received the Governor's assent on October 11, 1982 and that of the President on August 25, 1983 - excludes the Chief Minister but is, in a sense, more extensive than the Karnataka law. A sitting judge of a High Court can be appointed to the office.

The Karnataka Act maintains the distinction between 'allegation' defined to include failure 'to act in accordance with the norms of integrity and conduct' - and 'grievance' of injustice or hardship through mal-administration.

The Andhra Pradesh Act is confined to probe into any 'allegation' of abuse of position, improper motivation, corruption or 'lack of integrity. There was no provision comparable to the third schedule to the Central Bill of 1971.

Most State laws are variants on the 1971 model. The three innovations are real exercises in creativity and original thinking. The Uttar Pradesh Public Men Inquiries Ordinance, 1967, followed by a Bill the same year which lapsed, sought in essence to establish an Independent Commission of Inquiry as well as an independent directorate of prosecution.

It covered ministers, legislators, and the office holders of local bodies. Any one could prefer an 'accusation' of 'misconduct' against them; 'misconduct' was not defined but the word has been construed in judicial decisions and in reports of commissions of inquiry.

It provided for the appointment of a chief investigator of

the status of an Inspector General of Police and an investigating establishment under him. Any person could send to the governor a petition for instituting an inquiry into an accusation made by him. The governor had to prefer the accusation to a high court judge for preliminary scrutiny.

He could make such a reference *suo moto* as well. In making the preliminary inquiry, the judge could ask for the assistance of any minister or officer of the State governor or of the chief investigator. He could also give the person against whom an accusation has been made an opportunity to explain any matter. In case he came to the conclusion that the accusation was reasonably substantiated, he had to refer it to the governor.

The chief investigator had, then, to investigate into the matter and send his report confidentially to the governor. The governor could, then, refer the report to the Commission of Inquiry under this very law, consisting of one or two judges who, then, report their findings to the governor, and also pronounce them in public. If punishment was recommended, the chief investigator would pursue the prosecution.

The validity of the Tamil Nadu public Men (Criminal Misconduct) Act, 1973 was upheld by the Supreme Court in *M. Karunanidhi vs. Union of India & ANR* (1979) 3 SCC 431. Though it was repealed in 1977, it merits consideration as an innovative measure. It covered ministers and other public men including the Chief Minister and legislators.

The Act created a separate offence called 'criminal misconduct', which could be inquired into by a commissioner of inquiries with an additional commissioner of inquiries to be appointed by the governor on the advice of the Chief Justice.

The commissioner was to be of the status of a high court judge and the additional commissioner of a district judge. The term of the commissioner and additional commissioner was three years.

Any one could make a complaint within the limitation prescribed (within five years from the date on which the criminal misconduct was alleged to be committed or within one year from the date on which the public man ceased to be such public man, whichever was later). The commissioner could employ his own agency or depend upon other departmental agencies. He could suggest prosecution under the Criminal Law (Amendment) Act, 1952. The law was explicit.

If prosecution was recommended, 'the public man shall be prosecuted and tried under Section 6 of the Criminal Law (Amendment) Act, 1952.'

'Criminal misconduct' was defined to include acceptance of illegal gratification as well as abuse of position to obtain any valuable thing or pecuniary advantage.

The most successful of the State innovations was the Kerala Order of 1969; more successful, ironically, than the Kerala Public Man (Prevention of Corruption Act, 1983). The order was simplicity itself.

It covered the Chief Minister as well as the MLAs proving once again the spurious character of objections to their inclusion. It defined 'misconduct' to include corruption, favouritism, nepotism, 'abuse of position' or 'any act of omission' in the official capacity which *inter alia* is actuated by 'improper' motives.

Any citizen could set the machinery in motion. The government was bound to refer the complaint to a serving or retired high court judge. If he found that 'a *prima facie* case has been made out of that further investigation is necessary, he will report to the government accordingly.'

The order effectively surmounted the first obstacle. For the practice has been for the head of the government to decide whether or not a complaint against himself or one of his colleagues disclosed a *prima facie* case to warrant the setting up of a commission of inquiry under the Act of 1952; in other words, to sit in judgement of his own case, virtually.

The order, in truth, only formalised a practice which had come into vogue in the State largely because of the balance of political forces and high public awareness and ready recourse to inquire into charges against ministers which explain the several commissions of inquiry before the order was made. It's success was due also to the judge who worked the order.[17]

The order, was replaced by the Kerala Public Men (Prevention of Corruption) Act, 1983 which, in turn, was repealed by the Kerala Public Man's Corruption (Investigation and Inquiries) Act, 1987.

It was passed by the State assembly on December 13, 1987. Three annual reports were submitted under the 1983 Act, from 1985 to 1987. Sadly, the legislation got enmeshed in litigation and political strife.

The 1983 Act covered the entire range of "public men's from the Chief Minister and MLA downwards in the widest amplitude to include office bearers of a registered trade union.

Corruption was defined to cover receipt of illegal gratification as well as the abuse of position. The definition was far narrower than in the order of 1969. A three member commission was to be appointed by the governor 'in consultation with', rather than on the advice of, the Chief Minister and the Chief Justice of whom two were to be retired or serving high court judges.

The Commission was to make a preliminary investigation and subsequently, if a *prima facie* case was found, a detailed one. It's report went first to 'the government' and the next to the Governor if it was not satisfied with the action.

Like the Tamil Nadu Act, prosecution was mandatory if the Commission so recommended. It could also recommend that the public man vacate his post. But it was open to the government to reject this recommendation within three months of receipt of the report failing which the act obliged the public man to 'resign his office if he was Chief Minister, Minister or MLA. In other cases, he was 'deemed to have to vacate his office'.

Another innovation to empower the Commission (Section 16) was to call for a special property statement in the prescribed form from any public man who was under investigation. Preliminary investigations alone were to be in private and were confidential.

The 1987 Act introduced the concept of 'competent authority' for action 'the governor acting in his discretion', in the case of the Chief Minister. The definition of 'public man' was expanded to cover the office bearers of political parties, private schools and colleges and so was that of 'corruption'.

Yet, it fell short of the 1969 order in that acquisition of pecuniary gain was made an ingredient in the offence of abuse of power as distinction from 'improper motive', generally.

However, a new offence was added-possession by himself or any member of his family or any one else on his behalf of 'pecuniary resources or property disproportionate to his known sources of income'.

The three-member Commission was retained. So was it's two stage procedure but with an addition which is highly questionable. Existence of 'other remedies' could, in the Commission's discretion, justify a decision not to proceed further. Full powers to issue search warrants are conferred on the body.

Reports are to be submitted to 'the government' and 'the competent authority' is enjoined to intimate the action taken. If it is not satisfied with it, the Commission makes a special report to the governor. The power to order the public man to vacate his office was retained and strengthened by excluding the government's discretion to reject the recommendation.

Only office bearers of political parties and trade unions are exempted from this. What is more, the Commission itself is empowered to initials, rather than merely recommend, prosecution.

It is, however, not spelt out as to how and by whom such a prosecution is to be conducted. It is essential that the Commission should be endowed with a judicial personality.

Rathan than leave it to the Commission to call for property statements, the act obligates some public men, chief Ministers, ministers, MLAs etc. to submit it 'as statement of his assets and liabilities and those of the members of his family' once in two years (Section 25).

The act evoked a mixed reaction.[18] An important change was the Act of 1987 empowered the Governor to appoint members of the Commission only 'on the advice tendered by the Chief Minister in consultation with' the Chief Justice and the leader of the opposition. This was invoked to challenge the appointment of the members, in the High Court on March 13, 1990.[19]

This resume, which is illustrative and neither definitive nor exhaustive, demonstrates the obsolescence of the 1971 model and also exposes the spurious character of objections to the inclusion of the head of government or the legislators. If the offices of the *Lok Pal* and the *Lok Ayukt* are to have any meaning these exclusions must be abandoned for good.

A good test is that the institution should be able to resist the indifference and even scorn of the executive of the kind to which, for instance, the Rajasthan *Lok Ayukt* has been subjected.[20]

No uniform pattern should be imposed on the States. They should be free to innovate. The Model Bill prepared for and presented at the 3rd All India *Lok Ayukt*'s Conference in 1991 can, at best, serve as a guide. However, both at the Centre and in the States, the institution must conform to certain minimal requirements in order to meet the tests mentioned in this chapter These are:

(1) The offices of the *Lok Pal* and the *Lok Ayukt* should have a constitutional status, as recommended by the Administrative Reforms Commission (ARC). As in the case of the Election Commission (Article 324 of the Constitution), the details can be laid down by the appropriate legislature (Article 327). But the legislature should not be left free to abolish the office itself or curb its authority.

(2) The constitutional provision should define the functions, the procedure for appointment to the office, the ambit of jurisdiction and the powers. This would make the minimal requirements mandatory. To this extent, uniformity will also be introduced.

(3) The functions should be to inquire into any "grievance" of "mal-administration" as well as any "allegation" of "misconduct" by a citizen or *suo moto*. It is extremely important that both should be considered at one place as the 1971 Bill provided in contrast to the bills of 1977, 1985 and 1989. Often, evidence of corruption comes to light when a grievance of mal-administration is inquired into.

(4) The definition of "mal-administration" in the 1971 Bill [Clause 2] (g)] is adequate but not so the definition of "allegation" [Clause 2 (a)] as pointed out in the chapter. Even so, it is far better than the definition of "complaint" in the 1985 Bill and especially in the 1989 Bill [Clauses 2(b) and 2(c) respectively]. The definition of "misconduct" in Clause 3 of the 1977 Bill is adequate.

(5) Whether the *Lok Pal* should be a single member or multiple member is a matter of opinion. Given the amplitude of his jurisdiction, a multiple-member body would be more appropriate.

(6) The procedure for appointment should be analogous to the appointment of judges of the Supreme Court and the High Courts as laid down in the Constitution 67th Amendment Bill, 1990 moved in the Lok Sabha on May 18, 1990 (it lapsed on the dissolution of the Lok Sabha later in the year).

It provided for a National Judicial Commission, to recommend the appointments, comprising the Chief Justice of India and other judges. In the case of the *Lok Pal*, the appointing body should comprise the Prime Minister, the Chief Justice of India, the presiding officers of both the houses of Parliament and the leaders of the opposition in the Lok Sabha. A similar body should appoint the *Lok Pal* in the States.

(7) The *Lok Pal* should be a former judge of the Supreme Court or a former Chief Justice of a High Court. No one should be appointed to the office who is merely "qualified to be" a judge.

(8) The *Lok Pal* and *Lok Ayukt* should respectively have jurisdiction at the Centre and in the State over every "public man" as defined in Clause 2(g) of the 1977 Bill as well as every 'public servant" as defined in Section 2(c) of the prevention of Corruption Act, 1988; this is wider than the definition of "public servant" in Section 21 of the Penal Code. Specifically, the definition of "public man" should include both the chief

executive as well as legislators (the Kerala Act of 1987 also provides a good guide to the definition of "public man".)

(9) The institution should have an independent staff of its own. As discussed in the chapter on Commissions of Inquiry, an independent investigation agency should be set up on whose services the *Lok Pal, Lok Ayukts* and Commissions of Inquiry can freely draw upon.

(10) The institution should have a juridical personality. It should have the power to launch prosecution without the sanction of the government and to order a public man or public servant to vacate office. In the latter case, the order would be amenable to writ jurisdiction anyway. It would be fair to provide an appeal to the Supreme Court.

(11) The *Lok Pal*'s jurisdiction should be confined to the Union's functionaries. The ARC's draft bill covered Ministers and Secretaries at the Centre as well as in the States (Clauses 2 and 7). The 1977 Bill included Chief Ministers in the definition of "public man". The 1971 Bill was confined to central ministers alone, bar the prime minister. So were the 1985 and 1989 bills (the latter included the Prime Minister). It would only be fair to have a clear demarcation of the *Lok Pal* and the *Lok Ayukt*.

(12) Public support is indispensable to success. The staff should assist the underprivileged who approach the *Lok Pal* or *Lok Ayukt*. NGO's and Public Interest Groups make people aware of the existence of the institution and help them to file the complaints. The proceedings of the institution should be opened to the public.

Public grievances arising from mal-administration were sought to be redressed by an authority called *Ombudsman* which was first conceived in Sweden in 1809 as an autonomous, independent inquisitorial authority to inquire into complaints of transgression of law by administrative authority in the course of handling administrative affairs, illegality or delays in reaching decisions, discourtesy or rudeness, unfairness, bias, incompetence, high-handedness, mistakes, failure to respond, furnishing misleading statements, etc.

Similar institutions of *Ombudsman* with some modifications regarding powers and responsibilities were established in Finland in 1819, Denmark in 1953, New Zealand in 1962, Norway in 1963, United Kingdom in 1966 and Australia in 1976.

Lok Pal Needed

On the recommendation of the Administrative Reforms Commission in 1966, a *Lok Pal* Bill was introduced in our Parliament in 1968-69 to set up an *Ombudsman*-type of body, but it lapsed with the dissolution of the *Lok Sabha*.

The Bill, in a revised form, was again introduced in 1977, but that also lapsed. The Bill was introduced for the third time in 1989 but even that has not been taken shape.

Some States like Orissa, Maharashtra, Rajasthan, Bihar, Uttar Pradesh, Andhra Pradesh, Karnataka, Madhya Pradesh, Gujarat and Himachal Pradesh have statutorily set-up inquiry authorities similar to *Lok Pal* to look into certain types of complaints of mal-administration in the State, but all the enactments suffer from the same drawback viz., non-availability of a truly independent and unbiased investigating agency to aid the inquiry authority.

A New Lok Pal Bill

There has been a lot of talk lately of introducing a fresh *Lok Pal* Bill. A mere rehash of the old drafts of the Bill will not do to meet the needs of present times. The new *Lok Pal* Bill should include the following ideas, concepts and arrangements:

(i) The *Lok Pal* should be set up as a standing judicial body in the nature of an *ombudsman* at the Centre with responsibility for making inquiries into complaints of corruption and misconduct against all Central ministers (including the Prime Minister), Members of Parliament and top level bureaucrats in the Government.

(ii) The *Lok Pal* may be a multi-member body with all its

members including the Chairman, being persons who are working or had worked or are qualified for appointment as judges of the Supreme Court.

(iii) The appointment of the Chairman and members of the *Lok Pal* shall be decided by the President in consultation with the Chief Justice of India, after obtaining the recommendations of a committee on the lines prescribed in Section 4(1) of the Protection of Human Rights Act (1993) for the appointment of Chairperson and members of the National Human Rights Commission.

The significance of this committee is that it includes the Leaders of Opposition in the Lok Sabha and the Rajya Sabha besides the Prime Minister. This will eliminate any possible political bias in the appointment process.

The *Lok Pal* shall be assisted by a permanent secretariat of its own, separately funded in the same manner as presently followed for the Comptroller and Auditor General of India.

Lok Pal Functions

The *Lok Pal* shall be statutorily provided with an investigating wing and a prosecuting wing which will be filled with personnel, specially selected by the Chairman of the *Lok Pal*, with due regard to their background of impeccable honesty, professional efficiency and integrity.

They may be drawn from the existing cadres of investigating agencies and prosecuting agencies at the Centre and in the States but they shall be permanently seconded to the *Lok Pal* and shall not be required to return their parent units while in service. Their pay and allowances shall be duly protected from any possible victimisation by *mala fide* administrative action in the government machinery at a later stage.

It shall be competent for the President, and the President alone, acting within his discretion and judgement, to examine the reports of inquiry by the *Lok Pal* and decide on the further course of action thereon, which may include;

(a) launching of prosecution in court against those found *prima facie* guilty of criminal offences, or

(b) department of those found guilty of any misconduct from standing for election to Parliament or State Assembly or any statutory body for any specified period as may be provided in the *Lok Pal* Act.

Prosecution for criminal charges which arise from the *Lok Pal*'s report shall be directly launched and handled in court by the prosecuting wing of the *Lok Pal* only.

LOK PAL AND C.V.C.

The proposal to have a separate investigating wing and prosecuting wing for the *Lok Pal* or CVC set-up raises the question whether it will be practicable to have investigators and prosecutors function within such a small closed system for their entire career. The answer may be found in the existing set-up of the CBI itself which has about 800 investigating officers and 200 prosecutors.

About 75% of the CBI staff are drawn on deputation from the State police, and after the deputationists prove their mettle in CBI work, they are permanently absorbed in the CBI and get the normal career benefits within the CBI.

Those who do not make the grade, are sent back to their parent State. This system has worked well in the CBI, and can be adopted for the staff of the *Lok Pal* or CVC also without difficulty.

Even though their number may not be large, a suitable hierarchical career structure can be designed for them. They may also be made eligible for higher level posts in the Ministry of Law, as a kind of career facility.

The scheme of having separate investigating and prosecuting staff permanently attached to the *Lok Pal* or CVC is viable and workable.

C.V.C. and Lok Pal Integration

The statutory arrangements proposed above envisage a *Lok Pal* to look after inquiries into corruption at high levels including the political executive, and a CVC to monitor vigilance and anti-corruption work done by the CBI and the set-up of VOs in all government departments. Since the essential and ultimate objective is the same for both.

It would be best to integrate the two institutions and have a common legislation which would make the CVC a member of the *Lok Pal* itself and perform the tasks proposed for the CVC as above.

A common secretariat, investigating wing and prosecuting wing can serve both, in the integrated set-up. This would facilitate better co-ordination and development of legal expertise in the long run.

LOK PALS IN STATES

The State-level *Lok Pals* should be similarly set up statutorily in each State or for a group of States by Central legislation, with jurisdiction to inquire into complaints of corruption and misconduct against top-level bureaucrats in the State government and State ministers including Chief Ministers.

Appointment of the State *Lok Pals* shall also be made by the President only. Procedural arrangements applicable to the *Lok Pal* shall, *mutatis mutandis*, apply to the State *Lok Pals*.

Commissions of Inquiry Act

In view of the proposed comprehensive set-up of the *Lok Pal*/CVC at the Centre and in the States as statutory bodies to deal with complaints of high-level corruption, there will be no need to have *ad hoc* commissions appointed under the Commissions of Inquiry Act to deal with the same matter.

However, the Commissions of Inquiry Act may continue to remain on the statute book to facilitate appointment of special commissions to inquire into any matter of public importance not involving corruption e.g., air - crash, train smash or collapse of a public-building or river dam resulting in several deaths, etc. The investigating and prosecuting staff of the *Lok Pal*/CVC may be deputed to assist such Commissions of Inquiry as and when they are set-up.

C.B.I. Monitoring Supreme Court or High Court Cases

In recent years, the CBI has had to take up some cases on specific directions from a High Court or the Supreme Court and report the result of the investigation to the Court. Though the number of such cases is not large, all have been very sensational and have, therefore, required concentrated and continuous attention from the CBI for thorough and expeditious investigation.

In the recent Hawala Case, the Supreme Court has been practically monitoring the progress of investigating from time to time. In fact, the Supreme Court has been doing the type of supervisory work, which, in the normal course, the Director of CBI can and should do if he was under no pressure, direct or indirect, from the political executive in the Government.

While an odd case may get such attention from the Supreme Court once in a while, it would not be a healthy dispensation for the Supreme Court or High Courts to take on such a supervisory role at the stage of the investigation itself. Investigation proceeds on the basis of information as well as evidence. Courts are used to dealing with evidence but not information.

Assessment of information and it's follow-up is a matter for intimate executive supervision. It does not seem appropriate for regular courts to trial and appeal to get involved in this field work. We have to look for some other arrangement for ensuring cleanliness of investigation in the midst of polluting politics.

C.B.I. Cases Monitored by C.V.C.

In the existing scheme of things, there is ample scope for politically motivated interference from the Government side at the stage of investigation, because the CBI is part and parcel of the Government establishment. The very appointment of the Director of CBI and all other personnel down the line, their career perspectives and several other service benefits are all within the domain of the Government only.

It is this circumstance that operates against the professional independence of the CBI. This handicap has to be remedied. However, we cannot possibly conceive of the entire CBI organisation functioning autonomously outside the Government and being answerable only to courts, because such an arrangement might encourage excesses by the CBI field staff down the line.

Further, the Government has its own primary responsibility to ensure honesty and integrity of it's personnel, and it requires an organisation like the CBI under it's own control and direction to handle the normal anti-corruption work for which the Government is responsible.

The intervention of an outside institution like the *Lok Pal* or CVC is called for only in regard to high-level corruption or other sensitive cases which are prone to draw political interference.

For normal anti-corruption work, we must have the existing CBI set-up continue under the Government's administrative control, at the same time eliminating the scope for Government interference with the professional independence of the CBI to conduct it's investigations.

One possible arrangement for this purpose could be to empower the proposed judicially-oriented CVC to monitor the progress of the CBI investigations on such selective basis as it may decide, to ensure thoroughness and correctness of the investigations. The CVC may prescribe it's own norms for identifying the types of cases which require such monitoring.

The law relating to the *Lok Pal* or CVC set-up may also provide for any person to make an application to the CVC for including any particular case in the monitoring list, even though it may not fall within the norms laid down by the CVC.

The point is whether such a case should be decided by the public interest involved and the scope for extraneous interference with the course of investigation.

Since the proposed CVC will be made-up of persons who are either sitting or retired or qualified to be judges of the Supreme Court, this arrangement would obviate the need for the Supreme Court's interference in such cases in future.

Prosecution Needs Sanction

There are provisions in some laws which stipulate that the prosecution of a public servant in a court for an alleged offence committed by him, while acting or purporting to act in the discharge of his official duty, requires prior sanction from certain specified authorities.

Under Section 197 Cr. P.C., a public servant, not removable from office except with the sanction of the Central or State Government, cannot be prosecuted for such an offence without prior sanction from the Central Government or the State Government concerned.

Under Section 137 of the Customs Act, prior sanction from the Central Government will be required for the prosecution of any customs officer of and above the rank of Assistant Collector of Customs for any alleged offence committed by the officer under the Act. In the case of officers below the rank of Assistant Collector of Customs, prior sanction for prosecution has to be sought from the Collector of Customs.

Under Section 19 of the Prevention of Corruption Act, prosecution of a public servant for an alleged offence under the Act requires previous sanction from the authority competent to remove him from office. If this requires the sanction of the Central or State Government, it has to be accorded under Section 19 by the concerned Government.

In the present scheme of things, if the CBI seeks sanction from the Central Government for prosecution under the Prevention of Corruption Act, the CBI report is routed through the Central Vigilance Commission (CVC) which advises whether it may be accorded or not. In most cases, the CVC's advice is accepted, but there have been instances where the Government had declined to accord sanction. Such decisions of the Government are based on their perception and appreciation of the evidence brought up by the CBI.

In very sensitive cases of high-level corruption involving political VIPs, the issue of sanction for prosecution assumes political overtones. The existing scheme of things gives scope for *mala fide* exercise of discretion and judgement in either sanctioning or not sanctioning prosecution.

The rationale behind such provisions in law which stipulate previous sanction for prosecution is that the officials in enforcement agencies require to be protected against malicious or vexatious prosecution in court which may be deliberately launched by professional criminals to wreak vengeance against them. Honest and upright officials have to be effectively protected against such malicious prosecutions under the Prevention of Corruption Act also, because it is not uncommon that false allegations are made and evidence is cooked up by dishonest and unscrupulous elements in the society whose activities are severely curtailed by such officers.

While appreciating the need for such a protective clause in the Prevention of Corruption Act, we should also guard against the same clause being availed of by a corrupt executive in the Government to thwart the prosecution of a corrupt and favourite subordinate official. It is, therefore, necessary to have a statutory arrangement spelt out in the Prevention of Corruption Act itself to ensure that:

(i) the competent authority makes the order sanctioning or refusing to sanction prosecution, within a specified time limit, say one month, and

(ii) if the competent authority refuses to sanction prosecution, it shall state the reasons for refusal which shall be embodied in the order of refusal and it shall be open to the investigating agency to appeal against the order of refusal of the component authority to the *Lok Pal* whose decision thereon shall be final and binding on the Government concerned.

Appropriate amendments to the Prevention of Corruption Act for this purpose have to be drafted along with the proposed legislation for the *Lok Pal* set-up which will include the Central Vigilance Commission.

Property Confiscated

Provisions exist in the Criminal Law Amendment Ordinance of 1944 for attaching the properties acquired by a corrupt public servant when an alleged offence under the Prevention of Corruption Act committed by him is under investigation. This Ordinance continues to be law under Article 372 of the Constitution.

The temporary attachment which can be ordered by the competent court under this Ordinance at the stage of investigation can be followed up by an order of forfeiture of the property to the Government if and when the accused person is convicted of the offence in the court.

Under the existing provisions, this forfeiture is limited to the property procured by the convicted persons by means of the offence for which he stands convicted.

If the prosecution is for the offence of possession of assets which is punishable under Section disproportionate 13(i)(e) of the Prevention of Corruption Act, the final order of forfeiture at the time of conviction can cover all the properties which are included in this disproportionate part of his assets.

It would serve the cause of anti-corruption work better if the law is substantially amplified to cover properties acquired by a corrupt public servant in the names of his family members and relatives also.

It is well-known that habitual corruption at high level results in acquisition of 'benami' (proxy) property by the corrupt person in the names of others under his control.

The Smugglers and Foreign Exchange Manipulators (Forfeiture of Property) Act of 1976 provides for an procedure for the investigation and ultimate confiscation of properties acquired by smugglers and foreign exchange racketeers not only in their own names but also in the names of their relatives as elaborately defined in the Act.

The criminal Law Amendment Ordinance of 1944 may now be replaced by a more comprehensive Act to deal with properties acquired by public servants by corrupt or illegal means not only in their own names but also in the names of their relatives and others under their control. The new law may follow the pattern of the Smugglers and Foreign Exchange Manipulators (Forfeiture of Property) Act, 1976.

Assessing Corruption Intelligence

Effective anti-corruption work requires a good intelligence back-up. It is intelligence that leads to evidence. Quite a lot of intelligence relating to corruption is services becomes available to different enforcement agencies like the Income tax, Customs, Central Excise, Directorate of Enforcement, Intelligence Bureau and State CID. They function under different authorities and pursue their alloted tasks separately.

The corruption aspect of the intelligence with them may get overlooked in this process. For example, the undeclared large assets of a public servant detected in an income tax raid may be pursued by them solely from the revenue angle of tax collection, wherever the corruption angle of possession of disproportionate assets can be and should be pursued by the CBI.

There is no institutional arrangement now for a coordinated assessment of intelligence with different agencies for effectively pursuing the corruption aspect. The *Hawala* Case is a typical example. We now have a Joint Intelligence Committee in the Cabinet Secretariat of the Central Government for a joint assessment of intelligence pertaining to national security.

On similar lines, a small group under the Cabinet Secretary may be authorised to convene periodic meetings with representatives from the other enforcement agencies for pooling all the available intelligence pertaining to corruption. Follow-up action thereon can be taken up by the CBI.

Role for Civil Services

In the early years of Independence, it was a sort of working convention among civil servants that the ministers would decide policy matters while the civil services would deal with executive matters arising from policy implementation. The then political leadership also functioned according to this convention.

In later years the ministers savoured the prestige and power behind executive orders which affect the service personnel in the entire system, and preferred to be (and have remained) the sole decision-makers in all matters, including postings and transfers of the lowest grade government servants. Such overriding powers at the level of political executive have facilitated enormous growth of all-pervasive political corruption, which is now perceived as the fountainhead of all other corruption. We have to seek a way out of this impasse which the civil services have got into.

Article 53 of the Constitution stipulates that the executive power of the Union shall be vested in the President and shall be exercised by him, either directly or through officers subordinate to him, in accordance with the Constitution. There is no reference to 'Minister' in this Article. But Article 77 requires the President to make rules for allocating among ministers the transaction of government business in various departments.

It is from these business rules that ministers derive their statutory power to decide all matters arising in the government. It is this provision which enables a minister officially to overrule the secretary to the government in any matter, however right the secretary may be on record and however unjust and unfair the minister's decision thereon be

The time has now come for amending Article 77 to facilitate allotment of certain aspects of business to the Union Civil Services at the higher levels in the Government Secretariat also. The allotment may be so made as to reflect the working convention mentioned in the above paragraph. Article 166 which deals with the same matter in regard to the States should also be amended likewise. These amendments would go a long way in checking high-level political corruption.

MPs and MLAs Defined as Public Servant in Law

MPs, MLAs and elected representatives in metropolitan councils, municipal corporations, municipalities, *panchayats* and such other statutorily-constituted local bodies should be included in the definition of 'public servant' in the Prevention of Corruption Act by a specific amendment for this purpose.

These public functionaries should be required by law to submit to a prescribed authority, an annual statement of assets held in their names as also in the names of their parents or sons, daughters and other close relatives. These annual statements should be made available by the prescribed authority for scrutiny by any member of the public who makes an application for it.

Code of Conduct for MPs and MLAs

In the present-day realities of public life, the MPs and MLAs and their henchmen play a large role in promoting contacts at high levels. The lifestyles of many among them and their acquisition of large assets, both personal and *benami*, within a short period, do not inspire public confidence about their integrity or propriety of their financial transactions.

It is their conduct that sets the standards for public life in the country. Recognising the need for evolving a Code of Conduct for the legislators to ensure their integrity and commitment to serve public interest, the Central Government started an exercise in 1975 to draft a code in consultation with the State Governments, but this was later given up in the atmosphere of 'Emergency'. It may be revived and a 'Code of Conduct' for MPs and MLAs brought into force without delay. A special committee designated as Ethics Committee may also be constituted in Parliament and each State Assembly to monitor the strict observance of the Code by all members.

Audit of the Accounts of Political Parties

Section 13A of the Income Tax Act which was introduced in 1979 states that all kinds of income of political parties registered with the Election Commission shall be totally exempt from income tax, provided the books of accounts are maintained any duly audited. In practice, all political parties get away with a total absence of accountability of their finance, and none of them is subjected to any assessment by the Income Tax Department.

With their penchant for handling black money, all political parties revel in this 'no accounts and no tax' status and deliberately generate and sustain a permissive atmosphere which breeds corruption all around. In the recent case of 'Political parties election expenses and maintenance of accounts,' the Solicitor General admitted before the Supreme Court the Government's failure to enforce the I.T. Act provision relating to political parties.

The Judgement delivered by the Supreme Court on April 4, 1996 in this case would, hopefully, ensure strict enforcement of the relevant provisions in the Income Tax Act and the Companies Act to make all political parties maintain proper accounts of their income and expenditure from now on. This would go a long way in curbing political corruption.

A special cell should be set up either under the Comptroller and Auditor General or the Election Commission to conduct periodically a regular audit of the accounts kept by all registered political parties. A clearance from this Audit Cell must be made statutorily necessary for a political party to claim exemption for its income under Section 13A of the Income Tax Act.

Comptroller and Auditor General

Audit has an important role in the overall scheme of anti-corruption measures. An effective and Independent audit system deters fraudulent practices in financial dealings in the government and the public sector.

Some important cases successfully investigated by the CBI in the past were based on information exposed in audit reports presented by the Comptroller and Auditor General (CAG).

Effective prevention of corruption requires the CAG to be a person highly reputed for his integrity, professional competence and independence, and free from bias of any kind. The incumbents of this post in the early years of independence were persons of impeccable integrity with a good background of audit work. In later years, senior IAS officers who had functioned as secretaries to the Government have been appointed as CAG on the eve of their retirement from service.

Public confidence in the audit system and it's credibility are badly eroded if an officer who had participated in deciding large-scale contracts for works and supplies on government accounts is later pointed as CAG to preside over the audit of such transactions.

There is an immediate need to lay down formally in law a procedure for the appointment of CAG to ensure that a person with a high reputation for integrity and known for his professional competence and independence, with a good background of audit work alone fills the post.

Police Reform

Effective investigations and prosecutions under the Prevention of Corruption Act cannot be conceived in isolation from the overall scenario of general law enforcement in the country. Police is the primary agency of the State for law enforcement

In the present dispensation, the police system has become increasingly vulnerable to interference by extraneous persons. Police performance is perceived by the common people to be increasingly partisan and politically directed.

This has seriously handicapped impartial, truthful and effective law enforcement. The National Police Commission (NPC), set up by the Central Government in 1977 with wide-ranging terms of reference for a complete overhaul of the police system to meet the aspirations and expectations of people in our democracy, has made several recommendations for police reform to secure an effective, impartial and honest police performance.

A very important recommendation made by the NPC is to free the police from the exclusive control of the Government which always has a distinct political colour and direction at any given time, and put the police under the control of a multi-member State Security Commission which would be a statutory body presided over by the Chief Minister with members including the Leader of the Opposition in the State Assembly, a retired high Court judge and a few other eminent public men including academics of repute.

Several other vital recommendations of the NPC follow from this basic recommendation of a State Security Commission to monitor police performance in the State. Any amount of focusing on radical measures in law and executive action for effective anti-corruption work will not be realistic unless the overall scenario of law enforcement, in general, becomes clear and bright.

Witnesses examined by the CBI and State ACBs in corruption cases are sometimes threatened by muscleman at the command of the corrupt official concerned. The growing nexus between criminals and politicians has further encouraged this trend in recent years.

Highhanded and intimidatory tactics adopted by corrupt persons to suppress the evidence against them can be defeated only if the police is effective in dealing with the aggressive and disorderly elements in the society. This requires a professionally competent police, free from extraneous interference Immediate implementation of the NPC recommendations for police reform should, therefore, be viewed as a 'must' for effective anti-corruption work also.

Proposed Reforms

The reforms and changes suggested above can be brought about only by necessary amendments to the Constitution and the enactment of separate laws for the envisaged purposes. The establishment of *Lok Pals* at the Centre and in the States along with their investigating wings and prosecuting wings and the procedure for the transaction of their business have to be incorporated in a separate law to be passed by Parliament.

The conduct of MPs and MLAs has also to be governed by a separate code drawn up by Parliament and State Assemblies. The appointment of *Lok Pals* at the Centre in the States has to be made by the President himself, in exercise of his discretion and judgement, without having to consult the Council of Ministers. This would require an appropriate amendment to Article 74 of the Constitution.

Drafting Legislation

A small working group under the lead of a retired Supreme Court or High Court judge held in high esteem should be immediately entrusted with the task of drafting a comprehensive Bill for the necessary amendments to the Constitution and the enactment of separate laws for the different purposes mentioned above.

Several ameliorative and welfare measures launched by the Government for the advancement of socially and economically backward classes are rendered ineffective by the creeping corruption in administration. The poor and uninfluential sections of the backward groups find that unless they pay bribes to the operating functionaries in the field, they will not get the full benefit of the welfare measures intended for them. Rural youth suffer most in this situation.

Their economic distress and enforced idleness without adequate job opportunities, drive them to despair and some of them take to violent extremism. This phenomenon further weakens our social structure and tends to destablise our society.

Subjected to the constant play of such divisive and disruptive forces within itself, our society can hardly gather itself to remain as strong unit and march towards economic prosperity.

In such a situation, corruption cannot be viewed as a mere moral issue. It is a vital economic issue which saps the production potential of the nation and induces people to discard the path of hard work and take to shortcuts for achieving short-term individual gain.

This ultimately brings down the quality of output in all fields of production. National economy gets disrupted. By corrupt means, the rich may become richer, but the poor become poorer, and the nation degenerates.

The rising generation should realise that this will be the resulting scenario in the coming years if the canker of corruption is not effectively stopped and cured right now. The seriousness and urgency of the matter have to be understood by the youth of the country.

NOTES & REFERENCES

1. Justice William O. Douglas, *United States vs. Wunderlick*, 342 U.S. 98 (1951).
2. *The Times*, May 27, 1992.
3. R.K. Dhawan, *Public Grievances and the Lok Pal*, Allied, 1981. p. 209.
4. Frank Stacey, *The British Ombudsman*, Oxford, 1971, p. 22.
5. See Frank Stacey, *Ombudsman Compared*, Oxford, 1978 for the studies of the Swedish, Danish, Norwegian, Canadian and the British *ombudsman* and also of the French *mediateur*.
6. Lok Sabha Secretariat, *Lok Pal* , New Delhi pp. 5-6.
7. *The Hindu*, August 4, 1995.
8. *The Hindustan Times*, December 7, 1995.
9. *Indian Express*, December 10, 1995.
10. *The Hindu*, September 30, 1995.
11. *The Hindu*, December 13, 1995.

12. *The Telegraph*, December 19, 1995.

13. Justice T.S. Mishra, *Lok Ayukt* and *Public Interest*, a Paper read at a Workshop at Patna on October 5, 1986.

14. *Everyman's*, September 1, 1973.

15. A.R. Antulay vs Ramdas Nayak & Anr. (1984) 2 SCC 500. See also *ibid.* p. 184 on the ruling that a legislator is not a "public servant" as defined in Section 21 of the penal code. Earlier in the same case (1982) 2 SCC 463 the court had ruled that in deciding whether or not to accord sanction for prosecution of a chief minister, the governor to accord sanction for prosecution of a chief minister, the governor must use his individual judgement.

16. The text was published in *Indian Express*, December 20, 1988.

17. See A.G. Noorani, *Minister's Misconduct* (Chapter 7) on Azhimathi in Kerala, Vickers 1973.

18. See K.P. Nair's article in *The Hindu* of December 9, 1987 for an able comparison of the 1987 Bill with the Act of 1985.

19. *The Hindu*, April 16, 1990. See also K.P. Nair's article in *The Hindu*, March 18, 1990.

20. *The Statesman*, January 7 and 8, 1996.

THE FUTURE

34

PREVENTING CORRUPTION

Starting from the political boss to the lowest, level of bureaucratic functionary, none seems to the either an exception or immune from the evil effects of corruption.

Corruption in public life and services has grown to alarming operations in recent years. It marks the performing style of all politicians in power, actively abetted by unscrupulous businessmen and aided by acquiescent bureaucrats. It is presently experienced by all sections of the people.

Mamool payments are extorted by most of the Government functionaries in the field even for discharging their normal duties and providing services to which the public are legitimately entitled. In public perception, every government department now seems to function as a conduit for the regular upward flow of bribe money to the top political levels.

At the time of Independence in 1947, the country inherited a power-oriented administrative system left by the British Raj. The people, at - large were used to a *maa-baap* government on whose benevolence they depended for their existence and progress in any sphere of activity. That the government in present times is actually an instrument of their own creation through the Constitution is not conceptually perceived by the people.

Since their overall attitude to the government has remained the same as it was during the British Raj, it has become natural and easy for the elected representatives after Independence to play a similar role as the British administrators did not make capital out of the system.

Anti-Corruption Measures

Measures for tackling the problem of corruption may be broadly classified under three heads:

(i) preventive,

(ii) punitive and

(iii) promotional.

Preventive measures will include electoral reforms and administrative reforms which would render the transaction of all government business more transparent and accountable to the people.

Punitive measures will relate to laws, rules and the mechanism for effective investigation, court trial, departmental disciplinary action and other means to deter the corrupt functionaries.

Promotional measures will cover encouragement of value-based politics, inculcation of moral and ethical principles among the younger generation in schools and colleges and the build-up of a kind of social ostracisation of corrupt people by the society.

Prevention of Corruption Act

A special law to deal with corruption was first enacted in 1947 in the form of Prevention of Corruption Act. It defined certain categories of public functionaries as 'Public Servants" under the Act, and spelt out the punishment for different acts of bribery and corruption by such public servants.

All personnel in service under the Central Government and the State Governments all employees of public sector undertakings under these Governments all ministers in the Government at the Centre and in the States, all judges and magistrates and other judicial officers and all employees of municipalities and corporations and other statutory civic bodies came under the definition of 'public servant' under this Act.

It was comprehensively amended in 1988 to include some

more public functionaries under the definition of 'public servant' for the purpose of the Act. For example, all employees of universities were brought under the purview of this Act in 1-88.

However, a matter of great significance is that while ministers fall under the definition of public servant as per the Act, MPs and MLAs do not, unless they happen to hold an office or occupy a position in government and get remunerated for it.

In other words, the people's representatives, viz. MPs and MLAs as such do not come under the purview of the Prevention of Corruption Act, even in it's amended form in 1988.

This is a very significant omission. An attempt had been made earlier in 1972 to include MPs and MLAs in the definition of 'public servant' in the Indian Penal Code Amendment Bill 1972, but a Joint Committee of Parliament rejected the proposal.

Santhanam Committee

In the early years after Independence, the Government's keenness to root out corruption was reflected in several administrative measures that were taken to discipline the conduct of public servants and effectively monitor their performance by the hierarchical command structure in each department.

The Santhanam Committee set up by Parliament in 1962 examined this matter and made a number of recommendations for strengthening the vigilance and anti-corruption machinery in the Government.

In the late '50s and early '60s, the Delhi Special Police Establishment had successfully investigated some cases involving high functionaries. The Government dealt with the reports of these investigations promptly and effectively, and a climate was brought about which was conducive to the containment of corruption in all public services; but this did not last long.

Political Corruption

The late '60s and early '70s witnessed a qualitative change in the political life in the country. Politics emerged as an alluring avenue leading to positions of enormous power and patronage.

Enforcement of regulatory measures in commerce and industry by the issue of a variety of permits, licences, certificates and so on at various stages and levels led to increased corruption all around, particularly at the political level where ministers could and did take decisions deliberately favouring or disfavouring parties for a consideration.

The phenomenon of political corruption, thus, came into being. The electoral process also lent itself to manipulations by muscle power and money power and, thereby, enlarged the volume of political corruption.

The existing scheme of anti-corruption work is based on three assumptions:

(i) Functionaries at the top-most level in the Government are sincere and keen on putting down corruption.

(ii) Supervisory officials in the administrative system at the middle and top levels will themselves be motivated by the status of their office to check corruption at the lower levels and at the cutting edge of the administration.

(iii) Special measures devised for the expeditious conduct of court trials and departmental proceedings against corrupt officials will ensure quick and severe punishment which would deter corruption.

The above assumption were valid in the early years after Independence. The Santhanam Committee's Report further enlarged and strengthened the anti - corruption measures based only on these assumptions. Unfortunately, the recent decades have witnessed the collapse of all the three assumptions.

Firstly, political corruption at the level of ministers has grown to monstrous proportions. No one believes that the leaders of any political party are sincere and keen in rooting out corruption.

Secondly, when ministers themselves become corrupt, the senior officers in their departments are rendered weak and ineffective to check and put down corruption among the subordinate officers who have political linkage.

A few officers of high integrity and strong commitment to the national good try to remain aloof from this quagmire of corruption and restrict and content themselves by merely being correct in what they personally do, record and advise in the files.

They have no power to over-ride or annual *mala fida* decisions taken at the minister's level despite the factually correct and administratively fair and just nothings and advice recorded in the files.

The prolonged continuance of such a state of affairs in the Government has resulted in a number of officers, even at senior levels, succumbing to the situation and joining the political game of money-making and sharing the spoils.

Thus, the entire administrative structure in the country has been considerably weakened, and is unable to render efficient public service as far as the common people are concerned.

Lastly, court convictions and punishments in departmental disciplinary proceedings in respect of corrupt officials have been relatively few, considering the wide spread of corruption as preceived by the people. Even these few convictions and punishments are badly delayed owing to procedural blocks and legal wrangles.

The slow on the potential bribe-takers. In this way, all the three earlier assumptions are no longer valid. Any effective mechanism for anti-corruption work in present times will, therefore, have to include new institutional measures which will draw their strength and support from the Constitution itself, either directly or indirectly.

Genesis of CBI

During the years of the Second World War (1939-45), the scope for corruption in the Central Government increased enormously with the landling of large contracts for construction works and supplies connected with defence.

It was, then, that the Government of India set-up, for the first time, a special investigating unit in the War Department to handle all inquiries relating to corruption.

This unit expanded later as the Delhi Special Police Establishment (DSPE), and was given a statutory basis by the enactment of the Delhi Special Police Establishment Act of 1946.

After Independence, it developed as a specialised investigating agency under the Central Government primarily to deal with allegations of corruption pertaining to Central Government employees and also be available for assisting the State Governments into the investigation of specific crimes which may have inter-state ramifications or some other special features which make it desirable that the investigations be done by a Central agency rather than the State Police.

In its expanded from the Delhi Special Police Establishment, was named the Central Bureau of Investigation (CBI), and has been functioning as such from 1963 under the control of the Central Government.

Powers of CBI

CBI derives it's investigating powers form the DSPE ACT, and can exercise them on it's own authority within the limits of Union Territories and Centrally- administered areas only. Even here, investigating powers are limited to the specific offences that are notified by the Central Government under Section 3 of the Act offences relating to bribery and corruption have been notified by the Central Government in this context.

As and when the CBI is required to investigate a case of murder, decoity, kidnapping, abduction or such other offences unconnected with bribery and corruption, a special notification is issued to enable the CBI do such investigations.

Such Section 5 of the DSPE Act, the Central Government may empower the CBI to investigate the notified offences even in the limits of any State, but such empowerment can be ordered only with the consent of the Government of that State.

Thus, legal stipulation arises form the fact that the DSPE Act creates a police agency, and 'police' is in the Union List, which permits the extension of the powers of the police in one State to another State, also prohibits such extension without the consent of the second State.

In the first few years after independence, there was no

practical difficulty in the functioning of the CBI within the limits of the States also, because the same political party was in power in the States as well as at the Centre.

The situation changed when different political parties got into powers in the States. Some of them started withdrawing the consent given by the earlier State Governments whenever they felt that an investigation taken up by the CBI was politically embarrassing or uncomfortable for them.

Such situations have so far been defused by mutual understanding. But the CBI's status as an investigating agency within a State continues to be unstable and dependent on the State Governments mercy. This is a serious handicap in planning any nation-wide network of investigating units for anti-corruption inquiries.

Nation-Wide Jurisdiction to CBI

The above difficulty can be overcome if the Central Government legislates a separate law to put the CBI on a statutory basis. In fact, the name 'Central Bureau of Investigation' figures in Item 8 of the Union List in the Seventh Schedule and, therefore, Parliament can enact a law separately for the CBI. The new law has to project the CBI as an investigating agency only and not a police agency as otherwise it will be hit by them 2 of the State List, which refers to 'police'.

In fact, there is no need to project the CBI as a 'police unit'. It has no role or responsibility regarding maintenance of public order or peace, regulation of traffic or a host of such 'law and order' duties of the regular police. The CBI is solely concerned with investigations of specific cases assigned to it under law.

Therefore, it would be sufficient if the new law spells out specifically the powers of arrest, search, seizure, summoning and examining witnessess which are presently available to the police whn they invtigate a cognizable case and centers these powers on the CBI to facilitate thier investigations.

We have an example in the Customs Act which confers on customs officers the power to arrest, search and seize in certain circumstances related to smuggling. Likewise, a comprehensive CBI Act can take care of all the requirements of investigation work of the CBI.

The subject of 'promotion and maintenance of integrity and efficiency in public service does not figure as a specific item in any of the Lists in the Seventh Schedule.

Parliament can, therefore, legislate the new CBI Act in exercise of its residuary powers under Article 248. An independent statutory basis for the CBI is very necessary for any effective anti-corruption scheme to cover the nation as a whole.

The Estimates Committee of the Fourth Lok Sabha in it's 78th Report had observed that' it is necessary to give a statutory basis to the CBI in order to place it on a sounder footing.' In the follow-up action, a draft CBI Bill was prepared in 1990 but no progress could be made because it impinged on Centre-State relations.

The Estimates Committee of the *Tenth Lok Sabha* noticed this impasse and recommended strongly in it's 13th Report (1991-92) that this legislation should be taken up without further delay.

The deadlock on the Centre-State aspect of the matter can be resolved if , as recommend earlier in this paragraph, the CBI is projected as an investigating agency and not a police agency. This matter has to be pursued urgently in the interest of effective anti-corruption work.

Bureaux in States

While the CBI functions as the investigation agency for anti-corruption work in respect of matters to which the executive power of the Union extends, the States have their separate anti-corruption bureaux (ACB) for handling vigilance and anti-corruption work with regard to state matters. The CBI functions within the framework of the WSPE Act, but the State ACBs are regular police units and derive their powers of investigation from the Police Act only.

However, in both cases, the investigating agency functions, under superentendence of the Central Government or the State Government concerned.While Section 2 of the DSPE Act enables the CBI to exercise the powers available to regular police officers while investigating any specific case, it also lays down that the exercise of such powers will be subject to any order which the Central Government may make in this matter.

Whenever there is public pressure for an enquiry into the misconduct of a minister, the Central or the State Government usually resorts to the Commission of Inquiry Act to set-up a Commission to inquire into specific allegations made against the minister. A Commission of Inquiry is normally headed by a Supreme Court or High Court judge either serving or retired.

Though it's proceedings are conducted more or less in the manner of a court it is only a fact-finding body and not a court of trial and, therefore, it does not have power to award any punishment to a person against whom an allegation may get *prima facie* established during the inquiry.

It merely presents a report about the facts ascertained during the inquiry and it is for the government concerned to decide the further course of action. If a person is to be prosecuted on the basis of facts brought out by the Commission, the matter is referred to the CBI or the State ACB for a regular investigation.

Once again, the process of examining all the witnesses in detail is gone through by the investigating agency and, then, the matter is put before a regular criminal court for trial.

At the trial stage, witnesses are examined for the third time and only then is the state reached for the awarding of specific punishment to the accused if found guilty. All this takes a very long time diluting the thrust of the entire exercise. The effect of quickly awarding a severe punishment to the guilty person is not achieved.

Since the same set of witnesses are subjected to examination by different bodies at different stages separated by long intervals of time, the accused persons invariably tend to exert their influence and power to pressurise the witnesses in a variety of ways and make them prevaricate while giving evidence into the final stage in the court. Thus, the course of law and justice is thwarted and ultimately nothing worthwhile is achieved.

Not a single CBI case involving ministers has ended in firm conviction in the court during the last 40 years. There are instances where cases against ministers have been withdrawn by the Government even at the stage of court trial, solely on the basis of fresh exculpatory statements obtained from important prosecution witnesses by the accused ministers themselves and presented before the Government, pleading for the withdrawal of the case on the ground that the prosecution was false and politically motivated.

The Commissions of Inquiry Act does not envisage a permanent Commission of Inquiry in office. It merely enables the Central and state Governments to appoint such a Commission, as and when required. The Act itself does not provide for a permanent body to function as the investigating arm of the Commission.

Under Section 5A of the Act, the Commission usually secures the services of investigating officers from the CBI or the State Police for a short term of deputation to assist the Commission in indentifying the relevant witnesses and getting their preliminary statements recorded before the Commission itself starts formally examining them in open judicial proceedings.

These investigating officers have ultimately to get back to their parent agencies under the Central or State Government after the Commission's work is completed. This circumstance makes it difficult for them to function with complete independence and objectivity while making inquiries under the Commission.

They are naturally inhibited by the prospect of victimisation on their return to the government fold, if their inquiries result in the exposure of misdeeds of a powerful person in the political establishment. This is an important factor which detracts from the ultimate quality of a Commission's inquiry when the accused happens to be a political VIP.

Interference with Investigations

In the present scheme of things, the CBI or the State investigating agency functions under the total control of the Central or State government concerned. Therefore, in all cases investigated by the CBI or the State investigating agency, the Government concerned has full scope even at the stage of investigation to acquaint itself with the details of evidence as and when discovered by the investigating agency.

This circumstances affords ample scope for the Government, which in reality means the ruling party, to interfere at the stage of investigation itself and thwart the course of truth and justice to the detriment of public interest. Cases against VIPs are specially prone to such interference. The Bofors case is a typical example.

Working procedures within the CBI provide for a considerable amount of preliminary scrutiny and assessment of any information or complaint received by the CBI before a case is registered for regular investigation.

The level at which this decision is taken within the CBI is determined by the rank of the official against whom the information or complaint is received.

For example, cases against gazetted officers will require scrutiny at the level of DIG. Cases against heads of departments will be decided at the level of the Joint Director or Director. By and large, in the 1950s and 1960s, the CBI enjoyed full powers for taking such decisions within the CBI itself.

As a matter of convention, the Director of CBI used to keep the Prime Minister/Home Minister informed after the registration of the case, if it involved a very high - ranking officer in the Government or a political VIP.

In later years, some restrictive procedures have been formally laid down by the Government in regard to registration of cases by the CBI. Presently, these restrictions require prior clearance from the Government before the CBI can take up any case for investigation against an officer of the rank of Joint Secretary to Government and above. All such restrictions seem to be based on the powers given to the Government under section 2 of the DSPE Act.

The State ACBs are also bound by similar restrictive provisions which are more or less of the same pattern in all the States. In Tamil Nadu, the State Directorate of Vigilance and Anti-Corruption cannot take up any inquiry against an All-India Services officer without prior permission from the Government.

Further, the Directorate does not have authority to scrutinise any file in the Government Secretariat except through the Secretary to the Government who may call for scrutinise the file himself in the first instance and, then, decide whether the Directorate may be permitted to see it.

There restrictive procedures at the Centre and in the States in regard to anti-corruption work are detrimental to prompt and proper verification of vigilance information against top-ranking functionaries in the Government.

This is a big drawback in the existing system, and has to be set right. In it's 13th Report (1991-92), the Estimates Committee of the Tenth Lok Sabha had strongly urged the Government to do away with these restrictive procedures in regard to anti-corruption inquiries.

Effectiveness of CBI Investigations

A critical analysis of the annual reports of the CBI from 1972 to 1992 reveals the actual volume, nature and ultimate effect of CBI investigations. Some significant features are noted below:

Collection of Information

The number of CBI cases started on regular complaints received by the CBI are relatively small, as may be seen from the following figures:

Item	*1972*	*1992*
(i) No. of complaints examined during the year	6,650	6,520
(ii) No. in item (i) which led to CBI cases of regular investigation	477	229

About 70% of the cases registered by the CBI are based on information collected by the CBI's own staff. Viewed against the growing power of corrupt elements in administration and their potential to cause serious harm to anyone who may attempt to expose their misdeeds, the reluctance of the victims of corruption to come up with formal complaints to the CBI is understandable.

The responsibility, therefore, lies on the CBI to take the initiative of activating it's own intelligence units and collecting information pertaining to corruption. The same observations apply to the state ACBs.

Action Recommended

The volume of new cases taken up by the CBI year after year has more or less remained at the same level. In fact, the figures for 1992 show a slight decrease compared to 1972. But the volume of cases whose investigation was completed during the years has gone down.

A majority of cases investigated by the CBI result in departmental disciplinary proceedings only. Relatively lesser number of cases are chargesheeted in the court. The figures are as follows:

Item	*1972*	*1992*
(i) No. of new cases registered during the year	1349	1231
(ii) No. of cases investigated and finalised during the year (including old cases)	1790	1412
(iii) No. of cases in item (ii) prosecuted in court	384	505
(iv) No. of cases in item (ii) referred for departmental action	887	652

Court Trials Results

Disposal of CBI cases in the court has also shown a decline. The percentage of convictions has come down to 69% in 1992 compared to 85% in 1972. At the end of 1992, there were 4,148 cases pending trial compared to 1,362 at the end of 1972. Among the 4,148 pending cases, as many as 3,000 have been pending for over four years and some for over 15 to 20 years.

The relevant figures are furnished below:

Item	*1972*	*1992*
(i) No. of cases disposed of in court during the year	352	237
(ii) No. in item (i) which ended in conviction	300	164
(iii) No. in items (i) which ended in discharge/acquittal	52	73
(iv) Percentage of conviction in court	85.2	69.1
(v) No. of cases pending in court at the end of year	1,362	4,148

Departmental Actions

The number of supervisory officers at the middle and senior levels, i.e., gazetted officers who have been either convicted in the court or punished in departmental disciplinary action as a result of CBI cases, is very small, taking the country-wide spread of government personnel and the perceived extent of corruption among them.

Even among the gazetted officers who have been punished in the departmental action, the number among them, who have been given severe punishment like dismissal/removal/retirement from service is very small. Out of 547 gazetted officers who were departmentally punished in 1992, there were only 62 dismissals. The relevant figures are furnished below:

Item	*1972*	*1992*
(i) No. of public servants convicted in court	194	85
(ii) No. in item (i) who were of gazetted rank	15	44
(iii) No. of public servants punished in departmental action	806	798
(iv) No. of item (iii) who were of gazetted rank	150	547
(v) No. in item (iv) who were dismissed/ removed/retired from services.	8	62

Assets of Public Servants

The common man's perception of a corrupt official is based on the visible assets acquired by the corrupt official disproportionate to his known source of income. While it is usually difficult to get evidence from the victims of corruption about the specific instances in which they had been forced to give bribe, it is relatively easier to secure evidence from third parties about the assets acquired by corrupt officials over a long period.

Under Section 13 (1)(e) of the Prevention of Corruption Act, the very possession of unaccountable assets by a public servant is a substant offence by itself, irrespective of the other specific offences of bribery which may or may not be proved against him.

A case of disproportionate assets, if properly investigated and established, is a strong weapon to deal with corrupt officials. The record of the CBI in handling cases of this kind is not very encouraging. The number of such cases taken up by the CBI is very small, and most of the cases finalised by it have resulted only in the departmental disciplinary proceedings.

Convictions in court have been very few, and even among those convicted, gazetted officers are much less. Even among those convicted, gazetted officers are much less. Even in departmental proceedings the ultimate result is not encouraging.

Out of the 27 gazetted officers punished in 1992, there were only two dismissals. The rest got away with minor punishments. The relevant figures are furnished below Cases of Assets

Item	*1972*	*1992*
(i) No. of new cases registered during the year	89	57
(ii) No. of gazetted officers involved in the item (i)	44	34
(iii) No. of items investigated and finalised during the year (including old cases)	94	77
(iv) No. in item (iii) which were prosecuted in court	11	24
(v) No. in item (iii) which were referred for departmental action	58	42
(vi) No. of cases disposed of in court	6	5
(vii) No. in item (vi) which ended in conviction	5	2
(viii) No. of gazetted officers involved in item (vii)	2	—
(ix) No. of cases decided in departmental actions	40	44
(x) No. in item (ix) which resulted in punishment	28	24
(xi) No. of gazetted officers involved in item (x)	9	27
(xii) No. in item (xi) who were dismissed/removed/retired from service.	1	2

Vigilance Officers' Set-up

A fundamental principle projected by the Santhanam Committee is that the primary responsibility for maintaining integrity and rectitude besides efficiency of a department of the government rests squarely on the head of the department. Any outside organisation like the CBI can function only as a supporting agency by conducting investigations in specific cases.

The preventive aspects of anti-corruption work has to be borne, in a large measure, by the head of the department and his staff down the line. In fact, vigilance work should be viewed as an integral part of the responsibility of every supervisory officer at every level.

In 1955, the Central Government introduced a scheme of having a Chief Vigilance Officer (CVO) at the top level in each department assisted by vigilance officers (VOs) down the line at middle level to assist the head of the department in providing guidance and maintaining a constant drive for the effective handling of all corruption complaints and disciplinary proceedings arising from such complaints.

They are also required to monitor the actual functioning of the department, particularly at it's cutting edge, constantly review the working procedures and streamline them from time to time to eliminate the scope for practice of corruption and the consequent harassment of people who come to transact work with the department.

Central Vigilance Commission

On the Santhanam Committee's recommendation, a Central Vigilance Commission headed by the Central Vigilance Commissioner (CVC) was set up by the Central Government by an executive decision embodied in a Resolution in the Ministry of Home Affairs dated 11 February, 1964. The powers and functions of the CVC, as detailed in the Resolution include the following:-

(i) To undertake an inquiry into any transaction in which a public servant is alleged to have acted for an improper purpose, or

(ii) To cause an inquiry to be made into:

(a) any complaint that a public servant had exercised his powers for improper or corrupt purposes.

(b) any complaint of corruption, misconduct, lack of integrity or other kinds of mal-practices on the part of a public servant including members of the All India services even if such members are, for the time being, serving in connection with the affairs of a state government.

(iii) To call for reports, returns and statements from all ministries, departments, or corporate Central undertakings so as to enable it to exercise general checks and supervision over the vigilance and anti-corruption work in the ministries, departments, undertakings.

(iv) To take over under its direct control, such complaints, information or cases as it may consider necessary for further action which may be either:

(a) to ask the CBI to register a regular case and investigate it, or

(b) to entrust the complaint, information or case for inquiry

(1) to the CBI, or

(2) to the ministry, department, or undertakings concerned.

Central Vigilance Commissioner

The Resolution Further provides that :

"1. The C.V.C.

(a) will be appointed by the President by warrant under his hand and seal;

(b) will not be removed or suspended from office except in the manner provided for the removal or suspension of the Chairman or a Member of the Union Public Service Commission;

(c) will hold office for a term of six years or till he attains the age of 65 whichever is earlier; and

(d) on ceasing to hold the office of the CVC, shall not accept any further employment under the Union or State Government or accept any political public office.

"2. The CVC will be attached to the Ministry of Home Affairs, but in the exercise of its powers and functions, it will not be subordinate to any ministry or department and will have the same measure of independence and autonomy as the Union Public Service Commission.

"3. The CVO in ministries and departments will be appointed in consultation with the CVC, and no person whose appointment as CVO is objected to by the CVC will be so appointed.

"4 The CVC will have the power to assess the work of the CVOs and VOs and the assessment will be recorded in the character rolls of the officers."

C.V.C.'s Role

The first CVC was former Chief Justice of a High Court and, therefore, it's work started with the required judicial independence and objectivity. Subsequent appointees have been drawn from the IAS with the appointments being made just when the officer was about to superannuate at the top-level in administration.

In actual practice, the CVC's role is now confined to tendering advice to departments on the action to be taken on CBI reports in regard to gazetted officers.

The CVC also adivses on the reports drawn up by the inquiry officers on the conclusion of departmental disciplinary proceedings arising from corruption cases against gazetted officers.

The CVC makes an overall review of the preventive work turned out by the CVOs, VOs in different departments and gives them necessary directions. Very rarely has the CVC given directions to the CBI for regular investigation of any sensational case which might have been slurred over otherwise.

C.V.C. Reports

The Resolution also provides for submission of an annual report by the CVC to the Ministry of Home Affairs about its activity drawing particular attention to any recommendation made by it which had not been accepted or acted upon.

A copy of this report, together with a memorandum explaining the reasons for non-acceptance of any recommendation of the Commission, has to be laid by the Ministry of Home Affairs before each House of Parliament.

In the actual working of the CVC, this provision could not gain any significant interest or attention from the Members of Parliament.

New Law for the C.V.C.

A qualitative change in the impact of the CVC and the entire set-up of CVOs can be brought about only when the CVC is set up statutorily with adequate provisions to ensure it's functional independence and judicial orientation.

The procedure for the appointment of the CVC may involve the Leader of the Opposition also on similar lines as adopted for the appointment of the Chairman and Members of the National Human Rights Commission. A person who is qualified for appointment as a Supreme Court judge alone shall be appointed CVC.

The new Act for the CVC should also provide for an investigating wing under the CVC's control, more or less on the lines provided for the National Human Rights Commission.

The powers exercisable by the members of the investigating wing for making effective enquiries which will include searches, seizures and arrests should also be spelt out in detail separately in the same Act.

State Vigilance Commission

CVC should also be involved in the process of selection and appointment of the Director, CBI. Similar arrangements may be brought into being in the States also. Just as the Protection of Human Rights Act has provisions which enable the states to constitute State-level Human Rights Commission with duties and responsibilities within the state. The new Central Vigilance Commission with a corresponding role for directing and supervising vigilance and anti-corruption work with the Shape. This will include monitoring the work of the State ACBs also on the same times as proposed for the CVC in regard to the CBI.

35

THE FUTURE OF THE BRIBERY AND CORRUPTION

Since the time of Roman Republic "to Corrupt" has meant both to seduce a woman and to pay off an office-holder. One betrayes a lover or an office. One is faithless to a spouse or a public trust

Moral concepts are ideas bearing on the pursuit of the Good, that which satisfies basic human needs. As these needs are both personal and social, earthly and transcending earth, so moral concepts have personal and social dimensions, worldy and transcendental aspects. What constitutes basic human needs and what contributes to their fulfilment have been matters of discovery, debate and development.

Moral concepts found enshrined in traditions do not stay the same. They undergo transformation. They are subject to investigation and criticism. They expand, shrink, or disappear. They depend on what reason can determine and what is perceived as the demand and example of the God. The bribe has had the life of a moral concept.

The ideas preceded the world. It was discovered in the Ancient Near East and entered into the commandments of Israel. It was developed in Greece and Rome and became a shibboleth of orator-politicians. It entered the religious and political life of the Roman Empire. It was imparted to bribes and peoples unused to the restrictions it generated. It was put on the banner of religious reform in the eleventh century and stayed there for over 500 years.

It found full articulation in the poetry of Dante, in the plays of Shakespeare, and in the invention of a vocabulary tailored to the thought. It became part of the common law of England. It expanded its sway from judges to high administrators to legislators. It entered the American Constitution and became the stuff of American political conflict.

It was adapted to social and familiar and psychological contexts. It began to be a serious element in the criminal law as actually enforced. It formed a standard known to every country in the world and was honoured by hyprocrisy where unobserved in conduct.

Is bribery more like slavery or more like usury? Or is bribery likely to shrink, to be applied only in cases of spectacular official greed as usury is invoked where rates of interest become bloated? The future of the bribe depends on whether bribery remains a matter of moral focus and judgement.

The Non-moral Nature of Exchanges with Office Holders.

By bribery is meant improper reciprocation with an office-holder for an act intended by society to be gratutious. Seven arguments exist why such exchanges should not now be subject to predominantly moral judgements.

1. Everybody does it. Wherever one looks, whatever time or place or country. Exchanges with office holders are found. From the mayors of Nippur and Nuzi in 1500 B.C. to the mayor of Lansing, Illinois in 1976, payoffs have been made. From the Roman Curia under Innocent III to the Supreme Court of the United States under Earl Warren such exchanges have been arranged.

   In religious representations as ancient as The Book of the Dead and in secular reporting as recent as the Wall Street Journal such exchanges are commemorated. No religion has banned exchanges with the divine office-holder. No government has ever ruled without exchanges by and with the rulers.

   "All sects, all ages smack of this vice". This observation, made apropos fornication in Measure for Measure, is equally apt here. Women, it is true, appear to amack of its less than men, for in the case of bribery special opportunities must be conjoined to appetite.

Only office-holders can be the objects of bribes, and women have been office-holders less frequently than men. The sex differential apart, there is no common denominator isolating those who do participate in bribery and those who do not.

Roman and Visigoths, Englishmen and Africans, Catholics and Jews, Pagans and Protestants, Capitalists and Communists, Imperialists and Patriots have engaged in these exchanges. It was done by office-holders in the England of Edward I and in the England of James I and in the England of George III. It was done in America of Abraham Lincoln and the America of Teddy Roosevelt. It has been a way of life in Iran and Indonesia. Italy, India and Japan, our state houses and our national capital.

What has been done everywhere at every time cannot be contrary to human nature or destructive of the human pursuit of the Good. Universal, vast, ineradicable, bribery is a practice that accompanies the human condition.

2. It is necessary to do it. Such a practice cannot be counter to basic human needs; rather, it must itself meet human needs. The second argument builds on the observation underlying the first argument. What is commonly done must be done if one is to live and act in the world.

3. Reciprocities are formally indistinguishable. The usury prohibition known to medieval Europe broke down because it became impossible in practice to distinguish unlawful usury ("profit on a loan") from lawful interest, lawful profit on foreign exchange, and lawful partnership income. A similar phenomenon can be observed here and is indeed implicit in the two preceding arguments that reciprocity with an office-holder is normal and necessary.

A multitude of reciprocal exchanges are generally accepted as legitimate. No satisfactory criteria exist by which these exchanges can be distinguished from what bribery prohibitions classify as bribes.

The difficulty to distinguishing bribes from gifts was signalled in antiquity by the language. *Shohadh, doron, munus*—are they to be translated gift or bribe? Wise ambiguity. We hesitate because the Hebrews, Greeks, and Romans hesitated. Who could be certain that the gift was a corrupt gift? The Greeks had a word for it, runs the proverb. The Greeks did not have a word for bribes because all gifts are bribes. All gifts are given by way of reciprocation for favours past or to come.

The difference between a bribe and a gift lies, for some, in the non-specific and tacit character of the request for reciprocity that accompanies a gift.

"Access payments, campaign contributions, tips, gifts—the ways in which exchanges with an office-holder may be made are so many that no exhaustive list can be made. Need one catalogue, the forbearances, the appointments, the promotions, the kindnesses to siblings and in-laws, the sexual favours paid for or voluntarily given or the business opportunities afforded, which constitute the common coin of reciprocity as must as cash.

And which, escaping legal condemnation, are morally indistinguishable as returns to office-holders? The perfect impossibility of making any but arbitrary definitions of what is morally acceptable and what is "bribery" is evident.

4. It is immorally enforced. A moral idea that lives by immoralities is a contradiction in terms. Such is the notion of the bribe. When certain exchanges are categorized as bribes, enforcement of their condemnation is inconsistent; intemperate; hypocritical; an expression of envy. The idea is made effective by technicalities, lies, and bribes.

When the anti-bribery ideal is invoked it is inconsistently applied. At the level of law, the great unevenness has been demonstrated. The crime of bribery needs two for completion; in it's inception in Israel the law (like the Prophets and Wisdom) only condemned the bribe-taker, the first fatal inconsistency.

A second inconsistency—the crime is more dangerous the higher the official; from ancient Israel to America the general rule has been, the higher the officials, the greater his immunity from prosecution for bribery,. If the bribe-taker has been high enough—the lawmakers of Israel, the Senate of Rome—he has been completely immune.

Hypocisy in the enforcement of the anti-bribery ethnic is common. Cicero, the great foe of bribery; will not subject his clients, the knights, to the bribery law. Richard Nixon, whose administration creates federal "common law" bribery to bring down the Kenny machine, plots to give bribes. The Watergate Committee, nearly all of whose members took money from Gulf, Judges Nixon.

5. The material effect of the exchanges commonly condemned is either trivial or undemonstrated. At best, the bribery rules, which have been so extravagantly expanded, are like the taboos on sexual intercourse, which were so extravagantly expanded by elaborate biblical provisions about certain classes of kin, virgins, and the menstruous, all of whom were shielded from sexual encounters.

   Purity rules of this kind, designed to impose order on chaos and prevent national catastrophe, rest on no rational basic and prevent no substantive harm. Taboos, they should be discarded when no actual injury which they avert can be identified.

The Arguments Evaluated

1. The first argument has shown illustratively, but not

exhaustively, that bribery has been practiced by some of the persons of every country, race or creed. It is essentially a quantitative argument, and it's failure to produce quantitative data is it's first deficiency. As the final argument on the same side contends, bribery has never been quantified. We have no statistics showing how many do take bribes or have taken them. The argument is unproved.

The argument suffers from a second deficiency, the assumption on which it rests—that what should be done is what is done. This assumption, particularly prominent in recent arguments on sexual morals, has no validity.

Many common practices—torture, religious persecution, the denial of rights to those born out of wedlock— are known to be wrong. It's ubiquity did not change it's moral character. The very question being examined is whether bribery is in the same category once occupied by slavery as a general but detestable custom.

2. The second argument does not show that bribery is necessary but that it has been thought necessary, just as the maintenance of slavery was thought necessary even by such critics of the system as Jefferson. What is perceived to be necessary is often a function of what risks one is willing to run.

   No absolute constraint compels a business to bribe, just as no force made any one a slave-holder. Companies such as Gulf and Lockhead, which have repented of their corrupt ways, are as prosperous as when they were the paymasters of politicians throughout the world.

   The plea of necessity is restated by those who insist that bribery has a social function. Functional observations prove too much if they are translated into moral argument. Functionally useful, bribes sometimes satisfy the wrong needs— for example, the need to make several million dollars without risk— and they do so by a method always destructive of trust. The social purpose a bribe serves does not make the breach of trust disappear.

One kind of necessity remains, the necessity to bribe to prevent oppression. It is a necessity alleged only on behalf of the bribe-payer. It is no defence at all for the bribe-taker. He must bear the full moral weight of being a bribee. As to bribers, relief of oppression is urged in mitigation or excuse.

Not merely the victim of extortion because he is the initiator actively seeking to pay, a Wittgenstein or a Lincoln urges superior moral obligations that outweighs the obligation not to bribe.

Where the right of war exists, so does the right of usury, ran a scholastic maxim. A similar rule holds of bribery. In actual warfare, bribery is a weapon, less lethal than a bomb, which justly be employed. Social orders may exist where the bonds of civic friendship have been so far dissolved that the state of society approaches warfare, at least as to the oppressed. The Germany in which Wittgenstein acted was in such a state. In such conditions it is necessary to 'buy back harassment'.

3. The Third argument pretends that no distinction can be drawn between bribes and other reciprocities. All are reciprocities; they must be ultra-Puritans or ultra-liberatarians who say there is no difference between marital and other sex.

   For the ultra-Puritan, all sex is condemned; for the ultra-libertarian, all sex is permissible. The distinctions on which civilized conduct depends disappear in a raw reductionism.

   Defensible definitions, not dependent on the lines drawn by legal statutes, can be drawn. To draw them, it is necessary to go beyond the words 'gift', 'tip', 'contribution', and 'bribe' and not to accept the use of the first three words to conceal bribery. It is necessary to sketch the salient characteristics of the transactions these words denote as types.

Absence of absolute obligation creates one difference between contributions and bribes. Size is, thus, a relevant characteristic. A large contribution can create an over-riding obligation; it's proper name becomes bribe.

A bribe is not an expression of love. The briber seeks to move the bribee to serve the briber's interest. The more impersonal the medium, as Simmel observed, the better; if sex is used, it is as a commodity. The bribe never belongs to the bribee but in equity and morals to the principal for whom the bribee had a duty to act. The bribe is necessarily secret. If it becomes known, the bribee is damaged, disgraced, incapacitated from delivering on the bribe.

Deceit and lies are the bribe's normal accompaniment, necessary to protect it's secrecy. The accountability of the briber and the bribee are not to the public but to each other. Equivalence and, hence, size are important. The larger the amount relative to the recipient, the greater the pressure created.

The bribe is intended to reflect or to create an overriding obligation. The briber pays because he feels he must reciprocate or must have reciprocation. The bribee delivers because he must. Angelo is double-damned because he takes a bribe and does not act upon it; so is Hog in Cicero's classic indictment. In the obligation created by the bribe, moral paradox abounds.

Reciprocity is basic to human society. To violate the trust put in reciprocity is, generally speaking, immoral. The briber relies on the general trust put in reciprocity to impose an obligation contrary to the special trust placed in the office-holder. The bribe creates a conflict of duties non-existent in the cash or the tip; a secret, absolute obligation different from the contribution; a loveless compulsion unknown to the gift.

'Bribe' is used today not only in it's primary sense of an exchange with an office-holder but in the sense of any inducement given to alter conduct that would naturally be otherwise. In this derivative usage some of the differences between a bribe and a gift disappear. In their primary senses, a bribe expresses self-interest; a gift conveys love. A bribe subordinates the recipient to the donor, a gift identifies the donor with the recipient. A gift brings no shame, a bribe must be secret. A gift may be disclosed, a bribe, decisive. A gift does not oblige; a bribe coerces.

A gift belongs to the donee; a bribe belongs to those to whom the bribee is accountable. When a parent gives something to a child to get him to do something, is it a gift or a bribe? Normally what is given belongs to the child, it is disclosed; no shame attached; sometimes love is expressed.

At the same time the child is subordinated to the donor; size is not irrelevant; coercive obligation is imposed. If we make no objection to what is given, we say gift. If we disapprove morally, we say bribe.

No injury is done a bribee photographed in the act. No injustice is done when bribers or bribees are punished for other crimes they have committed although their participation in unpunished bribery is the reason for their prosecution. Next to tyranny, corruption, corruption is the great disease of government. Skilful surgeons need more than a single way of curing the disease.

5. The fifth argument invites morality to overlook bribery as too trivial for it's high concerns. Joined to the first three arguments, it is hypocritical, pretending on the one hand that bribery is universal and necessary; and, on the other hand, that it is too small to notice. Isolated and taken on it's merits, the argument is morally obtuse. Using a quantitative measure, it doubts the effect of bribery on material goods.

But the common good of any society consists not only in it's material possessions but in it's shared ideals. When these ideals are betrayed, as they are betrayed when bribery is practiced, the common good, intangible though it be, suffers injury.

To take a bribe is commonly understood as a prostitution of one's office. To pay a bribe is to play the part of a professional seducer. Secrecy and deceit are the common badges of the bribe and must be practiced by the parties to it.

To accept a bribe is to take on the necessity of lying. Human beings do not engage in such acts without affecting their characters, their view of themselves, their integrity.

The question was asked if bribery as a moral concept was more like usury or slavery. The answer is that today it is like neither. Usury has little vigour as a moral concept; bribery has much. Slavery is indisputably immoral; the morality of bribery is debated.

Could the bribery ethic undergo the same decline so that only extortion and the exploitation of great disparities in bargaining power would remain condemned? The question, put now at the height or near the weight of the embodiment of the bribery ethic in law, seems preposterous. Does not the bribery ethic assure an essential condition of government while sexual sins are merely private acts.

But sexual morals once were thought to speak to issues more central to society than government. Privatization is only a symptom of their fall. If the bribery ethic were to be regarded as obsolete, it too would be privatized.

Historically, the tie between the ethics of bribery and sexual ethics are close. It is not simply that they were formed in the same religious millieu and taught by the same religious tradition and depended on the command of the same God. They have shared the same language.

'Corruption' is a state of civil graft or sexual depravity. Bribed judges are 'whores', who was at least a virgin in the king's affairs. 'Fig-leaves' covered his shameful acts of bribetaking. Even cynical rejections of the two ethics are alike in implying that true 'virility' cannot be confined by the feminine virtues the ethical standards incorporate.

36

CONCLUSIONS AND RECOMMENDATIONS

At this time the pursuit of bribe has become a national enterprise in the united states. Watergate is the consequence not the cause of the phenomenon.

There are four reasons why bribery is likely to continue to be morally condemned :

1. Bribery is universally shameful. Not a country in the world which does not treat bribery as criminal on it's law books. There are some laws such as those on gambling that are constantly broken without any particular sense of shame attaching to the offence. Bribery law is not among them. In no country do bribe-takers speak publicly of their bribes, or bribe-givers announce the bribes they pay.

   No newspaper lists them. No one advertises that he can arrange a bribe. No one honoured precisely because he is a big briber or a big bribee. No one writes an autobiography in which he recalls the bribes he has taken or the bribes he has paid.

2. Bribery is a sell-out to the rich. In any situation ruled only by money or it's equivalent, the deeper pocket will prevail. The judicial judgements could be brought and paid for. There would be a market in judgements as there is in soybeans and potatoes.

The same holds true of the decisions of regulatory agencies of public authorities, of government procurement officer, of legislators. If bribes were not morally objectionable, we would live in a world of pure plutocracy where wealth would be the measure of all things.

The advocate of the acceptance of bribery as a non-moral matter may say he does not go so far. His position is that bribery, like pornography, may be restrained if it thrusts itself too boldly on the citizenry, if it flaunts itself in public areas where decent conventions prevent it's acknowledgement, if it fails to pay rhetorical tribute to other values a society honours. To accept bribery is to accept the way things age, not to proclaim a regime where mammon is publicly enthroned as sole monarch.

3. Bribery is a betrayal of trust. Trust, that is, the expectation that one will do what one is relied on to do, is a precious necessity of every social enterprise.
4. Bribery violates a divine paradigm. The imitation of God lies at the root of the bribery prohibition. It is too religious because it depends on a belief in God and belief in a non-bribeable, gift-giving God. It will not work in a secularist society where belief in God is either not admitted or not acknowledged to have consequences.

From the perspective taken here, the shame of the briber and the bribee are true indices of violation of the human good; the acceptance in practice of plutocratic rule is abhorrent; the trust reposed in government is inherent in public office, which becomes raw power without it; and the divine paradigm is real.

Personal and social needs are furstrated by the act of bribery which violates the basic need to honour by action not mere words, values other than wealth, the basic need to trust one's government, the basic need to be like one's heavenly Father. The nature of bribery is contrary to the nature of the human person in it's full development.

Going beyond the data, I venture a prediction; as slavery was once a way of life and now, whatever analogues in economic duress remain, has become obsolete and incomprehensible, so the practice of bribery in the central form of the exchange of payment for official action will become obsolete.

The movement to restrict by law many forms of reciprocal exchange with office-holders incorporates the trust of a dominant moral idea. The conventions that give concreteness to the idea of the bribe will be refined and made responsive to the needs satisfied by human trust and human conformity to God's example.

Recommendations

The recommendations and reform proposals are made as follows :

(i) A new law may be elected in Parliament to give statutory powers to the CBI to function as a Central Investigation Agency on a nation-wide basis without having to secure the consent of the State Governments to make inquiries within the territory of State Governments.

(ii) The existing restrictive procedures prescribed for the CBI and the State ACBs for dealing with complaints of corruption against high-ranking officers in the Government may be reviewed and modified to give functional independence to these agencies for speedy verification of intelligence relating to high-level corruption.

(iii) The existing set-up of the Central Vigilance Commission (CVC) may be put on a statutory basis.

(iv) A *Lok Pal* may be set-up as a statutory body at the Centre for dealing with complaints of corruption against all Central ministers (including the 'Prime Minister'), members of parliament and top-level bureaucrats in the governments.

(v) The *Lok Pal* may be a multi-member body, with all members including the Chairman being persons who are working or had worked or are qualified for appointment as judges of the Supreme Court.

(vi) Appointment of the Chairman and members of the *Lok Pal* may be made by the President by a procedure similar to the one adopted for the appointment of Chairman and members of the National Human Rights Commission, in which the leaders of the Opposition in the Lok Sabha and Rajya Sabha have an effective role in the appointment process.

(vii) The statutory set-up proposed for the CVC may be integrated with that of the *Lok Pal* by making the CVC one of the members of the *Lok Pal*. The charter of functions of the CVC may be defined as a part of the charter of the *Lok Pal*.

(viii) A separate investigating wing and prosecuting wing may be set-up as a part of the establishment of the *Lok Pal*. Their services will be available for all inquiries and prosecutions launched by the *Lok Pal*.

(ix) The Central *Lok Pal* Act may also provide for a State *Lok Pal* /Vigilance Commission with a similar charter of functions in regard to all ministers (including the chief minister) and services in the State. The President shall be the appointing authority for the State level *Lok Pal* also.

(x) The existing Commissions of Inquiry Act may remain, since special commissions may still be required to inquire into matters of public importance other than those involving allegations of corruption. The investigating and prosecuting staff of the *Lok Pal* may be utilised to assist the Commissions of Inquiry also as and when they are set up.

(xi) CBI will continue to function under the administrative control of the Central Government and function as its primary investigating agency. Specific cases relating to high-level corruption may be notified by the *Lok Pal* /CVC, from time to time, for being monitored by the CVC even as the CBI proceeds with the investigation. This will eliminate the scope for *mala fide* interference by the Government or other extraneous sources in the investigation of sensitive cases involving VIPS, political or otherwise.

(xii) The definition of 'public servant' in the Prevention of Corruption Act should be amplified to include MPs and MLAs and all elected representatives in metropolitan councils, municipal corporations, municipalities, *panchayats* and such other statutorily constituted local bodies.

These public functionaries should be required by law to submit to a prescribed authority an annual statement of assets held in their names as also in the names of their parents or sons, daughters and other close relatives. The annual statements should be made available by the prescribed authority for scrutiny by any member of the public who makes an application for it.

(xiii) A Code of Conduct may be drawn up to govern the conduct of legislators to ensure their integrity and commitment to serve public interest. A special committee designated as Ethics Committee should be set-up in Parliament and each State Assembly to ensure strict observance of this Code by all members.

(xiv) Section 13A of the Income Tax Act should be strictly enforced to secure proper maintenance of accounts by all political parties. A special cell may be set up either under the Comptroller and Auditor General or the Election Commission to conduct periodically a regular audit of these accounts. A clearance from this audit cell may be made statutory necessary for a political party to claim exemption for its income under Section 13A of the Income Tax Act.

(xv) Articles 77 and 166 of the Constitution may be amended to facilitate allotment of certain aspects of business to civil servants also at the higher levels in the Government Secretariat. This would check whimsical, capricious or *mala fide* disposal of the Government business at the level of the political executive.

(xvi) A formal procedure may be laid down in law for the appointment of Comptroller and Auditor General to ensure that a person with a high reputation for integrity and known for his professional competence and independence with a good background of audit work alone fills the post.

(xvii) In regard to prior sanction for a prosecution under the Prevention of Corruption Act, existing provisions of Section 19 of the Act may be amended to ensure that:

(a) the competent authority makes the order sanctioning or refusing to sanction prosecution within a specified time limit, and

(b) if the competent authority refuses to sanction prosecution, it shall state the reasons for refusal which shall be embodied in the order of refusal, and it shall be open to the investigating agency to appeal against such an order to the *Lok Pal* whose decision thereon shall be final and binding on the government concerned.

(xviii) Any amount of focusing on radical measures in law and executive action for effective anti-corruption work will not be realistic unless the overall scenario of law enforcement, in general, becomes clear and bright. Immediate implementation of the NPC recommendations for police reform should, therefore, be viewed as a 'must' for effective anti-corruption work also.

(xix) The Criminal Law Amendment Ordinance of 1944 provides for attachment of properties acquired by a corrupt public servant when an alleged offence under the Prevention of Corruption Act committed by him is under investigation.'

This statute may be replaced by a more comprehensive Act to deal with properties acquired by public servants by corrupt or illegal means not only in their own names but also in the names of their relatives and others under their control. The new law may be modelled on the Smugglers and Foreign Exchange Manipulators (Forfeiture of Property) Act, 1976.

(xx) A small working group under the lead of a retired Supreme Court or High Court Judge held in high esteem should be immediately entrusted with the task of drafting a comprehensive Bill for the necessary amendments to the Constitution and enactment of separate laws for the different purposes mentioned above.

Movement for Reforms

Legislation for the proposed reforms and changes would require the willingness of MPs and MLAs and political leaders of the country to accept the need for such reforms and changes and, accordingly, move them in Parliament and State Assemblies.

Left to themselves, the political bosses, elected representatives and various government functionaries who are presently benefiting from the fast spreading corruption all round will not be inclined to adopt fundamental changes in the system which will atonce reduce scope for corruption.

The pressure for effecting changes has, therefore, to be built up by the people at large. Presently, there seems to be a wave round the world where the peoples of different countries are expressing their disgust at the wrong doings of unscrupulous politicians who have brought them to the *sorry* mess they are in.

Italy, South Korea and Japan are examples where people's anger against corruption-ridden governments has displaced discredited rulers by new men who hold out the promise of cleansing public life. A people's movement is now called for in our country to fight the war against corruption and save the nation from disintegration.

The younger generation in schools and colleges have a vital stake in this matter and should, therefore, deliberate and evolve a methodology for mounting pressure to bring about these reforms and changes in our system.

Electoral Reform

Cleansing the national and state election of money power is central to the reform of the political process. There is substantial agreement now among political parties and opinion leaders in the country on the need to use public funds to meet the election expenses of candidates. Re-imbursement by Government of the candidates election expenses in parliamentary and state election is a reform whose time has come candidates of recognized political parties, as well as independent candidates under specified conditions, should be eligible for such reimbursement from public funds. Such financing may be provided in kind (e.g. free but limited television or radio time) as well as in cash. Guidelines should be established to minimise election expenses.

The recent parliamentary elections have demonstrated the feasibility of holding modest and orderly elections. Details of the proposed reform can be worked out once it is decided to introduce State funding of elections. According to reasonable estimates,

State funding of election expenses will not impose an impossible burden on the exchequer.

State funding of elections should ideally be accompanied by a ban on donations to political parties and individual candidates by business enterprises. Private financing has inherent risks of abuse that can never be fully eliminated even the best of regulations. State funding of elections should be used to wean political parties away from any obligation to business groups.

If, however, donations by business groups cannot be banned, the conditions for such donations should be specified and strictly enforced on both the donors and recipients. Political donations have specified limits, may be made subject to approval at the shareholders' meetings of companies. All donations should be made known through the annual reports of companies.

Uncontrolled election expenditure has contributed substantially to corrupt practices. Several measures can be taken to keep election expenses within reasonable limits.

Reduction in the campaign period, curtailment of permissible items of expenditure (e.g. transportation of voters), and strict enforcement of expenditure ceilings are steps that merit special attention.

Ceiling should include expenditure incurred by all sources (viz. candidates, friends and well-wishers, and parties)). Election accounts submitted by candidates should be cross-checked with those furnished by their political parties.

The introduction of electronic voting machines can reduce the period of campaigning and, thereby, provide an important means of reducing expenditure for candidates as well.

There are several other steps which can be taken to reduce the scope for abuse and corruption in the conduct of elections. The use of electronic voting machines will partly eliminate rigging. Appointment of watch-dog committees in constituencies and polling stations may act as a deterrent to abuses and corruption.

The use of heliographed, multipurpose photo identity cards (despite the recent problems in its implementation) will minimise impersonation. Considering the vital role of clean elections in the political process, they need to be given high priority as their benefits far outweigh the costs involved.

The Anti-Defection Act needs to be amended as follows to ensure that legislators are not bought and sold, Some of the suggestions made in this regard :

(a) no defection should be recognised in a legislature party unless it is the result of a split in the parent party;

(b) a cooling-off period between leaving the one party and joining another should be specified;

(c) there should be a ban on taking office after defection to the ruling party.

The integrity of the political process is influenced greatly by the way politicians and political parties conduct themselves. Their organisational culture, discipline, and integrity are seen by, and influence, everyone else. It is, therefore, essential to enact a law for regulating the functioning of political parties.

This law should require political parties to

(a) hold regular organisational elections to various levels;

(b) maintain prompt and systematic accounts and submit audited accounts to the prescribed authority (e.g. the Election Commission or the Comptroller and Auditor General); and

(c) comply with income-tax regulations and guidelines.

A clearance from the Audit Cell should be necessary for a political party to claim tax exemption under the Income Tax Act. The Election Commission may be given the authority to derecognise political parties if they fail to observe the proposed law.

Greater transparency and compliance with the law by political parties will go a long way in reducing the scope for corrupt practices and other abuses in their day-to-day operations and, in the process, exert a positive influence on other public institutions.

A code of conduct needs to be adopted by Parliament to provide guidelines for the conduct of elected representatives and to take appropriate action when departures from accepted norms are observed. Such codes of conduct exist in other countries. Proposals for a code of conduct for legislators have been made in India too, notably by the late Mrs. Durgabai Deshmukh, but never acted on.

An Ethics or Conduct Committee under the chairmanship of the Speaker of the Lok Sabha or State Assembly will be necessary to monitor observance of the code and decide on the actions to be taken in case of violations.

Elected representatives should also be required to declare on oath or affirm every year the assets held by them and thier sources of income.These returns should be monitored by the Ethics Committee and appropriate action taken to ensure the integrity of legislators.

Elected representatives deserve to be compensated adequately so that they are able to devote their primary attention to public service. It is, also, in the fitness of things, that their monetary emoluments are increased to reflect the scale of their expenses from time to time.

More rational compensation and benefits, policies for elected representatives are desirable not only for the purpose of reducing the incentives and opportunities for corruption, but also for larger reasons of efficiency and effectiveness.

At the same time, action can be taken to reduce or eliminate their material and non-transparent privileges which lead themselves to easy abuse such as quotas for gas connections, petrol pumps, telephone connections and school admissions. The recent steps taken by the Government of India along these lines are commendable.

Though the Prevention of Corruption Act was substantially amended in 1988 to include more public functionaries under the definition of 'public servant', Members of Parliament (MPs) and Members of Legislative Assemblies (MLAs) are not with in the purview of this Act.

Early steps need to be taken to bring MPs, MLAs, and all other elected representatives of local governments and such other statutorily-constituted local bodies within the purview of this Act.

The Criminal Law Amendment Ordinance of 1944 should be replaced by a more comprehensive act to deal with properties acquired by public servants through corrupt or illegal means not only in their names, but also in the names of their close relatives and as *benami* (proxy).

There is considerable evidence in India of the close links between political corruption and criminalisation of politics. No person with a criminal conviction should, therefore, be permitted to contest in an election to the legislature. Legislators convicted for criminal offences during their tenure should be required to vacate their seats forthwith.

Government Machinery Needs Reorientation and Restructuring

A proper functioning of the government and it's institutional mechanisms is bound to reduce the scope for corruption in any society. The reality, however, is that the structure, systems and style of functioning of many of India's public institutions, and the orientation of the bureaucracy, have contributed directly and indirectly to the culture of corruption.

Bureaucracy can be divided into two categorise. One is primarily concerned with the planning and implementation of policies, programmes and the delivery of services. The other consisting largely of specialised agencies, is concerned with monitoring the resources and processes utilised in these activities wit a view to preventing abuses and enforcing the law.

From the standpoint of corruption control, we identify four important areas for the restructuring and reorientation of both these parts of the bureaucracy. The focus here is not merely on streamlining their functioning but more importability on augmenting their integrity and impartiality.

The interventions are strategic in the sense that once these reforms are in place, many other desirable changes in the functioning of public institutions and the behaviour of the bureaucracy may also follow.

The key reforms called for are deregulation and debureaucratisation, bounded discretion in decision-making, realignment of the government's audit, intelligence and investigating agencies to achieve better corruption control, and the insulation of key appointments and personnel decisions from undesirable interference.

Of these, deregulation of industry and commerce has already made notable progress since 1991. While not all observers are agreed on the details of these measures, most will concede that they have reduced the scope for corruption in government.

The challenge now is to adapt this approach to other sectors and activities where opportunities for corruption are widespread. The focus of reform needs to shift to the State and local governments levels where enterpreneurs as well as ordinary citizens are still heavily dependent on a variety of public services, approvals and licences.

Deregulation on a massive scale is not necessarily a prerequisite for corruption control. The trick is to identify areas for intervention where the payoff in terms of corruption control is likely to be the highest. A strategic approach will require that the focus of reform should be on the more corruption prone public agencies that also have the most interaction with people.

A second area for restructuring and reorientation pertains to the use of discretion in public decision-making. Administrative decisions on complex subjects may have to be based, for good reasons, on the use of discretion and judgement by public officials. However, non-transparency and lack of accountability in decision making have created opportunities for collusion and corruption.

Corruption control calls for discipline in this area through an explicit adoption of a set of guidelines for the use of discretion, and documentation of the specific reasons for discretionary decisions to be made available to the affected parties.

For important categories of administrative decisions, the concerned authorities should be required to issue clear instructions on the use of discretion. These should also be made available to the public. These arrangements should include tribunals to decide on appeals., pertaining to administrative decisions.

Thirdly, specialised public agencies with a watchdog function or which are directly concerned with the investigation of corruption cases and law enforcement need to be strengthened from the point of view of effectiveness and integrity. The scope for legislative and institutional reform and management improvements is substantial here.

Information-sharing and coordinated work among these agencies are much needed steps. New mechanisms for reporting and sharing pertinent audit findings can be devised to aid investigative processes.

The institution of *Lok Pal* which has been supported by all political parties should be given constitutional status and placed at the apex of a network of *ombudsmen* established at the level of the State Governments and other major public authorities.

This independent network should be accessible to all citizens who wish to register complaints about corruption and misconduct even against the highest public officials. It is of vital importance that the *Lok Pal* should be under-printed by an independent agency for investigation and prosecution.

The fourth area for reform concerns the process of making top level appointments to the sensitive and specialised public agencies referred to above and appointments and transfers in the higher levels of the bureaucracy. It is leaders who set the tone in their organisations and signal others on whether corruption and abuses will be tolerated or not.

Credible and transparent approaches to the selection and appointment of persons to these positions will go a long way in attracting persons capable of resisting corruption and preserving their autonomy. In bureaucracy, it is not only appointments, but also transfers that need to be insulated from arbitrary action.

While selection, appointments, transfers and promotions in the entire bureaucracy deserve a close look, from a strategic perspective, the right place to start is at the top. These changes will call for a major reorientation in the thinking of the top echelons of the political and administrative levels.

Other Recommendations

1. A major review of the regulations governing the transactions of public agencies at the State and local levels with citizens and business enterprises must be undertaken with a view to eliminating their scope for creating incentives and opportunities for corruption.

   The initial focus of the review should be on departments and agencies which citizens interact on a regular basis such as the police, general administration, public distribution system, utilities dealing electricity, after and telephones, and local bodies providing basic civic services. The need for reform is the greatest and maximum impact can be achieved at State and local levels.

   Clear guidelines should be provided to the public who seek services and approvals, while minimising the scope for officials to make case-by-case discretionary decisions and authorisations. Ensuring transparency and fairness is most difficult where the use of discreation and case-by-case approvals are involved.

Where case-by-case decisions are unavoidable, stricter supervision, checks and clearer guidelines need to be put in place. Decision-making in more open forums and public access to information on such decisions are necessary.

The objective of this reform is not to dilute the regulatory function of the government. Rather, it should improve the efficiency and effectiveness of regulation while making it less susceptible to corruption.

2. In all important areas of decision-making that entail the use of discretion, potential abuses can be minimised by issuing administrative instructions to guide the use of discretion.

   This is especially necessary where such decisions result in the allocation of substantial funds, entitlements or privileges such as contracts, building permissions and licenses.

   Instructions should state the policy in accordance with which discretion is to be exercised. Greater transparency and clarity on the reasons for decisions are measures that tend to minimise the scope for abuse of power and corruption.

3. There should be a provision for the public to challenge the decisions of administrative authorities in respect of matters like grant of exemptions, and privileges. This can be facilitated though the creation of tribunals for hearing appeals against such decisions. Such tribunals should follow inquiry procedures for fact-finding rather than resort to dilatory adverbial proceedings.

4. The primary responsibility of the civil service to uphold the rule of law needs to be unambiguously reaffirmed. Political neutrality of the civil servant must remain the cornerstone of the civil service.

   The Centre and the States should prescribe rules and

regulations for affecting transfer of officers to ensure a reasonable tenure in various posts.

Reasons for any departure from this norm should be conveyed in writing to the affected officer. For heads of major public agencies and departments, the term of service should be three to five years so that they are enabled to implement programmes and reforms necessary to ensure good performance.

5. It is necessary to encourage those who work in the government to 'blow the whistle' when they come across corrupt practices. They may hesitate to report such cases to the authorities, however, for fear of retribution.

   This lacuna can be remedied by providing legal protection to the staff who expose corruption and wrongdoing in the government through enactment of a law on the lines of the legislation adopted by other countries to protect 'whistle blowers'.

6. The overriding role that political executives play in personnel decisions such as the postings and transfers of even the lowest levels of officials has been a contributory factor to the corruption within the government. The remedy to this would be to empower intra-service committees headed by the senior-most civil servants to deal with postings and transfers.

   Any departure at the ministerial level from the recommendations of such committees should be for reasons which are to be recorded in writing. They would also be open to appeal in the hands of Administrative Tribunals or specially constituted Civil Service Tribunals.

7. The cornerstone of the arrangements for tackling high-level corruption in the Centre and in the States is the creation of the *Lok Pal* (at the centre) and *Lok Ayukt* (in the States). Both the institutions should be given constitutional status as recommended by the Administrative Reforms Commission (1966).

Their jurisdiction should extend to all ministers— including the Prime Minister and Chief Minister— and the higher echelons of public servants, whether serving in governments, statutory authorities, public sector undertakings, local bodies, aided institutions (such as universities) or those belonging to any other category of public servants as defined in the Prevention of Corruption Act, 1988 which may be notified for inclusion. The basic features of the legislation should be uniform for the Centre and the State, with the latter being free to introduce innovations and adaptations.

8. The *Lok Pal* should be appointed by the President on the recommendation of a body consisting of the Prime Minister, Chief Justice of India, the presiding officers of both Houses of Parliament and the leader of the opposition in the Lok Sabha.

   A similar practice should be followed for the appointment of the *Lok Ayukt* in the States. It may be pointed out that the need for a non-partisan a political approach to high appointments had already been recognised in the case of the National Human Rights Commission.

9. The *Lok Pal/Lok Ayukt* should be free to investigate any allegation relating to corruption or criminal misconduct made by a citizen or referred to it by the executive, legislative or judicial arms of the State or taken up *suo moto* by itself.

   They should be able to take up investigations and launch prosecutions without any prior sanction from any level in the government. They should also have the power to direct a public servant to vacate his office, if considered necessary or desirable in the interests of the effective pursuit of its proceedings. The functioning of the *Lok Pal/ Lok Ayukt* should be a model of transparency.

10. In recent months, the Supreme Court of India has taken steps to ensure that the investigations and pros-

ecutions of the CBI are insulated from political interference and pursued in a time-bound manner without fear or favour.

While judicial activism is welcome, we cannot continually depend on it in all cases. It is, therefore, necessary to institutionalize the impartiality and integrity of the CBI by providing statutory safeguards to its autonomy.

This will be possible only if the CBI, and its counterparts agencies in the States, are placed under the sole administrative control of the *Lok Pal/Lok Ayukt* in matters falling within the jurisdiction of the latter.

The Governments at the Centre and in the States can have separate agencies under their administrative control to deal with other cases of corruption and with serious crimes which are now being handled by the CBI and counterpart agencies in the States.

The powers of the investigating agencies at the Centre and in the States should be clearly laid down through legislation in respect of such matters as arrest, search, seizure, summoning and examining of witnesses. No restrictions should be placed on the investigating agencies initiating or pursuing investigations and prosecutions.

11. Disclosure and identification of financial and procedural irregularities in the course of audit should be followed up with investigations for possible corruption. For this purpose, a special cell should be established in each State Accountant General Office and in the Principal Central Audit offices to identify cases that need investigation.

    A monthly letter may be sent by the Head of the Audit Office, to the concerned secretaries to the government, drawing attention to such cases. Audit offices should also keep the Vigilance Commissioners and *Lok Pal* informed of these cases and act as a source of information and intelligence to them and other investigative agencies.

12. It is important to encourage close networking among the different agencies such as the *Lok Pal* CBI, Income Tax Authorities, Enforcement Directorate and CAG. Appropriate and effective institutional mechanisms to facilitate the sharing of information and intelligence and co-operation in investigations need to be put in place to improve their role in tackling corruption.

13. A procedure similar to that suggested in the case of the *Lok Pal* should be followed for appointments to other high level positions such as the Comptroller and Auditor General of India and the Chief Election Commissioner, which equally need to be insulated from possible political interference.

Most importantly, all corruption problems can be radically solved if all services in governments, statutory authorities, public sector undertakings, local bodies, aided institutions (such as colleges and universities) or those belonging to any other category of public servants, as defined in the Prevention of Corruption Act, 1988, which may be notified for inclusion, from time to time, should be declared as temporary overnight by an ordinance. And, all such services should function on contractual basis ranging from a three months, six months or to a one-year period according to the nature of work involved. Besides, new government appointments should be reduced and the existing bloated bureaucracy be trimmed drastically to make it more efficient, effective and accountable to the people and the nation. It will, thus, amount to greasing the wheels of progress.

The logic is that this provision would introduce an element of fear in all public services. Corruption will flee away and humans will work efficiently and effectively for their own survival, as this measure would serve as a great deterrant. Such a practice obtains in serval western countries involving both Civil Services, public agencies and private companies. Hence, every one is aware of their efficient and effective working in whatever they do, for the good of their people and the country. Thus, a 'Hire and Fire' Policy should be pursued as a State policy.

Such an action will serve as a panacea for all problems ari sen out of bribery and corruption.

Empowering Citizens

Corruption can be effectively tackled only when the reform of the political process and the restructuring of government machinery are complemented by systematic efforts to inform citizens about their rights and entitlements, and to enable them to monitor and challenge abuses of the system.

By reducing the opportunities for corruption, measures of deregulation and debureaucratisation will reduce the hardships that the people experience, given them more competitive options, and empower them in the process. But much more should and can be done to relieve citizens of corruptions.

There are four important directions for empowering citizens that deserve special attention. Firstly, the culture of secrecy that pervades the functioning of the government must be broken so that citizens have access to the information that they need to understand, assess and challenge the policies, programmes and specific actions of public authorities.

Withholding of information is often justified by the Official Secrets Act and other time honoured practices in government. That the right to information is fundamental to the working of a democratic society and that it can act as a deterrent to the abuse of power are still alien concepts to many of our political and bureaucratic leaders.

Secondly, in respect of most public services, opportunities for corruption arise partly because people do not know what they can expect in terms of service delivery. To alleviate this sense of helplessness and to empower people to demand public accountability, it is essential that service providers specify and announce the standards and norms they intend to meet in their areas of responsibility.

They should also indicate the remedies available to the public when the assured standards of service are not met. Dissemination of this information will go a long way in increasing transparency in the working of public agencies, and to empower citizens to resist abuses and extraordinary corruption by those in authority.

Finally, the inner urge and resolve of a person to combat corruption depend, in no small measure, on his or her basic moral values and beliefs. In the prevailing pessimistic atmosphere, it is all too easy to ignore the fact that there are public servants who resist corruption and are willing to pay the price for standing firm.

Some have quit their jobs in protest rather than compromise on the principles and values they cherished. Similarly, there are many people in our society whose values militate against corrupt practices.

The field studies conducted by the Public Affairs Centre in different parts of the country have shown that the vast majority of people (nearly 85%) believed corruption to be wrong and abhorrent.

Even in the world of business, which is often portrayed as a source of corruption, there are enterprises that are able to maintain their integrity and resistance to corrupt practices. An outstanding example is the Alacrity group of companies in Madras, who are known for their transparent and straightforward ways of doing business in fields such as housing and real estate.

These examples are a testimony to the power of values and beliefs in sustaining people and organisations in their resolve to resist corruption. An important lesson of this experience is that it has worked within the framework of the institutional imperfections in India. The real challenge is to see that this approach is replicated in the country on a large scale.

If, on the other hand, the guiding values of people tolerate corrupt practices and unethical behaviour, there is little hope that such individuals will revolt against corruption or help launch a collective assault on corruption in their community or society.

When there is no collective urge to uproot corruption, the institutional and legal reforms proposed by the author will not go far, and any impact they make is likely to be marginal from the larger social point of view.

Important Suggestions

1. By limiting the monopolistic power of public service providers, deregulation of economic activities will reduce the spread and severity of corruption that citizens face in their real daily lives. However, the ability of the latter to monitor corruption and seek remedies should be increased by decentralising resources allocations and service delivery wherever possible.

   It is true that decentralisation by itself cannot eliminate corruption and abuses. But greater proximity to decision-making and to remedy or appeal mechanisms may empower people to monitor abuses and to seek redress more effectively.

   The implementation of the 73rd and 74th Amendments to the Constitution should be accelerated and made effective so as to empower people along these lines.

2. As access to information is essential to the empowerment of people, the Official Secrets Act should be suitably reformed. A Freedom of Information Act should be passed which explicitly guarantees the right of access to official documents subject to the provisions of the law. Detailed proposals have been formulated in this regard by the Consumer Education and Research Centre (CERC), Ahmedabad. Categories of documents exempt from disclosure and the limits to the right to privacy must be kept to the minimum and clearly specified.

   Categories of exempt information proposed in the CERC bill are advice of Cabinet to the President, information that may damage national defence and security interests, disclosure harmful to international relations and law enforcement, and information that entails the privacy of an identifiable individual. The law must also be consistent with the right to privacy that could be claimed by persons holding public office.

3. All providers of public services and regulatory agen-

cies should be required to specify and widely disseminate information on their standards and norms of service and remedies available to the public if they are dissatisfied. Laws governing these public agencies should mandate that they fulfil this requirement.

A useful approach is to enact a law that mandates public authorities to disseminate and display essential information about their services, and to give opportunities to the public to participate in the rule-making process as was envisaged in the Karnataka Administrative Procedure Bill of 1991.

Public service providers should also be required to undertake periodic surveys of their customers to identify the problems faced by them and to take steps to eliminate such problems.

4. An important causes of corruption in some public services is the failure of service providers to match services to the differing requirements of customers, and their ability and willingness to pay for well-matched services. To reduce the scope for such corruption, wherever feasible and appropriate, service providers may be encouraged to design and offer service with the required attributes such as speed and reliability and to price them accordingly.

   While free or subsidised services may be justified from an equity point of view, thee is a strong case for a judicious blend of subsidised and cost-plus recoveries. The scope for corruption and diversion of benefits is substantial when highly subsidised or entirely free services and goods are provided by the State.

5. All the major public utilities and other service providers should appoint independent *ombudsman* whom citizens can approach to redress their grievances, delays, malfunctioning and inefficiency. Smaller agencies may share an *ombudsman* at the same location. These *ombudsmen* should specialise in specific sets of services. The Reserve Bank of India's *ombudsman* for banking services is a model to follow.

6. Empowerment of the people to resist and fight corruption will depend greatly on the values and beliefs underlying their behaviour. While behavioural changes are, by no means easy to engineer, systematic efforts to incalculate values of integrity, honesty and probity in public life need to be undertaken on a large scale at all levels in the country.

   In the final analysis, what people see and experience are those which influence them most. Good examples from all walks of life, therefore, need to be widely disseminated and replicated. A wide range of organisations, political, religious, social and professional, can play a catalytic role in this endeavour.

Public Pressure for Change

As noted above, legal institutional reforms for tackling corruption need to be reinforced by pressure from citizens whose values and beliefs militate against corruption. But the power of individual concern and commitment can be multiplied and leveraged through the deliberate efforts of organised groups to encourage collective action to monitor and fight corruption. Since corruption is not a problem faced by every citizen every day, it is not easy to sustain collective interest in this issue on a continuing basis.

Institutions of civil society have, therefore, to be actively involved in this mobilisation of public opinion and action in this context. The media, for example, can be a powerful source of information and education of the citizen for this purpose.

Dissemination of information of what different groups of people are doing and achieving in their fight against corruption can be both educative and inspirational to people in other parts of the country.

Other civil society institutions such as voluntary agencies, religious groups and research bodies may be able to support people's movements for corruption control. Documentation of such efforts and networking among the organisations involved to leverage their impact are other important steps that deserve support.

Further Steps Needed

1. The media is already playing a major role in exposing corruption and corrupt practices. Its influence on public opinion and values will be even greater if it can seek, emphasise and publicise the positive side of combating corruption. Dissemination of information to the public on the service standards, guidelines, and norms of major service providers will be an important service to the community. Those who are doing good work by resisting corruption or taking steps to eliminate corruption need to be recognised and appreciated.

   It is important that the media in India devote more attention to investigative journalism so that readers can benefit from well researched stories and their lessons. A good example is the publication of the results of the surveys of public service users with respect to the quality and reliability of services.

   The quality and depth of work in this area can be improved by the media linking up with specialised research institutions and related professional groups in order to draw upon their studies and insights. Media should also help disseminate information on new approaches and innovations in tackling corruption, especially experiences and lessons from other countries that are not so well known in our country.

2. Business organisations, especially associations of business and industry, can render a valuable service by making their position clear on the subject of corruption. Business is seen as ambivalent on this issue, and on the whole reluctant to participate in any public debate on the subject.

   The time has come for organised business to express a collective view on the subject of controlling corruption, an issue in which it can be expected to have a vital stake.

   An important initial step could be for leading associations and chambers of business to recommend to the government specific measures that can be taken to minimise corruption in business-government relations, on the lines that the International Chamber of Commerce and Transparency International have attempted.

3. The other institutions of the civil society such as voluntary agencies and religious groups are also critical to mobilising public opinion against corruption. They can act as support and catalytic groups to encourage individuals and communities to resist corruption and to reform the system.

The Government could consult them in the process of reviewing and redesigning policies and internal systems and practices. They can also play a major role in assisting the less-privileged citizens and their groups in accessing the mechanisms available to seek remedies when faced with situations involving extortion and corruption.

Public interest litigation is another initiative through which voluntary groups and peoples' movements can challenge and expose abuse of power and corruption.

Many voluntary organisations are already doing outstanding work in this area as is clear from the recent case of *Jan Sunvayi* in Pali District in Rajasthan which demanded access to information from the local government on public works and in the process caused a major change in the attitude of the State Government.

In the last analysis, it is the awareness, resolve and demand for reform by the people that will determine the success of the many legal, institutional and policy changes proposed here for controlling corruption.

ANNEXURES

ANNEXURE-I

FRAUDS IN COMMERCIAL BANKS

Two years after setting up supervisory bodies to counter frauds in commercial banks, the RBI has not only failed to publish a public statement but also to curb irregularities.

It may have controlled inflation and managed foreign exchange, but when it comes to the surveillance of banks, the Reserve Bank of India (RBI) seems to have come a cropper. After the Rs. 2,000-crore securities scam surfaced in 1992, the RBI set up a separate Department of Supervision (DoS) on December 22, 1993, with the objective of strengthening surveillance. Less than a year later, it established the Board for Financial Supervision (BFS) and the Advisory Council to further sharpen this supervisory mechanism.

But recent developments have placed a question mark over the DoS's ability to curb the rising menace of frauds. Instead of improving public confidence in the banking system, the RBI and its regulatory wings-the Dos and BFS—have become more secretive. There has been no public document about the situation prevailing in the banking system.

The number of frauds in various banks, the massive losses incurred by some of the profit-making banks due to non-performing assets, the erosion of the entire capital base of Indian Bank, the controversy over the Rs. 133-crore urea import scam involving the State Bank of India, have done nothing to enhance the image of the RBI as The Great Authority.

RBI Deputy Governor S.P. Talwar in-charge of DoS-while refusing to given an interview on these issues, admited in a written reply that in 1995-96, the number of frauds reported to the RBI by commercial banks other than the Regional Rural Banks increased from 2,076 in 1992-93 involving Rs. 152.39 crore to 2,157 cases involving Rs. 191.97 crore during 1995-96.

Besides, as a banker said, there is a scam behind each of the 4,000 defaulting commercial bank accounts—where over Rs. 40,000 crore of bank money is locked up. Even though the number of defaulting accounts dropped last year, the money (non-performing assets) locked up in such accounts has remained static.

But Talwar has a different story to tell. During the year 1995-96, the BFS held 11 meeting which reviewed the inspection reports of 84 banks. But instead of punishing the real culprits, the DoS transferred some of its own officials.

According to documents with The Indian Express, inspection reports of banks like the Punjab National Bank, Sangli Bank, American Express Bank, Oriental Bank of Commerce, Central Bank of India and Indian Bank have revealed grave irregularities on various fronts, including loans and advances in violation of RBI norms, undue favours to some parties, misuse of stock-invest (a cheque facility for payment towards public issue applications) and loans against shares.

But RBI correctives have not prevented some of these banks from repeating the mistakes. Indian Bank showed a profit last year, but reported a massive loss of over Rs. 1,300 crore this year. What went wrong in a year's time? Was the DoS monitoring the functioning of the Indian Bank?

While some RBI officers have been able to detect the irregularities committed by bankers, their inspection reports are lying unattended at the DoS. "RBI has at least one inspection report indicting almost all the banks-government, private and foreign but they are gathering dust in RBI vaults," said a source in the DoS.

In the urea scam, the RBI says "certain transactions relating to remittance of funds abroad in the guise of payment for imports are not reflected in the above data as these remittances do not cause a loss to the bank and are treated as FERA violations. But there is a loss of foreign exchange to the country".

Even when the bridge loan was banned by the RBI after the MS Shoes episode, several banks extended this facility, circumventing the RBI guidelines by diverting the loan to the stock markets. DoS, the investigating authority, has not taken any punitive action on the matter.

About the action taken by RBI in these cases, Talwar's reply says" "Prevention of frauds is a management function of a bank. The role of the RBI is to keep the bank's managements informed of various areas in which frauds occur and to suggest preventive steps required to be taken.

The RBI has been increasingly issuing instructions to banks relating to fraud". In a number of cases, however, the action has been nullified by interference from politicians.

Says the RBI spokesman : "high-level expert committee (Ghosh Committee) submitted its report in 1992 and suggested various measures for prevention of frauds. Most of the recommendations were given to the banks for implementation and banks have reported the implementation of almost all of them". But some bankers beg to differ. "Neither the DoS nor the BFS has been able to bring down irregularities. These bodies were set up to clean up the banking system. I don't think they have done that, said a retired senior banker.

The Central bank also claims that where frauds by borrowers are reported by the banks and *prima facie* evidence of cheating by the borrower is noticed, the RBI also issues cautionary notices to all commercial banks against the borrower/ group. It is a different matter that banks don't follow the RBI advice. At least a few banks are known to have extended loans to defaulting accounts even when they have been "blacklisted".

Frauds and Irregularities

February 1995 : Ten top banks, including the three major ones, had given bridge loans after they were banned by the RBI in the light of the MS Shoes scandal. The DoS regularised such loans.

September 1995 : RBI investigation proved that there was window-dressing at Sangli Bank. The bank fudged accounts and showed profits when it actually incurred a net loss. The bank also diverted funds to companies promoted by some of the bank's directors. However, the RBI has not taken action against those responsible, instead of removing the three accused, the DoS hurrledly transferred the inspecting officer from the job.

January 1996 : In the Rs.133-crore urea scam, the RBI knew about the foreign exchange sanction but no action was taken. RBI looked the other way when SBI allowed the foreign exchange remittances without getting adequate insurance cover.

March 1996 : Punjab National Bank, one of the most profitable banks, is now in the red; thanks to some questionable deals. RBI has not come up with an inquiry or specific action on PNB.

March 1996 : RBI investigated the stock-invest scheme which was misused by several banks and promoters. Several companies, including a leading Mumbai-based pharmaceutical company, used stock-invests to artificially subscribe public issues. DoS which investigated the matter is now sitting on the reports.

June 1996 : Irregularities worth Rs. 34 crore were detected at Oriental Bank of Commerce. Liberal advances were made without getting the board's approval. The RBI chief general manager (DoS), D.S.R. Simhudu, who investigated several such cases, was summarily transferred to an insignificant department.

July 1996 : When Indian Bank ran up a loss of over Rs. 1,300 crore this year, the RBI was a silent spectator. Had nominee directors from RBI and DoS been alert they could have averted the crisis. It is now blaming the bank's former management and auditors.

ANNEXURE-II

EIGHT STOCK SCAM CASES CENTRALISED

The Department of Revenue has centralised eight cases belonging to the bear cartel involved in the multi-crore securities fraud.

The bears—including Bhupen C Dalal, Hiten P Dalal, JP Gandhi, Amhay D Narotam (all brokers), Dhanraj Mills, TB Ruia (shareholder, MCB Ltd) and Excel & Coproprietor S Ramaswamy—have income tax liabilities totalling over Rs. 3000 crore, including interest and penalty.

According to sources in the revenue department, the move has been initiated to follow up on recoveries from the bear cartel. The department has recovered only Rs. 25.29 crore so far against total outstanding dues of over Rs. 3000 crore.

The cases, which were earlier with different assessing officers (AO) under the charge of commissioner of Income Tax (CIT) Central-I Mumbai, will now come under the ambit of assistant commissioner SG Savadi.

Savadi was appointed officer on special duty—(OSD)-II, Central Range-7, in September last year. He will function under CIT Central-II, Mumbai.

The core assessments of the bear cartel's case assessment years 1991-92, 1992-93 and 1993-94 have been completed. "The recovery of demands is *sub-judice* in as much as the recoveries to be made, if any, in these cases, will be through an order of the Supreme Court", a highly placed income Tax officer said.

The huge amounts to be recovered are, therefore, subject to the direction of the court and cannot be recovered from the assessee directly.

As regards amounts in the bear cartel, Hiten Dalal has the highest tax liability of about Rs. 1,300 crore.

This includes tax of around Rs. 652.65 crore and an interest of Rs. 645.19 crore. So far, Rs. 15.14 crore has been recovered by tax officials, following orders from the Supreme Court.

BC Dalal has a total liability of Rs. 749 crore, of which Rs. 347.64 crore is the tax component, while Rs. 401 crore is the interest. The department has recovered only Rs. 1.08 crore from Dalal.

AD Narotam has a total liability of around Rs. 503 crore, including Rs. 220 crore as Tax. The department has so far recovered only Rs. 0.43 crore.

In the case of Dhanraj Mills, the total dues stand at Rs. 122.34 crore, of which Rs. 8.59 crore has been recovered. JP Gandhi owes around Rs. 76 crore to the department, while TB Ruia has a Rs. 0.16 crore outstanding.

The eight assesses have been notified, and their assets attached by the custodian appointed under the Special Court (Trial of offences relating to transactions in securities Act, 1992).

The demands made on the bear cartel on account of the assessments are intimated to the special court through filing of miscellaneous applications.

The Asian Phenomenon

Graft knows no national boundaries

It has many *avatars*, but is as omnipresent as the Almighty. '*Dagdas-bawas*' is how the Filipinos refer to it, having minted this special term after the May 1995 senatorial elections which was marked by massive cheating. Other countries in the region may not have a unique word for electoral graft, but they are as agitated about its proliferation.

Japan faced this spectre as its Lower House did go to the polls recently. Under the single-seat constituency election system, political campaigns are supposed to revolve around policy debates.

But the recent campaign did not appear to have adhered to those noble strictures. Observers point out how in one district, a former bureaucrat from the construction ministry, backed by the ruling Liberal Democratic Party (LDP), and a former construction minister from the Opposition Shinshinto (New Frontier Party), sought to outmanoeuvre each other by promising new public works projects for the district.

LDP's Takeshi Hayashida was promising a bullet train line, nothing less. As also development of the surrounding area, all of which will cost trillions of yen. Shinshinto's candidate, Takeshi Noda, while attacking the opportunism of his opponent, falls into the same groove. His promise includes a new train station, a bridge and public buildings.

Taiwan has a strong Election and Recall Law, legislation that states that persons convicted of violating anti-bribery laws will never be allowed to register again as candidate. Which is political death for a politician. But a large number of those who buy or sell votes don't necessarily get jail terms, something that the Taiwanese press has drawn attention to, time and again.

In Thailand, Pollwatch, the organisation charged with the job of cleaning up the electoral system, is facing a tough terrain as despite rampant vote buying, no one wants to come forward with proof. This is because people are intimidated by influential forces and don't want to lodge a complaint. Moreover, Pollwatch is an electoral watchdog with no powers to arrest anyone. So there is little hope that the impending election which Banham Silpa-archa has called will be any cleaner than the last one, or the one before that.

The situation is no better in neighbouring Malaysia. When Malaysian Prime Minister literally broke into tears during the Umno party polls, his well-wishers hoped he was not weeping in vain.

For, 'money politics', as the Malaysians describe the vexed

issue, continues to raise its head, despite Mahathir Mohammad's firm action to ban it in the last polls.

Eight Umno members were disqualified from contesting in the recent party elections. No prizes for guessing why. And the latest news is that seven of them could be sacked from their government positions under the party's constitution, provided the big guns decide to implement the provisos.

The only silver lining, possibly a kneejerk reaction to the PM's emotional outburst, was the election of Abdullah Ahmad Badawi, widely nicknamed 'Mr. Clean', to the post of Senior Vice-President.

People in power are always faced with the temptation to salt away the millions that come their way by way of public funds and private kick-backs. It calls for tremendous restraint and commitment to say no to the wads of bank notes that powerful conglomerates flash before those who occupy the seats of governance.

ANNEXURE-III

EXTRACTS FROM 1996 ELECTION MANIFESTOS OF NATIONAL PARTIES RELATING TO CONTROLLING CORRUPTION

1. Lok Pal

BJP : Appoint a *Lok Pal* to entertain complaints of corruption against anybody holding public office, including the Prime Minister.

INC (I) : Establish *Lok Pal* with jurisdiction over all political offices, including that of the Prime Minister and Chief Minister.

JD : *Lok Pal* Bill will be adopted to enquire into complaint of corruption against Union Ministers including Chief Minister and Prime Minister and others holding high public office.

Multi-member *Lok Pal* will be appointed by the President in consultation with the Chief Justice of India, Speaker of Lok Sabha and Chairman of Rajya Sabha, and leaders of government and the opposition in the two Houses of Parliament.

CPI(M) : The immediate setting up of *Lok Pal* bringing in its purview the Prime Minister; to be appointed by an authority consisting of the executive, legislature and judiciary.

CPI : *Lok Pal* Bill, which includes within its scope legislators and also the Prime Minister, should be adopted.

Lok Pal institutions should be set up at the Centre and in the States to investigate corruption charges against ministers and bureaucrats.

2. Electoral Reforms relating to Probity of Legislators and Political Parties

BJP : Update and adopt the Goswami Committee report.

Make it obligatory on every elected representative to make public his entire income and wealth within 90 days of election.

Amend the anti-defection law whereby a member of any Legislature who changes parties will lose his or her membership of the House.

Grant statutory status to the code of conduct drawn up by the Election Commission and give it teeth.

Take steps to curb expenditure on elections by imposing a ban on advertisements, cut-outs, etc. introduce electronic voting machines.

Introduce a scheme of State funding of candidates to all egislatures. Provide suitable incentives for open, official corporate funding to all recognized political parties.

Make it mandatory for political parties to submit audited accounts for public scrutiny annually.

INC(I) : All members of Parliament, legislatures and local bodies to declare their assets when assuming office and leaving office.

JD : Legislative initiatives will be taken to organise wide ranging reforms based on Dinesh Goswamy Committee Report.

Statutory provision will be made so that all those holding public offices and offices of political parties declare their assets annually which shall be scrutinised by an independent commission. Janata Dal favours State funding of elections and legitimate activity of recognized political parties.

Public auditing of the accounts of political parties will be made a statutory requirement.

CPI(M) : Comprehensive electoral reforms to ensure the

elimination of money and muscle power from elections on the basis of the Dinesh Goswami Report.

Amend Section 77 of the Representation of People Act to plug loopholes in enforcing ceiling on election expenditure of candidates. Strict action against all manifestations of the criminalisation of politics.

CPI : The Representation of the People Act should be amended to

(i) curb money and muscle power

(ii) ensure State funding specially in the form of necessary election material.

Persons with known criminal records should not be put up nor allowed to contest as candidates in elections.

3. Vigilance Machinery, Accountability, Transparency and Preventing Abuse of Political Power

BJP : The BJP will address itself to this challenge and task (of curbing corruption) by adopting measures that are mentioned here under. We do not claim that this is either the ultimate blueprint for the reduction of corruption or the last word on it. It is an expression of our commitment; a first step to setting right a very great wrong of many years' malignancy; a beginning and that, too, with ourselves.

A Government that intrudes the least, we hold, governs the best. We will endeavour to combine this with open and transparent governance.

Introduce extensive regulations and requirements upon those who hold public office so that no conflict of interest is ever permitted to influence a proper discharge of their duties.

Take measures to modify and reform the methodology of Government approval for contracts, schemes and large money value agreements so as to make them more transparent.

The powers of patronage, the right to say 'Yes' or 'No' to simple daily requirements of the citizens will be reduced drastically.

Expeditiously deal with cases of corruption unresolved and in which no action has been taken in the past 10 years.

INC(I) : Appoint a high-powered commission consisting of eminent jurists, parliamentarians and administrators to recommend legal, administrative and enforcement measures to control and contain corruption and implement these measures within 6 months.

Reduce the amount of discretion obtaining in administrative decision-making, including at Minister's level, so as to render them public, transparent and accountable.

Review the work of the enforcement agencies at the Centre and in the States with a view to accord adequate autonomy and insulation from interferences in discharging their duties.

Strengthening of internal vigilance and anti-corruption mechanisms for preventive and punitive vigilance in all Government, Quasi-Government and Public agencies/organisations.

Involvement of the public in vigilance and control of corruption through public hearings, access to information and promotion of voluntary organisations in this area.

JD : Honest civil servants at all levels will be protected form harassment and high handedness.

Rules of business governing administrative work will be reviewed and role of peoples' representative work will be reviewed at all levels will be strengthened in relation to administrative processes.

Official Secrets Act will be drastically revised. Right of Information will be included in the list of Fundamental Rights of the Constitution.

Transparency will be introduced in all business dealings of government with foreigners and Indians including contracts of sale and purchase and granting of credit by public financial institutions.

The CBI will be freed from the control of the Department of Personnel and made autonomous. For investigation of white collar offences, a separate autonomous organization on the lines of the CBI will be set up.

CPI(M) : Streamline functioning of investigating agencies; protect them from political interference; ensure speedy disposal and appropriate action.

CPI : Transfers and postings which are a fertile source of corruption should be done by a committee of senior officials.

Citizens's Committees composed of personalities of well-known integrity to be set up at different levels for rousing public opinion and with right to initiate proceedings before *Lok Pal* institutions.

There should be more transparency in government in all deals of contract and supply.

The Right to Information must be established so as to make administration more accountable to the people and their elected bodies.

ANNEXURE-IV

GLOBAL MEET TO COMBAT BRIBERY IN THE OFFING

An agreement was reached on November 21, 1997 in Paris among 34 countries of the Organisation for Economic Cooperation and Development (OECD) on the text of a binding international convention on combating bribery of foreign public officials in international business transactions.

On that occasion, the concerned nations signed the formal agreement in Paris. It is expected that the agreement will be ratified in April, 1998 and necessary national legislation would be implemented. The convention will criminalise business-related bribes to corrupt foreign public officials made through political parties and party officials.

The countries which join this convention were Australia, New Zealand, Japan, Korea, U.S., Canada, Mexico, Austria, Belgium, Czech Republic, Denmark, Finland, France, Germany, Greece, Hungary, Iceland, Ireland, Italy, Luxemberg, the Netherlands, Norway, Poland, Portugal, Spain, Sweden, Switzerland, Turkey and the U.K.

In addition the following non-OECD countries also agreed to take part in the convention—Argentina, Brazil, Chile, Slovak Republic and Bulgaria.

It is hailed that this convention on the part of OECD countries would help to promote good governance in developing countries by discouraging bribes. Bribes undermine good governance harm economic efficiency and development, distort trade and penalise consumers. However, the bribes are not practised only in the developing world.

They are prevalent in the industrialised countries as well as the famous lockheed case demonstrated. The bribe-takers included the Japanese Prime Minister, Mr. Tanaka, Prince Bernhardt of the Netherlands and German politicians. There have been reports of sharing of kickbacks between the politicians of the developed and developing countries in major arms transactions. In that sense this convention should contribute to good governance both in developed and developing countries provided it is implemented in good faith.

The Americans passed their Foreign Corrupt Practices Act some 20 years ago and they now claim credit that 33 more countries have joined the fight against corruption. One wonders how many in the world believe that in the last 20 years US firms have not been paying bribes to secure contracts abroad.

One may recall that after the enactment of the law prohibiting company donations for campaign funds for political parties, all that happened was donations were in black money instead of white. Similarly, one wonders whether such a convention against bribery would eliminate bribery altogether or would only convert it into black money transactions both for the giver and taker of the bribe.

One company bidding for a multi-billion contract earmarked tens of millions of dollars for 'educational expenses' and justified it on the ground that the people in the country where the project was to be executed had to be educated on the benefits of the project. The effectiveness of the convention and it's impact will have to be evaluated after several years of experience.

The detailed provisions for the transparency in contracts, procedures for complaints and penalties for violations will need to be examined before arriving at a judgement,

Everyday instances come to notice how various regulatory mechanisms are circumvented in the banking and financial sectors in the developed countries. If in-spite of this convention bribes are paid and received those transactions will be associated with black money generation and possible money laundering.

The money may not necessarily be laundered, but may be utilised in the black money sector—such as election expenses of political parties or for disbursements which are never accounted for.

Inspite of all such possible difficulties in enforcing this convention it is to be welcomed as indicating a move to promote genuine competition. However, it is well known that in spite of professions of commitment to free market and good governance, there is a wide gap-between declaratory intentions and practices. In due course we will know how wide this gap is.

ANNEXURE-V

LIST OF SOME SCANDALS/SCAMS IN INDIA

During the year 1995-96, 69 cases relating to the following scams were registered by the C.B.I. for investigation.

No. of Cases	*Name of the Scam*
(i) 11	Urea Scam
(ii) 17	Housing Scam
(iii) 44	Animal Husbandry Scam
(iv) 7	Bank Securities Scam
Total 69	

Out of these 69 cases, 64 cases are still under investigation.

The list of prominant scandals/scams in the country are given below :

Sr. No.	*Project Name*	*Amount in (Rs.)*
1.	Share Scam	1000 crores
2.	Sugar Scam	650 crores
3.	Bofors Scam	65 crores
4.	Hawala Case	65 crores
5.	Housing Scam	18 crores
6.	M.P. Trading	32 crores
7.	Fertiliser Scam	133 crores
8.	Medicine Equipment Scam	5000 crores
9.	Telecom Case	1200 crores
10.	Newsprint Case	20 crores
11.	Indian Bank Scam	1336 crores

/contd. /

Annexure V (contd..)

Sr. No.	Project Name	Amount in (Rs.)
12.	Fodder Scam (Bihar)	1000 crores
13.	Land Scam (Bihar)	400 crores
14.	Bitumen Scam (Bihar)	100 crores
15.	Medicine Scam (Bihar)	100 crores
16.	Forest Case (Meghalaya)	300 crores
17.	Ayurveda Sc. (U.P.)	32 crores
18.	Dhoti Saree Sc. (Tamilnadu)	11 crores
19.	Coal Sc. (Tamilnadu)	750 crores
20.	Forest Reserve Sc. (Meghalaya)	75 crore
21.	Wakof Scam (West Bengal)	1600 crores
22.	Dental College Case (Karnataka)	50 lakh
23.	State Bank of India, Case (1971)	60 lakhs
24.	Tandoori Kand	
25.	Shikh's Hattykand, Delhi	
26.	LIC Cheating Case (TTK-Mundada) (1957)	1.25 crores
27.	Jeep Scandle (1960) (Raised by H.V. Kanath	
28.	Tulmohan Issue (1974) (Raised by Madhu Limaye)	
29.	Purchase of German Subu	
30.	Churhat Lottery issue	
31.	Purchase of Zei Pistols	
32.	Purchase of Aeroplanes	

ANNEXURE-VI

LIST OF SOME WORLD SCANDALS

1. The Cost of Diplomacy. The extravagance of ambassadors (1840s).
2. The Cleveland Street Scandal. Aristocracy and homosexuality (1880s).
3. The Tranby Croft Affair Car-cheating scandal (1890s).
4. Chicago's First Ward Ball Protectionism and racketeering in Chicago (1909)
5. The Teapot Dome Scandal. Sale of US government leases on oil reserve
6. William Hickey's Closest Shave Tom Driberg's misadventures (1942).
7. Professor C.E. M. Joad's railway ticket fraud (1948).
8. The Rogue's Guide to Tangier Scandal in Tangier (1950s-1970s).
9. The Profumo affair (1961).
10. Northern Corruption Poulson's corrupt architectural practice (1960s-1970s).
11. The illegal domestic spying of the CIA (1970s).
12. Prince Bernhard of the Netherlands and the Lockheed scandal (1970s).

13. The Watergate Scandal (1972).
14. Charges of bribery against Spiro Against (45 vice-President (1973)
15. The case of the Exploding Cigar. CIA plot to assassinate Fidel Castro (1975).
16. Hoax story wins Janet Cooke a Pulitzer (1980)
17. Iran-Contra Story. Colonel Oliver North helps fund arms to Nicaraguan Contras (1987).
18. The Battle of the Quality Sunday Giants Pamella Bordes, Andrew Neil and Donald Trelford (1989).
19. Recruit Scandal. Japanese financial corruption (1990).
20. Saying the Unsayable about the Germans Nicholas Ridley's Spectator interview (1990).
21. Australian horse-racing scandal—the Fine Cotton affair (1991).
22. The largest Bank Fraud in world History. The collapse of BCCI (1991).
23. The Savings & Loans scandal in the US (1991).
24. Sir Joh Bjelke-Peterson charged with corruption (1990).
25. The Whitewater Affair. The Clintons' shady business dealings (1992).
26. The extravagance of Jacques Attali (1993).
27. The Mother of Scandals: Financial scandals swamp Italy (1993).
28. Manning Clark. The flaws of Professor Manning Clark, as revealed by his publisher (1993).

Source : The book of Modern Scandal from Byron to the present day edited by Bruce Palling [Weiden field & Nicolgon, London].

ANNEXURE-VII

LIST OF SOME BRIBES IN FOREIGN COUNTRIES

Year	*Official*	*Amount*	*Discussion: Chapter*
74 B.C.	Senator (Rome)	40,000	2 at note 12
73 B.C.	Governor (Sicily)	80,000+ sesterces	2 at 58
431 A.D.	Grand Chamberlain (Byzantium)	200 Gold Pounds	4 at 80
1204	Pope	100 Silver Pounds	7 at 53
1618	Chancellor (U.K.)	50-1,000	12 at 95-104
1664	Clerk, Naval Board (U.K.)	300 Pounds per year	13(17.16.64)
1694	Speaker of House	1,000 guineas	13 at 35
1780	Governor (Bengal)	40,000 pounds	14 at 36
1795	Legislator (Georgia)	$600-$1000	15 at 31
1813	Secretary of State (U.S.)	$5,000 (loan)	15 at 51
1862	Senator (U.S.)	$50,000	15 at 84
1867	Committee Chairman (U.S. Congress)	$80,000	16 at 70
1868	President (U.S.)	$25,000	16 at 71
1871	Congressman (U.S.)	$2,500	16 at 80
1871	Speaker of House	$64,000	16 at 103
1871	Alderman (New York)	2½%	17 at 44

[contd.]

Annexure VII [contd..)

Year	*Official*	*Amount*	*Discussion: Chapter*
1905	Supervisor (San Francisco)	$475-750	17 at 48
1905	Boss (San Francisco)	$115,000+	17 at 48
1905	Senator (U.S.)	$2,500	18 at 117
1908	Voter (Connecticut)	$2.50-2.75	17 at 73
1922	Cabinet Officer	$100,000	18 at 5
1932	Mayor (Boston)	$35,000	18 at 40
1932	Circuit Judge (U.S.)	$250,000 (2½%)	18 at 19
1937	District Judge (U.S.)	$250,000	18 at 33
1959	Councillor (Massachusetts)	$2,500	18 at 44
1965	Prince (Netharlands)	$1,000,000	20 at 36
1966	Supreme Court Justice (U.S.)	$20,000/year for life	17 at 147
1966	Governor (Illinois)	$159,000	18 at 85
1967	Governor (Maryland)	$20,000	18 at 58
1970	Sheriff (Illinois)	$6 per car towed	18 at 96
1970	Mayor (Illinois)	$85,000	18 at 109
1970	President (Korea)	$3,000,000	19 at 46
1970	Redevelopment Authority Director (Massachusetts)	$25,000 (10%)	18 at 78
1972	Presidential Candidate (U.S.)	$100,000	19 at 24
1972	Vice-Presidential Candidate (U.S.)	$25,000	19 at 25
1973	Prime Minister and associates (Japan)	$12,000,000	20 at 58
1974	President (Honduras)	$2,500,000	20 at 8
1978	Governor (Oklahoma)	$50,000	18 at 82
1979	Congressman (U.S.)	$50,000	18 at 141

Caveat

It is impossible in tabular form to discuss whether, beyond a reasonable doubt, the price was paid and whether, by some standard of the culture involved, it was regarded as a bribe. Consult the chapters listed for discussion.

BIBLIOGRAPHY

Adamany, David (1972). *Campaign Finance in America*, North Scituate, Massachusetts, Duxbury Press.

Alatas, S.H. (1980). *The Sociology of Corruption: The Nature, Functions, Causes, and Prevention of Corruption.* Singapore, Times Books.

____(1993). 'Corruption' in *Oxford Companion to Politics of the World*, Oxford, Oxford University Press.

Alexander, Herbert (1972). *Money in Politics*, Washington DC, Public Affairs, Press.

Alexander, Herbert and Rei Shivatori (eds.) (1994). *Comparative Political Finance among Democracies*, Boulder Colorado, Westview Press.

Andreski, S. (1996). *Parasitism and Subversion*: The Case of Latin America, London, Weidenfeld and Nicolson.

____(1968). *The African Predicament*, New York, Atherton Press.

Banfield, E.C. (1979) 'Corruption as a Feature of Government' in Ekpo (1979).

Baxi, Upendra (1989). *Liberty and Corruption, The Antulay Case and Beyond*, Lucknow, Eastern Book Company.

Benson, G.C.S. (1978). *Political Corruption in America*, Lexington, D.C. Health and Co.

Bhagwati, Jagdish N. (ed.) (1974). *Illegal Transactions in International Trade*, Amsterdam, North Holland-Elsevier.

Bhagwati, Jagdish N. (1982). 'Directly Unproductive, Profit-Seeking (DUP) Activities', *Journal of Political Economy*, 90.

Bhalerao, C.N (ed.) (1972). *Administration, Politics and Development in India*, Bombay, Lalvani.

Buchanan, J., Tollison, R. and Tullock, G. (eds.) (1980) *Toward a Theory of the Rent-Seeking Society*, Texas, Texas A and M University Press

Carino (ed.) 1986). *Bureaucratic Corruption in Asia: Causes, Consequences and Controls*, Quezon City, JMC Press.

Chuch, R.L. and Uppal, J.S. (1986). *Black Economy in India*, New Delhi, Tata Mc Graw Hill.

Clarke, M. (ed.) (1983). *Corruption: Causes, Consequences and Control*, New York, St. Martins Press.

Consumer Education and Research Centre, Ahmedabad (1995). *Judicial Pronouncements on Access to Information*, Ahmedabad.

____(1995). *Access to Information Bill (Proposed)*, Ahmedabad.

Doig, A. (1984). *Corruption and Misconduct in Contemporary British Politics*, Hammondsworth, Penguin.

Dunn, Delmer. (1972). *Financing Presidential Campaigns*, Washington DC— The Brookings Institution.

Ekpo, Monday U. (1979). *Bureaucratic Corruption in Sub-Saharan Africa: Toward a Search for Causes and Consequences*, Washington DC, University Press of America.

Gardiner, J.A. and Olson, D.J. (eds.) (1968). *Theft of the City : Readings on Corruption in America*, Bloomington, Indiana University Press.

Government of India, Ministry of Home Affairs, (1964). *Report of the Committee on the Prevention of Corruption (Santhanam Committee)*, New Delhi.

____Administrative Reforms Commission (1966). *Report on the Problems of Redress of Citizens' Grievances*, New Delhi.

____Ministry of Finance (1978). *Report of the Committee on Controls and Subsidies*, New Delhi.

____(1985). *Aspects of the Black Economy in India*, New Delhi.

____Ministry of Law (1988). *Prevention of Corruption Act*, 1988, New Delhi.

____Lok Sabha Secretariat (1992). *13th Report of the Estimates Committee (1991-92), Tenth Lok Sabha on Central Bureau of Investigation*, New Delhi.

____Ministry of Home Affairs (1995), *Vohra Committee Report*, New Delhi.

HMSO (1995). *Standards in Public Life, First Report of the Committee under Chairman Lord Nolan*, London.

Harriss-White, B. and Gordon White (1996). *Liberalization and Corruption*, Sussex, Institute of Development Studies Bulletin, 27:2.

Heidenheimer, A.J. (ed.) (1970). *Political Corruption: Readings in Comparative Analysis*, New York, Holt, Rinehart and Wilson.

Heidenheimer, A.J., Michael Johnston and Victor T. Le Vine (eds.) (1989). *Political Corruption: A Handbook*, New Brunswick, New Jersey, Transaction Publishers.

Hurstfield, Joel. (1973). *Freedom, Corruption and Government in Elizabethan England*, Cambridge, Harvard University Press.

Jagannathan V. (1987). *Informal Markets in Developing Countries*, Oxford, Oxford University Press.

Kernaghan, K. and Dwivedi, O.P. (eds.) (1983). *Ethics in the Public Service: Comparative Perspectives*, Brussels, International Institute of Administrative Sciences.

Klitgaard, Robert (1983). *Corruption in Mexico*, Cambridge, Harvard University Press.

____(1988). *Controlling Corruption*, Berkeley, University of California Press.

____(1990). *Tropical Gangsters*, New York, Basic Books.

Kohli, Suresh (ed.) 1975). *Corruption in India*, New Delhi, Chetana Publications.

Krueger, A.O. (1974). 'Political Economy of the Rent-seeking Society'. *American Economic Review*, 64:3.

Leff, Nathaniel H. (1964). 'Economic Development through Bureaucratic Corruption', *American Behavioural Scientist*, 8.

Levi, Michael and David Nelken (eds.) (1996). *The Corruption of Politics and the Politics of Corruption*, Journal of Law and Society (Special Issue), March, Oxford, Blackwell.

Le Vine, V.T. (1975). *Political Corruption: The Ghana Case*, Stanford, Hoover Institution Press.

Mac Mullen, Ramsay (1988). *Corruption and the Decline of Rome*, New Haven, Yale University Press.

Mauss, Marcel (1990). *The Form and Reason for Exchange in Archaic Societies*, London, Routledge.

Monterio, J.B. (1966). *Corruption*, Bombay, Manaktalas.

Montias, J.M. and Susan Rose-Ackerman (1981). 'Corruption in a Soviet-type Economy: Theoretical Considerations' in Steven Rosefielde (ed) *Economics Welfare and the Economic of Soviet Socialism: Essays in Honour of Abram Bergson*, Cambridge, Cambridge University Press.

Myrdal, Gunnar (1968) 'Corruption: Its Causes and Effects', Asian Drama: An Inquiry into the Poverty of Nations, Hammondsworth, Penguin, Vol II.

Nader, R. Petkas, P.J. and Blackwell, K. (eds.) 1972) *Whistleblowing: The Report of the Conference on Professional Responsibility*, New York, Grossman Publishers.

Nehru, B.K. (1986). *Thoughts on Our Present Discontents*, New Delhi. Allied Publishers.

Noonan, J. (1984). *Bribes*, New York, Macmillan.

Noorani, A.G. (1973). *Ministers' Misdeeds*, Delhi, Vikas Publishers.

____(1996). 'Rao & Scam', I, II and III in *Statesman*, New Delhi, March 10, 11 and 12.

Nye, Joseph S. 1967). 'Corruption and Political Development : A Cost-Benefit Ana ʾsis', *American Political Science Review*, 61.

Onoge, O.F. (1' 32). 'Corruption in Development', Zaria, Nigeria, *Ahmada Bello Univc ity*.

Padhy, K.S. an Muni, P.K. (1987). *Corruption in Indian Politics : A Case Study of a Indian State*, Delhi, Discovery Publishing House.

Palmier, Leslie I. (1985). *The Control of Bureaucratic Corruption*, New Delhi, Allie Publishers.

Paul, Samuel (995). *A Report Card on Public Services in Indian Cities: A View fro Below*, Bangalore, Public Affairs Centre.

Rogow, Arnol and Harold D. Lasswell (1963). *Power, Corruption and Rectitude*, glewood Cliffs, New Jersey, Prentice-Hall.

Rose-Ackerma Susan (1978). *Corruption: A Study ion Political Economy*, New York Academic Press.

____(1987). 'ribery' in John Eatwell, Murray Millgate and Peter Newman (eds). *The New Palgrave, The World of Economics*, London, Macmillan.

Roy, Bunker (1996). 'Right to Information: Profile of a Grass Roots Struggle', *Economic and Political Weekly*, Bombay, May 11.

Sathe, S.P. (1991). *Right to Know*, Bombay, N.M. Tripathi.

____(1991). *Administrative Law*, Bombay, N.M. Tripathi.

____(1996). *Tribunal System of India*, Bombay, N.M. Tripathi.

Scott, James C. (1972). *Comparative Political Corruption*, Englewood Cliffs, New Jersey, Prentice-Hall.

Senturia, J.J. (1931) 'Corruption, Political", *Encyclopaedia of the Social Sciences*, Vol. IV.

Singh, L.P. (1986). *Electoral Reform*, New Delhi, Uppal Publishing House.

Singh, N.K. (1996). *The Plain Truth*, Delhi, Konark Publishers.

Stacey, Frank (1971). *The British Ombudsman*, Oxford, Oxford University Press.

Tanzi, Vito (ed.) (1982). *The Underground Economy in the United States and Abroad*, Lexington, D.C. Health and Company.

____(1994). *Corruption, Governmental Activities and Markets*, Washington DC, International Monetary Fund.

Theobald, Robin, (1990). *Corruption, Development and Underdevelopment, Durham*, North Carolina, Duke University Press.

Transparency International (TI) (1996). *National Integrity Systems: The TI Source Book*, TI Berlin, Germany.

Tullock, Gordon (1987). 'Rent Seeking'', in John Eatwell, Murray Millgate and Peter Newman (eds.) *The New Palgrave, The World of Economics*, London, Macmillan.

Wade, Robert (1982). 'The System of Administrative and Political Corruption: Canal Irrigation in South India", *The Journal of Development Studies.* 18:3

____(1985). 'The Market for Public Office :Why the Indian State is not Better at Development', *World Development*, 13 :4.

____(1989). 'Politics and Graft: Recruitment, Appointment, and Promotion to Public Office in India' in Peter M. Ward (1989).

Ward, Peter (1989). *Corruption, Development and Inequality, Soft Touch or Hard Graft?*, London Routledge.

Williams, R. (1987). *Political Corruption in Africa*, Aldershort, Gower.

World Bank (1992). *Governance and Development*, Washington DC, World Bank.

Wraith, R. and Simkins, E. (1963). *Corruption in Developing Countries*, London, George Allen and Unwin.

Zwart Frank de (1994). *The Bureaucratic Merry-go-round, Manipulating the Transfer of Indian Civil Servants*, Amsterdam, University Press.

INDEX